HISTORY OF INDIA UNDER BABER

By

WILLIAM ERSKINE

ATLANTIC PUBLISHERS & DISTRIBUTORS

Published by
ATLANTIC PUBLISHERS AND DISTRIBUTORS
B-2, Vishal Enclave, New Delhi-27
Phone 5413460

Sales Office
4346/4C, Ansari Road, Darya Ganj,
New Delhi-110 002
Phone 3273880, 3285873
Fax 91-11-3285873

ISBN 81-7156-032-6

Typeset at
APD Computer Graphics
B-2, Vishal Enclave, New Delhi-110 027
Printed in India at
Print India
New Delhi

NOTICE.

The work now published occupied the attention of the late Mr. Erskine, as he mentions, through many years, being pursued with that carefulness and deliberation, with that anxiety to be accurate, which characterised all his literary labours: the object he had thus perseveringly in view is sufficiently explained in the following preface, which he himself prepared, — that of constructing the history of some of the most important periods in the annals of India on a wider and more comprehensive basis than the sole authority of the compilation of Ferishta, to which, almost exclusively, European writers had hitherto had recourse. That more ample materials existed for the elucidation of Indian history in all its stages, — materials even more abundant than those employed by Ferishta, — Mr. Erskine's studies made him fully aware; and his thorough acquaintance with the language of the authorities that were available enabled him to derive from them all the information they were calculated to afford. The consequence has been the present authentic record of an interesting and important period of Indian history.

The design of Mr. Erskine originally contemplated the whole of the reigns of the princes of the dynasty of Taimur in India, from the accession of Báber to the end of the sovereignty of Aurungzíb, including the previous occurrences of the life of Báber, and a general account of the Tartar tribes of Transoxiana. Ample materials had been collected by him and translated for this purpose, but he had found time only for the completion of the first portion of his task, — the lives of Báber and Humáyun,—the latter including a history of Shír Shah and the Pattan princes by whom Humáyun was, for a season, driven from his throne. The life of Báber has been in some degree anticipated by Mr. Erskine himself, in his valuable translation of that prince's autobiography; but in the present work we have the testimony of contemporary and subsequent authorities in addition to his own, and especially that of the great historian of the Mongol races, Haider Mírza, the author of the Taríkh-e-Reshídi — a work which Mr. Erskine recommends strongly for translation and publication. Other authentic writers are also now for the first time made to contribute to the elucidation of the reigns of Báber and his son; and we may consider this portion of the Mohammedan government of India as fully and finally elucidated.

AUTHOR'S PREFACE.

When there are already so many histories of India in the English language, it may reasonably be asked, why an attempt should be made to add another to the number.

The idea of the following work suggested itself many years ago, from observing on how limited a foundation most of our general histories of India were raised, the brief but judicious abridgment of Ferishta forming, in truth, the basis of them all. It seemed to me that a nation possessing such an empire as that of the British in India ought to have some ampler record of the transactions of the different dynasties which preceded their own in that country. The most natural and effectual means of supplying this want would certainly be a general edition of the historians of India,—a Corpus Scriptorum Historiæ Indicæ. But the least reflection shows that the necessary extent of such a work, joined to the very small number of readers, whether native or European, who call for, or are likely to avail themselves of it, if completed, makes it an undertaking, useful and desirable as it may be, that must be postponed to a distant period. Indeed, the ardour of British enterprise has not achieved such a collection even of the historians of our native land.

The various Histories of India that have been pub-

A 4

lished have been written with various objects. The volumes of Mill, as might be expected from any production of a man of his talents, are full of valuable materials, and, in spite of the disadvantage of being devoted to a particular system, evince an extraordinary union of acuteness, industry and ingenuity. But his narrative of early events is brief, and hurried over with rapidity. The later productions of different able writers, however useful, and however well adapted to their object as popular compilations, have added little to the amount of what was previously known.*

The History of India by the Honourable Mountstuart Elphinstone is indeed a work of a very different and much higher class. The rapid sketch of the early and Hindú state of India, contained in the first volume, exhibits such a concentration of a vast mass of reading and observation into a small compass, enriched by a perfect personal knowledge of the present state of the country, its inhabitants, and their habits of thought, as is hardly to be equalled in the whole range of literature. Nor are the views of the genius, character and government of the Musulmans in the subsequent part of the work, and the characters of the different agents who appear upon the stage, touched with a less masterly hand. With a rare union of wide research, profound reflection, and pregnant brevity, we everywhere mark the impress of the statesman, the moralist and the scholar. It will probably long continue to be the classical history to introduce the inquirer of every de-

* It is hardly necessary to remark that the works of Professor Wilson and Sir Henry Elliot had not appeared when this was written.

nomination to a correct knowledge of India. Had the narrative of the transactions of the princes of the House of Taimur, much of which is drawn from new and original sources, been as minute as it is faithful and interesting, the present work would never have seen the light. And yet, perhaps, the extent of narrative which it contains, is as much as the great majority of European readers may require or endure.

The object of the following pages is far more humble. It is to furnish, from a comparison of as many of the original historians of India as were accessible to the author, such a narrative of public events during the reigns of the first six Emperors of the House of Taimur, from Báber to Aurengzíb, as might be at once more minute and more authentic than, so far as the author knows, has yet appeared in any European language. During the two first of these reigns, — those of Báber and Humáyun, — there is rather a want of continuous contemporary authorities: and the desire to supply, as far as possible, the deficiencies of the ordinary histories may, by many, be thought to have led to the opposite extreme of too great detail, in the narrative now given of these reigns. For the four last reigns the materials are abundant, even to superfluity, so that there is less temptation to fall into such an error.

The period, commencing with the invasion of Báber, and ending with the death of Aurengzíb, was chosen as containing a very memorable portion of Indian history. The preceding periods are less perfectly known. The period that follows presents to our view the decline, and, in the end, the breaking-up of the Empire. A history of the period between these two,—that of the earlier princes of the House of Taimur, containing their original entrance into the country, and the gradual progress of their arms, till the empire reached its entire and most flourishing state,—seemed to form a natural foundation for the modern history of India, when those later contests with Europeans began, which have changed the whole face of things. The early transactions of the Portuguese and Dutch affected only the outskirts of the empire; those with the French and English, during the last century, affected its very centre, and, in their results, have shaken it to pieces. The materials for the history of the two first periods are still chiefly contained in the languages of the East, while those of the last may be best drawn from the relations and State papers of Europeans.

The author has indulged sparingly in any reflections on events, being rather desirous, by giving a faithful statement of facts, to let them speak for themselves.

The volumes now offered to the public contain the reigns of Báber and Humáyun. The whole life of the former was spent in camps. It was a period of transition, when the Government had not yet subsided into a regular form. Little progress towards settled institutions was made in the unquiet reign of his son. It was not till the time of Akber that a regular attempt was made to reduce to a system some portion of the rules and customs of the country, and to combine them by the principles of a just and impartial legislation. Even that great and enlightened prince had, however, many difficulties, religious and political, to encounter;

and as he was, in some instances, too much in advance of his age, and in others perhaps too fantastical, and had, besides, the misfortune to have a successor whose views differed from his own, many of his regulations died with himself.

To some readers the account of the Tartars of the Kipchák and of Moghulistán, contained in the Introduction, may seem to be too extended. But these tribes had great influence on the fortune of the founder of what has been called the Moghul Empire; and, without a considerable knowledge of their circumstances and transactions, much of the earlier portion of the history would be obscure.

The greater part of the volumes now published was written several years ago,—a circumstance which it may be necessary to mention, in order to explain why, in the course of the narrative, so little allusion is made to late events, such as those that have recently occurred in Afghanistán, or to the works of later writers.

As to the orthography of oriental words, that of Sir William Jones has in general been adopted. *K* has however been substituted for the hard *c; g* is used hard before all vowels, as in *gust; j* is soft, as in *just; ch* is used as in *chance; sh*, as in *ship*. Little distinction has been made of the letters peculiar to eastern alphabets; though *Kh* has been generally used for the Arab *khe*, as in *Khan;* and *gh* for the *ghain*, as in *Ghâzi*. The accent is often applied to mark a vowel as being long in a word, especially the first time it is used.

The author ought not to conclude without making his acknowledgments to John Romer, Esq., for the use of a manuscript of the Tabakát-i-Akberi in his collection: and to Horace Hayman Wilson, Esq., for that of the Taríkh-e-Reshídi, from which so much has been drawn. For an opportunity of consulting the Kholáset-ul-towáríkh, he was indebted to the kindness of the late Major William Yule. The other manuscripts quoted are chiefly in the possession of the author.

Bonn, May 28. 1845.

CONTENTS

OF

THE FIRST VOLUME.

PRELIMINARY REMARKS.

Page

Indian History. — Its three Periods - - - 1
Remarkable Era when the Kingdoms of Europe and Asia assumed a more permanent form - - 2
The States of Europe settle into a system - - ib.
Permanent Kingdoms formed in Asia - - - 5

INTRODUCTION.

Containing a general Account of the Tartars, especially of the Júji and Chaghatái Dynasties, and of the state of Transoxiana at the accession of Báber.

SECTION I.

GENERAL ACCOUNT OF THE TARTAR TRIBES.

Three grand Divisions, — Manchús, Mongols or Moghuls, and Túrks - - - - - 9
Conquests of Chengíz Khan and the Moghuls - - 12
Of the Túrki Tribes, and Taimur - - - 15
Difference resulting from the mode of settlement of the Tartars, in Tribes, or as Individuals - - 19

SECTION II.

CHENGÍZ KHÁN.

His conquests; Division of his Empire among his Sons 23
Their territories - - - - - 24
Júji Khan gets the Desht-Kipchák - - - 25
Conquests of his Descendants - - - - 26
Decline and division of their Kingdom - - 27
Rise of the Uzbeks, — and of the Kaizáks - - 28

SECTION III.

CHAGHATAI KHAN.

	Page
His extensive dominions - - - -	35
Decline of the power of the Chaghatái Khans - -	36
Division of their Empire into Moghulistán and Máwerannaher - - - - - -	37
Part I. Khans of Moghulistán and Amírs of Káshgar -	38
Toghlak Taimur and his Successors - -	39
Invasion of Taimur - - - -	41
Khizer Kwája and his Sons - - -	42
Yúnis Khan and his Sons - - -	44
Transactions of the Khans with the Mírzas of Máwerannaher - - - -	63
Part II. Khans of Máwerannaher - - -	66
Their decline and extinction - - -	67

SECTION IV.

New Túrki Dynasty under Mír Taimur -	69
His conquests - - - - - -	72
Shahrukh and Ulugh Beg Mírzas - - -	ib.
Abusaíd Mírza - - - - -	73
His death - - - - - -	74
Division of his dominions - - - -	ib.
Umersheikh Mírza, King of Ferghána - - -	ib.
His death - - - - - -	75
Succession of his son, Báber - - - -	76
Rulers of the neighbouring States at this period -	ib.

HISTORY OF BÁBER.

BOOK FIRST.

FROM BÁBER'S ACCESSION TO HIS FIRST EXPULSION FROM MÁWERANNAHER.

CHAPTER I.

CONQUEST AND LOSS OF SAMARKAND. — LOSS AND RECOVERY OF ANDEJÁN.

A. D.		
1494.	Accession of Báber - - - - -	78
	State of Ferghána, which is attacked on all sides -	79

A. D.		Page
1494.	Invaders repelled - - - - -	88
	Death of Sultan Ahmed of Samarkand - -	89
1495.	And of his Brother Sultan Mahmúd Mírza - -	92
	Revolutions of that Country - - - -	ib.
1496.	Báber invades it - - - - - -	99
1497.	Blockades the Capital - - - - -	101
	Huts his army in winter quarters - -	103
	Is attacked by Sheibáni Khan - - - -	ib.
	Takes Samarkand - - - - -	104
	Revolt in Ferghána in favour of his brother Jehángír -	107
1498.	Báber marches to quell it - - - -	110
	Loses Samarkand and Andeján - - -	ib.
	His distress - - - - - - -	111
1499.	He applies for succour to his maternal uncle, Sultan Mahmúd Khan - - - - -	113
	Gets possession of Marghinán - - - -	115
	Rising of the population of Ferghána in his favour -	116
	Recovers Andeján - - - - -	118
	Revolt of his Moghul Troops - - - -	120
	Success of Tambol - - - - -	ib.
	His defeat - - - - - -	123
	Campaign of Kásán - - - - -	124
1500.	Báber concludes a peace with Jehángír and Tambol -	126

CHAPTER II.

SHEIBÁNI KHAN.—CONQUEST AND LOSS OF SAMARKAND.

	Báber is kept under by his Minister - - -	127
	Affairs of Samarkand - - - - - -	128
	Báber invited there - - - - -	129
	He advances to the Capital - - - -	130
	March of Sheibáni to its relief - - - -	132
	History of that Chief - - - - -	133
	Flight of Báber by Hissár - - - -	141
	He resolves to attempt Samarkand - - -	145
	Takes it by surprise - - - - -	147
1501.	His Battle with Sheibáni and defeat - -	151
	He is besieged in Samarkand for five months - -	153
	Capitulation - - - - - - -	157
	He escapes to Uratippa - - - -	159

CHAPTER III.

SHEIBÁNI'S CONQUEST OF TÁSHKEND AND FERGHÁNA—EXPULSION OF BÁBER.

A.D.		Page
1501.	Báber visits the elder Khan - - - -	160
	His mode of life - - - - -	ib.
1502.	Revisits the Khan - - - - -	165
	Arrival of the younger Khan - - - -	168
	They invade Ferghána - - - -	170
	Báber surprised by Tambol, and wounded - -	172
	Tambol calls in Sheibáni - - -	175
	Affair of Akhsi - - - - -	ib.
	Báber driven out - - - - -	177
	His flight and danger - - - - -	ib.
1503.	The Khans defeated and taken prisoners by Sheibáni, who conquers Táshkend - - - -	184
	Tambol remains in possession of Ferghána - -	ib.
	The Khans are set at liberty - - - -	185
1504.	Tambol attacked by Sheibáni - - - -	187
	Besieged in Andeján - - - - -	184
	Surrenders, and is put to death - - -	188
	Báber abandons Ferghána - - - -	190
	Death of the younger Khan - - - -	ib.
	Subsequent history and death of the elder Khan in A. D. 1508 - - - - - - -	ib.

BOOK SECOND.

BÁBER'S TRANSACTIONS IN KÁBUL AND MÁWERANNAHER.

CHAPTER I.

CONQUEST OF KÁBUL.

	Báber passes through the Hissár Territory - -	194
	History of Khosrou Shah - - - -	196
	Báber joined by Báki - - - - -	202
	Crosses the Amu - - - - - -	202
	Sheibáni conquers Hissár and Kunduz - -	203
	Death of his brother - - - - - -	204

A.D.		Page
504	Báber joined by Khosrou's Moghuls - - -	207
	Submission of Khosrou - - - -	ib.
	Who is deserted by his followers - - -	208
	Báber marches against Kábul - - - -	210
	Besieges the City - - - - -	214
	Which surrenders - - - - -	216
	Description of the Kingdom of Kábul - -	217
1505.	Báber's circuitous campaign to the Indus - -	223
	Affairs of Badakhshán - - - - -	226
	Khosrou's death - - - - -	228
	Báber takes and abandons Kilát - - -	229
	Báki's dismissal and death - - - -	231
1506.	Jehángir flees from Kábul - - - -	ib.

CHAPTER II.

JOURNEY TO AND FROM KHORÁSÁN.—KHAN MÍRZA'S REBELLION.

1505.	Progress of Sheibáni - - - - - -	233
	He dreads the Moghuls in his army - - -	ib.
	Subdues Khwárazm - - - - -	237
	Besieges Balkh - - - - -	238
1506.	Báber marches to Khorásán - - - -	239
	Death of Sultan Husein Mírza of Herát - -	ib.
	Discord and want of spirit of his Sons, the Mírzas -	240
	Balkh surrenders - - - - -	241
	Báber returns home by the mountain-road - -	243
	His Danger in the snow - - - -	244
	Treachery of Muhammed Husein Mírza - -	249
1507.	Báber finds Kábul besieged by the faction of Khan Mírza - - - - - -	250
	Báber surprises the rebels - - - -	252
	Seizes the ringleaders, whom he pardons - -	254
	Sheibáni invades and conquers Khorásán - -	258
	Fate of the Mírzas - - - - -	260

CHAPTER III.

CONQUEST AND LOSS OF KANDAHÁR.—REBELLION OF THE MOGHULS.

	Affairs of Kandahár - - - - -	261
	Zúlnún's early life - - - - -	262
	Repairs to the Court of Sheikh Husein Mírza of Herát	ib.

A.D.		Page
1505.	He gets the Government of Zemín-dáwer	264
	And of Kandahár	266
	Connects himself with Badi-ez-zemán Mírza	269
	Hostilities with Sultan Husein	ib.
1506.	Death of the Sultan	274
1507.	Zúlnún becomes Minister to his Son	275
	His death	ib.
	Transactions of his sons with Báber	ib.
	Báber defeats them and takes Kandahár	278
	Sheibáni marches to their relief	279
	Alarm of Báber	ib.
	Kandahár retaken by Sheibáni	281
1508.	Báber assumes the Title of Padshah or Emperor	282
	Rebellion of Báber's Moghuls	283
	Quelled by his valour	285
	Affairs of Badakhshán	286
	Khan Mírza King	288
1509.	His indigent condition	291
	Sultan Saíd and Mírza Haider at Kábul	ib.
	Their reception	292

CHAPTER IV.

SHAH ISMAEL AND SHEIBÁNI.—BÁBER IN MÁWERANNAHER.

1509.	Sheibáni's unsuccessful Campaign against the Kaizáks	296
1510.	And against the Hazáras	297
	His quarrel with Shah Ismael of Persia	ib.
	Their correspondence	298
	The Shah invades Khorásán	300
	Marches to Merv, which Sheibáni defends	301
	Battle of Merv	302
	Death of Sheibáni	303
	Desertion of his Moghuls	305
1511.	Báber crosses the mountains	306
	His views on Máwerannaher	ib.
	State of the Uzbeks	309
	Ferghána recovered	310
	Operations in Hissár	312
	Báber defeats the Uzbeks	314
	Takes Bokhára and Samarkand	315
	Uzbeks expelled from Máwerannaher	318
	State of that country	319
	Religious feuds	320

A.D.		Page
1512.	New Invasion of the Uzbeks - - - -	322
	Báber defeated at Kul-málek - - -	ib.
	Abandons Samarkand and Bokhára - - -	ib.
	Joined by Persian Auxiliaries - - - -	323
	Advances anew towards Bokhára - - -	324
	Sack of Karshi - - - - -	ib.
	Battle of Ghazhdewán - - - - -	325
	Báber driven back to Hissár - - - -	ib.
1513.	Conspiracy and revolt of the Moghuls - -	327
	Their tyranny in Hissár - - - -	ib.
	Famine and pestilence - - - -	328
	Moghuls expelled by Obeid Khan - - -	329
1514.	Báber driven from Máwerannaher - - -	ib.
	Returns to Kábul - - - - -	ib.

CHAPTER V.

ARGHÚNS IN KANDAHÁR.

1514.	Báber returns to Kábul - - - -	334
	Rebellion of his Moghuls quelled - - -	ib.
1515.	He chastises the Hill Tribes - - - -	336
1519.	Takes Bajour - - - - -	337
	Swád submits - - - - - -	338
	Affairs of Badakhshán and of Kandahár - -	339
	Shah Beg submits to Shah Ismael,—is thrown into prison - - - - - - -	344
	Plot to deliver him—succeeds - - -	345
	He turns his Arms against Sind - - -	346
	Máh Chuchak—her story, captivity, and escape -	348
1520–21.	Báber's successive Campaigns against Kandahár -	352
1522.	Which is surrendered by convention - - -	355

CHAPTER VI.

ARGHÚN CONQUEST OF SIND AND MULTÁN.

SECTION I.

CONQUEST OF SIND.

Transactions in Sind - - - - -	357
Successive Dynasties - - - - -	358

A. D.		Page
1508.	Reign of Jám Firúz - - - - - -	360
	Misrule and rebellion - - - - -	ib.
1518.	Shah Beg called in - - - - -	363
1520.	He takes Tatta - - - - -	365
	Upper Sind ceded to him - - - -	366
	Revolt against the Arghúns - - - -	ib.
	Usurpation of Siláh-ed-dín, whom Shah Beg defeats and slays in battle - - - -	368
	Shah Beg's measures to settle the Country - -	370
	He makes Bheker his Capital - - - -	374
1524.	His death - - - - - -	ib.
	Character - - - - - -	ib.

SECTION II.

CONQUEST OF LOWER SIND AND MULTÁN.

1524.	Accession of Shah Hasan - - - -	378
	Revolt of the Jám - - - - -	ib.
	Shah Hasan takes Tatta - - - -	380
	The Jám flees to Kach and returns with an army -	ib.
	Is defeated - - - - - -	381
	Shah Hasan sole master of Sind - - -	ib.
	His desultory warfare with the Balúches - -	382
	He aims at the conquest of Multán - - -	384
	Previous history of that Country - - -	386
1525.	He takes Uch - - - - -	390
	Treaty. His territory extended to the Ghara -	391
	He takes Dirável - - - - -	392
	Is invited to Multán - - - - -	393
1526.	Besieges and takes the Capital - - -	394
	Leaves there a Governor — who is expelled - -	397
1527.	Multán occupied by Báber - - - -	398
	Shah Hasan defeats the Khankar - - -	399

BOOK THIRD.

BÁBER IN INDIA.

CHAPTER I.

INVASIONS OF INDIA.—BATTLE OF PÁNIPAT—AND SUBVERSION OF THE LODI DYNASTY.

	Early History of India	402
	Different Dynasties	403
	The Lodis	405
1518.	Reign of Sultan Ibráhím	407
	Internal troubles	ib.
1523.	Revolt of Behár—and of the Penjáb	412
	Báber's Four Invasions of India	413
1524.	His Transactions with Doulat Khan and Alá-ed-dín	417
1525.	Fifth Invasion of India	427
1526.	He takes Milwat	429
	Advances to Ambála	432
	Takes Hissár Firóza	ib.
	Battle of Pánipat	435
	Defeat and death of Ibráhím	437
	Báber enters Delhi and Agra	ib.
	State of India	441
	Inhabitants hostile to the Invaders	ib.
	Combination to expel them	442
	Báber's army disheartened	444
	His address to his Council	445
	Change in his prospects	446
	He acquires Sambhal and Ráberi	448
	Sends Humáyun to the Eastward	449
	Who takes Juánpúr and Kalpi	450
	Báber acquires Biána, Dhulpúr and Gualiár	452
	Attempt on his Life	455
	Multán submits	456
	Uzbeks invade Khorásán — take Balkh	ib.
	Affair of Mír Hámeh	458

CHAPTER II.

WAR OF RÁNA SÁNGA, AND CHÁNDÉRI.

Rána Sánga	460
His dominions and character	ib.

A. D.		Page
	Transactions with Báber	462
	Mutual recrimination	ib.
	His views of ambition	ib.
	He supports the Western Afgháns	ib.
1527.	Marches to Biána	ib.
	Is joined by Hasan Khan	463
	Báber marches to Síkri to oppose him	ib.
	Prowess of the Rájpúts	464
	Skirmish	465
	Discouragement of Báber's troops	ib.
	He lays waste Mewát	466
	Measures to reanimate his army	ib.
	He renounces the use of wine	ib.
	Remits the Temgha	467
	Address to his Council	ib.
	Its success	468
	Progress of the Afgháns in various quarters	469
	Báber moves onwards	ib.
	Prepares for battle	470
	Rájpút forces	471
	Battle of Kanwa	472
	Báber victorious	473
	Assumes the Title of Ghází	474
	Koel retaken	ib.
	Mewát reduced	475
	Humáyun sent back to Badakhshán	476
	The lost Towns in the Doáb, and Country beyond the Ganges, recovered	ib.
1528.	Campaign of Chándéri	478
	Medíni Rao	479
	His history	480
	Revolutions of Málwa	ib.
	Rána Sánga called in	ib.
	His victory and generosity	481
	Báber's proposal to Medíni rejected	ib.
	He takes the outer Town and Fort of Chándéri	482
	Massacre of the Rájpúts	483
	Death of Rána Sánga	484

CHAPTER III.

BÁBER'S CAMPAIGNS ON THE GANGES.

A. D.		Page
1528.	Báber marches to the East	485
	Passes the Ganges at Kanáuj	486

A.D.		Page
1528.	Disperses the army of Baban and Bayezíd	487
	Returns to Agra	ib.
	Transactions in Khorásán	489
	Invasion of the Uzbeks	ib.
	Obeid Khan besieges Herát	ib.
	The Shah defeats an Uzbek army	ib.
	Raises the siege of Herát	490
	Advances to Meshhíd	ib.
	Defeats the Uzbeks with great slaughter	ib.
	Temporary revival of Báber's designs on Samarkand	492
1529.	Balúch inroads	495
	The Eastern Afgháns acknowledge Sultan Mahmúd Lodi	496
	Rapid increase of his power	498
	Three Competitors for the Eastern Kingdom	ib.
	Báber takes the field	499
	Disperses the Afgháns	ib.
	Overruns Behár	500
	Affairs of Bengal	ib.
	Negotiations with that power	503
	Báber attacks and defeats the Bengal army	504
	Submission of the Afgháns	505
	Peace with Bengal	ib.
	Báber returns to Agra	507

CHAPTER IV.

BÁBER'S ILLNESS, DEATH, AND CHARACTER.

1529.	Báber's health declines	508
	Humáyun leaves Badakhshán	ib.
	Alarm of the Inhabitants	509
	Sultan Saíd called in	ib.
	Besieges Kila-Zefer	510
1530.	Makes peace, and retires	ib.
	Suleimán Mírza sent to Badakhshán	511
	Humáyun at Court	512
	His illness	513
	Báber's self-devotion	ib.
	Báber's dangerous illness	ib.
	Intrigues in favour of Mehdi Khwája	514
	His arrogance and fall	515
	Báber's dying advice to his Sons and Amírs	516
	His Death — Tomb	517

	Page
Character - - - - - -	519
Commentaries - - - - - -	522
Person - - - - - -	525
Children - - - - - -	ib.
Dominions - - - - - -	526
Their political situation—Taxes - - -	528
Landed Property - - - - -	529
Revenue—Customs—Post-houses - - -	530
Men of Letters - - - - -	530
APPENDIX A.—The Tartar Tribes—their Races and Origin -	533
„ B.—Khans of Moghulistán - - -	537
Amírs of Káshghar - - -	539
„ C.—Chaghatái Khans of Máwerannaher - -	540
„ D.—Amount of Báber's Revenues - - -	ib.
„ E.—Báber's Money of Account - - -	543

HISTORY OF INDIA.

PRELIMINARY REMARKS.

INDIAN HISTORY.—ITS THREE PERIODS.—REMARKABLE ERA WHEN THE KINGDOMS OF EUROPE AND ASIA ASSUMED A MORE REGULAR AND PERMANENT FORM.

It is the object of the following pages to present to the reader a History of the House of Taimur in India, but especially to give in some detail the history of the reigns of the first six princes of that race, from the invasion of Báber to the death of Aurengzíb, including a period of nearly two centuries.

History of India.

Its three periods.

The history of Northern India may be divided into three great periods. The *first* extends from the earliest times to the invasion of Sultan Mahmúd of Ghazni, in the beginning of the eleventh century, and may be called "The Hindú Period." The *second* reaches from that event to the invasion and conquest of Hindustan by Báber, in the beginning of the sixteenth century, a space of rather more than five hundred years, and may be denominated "The Early Muhammedan Period." It includes the conquests and ascendancy of the monarchs of Ghazni, and of various other Tartar and Afghan dynasties in India. The *third* period extends from the conquest of Báber to the present times, and exhibits to our view the sovereignty of "The House of Taimur," who have held the real or nominal power in India for the last three hundred years.

It is not intended in the present work to touch in any degree on the two first of these periods. Of the first indeed, interesting and curious as in many respects it is, very little is known, and that little but imperfectly. With the events of the second we are better acquainted, many native historians, some of them contemporary, having related with sufficient distinctness, if not the civil, at least the most important of the military occurrences of the times; and the valuable histories of Mr. Elphinstone and others have recently made the European reader acquainted with what is most worthy of notice in both of these periods. The history of much of the third period has never been written in any European language in detail; and yet a considerable acquaintance with it is perhaps necessary to such as would thoroughly understand the present state of India.

markable

It commences about thirty years after the discovery of the passage to that country by the Cape of Good Hope, at a remarkable era in the history of Man, when the governments of a great proportion of the various kingdoms both of Europe and of Asia, after numerous changes, began to settle down into that more permanent form which, on the whole, they have ever since retained, in spite of the conquests and revolutions to which many of them have been subjected.

Europe.
States
.le into a
.em.

In Europe the close of the fifteenth and beginning of the sixteenth centuries were marked by many striking events. Before that time most of the kingdoms of which it was composed, while acknowledging a king or supreme head, had been broken into a variety of independent or nearly independent states. Each country was occupied with its own internal concerns. There was no general system or balance of power among the kingdoms of Christendom, which might lead each to watch the events passing in the other as influencing itself. Each country was a separate system. Spain was divided into a number of different kingdoms acknowledging no supreme head. In France, the grand vassals or feudatories of the Crown held dominions that made them formidable to their sovereign, with whom they often waged war, and their dependence was in general little more than nominal. In England the Great Barons often controlled the King, and combated him in arms. But about the time in question, the various kingdoms in Spain, by conquest or by marriage, were united under one head; and the Moors who had long held the greater portion of the country were expelled. In France, the English having been expelled, the grand fiefs were gradually united to the Crown, and the whole of that powerful country was placed under the same head. In England, the long civil wars between the Houses of York and Lancaster had broken the power of the Great Barons; and the policy of Henry the Seventh, and of the princes of the House of Tudor, who took advantage of the depressed state of the Aristocracy, united the whole active force of the kingdom in the hands of the Crown. The spirit of war, of ambition or intrigue, that formerly (if we except the invasions of Italy by the German Emperors) had wasted itself in internal commotions in each separate kingdom, in bringing one portion of it to act against the other, in civil broils, or in private wars, now that the power of the community was consolidated in a single hand, and that each country enjoyed internal repose, took another direction, and sought for employment on a larger field and in transactions with foreign countries. Instead of a congeries of nearly independent systems scarcely acting on each other, Europe now presented one large system; and Christendom became to them all that sphere of action, which each had formerly been to itself.

This result was accelerated by the accident which, at this important crisis, placed in the hands of Charles the Fifth dominions more extensive than had for centuries been held by any one prince. The Netherlands and Dutch provinces, Austria, the entire kingdom of Spain, with its rich and extensive American possessions, Sicily, and a great portion of Italy, fell to him by hereditary descent; in addition to which he was early in life elected Emperor of Germany. The accumulation of territories so vast upon one head naturally excited the jealousy and alarm of the neighbouring Kings and States. This terror almost inevitably led to the idea, as it was the surest support, of the balance of power in Europe, which then began to be acted upon, and has influenced the conduct of its governments ever since, though sometimes with great deviations, occasioned by the blindness or the passions of its princes or people.

Great mental activity.

Various other causes excited and kept alive the mental activity for which this period was remarkable. The spirit of adventure which had led to the discovery of America, and of the route to India by the Cape of Good Hope, a spirit which in its turn was fostered by these discoveries that seemed to enlarge the powers of man, by offering new worlds for their exertion; the revival of ancient learning, in some degree hastened on by the taking of Constantinople by the Turks, an event that scattered many learned Greeks over the West, where their lessons were received with eagerness by men whose minds had already been awakened to a love of knowledge, and were prepared to receive them: the recent contemporaneous invention and active use of the Art of Printing, which secured and diffused all manner of knowledge, bringing it down to a lower class of society than it had yet reached, and gradually wresting it from the exclusive possession of monks and ecclesiastics, who for ages had been nearly its sole depositories; an invention which ere long, though it did not produce, secured the success of, the Reformation of Religion, and with that the stability and progress of all human knowledge; these and other events must make the period in question for ever memorable. From that time downwards, an understood Balance of Power existed among the States of Europe, and no considerable permanent enlargement or diminution of territory took place, till the ill-omened Partition of Poland, a flagrant act of injustice, which could have been accomplished only in a country whose political constitution was so irreclaimably bad, joined to the accident of that country lying in the outskirts of the European Commonwealth, where it was difficult for the forces of the Western Powers to act; and perhaps to the uncommon portion of sluggish and inert indifference which at that moment possessed the leading cabinets of Europe. But for about 300 years, each of the nations of the West, in spite of numerous wars and negotiations, continued to retain very nearly the same extent of dominion: an understood system of international law preserved the existence and, in some degree, the rights even of the weakest. **Permanence of its States**

Something of the same kind happened in Asia, though to a different extent. The immense conquests, first of Chengíz Khan, and next of Amír Taimur, achieved by the Tartars whom they led from the North, were gradually broken down into a variety of smaller states that carried on wars among themselves, conquering or conquered by each other. It was not till the beginning of the sixteenth century, that the fermentation and change of form of its various kingdoms subsided in the East, much in the same way as had occurred in Europe. **In Asia.** **Permanent kingdoms formed.**

The Ottoman sultans had long been extending their dominions with fearful rapidity; and, in the beginning of the sixteenth century, added Egypt and some other provinces to their empire. About this period, however, the farther progress of their arms was nearly checked, by the consolidation of the power of their neighbours, both on the side of Europe and of Asia. Shah Ismáel, the founder of the Sefvi dynasty, having subdued all the smaller potentates of Irák, Azerbáiján and Fárs, and conquered Khorásán, extended the Persian empire nearly to the limits which still bound it. The last great northern invasion was that of the Uzbek tribes, who expelled the descendants of Taimur from Transoxiana, and settled in that country, which they continue to hold to the present day. Báber, a prince, as he himself tells us, "born on the very farthest limits of the civilised world," being expelled from his hereditary dominions by this irruption and settlement, made himself master of Kábul and Kandahár, which had previously belonged to another branch of the family; and finally extended his conquests into India, which has remained, down to our own times, the real or nominal kingdom of his posterity.

These changes in Asia were nearly contemporary with those which have been mentioned as taking place in Europe; and, as the political system then introduced into Europe long suffered little alteration, the Musulman countries of the East, Turkey, Persia, Uzbekistán, and India, suffered no great change for centuries; except from the extended conquests of the Emperor of India to the south, which did not immediately affect his western neighbours; and at a later period from the conquests of Náder Shah, as transient as they were alarming. Kábul long remained attached to the Empire of India, as well as Kandahár, which last, however, was occasionally the battle-ground between the monarchs of Persia and Hindustan.

Conquest of India by the Tartars.

As the conquest of India in the sixteenth century was accomplished by Báber, himself a Tartar, by means of his Tartar chiefs and followers, and as the whole of the earlier part of his life was spent among tribes of that race, and many of the institutions of his later life affected by theirs, it is necessary, before proceeding to narrate the incidents of his reign, to offer some observations on the original condition and subsequent fortunes of these sons of the desert; and especially to give a short sketch of the previous history of the two great tribes of Moghuls and Uzbeks, who chiefly influenced his fortunes in peace and in war, that the reader may be the better able to understand the transactions of Báber himself, and his immediate successors, as well as to comprehend the peculiar spirit and principles of their government.

INTRODUCTION.

CONTAINING A GENERAL ACCOUNT OF THE TARTARS, ESPECIALLY OF THE JÚJI AND CHAGHATÁI DYNASTIES; AND OF THE STATE OF TRANSOXIANA AT THE ACCESSION OF BÁBER.

SECTION FIRST.

GENERAL ACCOUNT OF THE TARTAR TRIBES—THREE GRAND DIVISIONS, MANCHÚS, MONGOLS OR MOGHULS, AND TÚRKS.—CONQUESTS OF CHENGÍZ KHAN AND THE MOGHULS.—OF THE TÚRKI TRIBES AND TAIMUR.—DIFFERENCE RESULTING FROM THE MODE OF SETTLEMENT OF THE TARTARS IN TRIBES OR AS INDIVIDUALS.

SECT. I.

Tartar Tribes.

THE countries in the south of Asia as well as of Europe have, from the remotest ages, been subject to invasions from the north, the migratory inhabitants of which, pouring forward their hordes or tribes from their native wilds, have in some instances laid waste many of the most extensive of these more genial and favoured regions, and then disappeared; and in others have conquered and permanently settled in them. These invaders, in ancient times, were chiefly the Gauls, Germans, and Scythians; but, in later ages, in Asia, the Tartar tribes alone.

Under the general denomination of Tartar, a name known only since the twelfth century, European writers have comprehended the whole of those extensive tribes which range in the wide expanse of country stretching north of the Himalaya mountains, the Oxus, the Caspian, and the Black Sea, as far as the Northern Ocean, however much they may differ from each other in language or origin. Memorials remain of the incursions and conquests of these nations towards the south in very early ages: but their grand overflowings and permanent ascendancy in modern times occurred immediately before and after the tenth century, when large bodies of them traversed and settled in the dominions of the Khalifs; in the beginning of the thirteenth under Chengíz Khan, and in the end of the fourteenth under Amír Taimur, better known in the west as the great Tamerlane.

This name of Tartar, or more properly Tatar, which we apply to these numerous migratory tribes, is unknown to themselves as a general appellation, and never properly belonged even to any considerable proportion of them. It seems originally to have been the name of one division of a tribe of the race which we now, whether properly or not, distinguish as Mongols or Moghuls, and by one of those mistakes so common to foreigners, to have been erroneously applied to nearly the whole inhabitants of the north of Asia.

Grand races.

The tribes which we include under the name of Tartar consist chiefly of three great divisions or races, all differing from each other in manners, institutions, and language. 1. The Tunguses and Manchús in the east of Asia, north of China. 2. The Mongols, or, as they are called by the Persians, and Indians, the Moghuls, who occupy chiefly the middle portion north of Tibet, nearly as far west as Terfán, and part of the desert between that and the Yaik; and 3. The Túrks, who for many centuries have possessed the large regions that extend on the west of the Mongols from the desert of Kobi; having for their southern boundary the mountains of Káshghar and Pámer, Khorásán, the Caspian and Black Sea; the Don and Wolga on the west, and Siberia on the north. But some few tribes, both of Mongols and of Túrks, are to be found in the limits thus marked out as peculiarly belonging to their respective

SECT. I.

ranges. The Túrks are the most extensive and numerous of the three races.*

Each of these grand divisions is broken down into a great number of smaller tribes, generally nearly independent of each other, every one managing its own concerns; and it is not to be forgotten that though, for the sake of convenience, we designate the two former races as Tungus or Manchú, and Mongol, these general names are not used by the tribes themselves for that purpose, but each distinct tribe has its separate appellation. All who speak the Túrki language, whatever be their tribe, seem, however, to acknowledge themselves as being Túrks.

Their manners.

These Tartar tribes, as for the convenience of possessing a general name we may continue to call the whole of them, are all pastoral, and have each their own range, within which they move from place to place with their families, flocks, and dwellings, as the heat or cold of the season, the scarcity or abundance of pasture induce them. They live in tents or in movable huts, often carried in waggons, which their cattle draw from place to place, according to the movements of the tribe.† Their wealth consists in their flocks of cattle, sheep, and horses. Milk is their chief food, and the flesh of their flocks; but they kill their cattle sparingly and unwillingly. They are little addicted to cultivate the ground, and rather despise such of their neighbours as settle to breathe the polluted air of one spot, and to live on the top of a weed, as in contempt they de-

* The Túrki race occupies an important place in history. Europeans in general are chiefly acquainted with the Turks of Constantinople or Turkey, who are only one branch of the great tree. To distinguish the grand general race from the more limited one of the Ottomans, the former, in the following pages, are spoken of as Túrks and Túrki, with the ú accented. The usual unaccented form of the words (Turk and Turkish) is employed to mark the Ottomans or Osmanlis. For some further remarks on the Tartar tribes, see Appendix A.

† . . . . . Campestres Scythæ
Quorum plaustra vagas rite trahunt domos. — HOR.

SECT. I.

nominate corn. The care of the children, the preparation of food and clothing, and, in general, all domestic employments, belong to the women. The men delight in the chase, whenever the means of following it are presented. Living much in the open air, on horseback, exposed to fatigue and accustomed to long marches, and in older times often exposed to the dangers of war, and habitually on the watch against surprise, their mode of life made them hardy and bold, and gave them the habits of soldiers. Their government, though not uniform, is generally patriarchal; the whole tribe is regarded as descended from the same stock, and they willingly obey the head of a particular family as their hereditary ruler. But there is considerable variety in the internal government of different tribes arising from ancient usages, or the character of individual chiefs. Some are despotic, but in general the chief advises with the elders or heads of the leading families as a council; though on some solemn or important occasions it is usual to convene the whole tribe. Private disputes are settled by the Ak-sakáls (or Grey-beards, as they are called) * men of a certain age and authority, according to ancient usage.

Manchús.

Of these three races, the most eastern, the Manchús, about two hundred years ago conquered China, which they still continue to govern, as other tribes of the same Tungus family had already done in earlier times. But the race does not seem to be at all known to the historians of Persia or India, and has had no direct influence on the fortune of these countries.

Mongols.

The second race, the Mongols or Moghuls, chiefly occupy the country that lies between the other two, and have acted a very important part, though for a short period of time, in the history of Asia. For many ages the different Tartar races or tribes in the north had

* The Túrks and Afgháns call the leading men who form a sort of councillors in the tribe, *Ak-sakáls*, white (or grey) beards.

SECT. I.

Chengíz Khan. His conquests.

carried on war with each other, unknown to or unregarded by the conterminous nations, or known to their Chinese and Túrki neighbours alone, when Chengíz Khan, the chief of a small and till then unimportant tribe properly called Mongol, after a long series of struggles, such as in other instances have roused the genius and matured the talents of men destined to be conquerors, having by gallant exertions recovered the station of chief of his tribe, of which, in his youthful years he had been deprived, gradually subdued the tribes around, and subsequently extended his dominions in the Tartar waste, beyond the limits of his own race and language. Having subdued Pekin and the northern half of China, he led his Mongol hordes against the Oighurs and other Túrki tribes lying between Transoxiana and his own original country, most of whom, after severe conflicts, he compelled to acknowledge his sway. But his empire, great and mighty as it then was, would not have attracted much notice in Europe, had he not, crossing the Jaxartes, followed his Túrki enemies into the highly cultivated and, for that age of the world, civilised and refined country of Transoxiana or Mawerannaher, in which they had taken shelter among their brethren of the same race, who had long possessed the chief influence, and, since the decline of the empire of the Khalifs, held the reins of government in that extensive region. After besieging and sacking,
A.D. 1206–1227. with relentless cruelty, the numerous rich and populous cities with which the country of Transoxiana then abounded, he crossed the Oxus and poured the destructive inundation of his barbarians over Khwárazm, Bálkh, and Khorásán, ravaging on the one hand a large portion of Persia and Armenia, and on the other spreading desolation through Kandáhár and Ghazni as far as the Indus, over countries which for upwards of two centuries had been governed by rulers of Túrki extraction. Not content with this, he added the wide plains of the

SECT. I.

Khozars and Kumans beyond the Caspian to his own overgrown dominions.

Those of his descendants.

On his death, his mighty empire still went on extending its limits, under his immediate descendants, who not only continued the invasion of Southern China, but mounting the Wolga and passing the Don and the Nieper, conquered the Bulgarians, Russians, and Poles, and overran Hungary, Bosnia, Dalmatia, Silesia, and Moravia, threatening Vienna itself, and spreading consternation over all the kingdoms of Christendom.

Excessive cruelty.

The conquests of Chengíz Khan, and his immediate Moghul successors, were conducted with an exterminating cruelty and a cold contempt of human life and suffering of which history affords perhaps no other example. The Moghuls employed in their armies, and used as instruments of their conquests, the Túrki and other tribes of the desert whom they had subdued. But as they advanced farther from home, and left their deserts behind, the course of their march through more populous regions was marked by the burning of cities, the devastation and ruin of the country and the slaughter of all the inhabitants whom they did not carry off to sell as slaves. Their uniform plan was to convert the fields into a desert, and to leave behind them no human being that could rise on their rear, that could offer a moment's annoyance, or occasion the slightest risk to the invaders. By the barbarity of their massacres, in which age, and sex, and condition were alike disregarded, they spread horror and dismay around them on every side, and to remote regions. This habit of slaughter seems to have generated an unnatural and almost sportive thirst for blood, many harrowing instances of which are related by contemporary writers: and even in later times it would appear that no tribe has made less progress in humanity and civilisation than the Mongols.*

* The name of the horrible ogres of fable and romance was taken from the Oighurs, a tribe who were employed in the van of the armies that overran the east of Europe. The reckless cruelty and cannabalism of

SECT. I.

Their conquests in Europe they soon abandoned, Russia excepted, which they continued to hold for about a hundred and fifty years. Towards the end of the thirteenth century, their empire, which at one time stretched from the Sea of Korea to the Adriatic, began to fall into a number of separate kingdoms, and towards the close of the following century, disappeared altogether in the south of Asia, before the victorious arms of Amír Taimur.

Dissolution of the empire.

A.D. 1298.

A.D. 1400.

The dominion of the Mogols lasted therefore little more than seventy years as one great empire, and for about a hundred more in smaller independent kingdoms. But such was the influence of the power and name of Chengíz Khan, that, in spite of the comparatively short period of the Moghul ascendancy, the Musulman monarchs of Asia have ever since been eager to trace their families up to him as the grand source of sovereign authority; and though the number of Moghuls who since the decline of his family have sought their fortune in India is insignificant, compared with the Túrks and Persians, the term Moghul is still used in that country as a general appellation for all adventurers from the North; and has even given its name to the Moghul Empire, as it is called, though that empire was really founded by the Chaghatái Túrks, a perfectly different race. But so completely has the power of the Moghuls as a people, disappeared in the south of Asia, that perhaps the only direct remnant of the invasion of Chengíz Khan now to be found south of the Jaxartes is in the hills between Herát and Kábul, where some portion of the Hazáras or of the Aimáks seem to be the descendants

these imaginary beings were supposed, by the terror-stricken hearers of these tales, to present a faithful picture of the manners of the infidel Tartar invaders. D'Ohsson's learned Histoire des Mongols, tome i. (Paris, 1824), contains a lively account of the enormities of the Moghul invasion. But the Oighurs, though in the Moghul army, were of a Túrki family.

of a Moghul tribe settled in these highlands from the time of the great conqueror.

SECT. I.

The Túrks, their extensive range

The third and most numerous class of Tartars are the Túrks, whose ancient and peculiar territory has been already described as extending from the Desert of Kobi to the Wolga, and from the Oxus and the Caspian far into Siberia. This ancient extent of territory, partially broken by the intervention of some Moghul tribes, was much enlarged by conquests in different ages. Thus, in the west, they passed the Wolga and occupied not only the territory that afterwards became the extensive kingdoms of Astrakhan and Kásán, but the greater part of the northern shores of the Caspian and Black Seas, as far as Moldavia; and, on the south, the desert tracts which cross Khorásán and Persia, extending from Khwárazm to Kirmán, are possessed by the Iliáts or tribes of migratory Túrks, as indeed they have been from very early times.

and influence

Those desert and pastoral countries which they possess as sole occupants for the range of their herds and flocks are indeed extensive; but the most remarkable events of this history, and the most conspicuous display of the singular energy of the national character, occurred beyond the limits of the desert. The Túrks have in different ages extended their influence into the more cultivated regions of the East, sometimes acting individually unaided except by the inherent powers of their mind, sometimes acting in bands by direct force. Several of their smaller tribes, which found their way to the south, were at an early period entertained in the service of the Arabian Khalifs of Bagdad; and many private adventurers, generally little bands of their devoted followers, sought wealth and distinction by taking service in the armies of different Asiatic princes. Numbers of their hardy race were even purchased as slaves by these monarchs, and embodied as their life guards, or educated in their palaces as their

under the Khalifs.

SECT. I.

most trusty and confidential servants. These, in the course of time, rose to be their chief ministers, the generals of their armies, and governors of their provinces; and in the decline of the Khalifate, the principal revolutions effected in the empire, whether in the palace or the field, were conducted by them. In a similar manner, the kingdom of Ghazni came into the possession of Sebaktegín, a Túrki slave, whose son, Sultan Mahmúd not only extended his empire to the Oxus and Caspian, but carried his victorious arms many times into the centre of India. Towards the beginning of the eleventh century the celebrated Seljúki Túrks, leaving Transoxiana with their flocks, and being joined in their progress by kindred tribes from Khorásán, advanced westward, traversing the dominions not only of the Khalif of Baghdad but of the Greek Emperor of Constantinople. They gradually made the degraded khalifs mere puppets in their hands, and settled as conquerors both in Persia and in the western provinces of Asia Minor. From that tendency to division, however, so natural to the chiefs of independent tribes, they soon broke down into a number of smaller states and principalities; and the fragments into which they split, the Seljúki dynasties of Irán, Kermán, Damascus, Aleppo, and Iconium, as well as the Atábeks of Irák, Azerbáiján, Fárs, and Láristán, make a conspicuous figure in the history of these ages.

A.H. 390, A.D. 1000. In Ghazni, A.H. 429 A.D. 1038. The Seljúks in Persia,

The Túrki ascendancy was for a time interrupted by the Moghul invasion of Chengíz Khan and his descendants, which overturned the Seljúki and other Túrki Governments, and in the end, the Khalifate of Baghdad itself. But, the torrent soon passed over, and, on the ruins of Seljúki principality of Iconium, Othman, a Túrki Emír, founded a new state which in process of time, spreading on every side, grew into the Ottoman empire; and which, by the extent of its dominions and its success in war, in spite of the early shock that it received

A.H. 656, A.D. 1258. Osmanlis, A.H. 699, A.D. 1300.

SECT. I.

from the arms of Taimur, has overshadowed the fame of all the other Túrki monarchies, and carried the victorious crescent over a great portion not only of Asia and Africa, but of Europe itself.

Conquests of Taimur.

The conquests of Mír Taimur, in the end of the fourteenth and beginning of the fifteenth centuries, may be regarded as having re-established the direct Túrki government all over the countries south of the Jaxartes, the Caspian and the Black Sea;—Máwerannaher, Khwárazm, Khorásán, Persia, Syria and a great part of Asia Minor, besides the Afghán country, and India as far as Delhi, having submitted to his yoke. Since his time there has been no great Túrki invasion from the north, that excepted already alluded to, by which, in the age of Báber, the Túrki tribe of Uzbeks took possession of Máwerannaher and Bálkh; and that by which Báber himself transferred the government of India from the Afghans to the Túrks.

of the Uzbeks, A.H. 908, A.D. 1502.

of Báber, A.H. 932, A.D. 1525.

The subjection of various kingdoms of Hindustán, and, at a later period, of the Dekhan, to Túrki adventurers, may be added to the triumphs of the race.

Túrki Mamelukes in Egypt,

But the influence of the Tartar invasions was not confined to Asia and its governments. The intrepid and enterprising spirit of the Túrks was conspicuous wherever a certain number of individuals of their extraction was accidentally found. In Africa, numbers of Túrki prisoners taken by the followers of Chengíz, during the wars of that conqueror, having been purchased by the Sultans of Egypt, were embodied under the name of Mamelukes, or slaves, and trained as the body-guards of the prince. They, like all other Prætorian bands, soon discovered that by possessing the sword they possessed the government; and led on, in the ordinary course of ambition, they in the end deposed the ancient dynasty, raised one of their own number to the sovereign power, and for upwards of a hundred and thirty years continued to sway the sceptre of Egypt.

A.H. 648–784, A.D. 1250–1382.

SECT. I. During all that time they recruited their numbers by new purchases of slaves from the north. The throne continued elective among themselves, under the single restriction that the person who filled it should be of Túrkistán. The Túrki were succeeded by the Circassian Mamelukes, who pursued a similar system, till they were subdued by the Ottoman Turks. But the system of a Mameluke government soon revived, and was only brought to a close in our times by the atrocious perfidy of the relentless Muhammed Ali Pasha.

Circassian Mamelukes, A.H. 923, A.D. 1517.

Thus it appears that few races of men, at any period of the world, have acted a more distinguished part than the Túrki, who, in one form or another, for centuries ruled a great portion of the old world; and who, even at the present day, influence, directly or indirectly, the government, manners, and civilisation of mankind, from the Straits of Gibraltar to the deserts on the Yeneseí, and from the limits of Hungary and Poland to the farthest bounds of the empire of Hindustán.

These conquests, especially those of Chengíz Khan and of Taimur, produced several important changes both among the Tartar tribes themselves, and in the countries which they conquered.

Religion of Moghuls,

Before the age of Chengíz, the Mongol tribes had adopted from Tibet and India the religious tenets and observances of the Shamans, according to the sect of Buddhism prevalent in these countries; while the Túrki tribes, several of which inhabited on the borders of the Arab conquests in Transoxiana, and others were surrounded by Muhammedans or established in Muhammedan countries, had in general adopted the Musulman faith. Chengíz Khan and his first successors, who adhered to the old religion of their tribe, were therefore considered by their Muhammedan subjects as infidel Pagans. But they too, after being settled for a generation or two in Musulman countries, adopted the prevailing faith; whereas the Moghul tribes in their own

and Túrks.

country, down to the present day, in general retain their ancient religion. SECT. I.

Chengíz's plan of government.

When Chengíz deputed his sons or generals to govern any of the conquered countries,—and in this policy he was imitated by his successors,—he sent along with them an úlús or túmán, or some Moghul tribe or division of a tribe, to overawe the conquered. This policy was pursued as to the Túrki population as well as every other. The Moghul tribe so employed received an allotment of country, and placed themselves with their families and flocks in the pasture range of the tribes among whom they were sent. Though the Moghuls and Túrks differ in religion and language, yet by the inevitable intercourse that takes place between persons living under the same government, near to and in habits of intercourse with each other, by intermarriages, by traffic and in other ways, a considerable mixture of the two races took place, which showed itself both in their language, and in their features and bodily appearance. This was more particularly the case as to several of the Túrki tribes. The Moghuls, never having been conquered by the Túrks, have in general remained more unmixed; and in the intermarriages that have taken place between the two races, their features, which are the more marked, seem to have predominated over those of the Túrks. The intermixture of blood was, from civil and political causes, most frequent among the chiefs and leading men of the tribes.

Tartars settle

The condition of the Tartars who emigrated to the south was much affected by the accidental mode of their settlement; whether, for example, it was made by them as individuals or in tribes; whether they settled in the country or in cities. Thus their situation in Transoxiana and in Persia was considerably different from what it was in India.

in tribes,

Wherever circumstances have allowed, the Túrks have preserved their attachment to their original tribes and language, their fondness for a life of freedom, and their preference of the pastoral to the agricultural state. In regions not far removed from their original seats, and where there were deserts over which they could roam, as in Transoxiana, Khorásán, and Persia, they moved forward in tribes and in a body occupied the wastes and wilds that intersect these countries. In this way the Túrki tribes have become the possessors of nearly the whole of the deserts or pastoral plains of Tùrkistán, Máwerannaher, and Khwárazm, as well as of Khorásán and Persia, which they enjoy to this day; together with no small portion of Asia Minor, where the Turkoman tribes range from Syria as far as Smyrna and Nice. Hence too the language of the desert is different from that of the cultivated country. In Transoxiana, Persia, and Khorásán, the Persian, apparently the old language of these countries, continues to be that of the cities, of the villages, and of the cultivators of the ground, as well as of trade and commerce. But as the Túrks are the rulers in all these provinces, as the throne for some centuries has been filled and supported by Túrki families, as they with the mixture of a few Kurdish and Arab families are masters of the wilds, the Túrki, even in Persia, is the language not only of the desert, but of the court. In such circumstances the division into Túrks and Tájiks, — the latter the ancient agricultural and commercial population, the former the nomadic, the military and dominant race, — is in full force; and hence, throughout the Ottoman or Turkish dominions in Europe, Asia, and Africa, the Turkish, a dialect of the Túrki, is uniformly the language of the rulers; even when it happens not to be the language of the people, as in the greater proportion of the empire it is not.

or as individuals.

In India the influence of the Tartars was somewhat different. From early times the Tartars had been accustomed to resort to that country not in tribes but individually, as adventurers in search of fortune; and many of these adventurers of Túrki race, both in Hindustán and in the Dekhan, have risen to the greatest military and political eminence, and have even been elevated to the throne by their personal talents and energy of character. Some of them have transmitted their dominions to their posterity, and history accordingly presents us with various Túrki dynasties in these countries. The Túrks, however, never affected to monopolise all the authority of the kingdoms which they thus obtained. The natives of India, and adventurers of other tribes and countries, shared in the administration of the government and in military commands. The invasion of Taimur, who indeed entered India with immense military hordes, was only a sudden inundation that laid every thing prostrate before it, but soon passed away. Under his descendant Báber, on the contrary, the Túrks did not present themselves in tribes, but as parts of a regular army, or by individual emigration. They were mixed, in the army and in the court, with Moghuls and Persians. They found a country already populous, and its territories fully occupied by civilised inhabitants, as well as by a race of conquerors of their own religion. They had none of the exterminating ferocity of Chengíz, and were not so insane as to have a wish to expel the cultivators from lands, the value of which was owing solely to their labour, and which they themselves had no desire to occupy. The chiefs were rewarded with jágírs or landed estates, that is, with the government share of the produce; the inferior followers who were not provided for in the jágír of their chief, though they always showed a preference to a military life, gradually entered into the various branches of the public service. They willingly entered into the service of men of rank, rarely became merchants, hardly ever artizans or tradesmen, and were averse to agricultural pursuits. They claimed a superiority individually in

SECT. I. public and private estimation as belonging to the dominant class, but they did not herd together as a separate horde. The different races met and mixed in affairs of government, on their private business, in commerce and trade. But the foreign Musulman never entirely coalesced with the native Hindú. Religion continued always to keep them widely apart in their domestic intercourse, in their amusements, their customs and their habits of thinking. They were two different elements, possessed of repulsive qualities, which, however closely pressed together, never amalgamated. The language both of the country and the towns remained unchanged. During the two first reigns of the new dynasty, the Túrki continued to be the language of the emperor and his Túrki grandees; but the Persian by degrees became that of the court; at the same time that a different language, the Urdú Bhasha, the language of the horde or royal camp, composed in its elements of the language of Upper Hindustán, and of some other native Indian dialects, with a large infusion of Persian, became, even more than it had hitherto been, the medium of intercourse of the many separate nations and tribes which constituted the imperial army. Nor was it confined to the camp, but gradually came to be understood by the servants in the different departments of government, and by most of the chief village-officers in the whole extent of the many-tongued empire.*

* The period of the origin of the Hindustáni language is uncertain. It would seem to have begun under the earlier Túrki and Afghán dynasties, from the same causes that made it spread under the dynasty of Báber.

SECTION SECOND.

CHENGÍZ KHAN DIVIDES HIS EMPIRE AMONG HIS SONS. — THEIR TERRITORIES. — I. JÚJI KHAN GETS THE DESHT-KIPCHÁK. — CONQUESTS OF HIS DESCENDANTS. — DECLINE AND DIVISION OF THEIR KINGDOM. — RISE OF THE UZBEKS, AND OF THE KAIZÁKS.

SECT. II.

SUCH is a very general sketch of some of the grand leading distinctions of race among the wandering tribes of the north of Asia, of their original position in their deserts, and of the influence exercised on their character by the mode in which they afterwards settled in foreign countries. It still remains to give some idea of the early history and political divisions of the Uzbeks and Western Moghuls at the period of Báber's entrance into public life.

Chengíz Khan

Chengíz Khan, as we have seen, was a Moghul. In the history of his progenitors we meet with that infusion of fable and miracle which in ignorant times is deemed necessary to add dignity to the genealogies of illustrious men. Alankáwa, a virgin of the family of the chief of the Moghuls, by some undefinable intercourse with a celestial being, had three sons at a birth, from one of whom Chengíz Khan, the great hero of the race, was descended in the ninth degree, and Mír Taimur or Tamerlane, from another in the fourteenth.*

* Miles's Shajrat, pp. 46—48.; Abulghazi, Histoire Geneal. des Tatars, P. II. c. 15. The story is related with some variety of circumstances by all the Musulman historians. Abulghazi makes the lady not a virgin but a widow. The visitant is by some represented as a refulgent stream of sun-beams; by others as a man of an orange colour, with eyes of singular beauty. The date of the event, A. H. 111, (A. D. 729) is given in the Shajrat; but nine descents are too few to fill up the space from that date till Chengíz's birth.

SECT. II.

Chengíz Khan, at his death, left an empire that stretched from the Euxine to the Yellow Sea, and from the deserts of Mekrán to the farthest wastes of Siberia.

Divides his empire.

This mighty empire he, in his lifetime, had divided among his four sons. To the eldest, Júji*, he assigned the Desht, or Plains of Kipchák; but that prince dying some months before his father, the allotment was made over to his son Bátu. The territory of this prince comprised the country lying north of the lower course of the Sirr or Jaxartes, the Sea of Aral and the Caspian, including the rich countries on the Don and Wolga and part of those on the Black Sea. To the second son, Chaghátái Khan†, were assigned the wide extent of desert and pasture land between the Desht-Kipchák on the west, and the original residence of the Moghul tribes on the east, between the Tibet mountains, the Indus, and Mekrán on the south, and Siberia on the north: comprehending, besides the wide range of the northern desert, the countries of Káshghar, Khoten, and the Oighurs, as far as the desert of Kobi, Ferghana, and Tashkend on the Jaxartes, the whole of Transoxiana, with Badakhshán, Bálkh, Khwárazm, Khorásán, Ghazni, Kábul, and the other conquests of Chengíz in that quarter. To Oktái or Ogatái Khan, a third son, he allotted the original Moghul country, with the tribes immediately around it; and to a fourth, Túli, the possession of Khita or China.

To each of these four princes a force was assigned, to enable him to rule the dominions over which he was placed. This force consisted of some Ulus, or migratory hordes of Moghuls or other Tartars, which might be regarded as the standing armies of the different khans. Our concern is solely with the territories and successors of the two first, Júji and Chaghatái.

All the Moghul princes, in the first instance, ac-

* Called also, Chuchi, Zuzi, and Tushi.

† Or, Jaghatái.

SECT. II.

knowledged Oktái as the head of the empire; and, after his death, his place was supplied by election, the Grand Khan continuing to reside in the original Moghul country at Karakorum. In the course of some reigns, however, the dependence of the other princes on the Grand Khan became less and less, and finally ceased entirely. At what precise time this occurred in the case of the Júji and Chaghatái Khans, is not very clear. In Persia, Arghún Khan about A.H. 690 (A.D. 1291) joined his own name on the public coin with that of the Grand Khan; and Kázán Khan A.H. 703 (A.D. 1304) left out the name of the Grand Khan altogether. The change probably took place in the Júji and Chaghatái dominions about the same time; and the khans of these countries seem, thenceforward, to have been regarded as Khákáns or Grand Khans, each in his own territory.

The order of succession to the Khans was not strictly uniform. It was partly hereditary, partly elective. The Khan was always taken from the family of Chengíz; but on his death, if he happened to have a son of some talent who had assisted him in the government, the son was generally allowed to succeed; otherwise, the most distinguished of the brothers of the late Khan, or his uncle, or the relation who happened to have most influence in the tribe, was called to the government. Minors did not succeed at the time of their father's death; but the election was open to them at a future period, when they were of age.*

I. *Of Júji Khan, and the Desht-Kipchák.*

Júji gets the Desht-Kipchák, A.H. 624, A.D. 1227.

The portion of Júji Khan, the eldest of the sons of Chengíz, on his premature death, was transferred to his son Bátu. It was much enlarged by that prince in

* Miles's Shajrat-ul-Atrák, pp. 22—28.; Abulghazi Khan, Hist. Geneal. P. I. c. 2. &c.

SECT. II.

his celebrated expedition into the west, in which he took Moscow, reduced Russia and Poland to subjection, and extended his ravages into Silesia, Hungary, Bosnia, and Dalmatia, as far as the Adriatic. The operations of the Moghuls in their wide-extended invasions were conducted with their accustomed cruelty and barbarous contempt of human life and suffering. They exterminated, as far as they could, the inhabitants of the country which they overran, and spread consternation and dismay over the remotest parts of Christendom.* Bátu, on his return from this expedition, in which his brother Sheibáni had distinguished himself in a remarkable manner, made him a grant of some of the extensive provinces conquered from the Russians and other Christians, with a sufficient number of the Kuris, Naiman, Karlik, and Oighur tribes to keep them in subjection; and Orda-Itzen, another brother, made him a present of fifteen thousand Tartar families for the same purpose: but the brothers stipulated with Sheibáni, that he himself should take up his range between the territories of Bátu and Orda-Itzen, passing the summer near the Ural mountains and the Yáik river †, and the winter in the more southern countries on the Sirr and Sára-sú. In addition to this, Mangu-Taimur Khan, the brother and successor of Bátu, bestowed on Behåder, Sheibáni's son, the Ak-Orda, or White horde, probably a tribe of Moghuls. Hitherto the descendants of Chengíz Khan had been Pagans, but one of Bátu's successors, Uzbek Khan, having been himself converted to the Islam, introduced the Mahommedan religion among the tribes of Kipchák, which he ruled, and was so much beloved by the portion of his subjects who followed him in adopting the Musulman religion, that they assumed his name, and from him called themselves Uzbeks. He appears to have died about A.H. 751.

His successors.

Uzbek Khan, A.H. 720, A.D. 1320.

A.H. 751, A.D. 1350.

* See D'Ohsson, Histoire des Mongols, tome i. Paris, 1824.

† Or, Jaik.

SECT. II.

Civil Wars, and invasion of Taimur.

On the death of Uzbek Khan, a series of civil wars followed in the empire of Kipchák, ending in a general anarchy, during which several chiefs assumed independence. These disorders continued down to the time of Mír Taimur, who, when he had risen to power in Transoxiana, found two rivals, Urus Khan and Toktamish Khan, both descended of Júji, contending for the dignity of Great Khan of the Kipchák. Toktamish being worsted, sought the assistance of Taimur, who, after long wars, seated him on the throne of Seráichak on the Wolga. But a quarrel soon ensued between the allies; and Taimur, raising up Taimur-Kutluk, a third candidate for the Khanship, entered and overran the country of Toktamish, destroyed his towns and broke his power. But Taimur-Kutluk, like Toktamish, found it necessary, in his turn, to withdraw from the alliance of Mír Taimur, whom he probably found disposed to act rather as a master than an auxiliary. Mír Taimur, upon this, transferred his support to Kaúrchik, the son of that Urus whom he had humbled to place Toktamish on his throne. To aid his new ally, he placed in his service a powerful body of Uzbeks. There were, therefore, at this time, in the distracted country of Kipchák, besides inferior chiefs claiming independence, three Grand Khans, Toktamish, Taimur Kutluk, and Kaúrchik, all descended of Júji; and all of whom had successively been supported and opposed by Taimur. That great conqueror's policy was to rule by sowing discord among the tribes.

A.H. 777, A.D. 1375.

A.H. 797, A.D. 1395.

Rise of separate Khanships,

A.H. 808, A.D. 1406.

The family of Júji never recovered the shock which it then received from civil war and foreign invasion. Though a Grand Khan continued for some time after to be acknowledged, his power no longer prevailed over the whole wide extent of the Desht-Kipchák. Many of the heads of the remoter tribes disclaimed all superior authority, and acted for themselves. Three separate Khanships were gradually formed in the west, those of

SECT. II. Astrakhan, Kásán, and the Krim: while in the east, Kipchák became divided between the Khan of Tura and the Uzbeks. For a time, some one of the Khans descended of Júji continued to exercise authority over the Russians, and other races as far as Poland and Lithuania; issued his firmans as sovereign; and, when any quarrel arose, carried his mandates into execution with a high hand. Yet the Khan gradually ceased to be the same important personage that he had been. The arms of the Russians even began to encroach on his dominions, now broken into separate principalities, and province after province was swallowed up by their rising power.

The Uzbeks, A.H. 750, A.D. 1349. Our concern, in the following pages, is solely with the eastern division, that of the Uzbeks, whose range extended from the Yáik to the Sirr. In spite of their name of Uzbeks, their chiefs, though of the race of Júji, were not descended from Uzbek Khan, under whose khanship the tribe had been originally converted to the Musulman faith, but whose posterity had become extinct. It is said that such of the tribes of Uzbek Khan's extensive empire as had joined the Khan in the new opinions, withdrew to the countries between the Yáik and the Sirr. The Túrki tribes, who dwelt in Turkistán, led by their common origin and common faith, gladly united with them. Such tribes only as became Muhammedans took the name of Uzbeks. They did not amalgamate into one tribe, but continued in their many separate tribes as formerly.*

* Before the Khanship of Kipchák was broken into so many parts, and especially before the invasion of Taimur, a good deal of trade seems to have passed through the country. Arabshah complains that whereas formerly caravans used to travel in perfect safety from Khwárazm to the Krim, a three months' journey, and were hospitably entertained all along their route, none, in his time, ventured to make such a journey. (Manger, Arabshah, vol. i. p. 373.) He mentions that the Turki language was spoken with great elegance in Kipchák. It is obvious that the parcelling of a country among a number of independent sovereigns or tribes, must be unfavourable to the safe or easy progress of caravans or travellers.

SECT. II.

Abulkhair Khan.

About a century after the formation of this Uzbek confederacy, the sceptre of the tribes descended to Abulkhair Khan, an able and ambitious prince. In the course of his reign he made himself formidable to all his neighbours. He united many new tribes to his government, and, by the vigour of his character, ruled in the Desht-Kipchák with more absolute authority, and over a larger extent of territory, than any Khan had done for some generations. Not content with this, he engaged in the factions of Samarkand during the wars that followed the death of Ulugh Beg Mirza, and may be said to have placed Sultan Abusaid Mirza, then a young man and a fugitive, on the throne of Máwerannaher. Abulkhair, when he retired back into his deserts, loaded with booty, carried with him a daughter of Ulugh Beg Mirza, whom he married.

A.H. 855, A.D. 1451.

Secession of the Kaizák-Uzbeks.

The despotic superiority of Abulkhair was so sensibly felt by many chieftains of Kipchák, that several of them, especially some Sultans of the race of Júji who governed important tribes, knowing that they were objects of his suspicion, and believing that even their lives were in danger, moved away with their tribes from their ancient pastoral range, abandoned the Uzbek country, and seceded from his government. Among these were Gerái Khan, Jani Beg Khan and others, who fled towards Moghulistán.* This secession occurred while the khanship of the Moghuls was held by Isan-bugha Khan, Yúnis Khan's brother. Isan-bugha received the fugitives honourably, and assigned them a district on his western frontier. There, under his protection, they fed their flocks, free and unmolested, for several years.†

* The Uzbek Kaizáks are carefully to be distinguished from the Don Cossacks and other Russian Cossacks, who, whatever they may originally have been, have latterly become a very mixed race.

† The land allotted to these chiefs was Báshi near Jud-Kozi, which lies on the western limit of Moghulistán. Tar. Reshídi, f. 57. Our knowledge of the geography of the desert is so imperfect, that it is difficult to assign a precise situation to almost any of the places mentioned in the annals of Moghulistán.

SECT. II.

Fall of Abulkhair, A.H. 870, A.D. 1465-66.

Abulkhair had reigned many years as a victorious and fortunate prince, when a combination was formed, among the heads of the leading tribes in Kipchák, to humble his ambition and to set limits to his overgrown power.* He met the confederates in the field with his usual bravery; but being deserted by fortune, was defeated and slain with several of his sons. His defeat was followed by a separation of the tribes that had formed the Ulús of the Uzbeks. Many tribes resumed their independence, others formed new connections. A body of Uzbeks, to the number of twenty thousand men, migrating with their herds and flocks, joined Gerái Khan and Jani Beg, whose new confederacy soon acquired increase of strength, and speedily came to be formidable under the name of Kaizák-Uzbeks. A considerable body of Abulkhair's immediate retainers remained faithful to the family, and acknowledged Bárúj Ughlán, his eldest surviving son †, as their Khan. Burga Sultan, the cousin of Abulkhair, and head of a younger and separate branch of the family, though he had been employed with distinction and in offices of high trust by Abulkhair, availing himself of the general confusion that followed his death, took possession of a portion of territory which had belonged to the Khan; an act of

* Abulghazi, P. VIII. c. iv. The power of Abulkhair seems to have received a severe shock before this from an irruption of Uz-Taimur, the Taishí of the Kalimáks, who broke into his dominions at the head of a hundred thousand men. Abulkhair having refused to submit to the terms of peace that were offered, a battle ensued, in which the Khan was defeated, several of his principal chiefs slain, and himself forced to take refuge in his castle of Saghák. Being finally compelled to agree to the conditions proposed by the Táishi, the Kalimák inundation again flowed back from his country, but in its return wasted the rich provinces of Turkistán, Shahrokhía, and Tashkend. The Kalimáks, or Kalmuks, call their chief, Táishi; and from the terms Khan-Táishi are formed the word Contaish, by which he is generally known.

† Shah Bedágh, or Borák, the father of Sheibáni, is usually spoken of as the eldest son of Abulkhair. Abulghazi here calls Bárúj the eldest son. I have added the qualification "surviving," which was probably what Abulghazi meant.

ingratitude that was not forgotten by the grandson of Abulkhair.

SECT. II.

Rise of the Kaizáks.

The Kaizák-Uzbeks under Gerái and Jani Beg, supported as they were by the Khan of the Moghuls, became so powerful, that Bárúj Ughlan, Abulkhair's son, was unable to maintain himself in the ancient pastoral range of his father. Yielding therefore to necessity, he quitted the wide champaign that spreads on the north towards the Yáik, and retired to the south, into the plains of Turkistán, on the lower course of the Sirr, and the deserts to the north of that river. Here he had remained for some years in comparative seclusion and quiet, when he learned that Yúnis Khan, who now governed in Moghulistán, having been defeated in the East by the Kalimáks in a great battle, had retired before them, and with the Grand Ulus of the Moghuls, consisting of 60,000 families, had entered Turkistán, and taken up his winter-quarters at Kara-Tukái on the Seihun or Jaxartes. Barúj, burning with indignation at the protection afforded, first by Isanbugha, and now by his brother Yúnis Khan, to the Kaizák-Uzbeks, whom he regarded as refractory and rebellious subjects, resolved to gratify his revenge by beating up the quarters of the Moghuls.

A.H. 877, A.D. 1472-73.

Bárúj surprises Yunis Khan;

Having taken his measures with the greatest skill and secrecy, he set out at the head of a body of twenty thousand men, and by a sudden march completely surprised the encampment of the Moghuls. It happened that the whole of their men had that morning gone across the Seihun, which was frozen over, to enjoy a grand hunting party. Bárúj consequently found the camp quite undefended, and his people instantly began to drive off the flocks, and to seize and secure the property thus presented on every hand to their rapacity. When the alarming intelligence of this most unexpected attack was brought to the Moghul Khan, without waiting to collect his men, who were scattered in every

SECT. II.

direction over the country, he hastened to recross the river on the ice. He was at that moment accompanied by only six of his men, who bore the grand standard. He had along with him the great trumpet, which it seems none could sound like himself. As he drew near the camp, he sounded a blast, by which his friends at once knew that the Khan was at hand. The Moghul women, encouraged by the well-known sound, rose upon the intruders with the spirit that belongs to their race, and flew upon such of the men as had entered their tents, slaying or making them prisoners. The grand standard too, appearing in sight, no doubt remained that the Khan was approaching. The assailants, who were dispersed in all quarters in search of booty, thus attacked by the women within the camp, and expecting the more formidable onset of the approaching Moghuls from without, were seized with a panic. Bárúj Ughlán himself now attempted to mount his horse and to escape, but was stopped and made prisoner by a groom, assisted by some female servants. The Khan, on coming up, caused his head to be struck off, and raised on the point of a spear. Of the twenty thousand Uzbeks who had entered the camp, few escaped. Next day the Khan, pursuing his advantage, hastened to crush the remaining adherents of the family of Abulkhair, who, confounded by this new and unforeseen calamity, unable to resist, were entirely broken and scattered abroad, insomuch that a great proportion of them, compelled altogether to abandon the desert, retired into Máwerannaher.*

but is defeated and slain.

Shahi Beg leaves the desert.

Among those who then abandoned the desert was a man destined ere long to acquire a great name in the history of the times. Shahi Beg, or Sheibáni, was the grandson of Abulkhair Khan by that prince's eldest son Shah Bidágh Sultan. After Bárúj's disaster, he lin-

* Tar. Reshídi, ff. 57, 58. 64, 65. 209. 284.

gered for some time in the now inhospitable wilds and wastes of his forefathers, subjected to extreme misery, from hardships of every description; but at length, seeing no hope of effecting anything in the old dominions of his family, he found himself compelled to abandon them, and accompanied by a few faithful adherents, was one of those who repaired to Samarkand, which was then governed by Sultan Ahmed Mirza, there to await some favourable turn of fortune.*

The Kaizáks.

By the ruin of the old Uzbeks the new confederacy of Uzbek-Kaizák or Kaizák Uzbeks became the ruling power in the eastern district of Kipchák. As long as Gerái Khan lived he always retained the chief power, and on his death his authority descended to his son Berendúk Khan, who continued to reign for several years. But the influence of Kásim Beg, the son of that Jani Beg who had accompanied Gerái in the original secession, gradually extending itself among the tribes, Berendúk, finding at last that he had little left but the name of Khan, retired to Samarkand. Kásim Beg Khan, pursuing his advantage, became more powerful than Abulkhair had been, extended his power over nearly the whole Desht, and especially over the range which had formerly belonged to that prince and the elder Uzbeks, and is said to have had at his command an army of a million of men. But these events belong to a later period.

Gerái. Berendúk. Kásim Beg

Political State of the Desht.

When, in consequence of the ruin of the Elder Uzbeks, Sheibáni abandoned the desert, an event that preceded by a few years the birth of Báber, the Grand Khanship of Kipchák was divided into several separate states. The Khans of Krim maintained their independence. The kingdoms of Kásán and Astrakhán had already begun to decline under the growing force of the Russians. The older branch of the Uzbeks had hardly

* Tar. Reshídi, f. 118.

SECT. II. a political existence; while the new confederation of the Kaizák Uzbeks was in all the vigour of youth, and even already had attained an extraordinary degree of strength. Their territory, besides the eastern parts of the desert of Kipchák reaching westward to the Yaik, included a portion of the western range of Moghulistán.

The language of most of the tribes of Kipchák, and in particular of the Uzbeks, was the Túrki.*

* The authorities for the history of the Khans of Kipchák are Abulghazi, parts VII., VIII.; Miles's Shajrat, pp. 220—241; Taríkh Abulkhair Kháni; Manger, Arabshah, vol. i. p. 367.; Alem-arái Abási, near the beginning; Tar. Reshídi, ff. 57. 68, 69.; D'Herbelot, art. Abusaid; Deguignes, Hist. des Huns, tom. iv. p. 434.; Petis de la Croix, Hist. de Genghis-can, p. 510.

SECTION THIRD.

II. *Of Chaghat Khan — his extensive Dominions.*

DECLINE OF THE POWER OF THE CHAGHATÁI KHANS. — DIVISION OF THEIR EMPIRE INTO MOGHULISTÁN AND MÁWERANNAHER.

SECT. III.

Chaghatái's dominions.

The dominions assigned by Chengíz to his second son Chaghatái Khan were very extensive, and consisted of countries differing from each other in every particular. 1. The great northern pastoral range beyond the Sirr and Káshghar, of several months' journey, was entirely a townless waste, full of deserts, but interspersed too with lakes and rivers, varied with hill and dale, and with plains and meadows, which in the spring and summer were covered with the most beautiful flowers and plants; and in these seasons the climate of the desert was peculiarly delightful; but the extreme cold of the winter compelled the roving inhabitants, during that season, to repair to the more southern and sheltered districts. 2. Káshghar and Yárkend were in a middle state between the deserts of the north and the wealth and population of the south. Though abounding in wilds, they possessed some considerable towns, such as Káshghar, Yárkend, Khoten, Aksu, Terfán, &c. 3. The countries immediately north of the Sirr or Jaxartes, as well as those as far south as the Hindú-Kúsh and Hazára mountains, Táshkend, Samarkand, Bokhára, Bálkh, and others, were rich and civilised kingdoms, abounding in cultivated fields and flourishing cities. The

SECT. III. successors of Chaghatái do not seem to have long maintained an influence over Khorásán or the dominions beyond the Hazára range.

Their discordant composition.

In the first of these divisions, the whole population were wanderers of the desert, enthusiastically attached to their wilds, which they regarded as the paradise of the earth, holding all men of towns and cities, or cultivators of the soil, in contempt. Their own wild and vagabond life they considered as the only one worthy of free and generous men. In the second, there was a mixture of settled and wandering races; while in the greater part of the third the inhabitants were chiefly settled and stationary.

The principal tribe in the Chaghatái desert was that of the Moghuls, whence the country was called Moghulistán. And this is the peculiar tract intended when Moghulistán, or the Khans of Moghulistán, are spoken of, in the writers of Persia, from the age of Chaghatái to that of Báber. The principal tribes of the Chaghatái Moghuls were the Doghlat, the Khírás, the Konchi or Kochín, the Begchak, Tekrít, and some others. The Kirghiz appear to have been a separate tribe of the same race, and connected with the Moghuls, but who afterwards became hostile to them.

The language of the wandering tribes was either Moghul or Túrki, according to their descent: that of the towns and of the cultivators of the ground was in general Persian. There was a strong line of separation drawn between the tribesman and the Tajík.

To the south-east of the Moghuls inhabited the Kalimáks (or Kalmuks), a numerous and powerful race who stretched towards the great wall of China. They were not in the Chaghatái allotment; and, though originally of the same extraction, were often in a state of hostility with the Moghuls.

An empire composed of so many and such dissimilar materials; was not likely long to remain united, unless held together by an able and powerful hand; and the custom of the Moghul Khans, according to which they allotted particular tribes or districts to each of their children, was calculated still farther to favour this tendency to disunion.

For many years, however, the vigour imparted to the government by the genius of Chengíz Khan continued to operate. Chaghatái, his son, resided chiefly in the desert at his own head-quarters of Bish-báligh, and sometimes with his brother Oktái at Karakorum. Much of the business of government was conducted by the Minister Kárāchár-Nevián or Nuián; by whose counsel later historians affirm that Chengíz, in his will, directed his son to be entirely guided. The immediate successors of Chaghatái continued to reside chiefly in the desert; but the ambition and discord so common among Asiatic, and among all princes, were not long of appearing. Within a century after Chaghatái's death, it had become much the custom for the Khans, instead of living in the desert among the tribes, to visit and linger in the rich and populous countries on the Sirr and the Amu, where they appear at last to have fallen into a state of thraldom in the hands of their ministers.

Division of the Khanship.

A. H. 721.
A.D. 1321.

Down to the first Isan-bugha-Khan *, in spite of some disputes and civil wars, we find no distinct trace of a double succession in the Chaghatái dynasty. He, we are told, was called from Máwerannaher, where he then reigned, by the inhabitants of Kashgar, Yarkend, Alátásh, and by the Oighurs, who found no one among them of the posterity of Chaghatái Khan, who might fill the throne which was then vacant. This certainly

* In the Taríkh Reshídi he is called Ais, or Isan-bugha; in the Shajrat, p. 378., and by Price (Mohammedan History, vol. iii. p. 7.), following the Kholáset-ul-Akhbár, Il, or Ail Khwája; by Sherfeddín, Petis's transl., tom. i. p. 26., Aimál; and by Abulgházi, "Aimal Khwája, who reigned in Máwerannaher under the title of Isan-bugha Khan," pt. v. c. 1 & 5. See also the note of the intelligent English translator, p. 167.

SECT. III.

Khans of Moghulistán, and of Máwerannaher.

looks as if a division had already taken place; and as if, even then, different Khans had been acknowledged in different countries. However that may be, from this time forward, we find the Grand Khanship of the Chaghatái Khans broken up, and two rival or at least separate Khans, the one of whom governed in the country of the Moghuls and Káshgar, the other in Máwerannaher. The latter, who reigned in a civilised country that produced so many able writers, have been noticed by all the general historians of Persia, and a very short notice of them will suffice. The former, on the contrary, for a knowledge of whom we are almost entirely indebted to Mírza Haider, who was himself descended from them, have been nearly unknown, and a fuller account of their annals may be allowed.

Part First.—KHANS OF MOGHULISTÁN AND AMÍRS OF KÁSHGHAR.—THEIR SUCCESSION.—HISTORY OF YÚNIS KHAN AND HIS SONS.—TRANSACTIONS OF THE KHANS WITH THE THE MIRZAS OF MÁWERANNAHER.

Isan-bugha Khan.

A. H. 721—730.

A. D. 1321—1330.

ISAN-BUGHA KHAN did not survive many years his election as Grand Khan of the Moghuls.* Having died without issue, and none of the family of Chaghatái being left in Moghulistán, as the tribes of the desert still disdained to be subject to the titular Khans set up and pulled down at the will of a minister in Transoxiana, discord and disorder universally prevailed. The usual evils of anarchy were soon keenly felt and loudly deplored. But the men of the desert refused to acknowledge as Khákán any but a descendant of Chaghatái, and none of the race was to be found.

Interregnum.

* Isan-bugha seems to have been called from Máwerannaher about A. H. 721., and to have reigned in Moghulistán till about A. H. 730; but the chronology of the times is very uncertain.

SECT. III.

At that time Mír Yúlaji Doghlat was the ruler of Káshghar. He claimed to be hereditary Ulús-begi (lord of the tribe), under the Moghul Khans, and governed in his own right extensive dominions, reaching from the desert of Kobi to Ferghána.

The influence which he enjoyed from the extent of his power, was increased by the energy of his character. Deploring the anarchy that prevailed since the death of Isan-bugha, he resolved that the masnad should not remain vacant; and in due time produced a youth, whom he announced as the son of Isan-bugha, and a lineal descendant of Chaghatái.

Story of Toghlak-Taimur.

The whole story deserves to be related, as illustrative of Moghul manners. The chief wife of Isan-bugha was Sátelmish Khátún, by whom he had no children. Among his female slaves was one Mánselik, with whom he cohabited. It happened that he was obliged to join the army in an expedition which kept him in the field for a considerable time. By the usages of the Moghuls, the chief wife has, it seems, the entire management of the household, and, as part of it, the allotment and disposal of her husband's women, keeping back and giving him such as she pleases, and disposing of them with absolute authority. Discovering that Mánselik was with child, and envious of her good fortune, she gave her in marriage to one Shiráwal Dokhtúi, a Moghul, enjoining him to carry her off to his own country.

The Khan, on his return from the expedition, inquired for Mánselik, and was told by Sátelmish that she had been given away. "The woman was with child by me," said the Khan, much vexed; but as his wife had in no respect acted in opposition to the customs of the tribe, he smothered his regret, and said nothing more.

On his death, when the Moghul tribes fell into the state of anarchy that has been mentioned, Amír Yúlaji, the Ulús-begi, at length, determined that a Khan should be found, dispatched one of his trusty adherents to

SECT. III.

seek out Shiráwal, and to investigate the alleged story of Mánselik's pregnancy; commanding him, if her issue had proved a son, to steal him away, and bring him off. The Amír gave his envoy three hundred goats, that he might live upon their milk in his dreary pilgrimage; or, if reduced to necessity, kill them for his support. His messenger had ranged all over Moghulistán, without having discovered the man of whom he was in quest, and his flock was reduced to a single goat, when, in a sequestered district, he fortunately reached the encampment of Shiráwal. He found that Mánselik's child by the Khan had proved a son; and that since then she had had another by her new husband. The Khan's son, who must by this time have reached his eighteenth year, he contrived to steal away, and carry to Aksú. On his way to that city, the precious youth, in passing a narrow mountain road, slipped down a precipice of ice, from which, with much toil and danger, he was at length extricated, and delivered to Yúlaji. By him he was speedily proclaimed Khan, and was joyfully acknowledged in Moghulistán or Jetteh, as well as in Káshghar, by the style of Toghlak-Taimur Khan.

who is proclaimed Khan. A. H. 748. A. D. 1347.

The new Khan, some years after, became a convert to the Musulman faith, which he succeeded in introducing into a part of his dominions. He twice invaded and overran Máwerannaher, in which he established his son Elías Khan. On the death of Yúlaji, to whom he owed the masnad, and who, as Ulús-begi, had exercised much of the authority of the government, Toghlak-Taimur, from gratitude or policy, bestowed the father's office on his son Amír Khodáidád, then only seven years of age. Against this nomination Kamreddín, a younger brother of Yúlaji, remonstrated, claiming the office as belonging of right to him and not to his nephew, by the usages of the Moghuls. The Khan persisted in supporting his appointment, as it had been made; though he acknowledged, that, had the claim been earlier preferred,

Becomes a Moslem, A. H. 754. A. D. 1353. A. H. 761—3. A. D. 1360—2.

it would not have been rejected. Kamreddín, compelled to conceal his indignation, inwardly brooded over his revenge.

Is succeeded by Elías Khwaja. A.H. 765. A.D. 1364.

Toghlak-Taimur Khan, who died soon after, was succeeded by his son Elías Khwája Khan, who was at that time conducting the war in Transoxiana, where he was opposed by a combination of chiefs of the country, headed by Mír Husein and by the illustrious Mír Taimur. The Khan, after combating the confederacy with various success, was at last defeated and compelled to take refuge in the desert of Jetteh, where, after a short reign of about two years, he was basely assassinated by Kamreddín, who in one day put to death eighteen males of the family of the Khan, resolved, if possible, to exterminate the very race: after which, though not a descendant of Chaghatái or of Chengíz, he assumed the style of Khan, and the government of the country.*

Usurpation of Kamreddín.

Division of the Moghul Tribes.

These violent proceedings were viewed with horror and alarm by the Amírs of the Moghuls, who had an hereditary reverence for the family of the great conqueror. Discord followed. Many of the Moghul tribes refused to acknowledge the usurper, and others were even led to join Mír Taimur, when that warrior, after a long and varied course of discomfiture and success, having at length overcome all his early enemies and reduced Transoxiana under his power, made six expeditions into the Jetteh country against Kamreddín.† He overran both Moghulistán and Káshghar to their

Invasions of Taimur.

* Sherfeddín, vol. i. pp. 1—26.; Miles's Shajrat, pp. 378—380.; Abulghazi, pt. v. c. v.; Deguignes, vol. iv. p. 317.

† Sherfeddín, vol. i. pp. 220—364.; Tar. Resh. ff. 28—41.; Abulghazi, pt. v. c. v. The Desht, or Desert, of Jetteh, is often mentioned in the history of the Persians and Tartars as late as the time of Taimur, and the name is applied to the country north of Ferghána and Káshghar, in that age inhabited chiefly by the Moghuls. See Żefernáma, *passim*. The name, which was probably derived from that of the Getæ and Messagetæ, who inhabited the country in ancient times, was retained probably long after these tribes had left it. It has been

SECT. III.

A.H. 768—794. A.D. 1367—1393.

farthest limits, and in the last campaign, Kamreddín, his armies having been routed and himself pursued over mountains and in forests like a wild beast, worn out with fatigue and disease, seems to have perished in a savage corner of the desert, where he had concealed himself, accompanied by only two attendants.

Death of Kamreddín.

Story of Khizer Khwája,

Some time before Amír Khodáidád was thus relieved from his powerful rival, he had gone in search of a lineal descendant of Chaghatái Khan, whom he might raise to the throne of the Khans, and in whose name he might govern the country. His story, which in some respects resembled that told by his father Yúlaji in nearly similar circumstances, was, that when Kamreddín put to death the family of the Khans, there was one son of Toghlak-Taimur who was still at the breast. Amír Khodáidad, aided by his mother, had concealed the child in Káshghar. In vain, it was said, did the usurper use every means to discover the boy, who, when twelve years of age, was conveyed to the hill-country between Káshghar and Badakhshán, then to the hills of Khoten, and finally to Sárígh-Oighur and Lob-Kanik, far in the east, where he remained for twelve years more. When Kamreddín's power was on the wane, the young man was brought back, was raised to the Khanship by Amír Khodáidád, under the style of Khizer Khwája Khan, and acknowledged by many of the tribes. After contending bravely against Taimur in the field, the Khan was fortunate enough to make peace with that conqueror; and this pacification he consolidated by giving Taimur his daughter in marriage.*

who becomes Khan.

A.H. 791. A.D. 1389.

made a question whether the Jats, so widely extended over the Penjáb, on the banks of the Indus, and in other parts of India, are descended of them.

* Deguignes, in his chapter entitled "Les Mogols de Kashgar," after mentioning Toghlak-Taimur and his son Elías Khwája, and that Khodáidád placed Khizer Khwája on the throne, adds: "Les Rois de ce pays, descendent de ce dernier; mais leur histoire, et même leurs noms, ne nous sont pas connus." Hist. des Huns, tome.iv. p. 337. D'Herbelot is equally at a loss. The

SECT. III.

Power of the Ulús-begi.

Khodáidád, while he affected to restore the ancient line, did not neglect to retain the real power of the government. He claimed, under various grants to himself and his ancestors, twelve privileges, which transferred to him the entire direction of affairs. By these he was constituted Hereditary Ulús-begi, or Director of the Tribe, with precedence over all others; he could nominate Amírs or Commanders of a Thousand, and dismiss them, without referring to the Khan; he was not to be liable to punishment till he had committed and been convicted of nine capital offences; and, finally, no order or firmán was to be valid to which he did not affix his seal, that of the Khan being to be afterwards placed above it. In this manner the Khan was as much as possible reduced to be a cypher in the hands of his minister; and Khodáidád boasted that, in his long reign of ninety years, he had made six Grand Khans.*

Muhammed Khan. Shír Muhammed Khan. Sultan Weis Khan.

Khizer Khwája Khan was succeeded as Grand Khan by his son Muhammed Khan; and he by his son Shír Muhammed Khan. The latter years of this last prince were disturbed by the ambition of his nephew Sultan Weis. He, having fled from court, and having collected in the desert a band of adventurous banditti, carried on

wish in some measure to supply this deficiency in the history of a race intimately connected with Báber, has perhaps made the account of the Khans of the Moghuls, and the Amírs of Kashghar, in this Introduction, extend farther than was strictly necessary. The materials are chiefly drawn from the Tarikhi Reshídi of Mirza Haider Doghlat, who founded his narrative on the oral traditions of the Moghuls which he carefully collected; and in the latter portion of the history on the information of his father and uncle, who were descended of the Amírs of Kashghar, and, by the female line, of the Khans of Moghulistán. The contemporary history of their times and of his own is extremely valuable. See Appendix B.

* These Grand Khans were, 1. Khizer Khwája; 2. Shumaa Jehán; 3. Nakhsh Jehán; 4. Muhammed Khan; 5. Shír Muhammed; and 6. Weis Khan. Tar. Resh. f. 50. The second, third, and fourth were sons of Khizer Khwája; the second and third are not mentioned in the regular succession of the Khans. They seem to have died before their father, in whose lifetime they may have possessed separate governments or khanships; or they may have been associated with him in the general government.

SECT. III. a predatory war with his uncle, on whose death he was elected Grand Khan. Being a prince of great energy, he assumed the management of his own affairs, and was not reconciled to Mír Khodáidád, who had adhered to his uncle. This quarrel with the overbearing Ulús-begi, seems to have made a permanent rupture in the Moghul tribe. Khodáidád, who had dependent on him at least twenty-four thousand families, finding himself hard pressed, called in Ulugh Beg Mirza to his aid from Samarkand. The allies were unable, with their united forces, to make any impression on the grand tribe; but Káshghar was delivered up to the Mirza by treachery, and continued in his possession about fourteen years.*

A.H. 821 or 824. A.D. 1418 or 1421. His death; disputed succession.

In the course of the wars arising out of Ulugh Beg's invasion, Weis Khan was accidentally slain by an arrow discharged by one of his own men. His death was followed by new disturbances and dissensions. He had left two sons, Yúnis Khan and Isan-bugha Khan, the former the maternal grandfather of the emperor Báber, but then only thirteen years of age. It was probably a misfortune to Yúnis Khan that his mother was not a Chaghatái Moghul, but the daughter of an Amír of Kipchák. Parties were formed, some of the tribes adhering to the one brother, and some to the other. The great majority, however, favoured the younger of the brothers; and Yúnis Khan, though supported by Mír Khodáidád, found himself compelled to abandon Moghulistán. He was accompanied by thirty thousand families of Moghuls, under Irazan, a beg of the Tumán of the Khirás who were attached to Mír Khodáidád. As an elder sister of Yúnis Khan had some time before been betrothed to Abdalázíz Mírza, the son of Ulugh Beg, the two friendly chiefs, relying on this connec-

Yúnis Khan expelled by Isan-bugha.

* Tar. Resh. pp. 50 — 55. Khodáiadád at the age of ninety-seven (lunar years) made the pilgrimage of Mecca, and died at Medina in or after A.H. 850 — A.D. 1446.

SECT. III.

tion, carried him to the territory of Samarkand, to solicit assistance from Ulugh Beg; while Isan-bugha Khan and his adherents remained in possession of the desert.

Fate of his adherents.

Ulugh Beg heard, and not without alarm, of the approach of a numerous and tumultuous host, whose ancestors had so often overrun the rich plains of Transoxiana. He advanced as far as Dizak, north of Samarkand, to watch their movements, and met them with every profession of friendship and of readiness to espouse their cause. Jealous, however, of a power which might so easily be turned to his ruin and to that of his country, he determined to deprive them of the means of injuring him. For this purpose he arranged that the Moghuls should all be introduced into the castle of Dizak, in separate households, that their names might be regularly inrolled, so as to admit of their being properly furnished with provisions and pay. As they entered the castle without any suspicion, in small numbers and in succession, the chiefs were put to death, and all the others made prisoners, and scattered over the country. Yúnis Khan, with a fifth part of the spoil, was sent to Sháhrukh Mirza, the fourth son of Taimur, who then reigned in Khorasan. The Mirza, with the generosity of a refined and cultivated mind, placed him under the care of Moulána Sherfeddín Ali Shirázi, the celebrated historian of Taimur, and one of the most eminent moralists and poets of his age. In his house Yúnis Khan remained at Yezd for twelve years, in useful retirement, improving himself in every liberal study. To him many of the Moulána's verses are addressed. The misfortune of the Moghuls, and the massacre of so many chiefs, with the dispersion of their tribe, formed an era long remembered among them as "the calamity of Irazan." * A.H. 832. A.D. 1428–9

* Baber's Mem. p. 11.; Tár. Resh. ff. 53, 54.

SECT. III.

Isan-bugha, Khan of Moghulistán.

Meanwhile Isan-bugha Khan, the younger brother and successful rival of Yúnis Khan, supported by the principal tribes of the Moghuls, was acknowledged, though still a boy, over the wide extent of the Chaghatái desert. When this power was somewhat settled, Mír Syed Ali, the grandson of Khodáidad and who had sided with the Khan, asked and received his permission to recover his family government of Káshghar from the hands of the generals of Ulugh-Beg. He was a man of great energy, who had adopted a different line of policy from his grandfather, having joined Sultan Weis when he roamed as a brigand in the desert, and married his sister. The efforts of Mír Syed Ali, in the course of three brilliant campaigns, were crowned with success; and he became master of Káshghar and its territory.

Separation of the Moghul Tribes.

The extreme youth of Isan-bugha Khan for some time did not admit of his taking much share in public affairs; but, as he grew up, an act of violence as cruel as it was imprudent,—the assassination of Taimur Oighur, a chief of note, the effect of some party intrigue,—spread universal horror and disgust among his adherents. With one consent the tribes abandoned him. Mír Syed Ali, his faithful friend, on hearing of his danger, hurried from Káshghar, and conveyed him from Moghulistán to Aksu, treating him with every mark of honour and respect. Meanwhile the tribes, no longer bound by one common tie, dispersed in all directions, each acting independently for itself. Some bent their course towards the Kalimáks on the east; others went westward to the frontier of Kipchák; one body even joined Abulkhair Khan, the potent ruler of the Uzbeks, who at that period still held the deserts from the Yáik to the Sirr. Some chiefs built forts on the borders of Andeján, Turkistán and Seirám, and commenced a regular system of predatory incursions into these flourishing provinces. The Konchi Amírs, and a few others, continued to wander as before in the deserts of Moghulistán. All was disunion and anarchy, and threatened the permanent dissolution of the Chaghatái Khanship.

SECT. III.

Isan-bugha Khan, who now saw the full extent and the natural consequences of his crime, exerted every means in his power to evince his contrition, and to soothe the injured feelings of his subjects. He found means gradually to conciliate several of the heads of tribes, who, accepting his professions of regret, returned to his banner which they had unwillingly deserted.

Civil wars in Samarkand. A.H. 850–3. A.D. 1446–9.

The factions that prevailed in Transoxiana on the death of Sháhrúkh Mirza, and especially the civil wars between Ulugh Beg and his sons, which ended in his murder, were favourable to the Moghuls; as the employment thus furnished to the sovereigns of Samarkand at home, prevented them from thinking of any new attempt on the Khans, or their country. On the other hand, Isan-bugha, who had now in part recovered his strength, availing himself of the opportunity afforded by these troubles, entered Táshkend, Seirám, and the fruitful provinces that belonged to Samarkand north of the Jaxartes, with his shoals of Moghuls, plundered and laid them waste on every side, and then retreated to the desert, loaded with booty. When, however, some time afterwards, he repeated his invasion, he found Sultan Abusaíd Mírza, who in the interval had vanquished all his competitors, seated on the throne of Samarkand. No sooner did that active prince hear of the inroad, than, collecting a body of troops, he pursued the Khan in his retreat, and overtook him at Táráz.* The Moghuls, whose object was plunder and not war, fled without fighting; and the Sultan having expelled them, returned home, unable to retaliate. Sultan Abu-

Isan-bugha invades Táshkend,

A.H. 855; A.D. 1451.

is defeated by Abusaíd;

* Báber says that Abusaíd advanced beyond Yangi and gave Isan-bugha a severe defeat at a town in Moghulistán called Aspera. Mem. pp. 11, 12. Mirza Haider makes him overtake the Khan at Masíki, in books called Táráz, and says that the Moghuls fled without fighting. Tar. Resh. f. 57. Otrár is known by the names of Táráz, Yangi (or Yangi Kent), and, it would appear, of Masíki.

SECT. III.

said, having in the course of his successful wars conquered Khorásán, took up his residence at Herát. Isanbugha, encouraged by his absence from Samarkand, again entered his territories, invaded Andeján with a powerful force, and laid siege to the capital of that name. So numerous was his army that he is said to have inclosed the city with a triple line of troops, and to have run mines at once on every side of it. The town was taken; but the governor retired into the citadel, where he was soon glad to conclude a capitulation, by which he paid a heavy contribution for his safety. The Khan, after visiting the adjoining country, returned to his own deserts, but loaded with treasure, and driving multitudes of captives before him. "Down to the present day," says Haider Mirza, "many of the descendants of the people who were then made prisoners and carried off are still to be found in Káshghar, and are become perfect Moghuls." *

renews his inroads.

Abusaíd sets up Yúnis.

The news of this invasion was most unwelcome to Abusaíd, who was then in Khorásán preparing for an expedition against Irák. He was at a loss in what manner to deal with the Khan. If he were to advance into Moghulistán, he knew that his enemy, instead of meeting him in the field, would retreat into the most remote parts of the country, where it was impossible for the Sultan with his army to follow him; and that no sooner should he have commenced his retreat, than the Khan would follow close on his track, surround him with his swarms of horse, harass him in every march, carry off his stragglers and baggage, and disappear when he turned round to bring him to action. Abusaíd, eager as he was to march for Irák, could not leave behind so troublesome and so dangerous an enemy.

In this exigency the Sultan resolved to secure his

* Tar. Resh. f. 57.

own dominions by giving Isan-bugha employment at home, and to raise up against him, among his own subjects, a rival or master. Yúnis Khan, the elder brother of Isan-bugha, after the death of Moulána Sherefeddín Ali, had left Yezd, and travelled first to Tabríz, and afterwards to Shiráz, where for about fifteen years he remained in the service, first of Ibráhim Sultan Mirza, and then of Abdalla Mirza, the son and grandson of Sultan Sháhrúkh. Abusaíd now invited him to Herát, that he might set him up as Khan of the Moghuls; trusting that though eight and twenty years had elapsed since he left Moghulistán, such of the chiefs or tribes as were on bad terms with Isan-bugha would be glad to join his elder brother, and that thus a diversion would be produced, which could not fail to be favourable to the Mirza's interests. He probably did not wish either brother to gain a decided ascendency over the other. It might be more convenient for his views that Moghulistán should be distracted by parties, and kept in a state of combustion and weakness.*

Who comes to Herát.

When Yúnis arrived at Herát, he was received and entertained with great magnificence by Sultan Abusaíd, who acknowledged him as Grand Khan of the Moghuls, and entered into a treaty with him in that capacity. A grand festival was held on the occasion, in a stately kiosk or summer-palace in the Bagh-i-Zághán, where the Khan was introduced with much ceremony, and seated on a throne. The Sultan then addressed him in a long speech, in which he is said to have explained his views without disguise. He observed that when the great Taimur conquered the Khan of the Moghuls, many of his Amírs advised him to put an end to the dynasty of the Khans: that Taimur, however, seeing that some were partial to the old system, and having no wish to destroy it, raised Syurghatmish to the

* Tar. Resh. ff. 58—60.; Báber, p. 11.

SECT. III. Khanship, issuing all firmans in his name, but keeping him entirely in his power; that on his death, Mahmúd Khan was made Khan in his place *; that down to the time of Ulugh Beg Mirza, there continued to be a Khan, but that his power was merely nominal: that, at this last period, the Khalifs and Khans who claimed superiority over Taimur Beg's family became extinct, and that now the Mirza was altogether independent; that he had called Yúnis Khan from a low estate to make him a prince; that the Khan must however renounce the old pretensions of the family, must call himself his friend, and comport himself as such; and that in future, the sovereign mandates should be issued in the dominions of the Sultan in his own name, and in the name of his descendants. To these conditions Yúnis agreed, and confirmed them with an oath; from this time therefore the Mirzas of Transoxiana were independent of the Chaghatái Khans in form, as they had long been in reality. All the Moghuls who were scattered over the Sultan's territories were now commanded to join Yúnis Khan, who soon after set out to recover his kingdom.

His agreement with Abusaíd.

His character.

Yúnis Khan had now reached the age of forty †; but, though a man of talents, the training which he had received in the last twenty-eight years of his life, while it made him an amiable and learned man, and earned

* Tar. Resh. ff. 58, 59. 123. The author of the Shajrat gives us the same information. "On the death of Syoorghunumush Khan, the great Ameer Timoor raised to the throne his son, Sultan Mahmood, and his name was written at the head of state-papers as long as the great Timoor lived, and to the period when Timoor departed this life, at the town of Otrar, on his expedition against Khutai, the *Khani* or sovereignty of Sultan Mahmood was indisputed and independent." Colonel Miles's Shajrat, p. 383. The account of the descendants of Chengíz Khan in the Shajrat, being taken from Ulugh Beg Mirza's work on the four Ulús or tribes, closes with Sultan Mahmúd. The Tar. Resh. f. 123., informs us, that these khans were styled emperors (padsháh), but were mere prisoners. It is to be noted, that all the khans alluded to by Abusaíd were those of Máweran-naher, not of Moghulistán.

† His age was forty-one lunar years.

SECT. III.

for him the title of Ustád, or Doctor, in the refined society of Shiráz, was not equally fitted to make him popular or happy among the rude rangers of the desert. On entering Moghulistán, he was joined by several tribes who were disaffected to his brother, and especially by Mír Kerím-Berdi, who was a Doghlat, and by the Konchi and Begchak Moghuls. To strengthen his interest he married Ais-doulat Begum, the daughter of the Chief of the Kenchi Tumán, and the grandmother of Báber.* His followers soon formed a considerable body; but their chiefs had for so many years been accustomed to act for themselves as independent, that they yielded but a very imperfect obedience to their new ruler. Unable to command, he was compelled to use every art of conciliation, and to work upon them by such means as were in his power.

He re-enters the desert.

The two first years of his new reign present a varied scene of success and disaster. Encouraged by the numbers who joined his standard, he ventured, in the second year after his return, to advance against Káshgar, which was held by Amír Syed Ali, an able and popular prince, who, as we have seen, had adhered to his rival, but was now aged and unable to sit on horseback. Amír Syed shut himself up in the town, which Yúnis besieged. Isan-bugha, who was then at Yúldúz, the farthest eastern extremity of his dominions, on hearing of this attempt, collected his forces, and set out with sixty thousand men to the relief of the Amír. Such was his speed, that in eleven days he arrived, but attended by only six thousand, all the rest having fallen behind. He was joined by the Amír of Káshghar, with thirty thousand of his followers. A desperate

His attempt on Káshghar

* Ais-doulat Begum was the daughter of Shír Háji Beg, the greatest of the Saghíríchi Begs (probably a branch of the Konchi or Kochin). He was, on this occasion, seated along with her on a white felt, and with great pomp, proclaimed Khan by the tribes. Báber, p. 12. She is represented by Báber as a woman of great talents and influence.

SECT. III.

defeated.

battle was fought, about twelve miles from Káshghar, on the side of Aksú, where Yúnis Khan was completely defeated, and all his baggage, with his wife and eldest daughter, then at the breast, fell into the hands of the victor. The Amír entertained them honourably, and sent them back to the Khan. Yúnis, on this discomfiture, was deserted by the tribes that had joined him, but which now separated, each to consult for its own safety. Seeing himself thus deprived of all means of carrying on any active operations in Moghulistán, he left his family with their friends in the desert, and again repaired to Khorásán.*

His distress.

To such distress was Yúnis Khan now reduced, that on his arrival at Herát, he did not possess the means of providing even the customary offering which in the East it is necessary to make on approaching a prince. In this distress, he prevailed upon one of the officers of his household to allow himself to be presented to the Sultan as a slave. Abusaíd, desirous to keep up the intestine wars in the desert, and wishing to inspire the Moghuls with some confidence in the Khan, bestowed on him the territory of Masíkhi, a small hill-country dependent on Andeján, and bordering on Táshkend, and sent him to renew the contest. On his taking leave, the faithful servant, whom he had presented to the Sultan, finding himself left alone in a foreign land, was no longer able to repress his feelings, but broke out into loud lamentations. The Sultan, who inquired what was the cause of the man's distress, on discovering the truth, caused the honest Moghul to be properly accoutred, armed, and mounted, and sent him to follow his master.†

Death of Mír Syed, A.H. 862, A.D. 1458,

It happened fortunately for the Khan that Mír Syed Ali of Káshghar died soon after his return; and that about four years afterwards Isan-bugha also died, and

* Tar. Resh. f. 60.

† Ibid. f. 61.

SECT. III.

was succeeded by his son Dost Muhammed Khan, a man of a violent and imprudent character. Of the two sons of the Amír of Káshghar, the one sided with Dost Muhammed, and the other, of course, with Yúnis Khan, who, having been previously joined by many of his former adherents, and by some Moghul tribes, now became more powerful than he had yet been. He moved eastward, and several times entered Káshghar, being fond, we are told, of cities and of cultivated countries, and of living in houses; but the murmurs of the tribes who disliked and shunned all towns and settled habitations, preferring to dwell under tents, to live the free life and to breathe the free air of the desert, compelled him as often to retire back into Moghulistán. Dost Muhammed Khan, his nephew and now his rival, reigned only four years. On his death, Yúnis Khan, being joined by the chief men who had hitherto adhered to his brother's party, became all-powerful. A few of the immediate followers of the family carried off Dost's son, Kepek Sultan, then a boy, and fled with him to Terfán, at the eastern extremity of the country. It was now the wish of Yúnis Khan to have taken up his residence at Aksú, "which compared with Moghulistán was something of a town," but he speedily found that if he indulged this taste, the tribesmen would go over in a body to his grand-nephew Kepek Sultan. Compelled by necessity therefore, he returned to the wilds of Moghulistán with all his followers.*

and of Isanbugha, A.H. 866, A.D. 1462.

And of Dost Muhammed, A.D. 1465–6, A.H. 870.

Success of Yúnis Khan.

Just at this time occurred the disastrous expedition of Sultan Abusaíd Mirza into Irák, where he perished with his mighty army. Three of his sons succeeded him, in different kingdoms, in Máwerannaher; Sultan Ahmed Mirza in Samarkand; Sultan Mahmúd Mirza in Hissár, Kunduz and Badakhshán; and Sultan Umer-

Calamity of Irák; A.H. 873, A.D. 1468–9.

* Tar. Resh. ff. 61—64.

SECT. III. sheikh Mirza in Andeján and Ferghána. Yúnis Khan, in fulfilment of an engagement with Sultan Abusaíd, bestowed three of his daughters on these three Mirzas, with a view at once to strengthen the friendship between the two families, and to put an end to the enmity which had long subsisted between the Moghuls of the desert and the Chaghatáis of Máwerannaher.

Yúnis defeated by Kalimáks, A. H. 877, A.D. 1472–3.

Not very long after, in the course of A.H. 877, a Kalimák chief (expelled from his own country by intestine feuds), entered Moghulistán, on the east, with three hundred thousand followers. Defeated on the banks of the Ili, by the overwhelming force of these invaders, Yúnis Khan retreated westward to Turkistán, and passed the winter at Kara-Tokái. It was there that he was surprised by Bárúj Ughlan and his Uzbeks, who seized and plundered his camp, as has been mentioned, when he attacked them in turn, and inflicted on them an exemplary revenge. In the spring he moved to Táshkend. The governor of that province was Sheikh Jemáleddín Khar, nominally under the Sultan of Samarkand, but in the unsettled state of the country that followed Abusaíd's disaster in Irák, he yielded but an imperfect obedience to any superior. As Yúnis Khan approached Táshkend, the Sheikh came out in state with a numerous retinue, as if to meet and do him honour.* The Khan saw, with surprise, his own followers suddenly disappear from his train; nor was he much reassured when told that they were gone forward to receive Sheikh Jemál. Being soon left nearly alone, he was seized by his own people, at the command of the Sheikh, and thrown into prison, where he languished a whole twelvemonth.

Defeats Bárúj;

made prisoner by Sheikh Jemál, A. H. 878, A.D. 1473.

It appears that Yúnis Khan's Amírs, being discontented with him, had entered into a conspiracy with Sheikh Jemáleddín, to whom the whole Ulús of Moghuls sub-

* In "Istakbál," as it is called.

SECT. III.

Anecdote of Ais-doulat.

mitted as their chief. The Sheikh, to add insult to injury, bestowed Ais-doulat Begum, the Khan's wife, and mother of the betrothed wives of the Sultans of Samarkand and Ferghána, on one of his officers. The Begum, when this unseemly transfer was notified to her, uttered not a word. Her intended husband, arriving in the evening, entered the house; his attendants remaining without. The Begum's female slaves closed the doors behind him, and barred them within. They then fell upon the unhappy bridegroom and put him to death with their knives. In the morning his body was ignominiously cast out of the house. When Sheikh Jemáleddín sent to call the Begum to account for this murder, "I am the wife of Yúnis Khan," she replied, "and of him only. Sheikh Jemál has thought fit to give me to another. He knows whether this is in accordance with religion and law. *I* have killed the man; let Sheikh Jemál kill *me*, if he chooses." Jemál was loud in her praise, and allowed her to return with honour to her husband.

Yúnis released.

It was about a year after these transactions when Amír Abdal-kadús, with a small body of men, fell upon Sheikh Jemál, slew him, and brought his head to Yúnis Khan whom he released from his prison. All the Moghul chiefs who had joined the Sheikh now returned to their allegiance to the Khan. They protested to him that they had left him solely on account of his fondness for cities and cultivated countries, which to them were odious. The Khan promised that henceforward he would entirely give them up, and live and breathe in the pure air of the desert. As the Kalimáks had by this time returned to their own country, the Khán moved back with all his camp to the steppes of Moghulistán. Not long after his return, the servants of Kepek Sultan Ughlan, Dost Muhammed's son, who had been carried to Terfán, slew him and brought his head to Yúnis Khan. Though in a state of hostility with Kepek

SECT. III.

Sultan, the Khan was indignant at this act of treachery, and gave up the murderers to undergo the penalty of the Muhammedan law of retaliation. Yúnis Khan, thus relieved from all domestic enemies in the desert, remained in Moghulistán for several years, never even hinting a wish to visit any town; and, during that time, by his amiable manners and by his compliance with the usages of the tribes, succeeded in a very great degree in gaining their attachment. But though he thus became sole Khan of Moghulistán, the horde of the Moghuls never appears perfectly to have recovered that degree of unity, or the Khans that degree of power, which they had enjoyed before the death of Weis Khan and the calamity of Irazan. Habits of disunion and discord, long indulged, prepared them for new misfortunes.

Becomes sole Khan.

Some of the most important events of Yúnis Khan's later years, were his campaigns in Káshghar, and his transactions with his sons-in-law the Sultans of Maweran-naher. The former may be but briefly noticed, the latter are more nearly connected with the history of Samarkand.

Affairs of Káshghar,

Muhammed Haider Mirza, Doghlat, was the Amír of Káshghar, who had joined the party of Yúnis, and was protected by him. The Amír had married Jemák, the widow of his elder brother, to whom she had born a son called Ababeker. This young prince, aided by the intrigues of his mother, who completely directed her weak and uxorious husband, succeeded in wresting Yárkend from his uncle and stepfather. By his adventurous spirit and the unsparing prodigality with which he lavished on his followers whatever fell into his hands *, he soon attached to him a resolute band of chosen youths, drawn from the highest families in the

* When unprovided with the means of satisfying his followers, he sometimes gave up to them his tents, and the whole of his most valuable property, to be pillaged.

SECT. III.

tribes. Aided by them, and with the sanction of the Amír himself, he took possession of Khoten under circumstances of the blackest treachery *: and, rendered bold by success, at length advanced to occupy Káshghar itself, the seat of the Amír's government. Twice did the Amír oppose him in the field, and twice did Ababeker, with a handful of resolute troops, defeat his numerous armies. The Amír, in his distress, applied to Yúnis Khan, who hastened to his succour with fifteen thousand men. The combined army of the Khan and Amír, amounting in all to forty-five thousand men, advanced towards Yárkend, the seat of Ababeker's power, but was met and defeated by that enterprising prince, with a force of little more than three thousand men. Next summer the Khan again advanced to the assistance of his ally, with sixty thousand of his Moghuls: but the combined army, amounting to ninety thousand, was once more completely routed by Ababeker, who relied chiefly on five thousand well-trained troops. The immediate result of this battle was the occupation of Káshghar by Ababeker. The Khan and the Amír fled to Aksu, where the Amír drew the Khan's younger son Sultan Ahmed into a conspiracy against his father, which was with some difficulty defeated. In spite of this perfidy of his ally Yúnis Khan was preparing to march anew, to restore the Amír to his dominions, when he was called away to protect Ferghána.†

which is conquered by Ababeker.

A.H. 884, A.D. 1479.

A.H. 885, A.D. 1480.

Much of the later part of Yúnis Khan's life was occupied by his transactions with his sons-in-law, the Sultans of Samarkand and Ferghána. On the present occasion he found the brothers in a state of mutual hostility, and Sultan Umersheikh apprehensive of seeing his territories invaded and overrun by his brother the Sultan of Samarkánd. As the Khan approached Ferghána, he was met by his son-in-law the Sultan of that

Yúnis Khan in Ferghána.

* Tar. Resh. ff. 56—70. † Tar. Resh. ff. 56—70. 68—80.

SECT. III.

kingdom, who assigned to him the little province of Ush, east of Andeján, for his quarters. The Khan laboured zealously to effect a reconciliation between the brothers; but, as he found it a work that required time, he prudently sent back the great body of Moghuls into the desert, under his eldest son. By his friendly intervention the intended invasion was prevented. At the end of winter, when the Khan returned into his own country, he left Muhammed Haider, the deposed Amír of Káshghar, in the government of Ush, promising to come back and rejoin him at the proper season. But this arrangement was not agreeable to Sultan Umersheikh, who, on the Khan's departure, divested the Amír of his authority. Muhammed Haider, unable to stay where he was, or to go to Moghulistán, repaired to Káshghar, flattering himself that Ababeker, who was at once his nephew and step-son, would grant him a favourable reception. Immediately on his arrival, however, he was thrown into prison, where he languished for a year; when, by a clemency very unusual with Ababeker, he was allowed to leave the country and proceed to Badakhshán. Thence he went to Samarkand, where he remained two years; and afterwards joined Yúnis Khan on that chief's earnest invitation, and was with him on his death-bed, assisting him by his skill in medicine, for which the Amír was celebrated in his own country. Ababeker Mirza was thus left in possession of Káshghar, with all its dependent provinces, which that able but blood-thirsty and unscrupulous tyrant ruled nearly fifty years, and continued to hold at the accession of Báber.*

Yúnis Khan was never sorry to have a pretext for lingering near the Sirr. He was particularly attached to Sultan Umersheikh Mirza, the father of Báber. They are represented as having lived together on the most familiar terms. The Khan sometimes carried the Sultan

* Tar. Resh. ff. 68—80. 193—195.

to Moghulistán to visit him, and entertained him for a month or two in his tents; and, in return, accompanied the young Sultan to Andeján, passing an equal space of time in his palace. Umersheikh, who was ambitious and restless, made every exertion, but in vain, to induce the Khan to assist him in the conquest of Samarkand. With his own inferior forces he repeatedly invaded that kingdom. His brother, Sultan Ahmed Mirza, retaliated by frequent invasions of Ferghána. To defeat these invasions Umersheikh, year after year, called in Yúnis Khan, assigning to him some portion of his dominions, in which he took up his residence during the winter with his household and immediate followers, while the great body of the Ulús remained with their flocks in the wide-spreading steppes of their country. On the return of spring, when the Khan visited Moghulistán, the Sultan resumed possession of his districts. This armed mediation of the Khan prevented the success of Sultan Ahmed's plans against Andeján.

On one occasion, however, a serious misunderstanding arose between the two friends. Umersheikh had given up to the Khan the province of Akhsi for his winter quarters. Sultan Ahmed Mirza, who was ready to invade the country, on hearing of the Khan's movements, desisted from his hostile intentions. Umersheikh, thus relieved from his apprehensions, was impatient that the Khan should withdraw from Akhsi, which was the principal district of his kingdom; and, the Khan delaying and putting off his departure from time to time, the Sultan at length, losing patience, advanced to expel him by force. All the Khan's attempts to soothe him proving ineffectual, a battle ensued at Tíka-sakaratha, when the Sultan was defeated, taken prisoner and brought in bonds before Yúnis Khan. The good old Khan rose as his son-in-law approached, advanced to meet him, made his bonds be removed, loaded him with presents, and set him at liberty; telling him to hasten straight

SECT. III. home to prevent such disturbances as might be expected to ensue from the news of his discomfiture and supposed captivity; and promised himself to follow without delay. The Khan then proceeded to send off such of the tribes as were still with him to Moghulistán, and soon after, with his private household and a few followers, set out for Andeján, where he spent two months with the Sultan in his palace, and conducted himself in so frank and friendly a manner that no trace of soreness was left in the mind of either.

Obeid's account of the Khan.

It was in the course of one of the many quarrels that arose between the sovereigns of Samarkand and Ferghána, that Khwája Nasíreddín Obeidulla, a holy man of great celebrity, was called in from Samarkand to mediate a treaty of peace between the Khan and Umersheikh on the one part, and Sultan Ahmed on the other, and was received with much distinction by them all. "I had heard," said he, in relating the circumstance, "that Yúnis Khan was a Moghul, and I concluded that he was a beardless Moghul, with the rude manners and deportment of an inhabitant of the desert. On the contrary, I found him a handsome man, with a fine bushy beard, of elegant address, most agreeable and refined manners and conversation, such as are very seldom to be met with in the most polished society." One happy consequence resulted from this meeting. The venerable Khwája addressed letters to all the Sultans around, with whom his influence was very great, to inform them that he had seen Yúnis Khan, the Moghul. "The followers of such a man," said he, "are not to be carried off as booty. They belong to Islam: and," continues our author, "from that time forward, in Máwerannaher and Khorásán, none bought or sold captive Moghuls, who previously had been purchased in the same way as all Káfirs (infidels) are." *

* Tar. Resh. ff. 66—68.

SECT. III.

A.H. 879, A.D. 1474.

After the death of Sheikh Jemál, Sultan Ahmed Mirza of Samarkand had resumed possession of Táshkend and Seirám, which he made over to his brother Umersheikh (the father of Baber), who possessed them several years. On the occasion of a new quarrel between the brothers, however, Sultan Ahmed raised an army to recover these territories. Umersheikh, as usual, called in Yúnis Khan to his aid, and as the price of his alliance ceded Seirám to him. When the Khan entered the civilised country in which it lay, with the intention of taking up his winter quarters, a number of the Moghul tribes, always attached to the life of the desert, and jealous of their Khan's fondness for cities and agriculture, separated from his camp, deserted, and went home. The pertinacity with which Yúnis Khan so often went in the teeth of their predilections may seem inconsistent with his acknowledged talents; but, besides the natural influence of his learned education and early habits, he was affected by religious motives. His subjects were still in general pagans, or inclined to paganism; and his piety led him earnestly to desire that he could induce them to cultivate the ground, being firmly persuaded, says his historian, that until they settled and inhabited towns, he could not thoroughly introduce the Moslem faith.* Hence his repeated though ineffectual attempts to lead them to a more settled life. On the present occasion, the more refractory and resolute of those who adhered to their ancient faith and usages, and they seem to have been the great majority of the Moghuls, separated from him altogether, and returned into their deserts, carrying along with them, and putting at their head, his younger son, Sultan Ahmed Khan. But, as the extinction of his brother Isanbugha's family had now left Yúnis

A.H. 890. A.D. 1485.

Secession of some Moghul tribes,

* Tar. Resh. f. 112. A similar observation has repeatedly been made by Christian missionaries.

SECT. III. Khan without a rival, this defection affected him less seriously than it would have done at an earlier period, as the ascendency of his own family in Moghulistán was still left secure.

That winter the Khan passed in Seirám. The army of Sultan Ahmed having moved from Samarkand to recover the disputed provinces, Yúnis Khan sent his eldest son Sultan Mahmúd, with thirty thousand men, that he might form a junction with Umersheik, who was on his march from Ferghána, at the head of fifteen thousand men, to attack the common enemy. When the three armies had approached near each other, and a bloody battle was on the eve of being fought, Khwája Nasíreddín Obeidulla, hastening from Samarkand, sent forward expresses to announce his approach. The three potentates, obedient to the voice of the saintly man, halted the moment the messengers reached them. The Khwája brought the princes together into one apartment, and sitting down along with them, mediated, or rather dictated, the conditions of a peace. Táshkend, as well as Seirám, was given up to the Khan by the consent of the hostile brothers; and for some years continued to be the usual residence of one branch of the Moghul Khans.

Táshkend and Seirám ceded to the Khan.

A. H. 892, A. D. 1496–7. Death of Yúnis Khan.

About two years after these events, Yúnis Khan died, at the age of seventy-four. None other of the Chághatái Khans had attained to that age, says the historian; nay, hardly any of them had attained to forty.* He was an accomplished, brave, and generous prince; but, in his later years, placed in a situation much at variance with the previous habits of his life.

His sons succeed;

On his death, his elder son, Sultan Mahmúd Khan, generally called in this history "the Elder Khan," was proclaimed his successor as Grand Khan, and reigned over the tribes which had entered Táshkend and Seirám,

* These are lunar years. Tar. Resh. ff. 68. 80. 110.

SECT. III.

or that dwelt in the neighbouring steppes; but his younger son, Sultan Ahmed Khan (called hereafter "the Younger Khan") continued to govern the tribes that ranged in the more distant and much more extensive wilds of Moghulistán, reaching far to the north and east.

Mahmúd Khan defeats the Sultan of Ferghána,

No sooner did the death of the Khan become known to the Sultans of Ferghána and Samarkand, than they hastened to recover what they had lost. The former having pushed on a considerable force under his most distinguished officers, succeeded in getting possession of Ushter, a strong fortress in Táshkend. The loss of the conciliating spirit of Yúnis Khan was now felt. Ushter was immediately afterwards attacked and stormed by the new Khan, and all the Sultan's brave adherents put to the sword. As they consisted of his best troops, this reverse entirely broke his strength, which never had been great.*

and of Samarkánd. A. H. 893.

Nor was the Sultan of Samarkand more successful. In the course of the following year he led an immense army, said to consist of no less than an hundred and fifty thousand men, to recover Táshkend, was met by the elder Khan on the Chirr, a river which passes Táshkend on its way to the Sirr, and there completely routed, crowds of his army being drowned in attempting to recross. Mahmúd, pursuing his advantage, took possession of the country of Turkistán, lower down the Iaxartes, which had been occupied by the Sultan of Samarkánd, for whom it was then held by Muhammed Mazíd Terkhán, that prince's maternal uncle.† The Terkhán was himself taken and kept as a prisoner, and was afterwards useful in negotiating a peace. The government of Turkistán was bestowed, as a reward for some important services, on Sháhi-Beg or Sheibáni Khan, who had now entered the service of the Khan.

Seizes Turkistán, which he gives to Sheibáni.

* Tar. Resh. f. 81. Báber does not allude to this loss at Ushter.

† Báber's Mem. p. 21.; Tar. Resh. f. 80.

SECT. III.

The loss of Turkistán was not the only consequence of the disaster on the Chirr. When the news of it reached the Governor of Uratippa, in alarm, he gave up that valuable district to Umirsheikh Mírza of Ferghána, who continued to possess it till his death.

Consequent quarrel with the Kaizáks.

Sheibáni, now Governor of Túrkistán, gradually acquired a singular ascendency over the elder Khan, his patron; the natural influence of a powerful over a weak mind.* No sooner was he established in his government, than the scattered Uzbeks who were attached to the old dynasty, began to assemble from all quarters, under the banners of the grandson of their ancient chief. The patronage thus afforded by the Khan to the family of their mortal foe, led to keen remonstrances on the part of the sons of Gírái Khan and Jáni Beg Khan, the founders of the new confederacy of the Kaizák-Uzbeks. The Moghuls and Kaizáks had always hitherto been connected as friends and allies, the Kaizáks having received from the Moghuls a tract of their country, when they originally fled from the oppression of Abulkhair Khan and renounced his government. The Kaizáks now complained, that, to bestow Turkistán on Sheibáni Khan, their hereditary enemy, was bringing him into direct collision with them. This

Mahmúd defeated.

quarrel produced a rupture, which terminated in a war between the Kaizáks and Moghuls, in the course of which Mahmúd (the elder Khan) suffered two great defeats. These discomfitures of the Khan were, however, somewhat connected with another part of the internal policy of his government. "Yúnis Khan,"

Alleged cause.

says the historian, "had always been the khan of the great chiefs. Men who succeed to power without any effort frequently do not attend to, or do not know the worth of men of merit; nay, they vainly imagine that any whom they think fit to patronise or favour thereby

* Báber's Mem. pp. 9, 10.

SECT. III.

become men of worth. In conformity with this pernicious maxim, the new Khan, forsaking his father's policy, protected and patronised persons of low degree, who constantly employed themselves in undermining and subverting the old and dignified chiefs; so that, at last, the Khan proceeded to put to death five great Amírs, who were heads of departments, and extirpated their families, placing five others of low rank in their places. When the differences arose between the Khan and the Kaizák Uzbeks, on the subject of Sheibáni, and went on till they ended in war, these five mean creatures were his ministers. Hence," continues the historian, "defeat ensued; and the fame of the Khan and the terror of his name, which had settled on the hearts of the Sultans around, through the exertions of their predecessors in office, were entirely dissipated." * But the power of Sheibáni continued to increase, and he daily became more and more independent in his government of Turkistán.

Sultan Ahmed Khan of Moghulistán, A. H. 890, A. D. 1485.

His character.

The younger Khan, who ruled in eastern Moghulistán, was a man of much greater energy and capacity than his brother. When in his father's lifetime he retreated into the desert from Tashkend, accompanied by the discontented Moghuls, his first and most earnest concern was to reduce the power of the heads of tribes, by whom his father's plans had often been thwarted. To this task he devoted himself for ten years; in the course of which time he attained his purpose, by weakening some and destroying others. In the prosecution of this design he made many long and rapid marches, and fought many bloody battles; and it was only by his uncommon bodily strength and prowess, and by his skill in the management of his sabre, that he escaped, though not unwounded, from the attempts made by the indignant and refractory chieftains to assassinate him. In the end, however, he overcame every opposition, and

* Tar. Resh. f. 83.

SECT. III.

was implicitly obeyed by all. He made successful inroads on the Infidel Kalimáks, whom he defeated in two bloody battles, which earned for him the name of Ilachi Khan, signifying in their language "the slaughtering Khan," a designation by which he was ever after popularly known. When his brother Mahmúd (the elder Khan) was defeated by the Kaizák Uzbeks, Ahmed marched to his assistance, invaded their territory, thrice drove them from the field, and plundered their country. He kept Moghulistán in such order, we are told, that, for the extent of seven or eight months' journey, not a Kalimák or Kaizak dared to set foot on his territory.*

Such was the state of Moghulistán, and its Khans, on the accession of Báber.

Part Second. CHAGHATÁI KHANS OF MÁWERANNAHER. — THEIR DECLINE AND EXTINCTION.

Khanship divided.

A. H. 721, A.D. 1321.

We have seen that the Chaghatái Empire came to be divided into two great parts, Moghulistán and Máwerannaher, from the time of the first Isan-bugha, if not earlier. The history of the Khans of Moghulistán we have briefly traced. The territory lying between the Sirr and the Hazára mountains, with its inhabitants, more particularly and almost exclusively acquired the name of Chaghatái; a name afterwards still farther restricted to the portion of that territory lying beyond the Amu. The earlier succession of the Khans of Máwerannaher was troubled and uncertain; the strongest proof of which is, that, after Isan-bugha's departure for Moghulistán, of the ten who occur between him and Kásán Sultan, from A. H. 721 to A. H. 733, in the short space of twelve years, two are not of the Chaghatái line, (one

Máwerannaher.

A.D. 1321–33.

* Tar. Resh. ff. 84—86.; and Báber's Memoirs.

SECT. III.

being descended of Tuli and one of Oktái,) while the names of four are not contained in the lists of several historians of the dynasty.

Kázán Khan, A. H. 733, A. D. 1332-3.

Kázán Sultan Khan, who reigned about fourteen years, was the last of the Khans of Máwerannaher who was not a mere puppet in the hands of the Minister. Having put to death several Amírs and Núiáns, his tyranny or severity excited revolt among the chiefs of the different districts of his dominions. Mír Kazaghan, the head of a Moghul tribe settled in Khutlán on the Amu, was placed at the head of the confederated insurgents; and, after a war carried on with various success, Kázán Khan fell in battle, about a hundred and four years after the death of Chaghatái. By these events the power of the Khans of Máwerannaher received a fatal blow. "After him," says Abulghazi Khan, "there were indeed other khans in that country, but they were such as only bore the name of Khan without having the power, each head of a tribe assuming the liberty of doing what he pleased, and obeying the Khan as much as he thought fit."*

His death, A. H. 747, A.D. 1346.

Titular Khans.

It is unnecessary to follow the series of Chaghatái Khans who succeeded, princes possessed of no real authority, employed merely to sanction the acts of ambitious ministers, and most of them raised to the throne and dragged down and murdered, as state policy or the minister's caprice happened to suggest. Transoxiana fell into a state of anarchy, and to the calamity of intestine war was added that of Tartar invasion from the north. From all of these evils it was relieved by the final success of the great Taimur; who, having overcome all his competitors, reduced the country to order, and ruled with uncontrolled power. He retained, however, the still venerated name and dignity of the Khans;

* Abulghazi, Hist. Gen. pt. v. c. ii. A list of the Chaghatái Khans of Máwerannaher, who succeeded Kázán Khan, is given in Appendix C.

SECT. III.

though, for whatever cause, he changed the family; instead of a descendant of Chaghatái setting up one Syurghatmish, of the race of Oktái Khan, in whose name as Khákán or Grand Khan, and not in that of Taimur, all edicts and commissions were issued. Though this deference was paid to ancient usage, the Khan was carefully deprived of all real authority, and his office was a mere name. Syurghatmish dying in the lifetime of Taimur, the title was bestowed on his son Sultan Mahmúd Khan, who has acquired a place in history from being the person by whom the Ottoman emperor, Bajazet Ilderim, was made prisoner at the great battle of Angora. Sultan Mahmúd appears to have held the dignity of Khan as long as Taimur lived. The future succession is uncertain. Tumán Kutluk Ughlan is said to have succeeded Sultan Mahmúd. But with them the Grand Khans acknowledged in Máwerannaher probably ended. In the time of Ulugh Beg Mirza, Taimur's grandson, the monarchs of Samarkand began to issue firmans in their own name. Though the names of Toghlak-Taimur and of his son Elias Khwája, Khans of Moghulistán, are found in the list of Chaghatái Khans contemporary with Taimur, these princes were never recognised to the south of the Sirr, except for a brief period of four or five years, when their armies were in the temporary possession of the country.*

Their extinction.

When the dynasty of the Chaghatái Khans became extinguished in Máwerannaher, it was succeeded by that of Taimur; to whom, down to the present day, the monarchs of the East delight to trace up their origin.

* The principal authorities for this period are Sherfeddín, the Shajrat, Abulghazi, and Deguignes.

SECTION FOURTH.

NEW TÚRKI DYNASTY OF MÍR TAIMUR.—HIS CONQUESTS.—SHÁRÚKH AND ULUGH BEG MIRZAS.—ABUSAÍD MIRZA.—HIS DEATH.—DIVISION OF HIS DOMINIONS. — UMERSHEIKH MIRZA, KING OF FERGHÁNA. — HIS DEATH. — SUCCESSION OF BÁBER.

SECT. IV. Dynasty of Mír Taimur.

TAIMUR BEG, the founder of a new dynasty, was born in Transoxiana, at Shehr-sebz, or Kesh, thirty miles south of Samarkand, on the 25 Shábán A. H. 736 (A. D. 1336, April 9.).* He was the son of the Chief of the Birlás, a tribe of the purest Mongol origin, but the scattered individuals of which, from long residence in Túrki countries, had become Túrks in manners and language. His extraction, like that of all other great monarchs, has been traced back into fabulous times. As Chengíz Khan was the conqueror whose family for a century and a half had given rulers to all the principal countries of Tartary and Persia, a connection with it was courted as a mark of dignity and importance; and a pedigree connecting him with that family was easily discovered for the successful warrior. The period of time which had elapsed between Chengíz Khan and Taimur was too short, and the descendants of the great conqueror were too well known, to admit of any claim on the part of Taimur to a direct descent from him. But flattery found their common ancestor in the holy Alankáwa, and Taimur could claim as well as Chengíz, the honour of a heavenly descent. Whether he really did so, or whether the claim was made for

His origin.

* Abulghazi, pt. v. c. III. and IV.

SECT. IV.

Claim to be Hereditary Prime Minister.

him at a later date, is not very clear. He certainly, however, if the memoirs ascribed to him are authentic, did claim to be of the same family as Chengíz, and even to have pretensions to be hereditary Prime Minister of the dynasty.

The Altamghá of Tumana Khan.

The story was that Tumana, one of the ancestors of Chengíz, had twin sons, Kábul and Kájuli. The eldest one night dreamed that he saw a blazing star between the heaven and earth, the brightness of which gradually increased till it obscured all the other stars, and filled the whole earth with its splendour. The younger brother had the same dream, only his star was smaller, and its effulgence less brilliant. Interpreters of dreams were consulted, who predicted that from the race of the elder a mighty monarch would arise, who should conquer the whole earth, which his posterity would rule for ages; and that the younger brother and his descendants were to be their prime ministers. To carry into effect this declared will of heaven, the two brothers, it is pretended, entered into a covenant, styled "the Altamghá of Tumana Khan;" by which it was agreed, that, while the princes of the elder branch of the family were to be invested with all the honours of the sovereignty, the active cares of the administration were to devolve on the family of the younger brother. From Kábul, the elder brother, was descended Chengíz; and from Kájuli, the younger, came Mír Taimur.* Káráchár Núian (or Nevian) was the Atálik

* The genealogy given in the Jami-it-towáríkh and the Moiz-ul-ansab (Hist. des Mongols, p. 679.) differs in its earlier stages from that in Abulghazi, Hist. Gen. pt. IV. c. XV. The dream, as related in the Shajrat-ul-Atrak, is much more specific and more minutely prophetic, pp. 55—57.; see also, pp. 353. 367, 368. The more important question, regarding the grants of the Visiership to Taimur's family, is not free from difficulty. It is not clear when they are first mentioned, and there seem even to be discordant claims. In Taimur's Institute, as published by White, Taimur states that the agreement between Kábul Khan and Kájuli Behâder was shown to him by Toghlak Taimur himself; pp. 22—25. This is the more singular as we have already seen that a claim

or Minister of Chengíz, during his minority; in pursuance, it is asserted, of this ancient compact, which Chengíz afterwards renewed. That prince is said to have left Káráchár Núian as Prime Minister to his son Chaghatái Khan, who, on his part, at his death also committed to that able politician the execution of his will and the care of his children. It seems more certain that an agreement in writing was entered into between Dáwa Chichan, a descendant of Chaghatái, when he became Grand Khan of the Moghuls, and Alengíz Núian, a grandson of Káráchár, confirming the two alleged prior contracts. From Káráchár, Taimur is said to have been the fifth in descent. At all events, to be born like Taimur of the family of the Chief of the noble tribe of Birlás, was no mean origin. Its renewal.

But whatever was Taimur's descent, his high elevation was due to his own transcendent talents. His Taímur's rise

similar to that made for Taimur, to be Prime Minister to the Khan, was set up for Yúlaji, the very person who had placed Toghlak Taimur on the throne. Yet Taimur was a Birlás, Yúlaji a Doghlat. Mirza Haider, a descendant of Yúlaji and a man of veracity, informs us that he saw the firmans that had been issued in favour of Khodáidád, confirming the previous grants made to his family by Chengíz Khan and Toghlak Taimur, in his father's possession; that they were dated in spring, in the year of the Hog, at Kunduz; and that they were destroyed in the confusions consequent on the wars with Sháhi Beg Khan. Tar. Resh. f. 42. It would seem, therefore, as if claims were made by different families. The diversity between the representations of Taimur and Mirza Haider is curious, and may be considered as casting some doubt on the authenticity of the Institutes and Túzúk of Taimur. Gibbon, with his usual critical acumen, remarks, on occasion of the term *Uzbek* used in them, as applied to the invaders of Transoxiana, under Toghlak Taimur and his son, that were he assured that it existed in the original (Túrki) Institutes, he would boldly pronounce them a forgery. It may be remarked that neither Báber, a descendant of Taimur, nor Mirza Haider, Baber's cousin, both of them princes who wrote commentaries of their own transactions, the one in Túrki, the other in Persian, ever allude to Taimur as the author of a similar work. It is not impossible that his Commentaries were known only in that branch of his family that reigned in Irák and the West. I throw out these remarks rather for the purpose of exciting investigation than of delivering an opinion. At the same time, a critical examination of the Túzúk and Institutes would be a valuable contribution to Oriental History.

SECT. IV. first contests, like those of Chengíz Khan, had for their object to gain the direction of his own tribe, which, after many vicissitudes of fortune, he attained; and, following up his success, after long and painful exertions he became the undisputed ruler of all Máwerannaher, and had the glory of restoring to peace and to prosperity its various provinces, which had long been a prey to anarchy. After this success at home, he led his victorious troops not only into the deserts of Kipchák and of Moghulistán, but through the richest provinces of Asia, which one after another he reduced under his power, from the Dardanelles to Delhi; and left at his death one of the greatest empires the world ever saw. The troops by which he effected his conquests were chiefly drawn from the Túrki tribes beyond the Oxus.

and conquests.

His death, A. H. 807, A. D. 1405.

The history of Taimur and his earlier descendants is well known. It is only necessary for the present purpose to follow the history of the province of Máwerannaher. Soon after Taimur's death, his mighty empire was divided into many separate kingdoms. Máwerannaher became the portion of his son Sháhrúkh Mirza, who long held it. Taimur's third son, Mirza Miránshah, from whom Báber was descended, had for his share Azerbáiján, Syria, and Irák. He lived chiefly at Tabríz, the climate of which suited his constitution. But he fell, not long after his father's death, in a battle with Yusef, the chief of a Turkoman horde, near Tabríz.

Mirza Mir-ánshah, his third son.

Mirza Sultan Muhammed,

Mirza Miránshah's eldest son, Mirza Sultan Muhammed, at the time of his father's death was residing in Samarkand, where he was treated with great kindness by his uncle Sháhrúkh Mirza, and by that prince's son Ulugh Beg Mirza, more celebrated for his encouragement of science, and especially for the Astronomical Tables constructed under his patronage, than for his extensive dominions. Mirza Sultan Muhammed

SECT. IV.

Sultan Abusaíd Mirza,

does not appear to have taken any active part in public life. When visited on his death-bed by his cousin Ulugh Beg, he took his son Abusaíd's hand, and placing it in that of Ulugh Beg, recommended the young man to his protection. The trust thus committed to him, Ulugh Beg faithfully fulfilled; and Abusaíd, for some years, served him with diligence and affection. But when one of the sons of Ulugh Beg rebelled, and his father marched from Samarkand to chastise him, Abusaíd Mirza, led by a guilty ambition, having secretly formed a party, occupied that capital. Ulugh Beg, hurrying back to quell this unlooked-for revolt, was followed and defeated by his rebellious son, by whose order he was soon after murdered, though the decree for his execution is said to have borne the name of the titular Grand-Khan.* The parricide next defeated Abusaíd and made him prisoner, yet survived but a short time, and was murdered in his turn. The young captive being released from custody, after various reverses of fortune, joined Abulkhair Khan in the wilds of Kipchák, and induced him to lead a body of his Uzbeks into Máwerannaher. Escaping from the Khan's camp, after a victory gained by the Uzbeks near Samarkand, Abusaíd suddenly entered that capital, as has been mentioned, and was received with acclamations of joy by the inhabitants, who above all things dreaded the entrance of the barbarians, and gladly raised him to the throne.† In the course of an active and vigorous reign, he not only subdued Máwerannaher, but extended his kingdom over Khorásán as far as Mekrán and the Indus. But having engaged in an expedition into Azerbáiján, to support one tribe of Turkomans against Uzan Hasan the chief of another, who aimed at subjugating the province, he was sur-

A. H. 853, A. D. 1449.

* This was probably one of the last instances, perhaps the very last, in which the Grand Khan's name was employed.

† See before, pp. 29. and 47.

SECT. IV.

His death, A. H. 873, A. D. 1469.

rounded by that chieftain's army in the defiles of the mountains near Ardebíl, and perished with the greater part of his immense host. This event formed an era that long continued to be remembered as "the calamity of Irák."

Division of his dominions.

On the death of this powerful prince, the grandfather of Báber, his extensive dominions fell to pieces, and were occupied partly by his sons and partly by strangers. Of his sons, four became independent princes. The eldest, Sultan Ahmed Mirza, became sovereign of Samarkand and Bokhára; Sultan Mahmúd Mirza, his third son, gained possession of the provinces lying between the Hindu-kúsh and Asfera mountains, a tract comprising Badakshán, Khutlán, Turmez, and Hisár-shadmán; his fourth son, Umersheikh Mirza, the father of Baber, continued to rule the small kingdom of Ferghána or Andeján, lying on both sides of the upper course of the Sirr, which he had governed in his father's lifetime. A younger son, Ulugh Beg Mirza, retained possession of Kábul and Ghazni, which also had been given him by his father. The rich country of Khorásán, after a long series of revolutions, was at length conquered and enjoyed in peace by Sultan Husein Mirza, Baikera, also a descendant of Taimur, the greatest prince of his time, and an eminent patron of learning and learned men, as well as of all the fine arts.

Ferghána; Sultan Umersheik Mirza.

Sultan Umersheikh Mirza, Báber's father, had received the little country of Ferghána from his father in early life. He was, as we have seen, of an ambitious, restless disposition; and made repeated attempts to conquer Samarkand, the kingdom of his eldest brother, who in return as often invaded his dominions. Both married daughters of Yunis Khan, the Grand Khan of the Moghuls, who on different occasions marched to the assistance of Umersheikh, his favourite son-in-law, and mediated a peace between the brothers. Besides

A. H. 890, A. D. 1485.

Ferghána, the Mirza for some time possessed the fruitful

provinces of Táshkend and Seirám, which passed from him into the hands of the Moghul Khans. He also held for a short time Shahrokhía; and when Sultan Ahmed Mirza suffered his great defeat on the Chirr, the governor of Uratippa surrendered that place to Umersheikh, who kept it till his death. A.H. 893, A.D. 1488.

The Sultan had long reigned in his little kingdom, when, in A.H. 899, Sultan Mahmúd, the Khan of the Moghuls, and Sultan Ahmed Mirza, the King of Samarkand, who had taken umbrage at some part of his conduct, entered into a confederacy to deprive him of his dominions; and cemented their union by the marriage of the Khan with a daughter of the Mirza. The more effectually to carry their purpose into effect, it was concerted that the Khan should enter Ferghána on the north and seize the provinces beyond the river; while the Mirza was to enter the kingdom from the south and seize those on the left bank of the river. Accordingly, Mahmúd, advancing from Táshend with a large army of his Moghuls, penetrated into Akhsi, the chief of the northern provinces; and the Mirza at the same time marching from Samarkand, took the direction of Andeján, the capital of the provinces of the south. A.H. 899, A.D. 1494. His dominions invaded.

It was at this crisis, when his country was a prey to invasion, that Sultan Umersheikh Mirza was carried off by an unforeseen accident. His palace stood on an eminence in the castle of Akhsi. Like many princes of the age, he amused himself with training tame pigeons. Happening one day to go into a pigeon-house that was constructed within the palace, on the edge of a steep cliff overhanging the river below, the foundation gave way, he was precipitated down the cliff along with the building, and killed on the spot. This event happened in the thirty-seventh or thirty-eighth year of his age, when he had reigned about twenty-six years, reckoning His death;

SECT. IV.

from his father's death.* He is described by his son as a brave, good-humoured prince, of a sweet temper, elegant and refined in his manners and conversation, fond of letters and remarkable for his justice. In his external policy he was ambitious, restless, and unsteady. He left three sons, Báber Mirza, by Kutluk-nigár Khanum, the second daughter of Yunis Khan; Jehángír Mirza, by Fátima Sultan, the daughter of a chief of the Moghul Tumáns; and Násir Mirza by Umeid of Andeján, a concubine. He had five daughters, two of them posthumous.

his children.

It may not be unnecessary to mention again in this place what were the states that bordered upon Ferghána, and what princes reigned in them at this period.

Neighbouring princes.

Moghuls.

The Ulús of Moghuls on the Sirr, had for its grand Khan, Sultan Mahmúd Khan, the eldest son of Yúnis Khan, and Báber's maternal uncle. Besides the provinces of Táshkend, Seirám and Shahrokhía, he possessed some extent of territory in the desert.

But the wide desert of Moghulistán was held by Sultan Ahmed Khan, Mahmúd's younger brother; and the tribes that acknowledged him, fed their flocks in a range of country, three months' journey in extent, reaching from Tashkend to Yeldúz.

Older Uzbeks.

Of the territory of Júji Khan, the Desht-Kipchák, the eastern part was held by the Uzbeks. There had been a rupture in their tribes. On the defeat and death of Abulkhair Khan, the power of his family was broken. His son Bárúj Ughlán had soon after shared a fate similar to that of his father; and his grandson Sháhi Beg Khan, had been compelled to quit the desert, and after having lived as a refugee at Bokhára, was now in Turkistán, which he held under the protection of Sultan Mahmúd Khan, and strengthened himself by collecting the scattered remnants of the tribe that continued to be

* A. H. 899, Ramzan 4 (A. D. 1494, June 9.). He was thirty-nine lunar years old.

attached to his family, and such other Uzbeks as were discontented with their new rulers. SECT. IV.

Kaizák Uzbeks.

The other branch of the Uzbeks, (who got the name of Kaizák Uzbeks,) from having been originally a small predatory body, had by the course of events become the most powerful division of the two; and occupied the entire desert north of Turkistán as far as the Yáik. Their Khan at this period was Berendúk Khan, the son of Gerái. That country, by the writers of the time, is often called Uzbekistán.

Káshghar.

Káshghar was governed by Ababeker Mirza, a prince of great courage, but infamous for his tyranny and cruelty.

Samarkand.

In Máwerannaher; Samarkand and Bokhára, with Shehr-sebz and Karshi, were held by Sultan Ahmed Mirza, Umersheikh's elder brother.

Hisár.

Hisár, Khutlán, Badakhskán, and Kunduz were in the possession of Sultan Mahmúd Mirza, the immediate elder brother of Umersheikh.

The three brothers, Ahmed, Mahmúd, and Umersheikh, had each married a daughter of Yúnis Khan.

Kábul.

The more distant kingdoms of Kábul and Ghazni continued to be held by Sultan Ulugh Mirza, a fourth brother of the Mirzas.

Khorásán.

Khorásán obeyed Sultan Husein Mirza Baikera, who at that time was by far the most powerful of the princes of the House of Taimur. His capital was Herát, which for the space of nearly half a century was the most magnificent city of the East, and celebrated not merely for the splendour and dignity of its Court, the architectural beauty of its mosques, tombs, colleges, and palaces, but as being the resort of the greatest Divines, philosophers, poets, and historians of the age, who received the most liberal patronage from the Khákán and his Amírs.*

* The materials for this chapter are supplied by the Rozet-us-Sefa, the Taríkhi Reshídi, and Báber's Memoirs.

BOOK FIRST.

FROM BÁBER'S ACCESSION TO HIS FIRST EXPULSION FROM MÁWERANNAHER.

CHAPTER FIRST.

CONQUEST AND LOSS OF SAMARKAND.—LOSS AND RECOVERY OF ANDEJÁN.

ACCESSION OF BÁBER.—STATE OF FERGHÁNA, WHICH IS ATTACKED ON ALL SIDES.—INVADERS REPELLED.—DEATH OF SULTAN AHMED OF SAMARKAND, AND OF SULTAN MAHMÚD, HIS BROTHER.—REVOLUTIONS OF THAT COUNTRY.—BÁBER INVADES IT.—HE BLOCKADES THE CAPITAL.—HUTS HIS ARMY IN WINTER QUARTERS.—IS ATTACKED BY SHEIBÁNI KHAN.—TAKES SAMARKAND.—REVOLT IN FERGHÁNA, IN FAVOUR OF HIS BROTHER JEHÁNGÍR.—BÁBER MARCHES TO QUELL IT.—LOSES SAMARKAND AND ANDEJÁN.—HIS DISTRESS.—APPLIES FOR SUCCOUR TO SULTAN MAHMÚD KHAN.—GETS POSSESSION OF MARGHINÁN.—RISING OF THE POPULATION OF FERGHÁNA IN HIS FAVOUR.—RECOVERS ANDEJÁN.—REVOLT OF HIS MOGHUL TROOPS.—SUCCESS OF TAMBOL AND HIS DEFEAT.—CAMPAIGN OF KÁSÁN.—BÁBER CONCLUDES A PEACE WITH JEHÁNGÍR AND TÁMBOL.

BOOK I.

Báber's birth. 6 Moharrem, A. H. 888, Feb. 14. A. D. 1483.

ZEHÍR-ED-DIN MUHAMMED was born on the 6th day of Moharrem, A.H. 888. He was the son of Umersheikh Mirza, the sovereign of Ferghána, by his wife Kutluk-nigár Khánum, the daughter of Yúnis Khan, the Grand Khan of the Horde of Moghuls.* His name was

* Báber's genealogy, on the father's side, was;—Báber the son of Sultan Umarsheikh Mirza, the son of Sultan Abusaíd Mirza, the son of Sultan Muhammed Mirza, the son of Mirza Mirán-shah, the son of Amír Taimur Korkán.

On the mother's side, it was; Kutluk-nigár Khanum, the daughter of Yúnis Khan, the son of Weis Khan, the son of Shir Ali Khan, the son of Muhammed Khwája Khan, the son of Khizer Khwája Khan, the son of Toghlak-Taimur Khan, the son of Isan-bugha Khan, the son of Dawa Chichan, the son of Borák Khan, styled Ghiás-ed-dín, the son of Sukar, the son of Kámgár, the son of Chaghatái, the son of Chengíz Khan.

chosen for him by Khwája Nasír-ed-dín Obeid-ulla, at that time the most celebrated spiritual guide in Transoxiana. The Chaghatáis, we are told, having some difficulty in pronouncing the Arabic words Zehír-ed-din, called him Báber, a name which his parents adopted; and his official designation became Zehireddín Muhammed Báber.* At the period of his father's death he was little more than eleven years of age.

CHAP. I.

A.D. 1494.

A.D. 1494.

Ferghána.

The kingdom of Ferghána, now Kokán, to which he succeeded, and which has become so famous as his birthplace, though of small extent, was, as he himself informs us, rich in fruits and grain. It is surrounded on all sides by mountains, some of them covered with perpetual snow, except towards the south-west, between Khojend and Samarkand, where there is an opening between the hills and the left bank of the river Seihún. This river, called also the Sirr, and the river of Khojend, is the ancient Jaxartes†, which, flowing down from the mountains on the side of Káshghar, divides Ferghána into two parts, and afterwards proceeding by Táshkend and Turkistán, reaches the sea of Aral with diminished waters, after passing through a sandy desert.

The different ranges of hills that surround Ferghána do not seem to have any well-ascertained general names. Those on the south, covered with perpetual snow, which separate it from the little country of Karatigín, may be called the Asfera range: the mountains which separate it on the east from Káshghar, and on the north from the deserts of Tartary, seem to bear the name of Alatágh; while, on the west, a branch running from this last-mentioned range towards the Seihún, separates Ferghána from Táshkend, or Shahrokhía. The narrow opening already mentioned, between the Asfera hills

* Tar. Reshídi, f. 123. The Protector or Defender of the Faith, Muhammed the Lion.

† The Sirr is called in books, though not in the country, the Seihún, in the same way as the Amu is called the Jeihún.

BOOK I.

A.D. 1494.

and the south bank of the river, is opposite to the termination of this branch.

Its divisions.

The country was divided into seven principal districts, of which five were to the south of the great river, and two to the north. Of those to the south, the chief was Andeján, in which was the capital of the kingdom and the important fortress bearing the same name; the district of Usk extended to the eastward; that of Marghinán or Marghilán to the westward; Asfera stretched to the south and south-west among the mountains, occupying especially the glens and villages at their roots; and finally, Khojend, lower down the river, a strong place, within a bowshot of the stream, on the road to Samarkand. The districts north of the river were Akhsi * and Kásán; the former the second town and the strongest fortress in the kingdom. Umersheikh had made it his capital. Kásán stretched to the east and north of it.

As the little country of Ferghána possesses a rich soil, and lies in a temperate climate, though exposed in summer to violent heat, and in winter to severe cold, it abounds in corn and fruits, especially those of warm countries, such as the peach, the pomegrante, almond and melon. Its orchards and gardens were celebrated. Game is plentiful. The surface of the lower grounds is varied; while in the hills are delightful summer retreats, to which the inhabitants retire to avoid the heat of the weather. But though the country is in general fertile, it is intermixed with portions of ground that mark the neighbourhood of the desert.

Inhabitants.

In Ferghána, as in Transoxiana in general, the older inhabitants of the towns and of the cultivated country were Tájíks, and belonged to no tribe; but in later times the irruptions from the north had increased the number of tribesmen, both Moghuls and Túrks, so that

* Called also Akhsíkat.

the population of the open country, and a considerable portion even of that of the towns, was of Túrki race, and nowhere was the Túrki language thought to be spoken in so much purity. It was the language of the rulers, and was in such general use as to be understood even by the town's people, whose mother tongue was Persian.* It is but little known that the Túrki was at that period a cultivated tongue, in which much poetry and some history had been written. The poets were numerous, but Mír Ali Shér Nawái, a nobleman of the first rank in the Court of Herat, and a munificent encourager of learning, who flourished at this period, was generally acknowledged in his own age, and the judgment has been ratified by succeeding times as the most distinguished Túrki poet; the second place, by universal consent, being assigned to Báber. The commentaries of Taimur are supposed to have enriched this language; as did those of Báber at a subsequent time; and the Genealogical History of Abulghazi Khan, the Prince of Khwárazm, at a still later period.

It is not easy to convey any very correct idea of

* Baber's Memoirs, pp. 1—6. The Oxus was considered as the ancient boundary between the empires of Irán and Turán, the old Persian and Túrki monarchies. Yet there is good reason to believe that, in very ancient times, the whole cities and cultivated country between the Oxus and Jaxartes, with the rich and populous country north of the latter river, as well as the cities and cultivated plains of Káshgar, were inhabited by a race who spoke the Persian language; while the desert and champain of Transoxiana and Káshghar were traversed by wandering tribes, as they now are. The old inhabitants, who continue to be the artificers and cultivators, are called Tájíks, and sometimes Sarts. The term Tájík, which has excited so much discussion, and which is in use not only in Transoxiana but in Afghanistán, Persia, and Kurdistan, seems to be a corruption of "Tázi," *Arab*, being the name by which the invading Túrks distinguished the subjects of the Arabian government, who were the labourers and merchants, from themselves who belonged to wandering tribes, and were the rulers. Hence the familiar use of Túrk as opposed to Tájík; the former indicating a tribesman, the latter a townsman, a peasant. The term Tájík, in the mouth of a tribesman, was generally used as a term of contempt; while that of Túrk, employed by the Tájík, often signified a man of rough, unpolished manners. See Elphinstone's Caubul.

BOOK I. A.D. 1494. State of society, the state of society in Máwerannaher, of which Baber's little kingdom formed a part. The country being naturally rich, and when under the Aral dynasty, having been favoured by long peace, had become populous and highly cultivated; and the fields were, in many places, irrigated by canals, and improved by works of great labour and expense; so that the earlier writers represent it as a garden. As Samarkand had for ages been the seat of a powerful government, it had been richly adorned with the triumphs of Muhammedan architecture, palaces, mosques, colleges, and tombs. Of these some had been erected by Taimur, who, in the midst of his conquests, sent the artizans of Damascus and Delhi to labour in the improvement of his capital. Many other cities had shared the general prosperity. Trade flourished, to a certain extent, with the useful arts. Of their manufactures, those of paper and of crimson velvet were particularly celebrated. But the confusion and risks of war had recently interfered with every branch of national industry. The constant presence and learning. of a court had diffused through various ranks a certain refinement of manners. Learning, too, and knowledge, such as are found in Muhammedan countries, were cultivated. The instruction given in their schools and colleges, though deformed by bigotry, and though it sometimes taught a superstitious subjection to the commands of a spiritual guide, had, with all its defects, a tendency to exercise the reason, to elevate the imagination, and to mend the heart. In them they studied the Koran and its commentaries, containing the principles and the details of religion and of law; the Arabic and Persian Grammar and Logic; the Arabic, but especially the Persian, religious poets, with expositions of the abstruse and mystic passages. There were students in geometry, astronomy, and medicine, as well as of history; but the popular and almost universal taste was for the works of the national poets,

CHAP. I.

A.D. 1494.

especially the Shahnama, which were read with delight, and passages from them were familiarly quoted, not only in common conversation, but even in the transaction of business, and in official correspondence. Poetry was a favourite pursuit, and we hardly find any men of note in that age who had not cultivated the art to a greater or less degree. Few parts of the East had produced more distinguished men of science (especially while it remained under the Arabian government), or more venerated saints.*

Religious families.

There were particular families of holy men, reverenced for their piety; and some dark idea was entertained, that they were endowed with supernatural power, and superior influence with heaven. These men had numerous disciples and adherents, who followed their dictates with blind devotion. They had often a powerful effect even on public affairs: if they occasionally embroiled the country with their intrigues, it must be allowed that in other instances they protected the weak, prevented many individual acts of injustice,

* These writers employed the Arabic, at that period the language of science. Among them may be mentioned:—

Abu Ali Hasan ibn Ali, ibn Sina, better known as the Avicenna of the West, born at Bokhara, and eminently distinguished as a physician and as an expounder of the metaphysics of Aristotle (A. H. 370—428, A. D. 980—1036).

Sheikh Burkán-ed-dín Ali, a native of Marghinán (A. H. 530—591, A. D. 1136—1195), the author of the Hedáya, or Guide; a Commentary on the Musulman Law, translated by Captain Charles Hamilton, 4 vols. 4to, Lond. 1791; and of other works.

Ahmed (or Muhammed) ben Kothair Al-Ferghani, a native of Ferghana, as his name imports, who flourished in the end of the ninth century, in the time of the Khalif Almámon (A. H. 269, A. D. 883), and was celebrated as an astronomer and chronologist. Some of his works have been translated by Christomannus (Francof. 1590, 8vo) and by Golius (Amst. 1669, 4to).

Nor must we forget the astronomers who constructed the tables of the fixed stars, at Ulugh Beg's observatory at Samarkand. See Hyde's Syntagma, and the Geographical Tables; Graves in the Geographi Græci Minores.

To these authors may be added Al-Fárábi, a philosopher eminent in his own country, though less known in Europe, who was a native of Fáráb, beyond the Sirr, and who was murdered by robbers in Syria (A. H. 342, A. D. 954).

BOOK I. A.D. 1494. overawed the minds of fierce barbarians and of merciless tyrants, and softened the rigours of war. When no other person could venture to pass between hostile armies, they, from the sanctity of their character, often acted, first as mediators and afterwards as negotiators, in effecting a pacification.

It should at the same time be remarked that some of the Tartar nobles, who had been educated beyond the Sirr, were ignorant even of their letters; and that the want of political stability, and of any general or systematic means of diffusing improvement, confined knowledge to a few. Besides this, in later times, the arts and prosperity of Transoxiana were constantly exposed, not only to the ordinary vicissitudes of foreign war, and of internal discord, common to all countries, but to the more dreadful danger of being overwhelmed by the irruption of new hordes of ignorant and rapacious barbarians from the north, who threatened to sweep away the property, the personal liberty, and the lives of the inhabitants.

Art of war. As to their skill in the military art, displayed in the conduct of their large armies, they followed the practice and example of Taimur; dividing their host into several bodies, an advance, a centre or main-body, and a rear, besides flanking parties and reserve. The great bulk of the army consisted of cavalry: the arms in use were the bow and arrow, the cross-bow, the scymetar, spear, and mace; the defensive armour, the shield, coat of mail and helmet. The horses too were sometimes defended by cloth of mail or plate-armour. But the Tartars delighted much more in predatory inroads, in sudden attacks and surprises, raids and forays, than in regular warfare. With their horses, which were trained to endure fatigue and to subsist on little, they sometimes made marches of astonishing length. They trained themselves to the use of the scymetar, and much honour was gained by success in the single combats which were

CHAP. I. A. D. 1494.

often fought by champions in sight of the hostile armies. In conducting sieges they had little skill. They generally blockaded the place, trying to reduce it by famine. But escalade was also often resorted to; and they were not ignorant of the use of machines by which the wall was overtopped, or shattered. Little use seems to have been made of any engine for throwing stones, though they sometimes did employ the manjaníl or catapult. But they had studied the art of mining and countermining, which they sometimes employed with success. The use of heavy battering cannon was introduced by slow degrees, and very inartificially employed. The number of matchlockmen, small at first, increased from year to year.

Government.

Small as was Baber's kingdom, yet as he was a scion of the race of Taimur, he had around him a miniature court composed of the whole establishment of grand officers of state, and of officers of the houshold, such as belonged to the most splendid and powerful monarch. The instability of the times filled the courts of princes with crowds of bold and needy adventurers. The government was a despotism, shared with the heads of tribes, and mitigated chiefly by the influence of such holy and religious families as those already mentioned, and by the power of insurrection and revolt; a dangerous instrument, of most uncertain operation, but to which the evils of misgovernment and feelings of despair often drove the subjects in the turbulent times that ensued.

His father's death, 4 Ramzan, 899, 9. June, 1494.

The news of the death of Sultan Umersheikh Mirza, which happened at Akhsi on the 9th of June 1494, reached Báber the following day at Andeján, where he was then living. The young prince instantly took horse, with such of his followers as were at hand, and without delay rode to secure the neighbouring castle. He had reached the gate, and was about to enter, when Shiram Tagháí, one of the nobles who attended him, being seized with sudden apprehension for his safety,

BOOK I.

A.D. 1494.

laid hold of his bridle, and turned his course towards the public Id-gáh, or Prayer-Ground. In truth, Báber's situation was not free from danger. Sultan Ahmed Mirza of Samarkand was at that very time invading the kingdom with a hostile army; and it occurred to Shiram, that, if the young prince entered the castle, the Begs of Andeján, who would thereby have him in their power, might make their peace with Sultan Ahmed by seizing and giving up his nephew. No sooner, however, was it known in the fort that the young Sultan was drawing back, than Khwája Moulána Kazi *, a man of the first weight, and the Begs who were in the place, sent to invite him to enter, assuring him of their hearty loyalty, and warmest co-operation.

The Khwája was the head of a religious family of the greatest reputation, wealth, and influence in the country, which for many years had virtually held, by a sort of hereditary succession, the office of Sheikh-ul-Islam, or Judge in civil and religious cases, which in Musulman countries are alike decided by the Koran and its expositions. This family traced back its influence to Sheikh Burhán-ed-dín Kilij, a saint of much renown, and had long been regarded as the religious guardians and protectors of the country. The messenger of the Khwája and friendly Begs overtook Báber just before he reached the Id-gáh, and prevailed upon him, and his attendants, to return and enter the castle, as they had at first intended. A consultation was then held, when it was resolved to put the town instantly in a state of defence. Hasan Yákúb, a nobleman of high rank, and some other Begs, arriving a day or two afterwards, from a service on which they had been detached, joined them; and Hasan Yákub was made Master of the Household.

Báber enters Andejan.

The youthful monarch, on mounting the throne, found

* He is probably the same whom Mirza Haider calls Moulana Muhammed Sadr, Tar. Resh. f. 364.

CHAP. I.

A. D. 1494.

Confederacy against him.

that his situation was by no means an easy one; and that, small as his father's dominions were, he did not enjoy them by a quiet and undisturbed succession. We have seen that Umersheikh Mirza, not long before his death, had quarrelled with his brother, the Sultan of Samarkand *, who had, in consequence, entered into a league against him with Sultan Mahmúd, Khan of Táshkend To confirm this alliance, the Sultan had agreed to give the Khan one of his daughters in marriage; and it was concerted that while the Sultan invaded Ferghána to the south of the river, the Moghul Khan should enter it on the north.

Invasion of Sultan Ahmed Mirza.

In pursuance of this arrangement, the Sultan of Samarkand had already entered Umersheikh's country with his army, and had seized the western province of Uratippa, which lay beyond the proper boundaries of Ferghána; after which he had advanced into that kingdom, and had taken possession of the frontier district of Khojend. At the moment of his brother's death, he had added to these conquests the important town of Marghinán, in the heart of the country; and was now marching, with full confidence of success, towards Andeján, the capital of his nephew.

When he arrived on the banks of the Kába, only sixteen miles from that place, he was met by a mission,

* The princes of Taimur's family, even those who held the supreme power, had not yet assumed the title of *sháh* or *pádsháh*, king or emperor; they were called Mír or Mirza, and often Sultan. In the text, however, the ruling prince is often called King, for distinction's sake; following the usage of historians in general, and even of Báber himself. The title of Sultan was not confined to the sovereign, many chiefs, and children of chiefs, especially among the Moghul tribes, being called by that name, which is an Arabic term, nearly equivalent to Lord. The titles, Mír, Mirza, and Shah, came also, in process of time, to be very commonly given to religious guides and holy men, or mendicants, and, from a sort of flattery, were often continued to the descendants as part of the family name. The title of Mirza, in later times, has been lavished by common usage on secretaries and clerks; and in general on all who pretend to learning. Mirza is merely *mír-zadeh*, son of a Mír.

BOOK I. A.D. 1494. at the head of which was Khwája Moulána Kazi, who in Báber's name entreated the Sultan to withdraw from Ferghána, and to allow the young prince to retain the government of his father's kingdom; representing, in the true spirit of Asiatic remonstrance, that his nephew was at once his servant and his son; that the Sultan, even if master of the country, must necessarily exercise his authority by a delegate; and that, by leaving Báber in that situation, he would at the same time gratify his generous feelings, and most effectually promote his own interest. But Sultan Ahmed's ministers, by whom he was entirely guided, being averse to this arrangement, the proposal was rejected, and the army marched on.

The expedition, however, entirely failed of its object. The Kába which they had to cross in their advance, was a dark, muddy river, with a slimy bottom, and not fordable; so that it could be passed only by the bridge, which the invaders proceeded to cross, but in so disorderly a manner, that, numbers crowding over at the same time, all fell into confusion, and many of the horses and camels were pushed over into the river below and drowned. Something similar had happened to the army of Samarkand three or four years before, when the Sultan's troops were seized with a panic in crossing the Chirr near Táshkend, in consequence of which they had been totally defeated by a mere handful of Moghuls, and crowds both of men and horses had perished in the stream. This coincidence, which seemed ominous, disheartened the troops. To add to the impression thus made, a distemper broke out among the cattle of the camp, and carried off numbers of the horses. While they were thus dispirited, they found the men of Andeján, on the other hand, animated by the noblest spirit, resolute to defend their country and prince, and determined not to submit to the invaders. All these circumstances soon led to a negotiation, and terms of

CHAP. I.

A.D. 1494.

Pacification.

peace were agreed upon, when the invading army had advanced within four miles of Andeján. What these terms were is nowhere specified; but they were probably founded on the basis of the Sultan retaining his conquests, since Khojend, Marghinán, and Uratippa continued to remain for some time in the possession of the Sultans of Samarkand. Sultan Ahmed Mirza, whose health was fast declining, now returned homewards; but had made only a few days' march when he died, in the territory of Uratippa; having survived his brother, Báber's father, only forty days. He was succeeded in the kingdoms of Samarkand and Bokhara by his third brother, Sultan Mahmúd Mirza, the sovereign of Hissár.*

Invasion of the Khan of the Moghuls;

While these transactions were taking place on the south side of the Sirr, Sultan Mahmúd Khan, the Khan of the Moghuls of Táshkend, and Báber's maternal uncle had marched up the north bank of that river to fulfil his part of the treaty, had passed the hills that separate the territory of Shahrokhía from Ferghána, had entered that country, and laid siege to Akhsi. Báber's younger brother, Jehángír Mirza, was then in the town, which seems to have been his appanage. Some nobles, who happened to be in the neighbourhood, threw themselves into the place, which was very strong, and bravely defended it. Násir Mirza, the third brother, resided at Kásán, a district also on the north side of the river. His governor having some quarrel with certain other chiefs, they, influenced by party feelings, delivered up Kásán to the Khan, even before he approached it; but Násir Mirza was hurried off by his governor, and committed to the custody of Sultan Ahmed Mirza, his uncle, just before that prince commenced his march back from

* Báber's Mem. pp. 18, 19.; Tar. Resh. f. 83. Haider Mirza says (Tar. Resh. f. 83.) that Sultan Ahmed entered Andeján to prevent its falling into the hands of the Moghuls. This does not seem to be borne out by the facts, though it might have been the pretext. Ferishta (vol. ii. p. 5. Briggs's transl.) says that the peace was never ratified.

BOOK I.

A. D. 1494.

Andeján. Akhsi was the strongest fortress in Ferghána; the Khan's men were not at all fit for conducting sieges; and he himself happened to fall sick. When he found that the Sultan had made peace, and that there were no hopes of taking the town, he became disgusted with the war; and, like his ally, put an end to the campaign, and retired to his own country.

In another quarter the Khan seems to have been more successful. The province of Uratippa or Ushrushna, which his lower down the Sirr, to the westward of Ferghána, had for some years been in the possession of Umersheikh. Just before his death, it was seized by the troops of Sultan Mahmúd Khan; and the government bestowed on his most intimate friend, Muhammed Husein Mirza Doghlat, the eldest son of the late Haider Mirza, the Amír of Káshghar; and who, having married a sister of the Khan, and of Báber's mother, was honoured with the title of Korkán.*

and of Ababeker of Káshghar.

Nor were these the only attacks which the youthful prince had to sustain. His dominions were invaded, at this time, on the east also, by Ababeker Mirza Doghlat, the ruler of Kashghar; who advanced, plundering the country, as far as Uzkend † in the east of Ferghána, where he built a fort. But that irruption was checked with less difficulty than either of the others. An adequate force being sent against him, Ababeker was glad to conclude a peace and to recross the mountains of Káshghar. ‡

* Muhammed Husein had been brought up in early life with Sultan Mahmúd, who, we are told, could never bear his absenc , and always familiarly called him *Dásh*, which, in the Moghul language, means *friend*. Tar. Resh. f. 74. The Moghuls called the Chághatái of Máwerannaher, "kara dásh," f. 105. The term Gokaltash, or Kokiltash, which so often occurs in the history of India (frequently and more properly written *Gokaldásh*, foster-brother), seems properly to mean heart, or bosom-friend, from this Moghul term *dásh* and *gokal*, which signifies *the heart*. Of *Korkan*, various derivations have been given; but it seems originally to have meant *a son-in-law of the Khan*.

† Called also, Urkend and Aderkend.

‡ Báber's Mem. pp. 19, 20.

All foreign enemies being thus expelled, the chiefs who had defended Akhsi with so much success, now brought Jehángír Mirza and the late king's family across the river to Andeján, where the ceremonies of mourning for the deceased monarch were performed, and governments and other rewards assigned to such of the chiefs as had distinguished themselves in this successful defence of the country. The chief direction of affairs, and of the young prince, was vested in Hasan Yákúb, as Protector; who received the government of Andeján. This situation, however, that nobleman did not long enjoy. Intrigues agitate the court of a little Tartar prince as well as of the greatest monarch. An ambassador having come from Báber's uncle, Sultan Mahmúd Mirza, the new Sultan of Samarkand, bringing presents on the occasion of his eldest son's marriage, it was alleged, with or without foundation, and believed, that this ambassador had entered into a treasonable understanding with the Protector, who had suffered himself to be gained over to the interests of the Sultan. The ambassador took leave, "but," says the royal historian, "in the course of five or six months, the manners of Hasan Yákúb underwent a visible change. He began to behave very ill to those who were about me; and it became evident that his ultimate object was to depose me, and make Jehángír Mirza king in my place." * In consequence of these suspicions, a party was formed, headed by Ais or Isan-doulat Begum, Báber's maternal grandmother, the widow of Yunis Khan, a lady of high Moghul extraction and of great influence and talent. Having met privately and consulted together, the confederates resolved to seize Hasan Yákúb. That nobleman, however, getting intimation of their design, effected his escape: but soon after, when attempting to make himself master of Khokán †

CHAP. I.

A.D. 1494.

Hasan Yákúb, Protector.

A.H. 900, A.D. 1494.

* Báber's Mem. p. 27.

† Or, Khákend.

BOOK I.

A. D. 1494–5.

(at the present day called Kokán, and the capital of the whole country), he was intercepted by the troops sent against him, and slain in a nocturnal skirmish.

Death of Sultan Mahmúd Mirza, Rebí II. A. H. 900, January, A. D. 1495.

Sultan Mahmúd Mirza did not long survive his exaltation to the throne of Samarkand, having died about six months afterwards. He is represented as a prince of talent, but of incurably debauched and profligate manners.* The population of Samarkand, immediately on hearing of his death, rose upon Khosrou Shah, his prime adviser, who had accompanied him from his old principality of Hissár. The Terkhán Begs, who at this time possessed great influence in Bokhara and Samarkand, and other leading men, succeeded in allaying the tumult; and sent off Khosrou to Hissár, at that time held by Sultan Masáúd Mirza, the eldest son of the late monarch, to whom his father had given it when he removed to Samarkand. They then held a consultation, at which it was agreed to pass over Masáúd, and to call in Bayesanghar Mirza, his younger brother.

Bayesanghar succeeds in Samarkand.

That prince was accordingly sent for, from his government of Bokhara, and placed on the vacant throne of Samarkand.†

We have seen that Báber did not recover possession of Uratippa, nor of Khojend. Nor was his hold of the rest of his father's dominions altogether secure. At this crisis one Ibráhím Sáru, a Moghul, surprised the fort of Asfera, in the southern province of Ferghána, and declared for Bayesanghar. Báber marched against him; and after a siege of forty days, in the course of which he ran mines, and employed battering machines, reduced the place. Ibráhím, who had been long in the service of Báber's mother, came down from the fortress, and presented himself before the voung king, in the

* "Mirza Sultan Mahmúd, the most discreet and virtuous, according to our author" (the author of the Kholaset-ul-Akhbár), "of all the Sultan's (Abusaid Mirza) children," Price's Retrospect, vol. iii. p. 624. The instances adduced by Báber do not admit of this conclusion.

† Báber's Mem. pp. 28—33.

garb of a suppliant, with a scymitar suspended from his neck; and, by the intercession of Kazi Moulána, he was pardoned. From Asfera, Báber proceeded to recover the important country of Khojend; which, he tells us, was sometimes considered as no part of Ferghana; and, on his approach, it was surrendered to him by Bayesanghar's governor.*

CHAP. I.

A.D. 1495.

Báber recovers Khojend.

When at Khojend, Báber was not far from Shahrokhía, where his maternal uncle, Sultan Mahmúd Khan, the elder Khan of the Moghuls, then happened to be; and, undeterred by the unfriendly attempt which that chief had so lately made to deprive him of his dominions, he resolved to pay him a visit; in the hope of removing any misunderstanding that might still exist between them, and at the same time of conciliating his favour. Shahrokhía lies north of the Sirr, between Khojend and Táshkend. The Khan, a true Moghul, born and bred in the desert, and the genuine representative of Chengíz Khan, received him in state, sitting in a pavilion which was erected in a garden. "Immediately on entering," says Báber, "I made three low bows. The Khan returned my salutation by rising from his seat, and embracing me; after which I went back and again bowed once; when the Khan, inviting me to come forward, placed me by his side, and showed me every mark of affection and kindness." Having spent a few days with his uncle, Báber returned to Akhsi, by the right bank of the river, and then crossed over to Andeján.*

Visits Sultan Mahmúd Khan

On his return from this excursion, Báber was at a loss in what way to pay his troops. A tribe called Jagrak inhabited the wild and rugged country between Ferghána and Káshghar. Báber despatched a force against them, which entered the country and drove off about twenty thousand sheep and fifteen hundred horses, which he divided among his followers.

Plunders the Jagraks.

* Báber's Mem. pp. 33, 34.

† Ibid. p. 34.

BOOK I.

A. D. 1495–6.

Invades Uratippa,

Not long after, Báber made a sudden irruption into Uratippa, in hopes of recovering that district, which had belonged to his father. It was then held by Sultan Ali Mirza, under his brother Bayesanghar of Samarkand. As Báber approached, the Mirza retired, leaving Sheikh Zulnún in command, as governor. Báber sent Khalífa, a favourite officer, to communicate with Zulnún, and to bring him over to his interest. But the Sheikh, far from being shaken in his fidelity, seized the envoy and ordered him to be put to death. Khalífa, with great difficulty, effected his escape; and, naked and on foot, rejoined the camp. But the season was far advanced, and Báber, on entering the country, found that the inhabitants had taken in all their grain and provender; so that he was constrained to retire, from wanting the means of subsistence. Soon after his retreat, the Khan's people, crossing the Sirr, attacked and took Uratippa. Instead of restoring it to Báber, however, the Khan gave it to his brother-in-law, and particular friend and favourite, Muhammed Husein Korkán, Doghlat; who kept possession of it for nearly nine years, down to the time when Sheibáni Khan overran and took possession of that and of several of the neighbouring districts. This part of his father's dominions, therefore, Báber never possessed.*

which taken by the Khan.

A. H. 908, A. D. 1502.

Ramzan, A. H. 901, May or June, A. D. 1496.

Sultan Husein invades Hissár.

It was after Báber's return from this expedition that he was joined by a body of Uzbeks and Doghlat Moghuls, who for some time past had been settled in Hissár. They had just been driven from that country, by the invasion of Sultan Husein Mirza, the Sultan of Khorásán. That able and ambitious prince, probably wishing to take advantage of the death of Sultan Mahmúd Mirza, for at this period the death of any prince seems uniformly to have led to a scramble for his dominions, had advanced with a powerful army into the terri-

* Báber's Mem. p. 35.; Tar. Resh. f. 83.

tories of Sultan Masáúd Mirza, who now possessed Hissár-Shádmán, and the other states which had been enjoyed by his late father before he succeeded to Samarkand. Masáúd collected an army beyond the Amu, marched to Turmez, and for some time prevented the Sultan from crossing the river. But no sooner had a detachment of his army effected a passage by stratagem, than Masáúd, in spite of the remonstrances of Wáli, his minister, Khosrou Shah's brother, who proposed a rapid attack on the small party that had crossed, fled in alarm to Hissár; and, on hearing of the Sultan's approach, instantly, without even an attempt to face his enemy, abandoned his kingdom, fled disgracefully, and took shelter with Bayesanghar Mirza, his younger brother, in Samarkand.

Sultan Masáúd flies.

In consequence of this imbecility, Masáúd's army was broken up; Wáli drew off towards Khutlán. His brother Báki Cheghaniáni, with other chiefs, fortified himself in Hissár. Khamzeh Sultan and Mehdi Sultan, who some years before had left Sheibáni Khan's service and entered Mahmúd's with a body of Uzbeks, and Muhammed Doghlat and Sultan Husein Doghlat, who with a body of Moghuls from Káshgar had settled in Hissár, retired into the mountains of Karatigín. The Sultan of Herat sent in pursuit of them a body of troops, who were defeated in the defiles of the country, and the leaders taken, but set at liberty. The Uzbek and Moghul chiefs then crossed the mountains to Andeján, as has been mentioned, and offered their services to Báber, who willingly accepted them.

Báki defends Hissár.

Meanwhile Báki, who had thrown himself into Hissár, was successful in standing a siege of two or three months, against all the efforts of the Sultan; and his elder brother Khosrou Shah, the prime minister of Masáúd, who took charge of the counties on the south side of the river, adopting on this occasion a bolder and more generous policy than his master, having

BOOK I. A. D. 1496.

and Khosrou, Kunduz.

fortified himself in Kunduz, resisted with equal success the attack of Badi-ez-zemán Mirza, the Sultan's eldest son, whom his father had sent with a division of his army to crush him, and whom Khósrou, with an inferior force, contrived to shut up in his camp. So effectually was the Mirza thwarted in his object, that he was at length glad to retreat; when the enemy hung on his rear, and harassed him in skirmishes. The Sultan, disconcerted by the bold defence of Hissár, and by his son's want of success, was content to patch up a peace, and to cover the shame of his retreat by negotiating a marriage between a sister of Sultan Masáúd and a son of his own. This well-timed and successful resistance was the immediate origin of the great power which Khosrou Shah afterwards attained.*

Bayesanghar defeats the Khans.

At this very period some events occurred at Samarkand, which had great influence on Báber's future fortunes. Bayesanghar Mirza, the new Sultan, had been rather fortunate in the commencement of his reign. A party in his capital, at the head of which was Sultan Juneid Birlás, a man of weight in the country, who felt their views of ambition thwarted by the ascendency of the Sultan's Terkhan ministers, had invited the elder Khan of the Moghuls, Sultan Mahmúd, who was ever ready to enter into any scheme that promised to increase his power, to enter the territory of Samarkand with a hostile army. Bayesanghar, with much expedition and energy, led out a well-appointed body of troops to meet the Moghul invaders. He fell in with them near Kánbái, a town of Samarkand; upon which the advanced body of the Moghuls, the flower of their troops, dismounted and began to discharge their powerful arrows against their assailants. But the cuirassiers of the Samarkand army, charging at full speed, broke their lines, trampled them down

A. H. 900, A. H. 1495.

* Báber, pp. 37—39.

under foot, and cut them to pieces. The main body, on seeing this slaughter, were seized with alarm and did not stand their ground. Numbers were slain, and many taken prisoners. These were brought before the Sultan's tent, and beheaded as they arrived; and such, we are told, was the number of Moghuls thus put to death, that the open space in front of it being again and again incumbered with the heaps of dead bodies, it was thrice necessary to shift the Sultan's tent to clear ground. The Khan hastened back to Táshkend, with the loss of three or four thousand men.*

Displeases the Terkhán chiefs,

But this success, though it defeated the machinations of the conspirators for a time, did not secure the Sultan from new dangers. He was so imprudent as to displease the leading men of Samarkand, and especially the powerful family of the Terkháns. Having probably been brought up in early life among the Begs and soldiers of Hissár, he showed them on all occasions a marked partiality. The two last sovereigns of Samarkand, the Sultans Ahmed and Mahmúd Mirza, were the sons of Sultan Abusaíd by his chief wife, who was a daughter of Urda-bugha Terkhán. Her brother, Derwísh Muhammed Terkhán, who was thus the uncle of these two princes, had during their reigns possessed the highest influence; and it was chiefly to him and to the Terkhán family, that Bayesanghar, who was a younger son, owed his crown. Derwísh Muhammed, indignant at seeing the principal direction of affairs committed to the hands of provincials, left Bokhara in disgust, and repaired to Karshi, where Sultan Ali Mirza, a younger brother of Bayesanghar Mirza, then was, declared him king, and marched towards the capital.

who proclaim Sultan Ali Mirza.

Bayesanghár seized

The issue of these proceedings was that Bayesanghar was seized by stratagem in his palace and conveyed to

* Báber, p. 33.

BOOK I.
A.D. 1496.

the citadel, where Mirza Ali also was. The rebels then consulted together and determined to send him to the palace of Gok-serái.* This was a palace in the citadel of Samarkand, said to have been built by Taimur. It was there that every prince of the house of Taimur, when he became king, mounted the throne; and there that every one who aspired to it unsuccessfully met his doom; so that to say that a prince had been sent to the Gok-serái, was perfectly well understood to intimate that he had been effectually disposed of. But while things were in this state, Bayesanghar, having been allowed, under some pretence, to enter a building in the garden of the citadel, contrived to force his way through a sewer or aqueduct; and he afterwards let himself down over the walls of the fortress, and escaped to a village in the suburbs, where he took refuge in the house of Khwájika Khwája, a person of high reputation for sanctity, and of the first influence in the kingdom. The Terkháns, after waiting for some time without, entered the garden-house, and ascertained that their prisoner was gone.

escapes.

Having traced him to the Khwája's house, they surrounded it, demanding that he should be delivered up to them. This, however, the Khwája firmly refused; and such was the singular influence of these religious families in that age and country, an influence which in no small degree has been preserved to them down to our own times, that even the despotic Terkháns were too much afraid of the populace to venture to use force to withdraw him from the protection of these venerated men. In the course of a few days, some Begs, who were attached to Bayesanghar, being supported by the

Insurrection in favour of

* Green-Palace. The Gok-serái palace is said, by Báber, to have been built by Taimur; yet the palace of Gok-serái is mentioned by Petis de la Croix, Hist. de Genghiz-can, p. 214., as existing in the time of that conqueror, apparently on the authority of Abulfaraj; see also the same history, p. 287. The palace may have been rebuilt by Taimur.

Bayeshanghar.

citizens, who rose tumultuously, repaired to the Khwája's house, and bore him off in triumph into the city. They at the same time blocked up Sultan Ali and the Terkháns in the citadel. That fortress, not being provided for a siege, could not stand out a single day. Sultan Ali fell into his brother's hands, along with Derwísh Muhammed and other Terkháns; the rest escaped to Bokhara. Derwísh Muhammed was put to death. Sultan Ali Mirza was sent, instead of his brother, to the palace of Gok-serái, for the purpose of being blinded by the fire-pencil. It accordingly was applied to Sultan Ali's eyes; after which, as being no longer qualified for public life, he was allowed to retire into the city. There he repaired to the house of Khwája Yahía, the brother of Khwájika Khwája who has been mentioned. Yahía, like his brother, had a high reputation for sanctity; but was the head of a different faction, and his rival. Sultan Ali had attached himself to him as his spiritual guide. He was hospitably and honourably received. Whether it happened from want of skill on the part of the operator, or from intention, yet so it was that Sultan Ali's sight had sustained no essential injury. This, however, he carefully concealed, and, in a few days, escaping to Bokhára, rejoined the Terkhán Beys.*

Sultan Ali taken; escapes to Bokhára.

Bayesanghar was soon informed of his brother's escape, and conscious of the danger he had to apprehend from the irritated Terkháns, led an army to expel them from Bokhára. But Sultan Ali marching out, attacked, defeated, and pursued him back to Samarkand.

Samarkand attacked on three sides.

These events, and the confusion and anarchy with which they were attended in the kingdom of Samarkand, did not escape the observation of Báber, who resolved to try his fortune also in that great scene of his ancestors' glory. At the same moment, and induced by the same motives, Sultan Masaúd Mirza, who had

* Báber, pp. 38—40.

BOOK I.

A. D. 1496.

Shawel, A. H. 901, June or July, A. D. 1496.

retured to Hissár on the retreat of the Sultan of Herát, also entered that kingdom at the head of an army, accompanied by Wali, the brother of his minister Khosrou Shah. His claim was founded on his being the eldest son of the late king, and the elder brother of two of the competitors, and was supported by the power of his extensive dominions. Thus that unfortunate city, unfortunate from its very wealth and former prosperity, saw itself beleaguered on three sides, at the same time, by the arms of three different potentates, who acted without concert; Báber having advanced towards it from Andeján, Masaúd Mirza from Hissár, and Sultan Ali Mirza from Bokhára. Sultan Ali now proposed to Báber that they should enter into a treaty of alliance and mutual co-operation, to which Báber willingly agreed; and these two Mirzas, actuated more by jealousy of their rival than by any confidence in each other, accordingly had an interview on horseback near Samarkand, in the midst of the river Kohik, into which they cautiously advanced from the opposite banks, each attended by a limited number of followers. But as the autumn was already drawing to a close, and winter fast approaching, and as the country round Samarkand, exhausted by the presence of so many armies, was altogether unable to furnish the requisite provisions and provender for the troops, all the invading princes were compelled to withdraw into their own territories. On this occasion the Uzbek chiefs who have been mentioned as having joined Báber from Hissár, finding perhaps that his little kingdom had nothing to feed the hopes or satisfy the rapacity of adventurers, instead of accompanying him back to it, separated from him, and went to Samarkand, where they were gladly welcomed; but, in a short time, finding that things were not managed there to their satisfaction, they left it also, and joined their native chief Sheibáni Khan, in Turkistán.*

* Báber, pp. 41, 42.

CHAP. I.

A. D. 1497.

Báber again blockades Samarkand.

Ramzán, A. H. 902, May, A. D. 1497.

It had been arranged between Báber and Sultan Ali, at the conference in the river, that as soon as the winter was over, they should return into the field, and, in conjunction, form the siege of Samarkand. In the following May, therefore, when the season admitted of military movements, Báber led his army into the territory of Bayesanghar Mirza, and, after various successes, encamped at Yám, a village not far from the capital. Some skirmishes followed. It is a strong proof of the comparative civilisation which then prevailed in Transoxiana, that, while the besieging army was encamped in that position, a number of traders and shopkeepers came from the town with their wares and goods to sell in the camp bazár. "One day," says Báber, "about afternoon prayers, there was suddenly a general hubbub, and the whole of these Musulmans were plundered. But such was the discipline of my army, that on my issuing an order that no person should presume to detain any part of the effects or property that had been so seized, but that the whole should be restored without reserve, before the first watch of the next day was over, there was not, to the value of a bit of thread, or a broken needle, that was not restored to the owner." *

From Yám Báber moved his camp to Yuret Khán, a station four or five miles from the city, where he remained forty or fifty days. Many severe actions took place with considerable loss on both sides. On one of these occasions, a party which, on the treacherous invitation of some of the townspeople, he had sent to surprise the city by night on the side of the Lovers' Cave †, fell into an ambush, by which some of his bravest soldiers were slain, and others taken prisoners, and afterwards put to death. While he remained there, however, the inhabitants of all the neighbouring country submitted, and surrendered their strongholds to him.

* Báber, p. 43.

† Ghár, or Moghár-Ashikán.

BOOK I.

A. D. 1497.

" So many of the townspeople and traders came from Samarkand, that the camp was like a city, and you could find in it whatever is procurable in towns." *

From the station of Yuret-Khán, Báber moved first to the meadow of Kulbeh, and next to the hill of Kohek, on a different side of the town. When the people of Samarkand saw the army on its march from the one position to the other, thinking that it was on its retreat, and elated with their supposed success, they sallied out, both soldiers and citizens, in great numbers, towards two bridges, which crossed the river Kohek in that direction. Báber, observing this movement, watched for the favourable moment, when he ordered a charge of cavalry to be made upon them. It was completely successful. Numbers were cut down, and many, both horse and foot, taken prisoners. The higher officers and the soldiers were treated with the usual courtesy of the time. The same indulgence was not extended to the citizens. " Of the lower order of townspeople," says the Royal historian, " there were taken Diwáneh, a cloth-weaver, and one nicknamed Kilmásúk, who were notorious as the chief ringleaders of the rabble, in fighting with stones and heading riots. They were ordered to be put to death with torture, in retaliation for the foot soldiers who had been slain at the Lovers' Cave.† This chastisement put an end to all sallies in future, and the effect was such that the besiegers were allowed to advance unopposed up even to the ditch, and to carry off provisions from under the very walls.‡

* Báber, p. 44.

† The feelings of Báber and his advisers, towards the fighting townspeople of Samarkand, may remind the reader of the similar feelings of the *preux chevaliers* of the Middle Ages towards the citizens and peasantry taken in arms. Both thought themselves justified in treating them with cruel severity, and for the same reason. They regarded the use of arms as a monopoly belonging to a privileged class, and punished the military exertions of the lower orders as a troublesome interference with the rights of their superiors.

‡ Báber, p. 47.

CHAP. I.

A. D. 1497.

Báber huts his army.

But while these protracted operations were going on, the summer was drawing to a close, and the weather began to show symptoms of severity. Báber called a meeting of his Begs, to consult what was expedient to be done. All were agreed that the city was reduced to great distress, and must probably fall in a short time, but that it was impossible to keep the army in the field when winter came on, unsheltered as it then was, and in a country where the winter is extremely severe. It was resolved, therefore, to break up from before the city, and to erect temporary huts for the troops in some neighbouring forts, by which means they could still keep Samarkand, in a great degree, in a state of blockade. The fort of Khwája Dídár was pitched upon for head-quarters; and the necessary erections were begun, in and around it, without delay. When they were finished, the army moved into them. Some officers, however, went with their men to towns at a greater distance to secure better winter accommodation, so that the army was rather scattered.

Irruption of Sheibáni.

The very morning after Báber had taken possession of his new cantonments, Sheibáni Khan, the Uzbek chief, arrived with a formidable army, in presence of the camp. Bayesanghar Mirza, seeing the distress to which his capital was reduced, had sent to invite him to come to his assistance, and the Uzbek, not unwilling, had hastened by forced marches from Turkistán, beyond the Sirr. Báber, though his forces were dispersed, resolved to show a bold countenance, put the troops that were with him in array, and marched out to face the enemy. Sheibáni, who had hoped to take him by surprise, finding him on the alert, did not choose to hazard an action, and drew off towards Samarkand. Bayesanghar Mirza, who had expected much more effectual relief, from so formidable a reinforcement, disappointed and vexed at the result, could not conceal his feelings, and did not give Sheibáni the favourable

BOOK I. A.D. 1497.

reception which he had expected; while the Uzbek, who in the course of his expedition, short as it was, had seen at once the richness of the prey, and the weakness of its defenders, returned back a few days after to Turkistán. This is the first hostile appearance in Máwerannaher, of that remarkable man, who afterwards exercised so powerful an influence on the fate of Báber and of Samarkand.*

Bayesanghar abandons Samarkand,

That city had now sustained a siege for seven months. Bayesanghar had placed his last hope of relief on the arrival of the Uzbek army. Seeing that too fail, he gave himself up to despair, abandoned the place and his kingdom, and, attended only by a few attached followers, took the road to Kunduz. That district, which lies beyond the Amu, between Balkh and Badakhshán, was then held by Khósrou Shah, who was nominally subject to Sultan Masaúd Mirza of Hissár; but with whom, since that prince's retreat from Hissár, he had quarrelled, and of whom he was in reality independent. Masaúd could have no wish that his brother and rival should be able to unite himself with a protector so formidable as Khosrou; and Bayesanghar, the fugitive prince, in passing through the territory of Hissár, escaped with difficulty from an attempt made to seize him, though not without the loss of several of his followers who fell into Masaúd's hands. He finally, however, did succeed in reaching Kunduz, where he was well received by Khosrou, who though he had been the chief minister of his father, being at that time engrossed with his own schemes of power and of conquest, regarded Bayesanghar as a fit instrument for his soaring ambition.

which is occupied by Báber,

No sooner did Báber hear of the flight of Bayesanghar, than he hastened from his cantonments towards Samarkand. "On the road," says he, "we were met

* Báber, pp. 47, 48.

by the chief men of the city, and by the Begs; and these were followed by the young cavaliers, who all came out to welcome me. Having proceeded to the citadel, I alighted in the Bostan-Serai, (Garden-palace); and towards the end of the month of the former Rebi, by the favour of God, I gained complete possession of the city and country of Samarkand." * Báber was then in his fifteenth year.

CHAP. I.

A.D. 1497. End of Rebi I. A.H. 903. End of Nov. 1497.

What share Sultan Ali Mirza had in these transactions does not appear, no mention being made of him during the siege. Báber, whether in consequence of special agreement, or of his superior activity, alone entered the city. Sultan Ali had previously, however, overrun some of the dependent districts, especially those in the neighbourhood of Bokhára, and continued to retain possession of them, as well as of that city.

The city of Samarkand, the possession of which thus rewarded the perseverance of the youthful Báber, was one of the richest and most populous at that time in the world. It had been the capital of the great Taimur, and still maintained its pre-eminence in the countries which he had conquered. Báber gives us an interesting account of its mosques, colleges, and palaces. It was also ennobled by the observatory of Ulugh Beg.† The astronomical tables there composed under the eye of that prince, excited wonder in his own time, and still enrich at least the history of science. The city was situated near the Rohik or Zir-efshán river, called also the Soghd, in a fertile and populous country, and in a delightful climate; and its territory was remarkable at once for its ample harvests and for producing

* Báber, p. 48.

† See his Tables of Longitude and Latitude of the Fixed Stars, in Hyde's Syntagma Dissertationum, tom. i. Oxon. 1768, 4to; and his Geographical Tables, published by Graves in the third vol. of the Geographi Minores Græci, Oxon. 1711, 8vo; see also La Lande's Astronomie, tom. i. pp. 126, 127. Paris, 1792, 4to.

BOOK I.

A. D. 1497.

the finest fruits in the world. Taimur boasted that in one of its districts, that of Soghd, which probably retained the original name of the ancient Sogdiana, he had a garden a hundred and twenty miles in length. Its manufactures of paper and of crimson velvet, which were celebrated wherever commerce extended, have been already mentioned. The whole country, from the Andeján and the Sirr, to the Amu, including Bokhára, Kesh, and Karshi, was understood to belong to it. The inhabitants were celebrated for the refinement of their manners, their love of learning, and skill in the arts. The Persian, we have seen, was the language of Samarkánd and of all the other large towns, while the Túrki tribes, who occupied parts of the open country, preserved their ancient tongue, and their ruder manners.

Discontent of his troops,

As Báber did not enter Samarkand by storm, but on the invitation of its inhabitants, and would not sanction the general pillage of a city which he intended should be his capital, the crowd of adventurers, both Begs and soldiers, who had looked forward to the rich plunder that it was to afford as the reward of the toils which they had endured in a long siege, were extremely discontented. Though he bestowed on them such rewards as he had to give, they considered themselves as defrauded of the fairest and most natural recompense of their labours. He intimates, however, that his troops had somehow acquired considerable booty in Samarkand; but that, as all the rest of the country had submitted voluntarily, no kind of pillage whatever had been permitted elsewhere. It is probable that obnoxious individuals, or refractory quarters in Samarkand were plundered; and, as the arrogance of a victorious army is not easily checked, other irregularities might have been committed. The city, however, worn out from the long continuance of the blockade, for which it was not originally prepared, or victualled; and the country, laid waste by the movements of hostile armies for two successive summers, had been reduced to a wretched condition; insomuch that, instead of any supplies being drawn from the fertile fields around, it was absolutely necessary for the government to furnish the inhabitants with seed-corn to sow their grounds, and with other supplies to enable them to subsist till the ensuing harvest. To levy contributions for his army from such a country was, as Báber himself remarks, quite impossible. His soldiers were consequently exposed to much distress, and he possessed no adequate means of satisfying their wants. The men began to drop off, and return home. The example set by the soldiers was soon followed even by the leaders. All his Moghul horse deserted, and in the end Sultan Ahmed Támbol, a Moghul nobleman of the first rank in Andeján, forsook him like the rest, and returned home.

which desert.

To put a stop to this defection, Báber sent Khwája Moulána Kázi to Uzun Hassan, who had now the direction of affairs in Andeján, that he might prevail upon him to punish some of the fugitives, and send the rest back. But it soon appeared that Uzun Hassan was himself the enemy most to be apprehended. After Támbol had joined him, he no longer showed any reserve. A party, at the head of which were Uzun Hassan and Támbol, openly stood up in favour of Jehángír Mirza, Báber's brother, insisting that as the Sultan had now got possession of Samarkand, he should give up Andeján and Akhsi to his brother. These countries were at the same time demanded by his uncle, Sultan Mahmúd Khan, the Moghul ruler of Táshkend. Both appear to have urged their pretensions under alleged treaties.

Jehángír claims Andeján.

There is some indistinctness in the account which Báber gives of the claims of his uncle and brother; and, if we may judge from the usages of the times and the few facts known to us, there seems to have been some justice in the demands of both. The custom which at

BOOK I. A.D. 1497. that period prevailed of giving each son a separate appanage or principality, led to constant civil wars. Báber and Jehángír were born of different mothers, both Moghuls, but of different tribes. Jehángír seems to have been in possession of Akhsí as his share of his father's succession; and the Moghuls of his mother's clan attached themselves to him, and were desirous to make him independent. Most of the misfortunes of Báber's early life arose from this cause. When he had the brilliant prospect of acquiring the dominions of Samarkand, it was very natural that to secure the active co-operation of Jehángír and his friends, who composed a considerable part of the strength of Ferghána, he should have promised that country to his brother, to be held of the great kingdom of Samarkand; and some cession of territory, in return for assistance required, was probably in like manner promised to the Khan, such as his father Yúnis Khan had formerly received. Báber indeed affirms that his uncle, the Khan, could have no claim, as during the two years that he had attacked Samarkand, the Khan had given him no assistance; while, in answer to Uzun Hassan's claim on behalf of Jehángír, he says, that as the countries of Andeján and Akhsi, though never promised to the Khan, had been demanded by him, were he now to give them up to his brother, it would lead to unpleasant explanations with his uncle; and he besides remarks, that when this claim was set up for Jehángír, he had himself not above a thousand men of every description with him at Samarkand; that the claim made at such a moment too much resembled a command, and was repelled as peculiarly offensive.* Certainly, if the demand was in conformity to the literal terms, it must be allowed to be very little in the spirit of the agreement. Everything was now unfavourable

* Báber, pp. 55, 56.

to Báber; he was not settled in his new conquest; and all the deserters who left him on arriving in Andeján sided with Jehángír, and to cover their desertion, became his most determined enemies.

Uzun Hassan, himself a Moghul, who was governor of Akhsi and at the head of Jehángír's party, on receiving Báber's refusal of the demand in that prince's favour, marched toward Andeján and openly raised the standard of revolt. He was joined by Sultan Ahmed Támbol, also a Moghul, who possessed great influence in Ferghána, and who had lately deserted Báber. Báber, anxious to prevent the Moghuls who were in that country from taking part against him, despatched one Tulun Beg, who was also a Moghul, and a brave partisan, to enter into communication with his countrymen, and to attempt to retain them in his interest. But Uzum Hassan and Tambol, learning the route which Tulun had pursued, sent a body of light troops to intercept him, by whom he was taken, and soon after put to death. The revolted leaders, with Jehángír at their head, now laid siege to Andeján. Ali Dost Tagháí was the governor, and was zealously assisted in all his arrangements by Khwája Moulána Kázi. This eminent person, who was the religious director of Báber's family, was warmly attached to the young prince's interests. He soothed and conciliated such of the troops as had absconded from Samarkand, and is said to have divided eighteen thousand of his own sheep among the soldiers who were in the place, and the wives and families of such as still remained with the Sultan, to keep them steady to his cause. Repeated expresses were despatched to Báber by his mother and grandmother, who were in the town, as well as by Khwája Kázi, to point out the difficult circumstances in which they were placed, and to urge his speedy arrival; informing him that the capital was ill prepared for defence, and, if not speedily relieved, must inevitably fall.

Lays siege to Andeján.

BOOK I.

A. D. 1498.

Illness of Báber:

While these despatches arrived fast upon each other, the young prince lay at Samarkand, slowly recovering from a severe illness. Unfortunately, the confusion of his affairs prevented his laying himself up, and a dangerous relapse was the consequence of his exertions. For four days the only sustenance he received was from having his tongue moistened with wet cotton. Even his most faithful Begs and servants, despairing of his recovery, and thinking that all was over, began to leave him. It was at this moment that an envoy arrived from Uzun Hassan. During the dejection and disorder that prevailed in the household, he was imprudently introduced where the young prince lay motionless, and was afterwards allowed to depart. It so happened, however, that in a few days the vigour of Báber's constitution prevailed. The violence of the disease abated, and he began to recover, but still the attack left behind a thickness or difficulty of speech. Yet, imperfect as was his recovery, so urgent were the letters from his beleaguered friends, that he resolved to abandon his recent conquest of Samarkand, in which he had reigned only a hundred days, and set out for Andeján. In a week he reached Khojend, and there he was met by the painful intelligence that just a week before, on the very day he had left Samarkand, the castle of Andeján had surrendered to the enemy.

he sets out for Andeján.

Rejeb, A. H. 903, March, A. D. 1498.

Surrender of Andeján.

It appears that Uzun Hassan's envoy, who had been admitted to the Sultan's sick chamber, reported, on his return, that he had seen him lying at the point of death, speechless, and kept in life only by having his tongue moistened by wet cotton. This information was without delay communicated to Ali Dost, the governor of Andeján, and confirmed upon oath by the envoy in his hearing, while he stood on the city-wall, near one of the gates. Confounded by the news, and imagining any farther resistance to be unavailing, he entered into a capitulation, and surrendered the place. The besiegers immediately entered, and considerable severities were exercised. The attachment of Khwája Kázi to Báber was punished by his being ignominiously hanged over the gate of the citadel, to the great horror of a population by whom he was venerated. His family and dependents were given up to be plundered. Báber had owed him much, and was sincerely attached to him " I have no doubt," says he, " that Khwája Kázi was a saint. What better proof of it could be required than the single fact, that, in a short time, no trace or memorial remained of any one of all those who were concerned in his murder? They were all completely extirpated. Khwája Kázi was a wonderfully bold man, which is also no mean proof of sanctity. All mankind, however brave they be, have some little anxiety or trepidation about them. The Khwája had not a particle of either."*

CHAP. I.

A. D. 1498.

Báber's distress.

Báber now felt himself in a most trying situation. " To save Andeján," says he, " I had given up Samarkand, and now found that I had lost the one, without preserving the other." His capital and his hereditary dominions were occupied by a hostile faction, in the name of his brother. The greater part of his army had left him. On no side did he perceive one ray of hope to guide him onwards. His situation too was new to him. It was the first time he had been so deserted. " I became a prey to vexation and melancholy," says he, " for, since I had been a sovereign prince, I never before had been separated in this manner from my country and followers; and, since the day I had known myself, I had never experienced such care and suffering." Uncertain what to do, being equally shut out from Ferghána and Samarkand, he turned for succour to his maternal uncle, Sultan Mahmúd Khan.

The Khan enters into Akhsi.

Since the flight and death of Hassan Yákub, the

* Báber's Mem. p. 58.

BOOK I. A.D. 1468.

office of prime minister to Báber had been held by Kásim Beg, Kochin, whom he represents as brave, a man of talents, possessed of a rich vein of humour and an elegant wit, though, by an accident not uncommon among nobles of the Tartar race, he could neither read nor write.* Kásim Beg was now despatched to Táshkend, to prevail upon the Khan to march against Andeján. He succeeded in his mission. The Khan, who, with the true Tartar love of spoil, was ever ready to put his army in motion, where a country was to be plundered, marched up the right bank of the Sirr towards Akhsi, the portion of Ferghána nearest to his territory. The hostile and confederated lords, on their part, hearing of his advance, recrossed the river from the Andeján side, and encamped so as to cover Akhsi. There they contrived to engage the Khan in a negotiation, and by their arts of persuasion, and, as Báber intimates, by their bribes to the negotiators, prevailed upon him to retire back the way he came.

But retreats.

The defection of his only ally rendered the situation of the young prince more desperate than ever. Several of the Begs and soldiers who still adhered to him had their wives and families in Andeján. Anxious for their safety, and seeing now no other way to protect them, such as were so situated separated from Báber to the number of seven or eight hundred men, and returned home, leaving only two or three hundred adherents to the late conqueror of Samarkand. "I was now reduced to a very distressed situation," says he, "and wept a great deal." He went on to Khojend, which still adhered to him. There he was joined by his mother and grandmother from Andeján, and by the families of several of those who were still attached to his fortune; and there he spent the month of Ramzán, the great

* Báber's Mem. p. 16.

CHAP. I. A.D. 1498.

Muhammedan fast.* He then renewed his application for assistance to his uncle, who was always sufficiently ready to put his troops in motion, though generally to no very great purpose. As the Khan's recent treaty probably prevented any new effort against Andeján, Báber determined once more to make an attempt on Samarkand. The Khan sent his son with four or five thousand men to assist him; but before Báber could join them in the Samarkand territory, they had heard of the approach of the Uzbeks under Sheibáni Khan, and had hurriedly retreated homewards: Báber, therefore, unable to accomplish anything with his own slender means, returned to Khojend.†

Visits the Khan.

The vigorous and elastic spirit of Báber was not to be broken by this series of disappointments and discomfitures. He once more crossed the great river, and repaired to the Court of his uncle, the Khan of the Moghuls, to crave his assistance in recovering his father's kingdom. Báber's mother, we have seen, was the sister of the Khan; Jehángír's, as has been remarked, was also a Moghul, but of a different tribe. The Khan, after some solicitation, granted the young Sultan a feeble and inefficient reinforcement of eight hundred Moghuls, with which he surprised and carried by escalade the fort of Násukh, about forty miles from Khojend. But, finding it too far off to be conveniently retained, he abandoned it, and returned back to that town.

As Khojend was a small district that could hardly support two hundred retainers, it was of importance to Báber to afford it some relief from the burden of maintaining even his small army. For this purpose he endeavoured to prevail upon his neighbour and maternal uncle, Muhammed Hassein Korkán Doghlat, who, as has

* A.H. 903, Ramzán, A.D. 1498, May. It was on the 22nd May, 1498, and while Báber was overwhelmed by misfortune, that Vasco de Gama arrived at Calicut, and completed the discovery of the passage to India by the Cape of Good Hope.

† Báber, p. 50.

BOOK I.

A.D.1498-9.

Goes to Bishágher; which he is compelled to leave.

been mentioned, had held Uratippa under the Khan for the last three or four years, to lend him the village of Bishágher, in the district of Yárailák for one winter. It had formerly belonged to the late Kkwája Kazi, and lying on the road to Samarkand, was particularly favourable to Báber's views. Muhammed Hussein was finally prevailed upon to consent to this arrangement, and Báber removed to Bishágher; where he exerted himself with such activity during the winter, that, by stratagem or negotiation, he got possession of a great part of the country of Yárailák.

A. H. 904, A. D. 1498-9.

When the young Sultan, after occupying Samarkand for a hundred days, had left it on his return towards Andeján, the imperial city was occupied by his cousin, Sultan Ali Mirza of Bokhára, who had been his ally and coadjutor during the siege. As Yárailák was dependent on Samarkand, Sultan Ali, now advanced with a large force to expel the intruder; and Báber, who had not three hundred men with him, deprived of all means of a successful resistance, was compelled to withdraw from the limited conquests that he had made, and altogether to abandon that part of the country. Unwilling by returning to Khojend, to oppress the inhabitants of that little district, who for nearly two years had supported him and his band of followers, he turned off to the Iláks, a hilly tract south of Uratippa, where, living the unsettled life of a fugitive, he spent some time perplexed and distracted with the hopeless state of his affairs.

Goes to the Iláks.

"One day while I remained there," says he, "Khwája Abul Makáram, who, like myself, was an exile and a wanderer, came to visit me. I took the opportunity of consulting him with respect to my situation and concerns — whether it was advisable for me to remain where I was, or to go elsewhere, — what I might attempt, and what I should leave untried. He was so much affected with the state in which he found me, that he shed tears, and after praying over me, took his departure. I myself was also extremely affected. That very day, about afternoon prayers, a horseman was descried at the bottom of the valley. He proved to be a servant of Ali Dost" (the governor who had surrendered Andeján). "He came with a message from his master to inform me that he had undoubtedly offended deeply, but that he trusted to my clemency for forgiving his past offences; and that if I would march to join him, he would deliver up to me the town of Marghinán, and would do me such service and duty as would wipe away his late errors and free him from his disgrace." *

Invited to Marghinán;

No sooner did the young Sultan receive this welcome message than he mount and set out for Marghinán. It was then about sunset. The next three nights and two days he and his followers rode without halting, except to refresh and feed their horses. Before sunrise, on the third morning, they had arrived within four miles of Marghinán, having ridden about a hundred. It was now only that they began to consider, that on a former occasion Ali Dost had joined the enemy; and, even at the present moment, held Marghinán for them; that there had been no mutual intercourse with him, by which his real sentiments could be ascertained; that he might at that very time be treacherous, and leading them into a snare. Báber and his friends consulted together; and, though they saw that their apprehensions were not unreasonable, still it was agreed that their prudence had come too late, their whole party being worn out, both men and horses; and besides, so desperate was their present condition, that it was worth their while to hazard everything. They therefore pushed on, and early in the morning reached the gate of the castle. Here they found Ali Dost, who received them standing over the gateway, the gate being shut.

* Báber's Mem. p. 65.

BOOK I.

A. D. 1499.

which he enters.

He asked terms, which were granted him, when he threw open the gates, made his submission to his sovereign, and conducted him to a house in the fort. Báber had about 240 followers with him on this journey.

Discontent in Ferghána.

The possession of Marghinán, which lay far advanced in Ferghána, placed him in rather a better situation than he had been for a long time past. He found that Uzun Hassan and Támbol, who directed the councils of his brother Jehángír, had resorted to some harsh measures, that their government had become unpopular all over the country, and that his own restoration was very generally desired. To take advantage of the prevailing discontent, he sent Kásim Beg with a small body of a hundred men to the highlands south of Andeján to attempt to raise the country; while Ibráhím Sáru was despatched with about the same number to cross the river towards Akhsi, and to try what could be done in the northern provinces.

Uzun Hassan and Támbol, on hearing of Báber's success, collected not only the whole of their own followers with the Moghuls who were attached to them, but called out every man in Andeján and Akhsi who was able to bear arms; and taking Jehángír Mirza along with them, marched to invest Báber in Marghinán.

Uzun Hassan invades Marghinán;

Though the flower of the Sultan's little army had been sent off with the detachments, he was not dismayed; but, with the few old followers still left with him, and such new ones as he could raise on the spur of the occasion, he assumed a bold attitude, marched out, faced the enemy as they advanced to the town in battle array and in great force, and engaged and harassed them with such effect as to hinder their advancing beyond the outskirts of the suburbs. On two following days, when they came on in force to drive him from his position, he was equally successful.

Meanwhile the two small detachments that he had sent out were daily making progress. That under Kásim Beg was joined, as well by the peasants as by the tribes, whether wandering or settled, in the southern hill-country; while the other under Ibráhím Sáru that had crossed the Sirr, found the inhabitants there also universally disgusted with the new government. On their approach, the townspeople of Akhsi, the second city of the kingdom, rose upon the garrison with sticks and clubs, drove them out of the town, forced them to fly into the citadel, and then called in Ibráhím. To add to this success, a body of troops sent by Báber's uncle the Khan marched up the river, and passing the defiles, joined the detachment in the town of Akhsi.

The news of these occurrences alarmed Uzun Hassan. He instantly sent back from his camp at Marghinán a body of chosen men, with orders to cross the river and relieve the troops who were shut up in the citadel of Akhsi. When this detachment arrived opposite that town, by some oversight, in not pulling sufficiently high up the stream, the boat in which they were ferried across the Sirr missed the intended landing-place, and by the force of the current was carried down below the works into shallow water, where it could be reached by the enemy's horse, who instantly rode into the river and attacked them. They were all put to death or taken prisoners.

When this misfortune was known in Uzun Hassan's camp, he saw that he could no longer maintain himself near Marghinán. The army was led back in great confusion to Andeján. But on reaching that capital the confederate chiefs found, to their consternation, that the governor had declared for Báber. This unlooked-for event entirely disconcerted them. The army broke up, each chief shifting for himself. Uzun Hassan reached the citadel of Akhsi, which he had long held, and where he had left his family. Sultan Ahmed Tambol hastened to the eastward, to Ush, which was his proper government; and, before he arrived there, was joined by Jehángír Mirza; who, in consequence of a plot

but retreats.

BOOK I. A. D. 1499.

originating in one of those factions and disputes at that time so common, had been carried off from Uzun Hassan by some of his servants and followers*, and was now delivered to Támbol, who was Uzun Hassan's rival.

Báber enters Andeján. Zilkadeh, A. H. 904. June, A. D. 1499.

On this change of fortune, Báber once more re-entered his capital, from which he had been excluded nearly two years. Many and severe as were the changes of fortune that he had undergone, he was still little more than sixteen years of age.

When Támbol arrived at Ush he found the citizens in the same state of ferment as the inhabitants of the rest of the country, and indignant at his misgovernment and oppression. On his entrance, he was furiously attacked by the commonalty with sticks and stones, and fairly driven out of the place, which declared for Báber. Támbol, with Jehángír Mirza and a few partisans who still adhered to them, was now compelled to retire northward to Urkend, near the mountains that border on Káshghar.

Pursues Uzun Hassan,

Báber, eager to improve his success, did not waste his time in Andeján. In the course of four or five days he followed Uzun Hassan, his most formidable enemy, to Akhsi. That chief, finding that it would not serve any good purpose to hold out the citadel, since all the country had become hostile to him, entered into a capitulation, by which he agreed to give up the place, bargaining only for the lives and property of himself, his family and adherents, and for liberty to leave the country. The citadel was accordingly surrendered to Báber.

who capitulates.

This flow of success placed the affairs of the Sultan in a more prosperous situation in Ferghána than they had ever before attained since his accession. He had recovered his native kingdom, and rebellion was quelled. Before returning to his capital he devoted some time to settling the northern provinces of Akhsi and Kásán.

* Báber's Mem. pp. 66, 67.

He dismissed the Moghul auxiliaries whom his uncle the Khan had sent to his assistance; and then returned to Andeján, carrying with him Uzun Hassan, his family and dependents. That chieftain was allowed to leave the country, in terms of the capitulation, and crossed the southern mountains to Kárátigin, on his way to Hissár, attended by a small retinue. All the rest of his former followers remained behind.

Báber's imprudence.

But one act of imprudence blighted the fair prospects which seemed to be opening to Báber, and plunged him once more in an abyss of danger and difficulty. The soldiers whom Uzun Hassan had left behind, especially the Moghuls, had been the instruments of various acts of severity committed under his orders, and probably of many more done on their own account. After his departure, they seem to have entered Báber's service, or at least to have acknowledged his sovereignty, trusting to the terms of the capitulation. Several of the native Begs and others, however, who detested these rapacious strangers, represented to the young Sultan, that they were the very men who, during the late disturbances, had pillaged his adherents and the followers of the faithful Khwája Kázi, and had been guilty of every enormity; and that he was not to expect fidelity from men who had abandoned their own chiefs. They therefore urged him to issue an order for pillaging these notorious plunderers: or, continued they, if it seems going too far to order a general pillage, let us at least not have the mortification to see them riding our horses, wearing our clothes, and killing and eating our own sheep before our eyes: it is but fair that we, who have adhered to you in all your changes of fortune, should be suffered to reclaim at least such part of our own property as we find in the possession of these marauders, who should be very thankful for getting off on such easy terms. Without due consideration, Báber was prevailed upon to publish an order to that effect, though

BOOK I.

A.D. 1499.

in favour of such only as had accompanied him in his campaigns. "Nothing," as he himself remarks, "could have been more imprudent. When there was a rival like Jehángír Mirza at my elbow, it was a senseless thing to exasperate so many men who had arms in their hands. From my issuing this single inconsiderate order, what commotions and mutinies ensued! It was in reality the ultimate cause of my being expelled a second time from Andeján." * Báber was one of the few princes who had sufficient wisdom to see, and sufficient superiority of mind to acknowledge and profit by, his errors. It was this frank and healthful spirit of observation that helped to carry him through all the difficulties of his chequered life.

Revolt of the Moghuls.

The Moghuls were not to be plundered with impunity. They were not only brave but numerous, amounting to three or four thousand fighting men. They immediately put themselves in a posture of defence, and sent to offer their services to Támbol and Jehángír Mirza, marching at the same time to the eastward to join them. The affair was treated by Báber's chief nobles as a slight matter, which did not call for the Sultan himself to take the field. It was therefore arranged that Kásim Beg, with some other officers, should lead a detachment of the army after them, and chastise their insolence; and the Beg accordingly set out on the service. But it turned out a much more difficult matter than had been anticipated. The Moghuls

who joins Támbol.

were joined by Támbol. Hardly had the Beg passed the Ilamish river by the ford of Yasi-kijet, when the two armies met face to face, and engaged. After a desperate action, Báber's army was completely routed, and a number of his Begs and officers fell into the hands of

Defeat of Kásim Beg.

the enemy. Kásim Beg, and the few who escaped, fled

* Báber, p. 68.

A.D. 1499.

to Andeján and were closely followed by Támbol, who advanced within a farsang of the place.*

This reverse was most untimely. The country, after a long season of uproar and confusion, was just beginning to recover its tranquillity and to fall into order. Several of Báber's principal supporters were at a distance, actively employed in their respective governments, and could not, at the moment, assist him. The decided ascendancy which he had just recovered, was lost again. Támbol and Jehángír, improving their victory, advanced several times insultingly towards the town, with their army ranged in order of battle; but Báber declined a general action, at the same time that, by posting his troops under cover, in the gardens, houses, and narrow roads in the suburbs, he always checked the enemy in their movements. They shifted their ground repeatedly from one side of the town to another, in hopes of gaining some adv ntage; but, after remaining about a month in the vicinity of the city, without effecting any thing, they were at last compelled to break up, and moved for Ush, the fort of which was held for Báber, by Ibráhím Sáru's men.†

Andeján threatened.

The Sultan, on being relieved from this danger, sent to collect the whole force of his little dominions which had been dispersed after the surrender of Uzun Hassan; and, when those nearest at hand were assembled, put his troops in motion towards the end of August ‡, and soon arrived near Ush; the enemy, at his approach, retiring to the northward. Next morning, as he was marching past the town to follow them, he learned with surprise that they had given him the slip, and were in full march for Andeján. He proceeded, however, in his route towards Urkend, in which district the strength of Támbol lay; and sent out detachments, who indeed

Báber marches to Ush.

18 Moharrem, 905, 25 Aug. A.D. 1499.

And Támbol to Andeján.

* A farsang is about three miles and three quarters, or four miles.

† Báber, p. 70.

‡ We are hardly ever informed of the positive strength or numbers of the hostile armies at this period.

BOOK I.
A.D. 1499.

plundered and laid waste the country, but did nothing effectual. Támbol, meanwhile, held on his course towards Andeján, hoping to surprise it. He arrived there during the night, and entered the ditch unperceived; but, while his men were planting their scaling ladders, they were observed, and the alarm given; so that the attempt failed, and he was forced to retreat. Báber, having returned from Urkend into the territory of Ush, attacked and took Mádu, one of its forts, in which was Khábil, a brother of Támbol, with some of his best warriors; a fortunate occurrence for such of the Sultan's officers and men as had been made prisoners at the defeat of Yási-kijet.

The armies lie face to face.

The two armies soon after approached each other, and lay for upwards of a month, with not more than three or four miles between them. During this time there were daily skirmishes. Báber, whose army was the weaker of the two, drew a trench round his position, and carefully guarded against surprise. While thus situated, a Moghul chief, with the branch of a migratory tribe which had been obliged to leave Hissár, in consequence of one of the revolutions so frequent in that age, crossed the Kárátigín mountains and joined him.* Encouraged by this unexpected aid, which placed him in a situation to meet the enemy in the field, he advanced towards their camp, to offer them battle. Having heard, however, of his increase of strength, they did not venture to await his coming, but retreated hurriedly, with the loss of part of their tents and baggage; so that Báber on coming up encamped on the ground they had quitted. Támbol, after marching about twelve miles in the direction of Andeján, halted at Khubán. Báber followed him; and Támbol found himself at last obliged to march out and

* This was Sultan Ahmed Kerá-wal, the father of Kuch Beg, with his clan.

A. D. 1499.

Báber defeats Támbol.

engage in a regular battle. But, such was the ardour and impetuosity of the cavalry in Báber's left wing, that, having charged Támbol's right, they broke and totally routed it, even before Báber's right had time to come up. The victory was complete, many of the enemy being slain, and many taken prisoners, whose heads were ordered to be struck off, according to the barbarous custom of the times. Báber halted at Khubán. This victory, in the first pitched battle that he had fought, delighted him much. Támbol and Jehángír Mirza escaped towards Urkend; and, as the winter was at hand and little grain or forage to be found in the country, Báber led his army back to Andeján.*

Winter campaign.

It soon, however, appeared that the enemy, though defeated, were still in great strength; and that it was necessary to take such a position as would straiten their quarters, and hinder them from overrunning the open country at will. Báber, therefore, in spite of the inclemency of the season, marched his army to the eastward, to Suárási, a favourable position between two rivers, where he halted his troops, and contrived not only to keep the enemy in check, but to make constant inroads and forays into their country. He, at the same time, indulged himself in hunting and fowling, in the fine sporting country in which he lay. Unfortunately Kamber Ali and some others of his chiefs began to tire of the severities of a winter campaign; so that, to prevent discontent, the Sultan was obliged to give them permission to return home; and the consequence was, that, after remaining six or seven weeks in that station, he was finally compelled, in consequence of his diminished strength, most unwillingly to break up his quarters and return to Andeján. "Had I remained all winter in these cantonments," says he, "there is every reason to believe that, by the return of spring, the enemy would

* Báber, pp. 72—74.

BOOK I. A. D. 1499.

have been reduced to the last extremity, without fighting." *

When Támbol perceived the superiority which Báber had acquired in the field, he felt the necessity there was for looking around him for additional assistance. He happened to have an elder brother who held a confidential situation in the household of Sultan Mahmúd Khan, Báber's uncle; and, through him, he contrived to prevail upon that restless prince, who seems to have been ever ready to assist indiscriminately all who asked his aid, to send him a body of auxiliaries. Támbol, at the same moment that he learned that Báber had broken up his cantonments, received information that a detachment of the Khan's men was certainly in motion to come to his succour. This intelligence emboldened him, in spite of the season, to assume the offensive, and to march from Urkend to Suárási.

The Khan's son enters Kásán,

As soon as the alarming news was brought to Báber that a son of the Khan, with five or six thousand men, had entered his northern dominions, and laid siege to the important town of Kásán, he lost no time; but with his characteristic activity instantly set out, taking along with him such troops as were at hand. He marched all night, and next day reached Akhsi. "It was the depth of winter," says he, "the cold during the night was intense, insomuch that several of my people were frost-bitten in the hands and feet, and the ears of some of them were contracted like a withered apple." † Crossing the Sirr at Akhsi, he hastened on to Kásán; but, when he arrived within a mile or two of that town, was met by intelligence that the Khan's army, on getting notice of his approach, without waiting to receive him, had made the best of their way back to their own country.

but retreats.

Campaign of Kásán.

Meanwhile Támbol, who was marching by Suárási, as soon as he knew with certainty that Báber had left

* Báber, p. 75. † Ibid. p. 76.

Andejàn, also crossed to the right bank of the Sirr, and hastened on by forced marches; hoping to reach Kásán, and join the besiegers, before the young Sultan could arrive. In the afternoon of the very day on which Báber came to Kásán, the approach of Támbol's army was descried from a distance. Disconcerted and disappointed, when met by information of the precipitate retreat of the Khan's troops, Támbol halted his men. Báber, with the ardour of a youthful warrior and the instinctive talent of a general, urged the necessity of attacking the enemy without delay, while they were yet surprised and dispirited. His older officers urged that, as the day was about to close, it was better to put off the attack till the morrow, and their advice prevailed. Early next morning they mounted and rode to the attack, but the enemy was gone. Támbol, aware of his danger, had made his troops retreat, fatigued as they were, as soon as the darkness had fallen; and did not permit them to halt for a moment the whole night. They were indeed pursued, and at length overtaken, but not till they had found shelter in the fortress of Arkhián. Here Báber faced them for five or six weeks, *he* not being strong enough to besiege the fort, and *they* not venturing to attack his lines.

At the end of that time, Támbol, being invited by a petty chieftain among the Andeján hills, who had revolted from the Sultan, decamped by night, and marched to join him. Báber hastened to intercept him in his march, but ineffectually. Támbol succeeded in reaching the fort of Beshkhárán, and encamped, protected by it. As there was only the distance of a mile or two between the camps, daily skirmishes and single combats took place. But Báber's chief Begs and officers soon began to be tired of this fatiguing and ineffectual warfare, and talked of peace. Under these circumstances, Ali Dost and Kamber Ali, the chiefs of greatest influence in his army, managed to conclude a treaty; Báber says, with-

BOOK I.

A.D. 1500.

Treaty between Báber and Jehángír.

out informing him or the Begs most attached to him, of its progress or its terms, till it was concluded, when acquiescence became a matter of necessity. The conditions were, that, the river Sirr should be the boundary between Báber and his brother Jehángír; Akhsi, Kásán, and all to the north of the river being given up to Jehángír; while all to the south, including Urkend, was to belong to Báber; that, time was to be allowed to Támbol and his followers to withdraw their wives and families from Urkend; that after the two princes had tranquillised and settled their respective dominions, they should march in concert together against Samarkand; on the conquest of which kingdom, Báber was to give up Andeján also to his brother. This treaty was concluded in the end of February A.D. 1500, and next day Jehángír and Támbol waited upon Báber, when it was confirmed. After this, Jehángír proceeded to Akhsi and Bàber to Andeján, and the prisoners on both sides were set at liberty.*

End of Rejeb, A.H. 905, end of Feb. A.D. 1500.

* Báber's Mem. pp. 75–78.

CHAPTER II.

SHEIBÁNI KHAN. — SECOND CONQUEST AND LOSS OF SAMARKAND. — BÁBER IS KEPT UNDER BY HIS MINISTER. — INVITED TO SAMARKAND. — AFFAIRS OF THAT COUNTRY. — HE ADVANCES TO THE CAPITAL. — MARCH OF SHEIBÁNI TO ITS RELIEF. — HISTORY OF THAT CHIEF. — FLIGHT OF BÁBER BY HISSAR. — HE RESOLVES TO ATTEMPT SAMARKAND. — TAKES IT BY SURPRISE. — HIS BATTLE WITH SHEIBÁNI, AND DEFEAT. — HE IS BESIEGED IN SAMARKAND FOR FIVE MONTHS. — CAPITULATION. — HE ESCAPES TO URATIPPA.

A.D. 1500. Báber's constrained position.

When Báber was restored to peace, with his territories thus diminished, he was just seventeen years of age. The Beg who had now the chief direction of his affairs was Mír Ali Dost, Taghái, a Moghul, and a near relation; probably the brother of his grandmother. This was the same nobleman who had surrendered Andeján to Uzun Hassan; but Báber was indebted to him for his restoration to his dominions, as it was by him that he was invited to Marghinán, from his uncomfortable residence in the hilly Iláks. Báber seems never to have liked him, however, and represents him as a man of disagreeable manners, covetous, factious, sour of visage, and harsh of speech. Such a person was not likely to win the affections of a generous and lively young prince. The Mír found various pretexts for sending away the servants to whom his master was most partial. Khalífa, whom Báber always treated as a friend, was discharged. Ibráhím Sáru was imprisoned, stript of his government and fined; and Kásim Beg, Báber's favourite minister, a man of wit and talents, was dismissed. Several others of the chief officers were deprived of their governments. In a word, Ali Dost,

BOOK I. A.D. 1500.

relying on the assistance of Támbol, with whom he maintained a close understanding, having removed all opposition, and made all power centre in his own person, acted in every respect with unlimited authority. His son, too, began to affect the state of a sovereign; and his whole style of living, his entertainments and levées, were those of a prince. "My situation was singularly delicate," says the royal historian, "and I was forced to be silent. Many were the indignities which I endured at that time, both from father and son." It was at this period that Báber married Aisha Sultán Begum, the daughter of his uncle Sultan Ahmed Mírza, the late Sultan of Samarkand, to whom he had been betrothed in his father's lifetime.*

Shaban, A. H. 905, A. D. 1500, March.

Affairs of Samarkánd.

But the state of Máwerannaher was too disturbed and unsettled to leave a long repose to any prince within its limits. We have seen that when Báber abandoned Samarkand to return to the protection of his hereditary dominions, that capital was occupied by his late ally Sultan Ali Mírza, who had previously advanced with his army from Bokhára, and seized a great part of its territory. This prince, who was Báber's cousin, and still young, was, like him, kept in a state of wretched constraint and insignificance, by his relations the Terkhán lords, to whom he owed his kingdom. They appropriated to themselves the whole revenue, and divided at pleasure the different governments among their sons and dependents. Muhammed Mazíd was the minister who had the immediate direction of the Sultan. That prince, having grown up to man's estate, naturally felt uneasy under such treatment, and entered into a plot to remove his domineering servants. Muhammed Mazíd, getting notice of what was in agitation, and probably uncertain to what extent the conspiracy against his power

* Báber's Mem. p. 78.

had reached, withdrew from Samarkand, and was followed by many of the chief men of the country, who were his adherents. CHAP. II. A.D. 1500.

It was at this time that Weis Mírza, better known as Khan Mírza, the youngest brother of Sultan Ali, whose mother was a sister of the Khan of the Moghuls, entered the territory of Samarkand on the north, attended by an army furnished him by his uncle, Sultan Mahmúd Khan, whose Moghuls, as usual, were ready at every call. Weis Mírza was the fourth of the brothers who had aspired to the throne of Samarkand. Many lords of Moghul families who were in the city went out and joined the invaders. Muhammed Mazíd Terkhán, the offended and fugitive minister of Sultan Ali, also invited the Moghul army to form a junction with him, and had a conference with its chiefs at Shádwár. But so little could they agree, that the Moghuls proposed laying hands upon him and his party; though he was fortunate enough to discover and defeat their intentions by a precipitate flight from their camp. Thus deprived of his co-operation, the Moghuls were forced to retreat; while Sultan Ali, availing himself of their distress, pushed after them, overtook them in the Yar-ailák territory as they were coming to their ground, and completely routed and dispersed them.*

Báber marches against Samarkand.

When Muhammed Mazíd Terkhán and his followers saw that all hope of returning to Samarkand by any co-operation with the Moghul Khan, or any reconciliation with Sultan Ali Mírza was over, they turned their eyes on Báber, and sent to offer him their services. Being then in the uncomfortable situation that has been described, under constraint and without influence in his own court, Báber eagerly caught at the offer. Samarkand had long been the grand object of his

* Báber's Mem. p. 80. ; Briggs's Ferishta, vol. ii. p. 14.

BOOK I.

A. D. 1500.

ambition, and it had been expressly presented to him as such, when the recent peace with his brother was concluded. Without hesitation, therefore, he gladly began his march for that city, with the few troops that were near him at the time, sending an express to Jehángír at Akhsi, to follow him without delay.

Zikadeh, A.H. 905, June, 1500.

It was now the month of June, the proper season for action: but Báber had made only four marches when he learned that Támbol's brother, Khalíl, who had lately been his prisoner, had seized the fortress of Ush. Khalíl, having been set at liberty by the late treaty, had been sent by his brother to bring away their families and property from Urkend. Instead of executing this commission at once, as he might have done, he contrived, under various pretences, to remain lingering day after day in the neighbourhood, till hearing that Báber had actually set out for Samarkand, and that Ush was but slightly garrisoned, he attacked it by night, and carried it by surprise.

Báber had not been prepared for this act of treachery; but he resolved not to be diverted from his great object by any inferior consideration. He was displeased with those who had the present management of his affairs, and justly believed that he could best shake them off, when he was not surrounded solely by their immediate dependents. Besides, as he had been invited by a powerful party of the nobles of Samarkand, it was necessary to avail himself of the favourable moment, or lose it for ever. The little kingdom of Andeján was not to be compared to that of Samarkand, and its magnificent capital, the seat of the representative of Taimur. He therefore continued his march, and on his route was joined by a number of his adherents, and of adventurers, from his own country. No sooner, however, was he fairly engaged in this expedition, than his unslumbering enemy Támbol entered his hereditary dominions, and left nothing undone, to seize all the castles and districts of Andeján, and its territory, which Báber had just left.* CHAP. II. A. D. 1500.

Báber meanwhile, advancing by Úratippa, reached Yurat-khan, about five miles from Samarkand, without opposition. On the road he learned that he was not the only foreign enemy in the field. Sheibáni Khan, the chief of the Uzbeks of Túrkistán, who had probably been invited a second time by Sultan Ali, having again crossed the Sirr, had defeated the Terkháns of Bokhára, and was in full march towards that city. At Yurat-khan Báber was joined by Muhammed Mazíd Terkhán, and the disaffected Begs of Samarkand. They assured him that if he could gain the cordial cooperation of Khwája Yahía, who has been already mentioned as a holy man of great note and influence in the city, he might enter it without a struggle. We have already seen the influence of these spiritual guides in Transoxiana, and the benefit which Báber derived from the aid of Khwája Mouláma Kázi in Andeján. At this time there were two rival saints of leading influence in Samarkand, Khwájika Khwája, and Khwája Yahía. They were brothers; but, like the royal brothers, political events and their own ambition had set them at variance. Both of them had numerous followers and adherents. When the Terkháns surprised Bayesanghar Mirza in Samarkand, and that prince contrived to make his escape from the citadel, he took refuge, as we have seen, in the house of the former, who was his spiritual guide, and who protected him from the violence of the Terkháns. These unscrupulous chiefs, with all their power, did not dare to touch him, in the sacred asylum which he had chosen; and, in a few days, the rising of the people replaced him on his throne. And, in like manner, when his brother, Sultan Ali, the present sovereign, a prisoner in his turn, had undergone the

Encamps near it.

Religious guides.

* Báber's Mem. p. 81.

BOOK I. A.D. 1500.

operation which was supposed to have deprived him of his eye-sight, and rendered him unfit for public life, he retired to the house of Khwája Yahía, his ghostly father, who soon enabled him to escape to Bokhára.*

Intrigues.

From that period a rivalship subsisted between the two holy brothers. Báber, anxious to gain over Khwája Yahía, who was perhaps more attached to the Terkháns than to Sultan Ali, employed persons to enter the city and confer with him in private. The Khwája was too cautious to commit himself by returning any direct answer. He said nothing, however, to make Báber despair of success, and quietly took every measure in his power to smooth the way for his entrance into the city. Báber now moved to the banks of the Derghám, still nearer to the town, and contrived to send his librarian to the Khwája, who at length told him to make his master advance, and that the city should be given up to him. But one of Báber's chiefs, having unfortunately deserted at this very moment, informed the enemy that a conspiracy was going on. Measures of precaution had in consequence been adopted, which baffled the attempt; and the troops, finding the garrison in a state of preparation, fell back upon the camp. To make up for this failure, Báber was joined by Ibráhím Sáru, and several of the old Begs who had lately been driven from his service by the hostility of Ali Dost, the prime minister. As they were all graciously received, Ali Dost and his son were much offended, and asked leave to retire, a permission which Báber joyfully conceded; whereupon they returned to Andeján and joined Támbol.

Hardly had Báber got relieved from his obnoxious ministers, when news of an alarming nature reached him from Bokhára. Sheibáni Khan, after defeating in the field Báki Terkhán, who had succeeded his father,

* Báber's Memoirs, pp. 39, 40.

Abdal Ali, in the government of that province, had advanced with his Uzbeks and taken possession of the city of Bokhára, and was now in full march towards Samarkand. It may be proper to give some farther account of the previous life of that extraordinary man.* CHAP. II. A. D. 1500.

Early life of Sheibáni.

Sheibáni Khan was descended, as we have seen, from Júji, the eldest son of Chengíz Khan. His grandfather was Abulkhair Khan, the formidable Uzbek chief, from whom the Kaizák-Uzbeks seceded, and who was finally defeated and slain by a confederacy of the chiefs of the Kipchák tribes. The immediate consequence of this event was the dissolution of what may be called the Old Uzbek confederacy. Some tribes joined the Kaizák-Uzbeks, who now occupied a large portion of what had been Abulkhair's peculiar range. Other tribes and some chiefs even of his own relations, among others Burga Ughlan, in like manner extended their territory at the expense of his family. The children of Abulkhair who escaped from the bloody field and the slaughter that followed, continued for a time to hold a limited extent of country towards the lower Sirr, on the skirts of the desert, and possessed a considerable body of attached adherents. But the new calamity occasioned by the defeat and death of Bárúj Ughlan, a son of Abulkhair's, in his attempt upon the encampment of Yúnis Khan on the Sirr, completely broke up the old Uzbek tribe and dynasty. Sheibáni, or Sháhi Beg, the son of Shah Bidágh Sultan, another son of Abulkhair, was then in the prime of life; but the tribe was too much shattered and dispersed to admit of being rallied, and the surviving chiefs and their followers, after enduring many hardships, abandoned the country of their fathers. Sháhi Beg, too, who had his share of suffering, A. H. 877, A. D. 1472.

* He is called by Báber, Sheibáni and Sheibák Khan; by Haider Mírza, Sháhi-Beg Khan; and by Abulgházi, or his translators, Shaacht (Shabakht) Sultan. He was the son of Shah Bidagh Sultan, called also, Budak, Borak, Bidagh, and Shabadakh; only different modes of writing the same name.

BOOK I.

unwillingly quitted the desert, and with about three hundred faithful followers, repaired to Bokhára.

He goes to Bokhára.

He was there received and entertained by Abdal Ali Terkhán, one of the chief Amírs of Sultan Ahmed Mírza who then reigned at Samarkand.* Abdal Ali had married the sister of Sultan Ahmed's mother, who was herself a Terkhán. He long governed Bokhára with nearly absolute authority, and had very numerous followers; and now patronised and protected Sháhi Beg, who owed much of his future rise to his favour. It was probably through his means that he returned to Túrkistán, which was then held by Abdal Ali's brother-in-law, Muhammed Mazíd Terkhán, under the government of Samarkand. When, with the assistance of the Terkháns, Sháhi Beg began to establish himself once more on the border of the desert, the old adherents of his grandfather hastened from the different quarters over which they had been scattered, and came to join his standard, so that by degrees the number of his adherents became considerable; and they were devoted men, confident in the ability and prowess of their chief.

It has been mentioned that among those who had appropriated to themselves portions of the territory of Abulkhair, and tribes of his followers, was Burga Sultan, his cousin, for whom the Khan had always shown a particular friendship, and whom he had occasionally placed in command of his armies. This injury was not forgotten by Sheibáni; who, however, after his return, artfully dissembled his resentment, and lived apparently on the best understanding with Burga; but he only waited for an opportunity for revenge. This opportunity at last came. Burga Sultan having unsuspiciously taken up his winter quarters on the banks of the Sirr, not far from his own, Sheibáni one night

A. H. 886, A. D. 1481.

* The Tárikhi Reshídi says that he took service with Abdal Ali; Báber, on the contrary, affirms that, though he lived with him, he did not enter into his service, p. 24.

ordered a number of his people to attend him under pretence of a great hunting match that was to take place on the following day; but at midnight he suddenly set out with them, and in a short time, turning towards the camp of Burga, declared his intention of attacking him, and commanded his men on no account to think of plunder, but to spare no exertions to secure the person of that prince. CHAP. II. A.D 1500.

Surprises Burga,

Having entered the camp at dawn he pushed on straight to the tent of Burga Sultan, who, however, was not to be found, though his people affirmed that they had seen him just before Sheibáni arrived. Parties were despatched in every direction to pursue and bring back the fugitive; and one of them accordingly returned with a person who acknowledged himself to be Burga Sultan. Sheibáni no sooner saw him than he discovered that he was not Burga. He was found to be one Munga, of the Oighúr tribe, a man of distinction. When questioned by Sheibáni what had induced him to assume his master's name, the Oighúr replied, that he lay under such obligations to that chief that he was willing to sacrifice his own life for his; trusting that, while he was carried back, the pursuit would be relaxed, and Burga might escape. While Sheibáni admired the generosity of the man, he ordered fresh endeavours to be made to discover the fugitive.

The truth was, that Burga, on hearing the noise made by the troops who entered the camp, had started from his sleep, and, throwing over him a fur cloak that was lying by, escaped by the opposite side of the tent; and had thrown himself into a small piece of water that was near at hand, where he remained hid among the long reeds. It had chanced to snow during the night; and the traces of a man's naked foot, marked with blood, were observed in the fresh snow, and followed. They were the footsteps of Burga, who had wounded one of his feet while making his escape. He was

who is slain.

BOOK I. traced out, discovered, and brought before Sheibáni, who now, convinced by his own eyes that there was no mistake, made him be put to death, and was joined by all his tribe. Sheibáni's uncle, Khwája Muhammed Sultan, married the widow of Burga, though she was then with child by her late husband. The offspring was Jani Beg, whom the Khwája, who was not remarkable for his wisdom, affected to consider as his own son.*

Betrays Sultan Ahmed.

On the death of Yúnis Khan we have seen that Sultan Ahmed Mírza of Samarkand led an immense army to recover Táshkend and Seirám from his son Sultan Mahmúd Khan, who defeated the invaders with immense loss on the Chirr. This disaster, according to Haider Mírza, was occasioned by the treachery of Sheibáni. After the Sultan had been stopped three days on the Chirr by the Khan and his Moghuls, Sheibáni, who was then in the Sultan's army, sent a message to the Khan, it is pretended, to ask a private conference. They met during the night, and concerted that in the battle which was expected to be fought next day, the Khan should direct his attack against Mír Abdal's division, in which Sháhi Beg was posted with his troops; the Beg on his part undertaking to abandon his ground, and throw the army into confusion. Next day, accordingly, an action did take place, the Moghuls directed their attack as had been concerted, Sháhi Beg fled, and plundered the baggage of his own army. A general panic ensued, the confusion and rout of the Sultan's army were complete, and numbers were drowned in the Chirr. Such is the account of Haider Mírza, an uncompromising enemy of Sháhi Beg, and therefore a partial witness, though he possessed the best means of information; but it may be remarked that no such insinuation is made by Báber, who was equally his enemy.†

A.H. 893, A.D. 1488.

* Abulgházi, pt. VIII. c. iv. Báber, pp. 21. 24, 25.

† Tar. Resh. ff. 80, 81. 108.;

Sultan Mahmúd Khan followed up the victory on the Chirr by the invasion and conquest of Túrkistán. Muhammed Mazíd Terkhán (the brother of Derwísh Muhammed, the Minister of Samarkand, and brother-in-law of Mír Abdal Ali of Bokhára), who was the governor, was taken prisoner, and used as the medium for negotiating a peace with the Sultan of Samarkand, who was also his brother-in-law. The Khan gave up Turkistán, an old possession of the Uzbeks, to Sheibáni; as a reward, it is alleged, for his conduct at the battle of the Chirr. This donation, we have seen, occasioned a misunderstanding and wars between the Khan and the leaders of the Kaizák-Uzbeks, who were hurt by this patronage of their enemy, and was the cause of breaking up the friendship that had long existed between the Moghuls and Kaizáks.* Gets Túrkistán.

While Mír Abdal Ali lived, Sheibáni remained under some degree of control: but on the death of that powerful chief, which happened nearly about the same time as that of his sovereign Sultan Ahmed Mirza, he entered more actively into the interests of the Khan. The influence which he acquired over him was quite extraordinary.† Sheibáni from an early period had habitually aimed at extending his territory, and never scrupled as to the means. He was totally without faith, and bound by no promise or engagement. If any plan which he pursued failed, as frequently was the case, he never wanted an excuse or ready apology. "In this way," says Haider Mírza, "frequent misunderstandings occurred between him and Sultan Mahmúd Khan. The wonder rather was how easily, when occurrences of that kind did take place, his excuses, such as they were, were accepted. To give an example; he was on a time in Túrkístan, and professed all manner of attachment and loyalty to the Khan, who at that

His father's success.

A. H. 899, A. D. 1494.

* Tar. Resh. ff. 83, 84.

† Ibid. f. 119.

BOOK I.

"time set out with an army against Támbol. When he had marched three days, some circumstances occurred which balked his designs, and he was obliged to retrace his steps. Meanwhile Sháhi Beg Khan got news, in Turkístán, that the Khan had begun his march; and, placing the foot of ambition in the stirrup of daring, he set out in person to occupy Táshkend, at the same time sending on Mahmúd Sultan against Seirám, which in old books is called Istijáb. While on his road to Táshkend, Sháhi Beg learned that the Khan was on his way back; upon which he instantly despatched a messenger to meet him; to explain, that, hearing that his highness had set out to punish his rebellious servant Támbol, he had made haste to protect Táshkend and his family, children, and followers; (though of a truth, except himself, there was no enemy to hurt them); that, however, as he had subsequently heard that the Khan was on his way back to his capital, he too would return home. He at the same time despatched expresses to overtake Mahmúd Sultan, and to enjoin him on no account to molest the country, but to hurry back. On the Khan's turning back, his army dispersed, and the various Amírs returned home to their governments. Mahmúd, not aware of what had happened, and believing Seirám to be unprotected, began plundering as soon as he entered the country, and before the messengers from Sháhi Beg could arrive. The governor of Seirám, Mír Ahmed, who was Támbol's uncle, but a faithful and attached servant of the Khan, hastened out to meet the invaders, attacked and routed them, taking Mahmúd Sultan himself prisoner, and carried him in bonds into the presence of Sultan Mahmúd Khan, with his hands tied round his neck. The Khan sent to call my father, who immediately came and interceded for his life, which was granted. My father having entreated him most kindly, sent him away.

This laid the foundation of a very close and intimate friendship between my father and Mahmúd Sultan." * CHAP. II.

The severe defeat which Sultan Mahmúd Khan sustained at Kanbái from Bayesanghar Mírza, in his invasion of Máwerannaher, did not diminish his desire to seize the throne of Samarkand; but his ministers advised him to change his policy, and instead of invading the country himself, to remain at home and support Sheibáni, till he gained possession of Samarkand and Bokhára; that thus all the trouble and warfare would fall on Sheibáni, who was his creature, while in the end the whole benefit would accrue to himself.

In consequence of this false and foolish policy, the Khan lent his countenance and support to Sheibáni, whose power daily increased. All the adherents of Abulkhair Khan, Sultans, Amírs, and others, who had been scattered abroad on the defeat and death of the great Uzbek chief, and were still wandering in the deserts of Kipchák, or in the neighbouring countries in a state of destitution and dread, hastened to join his grandson in Túrkistán. Bands of bold adventurers from other tribes, ardent for enterprise and greedy for spoil, soon swelled his ranks. He led them into the rich provinces of Transoxiana, which he and his followers had had ample opportunities of surveying as fugitives and exiles. These provinces they now found a prey to faction, and torn with civil war. The barbarians of the desert eyed with "grim delight" the fruits, the harvests, and the wealth of that more favoured region; and returned loaded with the spoils of what they considered as an effeminate population. The army of Sheibáni, which at first consisted chiefly of his own Túrki Uzbeks, in the course of successive inroads was swelled by auxiliaries from the Moghul Khan, and

* Tar. Resh. f. 122. Mahmúd was Sheibáni's brother.

BOOK I. A. D. 1500.

recruited by volunteers and adventurers out of every race between the Wolga and Káshghar.*

We have seen, that, when called in on a former occasion to the succour of Sultan Ali of Samarkand, Sheibáni had advanced close up to Báber's winter quarters, but had drawn off without fighting, to Sultan Ali's great disappointment, and gone home; that he had afterwards returned, defeated Báki Terkhán, the son and successor of his old patron Abdal Ali; had taken Bokhára, and was now in full march towards Samarkand.

Takes Bokhára.

Invades Samarkand;

Sultan Ali Mírza, the nominal ruler of Samarkand, was reduced to great distress, both by the foreign invaders of his kingdom and by his quarrel with the powerful Terkhán lords, who had called in Báber. His mother, Zuhri Begi Agha, who possessed great influence over a weak and inexperienced youth like her son, being herself an Uzbek, and probably feeling a partiality for her tribe, sent a messenger to Sheibáni, in this exigency, to propose to him, that, provided he would engage to marry her, she would make her son deliver Samarkand into his hands; Sheibáni, on his part, undertaking to restore it to him as soon as he recovered his own paternal dominions. The Uzbek chief made no difficulty whatever in acceding to these easy terms. On arriving at Samarkánd he encamped at a garden close to the city. Sultan Ali Mírza, the same day, came out to meet him, without the knowledge of his principal ministers or advisers. His attendants remarked with alarm that the Khan received him with very little ceremony. Khwája Yaḥía, on hearing what the Mírza had done, was filled with consternation, but seeing no remedy, he also, to save appearances, went out and waited on Sheibáni. The Uzbek, aware of his intrigues, received him without

A. H. 906, Moharrem, A. D. 1500, August.

* Báber's Mem., *passim*, Introd. pp. lvii. lix.; Abulgházi, pt. VII. c. ii., pt. VIII. c. ii.—iv., pt. IX. c. i.; Tar. Resh. f. 118.

rising, and showed his feelings by some bitter taunts which he let fall. Sultan Ali was not long of feeling acutely the degraded situation to which he had reduced himself. He refused, however, to attempt making his escape, and was unceremoniously put to death a few days after. Khwája Yahía was banished to Khorasán, but was waylaid by the Uzbeks and murdered on the road; and the wretched Zuhri Begi, as the reward of all this misery which she had brought on her family and their friends, felt herself degraded to be a mere common concubine in the harem of Sheibáni.* CHAP. II. A.D. 1500.

As soon as the approach of Sheibáni Khan from Bokhára had been made known to Báber, he at once perceived that, with his moderate force, it was in vain to think of coping with so formidable an antagonist. He therefore hurriedly broke up the blockade of Samarkand, and instead of attempting to fall back on his own hereditary dominions, now in the hands of his declared enemies, he crossed the rising-grounds to the south-east, and marched towards Kesh, to which place many of the Begs of Samarkand, who had joined him, had previously sent their families. Here he learned the surrender of Samarkand; and not thinking himself safe from the pursuit of Sheibáni even there, he marched eastward to the territory of Hissár-Shadmán, accompanied by Muhammed Mazíd and the other confederate Begs, their wives and families. On arriving at Cheghánián, the Samarkand Begs, separating from the little camp, entered into the service of Khosrou Shah, the powerful ruler of Hissár and Kunduz; and thus left Báber, with his few remaining adherents, to depend on his own exertions. Zilkajeh, A.H. 905, A.D. July, 1500. which he takes; Flight of Báber, by Hissár.

The young prince now once more felt himself in a most destitute and wretched situation, without army, or country, or home. He knew not which way to turn. Khosrou Shah, his power.

* Báber's Mem. pp. 83, 84.

BOOK I.

A.D. 1500.

A.H. 903, A.D. 1497. We have seen that when Bayesanghar Mírza fled from Samarkánd, at the time when that city was taken by Báber, he had passed through part of the dominions of his brother Masaúd Mírza of Hissár and had placed himself under the protection of Khosrou Shah of Kunduz. That ambitious chief soon after, displeased with Masaúd, took possession of Hissár, in which he set up Bayesanghar as king, with a nominal and short-lived authority. Sultan Masaúd meanwhile, who made his escape, repaired to Herát. There he was well received by Sultan Husein, whose court in that age was the great asylum of unfortunate princes. He soon after, however, most unaccountably left that monarch's pro-

A.H. 903, A.D. 1498. tection to go back to Khosrou Shah. That unprincipled man, though he had been the prince's guardian and governor, cruelly put out his eyes. In less than a twelvemonth afterwards, Khosrou Shah, having invited Bayesanghar Mírza from Hissár to join in an attack upon Balkh, treacherously seized him and his chief Amírs, while in his camp on their route to that city,

A.H. 905, 10 Moharrem, A.D. 1499, 17 Aug. and strangled them with the bowstring. He at the same time put to death all such of the chief and confidential servants of the murdered prince as could occasion him any uneasiness, and seized the whole territories of Hissár. This event, which happened little more than twenty months after Bayesanghar Mírza had been driven from Samarkand, left Khosrou Shah the undisputed ruler of all the extensive dominions that had belonged to Sultan Mahmúd Mírza, before he was called to the throne of Samarkand.*

Báber's distress.

The death of Bayesanghar had occurred not quite a year before Báber entered the territories of Khosrou Shah. To remain in the dominions of the murderer of one, and the unprincipled oppressor of several of his nearest kinsmen was revolting to Báber's feelings. It

* Báber, pp. 60—63.

gave him pain, he tells us, even to pass through them. Distracted by the difficulty of his situation, he thought of attempting, by traversing Karatigín, to reach the tents of his mother's younger brother, Ahmed or Ilacheh Khan, who governed the great body of the tribe of Moghuls, in the remoter wilds of Tartary. Finally, however, he made up his mind to return into the country which he had lately left, and with which he was familiar, and crossing the lofty mountains on the north-west of Hissár, to meet whatever fortune awaited him in the fields of Samarkand.

He crosses the hills.

Entering, therefore, the valley of the Kámrúd, Báber followed the course of the river in its windings and cataracts among the hills. Many of his remaining followers, worn out with the difficulties of the journey over these mountain barriers, discouraged by his ill success, and seeing no prospect of a change, forsook him and turned back. For four or five days, the few faithful friends and servants who still adhered to his fortunes, toiled over the dangerous roads that led along the edge of the deep precipices, and winded up the narrow passes and steep shelving banks of that mountainous tract. Many of their horses and camels failed from fatigue, and were left behind. At length they came to the Pass of Sir-e-ták, "and such a pass!" says Báber; "never in my life did I traverse paths so narrow and so precipitous. We travelled on, with incredible fatigue and difficulty, amid dangerous narrows and tremendous gulphs. Having surmounted these steep, straight, and murderous defiles, after incredible losses and suffering, we at length came down on the confines of Kán." *

When Báber descended these mountains on the west, the long circuit which he had made, for the purpose of avoiding his enemies, brought him down upon the town

* Báber's Mem. pp. 60. 63. 72. 85.

BOOK I. A.D. 1500. and district of Kán. Here he, at length, gained correct intelligence of all that had occurred since the arrival of Sheibáni Khan. He found that on the taking of Samarkand, all his own officers had retired from the neighbourhood of the city, and were dispersed in various quarters; that Ibráhím Terkhán had thrown himself into Shíraz, and that Kamber Ali, abandoning the fort of Khwája Didár as too near the capital to be defensible, had withdrawn to Yar-ailák, and attempted to put the fortresses there in a state of defence. Meeting with but an inhospitable reception from the Malek of the hill-country of Kán, Báber descended to the lower grounds, and, with his usual spirit, pushed on for Keshtúd, one of the nearest towns to Samarkand; hoping to surprise the Uzbeks who, he imagined, would be in possession of the place, and not looking for an enemy. On reaching it, however, he found Keshtúd in ruins, and not a man left in the town.

Approaches Samarkand, Advancing still, he at length halted on the Kohik, a river of Samarkand. He passed it by a bridge, and despatched Kásim Beg with a party to attempt to surprise Robát-Khwája. They were just applying their scaling ladders to ascend the walls, when the garrison was alarmed, which compelled the assailants to retreat at full speed. Báber himself meanwhile had continued his course to Yar-ailák, where he was joined by Kamber Ali, while Ibráhím Terkhán and some other Begs sent to offer him their congratulations, and to declare their steady adherence to his cause.

In spite of this assistance, his force was so small, and his situation so desperate, that none but a man of the most heroic ardour would have ventured to think of extricating himself from his difficulties, except by retreat. His army had been broken up and dispersed. His own dominions were in the hands of his enemies, so that he could look for no aid from them; since even such of his late subjects as were still attached to him,

CHAP. II.

A.D. 1500.

were too much dispirited by recent events to be expected to join him. If, when his army was entire, he could not face Sheibáni Khan, still less could he be expected to do so now that it was broken and scattered in every quarter. Sheibáni was encamped near Khwája Didár with seven or eight thousand men, and had a garrison of five or six hundred in Samarkand. Khamzeh Sultan and Mehdi Sultan, with their Uzbeks, who some years before had left Báber's service for Sheibáni's, were encamped close by, with a large body of their followers, amounting to about two thousand fighting men. Báber, on the contrary, with all his exertions could not muster more than two hundred and forty followers. But he saw that if he had any chance of retrieving his affairs, it could only be by bold measures; and of all the plans that suggested themselves to his imagination, the surprise of Samarkand, though a daring enterprise, was that which he cherished as offering the best prospect of success, and which he finally determined to adopt. With great sagacity he reflected, that as yet the inhabitants could have formed no connections with their barbarous conquerors, whom they must regard with hatred and disgust; and he trusted that, if he could enter the place, and get over the first difficulties, he would be hailed by the whole of the citizens as a warrior of the race of their ancient sovereigns, sent to deliver them from their barbarous enemies. If anything, however, was to be done, it must be while things were yet unsettled, and not a moment was to be lost.

which he resolves to surprize;

Intent on his plan, the very conception of which in a fugitive hunted from place to place, indicated that superiority of genius that distinguished him through life, Báber left his retired quarters about noon, and rode briskly a great part of the night. By midnight he had reached his old quarters of Yurat-Khán; but finding the garrison of the city on the alert, he did not

but he fails.

BOOK I. A.D. 1500.

venture to approach nearer, and regained Yar-ailák next morning.

His state of mind.

Some little circumstances mentioned by Báber show how much at this time his mind was absorbed with the great enterprise which he had conceived. "One day," says he, "I happened to be in the castle of Asfendek with some of my inferior nobles and officers, who were sitting on the ground talking around me. The conversation turned at random upon a variety of subjects. I happened to say, 'Come, let us hit on a lucky guess, and may God make it good! When shall we take Samarkand?' Some said, 'In the spring:' it was then harvest; some said, 'In a month;' some, 'In forty days;' some, 'In twenty.' Nevian Gokultásh said, 'We shall take it within a fortnight;' and the Almighty made true his words, for within a fortnight we did take it. About the same time I had a remarkable dream. I thought that the venerable Khwája Obeidulla had come to visit me. I went out to receive him, and the Khwája came in and sat down. Methought a table was laid for him, but not perhaps with sufficient attention to neatness; at which the holy man seemed to be somewhat offended. Mulla Baba, observing this, made me a sign. I answered him likewise by signs, that the fault was not mine, but that of the person who had laid the table-cloth. The Khwája perceived what passed, and seemed satisfied with my excuse. When he rose to depart, I attended him out; but, in the hall of the house, he appeared to take me by one of my arms, and to lift me up so high that one of my feet was raised from the ground, while he said to me in Túrki, '*Skeikh Maslehet berdi*' (Sheikh Maslehet prosper you.') A few days after this dream, I took Samarkand." *

Undeterred by his former failure, he resolved to

* Báber's Mem. pp. 86, 87. Sheikh Maslehet was a celebrated saint of Khojend.

CHAP. II.

A. D. 1500.

Another attempt successful.

hazard an attempt once more. He set out after noon from his quarters in the hills, and at midnight reached the bridge over the Meghák, which runs by the public pleasure-ground of the city. Halting there, he sent on seventy or eighty of his best men, with instructions to apply their scaling ladders to the part of the wall that was opposite to the place called the Lovers' Cave *; when they had gained the parapet they were to push on against the party that guarded the Firozá gate, of which they were to gain and keep possession, and then to apprise Báber of their success by a messenger. The escalade succeeded. The top of the wall was gained without alarming the garrison, and the assailants moved along the ramparts as concerted; attacked and slew the officer in command at the gate, with a number of the guard; broke the lock and bars of the gate with hatchets, and flung it open. At the same moment Báber arrived on the outside, and entered. So far his enterprise was achieved by his own immediate adherents; but his other followers soon joined him. When he entered the town, the citizens were fast asleep. On hearing the uproar, the shopkeepers, he tells us, began to peep out fearfully from behind their doors, but were delighted when they found what had happened. The citizens, as soon as they were informed of Báber's entrance, being heartily tired of their barbarous masters, hailed him and his followers with acclamations of joy. They instantly rose and attacked the Uzbeks who were scattered over the town, hunting them down with sticks and stones wherever they could be found, and put to death between four and five hundred of them. The chief men of Samarkand, as well as the merchants and shopkeepers, now hastened to congratulate the young Sultan at his quarters, bringing him offerings and presents, with food ready dressed for him and his fol-

* Mogh ári Ashikán.

BOOK I. A.D. 1500.

lowers, at the same time pouring out prayers for their success. Báber, therefore, repaired to the college of Ulugh Beg, and took his seat under the great dome to receive the congratulations of all who came to salute him. Here, about daybreak, news was brought that the Uzbeks, though driven from every other part of the city, were still in possession of the Iron Gate. Without delay he leaped upon his horse, and accompanied by fifteen or twenty of his men who happened to be near him, galloped to the spot; but, on arriving, found that the mob had already assailed and driven them out of the town. Just as the sun was rising, Sheibáni Khan, with about a hundred and fifty horse, was seen spurring on for the Iron gate, but found as he came near that it was no longer in the hands of his troops. In the rapidity of his approach, he had left the rest of his army behind. "It was a glorious opportunity," says Báber, "but I had with me only a mere handful of men." Sheibáni, finding that he was too late, rode back to meet his main body.

Báber, still only in his eighteenth year, was elated with this signal success, achieved by his own sagacity and heroic spirit. He compares it with pride to the surprise of Herát by Sultan Hussein Mírza, Baikera, of Khorásán *, the grand exploit of the most celebrated prince of the age, and justly gives it the preference. But though he thus saw himself in possession of a noble capital, the smallest part of his work was yet accomplished. It was necessary to defend his throne by the same activity and valour, by which it had been gained. His enemies were powerful, the country wasted, his own force but slender. Fortunately he had the affections of his new subjects. To relieve them, to have his followers more immediately under his own eye, and to watch the motions of the enemy, his first care was

* Memoirs, p. 88.

to march out of the city, and to encamp at a garden-palace in the suburbs. Here he was again waited upon by all the men in office, as well as by every person of consideration in the place, who all offered him their homage. The more polished and effeminate inhabitants of a great city viewed the rapacity, the rude manners, the strange and barbarous attire of the Uzbeks, fresh from their deserts, with mixed feelings of aversion and terror. The peasantry too, and the people of the villages, were naturally no less anxious to be delivered from the ravages of an insolent and marauding enemy. As soon as the young Sultan's success at Samarkand was known, many districts at once declared for him, several forts were put into his hands, and from many others the Uzbeks fled, without leaving a garrison. The inhabitants of some of the towns rose upon their Uzbek garrisons, whom they expelled; and repaired their walls to resist a new attack. At this crisis the wife and family of Sheibáni Khan, whom he had sent for from Túrkistán to settle in a richer country and a more propitious climate, arrived with their own heavy baggage, and that of the other Uzbeks. Sheibáni still lingered for some time near Samarkand; but at length finding the whole country hostile to him, and that the forts were rapidly falling into Báber's power, he called in his troops and marched for Bokhára, turning unwillingly his back on the splendid prize which had escaped from his grasp.

Sheibáni retires.

The tide of fortune had now turned against Sheibáni. In the three or four succeeding months, most of the fortified places in Soghd and Miánkál, provinces that lie between Samarkand and Bokhára, submitted to Báber. The districts of Khozar and Karshi, which are situated south of Samarkand, towards the Amu, were taken possession of by Báki Terkhán, the late governor of Bokhára; while that of Karakúl, which lies to the south of Bokhára, was seized by a force that came from Merv, from

BOOK I. A.D. 1500-1.

beyond the Amu. The Uzbeks were expelled in every quarter, retaining possession of Bokhárá alone.*

Báber's difficulties, A. H. 906, A. D. 1500-1.

But though Báber's affairs went on prosperously during the ensuing winter, he was far from being without anxiety or free from danger. The Uzbeks, though driven from Samarkand, possessed the populous city of Bokhára and its fertile territory, and could recruit their force by drawing repeated swarms of hardy barbarians from the deserts. Samarkand, that once wealthy, populous, and powerful city, the seat of the arts and of learning, which for more than a hundred and forty years had been the throne of Báber's ancestors, had, as well as its rich territory, recently suffered from misgovernment, from repeated revolutions, and the ravages of hostile and of friendly armies. Its resources were reduced, much of its wealth destroyed or removed, and time was required to repair its losses, and restore the credit and confidence of its inhabitants. As the military forces of the kingdom were, at the moment, very inadequate to its defence, the young king sent ambassadors to all the neighbouring princes to solicit assistance. From his own hereditary dominions Támbol sent him only one hundred men; Sultan Mahmúd Khán, his uncle, sent him four or five hundred from Táshkend; Sultan Hussein Mírza of Herát, the most powerful of them all, gave him no aid whatever; nor did he receive any from that prince's son, Badi-ez-zemán Mírza, of Balkh, or from Khosrou Shah of Kunduz. He was compelled, therefore, to depend entirely on his own limited resources.†

Sheibáni advances from Bokhára.

Though Sheibáni had found it expedient to retreat, his power was unbroken. Early in the spring he collected his army. The party that had occupied Karakúl was unable to maintain it. Sheibáni marched and invested the fort of Dabúsi in Soghd, took it by storm,

* Báber, pp. 86—89.

† Ibid. pp. 90, 91.

CHAP. II.

D. 1501.

and put the garrison to the sword. This success compelled Báber to take the field about the beginning of May. He proceeded by slow marches on the road to Bokhára, while Sheibáni Khan, advancing in the opposite direction, encamped about four miles from him. Báber fortified his camp with a palisade and ditch. Daily skirmishes took place between their advanced parties and pickets. Sheibáni attempted a night surprise, but found the camp too well fortified and guarded to be carried by a slight attack, and was forced to retire.

Shawal, A.H. 906, A.D. 1501.

The armies face each other,

A battle, however, seemed inevitable, and Báber's mind was evidently fixed on the preparations for it. Perhaps this state of excitement working on his military ardour rendered him too impatient, for he resolved to hazard an engagement, though reinforcements to the amount of two or three thousand men would have joined him in the course of two days. The delusions of judicial astrology lent their aid to mislead him. "The cause of my eagerness to engage," says he, "was that the sahs-yúldúz (eight stars) were on that day exactly between the two armies; and, if I had suffered that day to elapse, they would have become favourable to the enemy for the space of thirteen or fourteen days." "These observations," adds the Sultan, "were all nonsense, and my precipitation was without the least solid excuse."*

and engage.

The armies prepared for battle. Báber's marched out, the men clad in armour, the horses caparisoned and covered with cloth of mail. They were in four divisions, consisting of right wing and left, centre and advance, according to the fashion of the times. As they moved forward, with their right flank on the river Kohik, which runs from Samarkand towards Bokhára, they were met by the enemy drawn up ready to receive them. The hostile army was far the most numerous,

* Báber's Mem. p. 92.

BOOK I. A.D. 1501.

and the extremity of its right turned Báber's left flank, and wheeled upon his rear. This compelled him to change his position by throwing back his left; in doing which, his advance, which was posted in front of the centre, and composed of his best men and officers, was necessarily thrown to the right. The battle was nevertheless manfully supported, and the assailants in front driven back on their centre. It was even thought at one time, by Sheibáni's best officers, that the battle was lost; and they advised him to quit the field. Meanwhile, however, the enemy's flanking division, having driven in Báber's left, attacked his centre in the rear, pouring in showers of arrows; and the whole left of his line being thus forced in and thrown into disorder, that, with the centre, became a scene of inextricable confusion. Only ten or fifteen men remained around the Sultan. They, seeing that all was over, rode off towards the right wing, which had rested on the river; and on gaining its banks plunged in, armed as they were. "For more than half way over," says Báber, "we had firm footing; but after that we sank beyond our depths, and were forced, for upwards of a bow-shot, to swim our horses, loaded as they were with their riders in armour and their own trappings. Yet they plunged through it. On getting out of the water on the other side, we cut off our horses' heavy furniture and threw it away." * The enemy were not able to follow them. The royal fugitive kept for some time along the right bank of the river, and afterwards recrossing it higher up, reached Samarkand the same evening.

Báber defeated; reaches Samarkand,

No defeat could be more complete; many of Báber's bravest and most experienced officers, among others Ibráhím Terkhán, Ibráhím Sáru, and Khalíl, the brother of Támbol, with numbers of his best soldiers, perished

* Báber's Mem. p. 93.

in the field. The fugitives and stragglers were pursued, plundered, and cut off; an operation in which none were more active than the Moghuls of Báber's own army. The officers who survived the battle, persuaded that nothing could now resist Sheibáni Khan, scattered in various directions. Muhammed Mazíd Terkhán, who had once more joined Báber, fled to Khosrou Shah in Kúnduz; some escaped to Uratippa; Kamber Ali and others, after reaching Samarkand, hastily removed their families from it, as from a place doomed to destruction. A very few remained in the city, following the fortune of their prince.*

which he resolves to defend.

Báber lost no time in summoning a council of such Begs and officers as adhered to him after this great calamity. It was resolved to put the town in a state of defence, and to maintain it to the last extremity. The young Sultan fixed his head-quarters at the Grand Porch of Ulugh Beg's College, which was near the centre of the city; and, with Kásim Beg, was himself to command the reserve. The other Begs and officers had their stations assigned in different parts of the ramparts, and at the gates.

Skirmishes.

In the course of two or three days Sheibáni Khan made his appearance, and took up a position at some distance from the town. The idle rabble, on hearing of his approach, assembled in crowds from all the wards and lanes of Samarkand, elated, probably, with their former success against his garrison, in the street; hurried to Báber's head-quarters at the college, shouting aloud, "Glory to the prophet;" and then marched out clamorously to battle. Sheibáni Khan, who had his troops ready mounted at the time, and was just preparing to lead them to an assault, not aware, probably, of the composition of this motley body, did not venture to approach the place, as he had intended, and fell back.

* Báber's Mem. pp. 93, 94.

BOOK I.

A.D. 1501.

This only added to the presumption of the inexperienced mob. They had even the presumption to march out to a considerable distance from the gates, in spite of the remonstrances of the old and hardy veterans, who received nothing but abuse and insult in return for their advice.

One day, not long after, Sheibáni Khan made an attack on the side of the Iron Gate. The mob, whose confidence had been increasing in consequence of their having as yet met with no check, marched out farther than usual. Báber, afraid of the consequences, ordered a party of horse to follow them, and cover their retreat. The Uzbeks, watching their opportunity, suddenly attacked the undisciplined multitude, broke in among them, and cutting them down, chased the fugitives up towards the gate. Báber's cavalry, chiefly composed of his household troops, then interposed. "Kuch Beg, sallying forth on those Uzbeks who came up first," says Báber," attacked them sabre in hand, and made a gallant and distinguished figure, in sight of all the inhabitants who stood looking on. The fugitives, occupied solely with their flight, had ceased to shoot arrows, or to think of fighting for their ground. I shot from the top of the gateway with a cross-bow, and those who were along with me also kept up a discharge. This shower of arrows from above prevented the Uzbeks from advancing, and, in the end, they were forced to retire from the field." This event effectually checked the rashness of the well-disposed but undisciplined populace.*

Báber was now completely blockaded and the city in a state of siege. The rounds of the ramparts and other works were made regularly every night, sometimes by himself, sometimes by one of his principal officers; a business which occupied them from sunset to morning.

* Báber's Mem. p. 95.

Sheibáni Khan, whose activity never slumbered, on one occasion made an attack by day, between the Iron and the Sheikh-zádeh Gates. Báber, who happened to be then with the reserve, instantly led it to repel the assailants. But this was only a false attack; and, while the young prince was busy in repelling it, the real assault took place in an opposite quarter. There Sheibáni had placed seven or eight hundred men in ambush, who, when the attention of the besieged was wholly engrossed by the false attack, issued from their concealment, made a lodgment close under the rampart, and applied to the walls five or six and twenty scaling ladders, so broad that each admitted of two or three men mounting abreast to the assault. Kuch Beg, who had charge of that part of the rampart, had his quarters exactly opposite to the spot where they appeared. "As there was fighting on the other side," says Báber, "the persons in charge of these works were not apprehensive of any danger to *their* posts, and the men at these stations had dispersed on their own business, to go to their houses, or to the bazárs. The Begs who were on guard, had each only two or three of their attendants and servants about them. Nevertheless Kuch Beg, Muhammed Kúli Kochin, Shah Súfi, and another brave cavalier, boldly assailed them, and displayed signal heroism. Some of the enemy had already mounted the wall, and several others were in the act of scaling it, when these four persons arrived on the spot, fell upon them with the greatest bravery, sword in hand, and, dealing furious blows around them, drove the assailants back over the wall, and put them to flight. Kuch Beg distinguished himself above all the rest, and this was an exploit to be for ever cited to his honour. He twice during this siege performed excellent service by his valour. The alarm being given, the neighbouring posts were on the alert, and, after fruitless

CHAP. II.
A.D. 1501.
Escalade defeated.

BOOK I.

A. D. 1501

efforts, the Uzbeks retired completely baffied on all sides.*

Blockade continued.

But though, after this, Kásim Beg made a successful sally, beat back the Uzbeks, and, to use the language of the times, brought in a few heads, the situation of the town did not improve. The harvest had arrived, but no supply of corn had found its way within the beleaguered walls. The siege had now lasted a long while; the provisions originally in the place, which had never been victualled for a siege, were expended. "The inhabitants," says Báber himself, "were reduced to extreme distress, and things came to such a pass, that the poor and meaner sort were reduced to feed on dogs' and asses' flesh. Grain for the horses becoming scarce, we were obliged to feed them on the leaves of trees, and it was ascertained from experience, that the leaves of the mulberry and blackwood † answered best. Many used the shavings and raspings of wood, which they soaked in water, and gave to their horses."‡

For three or four months of this period, Sheibáni Khan, renouncing active operations, did not approach the fort, but kept every passage to it blocked up, and changed his ground from time to time. After this he approached by night, beating his kettle-drums and raising the war-shout, as if for an assault; so that the garrison, exhausted as it was, was constantly kept in alarm, and compelled to be ever on the alert. Night after night was this repeated, till the strength of the small garrison was quite worn out. Things now appeared desperate. None of the neighbouring princes seemed to take any interest in what was going forward; no provisions or supplies of any kind arrived. The soldiers and inhabitants lost all hope, and began to make their escape from the town in small parties.

* Báber's Mem. pp. 95, 96.

† Kara-igháj.

‡ Báber's Mem. p. 96.

Sheibáni Khan, knowing their distress, moved nearer to the city, and encamped near the Lovers' Cave; in consequence of which Báber also moved his head-quarters in the same direction, to be near and to watch him. At this unpropitious moment, when he could no longer be of use, Uzun Hassan, the grand instigator of the revolt of Jehángír Mírza, contrived to enter the town with ten or fifteen followers. The famine was already at its height. Even men about the Sultan's person, and high in his confidence, unable any longer to bear the grinding pressure of the misery by which they were worn out, began to let themselves down from the walls and make their escape. There was no longer room even to conceive any hope of a successful defence. In these circumstances, Sheibáni Khan proposed a capitulation on terms. "Had I had the slightest expectation of relief," says Báber, "or had any stores remained in the place, never would I have listened to him. Compelled however by necessity, a sort of capitulation was agreed upon; and about midnight I left the town, by the Sheikh-zádeh gate, accompanied by my mother the Khanum. Two ladies besides escaped with us, the one of them Bechega Khalífa, the other Mingelik Gokultásh. My eldest sister, Khanzádeh Begum, was intercepted, and fell into hands of Sheibáni Khan, as we left the city on this occasion." Of this capitulation Báber evidently speaks unwillingly, and in few words; but his cousin, Haider Mírza, informs us that the marriage of Báber's sister, Khanzadeh Begum, to the Khan, was one of the articles of the treaty, and part of the price paid for his unmolested escape. She married Sheibáni and had a son by him, who died young. Samarkand had sustained a siege of about five months, when it fell, probably in the month of September, A.D. 1501.*

CHAP. II

A.D. 1501

Capitulation.

A.H. 907, A.D. 1501.

* Báber's Mem. pp. 97, 98.; Tar. Resh. ff. 125. 156. Sheibáni Khan, when he took Samarkand the first time, had married Meher-nigár

BOOK I.
A. D. 1501.

Báber's account of his journey after he was driven from the capital, which for the second time he had enjoyed during so short a period, is lively and interesting. He was still only in his nineteenth year. In quitting Samarkand, "having got entangled among the great branches of the canals of the Soghd, during the darkness of the night," says he, "we lost our way; and after encountering many difficulties, passed Khwája Didár about dawn. By the time of early morning prayers we arrived at the hill of Karbogh, and passing it on the north, below the village of Khardek, we made for Ilán-úti. On the road I had a race with Kamber Ali and Kásim Beg. My horse got the lead. As I turned round on my seat, to see how far I had left them behind, my saddle-girth being slack, the saddle turned round, and I came to the ground, right on my head. Although I immediately sprang up and mounted, yet I did not recover the full command of my faculties till the evening; and the world, and all that occurred at the time, passed before my eyes and apprehension like a dream or a phantasy, and disappeared. The time of afternoon prayers was over ere we reached Ilán-úti, where we alighted, and having killed a horse, cut him up, and dressed slices of his flesh. We staid a little time to rest our horses, then mounting again, before daybreak next morning we alighted at the village of Khalíla, whence we proceeded to Dizak. Táher Duldái was at that time the governor. Here we had nice fat flesh, bread of fine flour well-baked, delicious melons, and excellent grapes in the greatest profusion; thus passing from the extreme of famine to abundance, and

Khanum, the eldest sister of Báber's mother, and consequently the maternal aunt of his sister Khanzádeh. Sheibáni now divorced the aunt that he might marry the niece. By Khanzádeh he had a son, Khurram, to whom he gave Balkh, but who died young. He afterwards divorced her also, being jealous of her partiality to the interests of her brother Báber, whose favourite sister she was.

from danger and suffering, to security and enjoyment." —"In my whole life, I never enjoyed myself so much." —"It has been my lot," he adds, "four or five times, in the course of my life, to pass in a similar manner from distress and suffering to enjoyment and ease; but this was the first time I had ever been so circumstanced, and most keenly did I feel the transition from the injuries of my enemy, and the gnawings of absolute hunger, to the charms of security and the delights of plenty. Having rested and enjoyed ourselves two or three days in Dizak, we proceeded on to Uratippa." By the road he turned aside to visit his old quarters at Besháger.*

* Báber's Mem. p. 98.

CHAPTER III.

SHEIBÁNI'S CONQUEST OF TÁSHKEND AND FERGHÁNA — EXPULSION OF BÁBER.

BÁBER VISITS THE KHAN. — RETURNS TO DEHKÁT. — HIS MODE OF LIFE. — REVISITS THE KHAN. — ARRIVAL OF THE YOUNGER KHAN. — THE KHANS INVADE FERGHÁNA. — BÁBER SURPRIZED BY TÁMBOL, AND WOUNDED. — TÁMBOL, HARD PRESSED, CALLS IN SHEIBÁNI. — AFFAIR OF AKHSI. — BÁBER DRIVEN OUT. — HIS FLIGHT AND DANGER. — THE KHANS DEFEATED AND TAKEN PRISONERS BY SHEIBÁNI, WHO CONQUERS TÁSHKEND. — ARE SET AT LIBERTY. — DEATH OF THE YOUNGER KHAN. — TÁMBOL REMAINS IN POSSESSION OF FERGHÁNA. — ATTACKED BY SHEIBÁNI: BESIEGED IN ANDEJÁN: SURRENDERS, AND IS PUT TO DEATH. — BÁBER ABANDONS FERGHÁNA. — SUBSEQUENT HISTORY AND DEATH OF THE ELDER KHAN. — DISPERSION OF THE TRIBE OF CHAGHATÁI MOGHULS.

BOOK I.

A.D. 1501.

Báber visits Uratippa,

As Ferghána was now in the hands of Jehángír Mírza and Sultan Ahmed Támbol, Báber did not venture to revisit his old dominions. Uratippa was possessed, under the Khan, by Muhammed Husein Mírza, Doghlat, the husband of Báber's aunt, whom the fugitive king visited, and who agreed to let him have the village of Dehkát for his winter quarters. In Dehkát Báber left

and the elder Khan.

his baggage, and in a few days set out for Táshkend, where he waited upon his uncle Sultan Mahmúd, the Khan, and saw a number of his maternal relations. The Khan was prevailed upon to give him Uratippa; but on the young Sultan's return to that country, Muhammed Husein, probably by an understanding with

His life at Dehkát.

the Khan, refused to give it up. Báber therefore was obliged to repair to Dehkát, the district which the Mírza had assigned to him. It lies on the skirts of a high mountain: the inhabitants were not Túrks, but

Sarts or Tájíks, and of course speaking the Persian tongue, though Báber remarks it as singular that they had large flocks of sheep and brood mares, like the wanderers of the desert. Their sheep might be about forty thousand in number. He and his followers lived in the houses of the peasants and shepherds. In this quiet retreat, his young and elastic mind soon recovered from the pressure of the misfortunes which had lately weighed upon it. "I lived," says he, "in the house of one of the head men of the place. He was an aged man, seventy or eighty years old. His mother was still alive, and had attained an extreme old age, being at this time a hundred and eleven. One of this lady's relations had accompanied the army of Taimur Beg, when he invaded Hindustan. The circumstances remained fresh in her memory, and she often told us stories on that subject. In the district of Dehkát alone, there still were of this lady's children, grandchildren, great-grandchildren, and great-great-grandchildren, to the number of ninety-six persons in life; and, including those deceased, the whole amounted to two hundred. One of her great-grandchildren was at this time a young man of twenty-five or twenty-six years of age, with a fine black beard. While I remained in Dehkát, I was accustomed to walk on foot all about the hills in the neighbourhood. I generally went out barefoot; and, from this habit of walking barefoot, I found that our feet soon became so hardened that we did not mind rock or stone in the least. In one of these walks, one day, between afternoon and evening prayers, having lost the road, we met a man who was going with a cow in a narrow path. I asked him the way. He answered, keep your eye fixed on the cow, and do not lose sight of her, till you come to the issue of the road, when you will know where you are. Kwája Ased-ulla, who was with me, enjoyed the joke,

BOOK I. A.D. 1501.

observing, 'What would become of us wise men were the cow to lose her way?'"* In some of these incidents we may trace a resemblance to the boyhood of Henri Quatre, wandering barefooted among the simple and hardy peasants of the mountains of his native Béarn; a training which he often acknowledged had fitted him more easily to endure and surmount the hardships of his future life. Adversity and difficulties in their early days have been, for obvious reasons, the best school for princes who were destined to become great. The stories told to Báber by the aged lady, in this remote village, concerning the wonders of India, probably fired his youthful imagination, and may have assisted in implanting that ardent desire, which he tells us, he felt, at a later period, of visiting that distant land; and the fulfilment of which led to the most celebrated achievement of his life.

It was now winter, and many of his remaining followers, whom the season hindered from going out on plundering parties, asked leave to go to Andeján. Kásim Beg, his chief minister, advised him to take that opportunity of sending some article of his dress to his brother Jehángír Mírza, as a present. He accordingly agreed to send him a cap of ermine. The Beg then asked him, "What great harm would there be in sending some present to Támbol?" "Though I did not altogether approve of this," continues Báber, "yet, induced by the pressing instances of Kásim Beg, I sent Támbol a large sword, which had been made in Samarkand for Nevián Gokultásh, from whom I took it. This was the very sword that afterwards came down on my own head, as shall be mentioned in the events of the ensuing year."†

While Báber was thus engaged, Sheibáni Khan having taken possession of Samarkand and the territories

* Báber's Mem. p. 100.

† Ibid.

A. D. 1501 -2.

Sheibáni invades Shahrokhía.

around it, a misunderstanding arose between him and the Moghul Khan, which speedily broke out into open hostilities. The Khan had hitherto supported Sheibáni in all his conquests, weakly persuading himself that they were made on his account, as they were made under his protection. He now probably began to discover that Sheibáni was acting for himself. However that may be, the Uzbek Khan marched in the midst of winter to attack his late patron and protector, and having passed the Sirr on the ice, ravaged Shahrokhía and Beshkent. No sooner did this intelligence reach Báber, than, accompanied by his small train of followers, he rode off to succour his uncle. "It was wonderfully cold," says he, "and the wind of Há-derwísh had lost none of its violence, and blew keen. So intense was the cold that in the course of two or three days we lost two or three persons from its severity. I required to bathe, on account of my religious purifications, and went down for that purpose to a rivulet which was frozen on the banks, but not in the middle, from the rapidity of the current. I plunged into the water and dived sixteen times. Its extreme chillness quite penetrated me." * When Báber had passed the Sírr and arrived at Beshkent, he found that Sheibáni had retreated, after plundering the country up to the walls of Shahrokhía. Despatching a messenger to the Khan with this intelligence, he went on to Ahengerán, where he received accounts of the death of Nevián Gokultásh, his foster brother, an event not unattended with suspicions of violence. "The truth," says Báber, "no man can know. His death affected me deeply. There are few persons for whose death I have felt so much. I wept incessantl for a week or ten days." It is very delightful to find such warmth of attachment in a young prince. But all Báber's social affections were

* Báber's Mem. p. 100.

BOOK I.

A.D. 1502.

naturally keen and ardent; and from the nature of his early life he had escaped that tendency to selfishness, which flattery and the indulgence of every wish as soon as it is excited, generate in every situation of life, as well as upon the throne. He now returned to his winter quarters in Dehkát.

Báber in Masíkha. A.H. 907, A.D. 1502.

With the return of spring, Sheibáni advanced against Uratippa. As Dehkát was in the low country at the foot of the hills, and therefore liable to be overrun by an invading enemy, Báber left it, and passed by Ab-burden, to the mountainous country of Masíkha, where he remained some time. There is so much interest in the various little incidents which Báber relates of his youthful wanderings, and it is so seldom that Asiatic history descends to such familiar incidents, that, in spite of the length to which this narrative has been extended, we may still continue to follow him for some time longer. "Ab-burden," says he, "is a village which lies at the foot of Masíkha. Beneath Ab-burden is a spring, and close by the spring is a tomb. From this spring towards the upland, the country belongs to Masíkha; but downwards from the spring it depends on Yelghár. On one of the sides of a rock which is on the brink of this fountain, I caused the following verses to be carved:—

"'I have heard that the illustrious Jemshíd
Inscribed these words on a stone, beside a fountain:—
Many a man, like us, has rested by this fountain,
And disappeared in the twinkling of an eye.
Should we conquer the whole world by our manhood and valour,
Yet what part of it could we carry with us to the grave?'"*

In these highlands, the practice of cutting verses and other inscriptions on the rocks is extremely common. While in Masíkha he had a visit from Múlla Hajári, the poet; and, to soothe the hours of his exile, he exercised

* Verses from the Bóstan of Sádi.

himself in poetical attempts in the Túrki, his native tongue.* CHAP. III. A.D. 1502.

Sheibáni ravages Uratippa.

When Báber was informed that Sheibáni Khan had actually advanced into Uratippa, in spite of the fewness of his followers and their bad equipment, leaving his household and baggage in Masíkha, he marched down from the hills, so as to reach Dehkát about the end of the night, intending to hover on the enemy's flank and seize any accidental advantage that offered. But he found that Sheibáni had retired immediately after laying the country waste. Báber therefore retraced his steps to his mountain abode.

Báber visits the Khan.

Here he naturally began to reflect upon his own situation. It was evident that to continue wandering an exile on barren mountains, without house or home, could lead to nothing, and was throwing away his time. He resolved, therefore, to visit once more his uncle the Khan, and to attempt to interest him in his behalf. In pursuance of this determination he proceeded by the pass of Ab-burden; was at Shahrokhía on the great Muhammedan festival of the Id-e-korbán; and joined the Khan at Táshkend, his capital. Kásim Beg, Báber's minister, who had a quarrel of blood with the Moghuls, not venturing to accompany him, left him and went to Hissár.

A.H. 907, 10 Zilhájeh, A.D. 1502, June 16.

Just at this time Támbol led his army against the Khan, and had advanced as far as the Dale of Ahengeran, when a conspiracy was discovered in the heart of his camp, at the head of which were Muhammed Hissári and Kamber Ali. The conspirators escaped, and fled to the Khan. Támbol on this retired, and recrossed the river, but soon after entered the territory of Uratippa.

A.H. 908, A.D. 1502.

This invasion drew the Khan from his indolent repose. He assembled his troops, and after a grand re-

* Báber's Mem. p. 101.

BOOK I. A.D. 1502.

view, led them up the Sirr.* It does not, however, appear that he entered Uratippa; and he soon returned home again. "This expedition of the Khan's," says Báber, "was rather an useless sort of an expedition. He took no fort, he beat no enemy; he went out and came in again." †

Such inactivity was little suited to the youthful ardour of Báber. His keen and ambitious mind preyed upon itself. To fill up the long intervals of leisure now afforded him, he devoted his mind to poetical pursuits, and he records with pride the time of his composing the first ghazel (or ode) that he ever wrote. ‡ But, though now, as at every future period of his life, he delighted to fill up with liberal and elegant studies the hours which he could steal from business, he had sat upon the thrones of Andeján and of Samarkand, and ambition was still his ruling passion. One of his thrones was now filled by a brother younger than himself, the other by his inveterate enemy. "While I remained at Táshkend at this time," says he, "I endured great vexation and misery. I possessed no government, nor had I hopes of acquiring any. Most of my servants had left me from absolute want; the few who still adhered to me were unable to accompany me on my journeys from sheer poverty. When I went to my uncle the Khan's diwán (levée), I was attended sometimes by one man, sometimes by two; but in one respect I was fortunate, that this did not happen among strangers, but with my own kinsmen. After having paid my compliments to the Khan, I was in the habit of going in to Shah Begum, his mother, bareheaded

* The particulars of this review are detailed with great spirit in Báber's Memoirs, and form a curious picture of the manners of the Moghuls. Mem. p. 103.

† Báber's Mem. p. 104.

‡ The commencement of this poem shows the state of the author's mind:—

"I have found no faithful friend in the world, but my soul;
Except my own heart, I have no trusty confidant."

CHAP. III.

A. D. 1502.

and barefoot, with as much freedom as a man would use at home, in his own house. At length, however, I was worn out with this unsettled way of living, and with having no house or home, so that life itself became burdensome to me. I considered with myself, that it was better to take my way and retire into some corner where I might live unknown and undistinguished, than to continue to drag on existence in the wretchedness and misery which I then endured; that it were far better to flee away from the sight of man, as far as my feet could carry me, than to exhibit myself as a spectacle in such distress and abasement. I had thoughts of going to Khita *, a country which, from my infancy, I always had had a strong desire to visit, but had hitherto been prevented, from my being a king, and from my duty to my relations and connections. Now, however, my kingship was gone, my mother was safe with her mother and brother; in short, every obstacle to my journey was removed." † His only difficulty was how to get away from his relations. To effect this, he represented to the Khan, through his friend Khwája Abul Makárám, that the conquests of Sheibáni Khan in Transoxiana had added so much to that chieftain's power, that Túrks and Moghuls had equal grounds for apprehension; that it was necessary to watch his progress with jealousy, and arrest his course before he succeeded in reducing all his neighbours under his sway, when it would be too late to think of checking him; that it would be well if the Khan, and his younger brother, Sultan Ahmed, who ruled that part of the Moghul tribe which was in the desert, could come to an understanding, and act in concert; that, as the Khan had not seen his brother for four or five and twenty years, and Báber had never seen him at all, that prince might visit the younger Khan, and act as a channel of

* China.

† Memoirs, pp. 104, 105.

BOOK I.

A.D. 1502.

communication between the brothers. It was Báber's plan, had he been allowed to depart under these pretexts, to have visited Moghulistán and Terfán, after which the reins were in his own hands to turn whither he would. But this design he communicated to nobody; well knowing that his mother, Kutlak-Nigár-Khanum, would not endure the mention of it, and feeling it painful to impart such a plan to the few steady friends who had followed him in all his wanderings, with very different hopes. The Khan and his mother, Shah Begum, at first agreed to the proposed plan; but, as on reflection it occurred to them that he had asked leave to go in consequence of the poor reception that had been given him, some demur ensued; besides this, the Khan perhaps thought it probable that his brother might pay a visit to Táshkend, as the rapid success of Sheibáni had made the brothers desirous of acting in concert with all their force against the common enemy. And accordingly, at that very crisis, a messenger did arrive with information that the younger Khan was already on his march to meet his brother. This put an end to Báber's project. A second express soon followed, bringing intelligence that he was close at hand; on which Shah Begum, his mother, with the Khan's sisters and other relations, and among the rest Báber, set out to meet him.

Arrival of the younger Khan.

This family party had advanced as far as some small villages between Táshkend and Seirám, without exactly knowing when the younger Khan would arrive. "I had ridden out carelessly to see the country, when, all at once, I found myself face to face with him. I immediately alighted, and advanced to salute him. The moment I alighted, the Khan knew who I was, and was much disconcerted, for he had intended to alight somewhere, and, when duly seated, to receive and embrace me with great form and decorum; but I came too quick upon him, and dismounted so rapidly, that there was no time for ceremony, as, the moment I sprang from my horse, I kneeled down and then embraced. He was a good deal agitated and disturbed, but at length ordered his two sons to alight, kneel, and embrace me." They then mounted, and all rode on to meet his mother, Shah Begum, and the Khanums, his sisters; and, after embracing them, "the party sat down, and continued talking about past occurrences and old stories till past midnight."*

CHAP. III. A.D. 1502.

Next morning the younger Khan presented Báber with a dress of honour, and one of his own horses ready saddled. This dress Báber describes as consisting of a Moghul cap embroidered with gold thread; a long frock of China satin, ornamented with flowered needle-work; a cuirass of Chinese work, of the old fashion, with a whetstone and a purse-pocket: from one side of this purse-pocket hung three or four articles, such as a perfume-case and its bag, with other trinkets, such as Eastern ladies wear at their necks, while as many dangled on the other side. When Báber returned back tricked out and disguised in all this Moghul finery, he relates with much glee that even his intimate friend Khwája Abdal Makáram did not kown him, and asked what Moghul Sultan that was.

Meeting of the brothers.

About twelve or fifteen miles from Táshkend, the elder Khan, seated under an awning erected for the occasion, received his brother in all the pride of Moghul state. The ceremony, as described by Báber, is curious. The younger Khan advanced right towards his brother, and, on coming near him in front, turned to the left of the elder Khan, fetching a complete circle round him, till he was again in front, when he alighted; and, on coming to the distance at which *Cornish* is performed, he knelt nine times, and then went up and embraced him; the elder Khan, as his brother came

* Memoirs, pp. 105, 106.

BOOK I.

A.D. 1502.

near, standing up and embracing him in turn; they stood a long time clasping each other in their arms. The younger Khan, while retiring, again knelt nine times; and, when he presented his tributory offerings, again knelt many times; after which he went and sat down. All the younger Khan's men were dressed in the Moghul fashion,—in rich clothes such as had been presented to Báber, with their horses caparisoned and bedizened in singular style.

The Khans march to Akhsi.

The younger Khan brought with him only about fifteen hundred men; but the brothers soon took their resolution to attack Sultan Ahmed Támbol in Andeján. As there was some danger that Sheibáni might move to the assistance of Támbol, or at least try to make a diversion by an inroad into Táshkend, Sultan Mahmúd's eldest son was left with a strong force to guard Táshkend, and a reinforcement was sent to Muhammed Husein Mírza at Uratippa, for the purpose of impeding Sheibáni's advance in that direction. The army under the Khans amounted to thirty thousand men, and crossed the chain of hills that bounds Akhsi on the west. To create a diversion, Báber was sent with a detachment of Moghuls to cross the great river, and, proceeding towards Ush and Urkend, to take in the rear Támbol, who was said to have collected his forces in Akhsi ready to face the Khans. Báber does not mention with what professed intention, so far as concerned himself, the Khans entered his country. From what followed, it seems to be probable that they intended to seize it for themselves, and wished to use Báber only as an instrument for forwarding their own purposes. We find nothing like conscience or honour among the chiefs on the Sirr or the Amu, in this age. Ambition sanctioned every degree of treachery and deceit, even towards their nearest relations. Báber, with his detachment, marching to the north of Akhsi, crossed the Sirr on rafts, and by a rapid march, sur-

Báber takes Ush.

prised and took Ush; on which, all the tribes who occupied the hills and plains to the east and south of Andéjan gladly declared for him. Urkend, a place of great strength, lying on the Káshghar frontier, and formerly the capital of Ferghána, also tendered its allegiance. The people of Marghinán, in like manner, expelled Támbol's garrison and joined Báber; so that, in a short time, the whole kingdom south of the Sirr, Andeján only excepted, acknowledged his authority. Támbol, meanwhile, undismayed, lay with his army near Akhsi, facing the Khans, in a strongly fortified position. Daily skirmishes ensued, with little advantage on either side.

Támbol covers Akhsi.

Báber advances to Andeján.

Báber, thus master of one portion of the south side of the river, understanding that the men of Andeján also were anxious for an opportunity to join him, advanced towards the place by night; wishing to introduce into the town some person who might confer with his friends, and concert with them a plan for surprising the place. This plan failed from one of those accidents to which night attacks are so subject. In consequence of a mistake of his Moghul auxiliaries as to the watchword,—a military practice to which they were not accustomed, — two parties of his troops, in the darkness of the night, engaged each other as enemies, and the whole were compelled to retreat. Báber, learning soon after, however, that Támbol's troops at Akhsi were disheartened, and beginning to desert from his camp, ventured to march openly from Ush upon Andeján. He was met at some distance from the suburbs by a brother of Támbol's, whose troops he charged without hesitation, driving them back into the fort. Báber, with his habitual ardour, was keen for making a push to enter the gates along with them, convinced that such an attack would certainly succeed; but the greater caution of the older leaders decided that it was too late in the day for hazarding such an attempt; at the same time holding it certain that the place must fall next

BOOK I. A.D. 1502.

morning, without loss to the army. The troops were accordingly drawn off, to encamp at some little distance.

Is surprised by Támbol.

The Sultan, with that frankness and magnanimity which distinguish his character, acknowledges that, after retiring from the town, his conduct was most incautious. News had already reached him that Támbol, obliged to abandon his ground near Akhsi, was in full retreat on Andeján; yet, instead of occupying the strong ground along the banks of the Jákán, he crossed that river, and encamped on a level plain, near a village on the other side, and went to sleep, in negligent security, without outpost or vidette. Just before dawn, an alarm was given that the enemy was upon them. Báber, springing from sleep, rushed out with about ten of his best men, who were at hand to check their progress. He drove back the party whom he first met; but soon after fell in with the main body under Támbol himself, whom he did not hesitate to attack with his arrows. In an instant, however, he was himself wounded by an arrow which pierced his right thigh, while Támbol, riding up, discharged full on his head a furious sabre-blow, which stunned him. The blow was inflicted by the very sword which Báber had so lately presented to him. Though the steel cap which he had on was not cut through, his head was severely bruised. In wheeling round he received another sabre-stroke, the force of which was luckily broken by falling on his quiver. The enemy were now fast gathering about him, and only three of his followers were near him, so that he had nothing left for it but to try to extricate himself by a hasty retreat. He plunged into a deep stream which he met with in his flight, and was fortunate enough to hit upon one of the few places where it was fordable; and, falling in with two or three of his men who joined him, by taking bye-roads he succeeded in reaching Ush. Many brave officers and men fell that day.*

* Báber's Mem. pp. 110, 111.

CHAP. III.

A. D. 1502.

Támbol was not able to avail himself of all the advantages which this success seemed to offer, as the Khans had followed close after him when he broke up from his camp at Akhsi, and now advanced to Andeján. Two days afterwards Báber joined them from Ush, and waited upon the elder Khan. On this occasion the Khan communicated his intention to give up to his younger brother, Sultan Ahmed Khan, the whole of Ferghána south of the river, comprising all the tract of country recovered by Báber, with Andeján when conquered; under pretence that it was necessary that the younger Khan, as he came from a distance, should possess some convenient station for himself and his troops, near enough at hand to enable him to act against Sheibáni Khan, to check whose growing power was now the grand object. Báber was, in the meanwhile, to have Akhsi; and, when matters were settled in Ferghána, both he and the Khans were to march in conjunction against Samarkand; in the event of that city's being recovered, the younger Khan was to get Akhsi also, while Samarkand was to be given up to Báber. All this was not very agreeable to the young Sultan, but he saw no remedy, and was obliged to submit. On leaving the elder Khan, he went to visit his younger uncle; who, being on this occasion better prepared than when they first met so unexpectedly, came out ceremoniously beyond the range of the tent ropes to welcome him; and, as Báber walked with difficulty and leaning on a staff, in consequence of the wound in his thigh, his uncle took him by the arm, and led him into the tent, telling him that he had behaved like a hero. As the younger Khan had passed all his life in the remoter deserts of Tartary, his manners were rude and his accommodations but indifferent. "The small tent in which he sat," says his nephew, "certainly was not distinguished for its neatness; it had much the air of a marauder's; grapes, horse-furniture, and melons were lying huddled about

Joins the Khans;

proposed arrangement.

BOOK I.

A.D. 1502.

in it, here and there, in rare confusion." He insisted on Báber's taking the aid of his surgeon to manage his wound, and the serjeant-surgeon, from the report of his patient, appears to have been a quack worthy of his tribe.

To assist in carrying into effect the arrangements which it had pleased the Khans to make, Báber was sent to the north of the river with a body of one or two thousand Moghuls, to reduce Akhsi and Kásan, the provinces that had been allotted to him, while the Khans employed themselves in the siege of Andeján. He soon got possession of Noukend, a castle on the road to Kásan; and of Páp, a very strong fort in the Akhsi territory.

The success of the Khans and of Báber had reduced Sultan Ahmed Támbol and his party to great distress. Támbol saw no hopes of retrieving his affairs, but by detaching Báber from his uncles; but he believed that, if that could be effected, it would be impossible for the Khans to keep their ground in the country. Sheikh Bayezíd, Támbol's younger brother, and governor of Akhsi, communicated on the subject with Báber, and invited him into the city. Báber, who did not wish to separate himself from his uncles, informed them of the proposal; they advised him to pretend to enter into the plan, to accept the invitation, and afterwards to seize Sheikh Bayezíd.

Támbol attempts to gain Báber,

Báber was not fond of this mode of proceeding, as it implied a breach of faith. He was, however, eager to get into Akhsi, and to have the co-operation of Bayezíd; hoping perhaps that in due time he might detach him from his brother's interest, or even use him to strengthen his party against the Khans. An agreement was accordingly entered into, the terms of which Báber does not mention; and he was in consequence received into the town, Sheikh Bayezíd coming out with Násir Mírza, Báber's youngest brother, to receive and do him

who is received into Akhsi.

honour.* He took up his quarters in his father's palace in the outer fort.

Támbol calls in Sheibáni,

But matters were drawing to a crisis in Ferghána. The two Khans in conjunction pushed on the siege of Andeján. Támbol, sensible of his weakness, and that his ruin was at hand unless he provided an immediate remedy, sent to Sheibáni Khan at Samarkand to solicit his aid against the Moghul chiefs, and offering to hold Ferghána under him as his sovereign. Sheibáni, to whom no proposal could be more agreeable, readily accepted the offer, and promised to march without delay to expel the invaders. No sooner did the Khans hear that he was on his march, than they abandoned the siege of Andeján; and, retreating by Marghinán, repassed the river at Khojend. The moment their retreat began, the inhabitants of Ush, Marghinán, and of the rest of the towns,—who had voluntarily submitted to Báber, but who had been miserably oppressed and plundered by the Moghul garrisons which had been placed among them,—rose upon their oppressors, drove them out of their towns and forts, and stript them of their booty. Indeed, the helpless inhabitants, in these unhappy times, invariably suffered from every change, whoever were their masters.

Retreat of Khans.

Proceedings at Akhs.

Báber was now perplexed. Though he had little confidence in the attachment of the Khans, he did not wish lightly to desert them, especially as he had as little to hope for from their opponents as from them. They were become, however, the weaker party; and, it was clear, could give him no effectual aid, even were they disposed. To add to his embarrassment, his brother Jehángír,—the nominal sovereign of Ferghána, under Támbol,—made his appearance, early one morning, having escaped from Támbol's camp at Marghinán.

* It would seem that Násir Mírza, as well as his brother Jehángír, was used to strengthen the party against Báber.

BOOK I.

A.D. 1502.

Even Sheikh Bayezíd himself was now at a loss how to act. Affairs had become complicated. Some of Báber's Begs advised him to seize Bayezíd, to occupy the citadel of Akhsi, and trust to his own strength and good fortune. Báber objected to this proceeding, as contrary to good faith; and, before they could come to any resolution, Bayezíd moved into the citadel, which he occupied, and which was thus lost. During the general confusion, Báber neglected to place a guard on the bridge that led into that fortress; and, before the sun was up next morning, Támbol, who had hastened from Andeján, arrived, attended by two or three thousand cavalry in complete armour; passed the bridge and entered the citadel without opposition.

Bayezíd seized.

Báber had not at this moment many more than a hundred of his followers with him, all the rest having been sent out on various missions, to collect the revenues, to take charge of districts, or to garrison forts. He was himself in the town, which was open towards the citadel. Defence might justly have seemed hopeless; yet Báber, whose temper led him never to despond, was busy posting his few troops at the extremity of the different streets, and in procuring supplies of military stores for their use, when Bayezíd and Kamber Ali came galloping out of the citadel, to propose terms of pacification on the part of Támbol. Báber conducted the envoys to his father's tomb, which was near at hand, and sat down with them in the portico, that they might confer together. He sent to call his brother Jehángír, to join them. That prince accordingly came, along with Ibráhím Chápuk; but they, after consulting together, had come to the resolution of making Bayezíd prisoner. Jehángír whispered their intentions to Báber. Things were so much changed since that plan was first proposed, the enemy being now in possession of the citadel, and having a powerful force there, while Báber's scanty numbers had not a wall to defend them, that he at once perceived that more was to be hoped for from negotiation than from force; and therefore told his brother that the time for that was gone by. Jehángír, upon this, made a sign to Ibrahim to desist; but he, either really misunderstanding the sign, or only pretending to do so, laid hold of Bayezíd, who was immediately surrounded and rudely dragged away by their rough retainers. There was now an end of all treaty. It only remained to take to horse and prepare for action.

Báber driven from Akhsi.

On observing this act of treachery, the soldiers in the citadel immediately attacked the town. They were far superior in numbers. The feeble force which Báber possessed, in spite of a gallant resistance, were driven from street to street. The combat was hopeless from the first. After brave but fruitless exertions, Báber's followers began to think of saving themselves by getting out of the place. They made a push for one of the gates, and forced their way through. Bayezíd had fortunately escaped in the confusion which followed the attack. When out of the town, Báber imprudently halted to wait for his brother and the stragglers. The force opposed to them by the enemy was overpowering. Only twenty or thirty men were left with the young Sultan. Convinced at last that all was over, he set off in full flight, without his brother; and had hardly crossed the bridge, when a large body of the enemy appeared at the other end, and followed them in keen pursuit. Man after man was overtaken and unhorsed; they had hardly ridden three miles, as far as the village of Sang, when their party was reduced to eight men in all. After passing that village they saw no more of their immediate pursuers. They rode up the banks of the river Sang for a long time, by a bye-path, among winding glens, remote from the high-road; and, then, leaving it before sunset, emerged from the broken country into an open plain. Here they saw something which they suspected

His flight.

BOOK I. A.D. 1502.

might be a party of men at a distance. Báber placed his companions under cover, and ascended a rising ground, in order to discern with greater certainty what it might be; when suddenly a number of horsemen were seen galloping up the hill behind them. Not knowing how many they were, they all again took to flight. The horsemen pursued. Again they were overtaken, one after another, and unhorsed; till at last, of the seven who had been left with the young prince, Mírza Kuli Gokaltásh alone remained, and the pursuit was still continued. "Our horses were too tired to admit of being put to the gallop," says Báber; "we went on at a canter; but the horse of Mírza Kuli began to move slower and slower. I said to him, 'If deprived of you, whither can I go? Come then, and be it death or life, let us meet it together.' I kept on turning from time to time, to look for Mírza Kuli. At last he said, 'My horse is completely blown; and it is impossible for you to escape, if you encumber yourself with me. Push on, and shift for yourself. Perhaps you may still escape.' My situation was singularly distressing. Mírza Kuli also fell behind, and I was left alone."*

At this alarming moment, two of the enemy, Baba Seirámi and Bandeh Ali, were gaining upon Báber, whose horse began to flag. There was a tract of rocky ground near at hand, and a steep hill about two miles off. He had only twenty arrows left in his quiver. He was divided between dismounting at the first, and there defending himself as long as his arrows lasted; or, of pushing on for the second, where he thought he might place a few arrows in his girdle, climb up the hill, and set his enemies at defiance. As he had great confidence in his own nimbleness and speed, this last seemed his best chance of final escape; and he spurred on his weary horse. It was too fatigued, however, to exert its speed;

* Báber's Mem. pp. 117, 118.

and his pursuers got within bowshot of him. He was unwilling to shoot any of his arrows, on which his safety might finally depend. The pursuers, on their part, seemed unwilling to engage in close combat, or to come nearer, but kept tracking him.

It was about sunset when he got near the hill. His pursuers then called out, and asked him, whither he meant to go, informing him that both his brothers were prisoners. This intelligence added to Báber's danger and alarm; for he well saw that if the enemy once had all the three brothers in their power, every restraint was taken away from them. He said nothing, but kept on his course. After some time they again addressed him in a humbler style, dismounting and leading their horses; but he still went on, and entered a glen, up which they continued to follow him. He came to a steep ledge of rock, and tried to mount it, but his horse lost its footing. Again they addressed him in a mild tone of expostulation; asking him, what end it could serve, in so dark a night (for the night had now fallen dark around them), to go on in a line were there was no pathway. They asserted, and confirmed their assertion with an oath, that it was Támbol's wish to place him on the throne. He replied that he had no confidence in Támbol; but that, if they really wished to serve him, they might do so by showing him some road by which he could join the Khans; if not, he entreated that they would go, and leave him to his fate. They replied that they could not think of leaving him in so desolate a situation; that they heartily wished that they had never come, and were ready to serve him and follow him, go where he would. He bid them swear by the Koran that they were sincere; and they swore.*

After this oath he began to show them some confidence, though his trust was far from being entire.

* Báber's Mem. p. 119.

BOOK I. A.D. 1502.

He made them go before him, to point out the way. They misled him, however; and about midnight pretended that, in the darkness, they had passed the road which he had wished to take; but offered to conduct him to the village of Ghiva, whence he could easily reach the Khan's dominions. About three in the morning they came to the Karnán river, when one of them went on to reconnoitre, and returned to report that there were a number of men passing along the road, so that it was not safe to venture on it. Báber was in the midst of enemies, and morning was coming on. He proposed to his companions that they should all conceal themselves in the hill, during the coming day, and, when night arrived, get something to refresh their horses, and then cross the Sirr, and make for Khojend. Bandeh Ali, who was Darogha (or chief magistrate) of Karnán, offered to go to that town, which was not far off, to procure some food for themselves, and provender for their horses, and get it conveyed to them. This was agreed to, and they all took the road of Karnán, and halted about a mile or two from the place, while the Darogha went in. He did not return till after the sun was risen, when he brought out three loaves for the party, but nothing for their horses. They went off to a hillock hard by, to eat their bread, tying the horses lower down in marshy ground, out of sight, and kept watch on different sides of the hill. They first saw a party of five, one of whom they knew, pass by, going to Akhsi. Báber did not venture to speak to them, knowing them to be indisposed to him; but, as they were likely to halt for the night at Karnán, he laid a plan for carrying off their horses. They next saw a single horseman riding over the plain, but did not think it safe to accost him. It was, as he afterwards discovered, a fugitive from the rout, one of Báber's Begs, lurking like himself. As their horses had had nothing to eat for two days and a night, it was necessary to go down to the plain to let them graze. About afternoon prayers, when they had gone down, they observed a horseman riding over the very height they had left. Báber recognised him for the Kilanter (or Head-man) of Ghiva, went up to him, and addressed him with kindness, tried to gain his good will, and in the end despatched him to bring provender for their horses, some food for themselves, and the tackle used in passing rivers. They engaged him to meet them on the same spot, at bedtime prayers.

Evening prayers were past, when they descried a horseman going from Karnán to Ghiva. They hailed him and he answered them. It was the very same horseman they had seen before; but, though he was a Beg who had been five years in Báber's service, and was well known to him, so successfully did he change his voice for the purpose of concealment, that Báber did not recognise him. On the contrary, he was so uneasy from this man's passing and repassing them in this suspicious way, that he was afraid to adhere to his assignation with the Kilanter. It was settled, therefore, that they should go to some retired garden-house near Karnán, and there get a person who might repair to the appointed place of meeting, and bring the Kilanter. To Karnán they all accordingly went; and, on their arrival there, as it was winter, they brought the Sultan a cloak made of year-old lambskin, with the wool inside and coarse woven cloth without, such as is used for warmth in that country. They also procured for him a homely mess of pottage of boiled millet flour, which he eat with much relish. On his inquiring if they had sent anybody to meet the Kilanter on the hill, they assured him that they had; but the truth was that they were playing false, and had not only met him already, but had despatched him on to Támbol, to let him know where the Sultan was to be found. At the same time, pretending great care for Báber's safety,

BOOK I.

A.D. 1502.

they waked him after a fire had been kindled, and, when he had enjoyed but a few moments' rest, made him get up, mount his horse, and ride to another house in the suburbs, which they represented as safer, from being more out of the town.

While the Sultan lay down to rest in his new quarters, Baba Seirámi, one of his late pursuers, went to the terrace roof of the house, to keep a look-out. A little before noon, he came down and reported that he saw one Yúsef, a Darogha, coming towards them. As this man was well known to be a magistrate in the service of Támbol, Báber desired Baba to go out and ascertain if he had come in consequence of hearing that the Sultan was there. On his return Baba reported that Yúsef had met a man at the gate of Ahksi, from whom he had learnt that the Sultan was there; that he had put the man in close custody to prevent his abusing his knowledge, and had hastened to the spot to meet his sovereign. Báber, who began to fear that he had all along been deceived, asked Baba earnestly what was his real opinion of the matter. He answered that they were all his servants, and that there was nothing left for it but to join Támbol and his party, who would certainly make him king. While they were yet conversing, Yúsef entered, and throwing himself on his knees, exclaimed, "Why should I conceal anything from you?" Sultan Ahmed Támbol knows nothing of the matter; but Sheikh Bayezíd has got information where you are, and has sent me hither." On hearing this, Báber gave up everything for lost, and entreated Yúsef, if all was indeed over, to inform him honestly, that he might, while there was yet time, perform his last ablutions, before prostrating himself in prayer, and thus prepare for his fate, like a brave man and a true believer. Yúsef swore again and again that he was sincere, but Báber did not believe him, and retired into the garden to spend the few moments yet left him, in religious meditation, and in preparations for another world.*

A chasm in Báber's own memoirs, at this interesting period of his life, prevents our knowing in what manner he was extricated from the painful situation in which he was placed. He did however escape, and succeeded in joining the Khans.

Advance of Sheibáni, A. H. 908, A. D. 1502,

When the two Moghul Khans marched from Táshkend for Ferghána, Sultan Mahmúd had left his eldest son, Sultan Muhammed Sultan, with a large army to defend that country, should any attempt be made upon it by Sheibáni during their absence: while Muhammed Husein Korkan, Doghlat, to whom another body of troops was assigned, had orders to keep Sheibáni in check, should he advance by Uratippa. The Khans had imagined that these two armies were sufficient to cover their operations against Andeján, and that it would be impossible for any force to pass them both. But Sheibáni, whose interpretation of the term impossible was not the same as theirs, regarded the whole arrangement as being in his favour, since it allowed him, by a little management and activity, to make his way between the two covering armies, and to come upon the Khans, while they had with them only a third part of their troops. Setting out from Samarkand, therefore, he advanced towards Ferghána by rapid marches, taking Uratippa on his route. Muhammed Husein imagined that the Uzbek had come to lay siege to his fort, and busied himself in putting every thing into the most perfect state of defence. In the afternoon of the day of his arrival, Sheibáni encamped near the town, as if ready to begin his operations against it, with the morning. But, no sooner had the sun set, and darkness covered his movements, than he silently decamped, and marched away with all possible speed. When the

to Uratippa.

* Báber's Mem. pp. 120—122.

BOOK I. A.D. 1503.

morning light returned, and it was ascertained that he was gone, and that his march was directed towards Andeján, express was despatched after express to give the Khans notice of his approach.

to Andeján;

The expresses and Sheibáni reached the army of the Khans nearly at the same time; and the armies neither of Táshkend nor of Uratippa had time to march to their succour. The Khans had still with them about 15,000 men; and, after their hurried retreat, on the first alarm, across the river at Khojend, into the Akhsi territory, were joined by Báber, who had escaped without followers. They now believed themselves for a time at least, to be in perfect safety; when of a sudden, the indefatigable Sheibáni, with 30,000 horse, burst in upon the camp. The Moghuls, taken by surprise, had hardly time to mount and draw up. Being in confusion, and borne down by superior numbers, resistance was unavailing, and the defeat complete. The horses of the Khans being worn out in the flight, they were both made prisoners. Báber effected his escape, and made his way to the southern hills of Ferghána.*

defeats the Moghuls.

and takes the Khans.

Sheibáni, after his decisive battle, lost no time in improving his victory. Bayezíd waited upon him from Akhsi, and both he and his brother Támbol expressed the deepest gratitude for his aid, and the most devoted attachment to his interests. The Uzbek, on his part, seemed quite satisfied with their professions, did not waste time by going back to Andeján, but, leaving them to complete the reduction and settlement of the rest of the country, moved down the Sirr, towards the dominions of the elder Khan.

Conquers Táshkend,

He met with no opposition. Consternation and dismay had marched before him. As soon as the news of the defeat of the Khans, and that they were both prisoners in the hands of Sheibáni, reached Táshkend,

* The disaster of Táshkend was in Cancer, A. H. 908 (June, 1503). See Tar. Resh. f. 117.

Sultan Muhammed Sultan fled with his family, children, and the Moghul Ulús, into the deserts of Moghulistán. Muhammed Husein, of Uratippa, regarding any opposition as unavailing, and likely to be fatal, abandoned that place; and, unable to make his way across the Seihun, fled to the mountainous region of Karatigín, with his followers and whatever he had time to carry away. Sheibáni meanwhile marched downwards by Shahrokhía, Táshkend, and Uratippa, occupying the country and the towns as he went along. He had formerly been ambitious of an alliance by marriage with the family of the Khans, but his wish had not been gratified. He now enlarged his demand to three intermarriages; and he himself, his son Taimur Beg, and his nephew Jáni Beg, married each a princess of the family. Sheibáni behaved to the Khans with great courtesy; and, after the conquest of Táshkend, set them at liberty, in consideration of the patronage he had himself received from the elder Khan; but he detained as many of the Moghuls as he could, and no fewer than 30,000 of them were added to the Uzbek army. He seems to have borne a particular grudge to Báber's old friend Khwája Abul-Mokáram. Immediately after the battle he despatched a messenger to Táshkend to announce that the two Khans were in his hands, and that Báber had fled the country; and to add, that, if the inhabitants had any wish to save the captive princes, they must prevent the Khwája's escape, and detain him in custody. He was accordingly thrown into prison, but in a short time after effected his escape. To prevent his being recognised, he submitted to the mortification of cutting off his beard. Unable, from his age and infirmities, to reach any place of safety, he was compelled to take refuge with a man who lived in a village near Tashkend. This person concealed him for a day or two, but afterwards gave him up, when the Khwája was carried before Sheibani, who on seeing him in-

releases the Khans.

BOOK I.

A.D. 1503.

quired, "What have you done with your beard?" The Khwája answered by quoting two Persian verses, "He who puffs at the lamp which God has lighted, singes his beard;" but the felicity of the allusion did not avail him, and he was put to death. Sheibáni, having placed Uzbek garrisons in the chief towns, returned straight to Samarkand; while the two Khans, seeing their power broken and their army destroyed or transferred into the ranks of their enemy, retired into Moghulistán.*

Sheibáni invades Hissár.

Sheibáni's stay at Samarkand was short. His ambition had been fired by success, and he now aimed at the conquest of Khorásán itself. But he saw, that, before venturing on such an attempt, it was necessary, in order to prevent any attack on his flank or from behind, to reduce not only Ferghána, but Hissár, Balkh, and other countries north of the Parapamisan range. Khosrou Shah, who now ruled Hissár, Kunduz, and other extensive territories on both sides of the Amu, fully anticipated such an attack, and used every exertion to be prepared for it. When Muhammed Husein Doghlat fled from Uratippa to Karatigín, Khosrou invited him to his court, and questioned him earnestly as to the power of Sheibáni, the composition of his army, and his military tactics. Khosrou did not expect an attack that year, but thought it likely that he might be invaded the year after. Early in the winter, however †, Sheibáni, who never slumbered over his projects, led an army into Hissár. His purpose was not to seize Khosrou or to conquer his territories, but merely to try by experience the extent of that prince's power, and the temper of his military force. He ravaged Khosrou's country, meeting with little resistance; and then marched down to Balkh, which was held for Badi-ez-zemán Mírza,

* Tar. Resh. ff. 113—119.; Rozet-es-Sefa, vol. vii.

† This expedition seems to have taken place in the winter of A. H. 909, probably in October or November, A. D. 1503. Tar. Resh. ff. 117, 118. Balkh continued to be besieged during the winter.

the eldest son of the Sultan of Herát. Here too he met with little to oppose him, and laid siege to the capital. Having thus gained experimental proof of the nature and extent of what he had to fear from the rulers of Hissár and Khorásán, he resolved, before going farther, to march back, and remove whatever might occasion him danger or annoyance from behind. He, therefore, returned to Samarkand, and soon set out once more with a strong army for Andeján.

Sheibáni invades Andeján. Spring of A.H. 909, end of A.D. 1504.

The pretext for this invasion does not appear: but Sheibáni wished to possess Andeján, and was never at a loss for a pretext. Sultan Ahmed Támbol, ever since the battle of Akhsi, had been busily employed in reducing the hill-tribes of Andeján; and was in the country of the Jageráks, in the south east of Ferghána, when he heard that Sheibáni had entered his territory. Without losing a moment, he hurried back to his capital, resolved to defend it to the last. For that purpose he called in all his garrisons, as well as the troops that were scattered in stations over the country. These proceedings Sheibáni saw with delight. His plan had been to lay siege in person to Andeján; to send out detachments in every direction to seize the castles, ravage the country, carry off the inhabitants and reduce it to a desert, and then to retire; he proposed next year again to spread his troops over the country in the same way, to carry off or destroy the crops, to ruin whatever had escaped the year before, and complete the devastation. These measures, the plan of operations adopted by Támbol unexpectedly shortened. Sheibáni saw the possibility of deciding the contest at one blow. As his troops approached Andeján, Támbol, who had concentrated his whole force, marched out with a considerable body of men to harass the advance; but discovering that, not the advance only, but the whole hostile army, was close upon him, he retired with precipitation; and his active enemy, following close behind, cut a number of his

BOOK II.

A. D. 1504.

Besieges Támbol,

troops to pieces, before they could re-enter the town. Sheibáni, thereupon, resolved to block up the army of Támbol thus collected at one point, and dispirited by the loss they had recently sustained; and at once to push on the siege vigorously to a conclusion.

The siege had lasted only forty days, when Támbol found that all his means of defence had failed. It would appear, that, trusting to his being able to keep the field with at least some part of his army, he had not made sufficient provision for the supply of the whole within the walls. He therefore began to think seriously of capitulating; and discovered, by accident, a mediator in the enemy's camp. Muhammed Husein Doghlat of Uratippa, whom Khosrou in the course of that winter had expelled from Karatigín, having, with a part of his followers, effected his escape over the snowy mountains of that country, had descended into the highlands of the Jageraks, with which tribe he had united in repelling the late attack of Támbol. He had subsequently repaired to Sheibáni's camp, under a promise of immunity. There he had been most hospitably entertained and feasted, by Sheibáni and the Uzbek chiefs. On the morning of the forty-first day of the siege, Támbol, finding himself reduced to extremity, and perceiving Muhammed Husein in the enemy's trenches, called out to him from the top of a lofty turret, "My Mírza, do not forget me, and think of the times when we sucked milk from the same breast. Tell me what I should do, and I will do it." Támbol had been his foster-brother, and Muhammed was much affected. He asked Támbol, why he stood out, if he had no hopes of success; and intimated that the only step left was to surrender at discretion. Taimur Sultan, Sheibáni's son, was standing by at the time. In a word, Támbol, compelled by necessity, at length came out, accompanied by his brothers. Conscious of his danger and filled with alarm, he threw his arms round his fosterbrother's neck. The Uzbeks

who surrenders and is put to death.

hesitated not a moment, but unrelentingly put them all to the sword on the spot. The gates of the town were, at the same time, closed; and not the slightest plunder or excess was permitted within the walls. Andeján was bestowed on Jani Beg Sultan, Sheibáni's cousin; and Sheibáni soon after retraced his steps to Samarkand, where he made every preparation for returning to subdue those countries on the Amu which last year he had only visited.*

Báber a fugitive in Andeján.

During all these transactions, and ever since the battle in which the Khans had been taken prisoners, Báber had been compelled to wander as a fugitive and an outlaw in the hill-country on the south of Andeján; and especially among the mountain recesses of Sukh and Hushiár, districts of the province of Asfera. In all his wanderings he was accompanied by his mother, by some individuals of his family and household, and by a few faithful followers, who adhered to him in the midst of all his misfortunes. After he had been subjected for nearly a year to the utmost extremes of hardship and suffering; hunted from village to village, and from forest to mountain; finding the toils of his pursuers closing around him; that his partisans in the low country were totally dispersed, and that not a chance of success was left; he held a consultation with his small but devoted band. There was little room for diversity of opinion. Their prospects were dreary and dark. The kingdoms of Samarkand and Bokhára, which had so long been held by his family, and the former of which he had himself twice occupied for a brief space, were now in the firm grasp of an Uzbek barbarian; the territories of his uncle, the elder Khan, had shared the same fate; and his own little kingdom of Ferghána, a kingdom which, if we examine his history critically, he cannot be said ever to have fully enjoyed, had in like manner

* Tar. Resh. ff. 118. 121.; Báber, p. 168.

BOOK I.

A.D. 1504.

been added to the overgrown dominions of his rival. Opposition was hopeless; and he could not expect long to secure even his life, if he continued to roam as an adventurer in a territory which he had once vainly called his own. Young and brave as he was, the world was before him; and he resolved, abandoning for a time his native country, to court in foreign lands that success which fortune denied him at home. The territory and court of Khorásán naturally presented themselves to his imagination. That kingdom was governed by Sultan Husein Mírza, a monarch of great power and reputation, and beyond comparison the most distinguished prince then living of the family of Taimur. Accordingly, in the summer of A.H. 910, Báber bade a last adieu to the land of his nativity, and the whole party set out to cross the lofty and snow-covered range of mountains that separate Andeján from Karatigín and Hissár.*

Sets out for Khorásán.

Moharrem, A.H. 910, June, A.D. 1504.

While bringing to a close this first period of Báber's eventful life, it may be proper to advert briefly to the fate of his uncles the two Khans. After they were released by Sheibáni Khan, both the brothers retired into the desert. The younger Khan, Ahmed or Ilachi, retired to his own dominions in the east of Moghulistán, where he spent a few months. His previous life had been a fortunate one; and his late disaster preyed upon his mind, and affected his health. He never regained his spirits, and died in the end of the following winter.† Haider Mírza relates, that, he had heard from Khwája Taj-ed-din Muhammed, a saintly man, whose family were the hereditary Sheikh-ul-Islams of that country, that, when the Khan was suffering much from dysentery, he had observed to him—that it was reported that Sheibáni had caused noxious herbs to be mixed with his food; and that, if such was his highness's wish, he

Death of the younger Khan,

* Báber's Mem. p. 127.; Tar. Resh. f. 125.

† End of winter of A.H. 909 probably March, 1504.

would procure the precious teriák, or antidote against poison, brought from Khita, and would administer it. The Khan replied with a sigh; "Yes, Shahi Beg Khan has indeed poisoned me; and I will tell you how. From a low degree of abasement he has raised himself to such a pitch of elevation, that he has been able to make us two brothers prisoners, and set us at large again. From this disgrace originates the disease that has preyed upon my frame. If you know any antidote for a malady of that nature, it may be useful."*

The death of Sultan Ahmed Khan was, as usual, followed by civil dissensions in Moghulistán. When that prince had set out from Aksu to assist his brother on the Seihun, he caused his eldest son Mansúr Khan to be installed as Khan of the Moghuls; and now, on his father's death, Mansúr continued to hold that high station. His uncle, Sultan Mahmúd, however, who was at the time in Moghulistán, secured the chief power among the tribes in the western range of the desert; while Mansúr exercised his authority at Aksu, and in the whole territory to the east, as far as Chálís and Terfán. But Mahmúd's reign in the western desert was not undisturbed. Dissensions and civil wars soon broke out. His nephews Saíd Khan and Khalíl Khan, the younger brothers of Mansúr, carried on against him a harassing warfare, in which defeats were in turn suffered on both sides, and the success was various. But the ardour and activity of his youthful competitors, who naturally drew into their ranks the more adventurous spirits of the tribes, in the end secured the ascendancy. Sultan Mahmúd, who was naturally indolent, had also much of his father Yúnis Khan's preference for fertile and populous countries; and, disgusted with the hardships and sufferings to which he was exposed,

* Tar. Resh. ff. 113—119.; Rozet-es-Sefa, vol. vii., MS. — Briggs's Ferishta, vol. ii. p. 22. Ferishta erroneously relates the anecdote as of the elder Khan.

BOOK I. declared, that the most wretched situation in Táshkend was better than the sovereignty of Aksu. He retired to Betikend in Moghulistán, where there was some cultivation. After lingering about five years in the country, which was then a prey to civil discord, finding himself hard pushed, he finally resolved to throw himself on the protection of Sheibáni. That chief was at Herát when the Khan returned towards his old do-
and of his brother. minions. The Uzbek was not of a character to expose himself to any risk, by harbouring a prince of high birth and pretensions, and whose restless disposition might cause him future trouble "I have shown him favour once already," said he; "to continue to lavish it, would be pernicious to my country." The Khan was accordingly seized at Khojend and put to death with
A.H. 914, A.D. 1508. five of his sons. The eldest, Sultan Muhammed Sultan, who had used every effort to prevent his father from putting himself in Sheibáni's power, did not accompany him, but remained in Moghulistán, and afterwards repaired to Berendúk Khan, and Kásim Khan, the chiefs of the Kaizák Uzbeks. The succession of Khans of the Moghuls was carried on for many years afterwards, in the family of the younger Khan, Sultan Ahmed.*

* Tar. Resh. ff. 84—116. 131. The history of the Khans of the Moghuls, and of the Amírs of Káshghar, subsequent to Taimur Toghlak Khan, is detailed at great length in the Taríkhi Reshídi of Haider Mirza; and indeed forms the proper subject of the two first books of that work. These details are the more valuable as the succession of the Moghul Khans and of the Amírs of Káshghar, from that period, is not contained in any other work with which I am acquainted; and the learned Deguignes, as has been already observed, omits the subject from want of materials; observing, that, even the names of the princes of Káshghar, subsequent to Taimur, were unknown. Hist. des Huns, tom. iv. p. 337. The Tárikhi Reshídi well deserves to be published in the original, or translated. It is the production of a learned and accomplished man; and, in the two latter parts, of a contemporary, intimately acquainted with the men and events that he describes. Central Asia was then in a transition-state, which ended in the settlement of the Uzbeks in Transoxiana, of the Kirghíz confederacy in Moghulistán, and of the Chaghatái Túrks in India. The minute details which the author gives of his own sufferings, and of the sufferings of his

nearest relations, during the period that followed the ascendancy of Sheibáni Khan in Máwerannaher and Khorásán, — of their escapes, adventures, successes, and discomfitures, — let us more into the condition of the country and feelings of the inhabitants of these states and of Káshghar at that crisis, than perhaps any other monument extant. A portion of the last book relates to the history of Káshmír and Hindustán, and the whole work is interspersed with geographical accounts of countries, especially to the east of Máwerannaher, little known in Europe. The rise and fall of several tribes, or associations of tribes, in the desert, are recorded with much clearness and a perfect acquaintance with their external and internal policy. It would form a most valuable accompaniment to the Commentaries of Báber, which it illustrates in every page. The two royal cousins are worthy of each other, and do honour to their age.

BOOK II.

BÁBER'S TRANSACTIONS IN KÁBUL AND MÁWERANNAHER.

CHAPTER I.

CONQUEST OF KÁBUL.

BÁBER PASSES THROUGH THE HISSÁR TERRITORY.—HISTORY OF KHOSROU SHAH.—BÁBER JOINED BY BÁKI.—CROSSES THE AMU.—SHEIBÁNI CONQUERS HISSÁR AND KUNDUZ.—DEATH OF HIS BROTHER.—BÁBER JOINED BY KHOSROU'S MOGHULS.—SUBMISSION OF KHOSROU, WHO IS DESERTED BY HIS FOLLOWERS—BÁBER MARCHES AGAINST KÁBUL, WHICH HE TAKES.—STATE OF KÁBUL.—BÁBER'S CIRCUITOUS CAMPAIGN ON THE INDUS.—AFFAIRS OF BADAKHSHÁN.—KHOSROU'S DEATH.—BÁBER TAKES AND ABANDONS KILÁT.—BÁKI DISMISSED.—JEHÁNGÍR FLEES FROM KÁBUL.

BOOK II.

A.D. 1504.

Báber enters the Hissár territory.

WHEN Báber felt that not a hope of success, or even of safety, was left for him, if he persisted in lingering in his native kingdom; and that it was vain to contend any longer against the overwhelming superiority of Sheibáni Khan and his Uzbeks; we have seen that he pitched upon Khorásán as the scene of his future exertions. That kingdom had been governed for nearly half a century by Sultan Husein Mírza, Baikera, a descendant of Taímur Beg, and consequently of Báber's own family. He was the most powerful monarch of his time; and his splendid court was the great resort of men of letters, of artists, of military adventurers, and of unfortunate princes. At the period when Báber set out on his perilous adventure*, in which he was

* Moharrem, A.H. 910, begins 14th June, A.D. 1504.

attended by his two brothers, as well as by his cousin Mírza Khan, he had only reached his twenty-second year. Crossing the lofty mountains to the south of Ferghána, and having cast a last look on his native country, he halted some time on the neighbouring frontier, to learn the result of a mission that he had sent forward to Khosrou Shah, who then ruled the extensive territory of Hissár and Kunduz, on which he was entering.

The fugitive prince's followers bore every external mark of having participated in his long misfortunes. They were, as he himself describes them, a motley band of between two and three hundred men, most of them on foot, miserably dressed and equipped, with brogues on their feet, clubs in their hands, and blouses or long frocks over their shoulders; and who carried on their persons all that they possessed in the world. They had only two tents in the whole party; Báber's own, which he gave up to his mother, who also accompanied him, and shared his exile and his fortunes; and an ordinary felt tent *, of a kind common among the Tartars, constructed of cross poles, which was easily folded up when struck, and as easily unfolded again, to be pitched at the next stage, and which served for head-quarters. Though bound for Khorásán, the young prince was not without hopes that, in the general confusion which prevailed all over the countries on the Amu, something favourable might cast up by the road. Separate adventurers daily joined his little band; and brought the report, to him by no means disagreeable, that the Túrki and Moghul tribes of Khosrou's country were in a very unsettled and discontented state.†

By the return of his envoy, Báber found that nothing was to be looked for from any friendly disposition on the part of Khosrou Shah; but his expectations from the migratory tribes were rather confirmed. He ac-

* Iláchak.

† Báber's Mem. p. 127.

BOOK II.

A.D. 1504.

cordingly moved forward; and, as he advanced, was met by an ambassador from Khosrou, who, though sent under pretence of doing him honour, was in reality commissioned to act chiefly as a spy on all his actions, and who prescribed to him the direction and length of each day's journey, and even the spots where he was to halt. Báber complains that though he twice, when in distress, passed through the territories of that chief, so famous for his liberality to others, he never was a sharer of it. And, indeed, it is certain that Khosrou, who had formed for himself a powerful principality on the ruins of one portion of the empire of the house of Taimur, did not feel much pleased at the visit of a prince of that family, of high pretensions, and, what to a successful usurper was still more alarming, of acknowledged talents, and warm with all the fire of youthful ambition.

Khosrou Shah; his early life,

Báber had a fixed abhorrence of Khosrou Shah; and not without reason. Khosrou was originally from Túrkistán, of a Kipchák tribe. He had been in the service of different Túrki chiefs, and finally of Sultan Mahmúd Mírza, one of Báber's paternal uncles, whom he accompanied in the disastrous expedition into Irák, in which Sultan Abusaíd Mírza, Mahmúd's father, lost his life. In the course of the retreat he did Mahmúd most essential service, and gained great influence over him. Khosrou accompanied him to Hissár, of which that prince became the sovereign; and, on the death of Sultan Ahmed Mírza, when Mahmúd succeeded his elder brother in Samarkand, Khosrou accompanied him to his new capital, where he was his principal minister and adviser during his short and unpopular reign in that city On Sultan Mahmúd's death, Khosrou for some time concealed the event, and seized on his master's treasure. But no sooner was the demise of the Sultan known, than Khosrou was forced to fly from Samarkand, by the popular commotions that ensued,

CHAP. I.

and which were in a particular manner directed against himself, as the prime instrument or abettor of his master's gross licentiousness and tyranny.

Gains Kunduz.

Sultan Mahmúd, on succeeding to the throne of Samarkand, had given the country of Hissár to his eldest son, Sultan Masáúd Mírza, who had, in consequence, taken charge of it. Khosrou Shah had enjoyed the government of the rich province of Kunduz, to the south of the Oxus, before Sultan Mahmúd's death; and even then had already attained such importance that he numbered not less than five or six thousand men among his private retainers. Availing himself of favourable circumstances, as they presented themselves, he went on increasing his power and territory; till he had gained possession of the whole country between the Amu and the Hindú-kúsh mountains, and from the mountains of Badakshán down to Balkh; and drew the revenues of it on his own account. He paid great attention to financial matters; of which, says Báber, though a Túrk, he understood the details; and he made a liberal use of his wealth.* He was fortunate also in his wars. When Sultan Husein Mírza of Herát led an army against Hissár, Khosrou, as we have seen, bravely maintained himself in Kunduz; sending his brother Wali to support Masáúd Mírza on the Hissár bank of the river. Sultan Husein, though baffled for a time, at length found means, by a stratagem, to effect the passage of the Amu; upon which Masáúd, seized with unreasonable alarm, could not be prevailed upon to remain and keep his ground, in his own territories, but crossed the hills, and fled to his younger brother, Bayesánghar, the Sultan of Samarkand; while Wali, thus deserted, retreated into Khutlán.

A.H. 901, A.D. 1496.

Repulses Sultan Husein.

Sultan Husein, finding the field clear, laid siege to Hissár, a very strong fort; and at the same time sent

* Báber's Mem. p. 31.

BOOK II. his eldest son, Badi-ez-zemán Mírza, to attack Khrosrou in Kunduz. Hissár, deserted by its sovereign, was bravely defended for several months by Baki Cheghániáni, another of Khosrou's brothers, assisted by some officers of Masáúd. Badi-ez-zemán, meanwhile, marched against Khosrou; who, on his approach, concentrated his force at Kunduz. The Mírza advanced within ten or twelve miles of that town; upon which Khosrou, though inferior in numbers, boldly marched out, and offered battle. This Badi-ez-zemán declined, and kept within his trenches; but soon after, leaving Kunduz behind, he advanced with his army higher up the country to Talikán. Khosrou despatched detachments after him, which watched his movements, gained several advantages over him, and straitened his operations by repeated skirmishes. The old Sultan, observing how matters went, began to be uneasy about the result; especially as the spring rains were at hand, which would render his situation beyond the river uncomfortable, and the passage of it difficult, if not dangerous, for his army. He was glad, therefore, to save appearances by agreeing to a peace; which was confirmed by the marriage of one of his sons with a daughter of Masáúd Mírza. Having thus a pretence for retreating, he raised the siege of Hissár; and, recrossing the Amu, directed his efforts against Khosrou Shah, all whose detachments he drove in; and he was preparing to lay siege to Kunduz, when, by the mediation of Badi-ez-zemán, a peace was concluded; and the prisoners that had been taken, on both sides, restored. After this, the Sultan bestowed the government of Balkh on his son Badi-ez-zemán Mírza, and returned to Khorásán.*

The success thus obtained against a sovereign so able and so powerful as Sultan Husein, added wonderfully to Khosrou Shah's reputation. When, in the following
A. H. 902, A. D. 1497. year, a misunderstanding took place between the Sultan

* Báber's Mem. pp. 35—39.

CHAP. I.

and his son, which ended in a civil war, in the course of which the Sultan expelled Badi-ez-zemán from Balkh, Khosrou Shah gave the young prince a favourable reception, and supported him, and all his followers, in so handsome a manner, that, we are told, hardly any difference could be perceived between their new style of equipment and their former one at Herát, the most splendid court of the age.* Khosrou having quarrelled with Sultan Masaíid, who had returned to Hissár on the peace, sent Badi-ez-zemán Mirza, with two of his own brothers, to conquer that country. But this having been speedily composed, the Mírza, leaving Khosrou, crossed the Hazára mountains, and joined Zulnún Beg Arghún in Zemin-dáwer.

A. H. 903, Rebi 1. A. D. 1497. Nov.

It was not long after this that Báber took Samarkand the first time; when Bayesanghár Mírza, driven from his throne, fled through his elder brother Masáúd's territories, and sought refuge in Kunduz with Khosrou Shah, under whose tuition he had at one time been. Khosrou saw the use that could be made of the Mírza, as a fit instrument for gratifying his own ambition. He despatched an envoy to Sultan Masáúd, proposing that they should march in concert, with all their forces, to retake Samarkand; and that, when they had conquered it, Masáúd should fix the seat of his government in that capital, and give up the inferior principality of Hissár to his brother Bayesanghár. By these negotiations, Masáúd was thrown completely off his guard; while Khosrou, accompanied by Bayesanghár, advanced as if on their route to Samarkand, till they reached Cheghánián near Hissár, where they halted, under pretence of waiting till they were joined by Masáúd and the Hissár army. It happened that Masáúd, just at that time, had deprived some of his Begs of their jágírs or estates, a circumstance that had excited violent discon-

Surprises Hissár.

* Báber's Mem. pp. 44—46.

BOOK II. tent among them; in consequence of which some of them had already left him, and joined Bayesanghár. Khosrou, availing himself at once of this dissatisfaction and of the state of thoughtless security into which he had lulled Masáúd, by a sudden march surprised and took possession of the fort of Hissár. Masáúd himself escaped with difficulty, and sought refuge with Sultan Husein Mírza in Khorásán.

A. H. 903, A. D. 1498.

After this success, Khosrou placed Bayesanghár in Hissár; and bestowed Khutlán, a portion of Masáúd's territory, on his own brother, Wali. He then marched to invade Sultan Husein's dominions, that he might co-operate with Badi-ez-zemán and Zulnún Beg Arghún, who had revolted in the south. He laid siege to Balkh, at the same time sending on Wali to make an inroad towards Shiberghán, from which he brought back a hundred thousand sheep and three thousand camels. Sultan Husein had marched in person towards Kandahár against his rebel son, and had taken Bíst; but, having failed to reduce Zulnún, the powerful chief by whom that prince was protected, he found himself compelled to retreat. The rebels were encouraged, by the failure of this expedition, to hazard a bold enterprise, and pushed forward a large body of troops, which had nearly taken Herát by surprise. The declining years of the Sultan were embittered by the rebellion of his sons, and by civil wars. The fugitive Masáúd, meanwhile, was well received by Sultan Husein, who gave him one of his daughters in marriage; but he had afterwards the unaccountable weakness to yield to the solicitations of Báki Cheghániáni, Khosrou's brother, who had taken refuge along with him in the Court of Herát, to flee from that city, without taking leave of the Sultan, his father-in-law, and to rejoin Khosrou.

Blinds Masáúd.

Khosrou Shah, on the arrival of Masáúd, sent to call Bayesanghár Mírza from Hissár. He had now in his camp three princes of the house of Taimur; Sultan

Masáúd, the late sovereign of Hissár; Bayesanghár, his younger brother, lately Sultan of Samarkand, and now the nominal prince of Hissár; and Mirán-shah Mírza, the son of Ulugh-Beg Mírza, the Sultan of Kábul, who had quarrelled with his father, and fled to Khosrou for protection. Some of his counsellors advised him to put all the three princes to death, and at once to proclaim himself an independent sovereign. He did not act upon this advice, but Masáúd's imprudence met with a severe punishment; for Khosrou, soon after, commanded his eyes to be put out, and the young prince, no longer an object of political jealousy, was carried away by some of his faithful foster-brothers and household servants to the Court of Herát. This barbarous act excited universal indignation, even in that age of rapine and violence; for Khosrou Shah had been selected by his benefactor, the father of the young prince, as the governor of this his eldest son, of whom he had had the charge from his infant years. After this outrage Khosrou, hypocritically expressing the deepest penitence and regret, excused himself to Bayesanghár; protesting, in the most emphatic terms, that he had acted in all that he had done, only impelled by the imminent danger of his own life, as Sultan Masáúd had laid a plot to put him to death; but that, by his whole future conduct, he would wipe off the stain brought upon his character, and serve him as never subject had served prince. Having soothed and quieted his alarm by these representations, Khosrou proclaimed Bayesanghár king, and sent him back to Hissár. He, at the same time, despatched a strong auxiliary force along with Mirán-shah Mírza, to forward his views on the side of Kábul.*

In the following year Khosrou again invited Bayesanghár Mírza to Kunduz, under pretence of making a

* Báber's Mem. pp. 60—63; Tar. Resh. f. 117.

BOOK II.

A.D. 1504.

Murders Bayesanghár, 10 Moharrem, A.H. 905, 17 Aug. A.D. 1499.

new attack on Balkh: but, as his plans were now ripe for execution, and his own power firmly established, he threw aside all disguise, and caused that amiable and accomplished prince to be strangled; after which he usurped the sovereignty of the whole country from Karatigín to the Kindú kúsh mountains, and from Balkh to Badakhshán. This power he had already enjoyed for about five years, when Báber arrived for the second time in his dominions. When Khosrou was at the height of his power, his army amounted to between twenty and thirty thousand men. He was a prince of great capacity, liberal to his dependents, fond of show and magnificence, an able administrator; but heartless, profligate in his manners, totally unprincipled, and a slave to ambition.*

Báber joined by Báki. A.H. 910, A.D. 1504.

In marching through the territories of Khosrou Shah, Báber, as has been observed, was attended with jealous watchfulness by that prince's officers. When he arrived at Kabádián a city on the Amu above Turmez, he was met by an envoy from Báki Cheghániáni, a younger brother of Khosrou, and who held the government of Cheghánián, Turmez, and other districts north of the river. Báki, as seems to have been the invariable custom of the age, was then on indifferent terms with his brother; and the envoy assured Báber of his master's readiness to join him, and to acknowledge him as his sovereign. Báki himself soon after waited on Báber, while he was crossing the Amu at a ferry near Ubáj; and, having conferred with him, invited him to move down the left bank of the river, till he was opposite to the town of Turmez, where he promised to meet him. There Báki accordingly brought across his whole family, and his most valuable property; and then proceeded, in concert with Báber, towards Kahmerd, a district lying high up in the mountains between Eibák and Bamián, and at that time governed by Ahmed Kásim, a

Crosses the Amu.

* Báber's Mem. p. 72.; p. 31.

nephew of Khosrou. It was the intention of the confederates to deposit their women, and Báki's heavy baggage, in Ajer, a fort in that territory; after which they would be free to follow their fortune, wherever it might call.*

Joined by many of Khosrou's dependents.

The influence of the youthful Báber's fame and family, which Khosrou had so naturally dreaded, soon began to be felt. Every day, while on their march, they were joined by men of note, who deserted from Khosrou, and who brought assurances that all the Moghuls in his service, a numerous and powerful body, only waited a favourable opportunity to declare for Báber. It happened that, at this crisis, all the wandering tribes in that country, of every race, were dissatisfied with Khosrou; though the leading causes of the general disorganisation that prevailed were assuredly the terror inspired by the rapid progress and conquests already made by Sheibáni and his Uzbeks, and their advance towards Hissár.

Sheibáni takes Hissár.

Sheibáni, after the reduction of Andeján and the death of Támbol, returned to Samarkand. There he was occupied for some time in preparations for reducing Hissár, and for attacking the dominions of Khorásán. His army, by the addition of the Moghuls, was now nearly doubled; and the experience of the preceding winter had convinced him, that he would have little trouble with Khosrou, "whom he could drive away like a fly from its dish by a wave of the hand." He marched first to Hissár, which was bravely defended by Shiram, Chehreh, a servant of Khosrou's. Sheibáni in person superintended the operations of the siege; and Shiram after a time, surrendered by capitulation, on the promise of being allowed to leave the place in safety; a promise that was faithfully observed. †

While the siege was going forward, Sheibáni ordered

* Báber, pp. 127, 128.

† Tar. Resh. ff. 118. 121.; Báber, p. 168.

BOOK II.

A.D. 1504.

Sends his brother against Kunduz,

his brother Mahmúd Sultán* to take what number of men he chose, and advance against Kunduz. It was the stronghold of Khosrou, who, for many years past, had been filling it with magazines of provisions and military stores, as well as treasure, and had loudly proclaimed that he had laid up such abundance of everything, that, if all else failed, he could at least defend himself for twenty years in the castle of Kunduz. In the midst of this boastful trifling, news arrived that Sheibáni was besieging Hissár, and that Mahmúd Sultan was on his march to cross the Amu. That same hour, abandoning all his stores and preparations, he packed up his treasure and such of his valuables as were at hand, and fled in dismay from the town, to seek shelter and safety in the recesses of the neighbouring mountains. Hardly had he quitted Kunduz, when Mulla Muhammed Túrkestáni, one of his old and confidential servants, took possession of it, and declared for Sheibáni; and, two days after, Mahmúd Sultan arrived and occupied it with his army.†

which he takes.

Death of his brother.

After the surrender of Hissár, and when news of the reduction of Kunduz had reached him, Sheibáni, having committed the government of Hissár to Khamzeh Sultan, and of Cheghánián to Mehdi Sultan, began to march leisurely home. As the direct road by the Derbend Ahenein (the Iron Gate)‡ was narrow and difficult for so numerous an army, incumbered with plunder, he led his troops by way of Buyeh and Turmez; an easier though more circuitous road. An incident that occurred on this occasion, and which is illustrative of the character of Sheibáni, may be best given in the words of Sultan Saíd Khan, a son of the

* The Alim-Arái-Abási calls Mahmúd Sultan the uncle of Sheibáni; but the Tar. Reshídi and Abulgházi mention him as his brother.

† Tar. Resh. f. 121.; Báber, p. 130.

‡ This defile is also called Kahluga.

younger Khan, and afterwards a very distinguished ruler of Káshghar, who was then a prisoner at large in Sheibáni's camp. "After we reached Buyeh, I was sitting one day about noon in the Audience Pavilion. It was before people had come in any numbers, and only a few were present, composed chiefly of the Khan's immediate servants and dependents, when a man arrived in great haste with a face of terror and dismay, and laid a letter at the foot of the dignified throne. While he was engaged in reading the letter, a great change came over him. He rose up before he had finished it, and retired into the Haram, commanding his horse to be brought. He made some stay in the private apartments, which he left after noon-tide prayers and mounted. Great numbers attended him. It became known that Mahmúd Sultan had died at Kunduz, and that they were bringing his body. After he had left the camp and advanced to a distance, we saw a great crowd, as of mourners covered with black and drowned in grief and lamentation, who had laid down the bier and were standing behind it in rows. On perceiving this he made a sign, and all the Sultans and others dismounted and came to attend him. The men who have been mentioned raised a cry of mourning; and those on our side also raised a shout of sorrow. As he approached nearer he made another sign, when all the men who were with him formed themselves into a line and stood still, while he rode forward alone, till his horse's head was over the bier. He made another sign, when all became silent; and the men who had attended the bier, ceased from tearing their clothes and beards. He then called one of Mahmúd Khan's Amírs, and asked him such questions as are usual at ceremonies of mourning, when he remained silent for about an hour*, showing no alteration in his visage and ut-

* *Saat.*

BOOK II.

A.D. 1504.

tering no groan or sigh. After this he raised up his head and said, "'Twas well that Mahmúd should die. Men said, the power of Shahi Beg is supported by Mahmúd. Now let it be known that Shahi Beg depends on no man. Carry him away, and bury him.' All were filled with astonishment at his sternness and composure. The death of Mahmúd Sultan, Moghul, was a severe loss, as he was in every respect a thorough Moghul."* Sheibáni, who never rested, and who no sooner accomplished one undertaking than he prepared for another, on his return to Samarkand, got everything in readiness for attacking Khwárazm, which belonged to Khorásán.

Báber reaches Ajer,

Meanwhile Báber, having executed his intention of marching to Ajer, rested there a few days. The news of Sheibání's advance to Hissár had not yet reached him; and it was still doubtful in what direction the destructive torrent was about to flow. While lying there, he received letters from Sultan Husein Mírza of Herát, which grieved and alarmed him. That powerful prince, the only one who was now equal to meet the Uzbeks in the field, instead of concentrating his force for active operations, proposed to confine his exertions merely to the passive defence of the banks of the Murgháb, and of the line of fortresses that lay along the bottom of the Parapamisan hills; and invited Báber and Khosrou Shah to adopt a similar defensive plan of operations. This, Báber believed, must prove not only totally inefficient, but ruinous. But hope sprang up to him from another quarter. The Moghuls in Khosrou's service, who were encamped near Talikán, a powerful and fickle tribe, had openly quarrelled with him. Báber, to be at hand to take advantage of this occurrence, leaving in the fort of Ajer such of his men and horses as had been worn out by the fatigues of his long

* Tar. Resh. f. 130.

CHAP. I.

A.D. 1504.

journey, with the families and baggage of Báki and of some Aimáks who had recently joined him, set out to retrace the hill-road by which he had advanced.

is joined by Khosrou's Moghuls.

As he proceeded, various reports of the deepest interest reached him in rapid succession. He soon learned that the Moghuls were in full march from Talikán, by Ishkemish, on their way to meet him. As he advanced on his route, the farther information arrived, that Sheibáni and his brother were hastening to Hissár and Kunduz; and he soon after received the important intelligence that Khosrou Shah, believing that in the present distracted state of his affairs, and weakened as his army was by intrigue and defection, he had no chance of resisting so powerful an enemy as Sheibáni, had abandoned Kunduz, which was immediately taken possession of, by the Uzbeks; and that now that chief had withdrawn from his dominions, and was on his march for Kábul, with such of his troops as still adhered to him. When Báber reached the Surkháb, a river which flows through deep valleys by Doshi and Kunduz, and one branch of which rises near Kahmerd, he was met at length by the Moghuls of Hissár and Kunduz, who, to the number of three or four thousand families, joined his camp, and acknowledged him as their sovereign.*

Khosrou submits.

Khosrou, who had advanced from Kunduz, by Ghúri, on his road to Kábul, by the deep and narrow valleys of that mountainous tract, now found himself not far distant from Báber's encampment. Though still attended by a large body of troops, he perceived that the game was up. Seeing no hope of success from meeting his adversary in arms, he sent to propose an accommodation. To this Báber was prevailed upon by Bákí, Khosrou's brother, to agree; and a compromise was entered into; by which, on Khosrou's resigning all his

* Báber's Mem. pp. 127—130.; Tar. Resh. f. 121.

BOOK II.

A. D. 1504.

Treaty.

territories, his life and his private property were secured to him. Báber now marched down the Surkháb, to its confluence with the Anderáb, which he crossed and encamped in the district of Doshi. Khosrou, whose camp was not far off, here waited upon Báber, who received him, seated under a tall palm-tree. Having made his submission, as to his superior lord, he returned back to his quarters. When the conference was over, Báber, whose abhorrence of Khosrou was as deep as it was just, ordered his treasurer to send back the treasure, horses, and whatever else had been presented to him, just as they were; although, says our author, the king had only one horse suitable for a person of his rank, and that was used by his mother.*

Is deserted by his followers.

But the blow was struck. The act of submission, of a chief so haughty as Khosrou, sufficiently explained to the world the extent of his humiliation; and, that same day, even those adherents who till now had remained faithful to him, began to desert, and passed over in crowds to Báber; so that, before the evening of the following day, hardly a man of any consequence remained in his camp. Without loss of time Khrosrou, having loaded a number of mules and camels with his jewels, gold and silver plate, and other valuables, — for he was celebrated among the chiefs of the time for his wealth and magnificence,— set out for Khorásán, under the protection of a guard furnished him by Báber. Some part of his least portable property was probably left behind, and fell into the hands of Báber's followers†; as well as the whole of his military equipments, horses, and arms; of which the young king took possession. It was not one of the least remarkable of the numerous reverses of fortune in that unsettled period, that a prince, who, but a few days before, had had at his command

* Tar. Resh. f. 126.

† Khafi Khan speaks of much treasure and rich jewels acquired by Báber, which is inconsistent with that prince's narrative, as well as with that of the Taríkhi Reshídi.

CHAP. I. A. D. 1504.

twenty or thirty thousand troops, was obliged to avail himself of the protection of a youth who had so lately entered his territories as a fugitive and a wanderer, with not three hundred naked and unarmed followers.*

Mírza Khan's claim of blood.

On the evening of the interview with Khosrou Shah, Báber's cousin, Mírza Khan, the only surviving son of Sultan Mahmúd Mírza, Khosrou's old master, and the brother of the two unfortunate princes, one of whom had been put to death, and the other blinded, by Khosrou, came into Báber's presence with his charge of murder; and claiming the retaliation of blood, as allowed by the Muhammedan law. But Báber, deeply as he detested Khosrou, pleaded his faith, pledged by the convention, as a ground for sending him away in safety; and, by expressing the most heartfelt sympathy for the Mírza and his wrongs, soothed his wounded feelings, and prevailed upon him to desist from his legal claim of blood.†

Báki's advice.

From the time that Báber was joined on the Amu by Báki Cheghániáni, that nobleman became his chief minister and adviser. He now strongly urged Báber to send away his brother, Jehángír Mírza, into Khorásán; representing to him, that, in the confusion in which the whole country then was, with a number of different chiefs all striving for pre-eminence, that prince would certainly be pitched upon, by some ambitious man, as a convenient person to be set up in opposition to himself. But, whatever truth Báber saw in these remonstrances, the generous feelings by which he never ceased to be animated, prevailed. Though almost from the hour when he first mounted the throne Jehángír had been set up against him as a rival, and had even deprived him of his hereditary kingdom, he resolved, whatever had been the jealousies and heartburnings which had

* Báber, pp. 129—131.; Tar. Resh. ff. 125, 126.

† Báber, p. 132.; Tar. Resh. f. 126.

BOOK II. A.D. 1504.

formerly existed between them, on these accounts, or whatever the prospect of future feuds likely to arise from the same source, that he would not treat with unkindness a brother who had left his country to accompany him in his exile. He acknowledges, however, that everything happened precisely as Báki had predicted. At the same time, at Báki's solicitation, Kamber Ali Moghul, Jehángír's chief adviser, was sent away from the camp.*

Báber sets out for Kábul.

Although Báber's force had been so much increased by the numbers of Khosrou Shah's followers who had joined him, and especially by the accession of the Moghuls,—a brave, though turbulent race,—he did not venture to return back towards Kunduz or Hissár, where he must have measured his strength in an unequal contest with the Uzbeks, who were rapidly spreading over all the country between the Ama and the Hindú-kúsh mountains. A detachment of them, which had penetrated into the hills, was at that very moment ravaging the territory of Doshi, not far from Báber's camp. Báber had lost nothing of his hatred of his inveterate foe; nor had adverse circumstances damped his activity. A party of horse that he sent out fell upon these plunderers, routed them, and brought in a number of their heads. But he saw that in the present condition of his own affairs, and in the disorganised state of the country in which he was, it was not possible to offer any resistance on a large scale to the progress of the invader; that it was necessary to yield to circumstances; and would be prudent, for a time, to interpose the barrier of a mountain range between him and his victorious enemy. Kábul seemed to offer a more promising field for his exertions. His cousin, Abdal-rizák, the king of the country, had only recently been expelled by Mokím, a son of Zulnún

* Báber, pp. 128. 130—132.

Arghún, whose government was probably still unsettled. Having, therefore, divided among his troops the arms and armour which Khosrou had left behind him in his camp, among which were eight hundred coats of mail, and suits of horse-furniture, he set out with ardour upon his new enterprise.

A.D. 1504.

For some days he pursued his toilsome march among the precipices, and over the steep and painful passes by which the Hindú-kúsh mountains are crossed. Having surmounted the northern ascent, he proceeded to descend by Ghurbend. On reaching Ushter-shehr, he learned that Shirkeh Arghún, a favourite officer of Mokím Arghún, had taken post with a considerable force on the Bárán river, for the purpose of intercepting any fugitives or auxiliaries who might attempt, by the route of Penjshír, to join Abdal-rizák, the expelled monarch, who was then in Lamghán; and that he was still quite ignorant of their approach. Upon this Báber resolved to march forward for the purpose of surprising him. He set out in the afternoon, and rode all night. The appearance of the stars of the southern hemisphere showed that he had entered upon another clime. "Till this time," says he, "I had never seen the star Soheil (Canopus); but on reaching the top of the hill, Soheil appeared below, bright in the south. I said, 'This cannot be Soheil.' They answered, 'It is indeed Soheil.' Báki Cheghániáni repeated the couplet [of an eminent Persian poet] :—

"'O Soheil! how far dost thou shine, and where dost thou rise?
Thine eye is an omen of good fortune to him on whom it falls.'"

"The sun," continues Báber, "was a spear's length high, when we reached the foot of the valley of Senjed." The troops in advance fell in with Shirkeh, below Kara-bágh; instantly attacked him, and kept harassing him with a skirmishing fight, till reinforcements came up, when the whole detachment charged and routed his

BOOK II.

A.D. 1504.

troops, and made him and some of his best men prisoners.*

Is joined by other tribes.

When Khosrou Shah retired from Kundúz, he seems to have set out attended only by his household and regular troops, without incumbering himself with the irregulars and the wandering tribes whe were in his service, with some of whom, indeed, he had quarrelled. The various tribes, which differed from each other in race and in manners, formed, with the irregulars, five or six separate bodies. Of these, the Moghuls, we have seen, joined Báber. The others also hastened to cross the mountains, to try their fortune in a more favourable region. Two bodies,—one of them the Hazáras of the Desht or wilds, who had advanced by the Penjshír pass, while Báber had taken that of Kipchák; another consisting of some clansmen of Yusef and Behlul Ayub,—now arrived and joined the king below Senjed. Other two divisions, — the one from Khutlán, under Wali, Khosrou's brother; the other composed of Nukderis and Aimáks who had ranged about in Kundúz,—advanced up from the lower countries by the Anderáb and Seiráb, intending also to pass by the defiles of Penjshír. The Aimáks, who reached Seiráb before Wali's division, took possession of the defiles, attacked, defeated, and plundered Wali's troops as they came up, and forced Wali himself to fly back to the Uzbeks, by whom he was sent to Sheibáni, who made his head be struck off in the public market of Samarkand. Both the Aimáks and the scattered remnants of Wali's force now arrived and joined Báber, who marched down to Akserái near Karabágh, twelve or fourteen miles west of Kábul. The number of Khosrou's fighting men of various classes who joined Báber, is said to have amounted to twenty thousand.†

Báber, observing the motley composition of his new

* Báber's Mem. p. 133.

† Tar. Resh. f. 126.

army, made up principally of hereditary marauders, who, while in Khosrou's service, had been indulged in the most unlimited extent of licentious violence and plunder, resolved, in justice to the peaceful and more civilised inhabitants of the country on which he was entering, to take the first opportunity to check these excesses, and to reduce his followers under the rules of discipline. Nor was an occasion long wanting. An active retainer of Sídim Ali Derbán a Hazára chief, having carried off a jar of oil by force, from one of the inhabitants, was ordered to be seized and beaten with sticks, according to the practice of the country. He expired under the punishment; and this prompt and stern example, joined to an assurance of Báber's determination to defend the natives from oppression, at once put an end to such practices. But the want of a national force, and the necessity of employing bodies of banded adventurers of different tribes, was always one of the great difficulties which Báber had to encounter; and, on several occasions in the course of his future career, exposed him to the most imminent danger.*

whom he reduces to order.

As Kábul was now so close at hand, it became necessary to decide upon some plan of operations. Some of his officers were of opinion, that, as the season was far spent, it was most advisable to go down to Lemghán, to pass the winter there, and make up their minds at leisure as to future operations. Báki Cheghániáni, on the other hand, advised him at once to march upon the capital, and this advice he adopted; in consequence of which the camp was once more moved one stage forward, and pitched in the park or meadow of Ama, close by Kábul.

Encamps near Kábul.

Here Báber was joined by his mother, and by the families of his troops that had been left at Ajer. When he set out for Kábul, he had commissioned his mother's

Joined by his family.

* Báber's Mem. pp. 132—134.

BOOK II. A.D. 1504.

relation Shiram Taghái to conduct Khosrou a certain way on his road to Khorásán; after which he was to return by Ajer, and to bring on the household. But Shiram had not gone far when he discovered that Khosrou was no longer under his control; and his prisoner, instead of proceeding on his journey, insisted on accompanying him back to Kahmerd. On reaching that place, Ahmed Kásim, the governor, was induced by his uncle Khosrou to behave very harshly to the families that had been left in the district. Many of them were Moghuls, who were not disposed to submit quietly; and, in concert with Shiram Taghái, laid a plan for seizing both Khosrou and his nephew; who, having discovered the plot, fled by the valley of Ajer towards Khorásán. Thus relieved of all apprehensions from Khosrou, the detachment left Ajer with the families under their charge. But they had new dangers to encounter; for, the clans that inhabit the hills, roused by the rich booty presented to their rapacity, were all in arms to seize and plunder the numerous stragglers, and bands that were now crossing the mountains in every direction, from Kunduz and the north; and had occupied all the passes. The detachment from Ajer, with its convoy, going on by Kahmerd, shared the common danger. Many followers both of Báber and of Báki were made prisoners; others were pillaged and dispersed. Báber's family and houshold, however, made their way by the Kipchák pass, and, after many dangers and distresses, at length reached him at Ama.

Besieges Kábul.

From Ama, Báber next proceeded to the meadow of Chálák; and, having now determined upon the siege of Kábul, he made the army take up its ground on the different sides of the city.*

State of the kingdom,

The country of Kábul, the conquest of which Báber now determined to attempt, was hardly more tranquil

* Báber's Mem. pp. 134, 135.

CHAP. I.

than the miserable and plundered provinces which he had left behind; though from a different cause. After Sultan Abusaíd's death in Irák, Ulugh Beg Mírza, Kábuli, one of his sons, and Báber's uncle, became Sultan of Kábul and Ghazni; and had continued to govern these kingdoms till his death, which occurred about three years before Báber made his appearance on the south of the Hindú-kúsh.

Factions at court.

A. D. 907, A. D. 1502.

That prince was succeeded by his son Abdal-rizák Mírza. What became of his other son, Mirán-shah Mírza, whom we have seen a few years before in his father's lifetime, and in arms against his authority, we are not told. Abdal-rizák being young, his minister Shiram Ziker* ruled him and his territories with absolute power, and might really be said to have usurped the government; an occurrence at this period common to all the different descendants of the family of Taimur, who, educated for a throne in ease and effeminacy, were kept away from that knowledge of men and things which could alone qualify them to fill it with honour.

Shiram did not long maintain his ascendency. The court of the young prince soon became a scene of faction and intrigue. A conspiracy was formed against the minister by some of the first men among the nobles, who suddenly entered the capital with three hundred followers and murdered him as he was sitting at table in the Presence-Hall of the palace, at a great Muhammedan festival, when he had enjoyed his power about a twelvemonth. But, as none of the conspirators was so much more distinguished than the rest as to enable him to take a decided lead, the kingdom on this event became a prey to all the evils of anarchy.

A. H. 908, 10 Zilhájeh, A. D. 1503, 6 June.

Mokím surprises Kábul.

Encouraged by this state of affairs, Muhammed Mokím (a son of Zulnún Arghún, the governor or rather ruler of Kandahár), who held for his father the Germ-

* He is called Zaki Beg by Ferishta, ii. p. 24.

BOOK II. A. D. 1504

sír, (a considerable province on the Helmend,) supported by the Hazáras,—who inhabit the hills that lie along the upper course of that river, nearly as far as Kábul, and who were much attached to his father,—passed secretly through that mountainous tract, after a rapid march appeared suddenly before Kábul, and made himself master of the town. Abdal-rizák Mírza fled, and found refuge among the Turkoláni Afgháns in Lamghán; while Mokím, with little opposition, occupied the kingdoms of Ghazni and Kábul; and soon after, to assist in consolidating his power, married the daughter of Ulugh Beg Mírza, the late Sultan. Mokím's father, Zulnún Beg, when informed of what had happened*, wrote to his son, disapproving of the enterprise; but at the same time advising him, as the best means of retaining the acquisition he had made, to be ever watchfully on his guard, and especially to retain none of the old nobles of Kábul about him. In compliance with this advice, Mokím dismissed most of the old officers, and filled their places with creatures of his own. Abdal-rizák made several unsuccessful attempts to recover his father's dominions; and Mokím still continued to govern them, when Báber descended from the northern mountains and invested his capital.†

Surrenders it to Báber.

The advance and attack of Báber being wholly unexpected, Mokím had made no provision against such an event; and, from the suddenness with which the town and castle were blockaded, he found himself totally unprovided with the means of supporting a siege. The citizens, too, were all in favour of Báber. Mokím therefore saw no hopes of safety but in a capitulation, which soon followed, and by which it was stipulated that he, his family, and followers, were to march out with their effects, and to be permitted to return home uninjured.

* The author of the Taríkhi Sind makes the news of Mokím's conquest reach his father, Zulnún, when he was on the Amu with Badi-ezzemán, f. 90. v.

† Báber's Mem.; Taríkhi Sind.

CHAP. I.

A.D. 1504.

The place was accordingly surrendered after a siege of only a few days.* Although Báber had placed Mokím and his family under the protection of his own household troops and servants, commanded by his two brothers, whom he had ordered to guard them as they left the town, yet such was the violence and crowding of his unruly followers, pushing forward, eager to plunder the rich prey which Mokím's baggage was supposed to offer, that the Sultan himself was hastily sent for to appease the tumult; and this he could not accomplish till he had ordered several of those most active in the sedition to be shot by his archers, and others to be sabred. This constant determination in the young prince to maintain discipline and to prevent pillage, though it endeared him to his subjects, had not the same effect upon his needy and rapacious followers. Mokím, after this exercise of authority in his behalf, proceeded on his march, and arrived safe in his own government. And thus Báber, in the beginning of October, A.D. 1504, little more than three months after leaving, as a houseless exile, his little kingdom of Ferghána, saw himself sovereign of the far more extensive and powerful kingdoms of Kábul and Ghazni.†

Kingdom of Kábul.

The kingdom of Kábul which thus fell into the power of Báber, which became his favourite residence during the greater part of his future life, and which for two centuries remained annexed to the empire of India, was by no means so extensive as that which, under the recent Afghán dynasty, has passed under that name. It was confined to the provinces of Kabúl and Ghazni, and has been described with great minuteness and accuracy of detail by Báber himself in his invaluable commentaries. It consisted chiefly of a very elevated table-land, rising at an average about six

* End of Rebi ii., A.H. 910, beginning of October, A.D. 1504.

† Báber, pp. 135, 136.

BOOK II. A.D. 1504.

thousand feet above the level of the sea; and was bounded, on the north, by the lofty Hindú-kúsh mountains; on the west, by them and by the range which runs between the Hindú-kúsh and Khorásán; on the east, by those mountains which run from the lofty peak of Sefíd-koh, to the east of Gurdíz, past Sir-efzá and the sources of the Gomal, towards the plain of Ab-istádeh, supporting the lofty table-land of Ghazni and Kábul; and, on the south, on which side its limits are indistinctly marked, being probably bounded by the hills that enclose the basin of the Ab-istádeh lake. Even over this extent, the inhabitants of the plains and cultivated valleys alone yielded a regular submission. The hills were, in general, inhabited by independent and refractory tribes or clans, as were also some parts of the more desert plains; insomuch that even the high road between Kábul and Jagdalak, which formed the chief communication between the country of Kábul and the rich province of Lamghán, Pesháwer, and the Indus, was infested by hostile and predatory tribes within a day's journey of the capital.*

The kingdom appears, at that period, to have comprehended; I. the long and narrow plains running nearly from south to north from Ghazni to Kábul; II. the valleys that run westward into the Parapamisan mountains, especially that of Koh-dáman; III. the Kohistán or Highlands of Kábul, which lie to the north and north-west of that city, chiefly beyond the Ghurbend and Kábul rivers, and which are formed of the high and low lands of Ghurbend, Penjshír, and Nijrow, that run along the slope of the hills, and deep under the precipitous heights of Hindú-kúsh. IV. Lamghán or Laghmán, divided into two parts by the Kábul river. The portion on the north contained the valleys of Alishing and Alingár, that also run among

* Báber's Mem. pp. 232—278.

the mountains of the Hindú-kúsh range, and uniting, form that of Mandráur, which opens on the Kábul river. The portion on the south of that river contained the great district of Nang-nihár, which, besides its ample extent to the south, stretches down the deep descent of the mountains that buttress the table-land of Kábul, and comprehends, in its lower extent, the rich and warm valley of Adína, now Jelálábád. Besides these districts which lie on the Kábul river, the province of Lamghán was considered as comprehending Kuner and Núrgil, with Dera-Núr and Cheghán-serái, which lie on the Cheghánserái river. But Lamghán-Proper was strictly held to be confined to the divisions north of the Kábul river, and to be bounded by it and the Cheghanserái rivers on the south and east. V. Lohger and some districts to the south of Lamghán.

Such being the restricted limits of Kábul an Ghazni, all the territory between Cheghánserái and the Sind, such as Bajour, Swád, Pesháwer, &c.—were excluded. These were districts which had not long been occupied by the Afgháns. The whole extent of country reaching from the eastern limits assigned to Kábul as far as the Indus, west and east, and from the lower Kábul river below Adína to the countries of Síwí and Sind, north and south,—a tract which seems to have been the original seat of the Afgháns,—was also excluded. Both these divisions were, at this period, inhabited by tribes principally Afgháns; though, towards the north, and at the roots of the Hindú-kúsh range, several of the aboriginal tribes still remained nearly independent under their hereditary native chieftains. Indeed, though the Sultans of Ghazni and Kábul, when in the height of their power, had claimed them as subjects, and rendered them tributory, yet, beyond the occasional compulsory payment of tribute, the subjection both of these tribes and of the Afgháns of the wilds and the mountains, had been little more than nominal.

BOOK II.

A.D. 1504.

To the west of Kábul were the Hindú-kúsh and Hazára mountains, of which the latter extended to Khorásán near Herát. They also were principally inhabited by independent tribes; on the south and south-east by the Hazáras, a brave and numerous race; and on the north and north-west by the Aimáks, who, like the Hazáras, were wanderers and shepherds. The latter tribe held the tract from Zemín-dáwer up the Helmend to the lofty mountain of Koh-Bába, west of Kábul, with the hills immediately to the south of that line; the Aimáks held the country on the north of the Hazáras, from near Bamián towards Herát. It would seem that the Nukderis, who were Aimáks or allied to them, occupied the mountains between Zemín-dáwer and Herát, on the south-west range towards Farra.

Kandahár and the neighbouring provinces, to the south, acknowledged the sovereignty of Sultan Husein Mírza of Herát; but were in reality governed, nearly as an independent state, by Zúlnún Beg Arghún and his family; who had also acquired great influence among many of the hill-tribes to the north.

The towns and richer plains of the Kábul territory were inhabited and cultivated by Tájíks, who spoke the Persian tongue, and who, if not of Persian extraction, had at least been, in ancient times, for centuries under the Persian monarchy. The hills, with which the whole country abounded, were occupied by Hazáras, Afgháns, and other unsettled tribes, who sometimes possessed, and always infested, the plains and high-roads. The tribes in whose range lay the long and difficult passes between India and the upper country, considered them as part of their revenue; and when they did not plunder, levied taxes or contributions on caravans and travellers, in the same manner as is done by the Arabs of the desert.

The diversity of the inhabitants of these tracts, and of their languages, is well described by Báber. "In

CHAP. I.
A. D. 1504.

the country of Kábul," says he, "there are many and various tribes. Its valleys and plains are inhabited by Túrks, Aimáks, and Arabs. In the city, and the greater part of the villages, the population consists of Tájíks. Many others of the villages and districts are occupied by Pasháis, Peráchis, Tájíks, Berekis, and Afgháns. In the hill-country to the west, reside the Hazáras and Nukderis. Among the Hazára and Nukderi tribes are some who speak the Moghul language.* In the hills to the north-east lies Kaferistán, and such countries as

* That intelligent and successful traveller, Sir Alexander Burnes, takes notice of the peculiar appearance of the Hazáras, whom he met with in his journey from Kábul to Khulm. "The Hazáras," says he, "are a simple-hearted people, and differ much from the Afghán tribes. In physiognomy they more resemble the Chinese, with their square faces and small eyes. They are Tartars by descent, and, one of their tribes is now called Tatar-Hazára. There is a current belief that they bestow their wives on their guests, which is certainly erroneous. The women have great influence, and go unveiled." Burnes's Travels, vol. ii. p. 153., and iii. p. 224.

An account of the origin of the Aimáks, of Moghul race, is given in the Shajrat-ul-Atrák. During the invasion of Chengíz Khan, Sultan Rukn-ed-dín, a son of Sultan Muhammed Khwárazm-Shah, gallantly defended the strong fortress of Firúz-Koh, in the hills east of Herát, against a powerful army commanded by Huláku-Khan, the grandson of Chengíz, for a period of six months. "It is related that when Huláku left his grandfather to proceed by the road of Pasi-koh to Firúz-koh, from the rugged and stony nature of the country, and the steepness and difficulty of the hills, many of his horses were so knocked up that they could not move a foot, insomuch that he was obliged of necessity to leave them behind, appointing however a detachment composed of men out of each division to take care of them, with orders not to quit the place until he returned. When, six months after, the fort of Firúz-koh was taken, as well as Rukn-ed-dín, its brave defender, Tuli Khan, Huláku's father, arrived in Khorásán, and Huláku went by the route of Chisht Saflan and Ubek to meet him, and the men were forgotten. These people, not daring to leave their station without a yarlígh or mandate, continued to dwell there; and took women and girls from the neighbouring Hazáras, with whom they contracted marriages; so that, in a short time, they had a numerous issue and descendants; and that tract became known as Muri Saturgái; *muri*, in the Moghul language, signifying a horse, and *saturgái*, lame; being so called in memory of their settling there." Shajrat-ul-Atrák, MS. They were called *Aimáks* from the Moghul and Túrki word signifying *Tribes*. It is easy to see how they are sometimes called Aimáks, sometimes Hazáras.

BOOK II. A. D. 1504.

Kattór and Gebrek. To the south is Afghánistán. There are eleven or twelve different languages spoken in Kábul; Arabic, Persian, Túrki, Moghuli, Hindi, Afgháni, Pashái, Paráchi, Geberi, Bereki, and Lamgháni. It may be doubted whether so many distinct races, and different languages, can be found in any other country."*—"The various districts of Kábul lie amidst mountains which push out like so many mounds, with the valleys and level plains expanding between them; and the greater part of the villages and of the population is found on these intermediate spaces."†

Though the country of Kábul lies chiefly between the 32° and 35° of north latitude, yet, from the great height even of the valleys above the sea, the climate is temperate, and allowed to be one of the most delightful in the world. Kábul abounds in rich pasture and in delicious fruits, and is remarkable for its profusion of flowers. Though possessing some fertile arable country, it is still richer in flocks. The winter is often severe, and the snow lies deep. The height of the mountains, and the sudden descent of the land on the east, makes it easy at all seasons to command a change of climate; and, in some instances, to pass from summer heat to winter snow in the course of a few hours.‡

When Báber saw himself master of this valuable conquest, he proceeded to reward the chiefs and their followers, who had assisted him in the expedition. To his brother, Jehángír, he gave Ghazni; to Násir Mírza, Lamghán and Nijrow; to the greater chiefs, he allotted different provinces of the kingdom; while he rewarded the inferior officers by assignments of land, and by other gratifications. He levied a contribution of thirty thou-

* Mem. p. 140.

† Ibid. p. 153.

‡ See Báber's Mem. pp. 136—155.; Elphinstone's Account of the Kingdom of Caubool, still the most comprehensive and distinct; and Burnes's Travels; to which may now be added the works of Mr. Masson, who had an opportunity of visiting more of the country than any previous traveller.

sand loads of grain from Kábul, Ghazni, and their dependencies; to be bestowed on the wives, families, and followers of the wandering tribes, to enable them to accompany him on his expeditions and wars. "As I was at that time very imperfectly acquainted with the revenues and resources of Kábul, the amount was excessive, and the country suffered extremely." * CHAP. I. A.D. 1504-5.

In a short time afterwards, Abdal-Rizák Mírza, the late sovereign of Kábul, submitted to Báber and waited upon him: a circumstance which contributed to the stability of his government.†

Báber had been in Kábul but a short time, (which he had employed in chastising the Masáúdi Hazáras, who refused to pay a contribution of horses and sheep imposed upon them,) when Yar Husein, a son of Deria Khan, came from his father's government of Bhéra, a district lying beyond the Indus, on the south of Jélam, to invite him into that country. The offer was so much in unison with the young Sultan's wishes, that, a few days afterwards, an incursion into India was resolved upon.

Expedition to the Indus.

Although Báber did not, on this occasion, enter any part of what we now denominate India, this expedition is by historians regarded as his first invasion of that country. After having mustered his forces, and made the necessary inquiries, he set out from Kábul in Shaban, A.H. 910; and, having marched by Jagdalak, in six days reached Adína-púr, now Jelálábád. Here he was struck with the total change, both in climate and in the appearance of the country, that at once took place on his descending from the lofty table-land of Kábul,—from the temperate into the torrid clime. "I had never before seen the Germsíl (or countries of warm temperature), nor the country of Hindustán. On reaching them, I all at once saw a new world; the vegetables, the plants, the

A.H. 910, Shaban. A.D. 1505, January. Adína-púr.

* Báber's Mem. p. 156. The load is 700 lb. Avoirdupois.

† Tar. Resh. f. 159.

BOOK II. A.D. 1505. trees, the wild animals, all were different. I was struck with astonishment, and indeed there was room for wonder.* He proceeded by the Khaiber-pass to Bekrám, now Pesháwer. There a consultation was held as to crossing the Indus, as had been originally intended, when that plan was abandoned, and the army was led on a marauding and exploring expedition to the southward, through Kohát, Bangash, Bánu, and Desht Dáman, plundering all the way. Below this, they came on a small dependency of Multán, lying on the right bank of the Indus. After marching for some days along the banks of that river, Báber, leaving it, turned westward and north; and, proceeding along the borders of Siwístán, by Chotiáli and through the Duki country, at length reached known ground at the lake of Ab-istádeh; whence he went on to Ghazni, and then to Kábul, where he arrived in the month of May; having employed about four months in this very extraordinary and arduous circuit. In the first part of it, through the Afghán country, as far as Desht Dáman, and till they reached the Indus, the troops had many severe actions with the brave but barbarous Afgháns, who inhabited the hills and wilds; but they obtained very little booty. In the rich countries lying upon the Indus, on the other hand, so abundant were the cattle, that the meanest retainer in the army sometimes got possession of three or four hundred; most of which, from their very number, they were forced to leave behind. From the Indus to Ab-istádeh, cultivation nearly ceased; and the country was so barren and waste that the horses, already much exhausted by the length of the foray, began rapidly to fail. It was impossible to find corn, even for Báber's; and he was in the end compelled to leave his own tent behind, for want of carriage. Their difficulties in the latter part of their march were much increased by the

Circuit taken by Báber.

A.H. 910, Zilhájeh, A.D. 1505, May.

* Báber's Mem. p. 157.

CHAP. I. A.D. 1505.

heavy rains, which swelled the watercourses and filled the ravines. This expedition, undertaken by Báber so soon after he had gained possession of Kábul, whatever other consequences may have attended it, made him intimately acquainted with the nature of the greater part of the country west of the Indus.*

Plot against Báber.

It was in the course of this expedition that the first symptoms of Báki Cheghániáni's ambitious intentions began to appear. In joining Báber, he had probably reckoned upon finding him tractable and careless in business; he may have hoped to direct everything with absolute power, as his brother and the other ministers in the courts of Báber's cousins in Máwerannaher and Kábul had recently, without exception, been accustomed to do. On the contrary, he had even already found, in his own sovereign, a brave and active prince, of brilliant talents, inquisitive and intelligent in business; who listened, indeed, to advice, but decided and acted for himself. Before him, Báki's ambitious views stood checked; and he turned his eyes on Jehángír Mírza as a fitter instrument for his purpose. He proposed to him, to allow himself to be set up against his brother, who was to be seized and sent across the Indus. Jehángír declined taking the part assigned to him, and revealed the plot to his brother. Báki, however, was too strong in the number of his own immediate followers, and had too much influence in the army, to be dealt with rashly. Báber, therefore, dissembled; but, from this time forward, watched for the earliest safe opportunity of dismissing from his service so dangerous a minister.†

* Báber's Mem. pp. 156—166. Mírza Khan says that this expedition was undertaken by Báber, from finding that Kábul was not sufficient to support the numbers who had deserted Khosrou Shah, which made him think of carrying them into Hindustán; and that the cattle of the army were ruined in the course of it. Tar. Resh. f. 159.

† Báber, pp. 164, 165.

BOOK II. A. D. 1505. Násir Mírza marches for Badakhshán.

It was not till Báber had reached Kábul that he was informed of the events which had taken place in his absence. He found that his brother, Násir Mírza, instead of following him, as he had been ordered, had crossed the Hindú-kúsh range, and was engaged in operations on his own account, in Badakhshán. Various circumstances led to this. We have seen that Khosrou Shah, when sent towards Khorásán, had contrived to overpower his guard, and to return back to his nephew, Ahmed Kásím, at Kahmerd. Discovering very soon that he could effect nothing in his former dominions, he again set out for Herát. Before reaching that capital, he met with his former ally, Badi-ez-zemán Mírza and Zúlnún Beg, and accompanied them to Herát. All of them had, not long before, been at open war with the Sultan. Báber truly remarks, that, his success against Khosrou and Mokím, Zúlnún's son, had been the means of bringing all these proud and powerful men, in a humble condition, into the presence of their sovereign. After remaining for some time in the court of Sultan Husein, who gave him a gracious reception, Khosrou became anxious once more to try his fortune in the scene of his former glory, at Kunduz. Such an attempt was represented to him as being quite ridiculous, in the present shattered state of his affairs; and he was advised to wait for a more favourable moment; but, being impatient, he persisted and set out.

Sheibáni Khan had given the government of Kunduz to Kamber-Bi, of Merv, an Uzbek, who, in obedience to his master's commands, had entered Badakhshán, and taken possession of a great part of the country. But the natives of that rugged and mountainous province, who had never been completely reduced by Khosrou, and who detested a foreign yoke, rose upon the Uzbeks in several quarters at once, recovered Kila-Zefer, the principal fortress, beat back the invaders, whom they defeated several times with great slaughter, and sent to invite Násir Mírza to place himself at their head.* CHAP. I. A. D. 1505.

When Báber set out on the Afghán expedition, Násir had remained behind, though ordered to follow him; instead of doing which, he had spent the earlier part of the winter in expeditions planned and conducted for objects of his own. He had driven a body of the Aimáks and other tribes out of Lamghán; and had followed them up to the Bárán river, where he was lying when he received the invitation to repair to Badakhshán. Thinking that something might be achieved, in the agitated state of that country, he resolved to try his fortune in that quarter; and, without consulting Báber, who had not yet returned to Kábul, he set out; advanced from the Bárán river, up the passes of Hindú-kúsh; and descended on the northern slope, near Dehána. Here he fell in with Khosrou Shah, who, after quitting Herát, had just arrived in the neighbourhood with a few hundred men. Khosrou, with his accustomed art, tried to fasten himself upon Násir Mírza, and to gain him over, hoping to effect something under the cover of his name. But the Badakhshán chiefs, though they had invited Násir, were not disposed to receive Khosrou. Yet, so perseveringly did he cling to the young prince, accompanying him in all his motions, that it was not till Násir had reached the territory of Ishkemish, and had drawn out his troops in battle-array against those of Khosrou, that he was able to get rid of his unwelcome companion. Khosrou, thus left to himself, proceeded, with hardly a thousand men, to besiege Kunduz. Kamber-bi, hearing of his approach, called in Khamzeh Sultan from Hisár, who despatched troops to his aid under the command of his sons. They attacked Khosrou the moment they arrived, slew his nephew and some of his best troops,

A. H. 910, A. D. 1505.

Joined by Khosrou,

whom he shakes off,

* Báber, pp. 167—169.

BOOK II. A.D. 1505.

Khosrou's death.

and easily defeated his handful of men. Khosrou-Shah was himself taken prisoner; his head was soon after struck off in Kunduz, so lately the seat of his power, and sent off to Sheibáni, in Khwárazm. Such was the end of this man's guilty ambition, and of all his magnificence and crimes.*

Násir becomes king of Badakhshán.

Násir Mírza was less unfortunate. By the influence of a party in Badakhshán, headed by Mobárek Shah and Muhammed Korchi, he was acknowledged as king, and governed that country for two or three years. During some part of his short reign, considerable success attended his arms. When Sheibáni Khan laid siege to Balkh, he sent three or four thousand men to ravage Badakhshán. Násir Mírza was then encamped near Kishem; Mobárek Shah, who acted in conjunction with him, lying not far off. One division of the Uzbeks came upon Násir by surprise, but the Mírza bravely charged and totally defeated them, killing some and making others of them prisoners; many were drowned in attempting to recross the Kishem river, which had swollen after they had passed it. He then marched against the other division, which, in the mean time, had attacked and defeated Mobárek Shah's army; and, with the assistance of the Amírs who poured down from the neighbouring hills, he totally routed it also. In this affair the Uzbeks lost a thousand or fifteen hundred men. Násir did not, however, long maintain his ascendency in Badakhshán. Muhammed Korchi, Mobárek Shah, and other Amírs who had raised him to the throne, offended with some of his proceedings, and still more with the conduct of his favourites, rose in revolt; and, having collected a large body both of infantry and horse, marched against him, and took up a strong position. Násir and his young advisers, who had with them a considerable force of cavalry, impru-

A.H. 912, summer of A.D. 1506.

* Báber's Mem. pp. 168, 169.

dently attacked the insurgents in the broken grounds on which their infantry were posted. After repeated unsuccessful charges, the insurgents assumed the offensive, and, charging in their turn, put their adversaries to flight. All who still adhered to the Mírza were plundered, and he was finally driven out of the country, and compelled to fly to Ishkemish and Nárín; whence, recrossing the hills by the Surkh-áb and Abderch route, he descended by Shibertu on Kábul, where he once more joined his brother, the Sultan.*

CHAP. I. A. D. 1505. A. H. 913, spring of A. D. 1507. but is finally expelled.

Báber, after his return from his circuitous expedition in the Afghán country, had planned a more important one against Kandahár. But this was delayed; first, by an attack of fever from which he soon recovered, and next, by a violent earthquake, which did much damage all over the country of Kábul, throwing down many houses, and making breaches in the walls of the castles and fortified towns. In some places it formed deep cavities in the earth, and in others levelled considerable eminences with the ground.† After devoting a month to repairing the fortifications of the towns that had been injured, and to alleviating the sufferings of the inhabitants, with an activity and kindness by which he is said to have gained their affection, he led his army to the south, hesitating between attacking Kandahár, and plundering the hill-tribes. His brother Jehángír and Báki Cheghániáni advised an attack on Kilát‡, a strong fort on the road from Ghazni to Kandahár. It was accordingly attacked and carried by storm, though not without considerable loss. But all the blood spilt in the conquest was thrown away, as it was found impossible to retain it; probably in consequence of its being insulated from the rest of Báber's dominions.

Earthquake, A. H. 911, A. D. 1505

Báber invades Kandahár;

takes and abandons Kilát.

* Báber, pp. 199, 200. 219, 220.

† This was probably the earthquake felt at Agra, 3 Sefer, A. H. 911, (5 July, A. D. 1505). Briggs's Ferishta, vol. i. p. 579.

‡ Now, Kilát-e-Ghilji.

Jehángír and Báki, to whom it was successively offered both declined to take charge of it.*

Báki's intrigues.

For some time past, Báber had been on uncomfortable terms with his minister Báki. Much of his success in gaining over Khosrou's troops, by means of which he effected the conquest of Kábul, had been due to that nobleman. Báber complains that he was mean and sordid; as an instance of which he adduces the fact that, in marching together when they first met, after passing the Amu, near Turmez, though Báki had thirty or forty thousand sheep along with him, and Báber's ragged and weary followers were starving, not a single one did he offer; and adds, that, even when they had at last reached Kahmerd, his generosity limited itself to a gift of fifty. Báber had also complaints of a different kind to make. It appears that Báki had made the kettle-drum be beat before his own tent; an unpardonable offence, that being a mark of dignity which, in a royal camp, is confined to the sovereign alone; and though Báber had bestowed on him the transit duties, which are the principal revenue of Kábul, with the property-tax levied from the Hazáras, and had made him governor of Kábul and Penjshír, as well as commander of the guards, with the office of chief-minister, still Báki was not satisfied. We have seen, that, in the course of the late expedition down the Indus, Báber had too much reason to believe that he had been guilty of direct treason, and that he had placed himself at the head of a conspiracy, the object of which was to depose his sovereign, and to bestow his throne and dominions on his brother.

Báber had prudently dissembled his knowledge of these intrigues; but the minister, believing that his services were indispensable, in order to add to his own importance and claims, affected discontent; and was

* Báber's Mem. pp. 170, 171.; Briggs's Ferishta, vol. ii. p. 25.

CHAP. I.

A. D. 1505.

onstantly asking leave to retire. This, Báber as often efused; which only adding to Báki's confidence, he enewed his tender of resignation in more urgent terms. Co his consternation, he found his petition complied vith. In alarm, he now altered his tone, and sent to reract his offer, and to remind Báber, that, when he joined im, that prince had engaged never to call him to acount till he had been guilty of nine offences. But Báber was steady to his purpose, and sent him a list of leven heavy offences, the justice of all of which he was, ne after another, forced to admit. Báki soon after, eeing that his influence was gone, set out for India ith his family and property, and proceeded by way of haiber. After crossing the Indus, he fell into the ands of Yár Husein of Bhíra, whose visit to Báber at ábul has been mentioned. Yár Husein had accomanied Báber, in his late expedition to the Indus, as far s Kohat; where, on the representations that he made, áber issued firmáns to the Dilázáks, the Yusefzais id Kagiánis, tribes inhabiting in that quarter, desiring em to act under his orders; Yár Husein on his part edging himself to extend Báber's dominion beyond e Indus. But that chief, abusing the firmán he had ceived, enlisted in his service a number of Yusefzai d Dilázák Afgháns, as well as men of the Ját and ujer tribes, and was now employed, as a freebooter, in undering the country and robbing on the highways the Penjáb. Into the hands of this merciless mauder, Báki and his whole party fell; when their prorty was seized and the wretched exile put to death.*

Báber accepts his resignation.

His death; A. H. 911, end of A. D. 1505.

Early in the following spring, Báber's brother, Jengír Mírza, either discontented with the extent of untry assigned to him, or having taken some other ence, and instigated by two Moghul chiefs, to whose idance he had completely surrendered himself, fled

Jehángír Mírza flies from Kábul, A. H. 911, A. D. 1506.

* Báber's Mem. pp. 171, 172.

BOOK II.
A.D. 1505.

from Kábul for Ghazni, without coming to any explanation with his sovereign. After committing some acts of violence and hostility, and taking and plundering Kila Báki *, he passed through the Hazára country, with all his retainers, towards Bámián. Those tribes of Aimáks who by this time had withdrawn from Násir Mírza, were now ranging to the north-west of that place; and he flattered himself with hopes that he might induce them to espouse his cause.† It was not long before the course of events brought Báber into the same quarter.

* Q. Kila Safi?

† Báber's Mem. p. 175.

CHAPTER II.

JOURNEY TO AND FROM KHORÁSÁN. — KHAN MÍRZA'S REBELLION.

PROGRESS OF SHEIBÁNI. — HE DREADS THE MOGHULS IN HIS ARMY. — SUBDUES KHWÁRAZM. — BESIEGES BALKH. — DEATH OF SULTAN HUSEIN MÍRZA OF HERÁT. — BÁBER'S MARCH TO KHORÁSÁN. — DISCORD AND WANT OF SPIRIT OF THE MÍRZAS. — BALKH SURRENDERS. — BÁBER RETURNS HOME BY THE MOUNTAIN ROAD. — HIS DANGER IN THE SNOW. — FINDS KÁBUL BESIEGED BY THE FACTION OF KHAN MÍRZA. — TREACHERY OF MUHAMMED HUSEIN MÍRZA. — BÁBER SURPRISES THE REBELS. — SEIZES THE RINGLEADERS; WHOM HE PARDONS. — SHEIBÁNI INVADES AND CONQUERS KHORÁSÁN. — FATE OF THE MÍRZAS.

CHAP. II.

A.D. 1505.

Kábul at peace.

THE removal of an imperious minister, and the flight of a restless and ambitious brother, afforded Báber a degree of security which he could hardly otherwise have enjoyed in his new territories. Still, however, he was far from being free from causes of anxiety. The torrent of Uzbek invasion was not stemmed. His mortal enemy Sheibáni Khan, having now subdued Hissár, Kunduz, and the neighbouring provinces, had returned to Samarkand, and was preparing himself for new conquests.

Further projects of Sheibáni.

Two objects chiefly engaged the attention of Sheibáni at this period; the conquest of Khwárazm, which he was resolved to attempt; and the breaking down and amalgamation with his army of the numerous Moghul clans now in his service.

His anxiety regarding the Moghuls.

He found the Moghuls a race by no means tractable or easily subjected to discipline. They were accustomed to submit to none but their own chiefs. He had now about thirty thousand of them in his army. The death of his brother, Mahmúd Sultan, who understood their

BOOK II. A. D. 1505.

character, and whom they had followed with pleasure, was a severe loss to him. He could not venture to raise any one individual to the chief command of them, without raising up a rival to himself. Several, who were men of note among the Moghuls, were now at Samarkand. Of these the most eminent was Muhammed Husein Korkán, the son of Muhammed Haider, who had for many years been Amír or Ruler of Káshghar. Muhammed Husein was the most intimate friend of the elder Khan, whose sister he had married, and who had given him the country of Uratippa. When expelled from it, during the short time that he shared the favour of Khosrou Shah, he had married Sultáním Begum, the daughter of the late Sultan Ahmed Mírza, the Sultan of Samarkand. By these intermarriages he had become closely connected both with Sheibáni and Báber*; and his reputation among the Moghuls stood very high. Sheibáni had granted a large assignment to his wife Sultáním Begum in Shehr-sebz. Another Moghul of note was Sultan Saíd, the younger Khan's third son, who had been left wounded in the field when his father and uncle were defeated and taken. He had afterwards been carried to Akhsi, and had fallen into the hands of Sheibáni, on the death of Támbol and his brothers. In addition to these, Shah Begum made her appearance at Samarkand. She was the mother of the two Khans, the mother-in-law of one and grandmother of another of Sheibáni's wives, and the mother of his son's wife.

* The connection was manifold. Báber's mother, Muhammed Husein's wife, and Sheibáni's wife, were three sisters, daughters of Yúnis Khan. Báber and Muhammed Husein had also married sisters, daughters of Sultan Ahmed Mírza of Samarkand; and Sheibáni had married a sister of Báber's. In addition to this, Sheibáni married a daughter of the elder Khan, the niece of Muhammed Husein, and first cousin of Báber. The connection was drawn closer still by the marriage of Sheibáni's son, Taimur Sultan, with the family of the Khans; he having married the youngest daughter of Yúnis Khan by Shah Begum, a half-sister of Báber's mother.

She was a woman of ability and intrigue, and had always despotically managed the weak mind of her son, the elder Khan. When the Khan retired into the desert, after he was released by Sheibáni, she found herself thwarted by his ministers, which produced a quarrel with her son. Unable to bear the contradiction to which she was now subjected, and to which she had never been accustomed, she repaired to Samarkand, under pretence of soliciting from Sheibáni some district as a settlement for the Khan; and she there appears to have passed her time very comfortably, in the society of her daughters, and of numerous female connections.*

CHAP. II.

A. D. 1505.

He sets out for Khwárazm,

A. H. 910, November, A. D. 1504.

Sheibáni Khan set out for Khwárazm in the beginning of winter, with his army composed of Uzbeks and Moghuls. All the Moghuls, the common tribesmen as well as the Sultans and Amírs, were full of uneasiness and apprehension. Since the death of Mahmúd Sultan, their confidence was gone, and no Uzbek supplied his place. Muhammed Husein, who from gratitude had always been strenuously supported by that chief†, felt his loss most severely. Before involving himself in this enterprise, Sheibáni resolved to put things on a new footing, and to break up the banded system of Moghuls. It was necessary for that purpose to deprive them of their leaders. While engaged in preparations for the conquest of Khwárazm, he had one day a conversation with Mír Januka, a friend of Muhammed Husein. He told him that he was resolved on no account to leave Khwárazm till he had taken it; that the siege would probably last long; that, while any of the old Moghul chiefs were left, he saw plainly that their adherents would never give up their attachment to them, to transfer it to any other master; but, that, if a convenient opportunity occurred, they would do by him as he had

* Tar. Resh. f. 130.

† He had interceded for and saved the life of Mahmúd Sultan, when he was taken prisoner in a foray on Seiram.

BOOK II. A. D. 1505.

done by them; that their chief man was Muhammed Husein Korkán, the thoughts of whom disturbed him day and night, for to kill him was like killing one of the Khans; that he would willingly avoid that extremity. "Do you, therefore," continued he, "let him know my purpose, and send him a private message to make his escape, without delay, while yet he may; for, when he is gone, I must make other Moghul chiefs drain the blood-stained cup." That same hour, the Mír sent off an express to Shehr-sebz, which reached it about noon-tide prayers. "By afternoon prayers," says Haider Mírza, "my father, choosing me from among his children, and taking not more than sixteen of his followers along with him, fled towards Khorásán. I remember these events as a dream and imagination."* When his flight was known there was considerable alarm in Samarkand.

Flight of Muhammed Husein,

and of Sultan Saíd.

Sultan Saíd, a son of the younger Khan, three days afterwards also made his escape, and reached Seirám; whence he went on to Betikend† in Moghulistán, and joined the elder Khan, his uncle. The rest of the Moghuls of rank, says the Mírza, he sent to their eternal home, or to hopeless imprisonment. He ordered Shah Begum to be sent to Khorásán, and took all her people with him to Khwárazm.‡

Muhammed Husein reaches Herát.

Muhammed Husein Doghlat, when he reached Herát, found it the scene of much pomp and splendour. All Sultan Mírza Husein's children who had been in rebellion, had now submitted, and surrounded his throne; united by dread of the common enemy. The Doghlat was received in the most honourable manner, and a place assigned him next in rank to the Sultan's eldest son. The Sultan wished to bind him to his family, and to a residence at Herát, by a connection in marriage. This the Doghlat did not think advisable for him, and

* Tar. Resh. f. 139.

† *Heft-deh.*

‡ Tar. Resh. ff. 131. 156.

contrived to avoid. The Sultan was now very old, enfeebled by palsy and gout; and the talents of his sons were not such as to enable them, when they came to the throne, to cope with Sheibáni. To escape from forming this connection, Muhammed Husein pleaded a vow to make the pilgrimage of Mekka. Soon after, Shah Begum arrived in Herát. Along with her came Mehr-nigár Khanum, who was her step-daughter and the eldest sister of Báber's mother, and of the Doghlat's late wife, the same whom Sheibáni had divorced to marry her niece. Other relations accompanied them. On their arrival Muhammed Husein altered his plan. These ladies were all strangers in Khorásán, where they did not find themselves at home; but they were all near relations of Báber's mother. Muhammed, therefore, asked leave to accompany them to Kábul; which was not refused. "Some days before they reached Kábul," says the Mírza, "Kutluk-nigár Khanum, Báber's mother, died. Her death was a severe affliction to our party. Báber received us with the utmost distinction, sent an honorary procession to meet us, and treated us honourably and kindly to the utmost extent of his ability. Here we all spent some time in the height of ease and enjoyment." *

CHAP. II.

A.D. 1505.

Goes to Kábul.

Moharrem, A.H. 911, June, A.D. 1505.

Meanwhile Sheibáni Khan, having got quit of the grand Moghul chiefs by flight, and of the inferior leaders and heads of clans by death or imprisonment, had incorporated the mass of Moghuls with his army, which, besides his Uzbeks, was composed of adventurers from every tribe and nation around. He now laid siege to Khwárazm, which belonged to Khorásán, and was defended with extraordinary skill and bravery by Husein Súfi†, the governor, for ten or eleven months; and many of the gallant exploits of the garrison long continued to be remembered by the Uzbeks. In spite

Sheibáni besieges Khwárazm,

* Tar. Resh. f. 156.; Báber, pp. 169, 170.

† Chain Súfi. Tar. Resh.

BOOK II. A.D. 1505–6. of his frequent calls for succour, not one man was sent to his aid. "When no hope of relief from any quarter appeared," says Báber, "some dastardly wretches among the inhabitants, having lost heart, entered into an understanding with the Uzbeks, and introduced them into the fortress. Husein Súfi, on hearing the alarm, repaired to the spot; charged those who had scaled the walls; and, while in the act of driving them out, was struck with an arrow and died. This put an end to the contest, and the place was taken. The blessing of God rest on Husein Súfi, who never hesitated for a moment, in the midst of danger and distress, gallantly to expose his life at the call of duty." *

takes it. A.H. 911, end of A.D. 1505.

Sheibáni now returned to Samarkand, and made preparations for attacking the dominions of Khorásán with his whole force. His territories were most extensive. He was master of everything between the Amu and the Sirr, besides the tract of cultivated country that lies beyond the Sirr, from the Káshghar mountains to the Lake Aral. In like manner he had conquered the Amu from Badakhshán to Balkh, as well as the kingdom of Khwárazm. He now laid siege to Balkh. Sultan Husein Mírza saw that no time was to be lost in stemming the torrent of invasion; and, old as he was, took the field in the beginning of summer, and summoned the whole force of his dominions to join him.† He at the same time invited such of the neighbouring princes as were friendly to him, and among the rest Báber, to join in an undertaking that was equally the concern of all. Báber readily consented to lend his aid; both, from a wish to check the overgrown power of Sheibáni; and, from the expectation that, on his route to Khorásán, he might be able either to beat up the quarters of Jehángír and prevent his having time to form new alliances that

Sheibáni besieges Balkh.

Sultan Husein Mírza invites Báber,

* Báber's Mem. p. 176.; Tar. Resh. f. 161.

† End of A.H. 911, April, A.D. 1506.

might be dangerous to him, or prevail upon him to return to his duty. He accordingly set out from Kábul in the month of Moharrem * (June) for Khorásán, taking the rout of Ghúrbend and Shibertu. From Ushter-Shehr he proceeded to Zohák and Gumbezek; descending, by Saighán and the Dendán-shiken pass, to Kahmerd. Jehángír Mírza, alarmed at his motions, fled from the vicinity of Bámián, where he then was, and withdrew farther into the recesses of the mountains.

who sets out.

Báber halted some time at Kahmerd, and sent out his troops to forage and to collect grain and cattle in various directions. By his presence he overawed the Aimáks, and prevented them from joining Jehángír. Sheibáni was then busy with the siege of Balkh, the capital of an important portion of the Khorásán dominions; and his plundering parties extended their ravages over all the low countries lying between the mountains and the Amu. It was while Báber was still at Kahmerd, that he learned, by letters from the envoys whom he had sent forward, that Sultan Husein Mírza, whom he was marching to join, was no longer alive, having expired in the course of the preceding month.†

Death of Sultan Husein.

This news did not stop his advance; he again set out, and proceeding by the passes of Balkh-áb, penetrated the hill-country of Sáf. Here, learning that the Uzbeks were plundering Sán and Chárek, not far from his line of route, he sent out a detachment, who cut a body of them to pieces, and brought back a number of their heads as trophies.

Báber proceeds,

Here the Aimáks from the neighbouring hills came and unanimously acknowledged Báber. The emissaries whom Jehángir had sent among them to draw them over to his interest, had failed of success. That prince,

* Moharrem, 912, begins 24 May, A.D. 1506.

† Zilhajeh, A. H. 911, which began 25 April, A.D. 1506.

BOOK II. A.D. 1506.

being now reduced to extremity, was compelled to leave the mountains to which he had fled, and to go down to the valley of Pái, to wait upon Báber, and to acknowledge him as his sovereign. Báber, displeased with his conduct, paid him no attention, and pushed on for Khorásán *; and, in the end of October, after a march of eight hundred miles, he joined the sons of Sultan Husein Mírza at their camp on the river Murgháb, where they lay with all their forces.†

reaches the Murgháb.

Affairs of Khorásán.

Here Báber found that the late Sultan's death had nearly been followed by a civil war, in consequence of the grand bane of Asiatic states, a disputed succession. To prevent this evil, at so dangerous a moment, when a foreign enemy threatened the very existence of the kingdom, a compromise had been entered into among the chief men, who guided the councils of the young princes. It was arranged that Badi-ez-zemán Mírza, the eldest son of the deceased monarch, and Mozeffer Hussein Mirza, the son of his favourite Sultána, who had secured great influence among the nobles and royal household, should be placed as joint kings on the throne of Herát; each having his own minister to manage his affairs, and each his own governor in the capital; "a strange arrangement," says the royal historian; "a joint kingship was never before heard of. The well known words of Sheikh Sádi, in the Gulistán, are very applicable to it. Ten dervishes can sleep on one rug, but the same climate of the earth cannot contain two kings." ‡

Two joint kings appointed.

Báber is royally entertained.

Báber was received by the Mírzas with great pomp, was amused with the most splendid entertainments, and with every kind of feasting and festivity. The

* Jehángír joined him, however, either on the road or in Khorásán. Tar. Resh. f. 158.

† 8 Jemádi ii. A.H. 912, 26 Oct. A.D. 1506. Báber's Mem. pp. 199—201.; Tar. Resh. f. 157.

‡ Báber's Memoirs, p. 199. Some copies read *two*, others *ten*.

court of Herát had for many years been the most refined and magnificent of any in Asia. Never had the fine arts been cultivated, in any Musulman country, with more success than at Herát, during the long reign of Sultan Husein Mírza. Poets, divines, philosophers, historians, architects, musical composers, singers, and musicians, painters and elegant penmen, (a class, who, in Persia, are deservedly ranked among the professors of the fine arts,) all abounded; and many of them attained the highest reputation in their various pursuits. But the country itself was on the verge of ruin. The Sultan, who in his earlier life had been so active and vigilant, in the latter years of his reign gave himself up too easily to sensual and voluptuous enjoyments.

Character of the Mírzas.

His sons, unfortunately, had been educated in the ease and the corrupting indulgences of an effeminate court. Báber describes them, as men of elegant manners and winning address, accomplished, and intelligent, but devoted to pleasure, and ignorant of affairs. He soon saw that the brave barbarian from the north was not to be vanquished by men like these. Their tents of state, their rich carpets, their gorgeous attire, and goblets of silver and gold, without adding to their own means of defence, were an incentive to the rapacity of the enemy. He found that they had already spent three or four months in merely marching from Herát, and in assembling their troops on the Murgháb, and had remained all that time without attempting any active operation; while the important city and fortress of Balkh, which had been besieged by the Uzbeks for many months, and defended during all that time most gallantly, was at length compelled to surrender for want of succour.

Balkh surrenders.

"The Mírzas," says Báber, "although very accomplished at the social board, or in the arrangements for a party of pleasure, and although they had a pleasing talent for conversation and society, possessed no knowledge whatever of the conduct of a campaign,

BOOK II. A.D. 1506.

or of warlike operations, and were perfect strangers to whatever related to the arrangements for a battle, or the dangers and spirit of a soldier's life. While we remained on the Murgháb, news came that Hak Názer Chápa, with four or five hundred men, had advanced, and was plundering the territory of Chichektú. The whole of the Mírzas assembled, and held councils; but, with all their consultations, they could not contrive to detach a light party to cut up the plunderers. Chichektú is ten farsangs (forty miles) from Murgháb. I asked permission to manage the matter; but, being afraid for their own reputation, they would not suffer me to move." * By this time the winter was at hand, and it was agreed that the army should break up, and each Mírza choose suitable winter-quarters for himself; but that all should be ready to meet and commence operations early in the ensuing spring. They urged Báber also to winter in Khorásán. But as he had conquered his own kingdom hardly two years before, by the aid of various unconnected bands of mercenary adventurers, over whom his power was but contingent, and who required the immediate pressure of authority to retain them in their allegiance; and as, besides this, the whole neighbouring countries swarmed with wandering tribes and houseless soldiers of fortune prowling about in search of plunder and revolution; he justly deemed it dangerous to be long absent from his capital, especially at the distance of a two or three months' march. Several of the royal Mírzas, however, waited upon him, and, by their urgent entreaties, extorted his consent. To make the most of his time, he visited Herát, its holy and learned men, its colleges, mosques, sepulchres, and palaces; and was again royally entertained. But he soon saw the necessity of attending to the affairs of his own kingdom; and, in the last days of December, set

Mírza's army breaks up.

Báber visits Herát.

8 Shaban, A. H. 912, 24 Dec. 1506.

* Báber's Mem. p. 203.

CHAP. II.

A.D. 1506.

out from Herát, on his return to Kábul, by the mountain road.*

Returns by the mountains.

The snow had begun to fall, and the road was difficult even in summer; but Báber's ardour of mind, and indeed his prudence, urged him to push on without delay. As he advanced, the snow continued to fall incessantly, and became deeper and deeper. It soon reached up to the horses' knees, and, after a few days' progress, even above the stirrups. To add to their difficulties, when they were far advanced among the hills, their guide lost the road, and was never able to regain it. Kásim Beg, who was now again Báber's prime minister, and who had recommended this hill-road † in preference to the low-road by Farrah and Kandahár, which was more circuitous, eager to save his credit, dismounted with his sons and their followers, and, treading down the snow, made a road by which the army advanced a little. Next day, the snow being very deep and the road still not to be found, the troops were forced to retrace their steps to a spot which they had passed, where there was plenty of firewood; and parties were detached in all directions to try to discover, in the valleys or more sheltered grounds, any of the Hazáras, or other inhabitants, who might be wintering there. But all their efforts were unsuccessful; and, in two or three days, the whole of their parties found their way back, without having been able, on these solitary wilds, to meet with even a single person to serve as a guide. All had abandoned the snow-covered mountains, for their winter range in the lower grounds.

Difficulties of the road.

As it was ruin to remain where they were, they were compelled once more to set out through the snow, by

* Báber's Mem. p. 208.

† This route was by Lenger-Mír-Ghiás, the borders of Gharjistán, Chekhcherán, Chiraghdán, Anjukán, Khaisal-Kotí, the Zírín pass, Yeke-Auleng, and Bámián; considerably to the south of that route by which he had marched to Khorásán.

BOOK II.

A.D. 1506.

the very way along which they had so lately been forced to return. For the first week they endured incredible hardships, without being able to advance more than two or three miles. Báber himself, Kásim Beg his minister, and some of their nearest relations and servants, to show a bold face and to support the sinking spirits of their men, went on, to the number of about twenty, in front of the rest, tramping down the snow. At every step they sank up to the waist, or sometimes to the breast, but nevertheless went on. When the strength of those in front was exhausted, another band advanced and took their place, proceeding forward in the same way. After this, a horse was brought on, which plunged forward on the space they had trampled down, and, when he was exhausted, another was dragged on in his room. In this way they laboured on, the greater part of the army chilled and dispirited, having given up all heart; "and it was no season," says Báber, "to talk of exerting authority."

Reaches the Zírín pass.

Proceeding in their toilsome march for two or three days longer, they at length arrived at the foot of the Zírín pass.* The storm that day was dreadfully violent, the snow deep, and the defile so narrow that only one person could pass at a time. The horses could hardly be brought on, and the days were at the shortest. Their situation seemed hopeless, and they only thought of meeting death together; when, those who were in advance, just as the light failed, reached a cave†, which they entered, and found that it would afford shelter to a few persons. When the darkness came on there was

* Báber's son, Humáyun, was placed in similar circumstances in a winter march from Kunduz to Kábul. "It was then the depth of winter," says his biographer, Jouher, "and such a quantity of snow had fallen, that the roads were quite blocked up; we were therefore obliged to ram the snow well down, after which the horses and camels were enabled to move on." Jouher's Mem. of Humáyun, p. 85.

† Called Khawal-koti.

an end of exertion, every man being obliged to halt and pass the night where he happened to be.

Danger of the army. He enters a cave.

The cave, when examined, seemed but small. The Sultan was invited, by those who had found it, to enter and enjoy such comfort as it could yield. But Báber, with that generous spirit which on all occasions, and most especially in the most trying and dangerous, led him to share the hardships of those whom he led,—a spirit that in all his difficulties ensured to him the affection and fidelity of his followers,—refused to enter, while the great body of his men were suffering without. Taking a kind of spade, he dug for himself a hole in the snow, near the mouth of the cave; and, sitting down in the opening thus formed, found some shelter from the fury of the storm. Though he had dug breast deep in the snow, still he had not come to the ground. The snow and drift, driven by the wind, continued to increase; and, before the hour of bed-time prayers, the snow had settled four inches high over his head and ears. Meanwhile, those who had first entered the cave, having found means to explore its extent, reported that it was large enough to hold them all. On this, Báber shook off the snow by which he was covered, and entered the cavern, with those who were near him; at the same time sending to call in those who were farther off, and ignorant of what had happened. Fifty or sixty men, who were nearest at hand, found their way in, and producing such provisions as they could command, all sat down together, and sheltered from the cold wintry wind and drifting snow, feasted with delight on their simple and scanty fare, defying the angry elements, and forgetting for a moment all their past sufferings.

Severity of the cold.

Next morning the snow and the tempest ceased. With renewed spirit they again began trampling down the snow as before, and continued their weary labour all that day. At night, though the snow was over, the

BOOK II. A.D. 1507.

cold was most intense, and the distress extreme. Many lost their hands and feet, from its severity. On the succeeding morning they descended into a glen. They knew that this was not the road, but kept on, passing over many deep gulphs and ravines; and, by the time of evening prayers, gained the mouth of the valley. They now, at last, came on an inhabited country. The natives, in astonishment, saw them descend from the high lands over passes, which, at such a season, none had ever been known even to think of attempting; and they now found that the excessive depth of the snow, which had cost them so much toil, and which they feared would have proved their destruction, was what had in reality saved them; as its drifts had filled up the hollows, and so enabled them to pass over precipices and ravines, which, but for that circumstance, would have opposed an insuperable bar to their progress.*

He gains the low grounds.

Yeke-Auleng.

The people of Yeke-Auleng, where they had now descended the mountains, received Báber and his army into their houses with the greatest hospitality, brought out and killed their fattest sheep for them, and supplied hay and grain for their horses. Large fires were kindled, and the troops halted a whole day, to rest and refresh themselves. They still had a long tract of hill-country to pass, but the level was lower and the climate warmer. After some days, having passed Bámián, and descended by the Shibertu pass, they found that the Túrkomán Hazáras, a pastoral and predatory tribe, who descend from the mountains in winter, to spend the season in a more temperate atmosphere, were encamped exactly in their line of march, little expecting an enemy to come upon them from the snow-covered mountains behind. They were scattered in huts over the country, for the convenience of pasture. Báber plundered the first parties of them upon whom he

Bámián.

Id of Ramzán, A.H. 912, 14 Feb. A.D. 1507.

Plunders the Túrkomán Hazáras.

* Báber's Mem. pp. 208—212.

came; when the rest, being alarmed, collected together, and seized a hill near the route by which he was descending. Here he attacked and defeated them, after some resistance; put numbers to the sword, and took many of them prisoners with their wives and children; after which his troops spread on all sides, driving away the herds of horses and flocks of sheep of the unfortunate Hazáras, wherever they could be discovered.

Approaches Kábul.

Báber had now advanced within a few marches of Kábul, and at length gained some intelligence of the proceedings that had taken place there, while he was employed on his expedition. He found that the apprehensions which he had entertained of the possibility of revolt or rebellion, during his absence, had been but too well founded.

Báber gives Muhammed Husein, charge of Kábul.

When Báber came to the resolution of marching for Khorásán, he had visited his uncle Muhammed Husein Mírza, Doghlat, the husband of his mother's younger sister, and had proposed to him to undertake the management of Kábul, and the rest of the kingdom, during his absence on the expedition. The Mírza respectfully declined the honour, pleading that, when in Khorásán, he had made a vow to perform the pilgrimage of Mekka, and that to accept such a trust would be a violation of it; but added that, if his Majesty should appoint any of his great nobles to fulfil that duty, he would advise and assist them to the utmost extent of his ability. Báber, desirous to secure the co-operation of a man of so much reputation, and so near a connection, soon after introduced to him Nizám-ed-dín Khalífa, Múlla Baba Bishágheri, Mír Ahmed Kásim Kohbur, and some other of his confidential servants; and, after complimenting the Mírza in the warmest manner, added, "Relying upon you, I am about to set out; these Amírs will save you the trouble of details, by conducting the different departments, under your general direc-

BOOK II.

tion;" and, after the strongest expressions of good-will on both sides, and of confidence on that of Báber, he commenced his march to Khorásán.*

Reports at Kábul.

For several months all went on well at Kábul; but, as the winter advanced and the weather became severe, all direct communication with Khorásán being interrupted by the snow, and by the dangerous state of the roads, which were infested by banditti, and especially by the Hazáras, various reports began to prevail; that Báber had been seized by the Mírzas of Khorásán, and sent to a state prison, from which he never would escape in life. These reports were encouraged and propagated by a powerful party in his very court and palace.

The Moghul, Yúnis Khan, had left five daughters and two sons; three of the daughters being by one wife, and the two sons and two of the daughters by another.

Faction in favour of Khan Mírza.

The daughters of Ais-doulat Begum, the elder wife, were,—Mehr-nigár Khánum, the widow of Sultan Ahmed Mírza of Samarkand, by whom she had no children. After his death, as has been mentioned, she married Sheibáni Khan, by whom she was divorced that he might marry her niece Khanzáda Begum, Báber's sister. She left Samarkand, along with her step-mother Shah Begum, and had accompanied her to Kábul, where she now was. The second daughter was Báber's mother, who died just before the arrival of the party from Khorásán. And the third was the wife of Muhammed Husein Mírza, Doghlat, who also died some years before.

Yúnis Khan's other wife was Shah Begum, the daughter of the king of Badakhshán. By her, Yúnis had two sons, the elder and younger Khans; and two daughters. The elder daughter was Sultan-nigár Khánum, who had married Sultan Mahmúd Mírza, successively Sultan of Hissár and of Samarkand, by whom she had

* Tar. Resh. f. 157.

an only son, Sultan Weis, or, as he was generally called, Khan Mírza; she afterwards married two Khans of the Kaizák Uzbeks in succession. Shah Begum's younger daughter married Taimur Sultan, the son of Sheibáni Khan.

From this statement it appears that Shah Begum, while she was the step-mother of Báber's mother, was the mother of Khan Mírza's. Khan Mírza had been educated at Táshkend, after his father's death, and had become the favourite of his grandmother and aunts, who were at the court of the elder Khan, as well as of his uncle Muhammed Husein. Shah Begum, the grandmother, Mehr-nigár Khánum the aunt, and Muhammed Husein Mírza, the uncle of Khan Mírza, were all now at Kábul, as well as Khan Mírza himself, who had remained behind with his grandmother, instead of accompanying his cousin Báber on his expedition.

Shah Begum gains the Moghuls.

Shah Begum, who was a woman of spirit and of intrigue, resolved to raise her favourite grandson, Khan Mírza to the throne. She gained over a body of the Moghuls, who had remained behind at Kábul, and who regarded with reverence the widow of their old Khan, and the mother of the two Khans, his sons. She also drew over to her interest Sultan Senjer Birlás, a chief of considerable influence, and her sister's son. The real head of the conspiracy, however, seems to have been Muhammed Husein Mírza, though he was anxious not to appear, and left the ostensible management of the affair to Shah Begum. Even in what we may suppose to be the partial statement of his son Haider Mírza, Muhammed Husein is far from being blameless;

Conduct of Muhammed Husein,

"When the emperor was reported to have been seized (in Khorásán), and Shah Begum proposed to my father, that Khan Mírza should be acknowledged in his place, he refused to lend his sanction to the proceeding. The altercation that ensued led to tears and heartburning; and, through Shah Begum, the Khánums, too, were of-

BOOK II. A. D. 1507.

fended, a circumstance which my father felt very severely. At last he told them, that there was no use in being offended at his refusal, as he had ceased to take any share in the management of state affairs. This resolution he formed after a month's wrangling. When the king's Amírs, who came daily out of the fort to wait upon him, visited him as usual, my father privately told them, that they need no longer come; upon which they shut themselves up in the castle, and my father went to Ab-bárán, a town a day's journey from Kábul, and withdrew from all business. Shah Begum and the rest of her party, composed chiefly of the Moghuls, now made the Khutba be read in Mírza Khan's name, and used every exertion to take the fort of Kábul. Many combats ensued. The Begum sent a person to call my father, and to remonstrate with him. As their remonstrances and entreaties were such as it was impossible to resist, my father came from compulsion. The fort of Kábul was besieged for four and twenty days, when the emperor suddenly arrived." *

who joins the rebels.

Báber learns their proceedings;

On descending the mountains, after his long and toilsome march, Báber, while plundering the Hazáras, was informed of these important events; and that Kábul was still bravely defended by Múlla Baba Bishágheri, Khalífa, Mohib Ali Korchi, Ahmed Kásim, and others of his gallant adherents. Without delay, having at once formed his plan, he despatched, from Lenger-Taimur-Khan, a trusty messenger, whom he instructed to spare no exertion to find his way into the town, to inform the officers who held out in it that he was approaching; and that he would lose no time in relieving them; that he was to descend by the Ghurbend pass, and to march to take the rebels by surprise; that the signal of his approach would be a blazing fire, which he would kindle after he had passed the Minár hill; that they were to

communicates with the garrison of Kábul.

* Tar. Resh. f. 158.

answer it by another fire on the top of the old Kiosk within the citadel*; and, on the signal being so answered, the rebels were to be immediately attacked on both sides, by his troops from without, and by theirs from within.

Having sent forward his messenger, Báber determined upon leaving the heavy baggage to follow with Jehángír Mírza, while he himself pushed on without delay. Jehángír, while in Khorásán, had indulged in wine to excess, and was affected with fever and dysentery so violently, that it was generally reported that Khadíja Begum, the late Sultan's favourite wife, had, "after her old fashion," administered poison in his wine. He was still so feeble as to be compelled to use a litter.† Báber, having made this arrangement, hastened forward with all his disposable force. He advanced and halted one night at Ushter-Shehr, descended the Ghurbend pass, and halted next night at Sir-e-púl; refreshed and bathed his horses, and set out again at noon-tide prayers. Till he reached Tutkáwel, there was no snow. After passing that place, the farther he went the snow lay the deeper. "Between Noh and Minár," says he, "the cold was so intense that, in the whole course of my life, I have seldom experienced the like." Here he sent on new messengers to prepare the garrison for his approach.‡

Kindles fires,

After passing the hill of Minár, the army, in the evening, was compelled by the cold to kindle fires to warm themselves; and, in the morning again marched on, with the snow above the saddle-girths, their horses sinking and plunging through it. Before reaching Kábul, they saw a fire blazing in the citadel; and at once comprehended that the garrison were on the alert, and that the night fires of the army had been mistaken

which are mistaken.

* The Bálá-Hissár.

† Tar. Resh. f. 158.

‡ Báber's Mem. p. 214.

BOOK II. A. D. 1507. Surprises the rebels.

for the signal. They pushed on, however, and in spite of this mischance, still took by surprise the enemy, who fled without attempting to form or oppose them regularly, and dispersed and hid themselves in all quarters. Báber's first efforts were directed to secure the persons of Khan Mírza, and of Muhammed Husein Doghlat. Khan Mírza had just time to mount on horseback and escape; Muhammed Husein Mírza also fled from his palace and concealed himself. There was much hard fighting among the palaces and gardens in the suburbs, in the course of which the king, from his habitual ardour, was exposed to imminent danger. In a short time, some of the principal leaders of the rebels were seized. Sultan Senjer Birlás was taken and dragged before the King, with a rope about his neck. He had been particularly distinguished by Báber, who had given him the valuable Tumán of Nangenhár. Being in great agitation, he exclaimed, "What crime have I committed?" "And what greater crime can there be," replied Báber, "than for a man of your note to conspire with rebels?" "But," continues the generous prince, "as Shah Begum, the mother of the Khans, my uncles, was his mother's sister, I ordered them not to drag him in that shameful way along the ground, but spared his life, and did him no harm." *

Checks plunder in Kábul;

The garrison, meanwhile, had sallied out to complete the victory; and, to add to the confusion, the townspeople and rabble had risen, and were pursuing the fugitives and plundering whatever came in their way, with very little discrimination. Báber's first care was to despatch parties to chastise and drive away the plunderers; and to station guards, to preserve and restore the public peace. He then hastened to the palace of Shah Begum, eager to re-assure the minds of the princesses. He alighted without ceremony, at the

visits the princesses.

* Báber's Mem. pp. 214—216.

place he was accustomed to do, when paying her an ordinary visit *, and went up to the Begum with his usual cheerfulness and good humour. "She was filled with confusion, and knew not what to do or say," says Haider Mírza, her grandson. "Báber, kneeling, embraced her in the most affectionate manner, and reading her thoughts, mildly observed, 'You have exerted your motherly affection and patronage in behalf of one of your children; why should that vex or offend another of them. The mother's authority over her children is absolute. But,' continued he, 'I have been awake all night; I have made a most fatiguing journey, and am very weary.' So saying, he lay down at the Begum's feet, placed his head on her lap, and composed himself to sleep." "This he did," observes Haider Mírza, "to restore confidence and ease to her mind. He had not yet fallen asleep when Mehr-nigár Khánum, his mother's sister, entered. He instantly leaped up, and most tenderly embraced his beloved relation. 'Your child, your wives, and family,' said the Khánum, 'are all longing to see you once more.' 'Go,' said he, 'and carry into the city the news of my coming.' He followed close after her. The Amírs and all the population poured out thanks for his preservation and return, and employed the dust under the feet of the beneficent King as collyrium to adorn their eyes." †

From the Begum's residence, Báber went to the Chehár-bagh, which Khan Mírza had occupied as his palace. There he wrote and despatched letters to every part of the kingdom, as well as to the Aimáks and wandering tribes, to announce his victory. He then entered the citadel.

* In visits in the East, whether among princes or people of rank, great stress is laid on the ceremonial part of them, and especially the alighting from horseback in the outer or inner court, or at a particular distance from the gate. The distance at which the person visiting is received by the one visited, is also much attended to, and often the subject of previous negotiation.

† Tar. Resh. f. 159.

BOOK II.

A.D. 1507.

Mohammed Husein seized;

It was not long before Muhammed Husein Mírza, who had been discovered hid in one of the Khánum's store-houses among some carpets, was brought before Báber. The Khánum seems to have accompanied him, and pleaded for his pardon. As they approached, the King advanced to meet the Khánum; "O soul of thy mother," said she, "I have brought thee my guilty and unfortunate brother. What is thy command?" and she pointed to the Mírza. On seeing him, Báber at once went forward with his usual alacrity, and smiling with perfect frankness, took him in his arms, made many attentive inquiries, and showed him every mark of kindness and respect.* Khan Mírza, too, was overtaken not far from Kabul, and was brought before his offended sovereign. "I was sitting," says Báber, "in a portico of the Old Hall of Audience, when he was brought in. 'Come,' said I, 'and embrace me.' From the agitation in which he was, he twice fell before he could come up and make his obeisance. After we had saluted, I seated him at my side, and spoke encouragingly to him. They brought in sherbet. I myself drank of it first, in order to re-assure him, and then handed it to him. As I was still uncertain of the fidelity of a considerable part of the soldiers, the country people, the Moghuls and Chaghatáis, who were yet unsettled, I sent Khan Mírza into custody at large in the palace of his sisters, with orders that he should not leave it. But, as the commotions and seditions of the migratory tribes still continued, and as it did not seem advisable that the Mírza should remain in Kábul, I permitted him, in the course of a few days, to proceed to Khorásán."†

and Khan Mírza,

and pardoned.

Báber's reflections on their conduct.

But though the forgiving temper of Báber was so amiably exerted, in overlooking the offences of the Begum and Khánum, and in pardoning the more griev-

* Tar. Resh. f. 159.

† Báber's Mem. p. 219.

ous crimes of the others, we must not believe that this conduct was the result of mere indifference, of easiness of temper, or of a weak compliance with female solicitation. His clemency was, indeed, founded on strong natural affections, and constitutional strength of feeling, which were attended and nurtured by a secret persuasion that finds a place only in generous minds, that while he gratified his own heart by yielding to the impulse of emotions connected with the highest moral and intellectual elements of his being, he did not ultimately injure the interests of his people. Yet his noble mind felt the injuries that had been done to him most deeply; and the extent of his self-control may be seen by his reflections on the hard usage which he believed that on this and other occasions he experienced from these ladies, and his other relations of the family of the Moghul Khans. "It was not my wish that they should feel uneasy; yet the faction which had been guilty of such excesses was composed of persons, who, beyond all doubt, were not disposed to neglect the suggestions of the Begum and the Khánum. Khan Mírza was the grandson, by birth, of Shah Begum, and night and day with her. If he did not follow the advice of these ladies, it was at least in their power to have hindered his leaving them, and they could have kept him by them, under their own eye. Nor was this all. On various occasions, when, from adverse circumstances and misfortune, I was driven from my kingdom and throne, and separated from my servants and dependents, I had fled to them for refuge and succour; my mother too had gone to them, but we experienced no sort of kindness or support. Khan Mírza, who was younger than I, and his mother Sultan-nigár Khánum, at that time possessed rich and fertile districts, while I and my mother could not boast the possession of even a single village, or a few fowls. Yet my mother, too was a daughter of Yúnis Khan, and I was his grand-

BOOK II.

A. D. 1507.

son. In spite of this conduct, however, to every one of that family who came within the sphere of my influence, I performed my duty; whether they were related to me by blood or connected by marriage. Take for an example Shah Begum herself, on whom I bestowed Pemghán, which is one of the choice districts of Kábul; and at no time did I fail in my duty to her, in any respect, as her son and servant. Sultan Saíd Khan, the Khan of Káshghar *, reached me on foot, with five or six naked followers. I received them as if they had been my own brothers, and gave him the Tumán of Mandráur, one of the districts of Lamghán. When Shah Ismael overthrew and slew Sheibák Khan in Merv, and I passed over to Kunduz, the men of Andeján began to turn their eyes towards me, and several of them displaced their Daroghas, fortified their towns, declared for me, and sent persons to invite me. I despatched Sultan Sáid Khan, with my Báberi servants and an additional reinforcement, to hold the government of my own native country of Andeján, and raised him to the rank of Khan; and down to this moment I have always continued to treat every man of that family, who has sought my protection, with as much kindness as my own paternal relations; as, for example, Chín-Taimur Sultan, Isan-Taimur Sultan, Tokhteh-bugha Sultan, and Baba Sultan †, are all at this instant with me, and I have received and treated them with more distinction than my own paternal cousins. I have no intention," continues he, "by these remarks to reflect on any one, but only to state the plain truth; nor have I the least design to praise myself; I have spoken of things just as they happened; and, in every

* Sultan Saíd was son of the younger Khan, and so a grandson of Shah Begum.

† The three former of these were sons, the latter grandson of the younger Khan, and so all descended of Shah Begum.

word that I have written, have most scrupulously adhered to the truth." *

A. D. 1507.

Muhammed Husein pardoned;

Muhammed Husein Mírza, though his life was spared, had shown himself to be too dangerous a person to be permitted to remain at Kábul. "He had conducted himself," says Báber, "in such a criminal and guilty way, and had been actively engaged in such mutinous and rebellious proceedings, that, had he been cut to pieces, or put to a painful death, he would only have met with his deserts. As, however, we were related to each other, he having sons and daughters by my mother's sister, Khub-nigár Khánum, I took that circumstance into consideration, and set him at liberty, allowing him to go to Khorásán." * He was accompanied by Khan Mírza, who went no farther than Kandahár; but Muhammed Husein went on to Farrah. Before reaching that place he was met by crowds of every class, flying in the utmost distress and confusion, who reported that Sheibáni Khan had defeated the Mírzas of Khorásán, and taken possession of the country. He halted three months at Farrah; when Sheibáni, whose family had made several intermarriages with his, hearing that he was in his dominions, sent for him, and treated him with great distinction. He accompanied that chief to Samarkand, where he remained quietly for some time. But when, about three years after this period, it was known that the elder Khan was returning from Moghulistán towards Khojend, Sheibáni sent for the Mírza to Kelát, which he was then besieging, and thence speedily hurried him off to Herát; and, as he was jealous of his influence with the Moghuls, who were so numerous in his army, and of whom he lived in continual dread, he made him be followed and put to death. A similar fate was destined for the Mírza's son, Mírza Haider, who was however concealed and carried off to Kábul, and lived to attain very great eminence.

received by Sheibáni.

A. H. 914, A. D. 1508.

His death.

* Báber's Mem. pp. 217—218. † Ibid. p. 218.

BOOK II.

A.D. 1507.

Famine in Kábul.

A.H. 912.

Such was the result of Báber's prudent resolution to leave Khorásán, and return to his own dominions. His presence at Kábul had become necessary on many accounts, as well as to quell the recent rebellion. The confusion that prevailed, in consequence of successive revolutions, and of the march and plunder of foreign and barbarous troops over the country, joined perhaps to unfavourable seasons, had reduced the inhabitants to the most afflicting state of distress, which it required all his active benevolence and energy to alleviate. About the same time died his brother Jehángír Mírza, from the effects of excessive drinking *; and that prince's government of Ghazni was bestowed on Násir Mírza, the surviving brother, who had just returned from his unsuccessful expedition against Badakhshán. †

Death of Jehángír,

Bond of fidelity.

Báber, at this period, when all the countries around him were in a state of anarchy or revolution, and the minds of men were unsettled, seems, among other means of confirming his power, to have resorted to the expedient of making the leading men of his kingdom sign a bond of allegiance and fidelity. ‡ The newness of his own government, the late revolt, the distracted state of the whole of Central Asia, seemed to justify his adopting a measure, which has always had greater importance in appearance than it was ever found to possess in reality. §

Sheibáni invades Khorásán, A.H. 912, A.D. 1506-7.

Meanwhile in Khorásán, after he left it, affairs were less ably conducted. Sheibáni, having subdued Khwárazm and reduced Balkh, returned to Samarkand, where he spent the winter. Early in the spring, he set out with an army of fifty thousand men,

* Jehángír had married the fourth daughter of Sultan Mahmúd Mírza of Hissár (the sister of one of Báber's wives). He had no son, but left a daughter, who afterwards accompanied her maternal grandmother, Khanzáda Begum, to Badakhshán.

† Tar. Reshidi, f. 160.; Briggs's Ferishta, ii. p. 27.

‡ Metamassuk.

§ Tar. Resh. ff. 160, 161.

and crossed the Amu. He soon made himself master of Andekhűd, and advanced towards Baba Khaki, where the army of Khorásán lay. The two kings of Khorásán, Badi-ez-zemán Mírza and Mozeffer Mírza, with their ministers Muhammed Berendúk Birlás, and Zúlnún Beg, had assumed the command; but all was indecision and uncertainty, as was to be expected from a divided authority. Berendúk, a man of talent, proposed that he and Mozeffer, whose minister he was, should occupy and defend Herát; while Badi-ez-zeman and his minister Zúlnún should take up a strong position in the adjoining highlands, and call in the aid of the chiefs of Sistán, Kandahár, and Zemin-dáwer, as well as of the Hazáras and Nukderis, when they might be able so effectually to harass the Uzbeks, whose veteran troops it was dangerous to face in the open field, that they might not only prevent them from acting with effect against Herát, but soon compel them to retreat back with loss, disappointed of their object. But Zúlnún was jealous of Berendúk's holding the capital, and threw obstacles in the way of this plan, which Báber considered as founded on deep consideration and foresight. No plan of operations was yet formed, and all was discord and intrigue, when, early in June, they learned with alarm, that Sheibáni had passed the Murgháb, and had advanced to Sirakhsh. The camp was a prey to a sudden panic, and the army broke up. Resistance was not even thought of, except by Zúlnún, who had the advance; and who, having kept his ground with a hundred or a hundred and fifty men, was soon swept away, taken prisoner, and his head cut off. The Mírzas fled to Herát, reached it late in the evening, and, having rested their horses till midnight, again set out — without carrying off even their mothers, sisters, and families, who were in the adjoining fort of Ekhtiár-ed-din; and without taking any measures for the defence of the capital. Sheibáni, on his arrival,

CHAP. II.

A. D. 1507.

A. H. 913, A. D. 1507.

Divisions among the Mírzas;

A. H. 913, Moharrem, A. D. 1507, June;

who are defeated.

BOOK II. A. D. 1507.

found nothing prepared to resist him. He took possession of the city at once; and in two or three weeks the fort also surrendered, with the whole Harams of the late sovereign, and the families and children, and all the treasures of the Mírzas themselves. These ladies, as well as the citizens of Herát, were plundered without mercy under the authority of Sheibáni.

Conquest of Khorásán.

The disunion and want of concert among the princes led to the consequences that might be expected. Each retired to his own government. Sheibáni sent detachments of his army against them. The contest was not prolonged, though several battles were fought in different provinces. The victorious Uzbeks marched in every direction over Khorásán, that was soon prostrate before them. All of the Mírzas fell in action, or were put to death when prisoners, in the course of the next year or two, except Badi-ez-zemán Mírza, the eldest, who fled to Shah Ismael of Persia, and, after various adventures, died at Constantinople about ten years afterwards.*

Such was the termination of the dynasty of Taimur in the powerful kingdom of Khorásán. The sovereignty passed to Sheibáni Khan and his Uzbeks, who, however, as will soon be mentioned, held it only four years.

* Báber's Mem. pp. 220—224.; Tar. Resh. ff. 161, 162.

CHAPTER III.

CONQUEST AND LOSS OF KANDAHÁR. — REBELLION OF THE MOGHULS.

AFFAIRS OF KANDAHÁR. — ZÚLNÚN'S EARLY LIFE. — HE GETS THE GOVERNMENT OF ZEMÍN-DÁWER — AND OF KANDAHÁR. — CONNECTS HIMSELF WITH BADI-EZ-ZEMÁN MÍRZA. — HOSTILITIES WITH SULTAN HUSEIN OF HERÁT. — DEATH OF THE SULTAN. — ZÚLNÚN MINISTER. — HIS DEATH. — TRANSACTIONS OF HIS SONS WITH BÁBER — WHO DEFEATS THEM, AND TAKES KANDAHÁR. — SHEIBÁNI MARCHES TO THEIR RELIEF. — ALARM OF BÁBER. — KANDAHÁR RETAKEN. — REBELLION OF BÁBER'S MOGHULS — QUELLED BY HIS VALOUR. — AFFAIRS OF BADAKHSHÁN. — KHAN MÍRZA KING — HIS INDIGENT CONDITION. — SULTAN SAÍD AND MÍRZA HAIDER AT KÁBUL. — THEIR RECEPTION.

CHAP. III.

Affairs of Kandahár.

THE success of Sheibáni's arms, first at Samarkand, Táshkend, and Ferghána, afterwards in Hissár and Kunduz, then in Khwárazm, and now in Khorásán, was alarming to all his neighbours. He was undisputed master of the whole extensive regions, from the Tartar deserts to the Hindú-kúsh, and Parapamisan mountains, and the farthest limits of Khorásán. This new invader from the north seemed, like Chengíz Khan and Taimur Beg, to threaten universal conquest. After occupying Khorásán, it was naturally expected that he would march into Zemín-Dáwer and Kandahár, provinces which were then dependent on that kingdom. In these valuable possessions, Shah Beg had just succeeded his father Zúlnún Beg, Arghún, a man who for many years had acted a conspicuous part at the Court of Herát; and who, as he laid the foundation of the power of a family which afterwards came into frequent collision with Báber and his sons, governed Kandahár

BOOK II.

for many years, and long swayed the sceptre of Sind, is entitled to some commemoration in this place.

Mír Zúlnún Beg, his early life.

Mír Zúlnún Beg, the son of Mír Hassan Basri, was descended of the noble tribe of Arghún, by a family that had long held a high rank under different princes, and which affected to trace back its origin, through Arghún Khan, to the great Chengíz himself.* While yet a youth, he had attached himself to the service of Sultan Abu-saíd Mírza, whose dominions extended from Tartary to Kirmán; and became distinguished above all the young nobles of the Court, for his brilliant courage and especially for his gallant exploits in single combat, several of which were performed under the

A. H. 873, A. D. 1468.

Khákán's own eye. On the calamitous discomfiture and death of that powerful monarch at Ardebíl, Zúlnún returned to Herát to his father, and was there for some time, in the service of Sultan Yádgár Mírza, one of the numerous competitors for the vacant throne. From Herát he afterwards repaired to Samarkand, where he was favourably received by Sultan Ahmed Mírza, the eldest son of Abusaíd, his former master. Here he remained some years; but the Arghún nobles at that Court, having quarrelled with the Terkháns, with whom the Sultan was connected by his mother, who was of their tribe; and the Terkhán lords having gained unlimited influence over that pious, but weak and indolent prince, Zúlnún returned once more to Herát, where the great Sultan Husein Mírza had now fixed himself, as undisputed Khákán or Emperor, by the overthrow of the last of his antagonists.†

Repairs to Herát;

Under this able sovereign, the Court of Herát was

* The genealogy of Zúlnún Beg upwards from Mahmúd Gházán, bin Arghún Khan, bin Abakán, bin Hulakú Khan, bin Tuli Khan, bin Chengíz Khan, as given by historians, is distinct enough; but the downward course from Gházán to Mír Hasan Basri, Zúlnún's father, though the most necessary for establishing his claim, I have not met with.

† Mem. of Báber, pp. 20—24.; Tarikhe-Sind, MS. fols. 72, 73.; Briggs's Ferishta, vol. iv. p. 432.

the general resort of adventurers of talent or ambition, in arms, in letters, or the useful arts, from every part of Asia. A soldier, who, like Zúlnún, had distinguished himself by his personal prowess and his martial ardour in every action in which he had been engaged, was sure to be gladly welcomed. In due course of time his peculiar talents were called into action. The Sultan bestowed on him the government of Ghúr and the Núkderi* country, lying east of Herát, on the south-west limits of the Parapamisan or Hazára range of mountains. The inhabitants, like the more numerous tribe of Hazáras, who lived farther to the east, in the hills that lie between these districts and Kábul, were a rude and barbarous race of highlanders, who regarded the lowlands around them as their inheritance, and who, in their incursions, not only plundered the cattle and property of the neighbouring cultivators of the soil, but robbed travellers and the caravans of merchants, whom they intercepted while proceeding on their way from one city to another; and especially such as passed between Herát and Kandahár. The booty so acquired they carried off into their mountain recesses, where they defied the arm of regular government. Near as their territory lay to the capital, they had baffled all former attempts to reduce them to order.

gets the government of Ghúr, A. H. 884, A. D. 1749.

Attempts to repress the Hazarás and Núkderis,

No sooner was Zúlnún appointed to the government, than he hastened to his command, attended by a small

* The Nukderis, called by D'Ohsson Négoudariens, are described as having been originally wandering Moghuls, who used to range in Sistán, but who were sent by Gházán to Irák Ajemi, where they had summer and winter stations assigned to them. Being, however, accused of continuing their old freebooting practices, and molested in consequence, they moved away without permission, and placed themselves under the protection of Melik Fakr-ed-dín of Herát, who employed them against such of his neighbours as he wished to subdue. He continued to protect them from the resentment of Gházán. D'Ohsson, Hist. des Mongols, tom. iv. p. 193—6. ed. 1834. The territory assigned them at that time near the Ghúsi and the Khilji, they have ever since retained.

BOOK II. band of faithful adherents. Followed by a mere handful of men, he fearlessly attacked and defeated large bodies of the restless Hazára and Nukderi tribes, wherever they were to be found. His personal courage, and extraordinary bodily powers, astonished and daunted the rude mountaineers. He often had not more than seventy or eighty of his trusty followers along with him, when he surprised them in their tents, slew their warriors, and drove off their flocks. When repeated and bloody discomfitures, in which they found themselves vanquished at their own warfare, had produced the natural effect on their minds, he followed up his measures of hostility by a steady course of conciliatory kindness. The tribes, when thus courted by the rough and hardy hero whom they dreaded and admired, willingly transferred to him their services. He, in the end, not only reduced them to order (and they never were kept in such order as by him), but so completely secured their attachment, that those barbarous tribes ever after, and under all changes of fortune, continued the unshaken supporters of Zúlnún and his family.

Gets the government of Zemín-Dáwer, A. H. 888, A. D. 1483;

His success in these difficult operations, which occupied him three or four years, was so acceptable to the Sultan, that he soon after bestowed on him the government of Zemín-Dáwer. This province, which stretches from the roots and valleys of the Hazára mountains, along the right bank of the Helmend till its union with the Arghandab river, which joins it from Kandahár, is one of the richest and most fertile countries in these parts. To this was added the district of Farrah, to the west, which lies between the hills and Sistán. He also extended his influence over the Germsír (or warm country), a province composed of the deep and narrow tract of low hot lands, lying chiefly along the lower course of the Helmend.

and of Farrah.

By these conquests, and by his influence with the Hazára and Kipchák tribes, who dwelt in the hills and wilds of Kandahár, the power of this able and successful chief had become very formidable. The fame of his exploits, and of his conquests, regularly reached Herát; and were at first so agreeable to the Khákán, that he honoured Zúlnún with the Túgh, or horsetail standard* or banner, which marked a high rank among the nobility. But, in a short time after, his continued progress and growing reputation naturally excited alarm in a jealous court, in an age when every successful leader aimed at independence. He was recalled; and, his plans not being yet ripe for execution, he at once obeyed, and appeared in the presence of his sovereign; where his respectful and prudent behaviour went far to gain the Khákán's good opinion, and to remove the doubts that had been entertained of his fidelity.†

Rewarded with the Túgh.

Recalled.

At this period, the intrigues in the royal Haram had given rise to several parties at the court of Herát. Badi-ez-zemán Mírza, the eldest son of the Khákán, was filled with apprehensions by no means groundless, lest his father, acting under the influence of Khadíja Begum, his favourite wife, might be induced to prefer to the succession, her son Muzaffer Husein Mírza, who was also the Sultan's favourite child; though, according to Báber, who knew him personally, he had nothing in his mind or manners to justify this partiality.‡ Zúlnún, who saw the unsteady footing on which he was placed at the court of Herát, rather encouraged the discontent of the elder brother, whom he gained over, and particularly attached to himself. By this prince's advice, Zúlnún now discharged all his followers, renounced every appearance of state, and lived in a private and retired manner; still, however, showing himself from time to time in the presence. This quiet and prudent demeanour produced its effect. At the

Parties at Herát.

* Rather *cowtail,* it being made of the tail of the kitás or mountain cow.

† Tarikhe-Sind, fol. 73, 74. Mem. of Báber, p. 186.

‡ Mem. of Báber, p. 179.

BOOK II.

end of about one year, his situation was at length taken into consideration, in the royal council; on which occasion Badi-ez-zemán, who was present, but afraid to appear directly to favour Zúlnún, proposed that he should forthwith be appointed to the government of Kandahár, which was then vacant; a situation which, he said, hardly any officer of rank would willingly accept of, as the climate had always hitherto, in the course of two or three years, cut off those who held it. And he added that, should the same fate attend the new governor, it might only relieve his majesty of a subject whom he could spare*; while, if he survived, means never would be wanting of reducing him to his duty. The proposal was approved of; the abilities of Zúlnún, for quieting the province, were undoubted; and the Mírza was commissioned to inform him of this mark of imperial favour, and to invest him, on the part of the Khákan, his father, with a dress of honour, accompanied by a horse richly caparisoned, a standard, and kettle-drum, marks of high distinction, usually granted on such an occasion. Zúlnún, sensibly alive to this active proof of the Mírza's friendship, granted him a writing by which he bound himself to support him with life and soul, and to attend on his call, without hesitation or delay, under any circumstances whatever,—evidently implying, even against the Khákán himself.

Zúlnún appointed to Kandahár.

Leaves Herát privately.

But Zúlnún had not yet had his audience of leave; and the suspicions of his fidelity, which had been evaded rather than quieted, might still prevent his being allowed to take possession of his government. Aware of this, he lost no time in despatching orders to his eldest son, Shah Beg, and several of his most trusty Arghún and Terkhán officers, to join him immediately in Khorásán. Their arrival, as they might

* The malady so fatal at Kandahár was the Marze-Vibâ. See Tarikhe-Sind, fol.

be considered in the light of hostages for his fidelity, tended in some degree to remove suspicions of any sinister intention. Still, however, delays were interposed by the suspicions of the Khákán; and the disorders of Kandahár went on increasing; till at length the princes his sons and the chief ministers were compelled to represent to him, that the troubled state of the province most urgently required the presence of a governor; a representation which was speedily followed by an intimation to Zúlnún that it would be necessary for him instantly to set out by himself, leaving his son and suite behind him at the court. Delighted with the pretext which this sudden notice afforded for his departure, he secretly, without taking leave, set out by night, accompanied by his son, his nobles and troops, but leaving all his heavy baggage and servants; and, having had everything previously prepared, hastened with all possible speed towards his government. Nothing was known of his departure for several days, when an officer sent to Zúlnún's house, to desire him to put off his departure till the festival of the Nuróz or vernal equinox was over, reported, on his return, that Zúlnún had already set out, with his family; but that his servants, camels, baggage, and equipage of every description, were still at his house. When some of the courtiers observed, that such being the case he would speedily return; "No," said the aged monarch, "I have seen Zúlnún for the last time."

Arrival in Kandahár.

The state of affairs in the court of Herát made it advisable rather to overlook than to punish this insult. A firmán followed Zúlnún, confirming him in the government of Kandahár, but requiring his presence at court. The messenger overtook him at Farrah. He received the mandate with affected devotion and humility, declaring that it was the most earnest wish of his heart, after visiting his family, who were only two stages off, to accompany the messenger back to the

BOOK II. foot of the throne. He, however, went on to Kandahár, where he assembled a council of his relations, his tribesmen, and the principal chiefs attached to his interest, and laid before them the imperial requisition; which all of them, of course, insisted on his declining. To their instances he affected unwillingly to yield. The messenger, who was present, was soon after honourably dismissed with rich presents and a respectful reply: and the Sultan well saw that no hopes were left of his finding an obedient or faithful subject in Zúlnún.*

Nature of his territory.

The Arghún chief now applied himself, for some time, to the task of consolidating his authority, and of organising his military resources. These were ample; but the great diversity both in the physical structure of his dominions, which stretched over savage mountains, rich plains, and sandy desert; and in the manners and habits of the tribes by which they were peopled, which in general were barbarous and unsettled, of various races and speaking different tongues, made the task no easy one. In this business he was ably assisted by his son Shah Shujaa Beg, who, when only a boy, had accompanied him in his most perilous forays and expeditions, in which he had displayed an ardent but regulated valour. They extended their territory to the south, over the wild tracts of plain and rugged and broken mountains that lie in that direction, reducing Pishín, Shál, and Mustung, as far as the very borders of the Balúch country, and of Síwistán.

Rebellion of Badi-ez-zemán, A. H. 902, A. D. 1497;

The intrigues in the Haram of Sultan Husein Mírza terminated at length in the rebellion of Badi-ez-zemán Mírza. That prince, who soon after his revolt was defeated by his father, fled, as we have seen, to Kunduz to Khosrou Shah, then in the height of his power; whence, after a short stay, he crossed the mountain to

who takes

take refuge with Zúlnún, by whom he was received with

* Tarikhe-Sind, fol. 75, 76.; Briggs's Ferishta, vol. iv. p. 432.

CHAP. III.

refuge with Zúlnún.

every mark of distinction; and, among other offerings, received from him a present of forty thousand sheep at one time. He was entertained with royal pomp, and ere long married the daughter of Zúlnún Beg, a connection which drew closer than ever the bonds of union between the Prince and his supporter. In the meanwhile the Prince's son, Muhammed Momín Mírza, who had been driven to revolt in Asterábád, having been defeated on the same day with his father, was taken prisoner, and carried to Herát. There he was closely confined in the castle of Ekhtiár-ed-dín; and soon after put to death, by an order said to have been procured by the favourite Begum from her uxorious husband, while in a state of intoxication.*

Sultan Husein invades Kandahár, A. H. 904, A. D. 1497.

Sultan Husein Mírza, offended at the princely reception given to his rebellious son by a subject of his own, marched into his territories with a formidable army, for the purpose of chastising him. Zúlnún, seeing no hope of success from open resistance in the field, ordered the whole grain, cattle, and provisions that lay in the line of march of the advancing army, to be carried into the strong forts of the country; and, making a desert of his own territory, presented only a barren waste to the invader. He appointed his eldest son, Shah Beg, to defend Kandahár; and Muhammed Mokím, another of his sons, to guard the Zemín-Dáwer; while he himself retired into the fort of Pesheng†, and Badi-ez-zemán into another stronghold. As the Sultan advanced, by Farrah to the Germsír and the Zemín-Dáwer, he found no enemy to encounter; but at the same time nothing was procurable by which he could subsist his troops. Scarcity began to prevail, and famine was about to follow. To retreat, through a bare

* Báber's Mem. pp. 44. 46. Tarikhe-Sind, fol. 78—81.

† Probably Sira Kila, or Kila Abdalla, in Pishín, near the junction of the *Lora* and Surkháb. He is said to have rendered it so strong that not even a pismire could crawl into it.—Tar. Sind.

BOOK II. waste with troops exhausted as his were, was impossible; and his great army was on the point of dispersing to shift every man for himself, when he was saved by the timidity of the governor of Bíst*, on the Helmend, who surrendered the fort entrusted to his care, on the very first summons. Had he held out only for two days, the ruin of the imperial army was inevitable. In this fort the provisions that had been driven in from the surrounding country were found collected; and the stores which it contained enabled the Sultan and his army to retrace their steps to the capital, through the wasted plains they had so recently traversed.†

Takes Bíst.

Forced to retreat.

A. H. 903, A. D. 1498.

Attempt to surprise the Khákán.

In the early part of the ensuing spring the Khákán allowed a number of his soldiers to return for a short time to their homes, to refresh themselves after this campaign, and to prepare for another which he had resolved to make; while he himself, in his camp at the Auleng-Níshín near Herát, indulged at his ease in all the usual pleasures and amusements of a voluptuous court. But he had to do with an active enemy. News of the careless way in which he lay having reached the Germsír, Badi-ez-zemán and Shah Beg formed the plan of taking him by surprise. Accompanied by three thousand chosen horse, in five or six days, they reached Sebzáwár, where their approach was discovered by Ferídún Husein Mírza, one of the Khákán's sons, who sent messenger after messenger to alarm his father. The news spread consternation in Auleng-Níshín. Orders were despatched to Herát, to put the city in a state of defence; and the charge of it was committed to the celebrated Amír Ali Shír, who combined in his own person the characters of a distinguished soldier, poet, and statesman. A ditch was hastily begun to be drawn round the camp, and strong bodies of troops posted in advance. Meanwhile, scouts and expresses

A. H 903, Shaban, A. D. 1498, April.

* Or Bost.

† Báber's Mem. p. 62., Tarikhe-Sind, MS. fol. 80, 81.

in rapid succession continued to bring word that the invaders were hastening on without slackening rein; and it was the general belief, that, had they gone straight on, while the alarm and confusion still prevailed, instead of halting at Isferáin, a whole night, to rest themselves, they must have succeeded in their attempt. In the course of the next morning two considerable bodies of men from different quarters unexpectedly joined the imperial camp; so that the invaders, when they came near it, saw, from the numbers and state of preparation of their enemy, that there was not a hope of success; and hastened, without loss of time, to make good their retreat; which they effected, by their own speed, or by the confusion into which their unexpected approach had thrown their enemy.*

Fails.

To atone for this disappointment, Zúlnún and the Prince soon after raised an army, composed of all the military strength of Kandahár, Zemín-Dáwer, and Ghúr, besides a body of Hazáras, Nukderis, and Kipcháks, and entered Khorásán, plundering and laying waste the country. The Khákán was preparing to meet them in the field, when a negotiation was opened, by some saintly men, the usual mediators of the time. A request was made on the part of the Prince to have Sistán granted to him. This the Khákán peremptorily refused, and hostilities were about to recommence; when Mír Ali Shír, who was a personal friend of the Khákán, hastening from Herát to the camp, prevailed upon him to agree to the terms, and to grant Sistán and Farrah to Badi-ez-zemán; after which the two armies separated, and the Prince proceeded to his new principality.†

The confederates invade Khorásán.

Pacification.

But the causes of dissension lay too deep to be instantly removed. No sooner had Sultan Husein marched from his capital for Asterábád, to quell the

They again invade Khorásán.

* Tarikhe-Sind, fol. 81—83. Báber's Mem. p. 62.

† End of Sefer, A. H. 904, Begg. Oct. A. D. 1498. Tarikhe-Sind, fol. 83—85.

BOOK II. rebellion of another of his sons, than the Prince and Zúlnún, availing themselves of his absence, once more issued forth at the head of an army, chiefly composed of Hazáras and other hill-tribes; drove off the cattle, and ruined the property of the Amírs in the interest of the Khákán, and of his favourite son Mozeffer; and approached Herát. Mír Ali Shír, who had been left governor of the place, had used every means that skill and activity could employ for fortifying and provisioning the city. Zúlnún, leaving Badi-ez-zemán with the bulk of the army at Ubeh, pushed on nearer to the capital; when various persons, who yet remained in the adjoining villages, waited on him with congratulatory offerings; and informed him, that, several armies were on their march from different quarters to protect the capital, and were at that moment near at hand. Zúlnún despatched an express to communicate this information to the Prince, who joined him in Likal-khána. The imperial troops issuing from Baghát*, Zúlnún attacked them in the Auleng-Níshín, and victory declared for the confederates. They now encamped at the Auleng-Níshín, the usual camp of the Khákán; but soon moved to Púl-Málán, and summoned the city. Mír Ali Shír, however, faithful to his trust, declared his determination to hold it out to the last extremity; and, during a siege of forty days, bravely repelled all attacks of the enemy. By this time, news of the emperor's approach was received at Herát. Mír Ali Shír, who was attached to Badi-ez-zemán, immediately wrote to inform him of the fact, advising him to raise the siege. He accordingly moved away to Púl-Sálár, and thence to the Murgháb; where he was soon after joined by the force of Badghis and Chichektú,

Besiege Herát.

* I know not whether there is a suburb called Baghát, at Herát; or, if the name is merely applied to the collection of suburban houses and "gardens" of the rich Hírwis.

Púl-Málán is the name of the river that passes near Herát, and probably of a village on it.

and by Shah Beg with a select body of men from Kandahár. The governor of Merv having refused to surrender, Shah Beg, with his mountaineers, assaulted the place with such fury, that, after an attack maintained from morning till noon, that important place was carried.

Take Merv.

Meanwhile the Khákán had returned to Herát; but the army which he had brought from Asterábád was quite disorganised, from the fatigue of a long continued and hurried march; and he found his other troops dispirited by their late discomfiture. The Prince, too, had probably a strong party in his father's council. Sultan Husein began to incline to peace, and a treaty was in due time concluded; by which the province of Balkh, which Badi-ez-zemán had formerly enjoyed, was bestowed on him anew, with the title of Humáyun Khákáni; while Sistán, the province he now held, was made over to Amír Sultán Ali, a brother of Zúlnún.

Peace concluded.

A circumstance soon occurred, however, which showed how unwillingly this sacrifice was made by the Khákán. The governor of the fort of Lash, a dependency of Sistán,—being discontented with Sultan Ali, his new master,—sent privately to the Khákán to inform him, that such was the general feeling in his favour, that, if one of the young princes were to appear in Sistán, the whole country would at once declare for him. In consequence of this invitation, Ibn Husein Mírza, one of the Khákán's sons, was despatched into Sistán with two thousand horse. He advanced and stationed himself at a town called Uki. But he had to do with an active enemy. Zúlnún had heard of his motions, and instantly pushed on towards him, accompanied by his son, Shah Beg. He got near the Mírza's camp in the morning, while he was yet asleep, and his troops dispersed to plunder or forage. The Mírza, when roused, advanced bravely to meet the enemy, with about three hundred of his cavalry, who happened to be still around him. He had hardly moved off his ground, when Zúlnún, with a

Invasion of Sistán.

A. H. 908, A. D. 1503.

Defeated.

BOOK II. superior force, closed in upon him on every side. Though thus taken as in a snare, the Mírza fought valiantly; but was wounded by Mír Fázil Kokiltásh, an Arghún officer, and forced to retreat. Zúlnún suffered him to escape, and directed that neither he nor his troops should be molested in their way back to Herát.*

High reputation of Zúlnún.

These repeated successes had spread far and wide the reputation of Zúlnún. This was farther increased by the expedition of his son, Muhammed Mokím, against Kábul, and the conquest of that kingdom,—events that extended the sphere of his direct influence, from the desert of Khorásán nearly to the borders of India; and from the Parapamisan mountains to Mekrán. It is said, however, that the hoary politician did not approve of this last extension of the power of his family. Kábul was not, like the other dominions which he possessed, dependent on Herát; but an independent kingdom, the throne of which had long been filled by princes of the family of Taimur. By the expulsion of one of these was it acquired; and, so venerable was the name of the great conqueror, in these regions, that the right to fill a throne was still considered as belonging almost exclusively to his race. Zúlnún might reasonably suppose, that the direct occupation of such a kingdom put him too much in opposition to the reigning families, and too soon unmasked his views of entire independence. But while, in public, he chided his son for the impolitic and unauthorised usurpation, he at the same time instructed him as to the fittest means by which his new acquisition could be maintained. We have seen that the possession of Kábul and Ghazni was but a short-lived triumph, as the arrival of Báber, from the north, soon after wrested them from his grasp.†

A. H. 909, A. D. 1504.

Conquest of Kábul, transient.

A. H. 910, A. D. 1505.

Zilhájeh, A. H. 911, May, A. D. 1506.

On the death of Sultan Husein Mírza, Zúlnún's im-

* Taríkhe-Sind. MS. ff. 88, 89.

† Taríkhe-Sind. ff. 89, 90. Báber's Mem. ut supra.

portance received an ample increase. He became the prime minister and chief adviser of Badi-ez-zemán Mírza during his short and divided sovereignty in Khorásán. Considerable additions were then made to his government, especially on the skirts of the mountains on the side of the Herát. We are told by Báber, who knew him, that, though a brave, frank, and hardy soldier, he wanted compass of mind, was profoundly ignorant, very deficient in judgment, superstitious, and ridiculously open to flattery. His weakness in this respect was partly the cause of his death. When he was minister at Herát, and the Uzbek invasion engrossed the thoughts of all, some servile holy men and Múllas assured him that they had had communication with the celestial spheres, and that the glorious title of "Lion of God"* had been bestowed on him by the divine decree; that he was predestined to defeat the Uzbeks, and to take the whole of them prisoners. Zúlnún, who was a slave to the superstition of his day, returned thanks to the Almighty for having been selected as the instrument of so noble an achievement, the certainty of which he unhesitatingly believed; so that, when Sheibáni, pushing into Khorásán, cut off the communication of the Mírzas with each other, and defeated the troops which fell in his way, Zúlnún resolutely kept his ground, with about a hundred and fifty horse, expecting the fulfilment of the prophecy. Sheibáni's profane barbarians, however, speedily surrounded, and, by immense superiority of numbers, disarmed him and his followers. His head was afterwards struck off, to be presented to the Khan. Such was the end of Zúlnún's active life. His sons succeeded him in his extensive territories, in which he had nearly become independent.†

CHAP. III. A. D. 1507. Zúlnún becomes a prime minister at Herát.

A. H. 913, A. D. 1507.

Is slain.

When the Arghún brothers,—his sons Shah Shujáa Beg and Mokím,—by the progress of Sheibáni's success,

His sons correspond with Báber,

* Hezéber Alla.

† Báber's Mem. pp. 186—222.

BOOK II. A.D. 1507.

saw the whole family of Sultan Husein Mírza dispersed or slain, and the throne of Herát occupied by a Tartar chief, who had hitherto laid prostrate whatever opposed him, they naturally looked around for some one able to protect them in the hour of danger; and Báber presented himself as at once the nearest and most efficient ally within their reach; recommended perhaps the more from the influence of ancient opinion, being now the only remnant of the house of the great Taimur that preserved even the appearance of power. While the Uzbeks were busy overrunning Khorásán, the brothers, he tells us, repeatedly despatched ambassadors to him, with letters containing humble professions of service and submission; and he adds, that Mokím, in one of these letters, explicitly called upon him to hasten to his assistance. The extent of this submission and invitation it is not easy to ascertain. In the alarm into which they had been thrown, they may have used terms of humility of which they afterwards repented; while, on the other hand, Báber may not have been unwilling to give to the submissive style of courtesy common in eastern letters and verbal communications, a literal interpretation, as implying a real intention to submit to his authority, which was not intended. However that may be, with all the ardour and impatience of youth and ambition, he listened to the call, taking it in the sense that he desired; and instantly obeyed.

who marches for Kandahár.

We have seen that the civil wars, which had changed the government of Kábul and Ghazni so often in the course of a few years, joined to the march and ravages of armies, had made the summer after Báber's return from Khorásán one of great scarcity and distress throughout his kingdom. But it was not his dominions alone that at this time suffered from the ravages of war. As he advanced on his march towards Kandahár, he was met at Ghazni by numbers of fugitives, the wreck of the army of Khorásán;

CHAP. III. A. D. 1507.

and by some of the females of the royal house of Herát, and among others his own affianced bride, who were flying from that capital. At Kilát* he came upon a caravan of Indian merchants, whom, contrary to the advice of his officers, but following his own invariable practice, and in compliance with sound feelings of justice, which in the end coincide with those of sound policy, as Báber found on this and on other occasions, he did not proceed to plunder as they expected; though, impelled by his necessities, he levied a contribution from them. After he had passed Kilát, Khan Mírza and Abdal Rizak Mírza his cousins, who had both lately been his rivals, and sat on the throne of Kábul, joined him; with many other persons of importance, who were flying before the Uzbeks. He now despatched envoys to inform the Arghún brothers of his approach, calling upon them to concert measures along with him against Sheibáni Khan.†

A.H. 913, A. D. 1507.

The Arghún chiefs submit to Sheibáni.

But the policy of these princes had undergone an important change. Soon after his victory, Sheibáni had turned his views to Kandahár, and the other possessions of the Khákán in that quarter. He had even advanced by Farrah, as far as the Germsír, to enforce his claims, when an embassy from Shah Beg reached his camp, tendering the submission of the Arghúns, and offering on their part to read the public prayer and strike the coin in his name. Sheibáni, satisfied with this readiness to acknowledge his sovereignty, accepted their submission, and marched in another direction, to reduce the other portions of the wide extended kingdom that had fallen under his power, as the fruit of his victories. To Báber's requisition, therefore, they returned such answers as showed that they had no intention of submitting to him as their lawful lord. On the contrary, they affected to treat him as an equal.

* Now Kiláte Ghilji.

† Báber's Mem. pp. 224, 225.; Tar. Resh. f. 160.; Ferishta, v. ii. pp. 26, 27.

BOOK II.

A. D. 1507.

Battle of Kandahár.

Báber's proposals for a compromise being thus repulsed, he prepared for action; and, as his army was not numerous, he proceeded with much caution. He directed his march along the course of the streams that flow towards Kandahár, till he came near Baba Hasan Abdal and Khalishák. He next moved to a meadow near Kandahár; but did not think of engaging there, the ground being broken by villages and trees. As his troops, in the march from Khilát, had suffered much from hunger, nearly a half of them had gone out to forage and to collect sheep, cattle, and what else was required. At this moment, the Arghúns were found to be advancing on them. Báber instantly put his men in order, without waiting for the foragers. His whole number of regular troops was only about two thousand, of whom one half were absent. The Arghúns, who had at least four or five thousand regularly armed, exceeded them many times in number, and had probably expected to come upon them unprepared as well as scattered. Báber says, that he never had his men better disciplined and trained than at that time. They not only stood their ground against the superior force of the enemy, who were commanded by Shah Beg in person, having under him officers of great experience; but charged them in turn, and in the end broke through and put them to flight; and, such was their success, that they cut off the communication of Shah Beg with the fort,—neither he nor his brother being able to regain the town, which soon surrendered to the victor, with all its treasures and the families of the vanquished. Shah Beg fled to his southern possessions of Shál and Mustung, in the desert; while Mokím retired westward to Zemín-Dáwer. The spoil of the city was magnificently rich. The wealth, collected in the course of the long and fortunate life of Zúlnún Beg, was brought out and liberally divided by Báber among his followers. The number of horses, camels, and mules, the quantity

Shah Beg defeated.

Kandahár surrenders.

Richness of the spoil.

of rich silk stuffs and fine linen, of tents with awnings of velvet, and other rich clothes, besides gold and silver coin, was immense. To save the trouble of counting the money and specie, it was divided by weight, and enriched all the army. Báber bestowed Kandahár upon his brother, Násir Mírza, and then hastened back with his army to Kábul. Sheibáni Khan was too vigilant an enemy, to render it safe to linger needlessly so near him.*

Sheibáni marches to Kandahár,

Accordingly, Báber had not returned more than a week to Kábul, when he learned that Sheibáni was busily employed in besieging Kandahár. When Mokím, after his defeat, retired to Zemín-Dáwer, he sent to invite Sheibáni to his succour. That active prince, without loss of time, hastened by forced marches through the hill-country between Herát and Kandahár; in hopes of surprising Báber, whom he trusted to find yet indulging himself in the conquered city, free from care, in the full enjoyment of his victory. His plan was in part defeated by the sagacity of Kásim Beg, Báber's old and favourite minister, who had advised the speedy march back to Kábul; but Sheibáni laid siege to Kandahár, in which Báber's brother, Násir Mírza, was shut up.

which he seizes.

Alarm of Báber.

This news filled the young Sultan, and his adherents, with well-founded alarm. The power and talents of Sheibáni were too well known to them, by long and painful experience, and their own weakness was too visible, to admit of a hope that he could be resisted in the open field, in the present state of Báber's affairs. The conquest of Khorásán had added immensely to the previous power and reputation of the terrible Uzbek. At a council,—held for the purpose of deciding what course ought to be pursued in this difficult emergency, —such was the alarm diffused by Sheibáni's prowess and power, that it was considered as hopeless even to at-

* Báber's Mem. pp. 220—230.; Taríkhe-Sind. ff. 91—94.

BOOK II. A. D. 1507.

tempt the defence of the country of Kábul; and it was, therefore, judged to be most advisable to escape the coming tempest, by trying the fate of an inroad either

who marches for India;

into Badakhshán or India. Opinions were divided between the two; but Báber's wishes, which turned towards India, decided the question. Leaving, in Kábul,

A. H. 913, Jemádi I. A. D. 1507, September.

his cousin Abdal Rizák, the late king, he marched down the Kábul river for the Indus. To leave his rival master of the capital, may look like the dictate of listless despair. But he probably thought, that the long connection of that prince's ancestors with the kingdom afforded the best chance, when the great body of his own troops were withdrawn, of uniting in his favour the force of the country; and Báber may have trusted to his own talents, and to the ascendency which he had gained over his rival by success, for recovering the throne, at a future time, in case of the retreat of the Uzbeks. Yet the influence regained at this period by Abdal Rizák may reasonably be supposed to have had some connection with the revolution which soon after followed in his favour.

by Khurd-Kábul,

When Báber began his march towards the low countries on the side of Lamghán, the robber tribes, who possess the intervening passes, seeing him apparently abandon his lately acquired kingdom, and in full march for the Indus, following their usual policy, attempted to obstruct his progress; in the very line of march which has since become so memorable by the disasters of a British army. "We proceeded on our route by way of Khurd-Kábul," says Báber; "on reaching Súrkh Rebát, we passed Kurúk Sái by the hill-pass. The Afgháns who inhabit between Kábul and Lamghán are robbers and plunderers even in peaceable times. Fervently do they pray to God for such times of confusion as now prevailed, but rarely do they get them. When

* Little Kábul.

they understood that I had abandoned Kábul and was marching for Hindustán, their usual insolence was increased tenfold. Even the best disposed among them were then bent on mischief; and things came to such lengths that the morning we marched from Jagdálik, the Afgháns, through whose country we were to pass,—such as the Khizer-Khail, the Shimu-khail *, the Khirilji, and the Khugiáni,—determined to obstruct our march through the Kotal (or hill-pass) of Jagdálik, and drew up on the hill that lies on the north, beating their drums, brandishing their swords, and raising terrific shouts. As soon as we had mounted, I ordered the troops to ascend the hill and attack the enemy, each in the direction nearest to him. They accordingly advanced, and making their way by any valley, ravine, or other approach they could discover, got near them; upon which the Afgháns, after standing an instant, took to flight, without even shooting an arrow. After driving off the Afgháns, we reached the top of the ascent." † Descending to the district of Nangenhár, he halted before the fort of Adínapúr, now Jelálábád; a name which has become memorable in the annals of British India. Here Báber separated his army into four divisions, which he sent in different directions, to plunder and lay waste the country of the Afgháns, who at that period seem not to have acknowledged even a nominal subjection to the crown of Kábul. In these operations he passed the time, waiting for news from the west. As the alarm gradually subsided, he sent back some troops to Kábul; while he proceeded, himself, to survey the country upon the Cheghánserái river, and to plunder the inhabitants. ‡

CHAP. III. A.D. 1507–8.

and Jagdálik.

He was not long of receiving news which determined his return to Kábul. Sheibáni Khan had no sooner appeared before Kandahár, than the city was given up,

Sheibáni takes Kandahár,

* Or, Himu-khail.

† Báber's Mem. p. 232.

‡ Báber's Mem. pp. 232, 233.; Taríkhe-Sind. f. 95.

BOOK II.

A. D. 1507–8.

besieges the citadel,

Násir Mírza and the garrison retiring into the citadel. This fortress was vigorously assailed; mines were run under the defences, and sprung; and the place must infallibly have fallen, in the course of a few days more, when Sheibáni learned that the fort of Nirehtu *, east of Herát, in which he had left the females of his family, had been surprised by a sudden rising in that neighbourhood. Without delay he made Násir Mírza proposals for an accommodation, which were readily agreed to, when he hurried back towards Herát. Násir, who had found his situation in Kandahár too full of difficulty to give him any prospect of successfully maintaining himself there, was glad to yield up the citadel, and retreated to Ghazni. By Sheibáni's orders, and perhaps as a consequence of the capitulation, the Arghúns were immediately restored to the possession of both the town and citadel; and all the rest of the province submitted to them once more.†

which capitulates,

Shag Beg recovers Kandahár.

Báber returns to Kábul.

Though it was now the middle of winter, Báber, on receiving the news of these occurrences, returned to Kábul, and abandoned the idea of advancing into Hindustán. He gave Ghazni to Násir Mírza, and Nangenhár and other districts of Kábul to Abdal Rizák Mírza. Khan Mírza, when Báber marched from Kábul for Hindustán, had, with his permission, set out for Badakhshán, in hopes of gaining for himself a settlement in that country. He was accompanied by a number of his friends and followers, and in particular by his grandmother, Shah Begum, who was a princess of the ancient royal family of that little kingdom.

Khan Mírza sets out for Badakhshán.

Báber takes the title of Padshah.

It was at this time that Báber assumed the title of Padshah, or Emperor.‡ Till then, as he himself in-

* *Nirehtu* or *Kaliún* was a strong fortress, not far from Herát, in the Bádghís district. It was situated on the top of a rock; and, in order to reach it, it is said to have been necessary to march along a path a league and a half in length, and so narrow that two men could not walk abreast. Hist. des Mongols, vol. i. p. 242.

† Báber's Mem. p. 233.

‡ Many descendants of Taimur

CHAP. III.

A. D. 1508.

forms us, none of the family of Taimur Beg, even when on the throne, had assumed any other title than that of Mírza. His reasons for this assumption he does not explain. But, as Sultan Husein Mírza, who had long been regarded as the head of the family of Taimur, was dead, and his children slain or dispersed; and, as he himself was the only individual of that great House who now filled a throne, it is probable that he imagined it might be advantageous to his interest, as it was flattering to his vanity, to assume some title that might mark the high eminence on which he stood as the head of so illustrious a dynasty.*

Discontent of Báber's Moghuls.

But fate was not yet tired of persecuting Báber. Not long after his return to his capital, he was involved in new dangers. He had owed his success in Kábul chiefly to the troops who had revolted from Khosrou Shah, and joined him, as he travelled with a handful of ragged and wayworn followers, from Karatigín to the Hindú-kúsh mountains. The most powerful body that had come over to him consisted of some tribes of Moghuls, who, under their native chiefs, had for some time possessed a great ascendency near Hissár and Kunduz. He had besides been joined by some unsettled Turkomans, and others, from the same quarter. All these, under Khosrou Shah, had lived nearly at free quarters, and had been unlimited lords of the country and its wealth. Báber, who during the whole course of his life observed a mild but steady discipline, and was scrupulous in defending his subjects from oppression, after taking these bands into his service, had upon many occasions been compelled to check their marauding habits, and to punish their licentiousness

had assumed the name of Sultan; but, that title being often used by secondary Tartar chiefs, and their sons, Báber probably considered it as inferior or common. *Khákán e Mansúr*, which was the title employed by Sultan Husein Mírza, nearly corresponds with that of Emperor.

* Báber's Mem. p. 233.

BOOK II. A. D. 1508.

with considerable severity. Whatever was the cause, however, they became tired of their new service and new master, — no extraordinary event at a period in which the common ties even of regular allegiance seem to have been loosened in a singular degree, in all the countries between the Sirr, the Caspian, and the Indus.

They conspire against him.

It appears that these Moghul chiefs, with the leaders of the Kundúzis and Hissáris, had not only resolved to renounce their allegiance to Báber, but had joined in a plot for his destruction. Their plan was to restore Abdal-Rízák Mírza, the late king of Kábul, to his throne and dominions; and, besides this, to put him in possession of Kunduz and Khutlán, on the other side of the mountains. They looked back with regret to those rich countries from which most of them had lately fled, and which they had ruled so long, under the authority of Khosrou Shah, so much to their own comfort, so little to that of the wretched inhabitants. The conspirators and their followers amounted at first to two or three thousand excellent soldiers, who were lying in the suburbs of Kábul, and in the neighbourhood. Báber's army was encamped not far from Kábul, after a successful expedition against the Mehmend Afgháns. He had been repeatedly put upon his guard, and hints of what was going on had been given him. But, with that frankness and freedom from suspicion which were a part of his character, he had refused to credit the reports. He was therefore taken by surprise. A party of the conspirators had been placed in ambush to seize him, while he was on his way, by night, from the Char Bagh palace, without the city, to another within the walls.* He made his escape with difficulty, and reached the camp. When the revolt of the Moghul chiefs was known there, the effect produced by the news was most unfavourable. Some of his followers

* Probably about Sefer or Rebi 1508). (A. H. 914, June or July, A. D.

were panic-struck, not knowing the extent of the defection; others were probably connected with the disaffected. In the course of the night following that on which the revolt of the Moghuls became known, so many both of the officers and men disappeared, that, in the morning, he could not muster more than five hundred horse. It was not personal fear or disaffection alone that led to this general defection. Many, even of his bravest and most attached troops, deserted and repaired to Kábul, to be near their families; anxious to save them from the outrages to which the wives and children of such as remained with the Emperor were likely to be exposed from the unbridled licence of the rebellious Moghuls. The camp bazár was plundered.*

Báber's valour.

The details of Báber's contest with the revolted chieftains have not been preserved. His own commentaries are interrupted at the moment of the breaking out of the conspiracy, and an hiatus of eleven years follows, which we can but imperfectly supply from any other quarter. It appears that, in spite of the reduced state of his force, he lost no time, but, with his accustomed spirit, marched straight against the insurgents. This was one of his most desperate rencounters; and much of the final success that crowned his arms was due to his singular skill in the use of his sword, to his bodily strength, and to his personal gallantry. After a long and desperate combat, which was fought hand to hand, he broke and routed the foe. Báber, in that action, is said to have engaged, in single combat, five different champions of the enemy most eminent for their prowess; and to have slain or put them all to flight in succession.† His heroism and

* Báber's Mem. pp. 233—235.

† The names of the five champions are given, with some variation, by different authors. They were Ali Beg Shebgúr, Muhammed Ali Sheibáni (or Sistáni), Názer Behader Uzbek, Yakub Beg Báberjeng, and Abdalla Sef-sheken (Fe-

BOOK II.

A. D. 1508.

The revolt quelled.

desperation appalled his enemies, and reanimated his followers. Success crowned his arms. The Moghuls were defeated, after a long and severe struggle; and fled from Kábul. Abdal Rizák, his rival, fell into his hands in the battle, and was pardoned. But, having soon after entered into new cabals, and again risen in arms, he was seized and put to death; and Báber once more reigned the undisputed sovereign of Kábul and Ghazni.*

Affairs of Badakhshán.

While he thus established himself more firmly than ever in his new dominions, his cousin, Khan Mírza, had succeeded in mounting the throne of Badakhshán. It has been mentioned, that he set out from Kábul for that country, when Sheibáni Khan was besieging Kandahár; and Báber, doubtful to which side to turn, had finally resolved on marching for the Indus. Badakhshán had long been in a state of confusion, and various competitors had aimed at the sovereignty. After the expulsion of Khosrou Shah, the Uzbeks had attempted to conquer it, and failed. Násir Mírza, Báber's youngest brother, had been more fortunate; having been joined by several chiefs, he was acknowledged as king, and for a short period governed the country; but, as we have seen, was finally expelled by the Amírs, for alleged misgovernment, not many months before this time. The troubles still continued; and Shah Begum, who was the daughter of Shah Sultan Muhammed, King of Badakhshán, incited her grandson, Khan Mírza, the son of her own daughter by the late Sultan Mahmúd Mírza of Samarkand and Hissár, to try his fortune in her father's hereditary dominions. Shah Begum was a woman of ambition. Her father's family boasted of their descent from Alexander the Great. She con-

rishta and Kháfi Khan). Most authors speak of them as having been all slain; Mírza Haider says, slain or put to flight.

* Tar. Resh. f. 161.; Briggs's Ferishta, vol. ii. p. 29.; Kháfi Khan, f. 20.

CHAP. III.

A. D. 1508.

tended that they had swayed the sceptre of Badakhshán for three thousand years; that, though herself a female, and so incapable of filling the throne, the same incapacity did not extend to her grandson, Khan Mírza; and that, beyond doubt, her countrymen, who were devotedly attached to their ancient race of princes, would gladly welcome him. Báber had given his consent, and Khan Mírza set out,—accompanied by his grandmother, as well as by Mehr-nigár Khánum, his aunt, who, in spite of her nephew Báber's advice and remonstrances, also insisted on accompanying him.

Khan Mírza sets out to conquer it; A. H. 913, A. D. 1507.

They found the country nearly partitioned into three parts. Mírza Ababeker, the ruler and tyrant of Káshghar, had seized all the Upper Hazáras of Badakhshán *; the low grounds and the plain towards Kunduz, the richest part of the country, were in the occupation of the Uzbeks; while, one Rázi-ed-dín, a Musulman heretic †, who had been called in from Sistán, possessed a large portion of the intermediate country, especially towards Khutlán. The portion that still remained in

Its divided state.

* *Hazáraját báládest*. The upper districts in Badakhshán were called *Hazáras*.

† Rázi-ed-dín was a Chirághkúsh (or lamp-extinguisher), a sect of the Maláhida, or heretics, which is described as the very worst of all heathenism. According to the imputations of their enemies, they held the world to be eternal, and did not believe in the resurrection, or in a future life; they said, that, in the prophet's time it was incumbent on all to follow the ordinances of the law; but that, at the present time, the only duty incumbent on man is to study the dictates of sound and honest reason, and to act in conformity to them; that all other commands are futile; that sexual intercourse is not dependent on marriage, nor is kindred a bar to it, whatever be the degree; travellers they put to death to ensure their final salvation. Tar. Resh. f. 171. 178, 179. There is evidently some inconsistency in this account of their tenets. Their name, of Chirághkúsh, was given from the practice said to exist at their religious meetings, where men and women met, by night, and where, on the lamp being extinguished, indiscriminate indulgence followed. This is a calumny with which many different sects have been assailed,—from the time of the ancient Christians, whose love-feasts were so misrepresented, down to that of the Manicheans and Anabaptists. The doctrines of these Maláhida bear a resemblance to those of the Ismáilía sect, of which they were probably a division.

BOOK II. A. D. 1508.

the power of the old inhabitants was held by a number of petty chieftains and highlanders, proud of their independence. These chieftains, on the failure of the direct male line of the ancient dynasty, had started up in that rugged and mountainous region, and acted each as an absolute prince, in his own domain of spreading strath or narrow glen, with its adjoining hills. Of these, the most powerful and the ablest, at this time, was Zobeir of Rágh, a man of no family, but who, by his conduct and valour, soon gained the ascendency over most of the others.

Khan Mírza becomes king.

Khan Mírza's first entrance into the country was not prosperous. He had pushed forward to meet with Zobeir, and to announce the coming of the Begum, when he fell in with a detachment of the army of Ababeker, which attacked and dispersed his few followers. He himself fled, and escaped to Zobeir. Shah Begum, his aunt, and the other ladies who followed behind, were surprised and carried off to Ababeker, in whose prisons they died, after much cruel suffering. Zobeir, at first, treated the Mírza with some honour and respect; but soon, finding probably that his presence, deprived of his mother's influence, did not add so much to the means of resisting the invaders as had been expected, ceased to show him even the most ordinary attention, reduced his establishment to two or three servants, and seems to have kept him as a prisoner at large. After some time, however, Yusef Ali Gokuldásh, an old and attached servant of Khan Mírza, formed a conspiracy against Zobeir, whom he assassinated by night, and succeeded in raising his master to the throne of Badakhshán, which he continued to hold for about twelve years, down to the period of his death.*

* Báber's Mem. pp. 231. 12.; Tar. Resh. f. 160, 161. 172. 178. 197, 198.; Ferishta, vol. ii. p. 3. Kháfi Khan, f. 20. He seems to have died A. H. 926, (A. D. 1520). Briggs's Ferishta, vol. ii. p. 37.; Tar. Resh. f. 284.

CHAP. III.

Visited by Khan Mírza.

Though Khan Mírza thus attained his immediate object, his situation in Badakhshán was far from being enviable. Most of the inhabitants, even in the districts held by Ababeker and the Uzbeks, as they detested the government of strangers, were indeed secretly attached to him, but dared not declare themselves. He maintained himself in Kila-Zefer*, a strong castle which had been built by Mobárek Shah, one of the chieftains of Badakhshán, on whose death it fell to Zobeir, by whom he was slain; and it had now come to Khan Mírza, who made it his capital. Here, about a year after his conquest, he was visited by two men who afterwards became remarkable in Asiatic history.

The one was Sultan Saíd Khan, a son of the younger Khan, who, when defeated by his brother, Sultan Mansúr, in the desert, had fled to Andeján; and afterwards, escaping from Jáni Beg Sultan, then the ruler of that kingdom, who had orders from Sheibáni to put him to death, had made his way to Kila-Zefer. Here he was received with kindness by his cousin Khan Mírza, who treated him as well as his very straitened circumstances permitted. He remained with him two or three weeks; and, during that short period a party who were about the Mírza, and considered him to be a weak man, and ill-fitted for governing such a country, offered the sovereignty of Kila-Zefer to the Khan, "not half a loaf," says the historian, "presented on the charger of solicitation." He declined it; saying, that, to accept their offer would be unjust and unkind to his cousin, who had already endured so many troubles; and continued his journey to Kábul.†

A. H. 914.
A. D. 1508.

And by Mírza Haider.

Eighteen days after Sultan Saíd's departure, arrived the other fugitive, Mírza Haider. When Sheibáni

* While Mobárek was building it, he was attacked by the Uzbeks, whom he defeated; hence the name, Kila-zefer, *Castle of victory*. He was of a family called Mozefferi, which formed another coincidence. Tar. Reshidi, f. 172.

† Tar. Resh. ff. 173—176.

BOOK II.

A.D. 1508 -9.

Khan made that prince's father be put to death in Khorásán, he despatched orders to his nephew, Obeid-ulla Sultan of Bokhára, to drown Mírza Haider, then only a boy, in the Amu, while on his way to Khorásán. Though Obeid-ulla had married Mírza Haider's sister, he durst not disobey the dreaded command. Intelligence of the father's death had, however, reached one of the great spiritual guides of that city; and, under his direction, Moulána Muhammed Kázi, his disciple, and the tutor of Mírza Haider, exposed himself to all the risk of carrying off the young orphan.* He succeeded, and, after many difficulties and dangers, reached Kila-Zefer, where they were received by Khan Mírza, who was Haider's cousin, with as much hospitality and kindness as his poor means allowed. They found him with the name of sovereign, indeed, but surrounded by factious and turbulent men, and with a very narrow
A. D. 1508 -9. territory. He passed his time in little comfort, and was sore tried and distressed. He got over that winter in the best way he could; and, in the beginning of next spring, Shah Rázi-ed-dín having quarrelled with his

* The secret information had reached Hazret Moulána, a spiritual guide of great fame. Mírza Haider's tutor, Moulána Muhammed, having called on him, was asked,—when he meant to set out for Khorásán,—and answered, "In the course of a few days." The saintly man bid him return in an hour, as he had something to say to him. In about an hour, when Hazret Moulána's levée had left him, and only his confidential attendants were present, he asked Muhammed,—how he had suffered Muhammed Husein Mírza to go to Khorásán? "And now the Mírza's son, too, was going the same road." Moulána Muhammed replied,—that he let him go, trusting to the protection of God. The answer of Hazret Moulána was full of true piety and sound sense. Citing the example of the prophet Muhammed, who, *trusting in God,* fled from the heathen of Mekka, he added, "My advice is this. Trusting in God take the Mírza's son, and flee with him; and if any alarm or danger follows, I am answerable for your security. But there must be no delay." Moulána Muhammed, struck with his words, instantly set about concerting means for the escape, which he so successfully effected. The circumstances of it, as well as those of Sultan Saíd's, as related at great length by Mírza Haider, are possessed of a very deep interest.—Tar. Resh. ff. 165—175.

followers, they cut off his head, and brought it to Khan Mírza.

CHAP. III.

A. D. 1509.

Khan Mírza's indigent circumstances.

This revolution increased his territory, and somewhat bettered his circumstances; yet we may judge of the difficulties of this petty king by the fact, that when, in the course of the ensuing summer, a firmán came from Báber, desiring Mírza Haider to be sent to Kábul, there was a long and troublesome search before a single respectable coat could be procured for him. In the end of autumn, however, when he had spent about a year in Badakhshán, he was despatched with seventeen followers. "We had two horses among us," says the Mírza, "but no furnishings for the journey; insomuch that I had nothing on which to rest at night. Moulána Muhammed, who was a sort of father among us, had only a common coarse shawl, such as is worn by the lowest class in Badakhshán; whence some notion may be formed of the condition of the others." *

A. H. 915, Rejeb. End of October, A. D. 1509.

Mírza Haider's reception by Báber.

Mírza Haider arrived in Kábul when Báber, having defeated the rebellion of the Moghuls, enjoyed, for about two years, more repose than at most other periods of his reign. It is seldom that, in such distant transactions, we have so full an opportunity of entering into the private life and character of an eastern prince, as, in this instance, the narrative of Mírza Haider affords us. Some allowance must be made for the ornate, and, sometimes perhaps, inflated style of oriental writing. "When we reached Kábul," says he, "Shiram Taghái, who was my maternal uncle, as well as the Padshah's, came out in Istakbál (honorary procession) to receive me; and conveyed me to his house, where I was honourably entertained. The Padshah also sent to announce, that, in three days. the fortunate hour for my being presented would arrive, when he would send for me.

"The full moon of my fortune was now freed from

* Tar. Resh. ff. 165—179.

BOOK II.

A. D. 1509.

eclipse, and began to rise on the ascendant to full prosperity. An order arrived for my waiting on the Emperor. When I came into the presence, his Majesty's happiness-diffusing eye, which fell on me, began, from excess of kindness and extreme affection, to shed its pearls and rubies of price and felicity upon me. He extended to me the hand of favour and of good-fortune. After I had bent the knee, I went forward, and he took me to the breast of affection, and clasped me to the bosom of fatherly love; and there held me for some time, not suffering me to fall back, and to show the accustomed marks of respect; but made me sit down by his side, and, with a strong feeling of tender-hearted emotion, still continued regarding me with the same benevolent look, while tears flowed as before. 'How much,' said he, 'have you endured, from the martyrdom of the distinguished Beg, and of the Khan your uncle, and from the slaughter of your other relations. Praise be to God! that you have at length reached me in safety. Do not allow yourself to be too much dejected by their loss; for, believe me, I stand in their place, and whatever favour or affection you could have looked for from them, that and more will I show you.' By expressions such as these he soothed me, so that the sense of loneliness, of ruin, and banishment was driven from my mind. 'And who,' said he, 'took and carried you away?' I answered, 'My tutor, Moulána Muhammed Sadr.' 'Send for him,' he said. The Moulána was brought. As soon as his eye fell upon him, 'And this,' he said, 'is Moulána Muhammed Sadr?' He called him forward, and loaded him with praises. He inquired the particulars of our adventures, which the Moulána detailed. He bestowed suitable favours upon him, and sent him away delighted. He then said to me, 'You have not yet waited on Sultan Saíd Khan,' and ordered one of his principal officers to show me the way to his residence. I accompanied him, and had the pleasure of waiting on the Khan also.

"When I took leave of his Majesty to go home, I still experienced the imperial favour. As I came out, a nobleman approached, and having saluted and embraced me with the utmost respect, said, 'The mansion which the Emperor has appointed for you, I will show you.' He led me to the palace assigned me, which was extremely elegant. The rooms were spread with carpets, and a masnad was fitted up with the utmost care and taste. Furniture of every kind, with store of provisions and clothes, servants and attendants to such an extent that everything was perfect, were all prepared and ready for my reception. It may be imagined how much I enjoyed this rapid transition to such plenty, ease, and abundance, from the bodily suffering and actual want, as well as the confinement of the mind, as to a cage, that I had so long endured. I possessed all that fancy could desire. How can I sufficiently thank God for the change.

"In this way, I remained with the Emperor, passing my time in the enjoyment of perfect quiet and happiness. He watched over my education; and ever, with kindness and courtesy, by the promise of favour, or the threat of some privation, incited me to the acquisition of knowledge and virtue; and if he saw in me, at any time, some little thing that was commendable, he praised it heartily, and showed it off to every one, inviting commendation. During that period, he treated me with such favour and kindness as a tender father shows his beloved son and heir. It was a sad day that deprived me of my father; but, through the unremitting attention of the Emperor, I never felt the loss; and, from this time till A. H. 918, during which I remained in his service, if he rode out, I rode beside him, or, if he enjoyed himself in society, I too was of the party. Indeed, on no occasion did he ever separate me from himself, but when I was at my lessons; and, as soon as my lesson was done, he sent some one to call me. During the

BOOK II. A. D. 1509-10.

whole time of my stay with him, he always conducted himself towards me in this manner, with parental observance and affection."*

Sultan Saíd's.

The same honourable testimony to Báber's amiable disposition, was borne by Sultan Saíd Khan, who at this time was a young man in the full vigour of life. "When the Khan reached Kábul," says his historian, "he was received by the Padshah in the most friendly and respectful manner. Often in future life did he say, 'During my residence at Kábul, I passed my days in such entire absence of care, as I never did at any other time, or do now.'" He proceeds to explain the uninterrupted delight in which, for upwards of two years†, he spent his days; occupied with a continued series of enjoyment, love, and wine, gardens, flowers, and banquets; no care but what was to be the next pleasing engagement, never a head-ache, but from the wine-cup of the preceding night; that all the cares of government were the Emperor's, his was the pleasure; that every person and circumstance was favourable, so that he let loose and unrestrained the reins of pleasure, forming such intimacies as he liked, while the Emperor befriended him and supplied the means; that, with Báber, he lived in the most perfect confidence, and even intimacy, as his comrade and friend.‡

These two portraits, different as they are, need no comment. They present the character of the young Emperor, still only twenty-six years of age, in the most amiable light, and prove how free he, and some at least of the fugitive princes who filled his court, were, from the jealousies and fears that infest Asiatic palaces. Nor should it be forgotten, that the youth and the boy whom he thus patronised and cherished, became two of the ablest and most accomplished men and princes of their age.

* Tar. Reshidi, ff. 180, 181.

† He was with Báber from Shaban, A. H. 914, to Ramzán, A. H. 916. (Nov. 1508, to Dec. 1510). Tar. Resh. f. 178.

‡ Tar. Resh. ff. 176—178.

CHAPTER IV.

SHAH ISMAEL AND SHEIBÁNI.—BÁBER IN MÁWERANNAHER.

SHEIBÁNI'S UNSUCCESSFUL CAMPAIGNS AGAINST THE KAIZÁKS AND THE HAZÁRAS.—HIS QUARREL WITH SHAH ISMAEL.—THEIR CORRESPONDENCE.—THE SHAH INVADES KHORÁSÁN.—MARCHES TO MERV, WHICH SHEIBÁNI DEFENDS.—BATTLE OF MERV.—DEATH OF SHEIBÁNI.—DESERTION OF HIS MOGHULS.—BÁBER CROSSES THE MOUNTAINS.—HIS VIEWS ON MÁWERANNAHER.—STATE OF THE UZBEKS.—FERGHÁNA RECOVERED.—OPERATIONS IN HISSÁR.—BÁBER DEFEATS THE UZBEKS—TAKES BOKHÁRA AND SAMARKAND.—UZBEKS EXPELLED FROM MÁWERANNAHER.—STATE OF THAT COUNTRY.—RELIGIOUS FEUDS.—NEW INVASION OF THE UZBEKS.—BÁBER DEFEATED AT KUL-MÁLEK.—ABANDONS SAMARKAND AND BOKHÁRA.—JOINED BY PERSIAN AUXILIARIES.—ADVANCES ANEW TOWARDS BOKHÁRA.—SACK OF KARSHI.—BATTLE OF GHAJHDEWÁN.—BÁBER DRIVEN BACK TO HISSÁR.—CONSPIRACY AND REVOLT OF THE MOGHULS.—THEIR TYRANNY IN HISSÁR.—FAMINE AND PESTILENCE.—MOGHULS EXPELLED BY OBEID KHAN.—BÁBER DRIVEN FROM MÁWERANNAHER; RETURNS TO KÁBUL.

CHAP. IV.

Sheibáni completes the conquest of Khorásán, A.H. 913, A.D. 1507.

BUT great events were now preparing in the West. Sheibáni Khan, after retiring from Kandahár, had marched to destroy such members of the family of Sultan Husein Mírza as were still left. He himself and the other Uzbek Sultans, in the course of the summer, spread their troops over Khorásán; and at Meshíd, Nishábúr, Asterábád, and Turshíz, had actions, in which the Chaghatái princes and their armies were uniformly defeated. Numbers were slain, and the survivors so dispersed as never to be able to assemble again in any force. Of all Sultan Husein's sons, Badi-ez-zemán alone survived; and he was driven into exile. In the course of the winter, Sheibáni repaired to Máweran-

BOOK II. naher, to check the Kaizáks, the old foes of his family,
A. D. 1510 who, from the Desht-Kipchak, had invaded his domi-
A. H. 914, A. D. 1508. nions; but he returned in the spring to Khorásán. It was during this summer that the death of the elder Khan and his family, and that of Muhammed Husein Doghlat, took place; as well as the flight of Sultan Saíd and of Mírza Haider. Sheibáni, on his return to the south, employed himself in the reduction of the strong fort of Kelát, in Khorásán, and in settling the country.

Campaign against the Kaizáks, A. H. 915, A. D. 1509.

Next year, the good fortune of Sheibáni, hitherto almost uninterrupted, seemed to be on the wane. He marched against the Kaizáks. Although at that time Berendúk was the Khan, the whole business of the government was conducted by Kásim Khan, who was Khan in effect. Sheibáni, in spite of the extent of his power, was not able to cope with him. At that time, Kásim's army amounted to above two hundred thousand men. When it was winter, the rival chiefs withdrew from the field, and each took up his quarters in some situation that afforded food for his cattle. Sheibáni, whose horses and men were quite exhausted by their many and long marches, took his station at Kuruk-Kabái. But he did not there enjoy the repose he looked for. Having on one occasion detached a party of the best mounted of his troops to proceed to a distance on a plundering expedition, they were at first successful, and took a considerable booty and some prisoners. One day, however, when the detachment had halted to rest and feed their cattle, a false report was somehow spread among them, that Kásim Khan was in sight. In a moment, deserting not only the booty they had got, but their own baggage also, they galloped back in the utmost disorder to communicate the information to Sheibáni. He, being unprepared to
A. H. 915, A. D. 1510. meet a foe so formidable as Kásim Khan, commanded an instant retreat; and the army, hurrying back, reached

Samarkand in the end of the winter, in a state of complete disorganisation. Early in the spring, he went on to Khorásán.* CHAP. IV. A. D. 1510.

Campaign against the Hazáras, A. H. 916, A. D. 1510.

In the beginning of summer, Sheibáni led an army against the Hazáras in the mountains east from Herát; but not a trace of them was to be found. They had disappeared, and withdrawn themselves within the recesses of their hills. Unable to discover their retreats, he began to march back. His route lay where the river Helmed flows deep, through the precipitous fissures of the mountains. It was difficult to descend to its stream at all; and, even where a descent could be effected, the paths were so extremely narrow that it was altogether impossible, by them, to bring up water in sufficient quantities to supply an army like his. For several days, the troops were compelled to march on, thus tantalised, and subject to intense suffering from thirst. Numbers of the cattle perished, and the army returned to Khorásán in a shattered condition. As the winter was at hand, and two of his armies had been thus severely treated, he granted a general leave of absence to his troops, allowing every man to return for the winter to his own country and home, however distant.†

Shah Ismael Sefvi, of Persia,

Hardly were his troops dispersed, when he received the unexpected and unwelcome news that Shah Ismael Sefvi, the potent ruler of Persia, was in full march towards Khorásán, with his well-disciplined and veteran army.

When Sheibáni, after the total discomfiture of the sons of Sultan Husein Mírza, took possession of all that prince's dominions, his troops, in the wantonness of success, had plundered some parts of Shah Ismael's frontier; and, in particular, had passed the desert and ravaged the province of Kermán. Shah Ismael had

* Tar. Resh. ff. 162—181. † Ibid. ff. 181, 182.

BOOK II.

A.D. 1510.

Sends an envoy to Sheibáni.

His ancestors.

in consequence sent an envoy, whom he instructed to ask redress; or, at all events, to take measures to prevent a repetition of the injury to what he happened to call his "hereditary dominions." The sovereign of Persia was descended of a family that had originally become known by their ascetic piety, as holy and inspired men, who despised this world and its goods. Their contempt of wealth made them rich; and their eminence as saints enabled them to connect themselves in marriage with the great potentates of the age. Hence, not only was Shah Ismael descended from the seventh Imám, — a descent which shed the halo of sanctity around him,—but he was related to some of the most powerful princes of his time; his mother being the daughter, his grandmother the sister, of the celebrated Uzan Hasan, the chief of the Túrkománs of the White Sheep, — a prince whose sway extended over all Persia and many neighbouring provinces. Yet, though Shah Ismael's father, Haider Mírza, had placed himself at the head of a considerable army, composed in part of devotees attached to him, and had fought and fallen in battle, Shah Ismael was himself the first of the family who had attained to great temporal power. In early life, he had shared the misfortunes of his father and brothers, and had fallen into captivity. After his father's death, he was kept four years in prison. On the death of his elder brothers, being again free, he was placed at the head of their adherents, and in less than four years made himself master of all Persia. When he first came into contact with the Uzbek chief, he was still only twenty-four years of age, had latterly been prosperous in all his enterprises, and was full of the ardour and confidence of youth.*

Sheibáni's answer.

Sheibáni Khan, rendered arrogant by long success, and having his rivalry embittered by religious zeal, — as

* The Alem-arái Abási, f. 17. which contains the Persian account. Tar. Reshidi, ff. 182, 183.; Ferishta, vol. ii. p. 31.

Shah Ismael, by his victories, had given the ascendency in Persia to the tenets of the Shía sect, over what Sheibáni considered to be the orthodox Sunni doctrines, —returned for answer to the remonstrances made to him, that he did not understand on what Shah Ismael founded his claim to hereditary dominions; that sovereignty descended through the father, not the mother, —through males, not females; and, that the unequal match between his family and the females of Uzan Hasan's could confer no right. He reminded him of the saying, the son should follow his father's trade, the daughter her mother's; and insultingly sent him, as a present, a lady's veil and a beggar's dish; adding, "If thou hast forgot thy father's trade, this may serve to recal it to thy memory; but, if thou wouldst place thy foot on the steps of the throne, remember,

'"He that would clasp to his breast, Royalty as his bride,
Must woo her in the battle-fray, athwart sharp scymetars.'"

In conclusion, he remarked, that, as he intended soon, like a good Musulman, to perform the pilgrimage of Mekka, he would make a point of seeing him in his way through Irák. Having dismissed the Persian envoy, Sheibáni set out to join the army, which was at that moment marching against the Hazáras.

Shah Ismael's reply.

The youthful warrior, who professed to feel a pride in his descent from a family of holy dervishes, that gloried in their voluntary poverty, received the Uzbeks' taunts with affected humility. He returned for answer, That if every man was bound to follow his father's trade, all being sons of Adam, must adhere to that of prophets; that if hereditary descent conferred the only right to sovereignty, he did not see how it had descended from the Peshdádi to the Kyáni dynasties of Persia, or how it had come to Chengíz, or to him whom he addressed.

BOOK II.
A.D. 1510.

> "Boast not thyself, O, vain youth, of thy father, who is dead;
> Pride not thyself on bones, as if thou wert a dog."

That he, on his part, proposed making a pilgrimage to the shrine of the holy Imám Reza, at Meshíd*, where he would have an opportunity of waiting on the Khan. In return for his present, he sent him a spindle and distaff; and, alluding to his quotation, that Royalty must be wooed in the battle-field, he concluded, "And so say I also. Lo, I have tightened my girdle for a deadly contest, and have placed the foot of determination in the stirrup of victory. If thou wilt meet me face to face in fight, like a man, our quarrel will at once be decided. But if thou wouldst rather slink into a corner, then thou mayst find what I have sent thee of some use.

> '"We have sparred quite long enough, let us now exchange hard blows in the field.
> He who falls, borne down in the combat, let him fall.'"

Shah Ismael marches to Meshíd.

Having despatched this answer, without loss of time or waiting for a reply, Shah Ismael put his army in motion, and entered the territories of his enemy; sweeping before him the small detachments of the Uzbek army, which had been scattered over the country for the purpose of keeping it in subjection. They, at first, fell back and retreated on Herát. But Sheibáni, who had recently dismissed his army, at once perceived that he was not then in a condition to meet his adversary in the field. When he heard, therefore, of Shah Ismael's march upon Meshíd, to which he at once bent his course, he left Jan Vafa Mírza in Herát, and, with such of his troops as were at hand, set off for Merv, a city in the northern part of Khorásán, not far from the Amu, where he could easily receive reinforcements

* The shrine of Imám Reza at Meshíd is well known as a place of pilgrimage for all pious Shías. See a description of it in Mr. J. Baillie Fraser's amusing and instructive "Travels in Khorásán."

from his northern dominions ; or from which, if necessary, he could retire across the great river. Jan Vafá was not able to defend himself in Herát, but found himself compelled very speedily to follow Sheibáni.

CHAP. IV.

A. D. 1510.

And to Merv.

Shah Ismael overran Khorásán, as far as Meshíd, with little interruption. He visited the tomb of Imám Reza, and the holy places, with profound reverence and humility, bestowed rich presents on the guardians and servants of the shrine, and distributed alms profusely to the poor; after which he hastened towards Merv, in pursuit of Sheibáni, having sent on before him a strong force to clear the way. When they reached the pasture-grounds of Merv, Jan Vafá encountered them near Takerábád, not far from that city. A well-contested action ensued, in which the Persian general fell; but Jan Vafá and his Uzbeks were defeated, and pursued with great slaughter up to the walls of Merv. Sheibáni, whose army had not yet been sufficiently reinforced to enable him to keep the field, retired into the fort and city. He despatched expresses to hasten the return of his generals and chieftains from beyond the Amu, most of them having already reached home with their troops and their plunder. Shah Ismael, on his arrival, advancing up to the very gates of the town, pitched his tents and pavilions within sight of it, at a short distance. As both armies were composed of brave and veteran troops, many sharp skirmishes took place under the walls, in which numbers fell on both sides. Shah Ismael, seeing that operations were likely to be drawn out to a great length, in a desert country, where it was difficult to find provisions and provender for his army, and where he would soon be exposed to an attack from the whole united force of Máwerannaher and Túrkistán, resolved if possible to draw Sheibáni out into the open field. He pretended, therefore, to be under the necessity of retreating. He wrote to remind Sheibáni, that he had been rather more punctual to his engagements

Sheibáni retires into Merv.

Shah Ismael retreats.

BOOK II.

A. D. 1510.

than the Khan had been; since he had visited Khorásán, and performed the pilgrimage of Meshíd, though Sheibáni had shunned meeting him; and had also failed in his promise to visit Irák; he added, that he was now returning home, but would still be delighted to meet him whenever he went to Mekka. He then drew off all his forces from Merv, and marched towards the south, through the broken ground near the city.

Sheibáni follows.

The feint succeeded. The pickets of the Uzbek army reported that the Kezelbashes*, the name by which the Persian soldiers were known, were in full retreat. Sheibáni, stung with the taunts he had received, and eager to wipe off the disgrace of the campaign, marched out of Merv, and followed Shah Ismael, with twenty-five thousand horse†, and a number of the chiefs and grandees who had already joined him. Mír Kamber-Bi, and some others of his most experienced officers, represented to him, that, as the troops of Samarkand and Bokhára, to the number of twenty thousand men, had arrived and encamped within a distance of little more than four miles, it would be advisable, before engaging in battle, to form a junction with them; that the enemy, who were now undoubtedly retiring, could not escape, and might, even without a pitched battle, be destroyed in detail, before they could reach Irák. But Sheibáni, whose passions were excited, and who was ardent for action, replied that theirs was a holy war; and that there was no use in sharing the glory and the plunder with the other Sultans; and the army marched on.

Battle of Merv.

A small body of a few hundred horse, who were artfully presented to the advancing enemy by Shah Ismael, were soon broken, and, flying in disorder, led the Uzbeks forward in pursuit, till they had cleared the broken ground and pushed on to a river ten or twelve miles

* Red-heads.

† The Tarikh Alem-a-rái says thirty thousand.

from Merv. Encouraged by the slightness of the opposition presented to them, the Uzbeks passed the river, and had advanced into the open plain, when they suddenly saw the enemy's army drawn up ready for action.* Shah Ismael, who had thrown a division of his army into their rear, to seize the bridge by which they had passed, now attacked them in front with a column of seventeen thousand cavalry. Sheibáni Khan, who had probably pushed forward in the belief that he could always fall back at pleasure, now felt himself compelled to engage. The battle was fought at Mahmúdábád of Merv. The Uzbeks, though surrounded, combated for some time with their usual bravery; but, in the end, the regulated valour of the well-trained Kezelbashes prevailed. The Uzbeks were driven back, and the rout was complete. Sheibáni Khan found his retreat cut off. Attended by about five hundred men, chiefly the sons of Sultans, the heads of tribes, and men of distinction, he was forced to take shelter in an inclosure, which had been erected for accommodating the cattle of travellers and of the neighbouring peasants. There they were closely pursued, attacked, and hard pressed. The inclosure had no gate on the farther side. When they saw no hope left of retrieving the day, the Khan and the other fugitives attempted to escape, by leaping over the wall of the inclosure towards the bank of the river; but fell in heaps on each other, and the Khan was overlaid and smothered by the numbers who crowded after him.

CHAP. IV.

A.D. 1510.

Death of Sheibáni;

When the contest was over, the body of Sheibáni was sought for, and was disentangled from the heap of slain by which it was covered. His head was cut off and presented to Shah Ismael, who ordered the lifeless trunk to be dismembered, and the limbs to be sent to different parts of his empire, to be exposed to the popular gaze.

his body dismembered.

* A. H. 916, Shaban 29 (A. D. 1510, Dec. 2.). The Leb-ul-towárikh makes the date Shaban 20. Friday.

BOOK II.

A.D. 1510.

The skin of his head was stuffed with hay, and sent to Sultan Bajazet*, the Turkish Emperor of Constantinople. The skull, set in gold, was made into a drinking cup, which the Shah was proud of displaying at his great entertainments. An anecdote, illustrative of the barbarous manners of the Persians, is recorded on this occasion. Agha Rustam Roz-efzun, who had made himself master of the province of Mazenderán, and who still held out in his mountain fastnesses against Shah Ismael, had been in the constant habit of saying, that his hand was on the skirts of Sheibáni Khan's garment; an idiomatic expression, to signify, that he clung to him for assistance and protection. One day, when that chief was sitting in state at a grand festival, surrounded by the nobles of Taberistán, a special messenger†, sent by Shah Ismael, advanced fearlessly into his presence, and, with a loud voice, delivered a message from the Shah, concluding, "Though thy hand was never on the hem of Sheibáni Khan's robe, yet his is now on thine;" and, with these words, flung the rigid hand of Sheibáni on the skirt of the Prince's robe, and withdrew through the midst of the assembly. Not a word was spoken by any one, nor an effort made to detain him; all remained fixed in astonishment, and he escaped uninjured. The incident is said to have made a deep impression on the health of the Prince of Mazenderán, who, soon after, was brought to yield one half of his territories to the Shah.

Such was the fate of Muhammed Sheibáni Khan, the man who had brought so many calamities on Báber, who had stripped him of his paternal kingdom, and sent him out an exile and an adventurer, into foreign lands.

Consternation of the Uzbeks.

When the fugitives brought news to Merv of the event of the battle, the greatest consternation prevailed; every man, who was able, fled with his family and chil-

* Bayezíd. † Yesáwal.

dren, while numbers, who had no means of transport, left them to their fate. Obeidulla Sultan, of Bokhára, and Taimur Sultan, of Samarkand, the nephew and son of Sheibáni, who had arrived near Merv, entered the fort, carried away the Haram of Sheibáni and of some other chiefs of note, as well as whatever of value they could at the moment collect, and hurried off the same night. Numbers, however, were left behind. All the Uzbeks that were found in the place were put to the sword by the Kezelbashes, the women were carried into bondage. The inhabitants of Merv were included in the general massacre.

CHAP. IV.

A.D. 1510.

Desertion of the Moghuls.

Sheibáni Khan, ever jealous of the Moghuls in his service, had sent a great number of them to Khorásán, that they might be farther removed from the Khans of Moghulistán. These unwilling allies, who had now reached the banks of the Amu, gladly seized the opportunity of recovering their independence; and, to the number of twenty thousand men, separated from the Uzbeks, and set out for Kunduz, plundering on all sides as they went along.

Shah Ismael goes to Herát.

Immediately after this decisive battle, the Uzbeks retired in every direction from Khorásán. Shah Ismael soon after repaired to Herát, where he spent the winter.

Persecution.

His first care was to introduce the observances of the Shía sect into his new dominions; and, as he was met by a bigotry and a firmness equal to his own, he did not accomplish that object without a severe and cruel persecution, in the course of which the blood of many men eminent for their piety and their virtues flowed, and many distinguished names were added to the list of martyrs for the pure Sunni faith.*

* The chief authorities for the quarrel with Shah Ismael, and the defeat and death of Sheibáni, are the Taríkh Alem-arái Abási, ff. 17—19.; and Tar. Reshídi, ff. 181—183. Besides these, Ferishta and Kháfi Khan, the Genealogical History of Abulgházi, p. ix. c. 1., and the Taríkhe-Sind have been consulted.

BOOK II.

A.D. 1510.

Báber gets news of the battle of Merv, A.H. 916, 29 Shaban, A.D. 1510, 2 Dec.

The battle of Merv was fought on the 2nd of December, and, in the course of the same month, a messenger arrived at the palace in Kábul, bringing by express a letter for the Emperor from Khan Mírza. His feet were frost-bitten and his strength exhausted, as he had crossed the passes of the Hindú-kúsh, though deep covered with snow. The letter communicated intelligence of the battle of Merv, and the defeat of Sheibáni, whose fate, when the letter was written, was still unknown. It added, that the Uzbek Amírs, on receiving the news, had abandoned Kunduz; and that nearly twenty thousand Moghuls had separated from the Uzbeks, after their defeat, and were arrived in Kunduz, to which place Khan Mírza had himself repaired. He added, that he was ready to join the Emperor with all his forces, to aid him in recovering the kingdom of his forefathers.

Crosses to Kunduz.

A.H. 916, 1 Shawal, A.D. 1511, 2 Jan.

Nothing could be more in accordance with the wishes of Báber. "All winter as it was," he set out, without hesitation, by the Ab-dera pass, which he supposed to be at that season the most practicable.* He spent the Id, or Festival for the conclusion of the fast of Ramzán, near Bámián; it being still only a month since the defeat and death of his grand enemy. He

* A circumstance that preceded the Emperor's departure from Kábul is worthy of notice, as marking his character. "Meanwhile," says Mírza Haider, "the Emperor resolved to march to Kunduz. It was now about the winter solstice, and the season had all the violence of December; so, speaking tenderly to me, he said, 'The difficulty of the roads and the intensity of the cold are excessive. You will therefore stay this winter in Kábul; and, when spring comes, and the severity of winter is over, you can come and rejoin me.' On hearing this, I remonstrated with him; 'Torn from my relations and country,' said I, 'I have supported the miseries of my lot by the help of your majesty's kindness. If separated from you, how shall I ever be able to exist, in my orphan loneliness?' When he perceived that grief at the prospect of being left behind in Kábul was preying upon my mind and breaking my heart, he ordered such arrangements to be made for my going as the time allowed, and carried me along with him to Kunduz."—Tar. Reshídi, ff. 204, 205.

reached Kunduz early in January; and, having halted there a short time to recover from the fatigue of the journey, and to mature his plans, towards the end of winter he crossed the Amu,—in order to seize the strong fort of Hissár-Shádmán, and to expel Khamzeh Sultan and Mehdi Sultan, two of the most eminent of the Uzbek Sultans, who were in possession of the country.

CHAP. IV.

A.D. 1511.

Marches of Báber and Khamzeh, A.H. 917, A.D. 1511.

When Khamzeh Sultan heard of his approach, leaving a garrison in Hissár, which he had put in a state of defence, he marched to Wakhsh. Báber, on reaching Desht Kulak, one of the chief towns of Khutlán, was informed of this movement, and the same night set out to surprise his camp. At sunrise, he arrived on the ground where he expected to find him; but no enemy was to be seen. Some peasants were at length found, who communicated the information that Khamzeh Sultan, getting notice, about afternoon prayers on the preceding day, that his Majesty was lying at Desht Kulak, had instantly set off for that place. Báber without loss of time followed, by the route that Khamzeh had taken; and, about noon-day prayers, reached the ground he had himself originally quitted. It had been a game of cross-purposes. Khamzeh, on his side, had reached about sunrise the ground left by the Emperor, had found him gone, had pursued in the track of his march, and regained his own ground at noon. The consequences were no less singular. Báber and his officers had imagined that Khamzeh was not yet strong enough to resist them; and Khamzeh on his side, imagining that Báber could have brought but few troops with him from Kábul, and that the Moghuls were not yet in a condition to take the field, expected an easy conquest. Both, finding themselves mistaken, were alarmed, and retreated the same night; the Emperor to Kunduz, Khamzeh to Hissár. Both, at the moment, believed they had made a great escape;

Báber recrosses to Kunduz.

BOOK II.

A.D. 1511.

and each, in a few days, heard of the flight of the other.*

Embassy from Shah Ismael.

While Báber lay at Kunduz, an embassy arrived from Shah Ismael, bringing the Emperor's sister, Khánzada Begum, with rich presents and tenders of amity. It will be recollected that when Báber was compelled to abandon Samarkand, after defending it bravely for five months, she had been left behind, and became the wife of Sheibáni, who had divorced her aunt that he might marry her. By the Uzbek Khan she had a son, Khurram-shah, a promising youth, to whom he gave the government of Balkh, but who died young, a year or two after his father. Sheibáni, who was jealous of the attachment the Begum was known to entertain for her brother, fearing she might join in intrigues to his injury, divorced her, and married her to Syed Háde, a member of a religious family. The Syed had fallen in the battle of Merv, and the Begum became a prisoner in the hands of the Persians. Being soon recognised as the sister of Báber, she was treated with the greatest respect by Shah Ismael, who was disposed to cultivate that prince's friendship He now sent her, with all her property and servants, under a proper escort, to her brother. Báber informs us, that, on hearing of her approach, he rode out to meet her, accompanied by a favourite servant well-known to the princess. But so great a change had ten eventful years produced on the appearance of them both, though the Emperor was yet only twenty-eight years old, that, even after he had addressed his sister, neither she nor her attendants recognised either of them. Khánzada Begum passed the rest of her life at Kábul, beloved and honoured by her brother, whom she survived many years.†

Báber's embassy to the Shah.

Báber, who at this very time was meditating to send an embassy to Shah Ismael, did not neglect the occa-

* Tar. Resh. ff. 185, 186.

† Báber's Mem. p. 10.; Tar. Resh. f. 186.

sion, which that prince's generous proceedings now afforded him, to despatch Khan Mírza, with presents, as his ambassador, to thank the Shah for his courtesy to the Begum, to convey Báber's congratulations on his splendid victory over their common enemy, and to dispose him to lend assistance in the attempt, which he now meditated, to recover the kingdom of Máweran-naher.* CHAP. IV. A.D. 1511.

State of the Uzbeks.

The Emperor had already discovered, that, though the Uzbeks had suffered a severe defeat, their power was yet unbroken. On the death of Sheibáni, the Uzbek chiefs assembled to elect a Supreme Khan in his place. Their choice, according to the usages of the Uzbeks, was decided by a mixed consideration of age and family. They did not raise to the dignity of Khan, Taimur, the son of Sheibáni, but Kuchum, a son of Abulkhair Khan, and who was the eldest Sultan of the family. Taimur Sultan, the son of Sheibáni, ruled in Samarkand; Obeidulla Sultan, the son of Mahmúd Sultan, and nephew of Sheibáni, possessed Bokhára; Jani Beg Sultan, a son of Sheibáni's uncle, held Andeján,—while Kuchum probably occupied Túrkistán, and his son Siúnjek, Táshkend. Khamzeh Sultan and Mehdi Sultan were still in full force in Hissár and Cheghánián. The master-mind of Sheibáni was gone; but the veteran captains, and the physical force of the Uzbeks, still presented a formidable barrier to the progress of Báber. Though each chief was nearly independent in his own territories, all were ready to act in union when any assault was made from without, against any one member of the confederacy.

They make peace with the Shah, A.D. 1511.

Early in the spring, Shah Ismael set out to invade Máwerannaher, and had advanced along the roots of the Parapamisan range as far as Meimúna and Kara-

* Mírza Haider says, that Khan Mírza was sent with tenders of obedience and observance, and a request for assistance and aid.—Tar. Resh. f. 187.

BOOK II. A.D. 1511.

robat, when he was met by a mission sent by Taimur Sultan and other Uzbek chiefs, who had advanced to the banks of the Amu, to oppose his progress. They brought rich presents, and made proposals for a peace. Shah Ismael had important concerns which called him back to Azerbáiján and the frontiers of Turkey. Terms were soon concluded, by which it was agreed, that the Amu should be the line of separation between their dominions, and that all to the south of that river should belong to the Shah.* By this arrangement, the kingdom of Khwárazm, which had long been subject to Khorásán, fell to Shah Ismael; but being separated from that country by a wide desert, and the communication with it being difficult, it was, at no distant period, again overrun by the northern invaders. After making peace with the Uzbeks, Ismael Shah returned to Herát.

Ferghána recovered

While Báber was waiting to learn the result of his application to Shah Ismael for aid, a messenger arrived, from Syed Muhammed Mirza (brother of the late Muhammed Husein Mírza of Uratippa, and uncle of Mírza Haider) with the pleasing information that he had expelled the Uzbeks from the country of Ferghána.

by Syed Muhammed.

When Sheibáni Khan defeated the two Khans and took Táshkend, Syed Muhammed was in Kashan, so that he escaped being made prisoner. He afterwards joined the elder Khan in the desert; and remained some time, first with him, and afterwards with his son. Having again rejoined the Khan, whom he offended by the honest freedom of his advice, he was banished from his court, and forced to seek refuge with Jani Beg Sultan, the chief of Andeján. On the defeat of Sheibáni, when Báber entered the country of Hissár, a general council of the Uzbek Sultans was held in the spring at Samarkand. Jani Beg, who attended it, carried the

A.H. 917, A.D. 1511.

* Tar. Alem-araí, f. 18.

Syed along with him. The Sultans, in the course of their consultations, came to a resolution, that not a Moghul should be left alive in Máwerannaher. To this Jani Beg would not consent, and allowed the Syed and all the Moghuls in his service to go to Andeján, to join their families. The Syed, who was apprehensive that Jani Beg might alter his mind, proceeded with all haste to Andeján; and, soon after, what he dreaded did happen, as Jani Beg sent after the Moghuls, who were still on the road, and killed every man that was overtaken. The Syed, however, effected his escape and reached Andeján; where, being joined by the remnant of the Moghuls and by the inhabitants of the town, he succeeded in driving out the Uzbeks.

CHAP. IV.

A. D. 1511.

Treachery of the Moghuls.

Just before the news of this revolution reached Báber, he had been exposed to a new danger. The leaders of the Moghuls who had escaped from the Uzbek yoke, had waited upon Sultan Saíd Khan, a son of the younger Khan, who was now in the Emperor's camp, and told him, that, if he was willing, they were ready to make away with Báber, and to lay the reins of government at his feet; that their followers amounted to nearly twenty thousand good and effective men, while the Chaghatáis did not amount to five thousand. The Khan, who declined their offer, made answer, that while the hurricane of Sheibáni's invasion lasted, Baber Padshah had presented Kábul to him as an island, under shelter of which he had escaped the fury of the tempest; and that, now that the shore of prosperity was in sight, he could not be guilty of the ingratitude and perfidy of turning on his benefactor. The Khan, however, represented to the Emperor, through Mír Kásim Kochin,—who was his prime adviser, and who, though he could neither read nor write, was a man of talent and had an ingenious and elegant vein of wit,—that, as the Emperor's affairs were now prosperous and new tribes were joining him every day, the Khan might be

Sultan Saíd Khan sent to Andeján.

BOOK II.

A.D. 1511.

sent where he could have a separate command, and where his operations might be advantageous to both. As the news of the success in Ferghána arrived at this crisis, the Khan was nominated to the command in that country, and soon set out attended by all who chose to join him.*

Convention between the Shah and Báber.

After Sultan Saíd Khan had marched for Andejan, Khan Mírza arrived, with a part of the auxiliary force which had been sent by Shah Ismael. The Shah already complained that the Uzbeks had broken the treaty, by predatory inroads into his territory; and he had entered into an understanding with Báber, that that prince should retain whatever he conquered in Máwerannaher. Thus strengthened, the Emperor renewed active operations, and entered the country of Hissár. The Uzbeks on their side were not inactive. As they had ascertained that Shah Ismael had conceded the possession of Máwerannaher to Báber, they no longer apprehended an attack from him in person; and, their whole force being now disposable, they took their measures accordingly. It was resolved that Kuchum Khan and Siúnjek Khan should, in concert with Jani Beg, recover possesion of Ferghána; that Obeidulla Sultan should remain at Karshi; while Taimur Sultan, and other chiefs, should assist Khamzeh and Mehdi Sultans in driving the Emperor out of Hissár. Nor were they slow in carrying the concerted measures into effect. When the Emperor reached Pul-Sangín † on the Surkhab, he found that Khamzeh Sultan from Hissár had occupied it. He discovered also that the Uzbek army was far more numerous than he had supposed, and commanded by chiefs of the first distinction; and that to meet them in the field would be extremely dangerous. The enemy on their part, when informed of the inferiority of Báber's force, passed the river

Uzbek plan of campaign.

Báber forced to retreat;

* Tar. Resh. ff. 187, 188.

† Stone-Bridge.

lower down than (Pul-Sangín) the stone-bridge, by swimming. Intelligence of this movement having reached him about afternoon prayers, he instantly put his army in motion, and marched for Abdera, where the passes in the hills are extremely narrow and steep. All that night, and the succeeding day till noon, he continued marching with the utmost celerity, when he at length arrived at a position which the most experienced leaders considered to be very strong, and there took his ground.

takes up a position.

Towards midnight, news was brought that the Uzbeks were advancing in full force. The troops were instantly ordered to their posts, and remained under arms till day-break, ready for action. About sunrise, the advanced pickets reported that the enemy were in motion, and preparing to attack. Báber rode to an eminence to reconnoitre. He saw that there was only one, and that a narrow road by which the enemy could attack the hillock on which he was posted. Close by this was another hillock, divided from the first by a broad and deep ravine; and to this hillock also there was only one road. After the enemy had drawn out their ranks on the level ground below, they perceived that it was no easy task to mount the hill. Taimur Sultan (Sheibáni's son) and several other Sultans, with about ten thousand men, separated from the main-body, and began to ascend the farther hill. The Emperor instantly despatched Khan Mírza, with a body of the best troops, to oppose them. At the same moment, his eye happened to light on a band of men who were standing hard by, and he inquired who they were. He was informed that they were Mírza Haider's followers; being a party, chiefly Moghuls, who had been attached to his father, and who, on escaping from Khorásán, had now joined the son. Turning to the Mírza, he observed; "You are still rather young for such rough rencounters. Stay beside me, with Mouláná Muhammed and a few more,

Báber's arrangements;

his position attacked.

BOOK II. — A.D. 1511.

and send the rest of your men to succour Khan Mírza."

They arrived at a fortunate moment. Khan Mírza's men, after coming to their ground, had been charged by the Uzbeks, who bore down all before them, and had nearly reached Khan Mírza himself. Haider's men, under Jan Muhammed Atkeh, as soon as they arrived, attacked them in front; and the fugitives rallying, returned to the fight, and succeeded in driving back the Uzbeks. Haider's men took an Uzbek chief, who was immediately carried before the Emperor. He received the offering with joy as a favourable omen, and on the spot ordered the first prize of valour to be inscribed in Mírza Haider's name. Still, however, the contest continued to be maintained on both sides with desperate valour, till the light began to fail. The violence of the battle had not reached the Emperor's position, the direct road to which was difficult, while it was not easy to go up or down from one place to another. Late in the afternoon, the men of note who were about the Emperor dismounted. At nightfall, the enemy found it impossible to remain in their advanced position, for want of water, which was three or four miles off; they therefore were obliged to retreat during the night, in order to encamp near water. As soon as they began to make a retrograde movement, the foot soldiers and such as had dismounted, raised a shout and rushed after them. The portion of their army that was opposed to Khan Mírza, having observed Khamzeh Khan and the main body in retreat, were also eager to retire. As long as the two divisions remained facing each other, neither could gain any advantage over the other; but no sooner did the enemy commence their retreat, than Khan Mírza's men made a general charge, and the Uzbeks at once took to flight. When the main body saw that division discomfited, they too lost their firmness, fell into confusion, and were soon scattered in

The Uzbeks retreat; are totally routed.

complete rout. "It was now night prayers, when Khamzeh Sultan and Mehdi Sultan were taken, and brought before the Emperor. What they had done to the Khákáns of the Moghuls, and the Sultans of the Chaghatái, that did he to them. From night till morn were the fugitives pursued, and from morn till night, to the entrance of the Derbend-Ahinein, (the Iron Gate)." The immediate consequence of this victory, was the fall of Hissár.* CHAP. IV. A. D. 1511.

Báber now collected the whole of his troops, near Hissár. He was soon after joined by an additional body of auxiliaries, sent by Shah Ismael, under the command of Mustafa Ali and Shahrukh Sultan Moherdar; and numbers of men joined from the tribes around, so that the army, horse and foot, amounted to sixty thousand men. The Kezelbash force was under the command of Ahmed Sultan Sefi (who was related to the royal House of Persia), Ali Khan Istijlu, and Shakrukh Khan Afshár; of whom the two former had served with great reputation against the Ottoman Turks. The Emperor, with this powerful army, advanced towards Kárshi. The principal Uzbek chiefs had met at Samarkand. Obeidulla Khan, the chief of Bokhára, had fortified himself in Kárshi. Báber's ablest officers were against besieging Kárshi; time, they said, was valuable; and, if he pushed on and took possession of Bokhára, Kárshi must fall of course. In this opinion the Emperor concurred, and he marched past it, and encamped, when his scouts reported that Obeidulla Khan had quitted Kárshi and was in full route for Bokhára. Báber hastened on by forced marches, and reached it

Báber collects his army; marches to Bokhára; takes it, and Samarkand,

* Tar. Resh. ff. 189, 190. Mírza Sekander, the author of the Tarikh Alem-arái Abási, f. 18., says, that Khan Mírza was now put in possession of Badakhshán and Hissár, in conformity with the agreement with the Shah; or, as he expresses it, in obedience to the royal grant. This is not improbable, as it is in unison with the practice of the time. Báber looked forward to the sovereignty of Samarkand and Bokhára.

BOOK II. A.D. 1511.

before the Uzbeks, who, finding themselves anticipated, went on to Túrkistán, plundering the country by the way. The Uzbek Sultans who were in Samarkand, being also filled with alarm in like manner, took refuge in Túrkistán; and thus the country of Transoxiana was for a time cleared of the Uzbeks, after they had held it about nine years.*

where he is joyfully received,

After the Emperor had been a short time in Bokhára, he proceeded to Samarkand. His route resembled a triumphal procession; wherever he moved, he was received with universal joy; high and low, citizens and peasantry, all testified their delight. At Samarkand, he was welcomed by processions of the chiefs of the law, and of the merchants; and the grandees and men of every class came out to receive him. The roads and streets were thronged with the population; the houses, bazárs, and public entries were hung with drapery of brocade, and of the richest stuffs, paintings, and wrought work. All was done that could testify their joy at the happy change, the expulsion of the detested Uzbeks, and the restoration of a sovereign of the ancient race of their princes. He was proclaimed King, at Samarkand, in the beginning of October, A.D. 1511, amid the blessings and prayers of the inhabitants, who looked forward to years of happiness, under the mild sway of an enlightened and beneficent sovereign. Having amply rewarded his Persian auxiliaries, he dismissed them, and then marched back to Khorásán.†

and proclaimed king.

15th Rejeb, A.H. 917, 8th Oct. A.D. 1511.

Sultan Saíd in Andeján.

While these events were passing in Bokhára and Samarkand, Sultan Saíd Khan had proceeded, accompanied by his Moghuls, from Kunduz to Andeján, where he was received by Syed Muhammed Mírza. Soon after his arrival, the grand council of Uzbek chiefs,

The Uzbeks besiege Káshán.

* Tar. Reshídi, as above.

† Kháfi Khan, following Mirza Sekander, makes Báber dismiss the Persian auxiliaries after the march to Samarkand; Mírza Haider makes them be sent away from Bokhára, which seems premature.

already mentioned, was held at Samarkand, when different scenes of action were assigned to the different Sultans. Kuchum Khan and Siúnjek Khan were named to assist Jani Beg Khan in driving the Moghuls out of Ferghána. They entered the country, on the west towards Akhsi, and laid siege to Káshán, which was not in a perfect state of defence. The garrison was soon reduced to straits. Sultan Saíd Khan, on learning this, sent the chief part of his army towards the hills near Káshán, to harass, if they could not face, the enemy. The Uzbeks were not the only enemy who now infested Andeján. Ababeker Mírza had availed himself of the confusion produced by the death of Sheibáni, to aim at the conquest of the whole country. He was already possessed of Urkend, Madu, and Ush, some of the best provinces of Ferghána; and, hearing of the detachments sent to the relief of Káshán, pushed on to besiege the capital itself, carrying with him a number of engines for attacking towns — such as manjaníls, swing-cranes*, and scaling ladders. The garrison in the town, which amounted to only two or three thousand men, was not sufficient for defending the walls, which were very extensive; so that both the Khan and the inhabitants were filled with alarm.

Ababeker Mírza besieges Andeján.

Meanwhile, the Uzbeks had made a breach in the walls of Káshán; and, applying scaling ladders, had made so desperate an assault, that the garrison, driven to extremity, made their escape, and rode off by the gate on the land side. As the Uzbeks had dismounted when they came on to the assault, and had not reckoned on the garrison attempting to flee, they were unable to follow; and much time was lost before they could go back to mount and pursue them. Such as remained behind, with the stragglers and the inhabitants, were put to the sword. The garrison, joining the troops in

Káshán taken.

* Manjaníl, tarázu.

BOOK II. A.D. 1511.

the hills, that had been sent to their succour, went on straight to Andeján.

Ababeker defeated.

They reached it at a favourable moment. The army of Ababeker had arrived, and encamped about a couple of miles from the town; and, having prepared all their warlike engines, had determined next morning to storm the town in different quarters at the same moment. In the course of the night, the army returned from Káshán. Towards morning, the enemy advanced to the assault, ignorant of their arrival. The Khan had marched out and drawn up his troops, ready to receive them. The conflict took place at the village of Tumluq *, and the field was obstinately contested. In the end, the Khan was victorious, and Ababeker completely defeated, with great loss. After the battle, all the prisoners were collected in the park of Andeján, and orders issued for putting them to death. The slaughter had begun, when Syed Muhammed on his knees entreated the Khan, on every plea of humanity and policy, to spare them; the more especially as this victory was the key to unlock the cities of Káshghar; and that these unhappy men, who were of that country, might assist in the enterprise which he already meditated. He succeeded in saving the lives of such as were left, amounting to three thousand men; who, says the historian, lifted up their hands in grateful praise and thanksgiving.

The Uzbeks expelled from Máweranuaher.

This great victory made the Uzbeks proceed with caution in their operations. Soon after, news arrived of the defeat and death of Khamzeh Sultan; which was followed, in rapid succession, by that of the Emperor's advance to Samarkand, and the retreat of the Uzbeks before him. In a short time, the communication between Samarkand and Andeján was renewed, and the whole of both countries was recovered, not an Uzbek being left in either. The Emperor bestowed Táshkend

* Or, Tutluq.

on Mír Ahmed Kásim Kohbur, and Seirám on Kitteh Beg, his brother. The Uzbeks were thus driven back into Túrkistán and the desert, which they had quitted as adventurers about twelve years before. CHAP. IV. A.D. 1511-2.

Extent of Báber's dominions.

Never, till his conquest of India, were the dominions of Báber so extensive as at this period. They stretched from the deserts of Tartary to the farthest limits of Ghazni, and comprehended Kábul and Ghazni, Kunduz and Hissár, Samarkand and Bokhára, Ferghána, Táshkend and Seírám. Kábul and Ghazni he now gave to his youngest brother Násir Mírza. When Báber became possessed of these extensive dominions he had reached his twenty-ninth year.*

State of Transoxíana, A.H. 917-8. A.D. 1511-2.

The ensuing winter Báber passed in comparative tranquillity, employed in settling the affairs of his kingdom, and in the enjoyment of his favourite amusement of hunting. To the common observer, all seemed to promise a long course of prosperity; but causes were already in active operation that were soon to deform these bright prospects. The great mass of the settled inhabitants of the countries on the Oxus and Jaxartes, had little influence in the choice of a ruler, and took little part in military affairs. The succession to the throne, and the conquest and revolutions of kingdoms, were effected by the various Tartar tribes, who fed their herds and flocks in these countries, or who from time to time invaded them. Hordes of Moghuls, Uzbeks, and Túrkomans possessed the chief power. The Kezelbashes of Shah Ismael seem to have been dismissed before Báber had time to form a regular or efficient army, for the defence of his new dominions. As he had relied chiefly on the assistance of the Shah for his success in Transoxiana, he is said, not only himself to have assumed the Persian dress, but to have issued an order that all his troops should adopt it, and parti-

* Tar. Resh. f. 190—193. f. 268.

BOOK II. A.D. 1511-2.

cularly the Persian cap. This is distinguished by twelve points, emblematic of the twelve Imáms; and by a long strip of red cloth, issuing from the centre and hanging down behind, whence the Persian soldier has the name of Kezel-bash, or red-head. It was therefore in reality a religious, as well as a military badge; and marked an attachment to the Shía sect, in opposition to the Sunni or old orthodox faith. The inhabitants of Máwerannaher, accustomed to a change of masters, might perhaps have borne the yoke of the Persians as patiently as they had done that of the Moghuls and Uzbeks; but now their religious feelings were touched; and nobles, soldiers, and above all the divines and Imáms, so important a class in every Musulman country, but especially in Samarkand and Bokhára, were deeply offended and scandalised at this distinction granted to a foreign and hostile sect, who daily, in the public mosques and in their private prayers, vent curses against the three holy companions and successors of the Prophet.

Religious zeal of the inhabitants.

The religious zeal of the inhabitants was inflamed. Máwerannaher, from the earliest ages of Islám, had always been distinguished for the untainted orthodoxy of its doctors and their followers, and the meanest of the populace felt a pride in the honourable distinction. Nor was there much in the character or conduct of Shah Ismael, to conciliate whom these innovations were introduced, that could soothe their apprehensions. Descended of one of the holy Imáms, and of a family that had risen to distinction by their attachment to the Shía doctrines, he was himself a strenuous and bigoted apostle of the tenets of the sect, which he had introduced by force as the established religion of all his dominions. The detestation which the orthodox Sunnis of Máwerannaher bore to the heretical Shías of Persia, and their alarm at having the doctrines of a sect which they regarded as impious forced upon them, were naturally increased by the violent and cruel persecution which Shah Ismael had commenced in Khorásán, from the moment of his victory. He had commanded divine service to be celebrated in the mosques of Herát, and had assembled all the heads of the religion, and the most eminent teachers, to be present in the grand mosque, while the Khutba or prayer for the sovereign was read in the new form; the chief preacher of the mosque having honestly refused to repeat the curses on the three companions of the prophet, and Aisha the prophet's wife, was dragged down from the pulpit, and cut in pieces on the spot. Next day, the Shah sent for the Sheikh-ul-Islám, who was the chief Musulman doctor and judge at Herát, and attempted to bring him over to the new opinions. Having failed, the venerable man was condemned to a cruel death, in inflicting which the Shah himself is reported to have taken an active part. This persecution raged against recusants of every rank, as long as Shah Ismael remained in Khorásán. We cannot, therefore, wonder that the inhabitants of Transoxiana, and especially the divines and teachers of religion, should feel much alarm at such manifest indications, as were now made, of a desire, not merely to tolerate, but to favour the Shía doctrines and forms. Besides polemical reasoning, they had recourse to the weapons of ridicule, which often are hardly less powerful. The new garb of the King, and his soldiers, were the subjects of unsparing sarcasm and derision. The popularity of the Emperor, which a few months before had been so high, now rapidly declined. He knew that he was unable to cope with the united force of the Uzbeks, without the aid of the Shah; and the compliances which this persuasion led him to make to that prince's religious opinions, deprived him of the confidence of his subjects beyond the Oxus, in spite of the known humanity and beneficence of his character.*

* There is a difference among historians, as to the sovereign in whose name the coin was struck, and the Khutba read, in Máweran-

BOOK II.

A.D. 1512.

Invasion of the Uzbeks, A.H. 918, A.D. 1512.

But a storm was already gathering beyond the Sirr, which soon poured down all its fury on the plains of Bokhára. On the arrival of spring, the Uzbeks, encouraged by hearing that Shah Ismael had returned to Irák, resolved to attempt the recovery of Transoxiana. They accordingly left Túrkistán; one body marching to attack Táshkend, while another, under Obeidulla Sultan, advanced towards Bokhára. Báber, having detached a body of troops to the relief of Táshkend, hastened, with such as he could collect, to check the Sultan's progress.

Báber defeated at Kúl-malek.

Obeidulla, hearing of his approach when near Bokhára, thought it prudent to retreat; but was followed by Báber, who overtook him at Kúl-malek.* A fierce action ensued, in which the Emperor, being defeated, was forced to fly back to Samarkand. The enemy now turned upon him, pursued him into his capital, began to occupy the country on every side, and threatened to encompass the city, which, with its granaries empty, at the end of winter, was in no condition to stand a siege.

abandons Samarkand,

Seeing no chance of a successful resistance, he once more unwillingly abandoned the imperial city, and made his way to Hissár.†

naher at this period. According to Abulfazl, Ferishta, Kháfi Khan, and the Indian historians, it was in Báber's name. Mírza Sekander, the author of the Tarikh-Alem-arái Abasi, f. 18., followed by the Persian writers, says, it was in that of Shah Ismael. Thus, Sheikh Muhammed Ali Hazin, in his Life, p. 277., observes, that Báber, in the whole course of his life, courted the support of Shah Ismael and his descendants, "sometimes," says he, "by giving currency to their Khutba and coin, as in Samarkand," sometimes by petitions and supplications. The ambition of Shah Ismael might have led him to aim at the conquest of Transoxiana, had not the Turks, his powerful antagonists on the west, compelled him to be constantly on the watch against their progress. Báber was probably acknowledged as the sovereign of Samarkand, which had been held by his forefathers, because it would have been nearly impossible for the Shah to have conquered and held it directly by his Persian troops. When Mírza Sekander talks of the *peshkeshes* sent by Báber to the Shah, on dismissing the troops, and uses other terms of humiliation, he probably only adopts the insolent style used by Persian writers in speaking of the kings of foreign countries.

* Sefer, A.H. 918, which begins 18 April, A.D. 1512.

† Mírza Sekander, who is followed by Kháfi Khan and the

He had not been long there, when he was attacked by a body of Uzbeks, led by some of their khans and sultans, who assembled at the Derbend pass, and marched to overwhelm him. Báber threw such of his Moghuls and soldiers as were at hand, with their property and families, into the town and suburbs of Hissár, and barricaded the streets. The Uzbeks, who advanced and reconnoitred the place, seeing that he was resolved to make a desperate defence, gave up their design, and fell back on Cheghánián.* CHAP. IV. A.D. 1512. defends Hissár.

Báber, meanwhile, had applied for assistance to Biram Khan Karamanlu, who commanded for the Shah, at Balkh, and who sent a detachment to support him; on the arrival of which, the Uzbeks withdrew from the country of Hissár.

But Báber, after the signal defeat which he had suffered at Kúl-malek, had sent directly to Shah Ismael himself, to solicit an effective force, by which he might be enabled to expel the Uzbeks finally from Máwerannaher. The Shah, accordingly, gave instructions to Amír Nijm Sáni, his minister of finance, whom he had entrusted with the settlement of Khorásán, to render assistance to Báber in recovering the dominions he had lately possessed. On reaching Balkh, Amír Nijm resolved to march in person into Máwerannaher, and, taking with him the governor of Herat, the Amirs of Khorásán, and Biram Khan, of Balkh, he passed the Amu, and was soon joined by Báber, when the combined army is said to have amounted to sixty thousand men.† Amír Nijm joins Báber, A.H. 918, A.D. 1512.

Indian historians, makes the Emperor's army small, and that of Obeidulla very numerous. Abulfazl, going beyond this, gives Báber the victory; but adds, that from untoward circumstances he was obliged to retreat. Mírza Haider, on the contrary, (Tar. Resh. f. 199.) who was Obeid's brother-in-law, makes him, with three thousand men, defeat the Emperor with forty thousand. His account of Báber's transactions, at this time, is strongly tinged with an adverse religious feeling.

* Báber's Mem. p. 305.

† According to the Taríkhe Be-

BOOK II.

A. D. 1512.

Karshi sacked,

Early in the autumn, the army advanced to Khozar, which was taken. It next proceeded on to Karshi, which had been strongly fortified and garrisoned by Obeidulla Sultan, the chief of Bokhára, who was in reality at the head of the Uzbeks, though Kuchum was the nominal khan. It was proposed to leave it behind, as had been done with success in the preceding campaign; but Mír Nijm, saying that it was Obeidulla's lair, declared that it must be taken. It was accordingly besieged and carried by storm; when Sheikhem Mírza, the governor, with all in the place, whether Uzbeks or inhabitants, to the number of fifteen thousand, were put to the sword, without respect to age, or sex, or sanctity. The circumstances of this massacre disgusted Báber, who found that he was condemned to play a subordinate part, in an army professedly acting under his authority. He had ardently desired to save the inhabitants, who were Chaghatái Túrks of his own race and sect; and he had earnestly besought Nijm Sáni to comply with his wishes. But the unrelenting Persian, deaf to his entreaties, had let loose all the fury of war on the devoted city. Moulána Binái, the poet, one of the most eminent wits of his time, who happened to be in the town, fell in the indiscriminate slaughter, with many Syeds and holy men; "and from that time forward," says Mírza Sekander, "Amír Nijm prospered in none of his undertakings." *

The Uzbek chiefs, after the massacre at Karshi, appear for some time to have retired and fortified themselves in

dáuni, f. 182., he was accompanied by an army of seventeen thousand Kezelbashes. Mírza Sekander says, that he held the Vikálat Diván-Ali, f. 18. Kháfi Khan calls him the Amír-ul-Omra. The total amount of the army is taken from the Indian writers. The Persian writers say, that Mír Nijm entered Transoxiana without orders from Shah Ismael. This may only be to save the Shah's credit.

* Tar. Alem-arái, f. 19.; Tar. Reshídi, f. 199.; Tar. Kháfi Khan, f. 23. Kháfi Khan makes Mír Nijm defeat Obeidulla Khan, and shut up his army, of fifteen thousand horse, in Karshi.

A. D. 1512.

their strongholds. Mír Nijm seems to have passed on to attack Ghazhdewán, on the border of the desert, without having taken Bokhára. The Uzbek sultans had now had time to assemble; and under the command of Obeidulla Khan, who was joined by Taimur Sultan from Samarkand, they threw themselves into the fort the very night that Báber and Mír Nijm had taken their ground before it, and were preparing their engines and ladders for an assault. The Uzbeks, in the morning*, drew out their army, which took up a position among the houses and gardens in the suburbs of the town. The confederates advanced to meet them. The Uzbeks, who were protected by the broken ground, and by the walls of the inclosures and houses, had posted in every corner archers on foot, who poured a shower of arrows on the Kezelbashes as they approached. Biram Khan, who had the chief military command of their troops, being wounded, and having fallen from his horse, the main body of the army fell into disorder. "In the course of an hour," says Mírza Haider, "the influence of Islám began to prevail over heresy and infidelity. Victory declared for the true faith. The invaders were routed, and most of them fell in the field; and the arrows of Ghazhdewán revenged the sabre of Karshi. Mír Nijm, and all the chief officers of the Túrkománs," continues the pious Musulman, "were sent to hell-fire. The Emperor, routed and discomfited, fled back to Hissár." It is said that the Kezelbash chiefs, disgusted with the haughtiness and insolence of Mír Nijm, did not use their utmost endeavours to assist him; so that he was taken prisoner, and put to death. Many of the Persian chiefs, who fled from the battle, crossed the Amu at Kirki, and regained Khorásán.†

A. H. 918, A. D. 1512, Battle of Ghazhdewán.

Báber totally defeated.

* Mírza Sekander says that the battle was fought on Sunday, 3 Ramzan, A. H. 918. The day of the week is probably a mistake, the 3d Ramzan, 918, falling on Friday. The Leb-al-Towárikh makes the day of the battle, 17 Ramzan, 918.

† Tar. Reshídi, f. 199, 200. The

BOOK II.

A.D. 1512-3.

The Uzbeks recover Transoxiana.

A.H. 919.
A.D. 1513.

Shah Ismael returns to Khorásán.

The Uzbeks now not only recovered the country which they had lost in Transoxiana, but made incursions into Khorásán, ravaging the northern part of the province. Shah Ismael, on hearing of this disaster, resolved to return. On his approach, the Uzbeks retreated in alarm. He caused several of the officers, who had escaped from the battle, to be seized; and some of them to be capitally punished, for deserting their commander. Certain inhabitants of the province, being accused of having shown attachment to the Uzbeks and

account given by Mírza Sekander, (Tar. Alem-arái Abási, f. 19.) is somewhat different. He says, that Taimur Sultan, and Abusaid Sultan, threw themselves into the town, which they defended bravely for four months; that, at the end of that time, provisions began to fail in the Persian camp, and the horses suffered for want of provender; that Obeid-ulla Khan and Jani Beg Khan, who were in Bokhára, marched out with their troops in the highest order, and being joined by Taimur Sultan and the garrison of Ghazhdewán, engaged the besiegers on Sunday the 3d of Ramzan, within sight of the town; that Biram Khan, who commanded the troops, having been wounded, the army fell into disorder, and the rout became complete; that Muhammed Báber Mírza retired from the flight, separated from the army, and fled to Hissár. The two accounts are not irreconcileable. Though Mírza Haider speaks of the Uzbek chiefs as arriving on the same day with the Persians, and while they were preparing their engines for attack, yet their arrival may have been after the place had been besieged four months; and when an assault was preparing. The scarcity in the camp is probable, though adduced to lessen the disgrace of the discomfiture. To the same feeling may perhaps be ascribed the alleged slackness of the Persian chiefs in supporting Mír Nijm, and the reflection cast on Báber. The defeat of Ghazhdewán seems to have hurt the pride of the Persians in a high degree. They openly ascribed it to the treachery of Báber; Humáyun, when a refugee in Persia, was often taunted with this treachery of his father, as having destroyed Mír Nijm's whole army. In the Tarikhe Bedáuni, f. 182., a couplet is given, which Báber is reported to have written, and shot into the town, tied to an arrow, to intimate his hatred of his allies. It is not improbable that Báber could not conceal his disgust at the massacre of Karshi, and at the slights shown to himself; that a misunderstanding ensued between him and the leaders of the Persians; and, that they were willing to shift the bad success of the campaign, off themselves, by laying it upon him. The lines were,

Serfe ráhe Uzbekán kerdem Sháhrá,
Ger gunáhi kerdem, pák kerdem rahrá,

and, it is added, that on the following day when the armies engaged, Báber, by drawing off his troops, caused the destruction of the Kezelbashes.

CHAP. II.

A. D. 1513.

their creed, and of having vexed the Shías, were consumed in the fire of his wrath. In truth, he was a stern bigot and a merciless persecutor; a consequence of the religious foundation on which he established his government.*

Conspiracy of the Moghuls against Báber,

The fatal battle of Ghazhdewán, the destruction of his Persian allies, and the numbers and power of the Uzbeks, seemed to leave Báber no hopes of again ascending the throne of Samarkand and Bokhára. But, much as he had suffered, his misfortunes were not yet over. When Sultan Saíd Khan was sent with the Moghuls to recover Andeján, a considerable number, both of those who had escaped from the Uzbek yoke and of those who had previously been in the country, entered into Báber's service. He repeatedly complains, in his Memoirs, that on all occasions he had found the Moghuls a turbulent and treacherous race, ever ready for rebellion, or to turn upon their friends when defeated, and to strip and plunder them. Whether at this time they had any special ground for complaint, or whether they merely considered Báber's as a falling cause, is not very clear. Ferishta says, that he gave them offence by reproaching them with their misconduct during the late expedition. At any rate a serious conspiracy was formed, at the head of which were the most eminent Moghul chiefs, such as Mír Ayub Begchik, Mír Muhammed, Yádgár Mírza, and Nazer Mírza, who formed a plan for cutting him off. In execution of this purpose, they fell upon Báber's quarters by night, killing or wounding all who came in their way. So sudden was the attack, that Báber, who, on the alarm, started from his bed, and rushed out, had difficulty in escaping, in the undress in which he slept, into the fort of Hissár. The Moghuls, on finding that they had missed their prey, plundered

at Hissár.

* Tar. Alem-arái, f. 19.

BOOK II. A.D. 1513.

whatever was without the walls, and then, marching away, took up a position on the hills of Karatigín. The Emperor, finding it impossible to keep the field with his remaining force, having left some trusty Amírs to defend the fort, retired to Kunduz; and the whole country of Hissár, with the exception of the fort itself, fell into the hands of the Moghuls.

Their proceedings in the country.

No sooner were they masters of the country than they began to exercise every kind of violence and excess, on the persons and property of the wretched inhabitants. Assignments were granted, without the least regard to the ability of those who were to discharge them. Whatever cattle, grain, or other property the peasantry possessed, was torn from the owners, and squandered in wasteful prodigality. A horrible famine ensued in the city of Hissár, and the few who survived supported life by the most loathsome and unnatural means. These disgusting scenes were succeeded by a pestilence, and thousands of women and children were sold into captivity among the Uzbeks. The country presented a scene of misery and desolation; and, to add to the general distress, the winter being uncommonly severe, the ground was covered deep with snow. Nor did the Moghuls themselves escape. They not only suffered from want of grain, but the snow, which buried the fields, speedily produced a want of forage for their horses.

Obeid Khan invades Hissár,

Obeidulla Khan, of Bokhára, hearing of their difficulties, resolved to expel the Moghuls from Hissár, and entered the country towards the end of winter. They were at a loss how to act. They dared not apply to the Emperor after their late treachery; nor durst they join Sultan Saíd Khan, in Andeján, sensible that he would not sanction their lawless proceedings; and besides, the state of the roads did not admit of their crossing the mountains. They, therefore, took up a strong position, having on one side the Surkháb river;

on the other two sides the Wakhsh hills; the remaining side, being covered by deep snow, they regarded as inaccessible. The Uzbeks, when they arrived, reconnoitred the ground on every side. In a few days, the increasing heat of the weather began to melt the snow, and Obeid Khan, effecting a passage by the narrow and broken ground, which had been considered as impassable, one day at early dawn reached their position, and fell upon the Moghuls. Thus surprised, they did not attempt to make a stand, but threw themselves into the river, which they tried to cross. Numbers perished in the stream, or fell by the sword, or were made prisoners. Such as escaped fled to the mountains, and a few, after enduring incredible hardships, reached Sultan Saíd Khan, in Fergána. "In a word," says the historian, "Hissár, by the villany of these Moghuls, was lost to the Emperor, and fell under the power of the Uzbeks."*

and defeats them;

As long as there was any chance of a change of fortune, Báber lingered at Kunduz; though, even there, exposed to much want and suffering. At length, finding that all hope had vanished on every side, leaving Khan Mírza in Badakhshán, he once more recrossed the Hindú-kúsh mountains, and returned to Kábul.†

Báber returns to Kábul.

While these events were passing in Hissár, Sultan Saíd Khan had retained possession of Báber's paternal kingdom of Ferghána. We have seen, that when the Emperor's success had enabled him to return to Samarkand, and the Uzbeks had fled into Túrkistán, he had given Táshkend to Mír Ahmed Kásim, and Sirám to Kitteh Beg, his brother; and, that when Obeidulla Khan again crossed the Sir to invade Bokhára, Siúnjek Sultan had marched with his Uzbeks to recover Tásh-

The Uzbeks recover Táshkend,

Spring, A. H. 918. A. D. 1512.

* Tar. Resh. ff. 200—201.

† Báber appears to have returned to Kábul, A. H. 919, or A. H. 920, in the end of A. D. 1513, or early in 1514, probably the latter. See Tar. Resh. f. 201 and 213.; Akbernáma, Ferishta, &c.

BOOK II. kend. After the unfortunate battle of Kúl-malek, Siúnjek besieged Táshkend with all his forces, and reduced it to great distress. Mír Ahmed, seeing that every hope of retaining the town had vanished, made a bold sally by night, burst through the lines of the besiegers, and effected his escape.*

Sultan Saíd invades Táshkend, — In the course of the summer, Sultan Saíd, understanding that Báber was about to enter the territory of Bokhára, assisted by Persian auxiliaries, resolved to make a demonstration in his favour, by affording occupation to the Uzbeks in their own dominions. He, accordingly, entered the Táshkend territory with five thousand men, and ravaged the country. He was soon met by Siúnjek Sultan at the head of seven thousand Uzbeks, when a battle was fought, in which Sultan Saíd was defeated and wounded. He returned to Andeján; but the Uzbeks, alarmed at the advance of the Emperor and Mír Nijm, turned all their attention to Bokhára and Samarkand, and did not follow Saíd into Ferghána.

defeated. A. H. 918, Rejeb, A. D. 1512. Sept.

Defends Ferghána, — When the issue of the battle of Ghazhdewán left the arms of Siúnjek once more at liberty, he advanced towards Andeján. The winter was severe, the famine great, and the misery of the country extreme. Sultan Saíd, seeing that it was impossible to meet him in the field, placed different Amírs with strong garrisons in Andeján, Akhsi, and Marghinán; while he himself retired to the hill-country on the south, so as to be prepared to harass and assail him, should he lay siege to any place. Siúnjek, on finding that he was to be so vigorously opposed, retired and made no new attempt during the winter.

Kásim. Khan of the Kaizáks, called in. — During all this winter, however, Kitteh Beg remained shut up and besieged in Seirám. As the revolt of the Moghuls in Hissár had taken place, and the Emperor's

* Tar. Resh. f. 208.

CHAP. IV.

affairs were in such a desperate condition that he could render them no aid, both he and Sultan Saíd began to look around for some one who could assist them in their present danger; and none seemed so fit for that purpose as Kásim Khan, the chief of the Kaizáks.

We have seen, that, in the time of the great Abulkhair Khan, the powerful ruler of the Uzbeks, Gerai Khan and Jani Beg Khan had separated from him, and formed a new confederacy in the desert; which, on the defeat and death of Abulkhair, when his followers were dispersed and his territories partitioned, had risen to great power under the name of Kaizáks; a denomination originally bestowed on them from their predatory life, and which they retained when more powerful.* On the death of Gerai Khan, his son Berendúk Khan succeeded; Jani Beg Khan had also several sons, and, among others, Uzbek Sultan and Kásim Khan. Kásim Khan not only gained the superiority over his brother, but, in the course of time, became the chief leader of the Kaizáks; leaving Berendúk nothing but the name of Khan. Such was the condition of the Kaizák tribes at this crisis. In a short time afterwards, Kásim Khan expelled Berendúk, who fled to Samarkand, where he died in exile. Kásim Khan, before his death, which happened five or six years after this time, overran the whole Desht-Kipchák; was said to be able to bring a million of men into the field; and to have been the most powerful prince who had been in that country since Júji Khan.

Plunders the country, A. H. 919, A. D. 1513,

When Kitteh Beg solicited the assistance of Kásim Khan, the army of that potentate consisted of three hundred thousand men. The Beg sent to present him with the keys of Seirám, and to ask him to take possession of the country. The Kaizák chief consented, marched with a large army by Táshkend, plundering

* Tar. Resh. f. 208.

BOOK II. A.D.1513-4. the country. This attack deranged the plans of Siúnjek. Sultan Saíd entered Táshkend, that he might form a junction with the Khan's army; but had not advanced far before he heard of Kásim's return to the desert. and retreats. On this the Sultan retreated, and soon after visited Kásim Khan, at a remote station in his native wilds. Siúnjek did not attack Andeján all that summer, apprehensive of another invasion of the Kaizáks.*

Sultan Saíd abandons Ferghána. A.H. 920. A.D. 1514. In the following summer, however, Kásim Khan being occupied with his conquests in a distant part of the desert, Siúnjek Sultan marched, with a large force of the confederate Uzbeks, towards Andeján. Sultan Saíd Khan convened a council of his chiefs. They were unanimously of opinion that, unsupported as they were, it would be absurd singly to contend with the mighty power of the Uzbeks, and that they had a much fairer chance of success by marching into Káshghar, and attacking Ababeker Mírza, whom they had once before defeated. This resolution was accordingly adopted, Rebi 1. A.H. 920, May, A.D. 1514. and, before Siúnjek had time to enter the country, the Khan, with all his Amírs, their families and baggage, set out from Andeján and advanced towards Káshghar, by the route of Moghulistán. Their enterprise was successful. Sultan Saíd expelled the tyrant Ababeker, and ruled Káshghar many years with honour and in prosperity.

In this manner was Báber driven from his old dominions, as he had previously been from Hissár. From this period, except for a moment near the close of his life, he seems to have lost all hope of regaining either the country of Máwerannaher, or his native Ferghána; and he was "led by divine inspiration," says the courtly Abulfazl (writing in the reign of his grandson), "to turn his mind to the conquest of Hindustán." But though he never revisited those countries, we find, from

* Tar. Resh. ff. 209. 211. 93.

his Commentaries, that they never lost their influence over his imagination and affections. He often speaks of them, and of the companions of his early life, and always with a warmth which proves how deep was the impression that both had made on his youthful heart.

CHAP. IV.

A.D. 1514.

CHAPTER V.

ARGHÚNS IN KANDAHÁR.

BÁBER'S RETURN TO KÁBUL.—REBELLION OF HIS MOGHULS QUELLED. —HE CHASTISES THE HILL-TRIBES.—TAKES BAJOUR.—SWÁD SUBMITS.—AFFAIRS OF BADAKHSHÁN—AND OF KANDAHÁR.—SHAH BEG SUBMITS TO SHAH ISMAEL.—IS THROWN INTO PRISON. —PLOT TO DELIVER HIM—SUCCEEDS.—HE TURNS HIS ARMS AGAINST SIND.—MÁH-CHUCHAK—HER STORY, CAPTIVITY, AND ESCAPE.—BÁBER'S SUCCESSIVE CAMPAIGNS AGAINST KANDAHÁR—WHICH IS SURRENDERED BY CONVENTION.

BOOK II. A.D. 1514–15.

Báber returns to Kábul. A.H. 920, A.D. 1514.

WHEN Báber, driven from Máwerannaher by the overwhelming force of the Uzbeks, returned to Kábul, his youngest brother Násir Mírza, to whom he had assigned that kingdom when he conquered Samarkand, came out to receive him with every mark of honour and of welcome, and at once resigned to him the government. He asked to be allowed to retain Ghazni, which he had held previously to the expedition against Máwerannaher, to which the Emperor willingly consented. He soon after set out for that city, loaded with many marks of the imperial favour; but, in the course of the following year, he fell a victim to the excess of his habitual indulgence in wine.*

Death of Násir Mirza. A.H. 921, A.D. 1515

Rebellion of Moghuls and others.

His death was the signal for a mutiny and revolt among the great Moghul chiefs, in which several Chaghatái nobles also took a part. The cause is not explained, but seems to have related to the succession to Ghazni and its dependent districts. Shiram Taghái, the uncle of his mother, and who had all his life been in the service, Mír Mazíd Wajkeh his brother, Kúl

* He left a son Yádgár Násir Mírza, often mentioned in the course of the following history.

Nazer, and in general all the Moghuls, rose in rebellion. They were joined by Moulána Bába Beshágheri, who had been in such favour with the Emperor that he had only three years before been made governor of Samarkand, Uråtippa, and the hill-country; by Mír Ahmed Kohbur, who so recently had been governor of Táshkend; by his brother, Kitteh Beg, the gallant defender of Seirám, and by many of the most distinguished nobles of the Emperor's court. As to the causes and the details of the rebellion, we are left much in the dark. The Emperor himself, in giving the character of Dost Beg, who died some years afterwards, incidentally remarks, that the Beg, having, in the course of this rebellion, been detached from Ghazni on a plundering expedition with two or three hundred men, was attacked by three or four hundred chosen Moghul horse, who were sent to chastise him. They encountered him near Shirúkán, when he completely beat them, dismounted and took a number of them prisoners, and brought back with him a quantity of heads.* We are informed, in general, by Mírza Haider, that, after several skirmishes, encounters, and intrigues, the two armies were drawn out, when a battle ensued; that, at this crisis, Amír Kamber Ali, the son of Amír Kásim Kochin, Báber's favourite minister, arriving from Kunduz with a considerable force, fell upon and routed the right of the rebels; many of whom were taken and met with the reward of their treason, while others fled and escaped to Káshghar. Shiram Taghái was, for some time, in the service of Sultan Saíd Khan, "but, unable to support himself," says Mírza Haider, "he returned back to the Emperor, who, with his usual benevolence, received him kindly, shutting his eyes upon his unworthy acts, and regarding only his past services. He soon after left this transitory world."†

CHAP. V.

A.D. 1515.

Quelled.

* Báber's Mem. p. 266.

† Tar. Resh. ff. 202. 274, 275.

BOOK II.

A. D. 1515 –19.

Báber subdues the hill-tribes.

The quelling of this rebellion, and perhaps the banishment of the turbulent Moghuls, left Báber some years of comparative peace. This period he employed in arrangements for the government of his kingdom, and in checking or reducing to subjection the various mountain tribes on every side, which had hitherto yielded an imperfect obedience, or none, to the throne of Kábul. To follow Báber in all his expeditions against the Hazáras, Aimáks, Afgháns, and other tribes in the hills and wilds, would lead into needless detail. The history of them all is nearly the same. He sets out secretly with a strong light force, marches without halting, comes upon the encampment of the tribe unawares, disperses or slays the men, and carries off the women, cattle, and valuables. Sometimes, however, the clans are on their guard, and he meets with a brave resistance, when, after considerable loss to both parties, victory in the end inclines to the side of disciplined valour. It is hardly possible for governments constituted like those of the East, and possessed of no regular standing army, to subdue, and still less thoroughly to settle, the erratic tribes of the mountains and deserts, who always govern themselves most easily and effectually. Báber, in some instances, forced them to acknowledge his supremacy, and to a certain degree restrained their inroads and subjected them to tribute; but, in general, down to the time when he conquered Delhi, the Afgháns maintained their independence, only sending tribute, with more or less punctuality, according as the means of enforcing it were nearer or more remote. The Hazáras he often plundered and discomfited; but, as the greater portion of them were safe in their broken and inaccessible mountains and glens, though often defeated and pillaged, they never could be said to be subdued; yet, like the Afgháns, they were restrained for a time from plundering, as they had for ages been accustomed to do, on the lower grounds and passes of his territories.

CHAP. V.

A.D. 1519.

Báber takes Bajour.

One portion of territory, which is at present comprehended in the Afghán country, though down to the period in question it had not belonged to the kingdom of Kábul, he did however subdue. The country between the Cheghánserai river and the Indus was overrun by Báber, about fifteen years after his conquest of Kábul. Thirty years before that last event, the Yusef-zai Afgháns, said to come from Khorásán*, had settled in the lower parts of that tract, expelling the Dilázáks, the former inhabitants. This territory, which lies at the southern roots of the Hindú-kúsh range, and was highly cultivated, had, in older times, been held by the Sultans of Swád and Bajour; a race of princes whose authority appears, at one time, to have been very extensive, especially among the rich cultivated valleys of that hill-country. The dominions of the Sultan of Swád, at one period, had even extended to both sides of the Sind. The Yusef-zais had succeeded in expelling the Dilázáks from part of the Swád territory, and had also encroached upon the Sultan, so that he had been compelled to retire into Upper-Swád. The Sultan of Bajour was still independent.† Báber, when he entered the country, was attended by several Dilázák chiefs, who served him as guides, and directed his vengeance against their deadly enemies the Yusef-zais. He first marched against the strong fort of Bajour, and the Sultan refusing to submit, he attacked it with engines of war, and with matchlocks, which were quite new to the garrison. The alarm which these produced, as soon as their effects were experienced, was employed to cover an escalade that proved successful. The whole male inhabitants, three thousand in number, including their sultans or chiefs, were cruelly put to the sword as infidels, and a pillar erected of their heads. The women

A.H. 925, A.D. 1519.

* It must be observed, that the term Khorásán is very indefinite, often including all the country west of Ghazni.

† Báber's Mem. p. 140.; Elphinstone's Caubul, p. 246.

BOOK II. A.D. 1519.

and children were led into bondage. Báber, seated in statè in the palace of the Sultan, bestowed the government of the country on Khwája Kilán.*

Swád submits.

Immediately on hearing of these transactions, Sultan Wais of Swád sent to offer his submission, which was accepted.† The Emperor then proceeded to plunder Penjkora, and some neighbouring districts. The Yusef-zais sent ambassadors to soothe his resentment; and as, from experience, he had found the difficulty of subduing them by open force in the rugged country which they occupied, he sought to conciliate men whom it was not always easy to chastise or to reach, by asking in marriage the daughter of Malek-shah Mansúr, one of their chiefs.‡ This union, which in the opinion of barbarians deeply imbued with all the feelings of clanship, gave him a strong and intimate connection with the tribe, assisted in checking the customary *raids* and outrages of several of its branches; for, with others, hostilities seem to have continued. The final agreement with the friendly Yusef-zais was, that they should make no inroads into Swád above Anúha, the amount of contribution (or black-mail), which they had been accustomed to levy higher up, being allowed as a deduction in the rolls of their revenue collections; and that the Afghâns, who cultivated lands in Bajour and Swád, should pay six thousand loads (about thirty-eight thousand cwts.) of grain, to the government.§

Convention with the Yusef-zais.

Báber's inroads on the Afghâns.

It may be imagined that it was no easy task to restrain tribes which, like those around Kábul, had for ages been accustomed freely to indulge in robbery and insubordination of every kind; and it should seem that hardly a year passed in which Báber did not make inroads into the country of some one or other of them, to chastise their licentiousness, to protect his more peaceable subjects, and sometimes, perhaps, for the less

* Báber's Mem. p. 246—248.

† Ibid. p. 249.

‡ Ibid. p. 250.

§ Ibid. p. 268.

laudable object of plundering them of their wealth, or of reducing them to subjection.* CHAP. V.

Affairs of Badakhshán.

During this period the subordinate kingdom of Badakhshán continued to be governed by Khan Mírza, whose circumstances had been considerably improved, by the freedom from Uzbek invasion afforded by Báber's invasions of Transoxiana. Some years afterwards, the Mírza had the misfortune to have a difference with Sultan Saíd Khan, of Káshghar.

Perhaps A. H. 909.

The ground of it originated long before Khan Mírza had taken possession of Badakhshán, and while Báber was still in Ferghána. In the latter part of Khosrou Shah's reign, over Kunduz and Badakhshán, Mírza Ababeker of Káshghar had seized some of the high mountain districts, or Hazáras, of the latter country, such as Sárigh-Juián, Perwáz and others. Before Khosrou could obtain redress, he fell before the superior fortunes of Sheibáni Khan, and Báber. When Sheibáni took possession of Khosrou's other dominions, the Mírza refused to yield these Hazáras to him, and many battles were

* Báber himself records several of his forays and inroads into the countries of the tribes around Kábul, such as that against the Sultan-Masaúdi Hazáras, south-east of Kábul, (A. H. 910, A. D. 1504.) Mem. p. 156. The most remarkable was the grand circuit already mentioned, which he made just after mounting the throne of Kábul, when he went, first against the Afgháns of Kohát, thence through Banu, Bangash, and Daman, down the Indus to the Multán territory, and the borders of Sind; in the course of which, he plundered the Isa-khail and other tribes, and returned through a desolate country by Chotiáli and Abistádeh to Ghazni, (A. H. 910, A. D. 1505.) Mem. p. 157—166. He next year (A. H. 911, A. D. 1506) plundered the Túrkomán Hazáras, near Bámián, seized numbers of sheep and horses, and slew many of the tribesmen.—Ibid. p. 173., and again, (A. H. 912, A. D. 1507), p. 212, 213. He beat the Khizer-khail, Shimu-khail, Khirilji, and Khugiáni Afgháns, when attempting to obstruct his march in the pass below Jagdalik, and plundered the Alishing Afgháns and the Kafirs. (A. H. 913, A. D. 1507) p. 232, 233. He plundered the Yuzef-zais and Muhammed-zais of the plains, (A. H. 925, A. D. 1519) p. 251. and 274. He plundered the Abdal-rahman Afgháns in Gurdíz, making a tower of the heads of the slain, p. 270.; and the Khizer-khail, p. 277.; imposed a tribute of four thousand sheep on the Khirilchi, and Shamu-khail. — Ibid. Other instances occur.

BOOK II. in consequence fought with the Uzbeks. Mírza Ababeker continued, however, to retain in his power all above the upper passes of Badakhshán.

At a future time, when Khan Mírza came into possession of a part of the country, we have seen that he was much straitened and kept down by the vicinity and power of the Uzbeks, and that he was unable to recover any of the usurpations of Mírza Ababeker, who continued to hold Sárigh-Juián and all the highlands above the narrows, which, for the space of twelve years, remained separated from Badakhshán and united to Káshghar.

Quarrel of Sultan Saíd and Khan Mírza,

When Sultan Saíd, driven from Ferghána by the Uzbeks, attacked and defeated Mírza Ababeker, and took possession of the territories of Káshghar, he divided these upper districts of Badakhshán among his Amírs, in the same way as he did the country of

A. H. 921.

Káshghar. Mír Beg Muhammed, who was sent as governor, claimed the districts of Wakhan and Derwáz, as belonging to the Káshghar Hazáras, as well as Sárigh-Juián; while the inhabitants of the two former asserted their right to belong to Badakhshán, and claimed protection from Khan Mírza.

The Mírza readily acceded to their request. He had long had an eye on these districts, which he considered as part of Badakhshán, or rather as being in reality Badakhshán itself, since from them the rest of the country took its name. Sultan Saíd, on the other hand, claimed them under a twelve years' possession, which, he contended, had broken the old right, and transferred them to Káshghar; adding, that Khan Mírza, in seizing them by force, had rendered it impossible for the Khan to yield them up to him as a friend and relation, even had he, from other considerations, been disposed so to do.

Saíd invades Badakhshán, A. H. 924.

The Khan followed up his remonstrances by leading an army into Badakhshán. Khan Mírza, totally unable to meet him in the field, shut himself up in Kila-Zefer, while Saíd ravaged the country. The Mírza, now heartily repenting his ill-judged enterprise, made the humblest submissions; and Sultan Saíd Khan, seeing his weakness, and unwilling that his dominions should be totally ruined, took pity on him and retired. No farther attempt was made, during Khan Mírza's life, to recover these Hazáras.*

but retires.

Khan Mírza died about A. H. 926, leaving a son, Suleiman Mírza, a child, whom Báber sent for and kept near himself; at the same time giving Badakhshán, as a dependent principality, to his eldest son, Humáyun Mírza. That prince went, took possession of it, and governed it nearly ten years. During that period, he seems to have resided much in the country. He left it in A. H. 932, when he attended his father, with the troops of Badakhshán, on his last invasion of India; from which, after the defeat of Rána Sanga, he led them back to their own country.†

A. H. 926, A. D. 1520.

A. H. 933, A. D. 1527.

From the period of Báber's return from Transoxiana the two great objects that engaged his mind were, the conquest of Kandahár, and that of Hindústan.

We have already seen, that he was hardly settled in the possession of Kábul and Ghazni when he attempted to add Kandahár to his other dominions; that he had very early succeeded in overrunning its territory, and had even besieged and taken the capital; but that Sheibáni had wrested from him his new acquisitions, and restored them to Shah Beg, the eldest son of Zúlnún.

Báber's transactions with Kandahár. A. H. 913, A. D. 1507.

The conquest of Kandahár was not an easy task. Shah Shujaa Beg, who now governed that country and several other dependent provinces, was a prince of great talent, a brave soldier, a prudent politician, popular both with the army and with his subjects, and an en-

Shah Shujaa Beg.

* Tar. Resh. f. 272, 273.

† Báber's Mem. p. 373.; Briggs's Ferishta, ii. p. 37.

BOOK II. lightened patron of letters and of learned men. It would appear, that, on his father's death, finding himself placed in Kandahár, between the force and activity of Báber on the one side, and the overwhelming power of Sheibáni on the other, he early saw that the physical resources of the provinces which he possessed were quite inadequate to resist either of these princes; the different parts of his kingdom being, from their local situation, unable to afford each other that ready help which is necessary, either for attack or defence, in time of need. He had therefore thrown himself on the protection of Sheibáni, and is said to have struck the coin and read the public prayers in his name. Sheibáni not only enabled him to recover Kandahár from Báber, but showed him other marks of favour, during his own transient possession of Khorásán.*

A.H. 884, A.D. 1479. It has already been observed, that soon after acquiring Kandahár, Zúlnún Beg had added to his possessions Shál and Mustung, which lie at some distance in the southern wilds.† About four years later, his son, Shah

takes Síwí. A.H. 890, A.D. 1485. Beg, besieged and took the fort of Síwí, which Beháder Khan then held for the Jám; and, having left there his younger brother, Muhammed Beg, returned to Kandahár. Muhammed seems to have pushed his plundering parties as far as Ikerí and Chandúka, in the territory of Sind. Jám Nanda, who was then the sovereign of that country, sent a large force, under Mobárek Khan, to protect his subjects. Mobárek encountered the Arghúns in a hot action, in which Muhammed fell, his

but loses it. army was defeated, and Síwí retaken.‡

* Tar. Sind. f. 94.

† About a hundred and fifty miles.—Tar. Sind. f. 73.

‡ Tar. Sind. f. 68. Chandúka Sitharja is Chand-koh; Ikeri or Ukeri, I do not know. It may be Lhari. Jám Nanda's force is said to have engaged Muhammed at Dera-Feríb, better known as Jilougír; both names with which I am unacquainted. Abulfazl calls Shah Beg's brother, Sultan Muhammed, Ayeen Akbery, vol. ii. p. 120.; as does the Tabakáte Akberi; Ferishta, vol. iv. p. 427., calls Shah Beg's conquest, the fort of Sewly; which

CHAP. V.

Desirous of invading Sind, A. H. 913, A. D. 1507.

When Báber afterwards took Kandahár, Shah Beg, driven from the more fertile and populous parts of his dominions, retired, as has been mentioned, to Shál and Mustung, where he was met by Fázil Beg Gokuldásh, and some other of his local officers, who introduced to him the heads of the tribes that occupied the hills and passes of that broken and difficult country. Shah Beg's authority over them, as well as over the portion of Síwí that acknowledged his sovereignty, was perhaps slight, except in the low lands, which were most easily overrun. These poor but free hill chiefs, whose allegiance was that of tributaries rather than of regular subjects, were but little pleased with finding that the Arghúns, a body of rapacious and overbearing strangers, intended to take up their residence among them. But when Shah Beg proposed to them an attack on Sind, an enterprise calculated at once to gratify their love of plunder and to free them from the grievous burden of entertaining their new guests, they all declared themselves ready to attend him. The speedy restoration of Shah Beg to the possession of Kandahár, by the advance of Sheibáni from Herát, put an end to this plan for the moment; but the events which followed, and which embroiled Shah Beg with both of his powerful neighbours, again, at no distant period, turned his attention that way, by proving how uncertain was the tenure by which he held Kandahár.*

seems to be an error of the copyist for Síwí, as it is properly named in the Tabakáte Akberi, his authority.

* The events that succeed are very uncertain. Some authors make Shah Beg send Mírza Isa Terkhán to revenge the death of Muhammed; and say that he encountered Mobárek, whom he routed and drove into Bheker, which Shah Beg himself took by capitulation; and that the Beg even reduced Sehwán. They add that Jám Nanda made repeated fruitless attempts to recover Síwí; but the prowess of the Arghúns had made such an impression on the inhabitants of Sind, that they did not willingly face them in the field. See Tab. Akberi, f. 507.; Ferishta, vol. iv. pp. 427, 428.; Ayeen-Akberi, vol. ii. p. 120. Altogether, the dates of the conquest of Bheker and Sehwan are very obscure. Shah

BOOK II.

In dread from Shah Ismael, A. H. 917, A. D. 1511.

When Shah Ismael defeated the Uzbeks and took possession of Khorásán, the Arghún chief, the principal part of whose dominions were dependent on that country, was once more filled with apprehension. Soon after the battle of Merv, the victorious Persian sent a detachment, which advanced as far as Sistán, on its route to Kandahár, for the purpose of enforcing the claims which he had over it, in right of his recent conquest. This brought matters to a crisis, and we soon after find Shah Beg holding a council of his nobles. To them he represented the difficult position in which, by the defeat of Sheibáni, his protector, he was placed, between the Persian and Chaghatái princes; and pointed out the impossibility of successfully resisting a monarch like Shah Ismael, then in the height of his power. He therefore declared that he had come to the resolution, as on the whole the best he could adopt, to accompany to the royal presence the general of the Persian troops that had been sent against him, on the guarantee of that officer for his safety; and to make his submission to the Shah, in person. At the same time he sent a mission to Kábul, to conciliate Báber.*

Resolves to submit.

Repairs to Herát.

On his arrival at Herát, he met with a gracious reception, was excused the ceremony of prostrating himself before the sovereign, according to what was now become the received etiquette of that court, and was only required to bend the knee, in conformity with the Chaghatái usage. After he had remained there some time, and seemed to have gained all that he had desired, it was settled that he was to take leave on his return home, at the approaching festival of the Noroz.† But before that day arrived, things took another turn. The Persian general was sent to the castle of Ekhtiár-eddín; and Shah Beg himself was thrown into prison

Thrown into prison.

Beg was certainly in possession of Kahan when Báber conquered Kábul.

* Tar. Sind. ff. 98, 99.

† The Persian new-year, at the vernal equinox.

in the fortress of Zefer *, and charged with having, by his pretensions to independence, attempted to deprive his sovereign of a portion of his dominions. His followers dispersed; some of them found their way back to Kandahár, while others lurked about in Herát; but all of them continued firmly resolved to seize upon any accident that might occur, to render assistance to their beloved master. CHAP. V.

Plot to deliver him.

Shah Ismael soon after quitted Herát, on his return to Irák; and Shah Beg was left to linger out his life in prison. But when some time had elapsed, Mahter Sambal, one of his attached slaves,—believing that the first vigilance of the gaolers was relaxed so far as to afford him hopes, by patient perseverance, to gain an interview with his lord,—repaired to the fort of Zefer; and, having learned how matters were then conducted, opened a pastry-shop, close to the tower in which Shah Beg was confined. In the course of his calling, by his conciliating manners, joined with occasional little presents of his sweetmeats and pastry, contriving to form an intimacy with the guards, he went quietly and steadily on, omitting nothing that could forward the design he had in view. By frankly associating and mixing with them, he lulled all suspicion; gradually gained ready admittance into the tower; and, having first put the prisoner on his guard by signs and hints, at length succeeded in speaking with him privately. Shah Beg being thus prepared, twelve of his faithful retainers bound themselves to each other by an oath, either to deliver him from prison and convey him to Kandahár, or to perish in the attempt.†

which succeeds.

When everything was arranged, the conspirators repaired to the castle, at different times; and were one by one received into Sambal's shop, where they lay concealed. At night, Sambal, who had prepared some

* Perhaps the name may be a Kila-Zefer, somewhere near Herát.

† Tar. Sind. f. 99.

BOOK II. sweetmeats and pastry for the occasion, in which he had mixed a strong narcotic, disposed of them as usual among the guards, who were thus in a short time rendered quite insensible. He then passed the sleeping guard, accompanied by two of his associates; made his way good to Shah Beg's room; and, by means of some ropes which they brought for the purpose, assisted him to descend on that part of the tower which opened on the outside of the fort of Zefer. The rope, however, having broken, he fell from some height, and, in the fall, his manacles, from which they had not been able to disengage him, knocked out one of his teeth. In spite of this accident, his friends, who were waiting below, got him mounted, and they all set out on horses, shod, it is said, backwards, to mislead the pursuers. They rode incessantly for two nights and a day, when, getting a change of horses, they resumed their route, and went on without halting, till they arrived on safe ground. As soon as the keepers of the tower recovered their senses, and found the prisoner gone, a hot pursuit commenced, but in vain. The fugitives were already too much ahead to be overtaken.*

Turns his views towards Sind.

It was now more evident than ever to Shah Beg, how little he could depend upon the favourable disposition of either of his neighbours. Fortunately, the occupation afforded to Shah Ismael by his wars against the Ottomans in the west, and the attempts of Báber, immediately after the overthrow of Sheibáni, to conquer from the Uzbeks the ancient possessions of his family beyond the Amu, withdrew the attention of both for some years from the kingdom of Kandahár; and afforded leisure to Shah Beg, who was sensible that this respite was but temporary, deliberately to consider his situation, and to mature his plans.

A.H. 917—920, A.D. 1511—1514.

Consults

When affairs were somewhat settled in Kandahár, he

* Tar. Sind. f. 100.

assembled his Arghúns and Terkháns, who had always preserved much of the original spirit and equality of their tribes, and addressed them on the danger of their position, between the kingdoms of Khorásán and Kábul; and pointed out the expediency, while there was yet time, of securing some place of refuge, which might receive them in case of necessity. His views were shared by them all, and the entire possession of Síwí was naturally pitched upon for their first attempt. It lay on the side most remote from their powerful neighbours; it possessed a natural barrier of rugged mountains, and of long and difficult passes; while, at the same time, the possession of it would be a step towards the ultimate conquest of the rich and extensive kingdom of Sind.

CHAP. V.

with his chiefs.

Takes Síwí.

Síwí or Síwistán, a name which seems then to have been applied to a larger portion of the territory between the Afghán and Balúch country than now goes under that denomination, was held partly, as we have seen, by Shah Beg, and partly by the family of Sultan Perowli Birlás *, of the old Túrki race, who, on hearing of Shah Beg's intentions, sent him a friendly mission, with such presents as he could command. They were accepted, but did not prevent Shah Beg from entering his territories, and coming by surprise on his town, also called Síwí, which he took, some of the inhabitants submitting, while others fled to Fatehpúr †, the most populous district of the province. After this success, Shah Beg, having sent back part of his troops to guard Kandahár, himself pushed on to Fatehpúr, which was fifty kos from Síwí, on the road to the Sind; but which, says the historian, is now desolate, though its walls and houses are standing. ‡ Here Sultan Perowli attacked him, with two or three thousand horse of the neigh-

* Also written Berávli and Herawali. I am by no means satisfied as to the date of these transactions.

† I know not where to look for Fatehpúr, unless it be the present Shikárpúr.

‡ He wrote A. H. 1009 (A. D. 1600).

BOOK II.

bouring tribes* that he had collected; but victory favoured the invaders, and such of the vanquished as escaped fled towards the Sind. Shah Beg now returned to Síwí, where he remained for some time; and, with a view to his future residence, gave directions for building some palaces, and for laying out gardens for himself and his nobles. He also erected a castle; after which, leaving proper officers to settle and govern the province, he hastened back to Kandahár.†

Máhchuchak. Her story.

It was on his return from one of the expeditions which he undertook at this time, for the purpose of extending his dominions towards the south, that an incident occurred which may deserve notice, both as connected with the history of Shah Beg and his successors, and as illustrative of the manners of the age. When Báber took Kandahár, the whole families of the Arghún chiefs fell into his hands, and among others Máhchuchak Begum, the daughter of Muhammed Mokím, Shah Beg's brother. This lady, as Báber himself informs us, was married, a few months after, to Kásim Gokultásh ‡, an officer of distinguished merit, to whom Báber was much attached, and to whom, at a subsequent period, he owed his life. But this alliance, formed in captivity, seems to have been painful to her relations, and was probably considered as not suitable to her rank. By Kásim she had only one daughter, Nahíd Begum, who afterwards became celebrated in the history of Sind.§

Plan for her escape.

The disgrace of having a princess of their illustrious house in a secondary situation, in a foreign land, rankled in the minds of the ladies of the haram. On Shah Beg's return from Síwí, in the midst of the re-

* These are specified to have been the Doulat-sháhis, Barghdáis, Korbáis, Lorgáhis, Balúches, and other tribes.—Tar. Sind. f. 96.

† Tar. Sind. f. 96.

‡ Mem. p. 233. The marriage appears to have taken place A. H. 913, in the winter of A. D. 1507–8.

§ Tar. Sind. f. 95.

joicings which took place on the occasion, Mokím's widow presented herself, in the garb of a mourner, standing upright, in the doorway of the palace, with a coarse black woollen cloth thrown over her head, in sign of her deep distress. She laid hold of the skirt of his garment as he entered, and with loud lamentation and tears besought him to have pity on her daughter, all that was now left of his beloved brother, and to release her from her shameful bondage. Shah Beg, moved by her misery, and by the remembrance of his brother, who had died not long before, thus forcibly brought to his mind, expressed his willingness to attempt whatever could be done to effect the object of her wishes. Success was not easy; and the consultations which he held with his nobles produced nothing satisfactory. A plan was, however, devised by the ladies in the haram, and met with his acquiescence. It was arranged that some one should be sent to open an intercourse with the princess; and, when she was fully prepared, that means should be taken to carry her off from Kábul into the hills of the Hazára country that were nearest that city; secure that, when once among the friendly mountaineers, she would soon find her way in safety to Kandahár.

In pursuance of this plan, Doulat Kitta, a female who had been a servant in Mokím's haram, was despatched to Kábul; but before setting out, in compliance with the demands of eastern decorum, she was married to one Doulat Khan. On arriving at Kábul, she contrived to introduce herself to the Begum, as a helpless stranger; and, when a safe opportunity offered, discovered herself and revealed the plan. The princess, surprised and alarmed, refused to enter into the plot, and expressed her fears that, should she reach Kandahár, her proud relations would consign her to the grave, to bury deep the stigma brought on them by her captivity. Doulat Kitta relieved her apprehensions, by taking the most solemn oath that no such intention was entertained; and that, on the contrary, the warmest welcome awaited her from her mother and her uncle. Máh Begum was at last prevailed upon to consent; the news was conveyed to Kandahár; and a select body of the first warriors and chief nobles of the kingdom was secretly despatched on the service. They took their way through the country of the Hazáras, and pushed on for the capital, having arranged with the chiefs of that tribe that they should take post on the point of their mountains nearest to Kábul, with a body of their followers, to be ready to support the party on its return. On getting near Kábul, they rested for two or three days, at a short distance from the town, to refresh their horses, and, it is said, to have them shod backwards.

which succeeds.

When everything was in readiness, Máh Begum, on the day fixed for the attempt, left her house about the time of afternoon prayers, to repair to the bath, the great place of recreation and freedom for Musulman women. Having waited till the moment when the streets were covered with the crowds leaving the mosques, she mingled with them; and, protected by the impenetrable disguise worn by Musulman ladies, which covers the whole body, leaving only an opening for the eyes, made her way, unnoticed, among the throngs that were passing to and fro. She reached in safety a convenient spot that had been fixed upon, where she was mounted on horseback, and conducted by Doulat Kitta to the party which waited her coming. Her daughter, Nahíd, then a child of only eighteen months old, and unable to bear the fatigue of the flight, was of necessity left behind. The instant she appeared, the whole party, delighted, leaped on horseback and set out along with her. All that night, and the next day, and the night following, they held on their way. In the course of the succeeding day, they arrived at their halting-place. Here, having rested awhile to recruit their exhausted strength, they went on for a day and night more, by which time they had escaped from the dangerous ground, and found themselves in safe quarters among the friendly Hazáras.

Máh Begum reaches Kandahár.

They now halted for a few days, that the princess might rest from her fatigues, and then went on to Kandahár. As she approached that place, the grand scene of her hopes and fears, Shah Beg came forth to receive and welcome her, with every demonstration of joy; saluted and embraced her affectionately as his brother's daughter, treated her with every mark of honour, conducted her to the palace, and there, taking her by the hand, placed her in the arms of her mother and her nurse. It was a day of general rejoicing, as for a great victory. All who had been engaged in the enterprise were rewarded with presents of horses, arms, or dresses of honour. In adventures and rescues such as these the Arghúns delighted, and their predatory habits taught them, like our borderers, to manage them with the utmost address and sagacity.

Anecdote of her husband.

For some time preceding these events, Máh Begum's husband, Kásim Gokultásh, had attended Báber in his wars beyond the Oxus against the Uzbeks. It happened, on one occasion, that the Emperor, while alone, was surrounded and taken by a party of the enemy. His troops were not near enough to assist him. The gallant Kásim, with admirable presence of mind, going up, and personating the Emperor, exclaimed, "How dare you touch a servant of mine? Do you not know your prince?" Deceived by his words, they let go Báber, to turn to what they supposed a richer prize; and, in the scuffle that ensued, the Emperor escaped. The Uzbeks put Kásim to death; but Báber ever after cherished and protected his family, and all his dependents, with the most affectionate care. After Kásim's death, — which, according to one authority, occurred about a year after her rescue, — his widow married her

BOOK II.

cousin, Shah Hussein, the eldest son and heir of Shah Beg; and, on his death, she married Mírza Isa Terkhán, who succeeded him in the kingdom of Tatta. Her daughter, Nahíd, Báber gave in marriage to Ma[illegible]b Ali, the son of his prime minister, Nízám-ed-din Ali Khalífa; and her name often appears, at a later period, in the history of Sind.*

Báber plans the conquest of Kandahár. A. H. 920, A.D. 1514.

The repose, which Báber's expedition against Bokhára and Samarkand had afforded to Shah Beg and the Arghúns, was at an end when the Emperor returned to Kábul, disappointed and discomfited. He had no sooner arranged the affairs of his kingdom, which he found in a state of disorder, than he directed his views, with more determination than he had ever yet done, towards the conquest of Kandahár. The time was favourable, as the attention of Shah Ismael was entirely and painfully occupied by his war in the west with the Ottoman Sultan, Selím, in which he had recently suffered a great defeat. We have seen, however, that Shah Beg was not taken by surprise. He had long anticipated such an attack, and had not only extended his dominions to the south, but had collected, within the strong town and citadel of Kandahár, all the warlike stores and provisions that he could command; and had also strengthened the defences, and manned them with his bravest and most experienced adherents. To avoid being attacked by surprise, on hearing that Báber had assembled a large army, he sent spies into the imperial camp, to bring him regular information of its numbers, and of the direction in which it moved. From them he at last learned, that a formidable army, under Báber himself, was on its march for Kandahár. As it approached that place, Báber was attacked with a dangerous illness, which so much alarmed his army, whose confidence was placed chiefly in him individually, that great trepidation

Marches against it, probably A. H. 923.

* Akbernáma, Abulfazl, f. 206.; Taríkhe-Sind, as above.

prevailed in the camp. Shah Beg, with much address, seizing the favourable moment for negotiation, sent a mission to the Emperor, composed of the chief men of Kandahár, who carried rich offerings, at the same time soliciting for a peace. Báber, as Shah Beg had foreseen, glad of a pretext for retreating with honour, accepted the presents, and, as if satisfied by his representations, sending him a dress of honour, took his way back to Kábul.*

Accommodation.

Shah Beg's alarms.

The Emperor's retreat gave some farther breathing time to Shah Beg, as the direct attempts on Kandahár do not seem to have been renewed for some years. But he is said to have declared that he clearly saw, that, independent of Báber's ambition, two circumstances would impel that prince never to desist till he had conquered Kandahár. The first was the mistaken policy of his brother Mokím, in seizing Kábul, a royal seat, held by a member of the family of Taimur, an insult which never would be forgiven; the second was the very great number of princes connected with the royal family, and of nobles of distinction, who filled the court of Báber, and for whom no provision could now be made, either in Máwerannaher or Khorásán.†

Death of Jám Nanda.

But while affairs bore this unfavourable aspect on the side of Kábul, the factions and civil wars which, in Sind, had followed the death of Jám Nanda, in consequence of the minority of his son Jám Firóz, and the consequent misery of the inhabitants, rekindled in Shah Beg the hopes which he had long cherished of effecting something considerable in that quarter. In the beginning of the winter of the following year, he dispatched, into the territory of Sind, a small detachment of a thousand horse, who plundered Kahan and Baghbán, two thriving and populous townships belonging to that country. It gives some idea of the extent of their cultivation to

Shah Beg plunders Kahan and Baghbán. A. H. 924, 18 Zikad. A. D. 1518, 21 Nov.

* Tar. Sind, ff. 100, 101.

† Tar. Sind, ut suprà.

BOOK II. A.D. 1519–20.

learn, that, from the last of these towns, the invaders, among other plunder, carried off no fewer than a thousand camels, which were employed in turning wheels to supply water for irrigation.*

His son flees to Báber.

It was about this time that Shah Hasan Arghún, Shah Beg's son, in consequence of some dispute with his father, fled to the court of Báber. He was courteously received and honourably entertained by that prince, with whom he became a favourite. Báber is said to have taken pleasure in initiating him into the arts of government, and to have predicted that he would one day become an eminent prince. He remained nearly two years with the Emperor, when, a reconciliation with his father having been effected, he returned home.†

Báber invades Kandahár. A. H. 925, A. D. 1519, A. H. 926, A. D. 1520.

The next year, Báber was employed in quelling the refractory Afgháns, and in invading the Penjáb; and the year following, he again entered the Penjáb, and had advanced as far as Siálkót on the Chenáb, when he was recalled by an invasion of his territory from Kandahár, of the particulars of which we are not informed.‡ As he had now made up his mind to his long-cherished and favourite design of invading India, an enterprise for which the circumstances of that country had become peculiarly favourable, he resolved, setting every other object aside, to exert the whole force of his dominions in the conquest of Kandahár, a measure which he considered to be an indispensable preliminary to the success of his Indian enterprise; since he could not, with safety, leave behind him an enemy so powerful and so able as Shah Beg. He therefore marched back from the Penjáb, and having expelled the invaders from his territory, at once advanced into theirs. He first of all ravaged the country of the Hazára and Nukderi tribes, who had probably been the immediate aggressors. A famine

Famine —

* Tar. Sind, i. 901. And Báber's Mem. p. 265.

† Tar. Sind, f. 102.; Báber's Mem. passim.

‡ Briggs's Ferishta, vol. ii. p. 37.; Kháfi Khan, f. 25.

CHAP. V.

A. D. 1520 –22.

at that time desolated the country of Kandahár. Nevertheless, he sat down before the capital, which he began to attack regularly by mining and by battering its walls. At the same time, he subjected it to a close blockade; and, the town being probably worse provisioned than usual, in consequence of the prevailing scarcity, the townspeople were soon reduced to the greatest distress for want of food. To famine succeeded pestilence, which, having spread into Báber's camp, early in the summer, compelled him to raise the siege, perhaps without altogether relinquishing the blockade.

Siege of Kandahár, turned into a blockade.

But Báber was fixed in his purpose; and, though Mehter Sambal, now became a favourite general of Shah Beg's, contrived to throw a supply of provisions into the town, yet Báber, next season, after marching over the country while the crops were yet on the ground, and carrying off and destroying the harvest, renewed the active siege of the town, and made the blockade closer than ever. Shah Beg, who meanwhile had been pushing on his operations in Sind with great success, and who, in the course of the year, took possession of Tatta itself, and completed the subjugation of the country, finding his affairs in Kandahár reduced to the last extremity, sent an embassy to the Emperor with proposals for peace. Negotiators from both sides having met, a treaty was soon concluded and signed; by which it was stipulated, that Shah Beg should hold Kandahár till the following year, when the city and all the dependent provinces were to be delivered up to the Emperor. The interval thus allowed, Shah Beg employed in removing his own family and effects, and those of his followers and adherents, in the first instance, to Shál and Síwí; and next year, when Báber again advanced to Kandahár, the keys of that capital, and of the citadel were presented to him by Mír Ghiás-ed-dín*, the nephew of the historian Khondemir, the

Báber lays waste the country, A. H. 927. A. D. 1521.

Convention for the eventual surrender of Kandahár,

which is finally given up to Báber. A. H. 928, A. D. 1522.

* The Tárikhe-Sind calls him the father of Mír Abul-Mokárem, f. 109.

BOOK II.
A. D. 1522.

celebrated author of the Habíb-es-Seir. The Emperor, at the same time, took possession of the whole country of Kandahár and its dependencies, including parts of the Germsír along the course of the Helmend; which formed the utmost limit that his empire ever reached in that direction.*

* In this account of the reduction of Kandahár we are not assisted by Abulfazl, and but little by Ferishta or Kháfi Khan. The Taríkhe-Sind is the principal authority, and its chronology is very perplexing. Ferishta says, (vol. ii. p. 37.) that the siege lasted three years; Kháfi Khan (f. 25.) says, four; and Mírza Haider (Taríkh. Reshidi, f. 275.) says, five. Operations were carried on for several years, probably rather by wasting the country and blockading the town, than by a regular siege.

CHAPTER VI.

ARGHÚN CONQUEST OF SIND AND MULTÁN.

SECTION I.

CONQUEST OF SIND.

TRANSACTIONS IN SIND. — SUCCESSIVE DYNASTIES. — REIGN OF JÁM FIRÓZ. — MISRULE AND REBELLION. — SHAH BEG CALLED IN. — HE TAKES TATTA. — UPPER SIND CEDED TO HIM. — REVOLT AGAINST THE ARGHÚNS. — USURPATION OF SILÁH-ED-DÍN, WHOM SHAH BEG DEFEATS AND SLAYS IN BATTLE. — SHAH BEG'S MEASURES TO SETTLE THE COUNTRY. — HE MAKES BHEKER HIS CAPITAL. — DEATH OF SHAH BEG. — HIS CHARACTER.

Transactions in Sind.

HAVING accompanied the Arghúns so long in their progress, during their rise and fall in Kandahár, it may be convenient, while their history is yet familiar to the reader, to follow the dynasty into the territory of Sind, to which they turned their arms, and thus prevent the necessity of interrupting the course of the narrative at a future period.

Shah Beg retires from Kandahár.

During part of the last years of his possession of Kandahár, Shah Beg had been employed in removing the families and property of his retainers to Shál and Síwí, beyond the limits of that kingdom. These became his place of arms in the invasion of Lower Sind, an undertaking which he had long meditated and now resolved upon. Indeed, the undisturbed and quiet way in which he removed from Kandahár, so unlike the ordinary transactions of the age, and the good terms

BOOK II. on which he and his successor appear to have subsequently lived with Báber, make it not improbable that his giving up Kandahár was attended with an understanding, that he was to be allowed unmolested to attack Sind, and provide for his numerous tribesmen and retainers, whom that event had thrown destitute, by estates which their sword could conquer on the fertile banks of the Indus.

Successive Dynasties of Sind.

Sind, the country in which Shah Beg, thus expelled from Kandahár, resolved to establish the seat of his government, though conquered by the Muhammedan Khalifs in the end of the first century of the Hejra, was not long retained by them. It was afterwards, for some time, governed by a race, who, as they are said to have been descended from the Ansaris, or companions of Muhammed, must have been Musulmans. To them succeeded the Sumras, a native tribe, who, with some intervals, reigned till about A.H. 740, when they were expelled by the Sammas, a tribe distinguished by the name of Jám. This dynasty, which sometimes was subject to Delhi, and sometimes shook off its yoke, still continued to reign when Shah Beg turned his eyes towards their dominions.

A.H. 740, A.D. 1340.

Extent of territory.

Jám Nanda*, who was the reigning prince in the time of Shah Beg's father, and for some time after his own accession, appears to have possessed an extensive territory, which originally reached from the ocean to the Multán territory, above Bheker, on the one side; and from the Rájpút desert and Kach, to the Bolán Pass and Balúchistán, on the other; comprehending, the Delta of the Indus and the country on both sides of the river to some distance from its banks, especially Sehwán, with Shíkárpore, Kach-Gandava, and part of Síwistán. Some portion of these dominions, we have

* They pretended that they were descended from the Persian Jamshíd, whence they called their Makádam or Kílanter, Jám. Tabakáte Akberi, f. 506.

however seen, had been wrested by the Arghúns from Jám Nanda, in his lifetime.* CHAP. VI. SECT. I.

* There is much confusion in the latter years of the Sind dynasty, and especially as to the date of the close of Jám Nanda's reign.

The dates on the margin of Briggs's Ferishta, vol. iv. pp. 423—430., are, I presume, those of the translator, carrying forward the reigns of the successive princes, according to the number of years allotted to them in the text. Jám Nanda's death is placed A. H. 894.

In all the lists of the princes of the Sama race, which I have had access to consult, the lengths of the reigns differ; especially that of Jám Nanda, the father of Jám Firóz, the last prince of the race. The Tabakáte Akberi gives him sixty-two years, the Ayín Akberi sixty years and some months, Ferishta thirty-two years, and the Taríkhe-Sind forty-eight years. But it is difficult to find a correct previous date from which to start.

The Tarikhe-Sind makes Jám Radhan assume the masnad, A. H. 858, Jemadi, i. 6. According to it, he reigned eight years and a half, when he was poisoned by Jám Sanjer, who succeeded, and reigned eight years. To him Nanda succeeded, A. H. ., Rebi i. 25. The year is confusedly written, but seems 8—4.

Now, eight years and six months from A. H. 858, Jemadi i. 6. would bring the commencement of Sanjer's reign to A. H. 866, Zikada 6, and the eight years of Sanjer's reign to A. H. 874, Zikada 6, within less than two months of A. H. 875; but, both the Tabakát and Ayín Akberi allow him a few months beyond the eight years, which would bring him into A. H. 875; and the forty-eight years assigned to Jám Nanda's reign, in the Taríkh, would bring his death to A. H. 823, the date assigned to it in the Tarikhe-Sind, f. 103. This is too late to agree with known facts. But if Jám Radhan's reign of eight years and a half be deducted, it brings us back to A. H. 914.

Abulfazl in his list, Ayín Akberi, vol. ii. p. 122., makes Jám Radman (Radhan) and Jám Sanjer the same person, and assigns only eight years and some months to both. None of the lists, except that of the Tar. Sind, gives a separate place to Jám Radhan; though the details presented in that work hardly admit of the supposition that they are the same person. If we strike out Jám Radhan's reign, preserving the date of his accession as that of Jám Sanjer's, Jám Nanda's accession would be A. H. 866, and his death A. H. 914.

The Kholáset-ul-Towáríkh, f. 344., following the Tar. Behader-Sháhi, makes Jám Siláh-ed-dín lead an army into Sind, A. H. 918. His last invasion, when he expelled Jám Firóz was in A. H. 926, immediately before the conquest of Sind, A. H. 927. (Ferishta, vol. iv. pp. 429, 430.) And Abulfazl in the Ayín Akberi, vol. ii. p. 122, gives Jám Firóz twelve years of reign, before his expulsion by Siláh-ed-dín. Taking this to mean the second invasion of A. H. 926, would bring Jám Firóz's accession to A. H. 914. Shah Husein took possession of Tatta in A. H. 927, though Jám Firóz maintained a contest for some time later.

On this hypothesis, Jám Nanda died about A. H. 914; Jám Silah-ed-dín invaded Sind, A. H. 918 and 926; Tatta was taken possession of by Shah Husein, A. H. 927.

In fixing on A. H. 927 for the

BOOK II.

Jám Firóz, a minor. Probably about A. H. 914, A. D. 1508.

On Jám Nanda's death, the country was exposed to all the evils of a disputed succession. His son, Jám Firóz, being a minor, Siláh-ed-dín, his relation, the grandson of Jám Sinjer, the predecessor of the late prince, openly aspired to the crown. But Jám Firóz, being supported by Deria Khan, the minister, and by the chief families and holy men of Tatta, was finally established on the throne. Siláh-ed-dín, compelled to flee, repaired to Gújrát, where he remained several years with Mozeffer Shah, with whom he was connected by marriage. During a portion of that time, Sind enjoyed repose; but, as Jám Firóz grew to manhood, like other princes educated in ease and pleasure, he gave himself up entirely to sensual and selfish enjoyment, neglecting the affairs of his government. The natural consequence ensued. His courtiers and the Sammas of his tribe were guilty of much oppression, both among the townspeople and the inhabitants of the country, who were of a different race from themselves; and the Jám, in spite of the repeated representations and remonstrances of his minister, having persisted in protecting the aggressors, Deria Khan, in despair of being able to conduct the public affairs with satisfaction to himself, or benefit to the country, withdrew from his charge, and retired to his jágír of Kahan, where for several years he gave himself up to the moral and religious studies of the times.*

Misgovernment.

Discontent; Siláh-ed-dín called in,

The inevitable effects of such misgovernment were soon visible. Discontent became universal, and oppression spread wider and became more audacious. The leading men of the older race of inhabitants, and the chief merchants, resolved to hazard every calamity

conquest of Tatta, we are supported by Ferishta and the numerical words *Kharábi-e-Sind*, mentioned in the Tabakáti Akberi.

Still, however, it must be acknowledged that the time of Jám Nanda's death is far from being certain.

* Tar. Sind, ff. 69, 70.

rather than continue in their present state of suffering. They, therefore, sent privately to invite Siláh-ed-dín to assume the government of the country, representing the time as most favourable, the Jám being a weak debauchee, while his late minister and great support, Deria Khan, had retired in disgust from public life. Siláh-ed-dín communicated to his relation, Mozeffer Shah, the letters and invitation which he had received; and, in a short time, by that prince's assistance, he was enabled to return to Sind at the head of a considerable army; and, marching incessantly, contrived to cross the Indus, and come upon Tatta, while Jám Firóz was quite unprepared to oppose him. That weak prince, without resistance, fled up the western bank of the river. The successful invader, having entered the capital, mounted the throne of Sind; and divided the property and possessions of the clansmen and adherents of his rival among his own supporters, the country in general observing the change with joy.

who ascends the throne.

Roused from his dream of pleasure by these decisive events, Jám Firóz looked around him, and saw no hope of retrieving his ruined affairs, but in the assistance of his late minister, to whom he dispatched his mother, to express his profound regret for his past misconduct, and to solicit his support and countenance. Deria Khan was easily moved to lend his aid; and, leaving his retirement, by the influence which he possessed over the whole western bank of the Indus, he soon collected a body of troops, chiefly from Bheker and Síwístán. Firóz's standard was joined by numbers from the Balúch and other neighbouring tribes; and it would appear that the Arghúns, too, lent a body of troops, under the command, it is said, of Mehter Sambal, originally the slave, and now the favourite general, of Shah Beg.* When all were ready, Deria Khan moved down to

Deria Khan joins Firóz.

* Tar. Sind, f. 108.

BOOK II. attack Jám Siláh-ed-dín; but was met by that prince's general, Háji Vasír, and, after a bloody battle, defeated and forced to retreat. From the field of battle, Háji Vasír wrote to inform Siláh-ed-dín of his success, and that affairs bore the fairest aspect. The messenger who carried his letter happened to fall into the hands of a party of the enemy, and, with the letter, was brought to Deria Khan. That crafty statesman substituted and forwarded a different letter, also written in the Háji's name, to announce that his army had been completely routed, that the enemy was advancing in full force, and advising his master to remove his haram and followers from Tatta without any delay, and to meet him at the town of Cháchgán, to which place he was himself directing his march. The stratagem succeeded. Siláh-ed-dín in dismay abandoned his capital by night, and crossed the river, to the total ruin of his affairs. He was afterwards met by Háji Vasír, when an explanation took place, but too late to repair the mischief that had been done; so that he was compelled once more to retire into Gujrát, after having reigned eight months in Tatta. Deria Khan, after having pursued him into the desert, returned to Tatta, on the morning of the grand Muhammedan festival that takes place on the conclusion of the feast of Ramzán, and replaced Jám Firóz on the throne.*

Battle.

9 Ramzán, A. H. 918.

Siláh-ed-dín retires to Gujrát.

Firóz restored. Id-al-Fitr.

Misrule.

Jám Firóz continued to reign for some years after he had thus regained his dominions; but the vices which had already excited discontent among his sub-

* Taríkhe-Sind, ff. 70, 71, 72.; Briggs's Ferishta, vol. iv. p. 429. The year in which these events took place is uncertain. The Kholáset-al-Towáríkh mentions A. H. 918, as the year in which Siláh-ed-dín invaded Gujrát, f. 344.; but other dates in the passage are incorrect. The Taríkhe-Sind, ff. 71, 72. mentions the 9th Ramzán as the night on which he quitted Tatta, and the Id-al-Fitr as the day on which Firóz re-entered it, but does not specify the year. Ferishta makes Deria Khan, in the first instance, join Siláh-ed-dín, but afterwards return to his allegiance to Firóz, and assist in expelling the pretender, which is far from being improbable.

jects, and driven him from his throne, produced the same effects once more. It was no time to slumber, when he had active and keen-sighted enemies on every hand. The prospect of the occupation of Kandahár, by Báber, was an event of the utmost importance to his affairs, as it was likely to bring the whole force of the Arghúns close upon his frontier. After Shah Beg had removed the families of his adherents to Shál and Síwí, as famine still raged in Kandáhar, they were exposed to great distress, from scarcity of food, in their new quarters.* It never had been his intention to confine his warriors to the barren residence of the desert, and he had sent spies into the richer and more civilised country of Sind, to discover what chance of success awaited him should he make an attempt on that province. They found everything favourable to his enterprise. The misgovernment of the Jám had spread universal discontent, and the ryots prayed for a change. The Doulat-sháhi and Turgáhi tribes, which Shah Beg, in his former expeditions, had expelled from Síwí, had been allowed to settle in one of the suburbs of Tatta; and they now invited their late enemy, promising to join him. Some Arghúns, who had fled from his camp for offences, or left it for other causes, and taken refuge in Sind, were also authorised by the malcontents to invite Shah Beg to invade the country; and he did not hesitate to obey the call.† Leaving sufficient garrisons in Shál, Síwí, Fatehpúr, and Ganjába to protect these forts, and the families and property

Shah Beg invited,

* It is usual for eastern princes to give assignments or drafts out of the revenues of their provinces, for the payment of the troops and officers. In the present instance, the distress was so great, that Shah Beg is said to have been compelled to give drafts to his troops, for a certain quantity of turnips, carrots, and other roots. Tar. Sind, f. 103.

† A.H. 925. (A.D. 1518). The Tarikhe-Sind, f. 72. reads 916, but probably *asher* (ten) should be read *asherein* (twenty). As, however, the date 11 Moharrem, A.H. 926, occurs soon after, I have ventured to make the date 925, the end of the preceding year.

BOOK II.

marches towards Tatta.

of his followers, which they contained, to the delight of his troops he led them towards the provinces on the Indus, the granary of that quarter. He was preceded by Mír Fázil Gokultásh, with two hundred and forty chosen horse, who, entering the Sind country, passed the town of Bághbán.* An army of Sammas had been collected by Mahmúd Matin Khan, at Tilhati †, on the left bank of the Indus, three or four kos from Sehwán, to oppose and watch the motions of the invaders. Shah Beg, with the main body of his army, followed Mír Fázil. As he approached, the head-men and inhabitants of Bághbán hastened to submit, and entered with zeal into his service.‡

Advances to the capital.

His great aim now was to induce the Sindians to submit without fighting, and, to attain that object, he lavished favours on all who joined him. But, finding the progress of revolt slower than he wished, he resolved on more active measures. Marching from the Lakhi hills, he left behind the hostile army at Tilhati, advanced rapidly towards Tatta, and soon encamped on the banks of the Khanwa, about three kos to the south of that capital. At that time, a great branch of the river flowed to the south of Tatta, and, from its depth, he found great difficulty in crossing, all the boats having been carefully removed. Fortunately, however, a herdsman was observed, who had effected a passage from the other side, and who, being examined, pointed out a ford, by which the whole cavalry was enabled to get over, leaving the baggage protected by a strong guard. Shah Beg then advanced towards Tatta; upon which Dera Khan, leaving Jám Firóz in the city, marched out with a large force to repel the invaders.§

11 Moharram, A. H. 926, 2 January, A. D. 1520.

* I know not what district is here called Baghbán; perhaps Larkhána.

† Probably the Titli-Mur of Burnes's map, which, however, is on the right bank of the river.

‡ Tar. Sind, ff. 103, 104.

§ Dera Khan is called the adopted son (piser-e khwándeh) of Jám Nanda.—Tar. Sind, f. 103. He may, however, be Deria Khan the minister.

In the battle that ensued Shah Beg's hardy veterans were successful. Dera Khan, with some other noblemen, and numbers of Sammas, were taken prisoners and put to death. Jám Firóz, filled with alarm, fled from the city, and crossed the Indus. The town of Tatta was entered by the victorious troops, and for days subjected to all the outrages and miseries that are the lot of a city taken by storm. Numbers of the wives and children of the inhabitants of all classes were reduced to slavery. Shah Beg, placing a guard on the palace, which Jám Firóz had abandoned, saved the honour of his family, who, from the suddenness of the calamity, had all been left behind, and treated his children and the females of his haram with the greatest respect. On the tenth day, when the lust and rapacity even of the merciless plunderers had been nearly satiated, Kázi Káz, a holy man, who, in the midst of the general ruin, had in vain been seeking in every quarter for his wife and children, sat down, and, with an eloquence that flowed from the heart, addressed a letter to Shah Beg, in which he described the intolerable misery endured by the inhabitants. It was conveyed to the Arghún chief, and touched his feelings. He straightway took an arrow from his quiver, and, delivering it to the Imám, who was the bearer of the letter, commanded one of his own attendants to accompany him round the city, with orders that the pillage should instantly cease, and that the persons and property of the inhabitants should thenceforward be respected. This ordinance, enforced by the respected symbol that accompanied it, met with unhesitating obedience, and an end was put to the barbarous scenes that afflicted a great and unfortunate city.

Defeats the Sindis.

Tatta sacked.

The pillage stopped.

Jám Firóz, on finding his women and family in the hands of Shah Beg, remained for some time at Purar, showing every sign of profound affliction. He deputed some of his chief officers to conciliate the victor. A

Treaty with Jám Firóz.

BOOK II.

negociation was soon entered into, and, as he made the humblest submissions, meanly laying the blame of the late war on the instigations of his ministers, and vowing eternal subserviency and gratitude to the invader, a treaty was not long of being concluded.* His family being sent back, he waited on Shah Beg, and it was finally agreed, that all the country from the Lakhi hills downwards, including Tatta, should remain the Jám's, while all the territory of Sind above these mountains was to be held by Shah Beg.

End of Sefer, A.H. 926, February, A.D. 1520.

Confederacy against the Arghúns.

The victorious army now marched out of Tatta, and encamped on the outside of the city; but the news from Sehwán † speedily recalled Shah Beg to that quarter. The regular form which the invasion of the Arghúns had assumed, did not seem likely to terminate in a mere political ascendency, leaving the wealth and property of the country much as before; but threatened to extend to a violent occupation of the very houses, lands, and property of the inhabitants, to support a numerous, rapacious, and famished body of Tartar adventurers, who were settling down like a swarm of locusts, devouring all they met with, and insatiate for more. The alarm spread on every side. A great assemblage of all the neighbouring chiefs and tribes, including the Safías and Sodhas, had met at Tilhati, and unanimously vowed to remain united, and never, while they had life, to desist from hostility to Shah Beg and his tribe.

Measures of Shah Beg,

Shah Beg hastened by rapid marches to Sehwán ‡, and, having reduced the castle, left a force, under some of his most trusty nobles, to defend the adjoining country. Bheker, he left in charge of Sultan Mahmúd

* Tar. Sind, f. 103—107. Suspicions were very generally entertained that Jám Firóz had joined in inviting Shah Beg into Sind, that he might free himself from the control of his minister.

† Síwístán,—by which name Sehwán is often called.

‡ Kila-Síwístán.

Khan Kokiltash, and proceeded to Shál, to bring down the families which had been left there. Kázi Káz, whom Shah Beg sent to Tilhati to Mahmúd Matin Khan, the brother of Dera Khan, as an envoy, to attempt to soothe the enmity of the confederates, was refused admission into the place. Shah Beg therefore found it necessary, on his return from Shál, to move against them, and encamped on the banks of the Indus opposite the Tilhati, where he halted three days. Here he learned that a difference of opinion, so fatal to confederacies, existed among the allies; that the chiefs were disposed to come to an accommodation, but were thwarted by the furious bigotry and intolerance of Mahdúm Bilál, a saintly theologian, who possessed the greatest influence on the popular mind. That very night, having secured some boats, Shah Beg effected the passage of his whole army. The allies pushed forward their advance, under Waran-mal Sodha, to check the Arghúns; but it was met and driven back by the gallantry and skill of Mír Fázil Gokultásh, who, pursuing his advantage, followed them close in their flight. Shah Beg, on coming up, found the battle won, and that his men had pushed forward to the very gates of the town. The rout was complete; numbers of the Samma army were intercepted and prevented from entering the place. Many were killed, and many threw themselves into the river and were drowned; others effected their escape and reached Sehwán.* For three whole days, the fighting and carnage continued in the town, every foot of which was desperately defended, till Waran-mal and his Sodhas perished to the last man. Few of the inhabitants were left alive. This decisive blow secured for a long time the peace of the surrounding country.†

who defeats the allies.

The treaty with Jám Firóz had not been long con-

Firóz's misconduct.

* Síwístán, Tar. Sind.

† Tar. Sind, f. 107, 108.

BOOK II. cluded, and the Arghún and Terkhán troops withdrawn from the province of Lower Sind, when the misgovernment and discontent inseparable from a falling state again became rapidly visible. The news of what was passing at Tatta, and the disasters, incapacity, and unpopularity of Jám Firóz, once more emboldened Siláh-ed-dín to attempt to recover a throne, his possession of which had formerly been so transient. He was now in high favour and power at the court of Gujrát, and was soon enabled, by the assistance of Mozeffer Shah, to enter Sind at the head of ten thousand horse, chiefly Jánijas *, Sodhas, Sammas and Kattis. He was favourably received; and the pusillanimous Jám, who had no resources in himself, and deserved nothing from his subjects, fled on the first alarm of his approach, and hastened towards Sehwán †, to claim the succour of the Arghún nobles, who, with a strong body of troops, had been left in that place, for the purpose of assisting him in case of need. Siláh-ed-dín quietly took possession of the capital, and of all the lower country, and at the same time dispatched a force in pursuit of his rival.

Siláh-ed-dín seizes Tatta.

When the Jám reached Sehwán, he found that Shah Beg was absent, anxiously engaged in settling his affairs on the side of Shál and Kandahár. But the Amírs who were left in charge of the province dispatched a messenger to inform him of what had occurred, and to ask his instructions. This messenger was accompanied by an ambassador from the Jám, craving his protection. The Beg, who well perceived how much it was his interest to support his own creature, ordered his Amírs to hold themselves in readiness to assist him, and dispatched from Shál his son, Shah Hasan, who in twenty days reached Sehwán, with a strong body of cavalry, and took the command. He was followed by repeated

Shah Beg moves to meet him.

14 Moharrem, A. H. 927, 25 Dec. A. D. 1520.

* So in the MS. Taríkhe-Sind, f. 108.; perhaps Jharijas.

† Síwístán, Tar. Sind.

reinforcements of men and supplies of warlike stores, and Shah Beg himself promised soon to join them.*

On hearing of this concentration of the Arghún troops, Siláh-ed-dín's army, which, under the command of Sarang Khan and Ran-mal Sodha, had pursued Jám Firóz into Sehwán, and was now watching his motions, retreated; and, crossing the Direh †, strongly entrenched themselves at Tilhati, where they maintained a threatening aspect. Shah Beg, leaving Kázi Káz, now become one of his leading counsellors, to bring on the women and heavy baggage, joined his army. On his arrival, he sent forward Jám Firóz under the guidance of Shah Hasan, and a strong detachment of troops, who, giving the confederates the slip, advanced on the road to Tatta. No sooner did Siláh-ed-dín hear of this movement, than he abandoned Tatta, crossed the Direh, and encamped at Jún; so that Jám Firóz, hastening forward once more, entered his capital, came out in grand cavalcade to receive Shah Hasan as he approached, presented him with rich offerings, and treated him with every mark of consideration and honour. By their joint efforts, they speedily brought into the field a formidable army, and moved to face Siláh-ed-dín. After a few marches the armies met, and Haibat, Siláh-ed-dín's son, who commanded the advance, having been attacked and surrounded by a superior force of the Arghúns, was slain. His father, informed of this misfortune, brought on his main body; and, thinking only of revenge, rushed furiously on the enemy, who received him with steadiness; and he fell fighting with desperation. The wreck of his army escaped to Gujrát. Shah Hasan, having halted three days on the field, returned back with Jám Firóz. The result of the battle was announced from Bághban by Shah Beg, not in the

defeats and slays Siláh-ed-dín.

* Tar. Sind, f. 109.

† I know not if the Direh or Dira be a particular branch of the Indus, or a Sindi corruption for *deria*, the river.

BOOK II. name of the Jám, but in that of his own son, Mírza Shah Hasan, a decisive mark of the insignificance to which the nominal sovereign of Sind had been reduced. And this period may be taken as the termination of the dynasty of the Sammas, and the commencement of that of the Arghúns, in Sind.*

Rebi II. A.H. 927, March, A.D. 1521.

Military licence.

An incident, which occurred at this time, may serve to show the mode in which military movements were conducted in that age and country. Shah Beg's men, who accompanied the families and property of the army, or rather of the tribe, on its way from Shál to Sind, had reached Machi, a considerable town; when, receiving or fancying some insult, they attacked and took the place, slew the inhabitants, seized their effects and cattle, and razed it to the ground.†

Shah Beg strengthens his forts.

The uniform success that had attended Shah Beg's enterprises on the Indus, now afforded him some leisure, which he employed in settling his conquests, and arranging his ulterior plans. For that purpose, he returned to Bághban, where he was met by Shah Hasan, who had left Jám Firóz in Tatta,—with a body of troops, who, under pretence of protecting him, in reality relieved him from the whole burden of government. Shah Hasan was accompanied by the main body of his victorious army, whom his father received with joy, and honoured with rewards. Shah Beg, leaving them there to rest after their fatigues, repaired once more to Sehwán, where he inspected the condition of the fort, which he repaired, and fitted both for defence and as a convenient depôt for the families of his followers. He commanded a large quantity of grain to be laid up in store, and enjoined each of his principal adherents to build a house for his own accommodation, marking out the ground for that purpose, as well as for the houses of the lower ranks. He then rejoined the army, which

* Tar. Sind, ff. 108—110.

† It lies in the present Kach-Gandava. Tar. Sind, f. 108.

marched for Bheker. After the first day's march, he dismissed Jám Firóz's ambassador with presents and letters, intimating his intention of soon marching to conquer Gujrát, and, when in possession of that kingdom, he promised to restore Sind to the Jám, in all its ancient extent.*

Affairs at Bheker.

On reaching Chanduka †, a confidential servant ‡ of Sultan Mahmúd Khan, who commanded in Bheker, arrived in the camp, to explain to Mír Fázil Gokultásh, his father, the difficult situation in which he was placed. When he was made governor of that important fortress, he was advised to conduct himself by the advice of the great Syeds of the place, who formed numerous and powerful families that had long had great influence in that quarter, and who had become responsible for the management of affairs; and Shah Beg had also directed some of the chief men of the Dharícha tribe to remain in the fort. The latter, having become discontented, fled from it, were now in a state of active hostility, and, to the utmost of their power, obstructed the governor's operations. The truth seems to be that the new rule of the Arghúns was not popular. Taxes and duties were imposed, which the people of the country positively refused to pay, and not only turned back with disgrace the officers sent to levy them, but assembled in force in the plain of Lohri, ready to offer battle to the governor. Sultan Mahmúd, Mír Fazil's son, then only twelve years of age, was eager to march out against them; but his boyish impetuosity was restrained by the Syeds, who, on two occasions, when the Dharícha men threatened to cross over, and seize both the fort and Mahmúd, manned the towers and ramparts, and, by the bold face which they presented, dispelled the danger.

* Tar. Sind, f. 111.

† Chandhoh, said to be thirty kos west from Bheker.

‡ Baba Chuchak, his Anka, or foster-father.

BOOK II.

Mír Fázil communicated this information to Shah Beg, and was directed to cross the river at Chanduka with two hundred horse. Having succeeded in allaying the fears of the kilanters and heads of villages, he induced them to come in, and accompany him in his march. On his reaching Beheri Alúr, not far from Bheker, his son intended to have come out to meet him in *iṣtákbál*, with an honorary cavalcade, but his father ordered him not to leave the fort, to be watchfully on his guard, and at once to throw into prison every person within it, of whose dispositions he entertained the smallest doubt.

Murder of the Dharícha and other chiefs.

When Fázil arrived in the vicinity of Bheker, Lula, the chief of the Dharícha Zemindars, waited upon him with his brethren; and the kilanters (or head-men) of different other townships, also, came in to tender their services; so that, on reaching Lohri, he had forty-seven of the leading men of the district in his power. The Arghúns had resolved to carry matters with a high and merciless hand, and at once to break the spirit of the country. They were looking round for lands in which to settle, and jágírs to hold, and wished to have no men of influence to interfere with or impede their measures. Mír Fázil put to death, in the first instance, twenty-seven of these men. As soon as Shah Beg heard of Mír Fázil's success, he pushed on for Bheker, and encamped in the plain, at the village of Sakhar. The town and fort of Bheker is situated on an island in the Indus, having the town of Lohri or Rohri on the left bank, and that of Sakhar on the right, immediately facing it. Sultan Mahmúd Khan, after waiting upon his father at Lohri, rowed across the river, and was presented to Shah Beg, who received him with distinguished favour. The Sultan having made his report of the state of the country and exposed his grievances, the Beg turned to Kázi Káz, who was present, and looked at him, as if to ask his opinion. The Kázi remarked, that, certainly the country was under water, and that, in consequence, a number of weeds had sprung up, which much required the assiduous use of the weeding hook. Shah Beg instantly gave orders that the rest of the Dharícha prisoners should be put to death. Sultan Mahmúd, whose cruel and tyrannical disposition was derived from a taint of insanity, or increased by it, received the commands with pleasure; and, returning into the fort, had them all murdered that same night, and their bleeding bodies cast over a tower, which was ever after called "the Bloody Tower."*

The Syeds forced to leave Bheker.

Soon after this barbarous execution, Sultan Mahmúd, accompanied by his father, brought the Syeds, to whom he had been so much indebted, and introduced them to Shah Beg. He represented their admirable conduct, and the obligations under which they had laid him. Shah Beg made many flattering inquiries into the particulars of the late occurrences, and complimented them in the highest terms on their fidelity and the courage they had displayed. After they had taken leave, he renewed his questions in private to Sultan Mahmúd, inquiring particularly regarding the Syeds, and received the same answer as before; but the Sultan, in concluding, remarked, that though these men were indeed well-disposed, and had been useful, yet that the residence within the fort of so many persons of the same class and family was any thing but expedient. Shah Beg smiling observed, "In sooth you give them right excellent commendation." Since they had now ceased to be necessary, he soon sent a civil message to let them know, that, as the Beg's men were about to enter the fort with their families, and were in want of room, it would be well if the Syeds confined themselves to two or three large houses. They understood what was meant, and, discovering that it was no longer ad-

* Burj-Khúni.

BOOK II.

visable for them to remain within Bheker, asked leave to quit it. That permission was readily granted, and they settled in the neighbouring town of Lohri.*

Shah Beg makes Bheker his capital.

Shah Beg was greatly struck with the situation of Bheker, which, from being placed in an island, besides its advantages as a nearly impregnable fortress, commanded the country on both sides of the river, and the navigation of the stream. He regarded it as admirably fitted to be the political and commercial capital of Upper Sind; and he bent all his attention to improve it to the utmost. He divided the houses and wards of the town among his Amírs and troops; and, having fixed on a plan of a castle, he divided the different portions of the fortifications among his Amírs, that they might superintend their completion. To furnish materials for the extensive works thus in progress, the fort and town of Alúr, formerly the capital of the country, but which had fallen into decay, were demolished, and the bricks transported to Bheker. The houses which had been built by many Túrks and Sammas, in the immediate neighbourhood of Bheker itself, shared the same fate. It is said that, when Shah Beg first laid down his plan for the defences, after making the proper survey, he remarked to his son, that, before beginning to work upon them, they must try to manage two rising grounds to the south, by which they were commanded. But after an hour's reflection, he observed that, what was of most importance was to complete the fort and houses without delay, since the place had very powerful means of defence; that the two eminences might be overlooked in the meanwhile,—since no prince with a shattered force, or whose affairs were in disorder, would be able to reduce it; and no great prince was likely to attack so small and remote a fortress with a strong army. The houses in the fort were soon finished, and a citadel

* Tar. Sind. ff. 108—113.

was erected, containing apartments for his household, for Shah Hasan, and a few Amírs of the first rank. Certain of his favourite officers had also lodgings assigned them there.*

Settles the country.

Shah Beg resided about a year at Bheker, to see his plans for the improvement of the town and fortifications carried into execution, and for the purpose of settling the surrounding districts. He found that large bodies of Balúches, a bold and hardy race of men, having crossed the Indus, had occupied large portions of the country on the left bank of the river, and harassed the old inhabitants by their predatory incursions, which he found it impossible to check. Determined to find a remedy, he adopted a measure, in the execution of which he was restrained neither by honour nor humanity. He made a certain number of his most faithful and resolute retainers take up their quarters in every village; who, remaining there till all suspicion was lulled to sleep, were ordered, on the same hour and day, to rise upon the Balúches, and put them to the sword. The plot was carried into execution with relentless cruelty and detestable treachery, and the inhabitants of forty-two Balúch villages were butchered in cold blood.†

Massacre of Balúches.

Death of Mír Fázil, A. H. 930, A. D. 1523.

Early in the winter of A. H. 930, Shah Beg moved from Bheker with a large army, to proceed to the invasion of Gujrát; and, as he moved down the Indus, cleared the country on both sides of the river, of such as he believed to be ill-affected to him. When he reached Chanduka, his old general and connection, Mír Fázil Gokultásh, was taken ill, and forced to return to Bheker, where he died. His death deeply affected Shah Beg, who spoke of it as a presage of his own. Leaving the camp, he returned to Bheker, where he staid a fortnight,

* Tar. Sind, f. 114. The author remarks, that the castle still subsisted in his time, A. H. 1009 (A. D. 1600).

† Ibid. ff. 114, 115.

BOOK II. to be present with the family of Fázil during the ceremonies of mourning, held so sacred by Musulmans. On rejoining his army, he proceeded to Sehwán, his troops ranging on both sides of the river as before. After provisioning that fortress, and putting it in the completest state of order, as a military station, he again renewed his march, and took the direction of Tatta. Having halted at the township of Akhím, he despatched officers to call Jám Firóz, and waited some time for his coming. The news which here reached him, of the advance of Báber by Bhíra and Khusháb, to the conquest of India, deeply affected his mind, already sore tried by his misfortunes, and by bodily suffering. He expressed, to some of his nobles, his apprehensions, that the Emperor would never suffer him to enjoy Sind, but would wrest it, too, from him and his family; that he must, therefore, appeal to another tribunal. This inward anxiety preying on a weakened constitution, he gradually sank away, till the 22 Shaban A. H. 930, when he breathed his last. His nobles and chiefs, after having tendered their allegiance to his son, and conducted everything, as we are told, according to the Chengízi usages, conveyed his body to Bheker. Three years afterwards, it was carried to Mekka, where a monument was erected over his grave.*

And of Shah Beg, 22 Shaban, A. H. 930, 25 June, A. D. 1524.

Shah Beg was an able and active prince, but cruel and unrelenting, a successful general, and a brave warrior. He was distinguished for his personal prowess. In battle, it was his custom to push forward before all his troops; and when remonstrated with, and told, that such impetuosity was not becoming in a general, the

* Tar. Sind, ff. 115, 116. The Tabakáte Akberi the Kholáset-ul-Towárikh, f. 344., and Ferishta, make the conquest of Sind and the flight of Jám Firóz in A. H. 927, and Shah Beg's death three years after, in A. H. 930. The Taríkhe-Sind makes his death 22 Shaban, A. H. 928. In this instance, I have ventured to keep all the dates of that work, except that of the year. The Ayín Akbéri, ii. p. 121., places the conquest of Sind in A. H. 929.

remonstrance produced no effect; he merely answered, that on such occasions he lost all self-command, and only considered how no one should stand before him. In his younger days, he had devoted a portion of his time to the study of the laws and speculative sciences of the Muhammedans. While at Herát, a city which then abounded with eminent men, he had weekly meetings at his house of the most learned of the theologians and lawyers. He himself wrote various works, which are said to have enjoyed considerable currency, such as notes on grammar and logic, some tracts on the laws of inheritance and on the fundamental articles of religion, as well as a few poems. But his pursuits had not elevated his mind to a humane and refined morality, and the barbarous institutes of his ancestor Chengíz Khan seem to have guided his practice. His approved piety gained him the respect and support of the divines and religious men, whose influence was at that time so powerful; and it was not supposed to be tarnished by his crimes. Religion threw her mantle over passions which were directed against unbelievers, and only violated the laws of morals and humanity. His treachery and barbarous massacres were but ill fitted to civilise the countries which he conquered.*

* Tab. Akberi, f. 508.; Tar. Sind, ut supra.

CHAPTER VI.

ARGHÚN CONQUEST OF SIND AND MULTÁN.

SECTION II.

CONQUEST OF LOWER SIND AND MULTÁN.

ACCESSION OF SHAH HASAN.—REVOLT OF THE JÁM.—SHAH HASAN TAKES TATTA.—THE JÁM FLEES TO KACH.—RETURNS WITH AN ARMY.—IS DEFEATED.—SHAH HASAN SOLE MASTER OF SIND.—HIS DESULTORY WARFARE WITH THE BALÚCHES.—HE AIMS AT THE CONQUEST OF MULTÁN.—PREVIOUS HISTORY OF THAT COUNTRY.—HE TAKES UCH.—TREATY.—HIS TERRITORY EXTENDED TO THE GHARA.—HE TAKES DIRÁWEL.—RECALLED TO MULTÁN.—BESIEGES AND TAKES THE CAPITAL.—LEAVES A GOVERNOR THERE, WHO IS EXPELLED.—MULTÁN OCCUPIED BY BÁBER.—SHAH HASAN DEFEATS THE THANKER.

BOOK II.

Accession of Shah Hasan.

WHEN the news of the death of Shàh Beg reached Tatta, it was received with every demonstration of joy. The inhabitants, who felt severely the burden and misery of the yoke under which they groaned, and who were keenly alive to their present sufferings, were willing, as the unhappy often are, to expect advantage from any change. The weak and restless Jám saw with triumph, in the death of his lordly ally, a prospect of liberty, which he wanted the spirit and talents to improve. With imprudent precipitation, he ordered the kettle-drum to be beat, to announce the joyful event, and resolved to assert his independence. This intelligence reached Shah Hasan* at Násírpúr, where he was

Revolt of the Jám.

* The name of this prince is sometimes written Hasan, sometimes Husein. In the Memoirs of Báber he is called Hasan, by later historians generally Husein.

performing the ceremonies of mourning for his father, and where he mounted the masnad as his successor. His nobles, the Kazís, and the holy men who were at his court, invited him on that occasion to read the Khutba, or prayer for the prince, in his own name; but *that* he declared he would not do, while any of the great Taimur's race remained; and he directed it to be read in the name of Báber. The intended expedition against Gujrát he at once gave up, and bent his whole force to punish the Jám for what he called his treachery. As soon as the fast of Ramzán was over he marched towards Tatta.

Shawal, A.H. 930, August, A.D. 1524.

Deputation to Shah Hasan,

The Jám, who was as unable to oppose as he had been ready to insult him, alarmed at the news of his approach, sent envoys with presents to meet him on the road, to condole with him on the death of his father, and to attempt to soothe and conciliate him, by the humblest professions of allegiance and fidelity. But the envoys, among whom was Kázi Káz, betrayed the master whom they did not respect, and in whose firmness they had no confidence. When privately interrogated, they acknowledged, that, though they had in public delivered the words of their employer, his real intentions were very different, and that he was busy collecting arms and warlike stores of every description, to enable him to expel the Arghúns. Shah Hasan dismissed the envoys, but soon followed them by long marches without intermission. On hearing of his approach, Jám Firóz, who, even if he had possessed courage and military talent, had destroyed the efficiency of his own army by his long reliance on foreign succours, without attempting to face the enemy, retired beyond the river and abandoned his capital. When Shah Hasan reached the branch of the Indus that ran to the south of the city, he found that Mánik Vazír, and some others of the Jám's officers, had collected boats, which they had filled with musqueteers and archers, to check his approach. These, for some time, by their activity,

who marches for Tatta.

BOOK II.

which he takes.

prevented the passage of his troops. But this obstacle was soon removed. These brave men were attacked and slain, and his army crossed over, and occupied Tatta. The Jám fled to Kach, where, by a profuse expenditure of money, and by the hopes of booty, which the invasion of the rich provinces of Sind held out to a race of bold freebooters, he speedily collected a large army*, from that country, and from the adjoining tribes of Gujrát.

The Jám collects an army in Kach.

Enters Cháchkán.

It was not long before, with this force, he entered Cháchkán and Rahíma, on the eastern frontier of Sind, spreading terror around. Shah Hasan took his measures with calm composure, to meet this danger. Leaving an adequate force to guard the capital, he crossed the river, and, with the main body of his troops, hastened to meet the invaders. They saw his sudden arrival with surprise; but the majority of their troops, being of the Rájpút race, kept their ground and remained firm and unshaken. As he approached, they were seen to take off their turbans; and, tying themselves to each other by their clothes and girdles, with their head and feet bare, waited prepared for the fight. Such is the practice of these tribes in those desperate cases in which they determine to conquer or die. Shah Beg pointed out to his troops this act of desperation, as an undoubted symptom of the terror inspired by his arms, and hailed it as an omen of victory. He ordered his archers to get their bows and quivers in readiness; and dismounting, bathed and purified himself according to the rites of his religion; after which, holding up his hands, he poured forth his orisons, praying aloud to God for victory over his infidel foes. The archers began the battle by discharging showers of deadly arrows; and when these had had time to take effect, he himself charged sword in hand at the head of his bravest troops. The battle lasted with desperate fury

Battle,

* It is called of fifty thousand men, probably by a great exaggeration.

from dawn till noontide prayers, when the field was strewed, it is said, with twenty thousand of the enemy, and all opposition was over. The Jám fled to Gujrát. Shah Hasan, after remaining three days on the field of battle, to refresh his troops and improve his success, returned to Tatta.*

gained by Shah Hasan,

By this decisive victory, which transferred the government of Sind from the Jám to the Arghún race in style and title, as for several years past it had already been in reality, Shah Hasan was left without a rival. He remained at Toghlakábád, one of the suburbs of Tatta, for about six months; a time which he employed in rewarding the Amírs and soldiers who had distinguished themselves, and in settling the rich and fertile districts of Lower Sind, whose inhabitants, chiefly composed of industrious cultivators, much as they regretted a change, were unable, from their habits of life, to offer any resistance. He then returned to Bheker, which was placed in a country, and amidst a population, of a very different description; being surrounded by deserts, inhabited by brave and independent tribes. In the course of his march, he was met by the chiefs of the neighbouring country, who, with tributary offerings, congratulated him on his success, and made their submission. He continued his journey, hunting all the way to the village of Baberlu, three kos from Bheker, where the chief inhabitants of his second capital came out in procession to welcome him. At Bheker he spent some time.†

who becomes sole master of Sind;

His chief attention, while at Bheker, was devoted to the improvement of the place, and to the more complete

and attempts to settle the country.

* Tar. Sind, ff. 118. 129. 131. Beháder Shah, of Gujrát, when on his way to the Dekhan, in Moharrem A. H. 935 was overtaken by the Jám, who complained, that the Arghúns had taken his country; Beháder gave him twelve lak of rupees, and promised to assist him in recovering his dominions. This would look as if he had made some attempt subsequent to A. H. 831.—Ferishta, vol. iv., Life of Beháder.

† Tar. Resh. f. 131, 132.

BOOK II.

conquest and pacification of the neighbouring country He was master of a great proportion of his territory only in name. The mountainous tracts and desert wastes around, harboured a hardy and independent race of men, who ill brooked any superior, and who were themselves accustomed to plunder and render tributary the more industrious population on every side. In the hills, they consisted chiefly of tribes who lived by their flocks, and shared the strong love of freedom and of tribe that belongs to such a life. Some, both there and in the lowlands, were of a foreign race, chiefly Balúches, introduced by conquest among the more peaceful cultivators,—a state of society in which, being the rulers, and relieved from the cares and personal labour required to gain a subsistence, they form a dominant class, who have much leisure, and are strongly attracted by the excitements and prizes of war. In such a situation, predatory inroads on their neighbours become the favourite occupation. These freebooters and warriors, both Shah Hasan and his father had laboured, though with imperfect success, to reduce to regular obedience. He now resolved, if possible, to put an end to their forays and robberies.

Desultory warfare with the Balúches.

It happened that at this time complaints reached him from the inhabitants of the districts of Mátila* and Mehr, east of the Indus, that they were incessantly molested by the inroads of their neighbours, the people of Ubára, Bhati and Ahen, who were of the Dehr and Machí race. This induced him to send Baba Ahmed, the eldest son of the late Mír Fázil, to check their incursions. Baba Ahmed advanced with a strong force, and, after having ravaged and plundered the territory of the offenders, marched back to the fort of Mátila. The Dehr men, enraged at this chastisement, represented to the Sewrái Balúches, that, if an outrage

* Mátila lies north-east of Bheker, about thirty miles. It is said to be Mírpúr.

such as this was to pass unnoticed, it would soon grow into a custom; and that the insult ought to be revenged in the very outset. The Balúches acquiesced in this reasoning, so consonant to their habits, and, pouring down in great numbers, wasted the district of Mehr. In their retreat, however, they were overtaken by Baba Ahmed, near Ubára, defeated, and some of the Dehr men taken prisoners. Shah Hasan had sent another division at the same time against the Balúches, which advanced as far as Kendi, plundering as it went; and, in returning, slew or made prisoners a number of the Machí men, dependent on Ubára, forced them to pay a heavy contribution, and to give a lady of the tribe in marriage to Baba Ahmed; a concession which only the greatest distress could have wrung from them. Ubára itself was reduced by Baba Ahmed, who, leaving a garrison in the town, returned to Bheker.

Baba Ahmed slain.

While the country was in this unsettled state, Shah Hasan's camels, which were feeding near Mátila, attended by some men of Dehr and Mehr, under the charge of his servants, were driven away by the Sewrái Balúches, and the Játs of the territory of Diráwer * and Fatehpúr, who had learned where they were. Baba Ahmed, immediately upon hearing of the foray, pushed after them, from Bheker, laid waste the Diráwer and Fatehpúr territory, slaying many of the inhabitants, and succeeded in recovering the camels. He had returned back as far as Bhati and Aken, when he was intercepted by the Sewrái Balúches and Dehr men, who had united to cut off his retreat. A sharp action ensued, in the course of which, Baba Ahmed, having received some severe wounds, was forced to quit the field; and, just as he reached the territory of Mátila, fell exhausted from his horse, and expired.

Death of his brother.

His brother Abdal Fitáh, burning with impatience

* Or Diráwal.

BOOK II. to revenge his death, got permission from Shah Hasan to succeed him in his command; but, to check the excess of ardour, which was likely to lead him into danger, Mír Kásim, whose daughter the youth had married, was sent to accompany him on the expedition. The body of Baba Ahmed was sent to Bheker. Abdal Fitáh remained for some time in the country, watching a fit opportunity for striking a blow. At last, he proceeded against the Rahmu Dehr tribe, slew a great number of Balúches and Dehrs, and advanced as far as Mou, committing great devastation, and dispersing the Balúches who lay along his route. They were at last glad to supplicate for peace, which was granted, on condition that Bhati and Ahen should become the limits of Sind. He took up his residence there for some time. But the predatory habits of the Balúches were too deeply rooted to be easily removed. One night, he was informed that they were driving off the cattle of Ubára. Abdal Fitáh, hastily buckling on his armour, rode in pursuit of them. The night was excessively hot and sultry, and he was suddenly and so severely affected, that he expired before he could be brought home. Sultan Mahmúd Khan, the brother of these two youths, afterwards mounted the throne of Bheker. These few details will give an idea of the ordinary warfare of Upper Sind.*

Shah Hasan's views on Multán.

But the ambition of Mírza Shah Hasan now aimed at higher objects than the reduction of a few villages in the desert. The state of parties in Multán, at this time, flattered him with hopes that he might be able to seize the reins of government in that country. Báber, who was at this time busily occupied in gaining an ascendency in the Penjáb, and whose views extended to the throne of Delhi itself, is said to have encouraged him to proceed with his enterprise. Shah Hasan acknow-

* Tar. Sind, ff. 131—133.

ledged him as his superior lord, and the diversion might in many respects be favourable to the Emperor. But before setting out on an expedition that might detain him long from his other dominions, he paid a visit to Síwí, which he reached with a thousand horse in one week, that he might examine how such of his Arghún, Nukderi and Hazára adherents, as had been left behind there with their families, were situated. He carefully examined and improved the fortifications, which he left under the charge of trusty officers. He returned by Chitrui Lohr, plundering the Rind and Maksi Balúches, made numbers of them prisoners, and reduced the rest to obedience. The kilanters and head men of the country waited on him in token of submission, and, on condition of the prisoners being set at liberty, suffered themselves to be carried to Bheker.

He visits Síwí;

chastises some Balúch tribes.

For accomplishing the ambitious plan which he had formed, it was of the utmost importance to Shah Beg, to have the active concurrence of Báber and his ministers. While he resided at that prince's court, he had formed an intimate connection with Nizám-ed-dín Mír Alí Khalífa, the prime minister; and an engagement had even been made for his marriage with a daughter of that nobleman. He now sent ambassadors to Báber, to assure him of his attachment, and at the same time he claimed from Khalífa the fulfilment of his promise. Accordingly, Gúlberg Begum, Khalífa's daughter, was conveyed with every mark of honour to Sind, where she married Shah Hasan. To bind still closer the alliance of the families, Nahíd Begum, the daughter of Máh Begum *, who, as we have seen, was left behind in Kandahár, when her mother effected her escape, was now, with the Emperor's approbation, married to Mohib Ali Khan, the son of Khalífa. These alliances greatly strengthened Shah Hasan's interest at the Em-

Matrimonial alliances.

* Máh-Chuchak Begum, after her first husband's death, had married Shah Hasan.

BOOK II. peror's court, and seemed to secure him in the possession of his recent conquests.*

State of Multán. The province of Multán, which, though lying among deserts, contains some of the most fertile and populous parts of the Penjáb, was then possessed by the dynasty of Langas. The first Muhammedan conquest of Multán, if we except a transient one under the early Khalifs, was made by Sultan Mahmúd of Ghazni and his successors; on the decline of whose empire it again fell under the native Hindús. It was afterwards conquered by the emperors of Delhi, under which kingdom it remained till the fall of the Toghlak dynasty, when A.H. 814, A.D. 1411-12. the whole empire fell to pieces, and new monarchies started up in every direction. The miseries endured in Multán, while this anarchy lasted, both from internal faction and foreign invasion, after being felt for some years, at length induced the inhabitants to assemble, in order to concert some means for removing them; Sheikh Yusef chosen ruler. when they agreed to confer the supreme power on Sheikh Yusef, the head of a great monastery near the capital, —a man to whom they were partial, both from the reverence in which his family had long been held, and from the sanctity of his own character. He acceded to their wishes, assumed the attributes of an independent prince, increased the military force of the country, made many wise regulations, and conciliated both his own countrymen and the neighbouring states.

Deposed by the Langas. Among these neighbours was Rai Sipehra, the chief of a tribe of Langas, who inhabited Rápri and the adjoining districts. By a long series of flattery and artifice, he contrived to lull any suspicions that Sheikh Yusef may have entertained of his designs; and, having succeeded in introducing a band of his tribesmen into A.H. 848, A.D. 1445. the city, seized Sheikh Yusef in his haram, sent him to

* See the Tabakáte Akberi, f. 516.; Ferishta, vol. iv. pp. 396. 435., and the Kholásat-ul-Towárikh, f. 253.; Taríkhe-Sind, ff. 134, 135.

Delhi, and himself occupied the vacant masnad, under the title of Sultan Kútb-ed-dín.

A. H. 864, A. D. 1460.

In spite of the treachery by which Sultan Kútb-ed-dín gained the throne, he reigned for sixteen years, died much lamented by his subjects, and transmitted the sceptre to his son, Husein Langa; and his grandson, Mahmúd, filled the throne, when Shah Hasan meditated an attack on the country.*

Extent of Multán.

Multán, during the eighty years it was held by the Langa dynasty, seems to have been a prey to the surrounding tribes of Gakers, Afgháns, Balúches and Sehna Jáms. Its territory reached from the Indus, near the Derra Dín-panáh, to the Rávi, and thence downward to Upper Sind. It contained much desert; but the lands on the banks of the Chenáb and the Ghara were richly cultivated, as well as some on the Indus; and Multán being the route which the caravans between India and Kandahár were accustomed to take, the union of commerce and agriculture had made Multán and Uch flourishing cities. Some bodies of Balúches, Sehna Jáms, and other tribes, had been received within the Multán territory at different times, some of them settling higher up than the capital, while others occupied the country lower down, about Uch, and between the Ghara and Indus.

Factions.

The invasion of Multán by Shah Hasan was much facilitated by a deadly quarrel that had arisen between the reigning prince, Mahmúd Langa, and two of his ministers of the Sehna tribe, who were patronised by Sultan Sikander Lodi, of Delhi; which had proceeded to such a length, that the hostile parties met in the field, and, Mahmúd being defeated, a division of Multán had taken place,—the minister Jám Bayezíd receiving the cession of the district of Sirwar, up the Chenáb, while

* Tar. Sind, ff. 135—138.; Ferishta, vol. iv. p. 381.; Tabakáte Akberi.

BOOK II.

Mahmúd retained the city of Multán and the country below it.

Shah Hasan marches from Bheker. A.H. 931, A.D. 1525.

When everything was prepared for the invasion, Shah Hasan marched from Bheker up the left bank of the Indus, which in that age was chiefly overrun by the Balúch tribes, and, as he approached the fort of Sewrái, plundered and laid waste the country, slaying all whom he met. The Balúches, terrified by the numbers of his army, fled to Uch, leaving a garrison in Sewrái, which was the strongest fort in that country. Sultan Mahmúd Bhekeri, who had been sent in advance with a small party, as he approached it, came upon a considerable body of the enemy, and, though accompanied by only eighty men, attacked them without hesitation, and put them to flight, killing two hundred of their number, thirty of whom, he boasted, had fallen under his own sabre. The enemy, confounded by this sudden attack, deserted the place without farther resistance. Shah Hasan, on hearing the result, loudly applauded the bravery of Mahmúd, in presence of all his court; but afterwards, sending for him in private, gave him, we are told, three friendly slaps on the cheek, at the same time reprimanding him severely for his rashness, in having exposed himself and his little party to needless danger.*

Takes Sewrái and Mou.

Having ordered the fort of Sewrái to be razed to the ground, he moved on to Mou, a place of considerable consequence. Here he was met by two reverend Sheikhs, who came out of the town to deprecate his resentment, and to express the willingness of the people in the fort to surrender. He sent in a party of his men, to take possession of the stores which it contained, and to make all the Langas and Balúches prisoners. Such of the inhabitants as took refuge at the shrine of Sheikh Hamad, he respected; the rest were seized as slaves. He halted there three days to visit the holy places; and

* These incidents are mentioned by the author of the Tarikhe-Sind, (f. 138.) to whom Sultan Mahmúd himself related them.

extracted from the Sheikhs, who had charge of them, a promise, to suffer his people freely to pass and repass, but to exclude his enemies. Sheikh Rúh-ulla, the most venerable of them, then sued for the pardon of the Rahmú-Dehris; but Shah Hasan referred them to Sultan Mahmúd, in the death of whose two brothers they had had a principal share. The holy man's intercession in the end prevailed; and the chief of the tribe, having presented himself before that prince as a suppliant, with a sword hanging from his neck, to signify that in *his* hands lay his life or death, was forgiven. As a seal to this pardon, the chief then asked that his niece might have the honour of being received into Sultan Mahmúd's haram, which was granted; and the sister of Jám Jiún Dehr was accordingly given to him, as a propitiation and atonement for the claim of blood.*

Advances to Uch.

Leaving Mou, Shah Hasan now sent forward a party of five hundred horse in advance, and, following, encamped on the frontiers of the Men of Lar. Nanda Dehr, a man of great weight at Multán, having waited on him and submitted, he proceeded on to Uch. The Langas and Balúches had now had time to collect their forces, and Uch was a town of such consequence that they resolved to hazard a battle in its defence. They were very much more numerous than the invaders, who, on their approach, were assailed by showers of arrows. But Shah Hasan's veterans, moving forward rapidly and undauntedly to the attack, broke and routed their opponents with great havock, and took a number of prisoners, some of them men of note, but all of whom they put to death, without discrimination. From the field of battle, the victors pushed on to the gates of the city, which they assaulted, amidst showers of darts and arrows discharged from the ramparts. The enemy defended themselves vigorously, till the heads of their

Defeats the Langas.

* Tar. Sind, ff. 138, 139.

BOOK II.

chief leaders, who had fallen in the battle or in the subsequent slaughter, were exhibited, raised aloft on spears, when they were seized with terror and fled. The Arghúns, entering, put to death every man whom they met that belonged to any of the tribes; while the wretched townspeople were exposed to all the horrors of a city taken by assault. At length, the most distinguished of the religious men of the city, — men who, from their habits, were disposed, and from their influence had the power, in many instances, to mitigate the horrors of war in these rude and barbarous countries, — waited upon Shah Hasan. Moved by their entreaties, he ordered the rapine and pillage to cease, and dispatched officers in different directions, with instructions, that the head of every man who disobeyed the command should be struck off, and brought to him on the point of a spear. He dismantled the fortifications, and destroyed many of the principal buildings, the timber of which he caused to be conveyed to Bheker.*

Takes Uch.

Sultan Mahmud Langa raises an army.

Sultan Mahmúd Langa, alarmed at the progress of the enemy, and the occupation of the second city of his dominions, strained every nerve to raise a powerful army to overwhelm the invaders. Within a month, his army, we are told with the usual exaggeration, amounted to eighty thousand men, composed of Balúches, Játs, Rinds, Dudáis, and other tribes. He marched out of Multán, proposing to meet Shah Hasan, who, on hearing of his preparations, had encamped on the banks of the Ghára. The Sultan, after halting a month close by Multán, to provide the necessary stores, ammunition, and arms, at length put his army in motion. But, at the very first station, he died suddenly; as was universally supposed of poison, — administered, according to some, by Sheikh Shujáa Bokhári, his minister and son-in-law, who dreaded his resentment for some acts of mis-

His death.

* Tar. Sind, ff. 138—140.

conduct; according to others, by Langer (or Leshker) Khan, a man of note, who had been a slave of the family; each faction probably throwing the crime on their rival.* CHAP. VI. SECT. II.

When his death was announced, the Langas and Balúches assembled and raised to the throne his son, Sultan Husein Langa, then a minor; and, seeing no hopes but in peace, sent Sheikh Behá-ed-dín, a man universally reverenced, to attempt to put an end to hostilities. He found Shah Hasan well disposed to listen to his overtures, and a treaty was soon concluded, by which the Ghára was declared to be the boundary between the two states. Peace. Sind extended to the Ghára.

To secure this large accession to his territory, Shah Hasan ordered the fort of Uch to be rebuilt, and, leaving a strong garrison in the town, marched back towards Sind. He was naturally anxious to reduce to obedience and to order the country on the east of the Indus, which had already cost him so much trouble; and for that purpose no place was of greater consequence than Diráwel†, a town and fort that lay at some distance within the desert. He was informed by Ekbál Khan, who had deserted to him from Sultan Mahmúd Langa, that it contained an immense quantity of treasure, which had been hid there by successive Sultans. A message was despatched to Ghází Khan, who held the place, inviting him to repair to the Arghún camp; but he declined obeying the call. Shah Hasan, eager to secure the treasure, and to reduce a chief, whom, since the treaty, he regarded as his subject, marched Shah Hasan.

* Taríkhe-Sind, ff. 140—142.; Tabakáte Akbere, f. 516. Ferishta, in his history of Sind (vol. iv. p. 435.) says, that Baber directed his generals in A. H. 931 (A. D. 1524) to reduce Multán; but that, on Mahmúd Langa's sending some officers to him, to entreat him to forego the conquest of the country, he consented, on the Langa's acknowledging fealty and paying tribute. Does this refer to Shah Hasan's expedition recorded (Ibid. p. 396, 397.) in the history of Multán, and to his subsequent retreat?

† Or, Diráwer.

BOOK II. towards the town. The tribe who possessed the country around were eminent for their valour. Sambal Khan was sent in advance, with a chosen body, to fix upon a proper place for a camp, and for raising batteries. He found the fort lofty and strong. To supply the want of water, which was likely to be one of the greatest difficulties the army would have to encounter, he set people to work, who dug three hundred wells in three days, so that the camp was abundantly supplied. The Mírza himself arrived four days afterwards, and reconnoitred the fort. The necessary batteries and works being constructed, he commenced a discharge from his artillery, as well as his bowmen. After a siege of some length, the defenders found themselves hard pressed, without prospect of escape or relief. Sambal Khan, having run mines in various directions, sprung two of them, which threw down the bastion and part of the rampart before the gate. The garrison, who saw the near approach of destruction, defended themselves with desperation, throwing rockets, and heaving down burning combustibles among the assailants. In the end, however, a resolute body of Arghúns, rushing on with their shields over their heads, gained the top of the breach, and were soon followed by the rest of the army, who made prisoners of all who were not slain. The Mírza, thus in possession of the stronghold, lost no time in employing every means to discover the wealth of which he had heard, and especially the hidden treasure; and great quantities were, in reality, found. One half of it, he retained for his own share; the other, he divided among the troops. He then marched down by the Uch territory for Bheker, which he reached in fifteen days; and there devoted some time to festive enjoyments in celebration of his victory.*

1 Rejeb, A.H. 931, 24 April, A.D. 1525. besieges and takes Dirávvel.

Minority of But Shah Hasan did not long remain inactive. The

* Tar. Sind, ff. 142—144.

state of Multán speedily recalled him into that country. Sultan Husein Langa, who had succeeded his father, Sultan Mahmúd, being still a minor, the entire direction of the government remained with Sheikh Shujáa Bokhári, and the ladies of the haram, who were strongly suspected of being concerned in the death of the late prince. In such a situation, the virulence of faction acquired even more than its usual force. The minister found himself quite unequal to the task of preserving or of restoring order. The leading chiefs and nobles retired, each to his own tribe or jágír, and strengthened himself there, while oppression and injustice stalked abroad unchecked. A general anarchy prevailed, and the suffering inhabitants, worn out by the immediate distress, were ready for any change.

the Sultan of Multán.

Anarchy.

Langer Khan*, one of the most powerful of the late Sultan's Amírs, was at the head of one of the parties. Seeing no prospect of gaining an ascendency over his rivals by his own unaided means, he repaired to Shah Hasan Mírza, and to him explained the disorder and misery of the country, and the factions into which it was divided, inviting him once more to invade it at the head of his army. Shah Hasan required few arguments to induce him to follow this advice. Without loss of time, he sent on Miskín Terkhán in advance, and himself followed. Alarmed at the news of his approach, the Langas deputed Sheikh Ismael Koreishi, one of the most venerable of their religious men, to deprecate his wrath. The Sheikh met him when he had reached Mou, was received with every mark of respect and reverence by Shah Hasan, who presented him with a large sum of money as an offering to an honoured guest. After some conferences, in which the Sheikh attempted to divert the Mírza from his purpose, the holy man, finding that he made no impression, asked permission to retire to Tatta to his friends; a request to which

Shah Hasan invited to Multán.

A. H. 931, A. D. 1525.

* By some writers he is called Leshker Khan.

BOOK II. Shah Hasan agreed, and at the same time bestowed on him a village in Uch.

which he besieges; From Mou, Shah Hasan pushed onwards to Multán; and the Langas, though they had collected in some force, seeing no hope of encountering him with success in the field, retired into the capital. Langer Khan, who was now at the head of a considerable body of men, having plundered the Tilhati Kehlu men, brought all their grain, cattle, and property to the camp; while Shah Hasan, without loss of time, sat down before Multán, and laid active siege to the place. A deputation from the city, headed by the prime minister's brother, now waited on the Arghún, to assure him of the devotion and attachment of the Sultan; but Shah Hasan told the ambassadors, that the most satisfactory proof of such attachment would be for the Sultan immediately to meet him in his camp and make his submission; a step which would allow him at once to settle the affairs of the country, to restore Multán to the Sultan, and himself to return home.

When the ambassadors carried back this report, the Langas, seeing no hope of an accommodation, made every preparation in their power for an effectual defence. In the beginning of the siege, they made a series of desperate sallies on the Sindians, and molested them in all their operations. But Shah Hasan, in spite of all their efforts, proceeded steadily in his plans, constructed his batteries and cannonaded the walls, at the same time that he kept the city in a state of blockade, and cut off all its supplies of provisions.

distress of the besieged. The siege was long, and much vigilance and valour were exhibited on both sides. At length, famine began to prevail in the city, though the Amírs, to make their grain last the longer, had issued a proclamation, that no flour should be baked into bread, but that it should be employed solely for broths and other messes.* Pro-

* The head of an ox sold for ten tangas; a mán of grain (Multan weight) for a hundred tangas. — Tar. Sind.

visions of every kind gradually failed, and the little that was left rose to the most exorbitant prices. The most disgusting and unlawful food was used; the hides of cows and other animals were steeped and ravenously eaten; if a cat or dog was found, says an eye-witness, it was considered like kid, or the greatest dainty. Shujáa-ul-Múlk had appointed one Jadeh, a Máchi, to the command of a sort of country militia, and gave him charge of the city. He and his men entered any house at pleasure, under pretence of searching for provisions, and plundered whatever fell in their way. Such was the general misery that many of the inhabitants threw themselves over the walls into the ditch, in hopes of effecting their escape; numbers perished; and Shah Hasan, pitying their deplorable condition, issued orders that no Multáni, while thus attempting to escape, should be put to death.

The place taken by storm.

When the siege had lasted a year and some months, and the garrison were worn out and reduced to skeletons, the Arghúns resolved to terminate it by a grand effort; and, after having slain a number of the defenders, and cleared the defences by a continued discharge of arrows and shot, made a general assault, and at the same time having broken open the Lahór gate with axes and hammers, about the dawn of day entered the place. A scene of indiscriminate slaughter and pillage ensued. The inhabitants, from the age of seven to seventy, except such as took refuge in the convent of the Sheikhs, were seized and reduced to slavery. After the pillage had continued for ten or twelve days, Mohib Terkhán proceeded to the monastery, which also he plundered and set on fire, after he had drenched it in blood. The greater part of the Langas, and of the army of Multán, perished in this calamity; and money, jewels, and other valuable property to a large amount fell into the hands of the victors. Shah Hasan at length put an end to the slaughter, directed that no creature

End of A. H. 932, summer or autumn, A. D. 1526.

BOOK II. should suffer any farther injury, and commanded deep pits to be dug to bury the dead. The young Sultan Husein and his sister were brought to him, and delivered to Miskín Terkhán, who married the lady and treated the youth as his own son; he is said to have died soon after.*

* Taríkhe-Sind, f. 145—147.; Tabakáte Akberi, f. 516.; Ferishta, vol. iv. p. 399.; Kholásat-ul-Towaríkh, f. 253. The Taríkhe-Sind, differing from the others, places the sack of Multán in A. H. 933, Rebi ii. 15. But the testimony of Moulána Saad-ulla Lahúri, an eye-witness, (Tabakáte Akberi), seems decisive. Fifteen months is mentioned as the length of the siege. Nizám-ed-dín Ahmed Bakhshi, the author of the Tabakáte Abkeri, cites part of the curious narrative of an eye-witness, some of which is also quoted by Ferishta, from a document in the narrator's handwriting. (Ferishta, vol. iv. p. 399.) The account of Moulána Saad-ulla Lahúri, who was an eminent man of letters of that age, says Nizám-ed-dín, is as follows;—"I was at that time in the fort of Multán. The siege had lasted several months, and Mírza Shah Husein's army had so completely prevented all entrance into, or issue from the place, that it was impossible for any living thing from without to afford assistance to the besieged; or for any of those within, to make their escape out, so as to reach a place of safety. Such gradually became the scarcity of food and victuals in the town, that, if perchance a dog or cat fell into the hands of any of the besieged, they ate its flesh as a dainty, or as if it had been kid. When the town had been besieged a year and some months, it was at last taken and given up to be plundered. All the inhabitants, from the age of seven to seventy, were seized as slaves. Such as were suspected of having money were subjected to every kind of suffering and torture. This calamitous event took place in the latter end of A. H. 932." He proceeds to relate some occurrences regarding himself personally. "When the town was taken by the Arghún army," he says, "a party entered our house, and one of them bound and carried away my father, Moulána Ibráhím Jamád, who, for sixty-five years, sitting on the masnad of instruction, had delivered lessons in various branches of knowledge; and, towards the close of his life, had become blind. He was placed in confinement; as, from the style and elegance of his house, they supposed that he must be possessed of wealth. They began to exercise severities upon him. Another of them laid hold of me, and took me to the Mírza's vazír, to whom he gave me in a present. It so chanced that the vazír was sitting on a wooden platform in the court of a serái, and desired a chain to be put on my leg. The other end of the chain they fastened to the foot of the platform. Not a tear stood in my eye, for myself; but I lamented grievously the misfortune of my father. In about half an hour, the vazír called for his ink-horn, and, having mended a pen, was preparing to write; but it occurred to him that, before writing, he should perform his religious

CHAP. VI. SECT. II.

Shems-ed-dín, the new governor:

Shah Hasan, after remaining two or three months in Multán, which is represented as having been so completely sacked and ruined that it was not supposed it could ever again be restored returned to Bheker, leaving Khwája Shems-ed-dín, one of his Amírs*, with two hundred horse, an hundred foot, and an hundred matchlock-men in charge of the city. Lenger Khan was joined with him in authority. The Arghún seems to have regarded Multán as a secondary concern; being probably well aware, now that Báber had succeeded in the conquest of Delhi, that he could have no hopes of being allowed permanently to retain an important province, so near Lahór. Great cruelties were exercised on such as were supposed to be wealthy, to make them discover their riches. Among others, large sums were

ablutions, and he went into the bath. Being now left alone, I went to the platform, and wrote a couplet of a Kasídeh, applicable to my circumstances, on the paper which he had made ready for writing upon; and then returned to my own place, while tears streamed from my eyes. In an hour (*saat*) he returned, and resumed his seat, and was proceeding to write, when he observed the couplet written on his paper. He looked around, but seeing nobody else, turned to me, and said, 'Did you write this?' I answered, 'I did.' He inquired, who I was. No sooner had I mentioned my father's name, than he rose, removed the chain from my foot, threw over me his own cloak (*pyráhan*), and the same instant mounted his horse, and went to the presence-chamber, where he presented me, and explained my father's situation. The Mírza gave orders to search for my father, and bring him.

"It so happened that, when my father was brought into the Mírza's court, in a very unseemly plight, they were reading the Hedáya. The Mírza ordered one dress of honour to be given to my father, and another to me. My father, in spite of the distraction of his spirits, expressed himself, when he began to speak, with such order, perspicuity, and force, that all present were amazed and delighted; and the Mírza, before the levee broke up, gave directions that my father should attend him in all his journies. He, at the same time, enjoined his officers to recover such of the Múlla's property as had been carried off, and to pay from the treasury what could not be recovered. My father observed, 'My life is drawing to a close. It is now time for me to be preparing for my last journey, and not to think of attending the Mírza.' And my father was not wrong; for, in the course of two months from that time, he became partaker of the mercy of God."—Tabakáte Akberi, f. 516—517.

* The Kholásat-ul-Towárikh calls him his slave.

BOOK II.

His tyranny.

daily extorted from Sheikh Shujáa-ul-múlk Bokhári, the late minister, till at last he sank under the tortures to which he was exposed. These severities were probably exercised chiefly by Shems-ed-dín; for Lengar Khan appears to have pursued a different course, and, having collected workmen from all quarters, gave them high wages, and restored a great part of the buildings of the desolate city; a conduct by which he earned much and just popularity. An oppressive foreign government, unsupported by a powerful military force, could not be expected long to maintain its authority.

The Arghúns expelled.

Langer Khan, disgusted with the management of affairs, left Multán, and repaired to Báber's court; upon which Shems-ed-dín was expelled by a popular insurrection headed by one Shemshír Khan, after the Arghúns had held it about fifteen months. Shah Hasan is said to have, in consequence, resigned the province to the Emperor; who seems to have bestowed it upon his son, Askeri, and to have sent him, accompanied by Langer

It is occupied by Báber.

Khan, to take possession of his government; and under the management of Langer Khan it remained, during the rest of Báber's reign.*

Its future revolutions.

On Báber's death, Humáyun found himself compelled to give up Multán, along with the whole of the Penjáb, to his brother Mírza Kámrán. That prince sent his own servants to take charge of Multán, and recalled Langer Khan to Lahór, where he was well received; and the Mírza assigned him a residence near the city, which afterwards became a part of it, and was called the Daireh of Lenger Khan, from his palace. He seems also to have been nominated to the government of Kábul, in

* The date at which Báber named Askeri to Multán is not precisely fixed; but it was probably about the end of A. H. 933, or very early in A. H. 934. The Emperor, before setting out against Chándéri (14 Rebi i., A. H. 934, December 9, 1527) had recalled that prince, to consult with him on the affairs of Multán. Báber's Mem. p. 374. Askeri rejoined him, 3 Moharrem, A. H. 935 (Sept. 18, A. D. 1528) p. 374., p. 382. Inroads of the Balúches are mentioned, pp. ibid., 382, 396, and 398.

exchange for Multán, though probably he was never allowed to visit his government. From Kámrán, Multán passed to Sher Shah, and his descendants. Under Akber, it was regained by the Imperial family.*

Shah Hasan defeats the Khankar.

When Mírza Shah Hasan reached Bheker, on his return from Multán, he found that the Khankar was threatening an invasion on the side of Gujrát. This induced him to repair to Tatta, where he received an embassy from the Khankar†, demanding reparation for the blood of his brother Amír Amráni, who had been slain in some border inroad by Shah Hasan's subjects. That chief proudly observed, that he had declined attacking the family and children of Shah Hasan, while he was engaged at a distance; but now that he was come back, he must either resign some portion of the territory of Sind, as an atonement for blood, or prepare for war. Shah Hasan replied, that his answer was contained in a single word, war; and insultingly added, that the blood of Amráni was still fresh on his garments; and that, instead of waiting at home to receive his enemies, he would hasten to meet them in the field.

Leaving part of his force for the protection of Tatta, he instantly marched with the remainder into Kach. Being there disappointed of supplies, scarcity made its appearance in his camp. This compelled him to adopt decisive measures for forcing on an engagement. He divided his army into four bodies, intending to surround and attack the enemy on every side. The Khankar, whose scouts informed him that Mírza Shah Hasan was advancing with but a handful of men, believing the division which that prince commanded to be the whole of the army, determined to anticipate his attack, and marched, with ten thousand horse and a large body of infantry, for that purpose. The sound of his kettle-

* See the Tabakáte Akberi, f. 516, 517. Tárikhe-Sind, f. 147. Ferishta, vol. iv. p. 399, 400 and 435, 436; vol. ii. p. 62.

† The Khankar seems to have been a chief settled in Kach and the adjoining desert.

BOOK II.

drum was heard at a distance in the desert by Sultan Mahmúd Bhekeri, who commanded another of the divisions of the Mírza's army; and a reconnoitring party having been sent to a rising ground not far off, descried the enemy's columns in full march to attack the Mírza. Mahmúd instantly dispatched messengers to inform the Mírza, and the commanders of the other divisions, of the enemy's movement; and that he was ready to assist them in a simultaneous attack. The divisions closed in. The Khankars, on seeing themselves surrounded, alighted from their horses; and, as was usual with their tribe, when brought into imminent danger, joining shield to shield, and tying together the hems of their girdles, stood spear in hand to receive the foe. The Arghúns were ordered to use their bows only, in the first instance, and to shower down arrows upon them. For an hour or two the slaughter continued, when the survivors of the Khankar fled in despair, and were met and cut in pieces by the division of Shah Hasan's army that had taken a circuit into their rear. The defeat was complete. The victors spent the night on the field of battle; and, next day, spread themselves over the whole surrounding country, plundering the inhabitants, pillaging their houses, digging up the floors and searching in their concealments, for their jewels, money, and other valuable effects. They, at the same time, carried away their camels, horses, cows, and other cattle, as well as the miserable inhabitants themselves, in droves; after which, the whole army returned to Tatta.*

Extent of his dominions.

Mírza Shah Hasan continued to rule for many years his extensive territories of Upper and Lower Sind and Síwístán, reaching from the limits of Kandahár, Afghánistán, and Multán, to the borders of Kach and Gujrát; and his history, at a future period, will be found mingling itself with that of Báber's son and successor, Humáyun.

* Tar. Sind., f. 147—9.

BOOK III.

BÁBER IN INDIA.

CHAPTER I.

INVASIONS OF INDIA.—BATTLE OF PANIPAT.

EARLY HISTORY OF INDIA. — DIFFERENT DYNASTIES. — THE LODIS. — REIGN OF SULTAN IBRÁHÍM. — INTERNAL TROUBLES. — REVOLT OF BEHÁR — AND OF THE PENJÁB. — BÁBER'S FOUR INVASIONS OF INDIA. — HIS TRANSACTIONS WITH DOULAT KHAN AND ALÁ-ED-DÍN. — FIFTH INVASION OF INDIA. — HE TAKES MILWAT. — ADVANCES TO AMBÁLA. — TAKES HISSÁR-FIRÓZA. — BATTLE OF PANIPAT. — DEFEAT AND DEATH OF IBRÁHÍM. — BÁBER ENTERS DELHI AND AGRA. — STATE OF INDIA. — POPULATION HOSTILE TO THE INVADERS. — COMBINATIONS TO EXPEL THEM. — BÁBER'S ARMY DISHEARTENED. — HIS ADDRESS TO HIS COUNCIL. — CHANGE IN HIS PROSPECTS. — HE ACQUIRES SAMBHAL AND RABERI. — SENDS HUMÁYUN TO THE EASTWARD, WHO TAKES JUÁNPÚR AND KALPI. — BÁBER ACQUIRES BIÁNA, DHULPÚR, GUALIÁR. — ATTEMPT ON HIS LIFE. — MULTÁN SUBMITS. — UZBEKS INVADE KHORÁSÁN. — TAKE BALKH. — AFFAIR OF MÍR HÁMEH.

THE latter years of the life of Báber were chiefly occupied with the most important enterprise of his reign, and that which has rendered his name most illustrious in history, the Invasion of India; and especially the conquest of Delhi and its dependent provinces. CHAP. I.

That invasion he undertook rather more than twenty years after his conquest of Kábul and Ghazni; at a time when, besides these kingdoms and the dependent principalities of Badakhshán and Kunduz, he was master also of Kandahár. But before proceeding to the details

BOOK III.

of that enterprise, it will be necessary to cast a cursory glance over the previous revolutions of Hindustán; and to explain such circumstances, in the internal situation of the kingdom of Delhi, as ultimately affected his success.

Early history of India.

The inhabitants of the vast and populous countries of India seem to have been doomed, from the earliest times, to be the prey of every invader who came upon them from the north; while they, on the other hand, never made conquests of any importance, at least in historical times, beyond what are considered as the natural limits of the country,—the Himalaya mountains and the Indus. Passing over the ancient inroads of the Persians and Greeks, they have, in modern times, been repeatedly invaded with success, on the land side, by the Muhammedans of Asia, and from the sea, by the Christians of Europe.

Hindu Period.

During the Hindu Period, which may be considered as reaching down to about the year one thousand of the Christian Era, all India was subject to races of men, whom, from our ignorance of their previous history, we may regard as native. From the Indus and the northern mountains on the one side, to Cape Comorin on the other, a variety of languages, differing from each other in a greater or less degree, were spoken; and the prevailing religions were, the Brahminical and the Bhuddist, including in the latter the Jaina.

This original state of things was violently altered by the irruptions of the Musulmans, who gradually gained a predominant influence over the whole of India.

First Musulman Period.

Their history, in that country, we have already divided into two periods; the one, of about five hundred years, extending from the invasion of Sultan Mahmúd of Ghazni to that of Báber; the other, of nearly three hundred, reaching from the invasion of Báber to our own times; which last is known as the Dynasty of the House of Taimur in India.

CHAP. I.

The former of these periods comprehends several dynasties.

Dynasty of Ghazni. A.H. 391, A.D. 1001.

Under the first of these, that of Ghazni, the repeated irruptions of Sultan Mahmúd, — which reached with desolating fury from the borders of Afghánistán through the Penjáb to Delhi, the Rájpút States, and the farthest extremity of the peninsula of Gujrát, — broke up, for a time, several of the native Hindu governments; most of which, indeed, resumed their authority, though some of them emerged under new forms, as soon as the torrent of invasion had swept by. But the Sultans of this dynasty retained possession of a great part of the Penjáb, especially of Lahúr and its territory, for about a hundred and ninety years; and, though several of these princes occasionally extended their conquests into Hindustán and Gujrát, the Penjáb may be considered as the boundary of their dominion, all to the south being still under Hindu government.

A.H. 582, A.D. 1186.

Of Ghúr.

The Ghaznevi was destroyed by the Ghúri dynasty; founded by Sheháb-ed-dín Muhammed Ghúri*, an Afghán of Ghúr, who, from the mountains of that country which lies between Herát and Kábul, overthrew the already tottering power of the Sultans of Ghazni. His armies, after occupying the seat of government, penetrated in repeated invasions through the Penjáb; advanced into Hindustán; and, in a great and decisive battle, defeated and broke the force of Rajasthán and Delhi. Muhammed Ghúri was succeeded by Eibák, one of his lieutenants, originally a Túrki slave, who, under his auspices, had conquered Delhi, and may be regarded as the real founder of the Musulman Empire

A.H. 589, A.D. 1193.

* This distinguished prince is by Ebn Batúta (Lee's transl. p. 112.) called Sultan Sheháb-ed-dín Muhammed ibn Sam el Ghouri; by Báber (Mem. p. 309.) he is called Sultan Sheháb-ed-dín Ghúri; the Tabakáte Akberi styles him Sultan Moiz-ed-dín Muhammed bin Sam, often called Sheháb-ed-dín Ghúri. In Briggs's Ferishta (vol. i. p. 161 et seq.) he is generally called Mahomed Ghoory; though (p. 168.) he is described as Moyiz-ood-deen Mahomed Ghoory.

BOOK III.

in India. The throne, now transferred into that country, was held, for nearly a hundred years, chiefly by successful generals and slaves of the Ghúris. They extended the Musulman sway far to the south; so that, besides the uniform possession of the territory of Delhi, the provinces of Bengál, Behár, Gualiár, Malwa, and various others were, from time to time, subject to them. They were essentially a Túrki dynasty, and supported by Túrks from the north.

Of the Khiljis. A. H. 687, A. D. 1288.

The Ghúri was succeeded by the Khilji dynasty; also said to be of Túrki extraction, but which seems rather to have been of an Afghán race; and it may be doubted if they are not of the Ghiljí Afgháns. They reigned, with great renown, over Delhi and a considerable part of Hindustán, for about thirty-three years; and even pushed their conquests beyond the Nerbáda into the Dekhan.

The Toghlaks. A. H. 721, A. D. 1321.

The Toghlak dynasty, originally descended of Túrki slaves, succeeded that of the Khiljis; and, for nearly a hundred years, ruled over Delhi and its subject provinces, though with diminishing power and distracted by factions. In the troubled reigns of some of its princes, most of the principal provinces of Hindustán separated themselves from the empire, and became governed as independent states. After the invasion of

A. H. 814, A. D. 1412.

Taimur Beg, or Tamerlane, the Toghlak kingdom, frail and disjointed before, was broken in pieces.

The Syeds.

The invasion of Taimur in India was, like a hurricane, short and terrible; but, though his conquests introduced a new race of princes into Transoxiana, Khorásán, and Persia, he left no prince of his own race to secure his conquests in India. An officer, whom he appointed to command in Delhi, did not claim the style of Sultan; which, however, was early assumed by his posterity, who are known as the Syed dynasty, and governed, after the Toghlaks, with a loose rein for about thirty-

CHAP. I.

eight years, when Delhi passed into the hands of an Afghán family.

The Lodis. A. H. 854, A. D. 1450.

Behlúl Lodi*, whose uncle had some time before usurped the government of Sirhend, was raised to the throne by a confederacy of six or seven great Afghán chiefs. At the period when this confederacy was formed, the empire of Delhi had really ceased to exist, having been broken down into a variety of kingdoms and principalities. Of all the former vast empire, Delhi alone, with a small territory around it, was held by the Syed Sultan, Alá-ed-dín, the nominal sovereign. The more considerable provinces, Multán, Juánpúr, Bengal, Malwa, and Gujrát, had each its separate king. The provinces around Delhi were in the condition emphatically called Malúke Tewáif, or governments of tribes. Mehróli and Mewát, to within seven kos of Delhi, were in the hands of Ahmed Khan of Mewát; on the opposite side, Sambhal, to the very suburbs of Delhi, was occupied by Deria Khan Lodi; Kol-Jalesir, in the Doáb, by Isa Khan Túrk; Ráberi and its dependencies, by Kutb Khan Afghán; Kampila and Patiáli, by Raja Pertáb Sing; Biána, by Daúd Khan Lodi. The names of these rulers will mark the degree of ascendency enjoyed by the different tribes, in the immediate vicinity of the capital. Behlúl himself possessed the extensive provinces of Lahúr, Dibalpúr†, and Sirhind, as far south as Panipat.

Divided state of India.

Sultan Behlúl; his conquests.

The accession to the throne of Delhi of Sultan Behlúl Lodi, the founder of the Lodi dynasty, and a prince of great energy, restored some portion of vigour to that monarchy. He soon reduced the petty states around the capital to narrower limits; he forced the neighbouring princes to own his supremacy; and, after a long-continued series of hostilities, conquered that part of the Sherki or Eastern kingdom of Juánpúr, which com-

* Or Bhelól.

† Often called Dipálpúr.

BOOK III.

prehended the countries lying north of Behár, and east of the Ganges; at the same time driving the King, Sultan Husein Shah Sherki, into Behár.

Sultan Sekander. A. H. 894, A. D. 1488. extends the empire,

Behlúl's son, Sultan Sekander Lodi, a prince of talent, in a reign of thirty years, enlarged the kingdom still farther. In the East, he subdued Behár, the last province that remained in the possession of the Sherki kings; and even advanced into Bengal, where Sultan Husein Shah had taken refuge. By a convention concluded with Sultan Alá-ed-dín of Bengal, it was agreed, that Sekander should retain Behár, Tirhút, Sirkár Sárán, and all that he had conquered; that he should not again invade Bengal; and that neither prince should support the enemies of the other. On the west, he gained possession of Dhúlpúr and Chándéri, and received the submission of the Raja of Gualiár and other princes; so that, at his death, his kingdom had attained a very great extent, containing the Penjáb, the Doáb, the provinces of Oud, Laknau, Juánpúr and Behár, besides a wide tract of country to the west of the Jamna, from the Satlej to Bandélkand. These extensive possessions, however, though under one king, had no very strong principle of cohesion. The monarchy was a congeries of nearly independent principalities, jágírs and provinces, each ruled by a hereditary chief, or by a zemindar or delegate from Delhi; and the inhabitants looked more to their immediate governors, who had absolute power in the province, and in whose hands, consequently, lay their happiness or misery, than to a distant and little known sovereign. It was the individual, not the law, that reigned. The Lodi princes, not merely to strengthen their own power, but from necessity, had in general committed the government of the province, and the chief offices of trust, to their own countrymen, the Afgháns; so that men of the Lodi, Fermuli, and Lohána tribes, held all the principal jágírs; which, from the habitual modes of thinking of their

which is composed of many smaller states.

race, they considered as their own of right, and purchased by their swords, rather than as due to any bounty or liberality on the part of the sovereign.

Sultan Ibráhím. A. H. 924, 7 Zikáda, A. D. 1518. 10 Nov.

The natural consequences of this state of things were felt on the accession of Sekander's son, Sultan Ibráhim Lodi.* On that event, a meeting of the principal Afghán leaders was held, at which the affairs of the state were discussed. These free and turbulent chiefs, who hated any superior, being struck with the danger of making the monarchy despotic, should all the executive power be vested by mere hereditary succession in one hand, came to the resolution of effecting a partial division of their acquisitions in India; by giving Ibráhím the kingdom of Delhi, with the chief power, and placing Jilál Khan, his brother, in the government of Juánpúr, as a subordinate prince,—a division which seems to have been intended by their father. Sultan Ibráhím, it would appear in the first instance assented to this arrangement; and Jilál Khan had accordingly set out for Juánpúr, to assume the government. But he halted for a few days at Kalpi, his old jágír, to enjoy the pleasure of the chase, where he strengthened his interest by making Fateh Khan Sirwáni, the son of Azím Humáyun, his prime minister. Meanwhile, Khan Jehán Lodi, a chief of the first rank, coming to congratulate Ibráhím on his accession, exclaimed loudly against the

Intended division of the empire.

* There is some difficulty as to the date of Sekander's death and Ibráhım's succession. Ferishta says, that Sekander died on Sunday, 7 Zikáda, A. H. 923 (21 Nov., A. D. 1517); and the Nisáb-náma-e Afghánán remarks, that Ibráhím succeeded on the 8th Zekada of that year. Báber, in his journal of Sefer, A. H. 925 (Feb., A. D. 1519), informs us, that he sent ambassadors to Ibráhím, whose father had died five or six months before. This would place Sekander's death in A. H. 924 (A. D. 1518). Now, the 7 Zikada, A. H. 923 (21 Nov., A. D. 1517) falls on a Thursday; whereas the 7 Zikada, A. H. 924 (10 Nov., A. D. 1518) falls on a Sunday. Ferishta's date seems, therefore, to have placed the occurrence one year too soon. The later date also accords better with the date, Friday, 15 Zihaj, A. H. 923 (924), the day of Ibráhím's grand entertainment.

BOOK III. proposed policy; and pointed out to him, and to the Afghán Amírs, that it would inevitably lead to civil war; and, in the end, prove fatal to the Afghán authority in India. In order to repair the error which had been committed, he prevailed upon the Sultan to despatch a messenger to Jilál, inviting him to an immediate personal conference, on matters that could not be settled by correspondence. Jilál, however, suspecting treachery, declined to return. A deputation of three of the most eminent nobles of the court of Agra, that was next sent to him for the same purpose, used every kind of persuasion to induce him to meet his brother; and, for that purpose, among other expedients, resorted to the use of magical charms, in the efficacy of which they had a faith common in that age and country; but he persisted in his refusal.

The Sultan, thus baffled, determined to resort to force. At the same time, however, he did not neglect the arts of intrigue; and, by his emissaries, soon succeeded in gaining over several of the great chiefs and jágírdars, connected with Juánpúr, who engaged to favour his interest, and to refuse submission to Jilál. Of this number were Deria Khan Loháni, governor of Behár; Násir Khan Loháni, the jágírdar of Ghazipúr; and the Sheikhzáda, who held Oud and Laknau; men of such high influence that, among them, they could bring thirty or forty thousand horse into the field.

A. H. 924, Zihaj 15, A. D. 1518, Dec. 18.

Jilál, king of Juánpúr.

To gain popularity, so necessary at such a crisis, Sultan Ibráhím, after his enthronement, gave a royal entertainment, at which, with a liberal hand, he not only bestowed offices, and rich presents, and dresses of honour, on the principal Afghán Amírs and chiefs, but distributed charitable donations among the religious mendicants, and the poor and needy of every description. His success was such that Jilál became alarmed, and openly charged Ibráhím with the design of wresting from him the apanage intended for him by his father, and confirmed to him by special agreement. He, therefore, threw off the mask, assumed the insignia of royalty, was proclaimed King of Juánpúr by the style of Sultan Jilál-ed-dín, and raised an army to maintain his pretensions.

These precipitate measures disconcerted the nobles who had originally intended to support him, but who were not yet prepared to declare themselves. While some of them still adhered to their engagements, others felt inclined to declare for Ibráhím. Azim Humáyun Sirwáni, a chief of great influence, but not well affected to Ibráhím, had, for some time previous to Sekander's death, been engaged in besieging Gualiár. Jilál, we have seen, had raised his son Fateh Khan to the office of his prime minister; and the father was prevailed upon to raise the siege and join in the revolt. He advised Jilál to march to Juánpúr, to establish and strengthen himself there; and he soon succeeded in driving out of Oud the governor, Saíd Khan, who retreated to Laknau.*

Ibráhím marches against him.

No sooner was Ibráhím informed of what was passing, than he set out to attack his brother. The great Afghán nobles had now, in general, become sensible of the danger into which they were bringing their dynasty, by attempting to raise up two independent and hostile princes. The greater part of them, accordingly, drew back, and joined Sultan Ibráhím. When that prince arrived near Kanauj, he was met by Azim Humáyun Sirwáni, and his son, Fateh Khan, Jilál's prime minister, who both now deserted him, and entered Ibráhím's service. This was decisive of the fate of Jilál; numbers imitated the example. Finding himself hard pressed, the unhappy prince resolved to make a desperate effort; and, leaving his family in Kalpi, advanced with

* There is considerable indistinctness, and some contradiction, in the account given of Jilál's proceedings, during his short career. It seems to be uncertain whether he ever went in person to Juánpúr.

BOOK III.

thirty thousand horse towards Agra. On reaching that city, instead of immediately forcing his way into it, he allowed the governor to amuse him by negotiations, till reinforcements had arrived, and the danger had ceased. Meanwhile, Kalpi was taken and plundered in his rear. Jilál, driven to extremity, concluded a treaty with Ibráhím's generals, by which he agreed to resign the insignia and dignity of a king, and to confine himself to Kalpi, his old jágír. This convention, however, Ibráhím, who had been successful in the interval, refused to confirm; and Jilál, in despair, fled and took refuge with Raja Mán, of Gualiár. But, an army being some time after sent to besiege that fortress, Jilál was compelled to leave it, and repaired to the court of Sultan Mahmúd Khilji, of Malwa. Even here he could not find a safe asylum. Being compelled to quit Malwa, in order to seek refuge elsewhere, he was taken by the Gonds, while passing through their country, and delivered into the hands of his brother, who put him to death.*

His death, A. H. 924, A. D. 1518.

Ibráhím wishes to humble the Afghán chiefs.

The suppression of a dangerous rebellion, which always strengthens the power of a sovereign, would have afforded Ibráhím a favourable opportunity of conciliating the great Amírs, many of whom were discontented. Unfortunately, however, his views had taken another direction; and he made it the grand object of his policy to humble them, and to extend the royal prerogative. Renouncing the homeliness characteristic of his nation, his great desire was to accustom his nobles to pay him the reverence which he deemed to be due to a king. All were commanded to stand motionless in his presence, with their hands crossed on their breast; and other corresponding changes were made in court etiquette. The Afgháns, who, in their own country, are remarkable for the freedom and blunt-

* Nisáb-náma-e Afgh., f. 72—7.; Kholáset-ul-Towárikh. MS. Briggs's Ferishta, vol. i. p. 591—5.;

ness of their manners, and who were accustomed to regard the prince as their chief, not their master—as the representative of the national force, raised to power and maintained in it by their support—could ill brook the change. Ibráhím, more perhaps from dislike to his nobles than love to his subjects, affected to view all below him with precisely the same favour, and as entitled to the same impartial consideration. But he soon learned that such maxims, however just in themselves, and however beneficially acted upon by a prince who governed either a despotic monarchy or one regulated by equal laws and fixed political institutions, were but ill suited to a foreign and military government, limited only by an aristocracy of rapacious and turbulent chiefs. Such a government, defective in its very foundation and principles, if it does not happen to have at its head a man of powerful and commanding talents, must be content to employ the ordinary grosser principles of fear and favour, and to purchase, at a high price, the support of partizans, by whose aid its own usurpations may be maintained. Discontent spread rapidly, especially among those who were most nearly on a level with the throne. Ibráhím, actuated by jealousy of all the leading nobles, even of those by whom he had been raised and supported, imprisoned some, and treated others with capricious cruelty. A revolt and civil war were the consequence; which, after much bloodshed, were quelled by the energy of Ahmed Khan Lodi, Ibráhím's general.

Revolt, quelled.

The Sultan, imagining that, by the successful issue of this second domestic contest, he had at length gained the object of his ambition, and presuming too hastily upon his power, ventured to put to death several of the most eminent of his father's Amírs. But these executions, far from quenching, added fuel to the flame of discontent. Disaffection spread more rapidly than ever. The whole monarchy was convulsed. In Behár,

Ibráhím puts to death some of his Amírs.

Revolt in Behár,

BOOK III.

A. H. 930, A. D. 1523.

Oud, Juánpúr, and the Sherki or Eastern provinces,—which had so lately been an independent kingdom, and where the Afghán nobles appear to have been always very powerful,—they flew to arms, under the direction of Násir Khan Loháni of Gházipúr, Maaruf Fermuli, and other Amírs; and, the rebellion having soon assumed a regular form, they elected for their chief Deria Khan Loháni of Behár, who, besides his own province, soon saw himself in possession of the whole country east of the Ganges. He defeated, in several engagements, the troops sent against him by Sultan Ibráhím; and, on his death, which happened not long before that of the Sultan, the revolted chiefs transferred the chief command to his son, Behár Khan Loháni*, whom they proclaimed king, under the style of Sultan Muhammed Shah. To quell this rebellion, Ibráhím had been obliged to send a powerful army, under Mustafa Fermuli and other officers.†

Deria Khan made king; succeeded by his son.

Doulat revolts in the Penjáb.

Nor was Ibráhím's policy more successful in the important province of the Penjáb. Doulat Khan, the governor of Lahúr, alarmed at the violent proceedings of the Sultan, which threatened his destruction, rose in open revolt. In addition to this, Alá-ed-dín, an uncle of Ibráhím, aiming still higher, fled to Báber, at Kábul, to solicit him to support his pretensions to the crown itself, against his sovereign and nephew. In a word, at the moment when Báber's views were definitively turned to India, faction, distrust, and open rebellion, were shaking the throne of Delhi on every side.

Alá-ed-dín aims at the throne of Delhi.

Báber called in.

We have seen that Báber, even before he was thus called upon, had long eagerly turned his eyes towards that country; and that he was hardly master of Kábul

* The Lohánis or Lohánas are often called Núhánis. It may, I think, be remarked, that, under the Lodis, the Afgháns who rose to eminence were chiefly those on the eastern borders, the Lohánas, Fermulis, &c.

† Báber's Memoirs, p. 335, and Nisáb-náma, f. 79.; Briggs's Ferishta, vol. i. p. 597.

before he was invited into the Penjáb. The chronology of his various invasions of India is not very distinct, but he himself tells us that he made four, previous to that in which he conquered Delhi. CHAP. I.

His first invasion of India, A. H. 925, A. D. 1519. Sefer 16, Feb. 17.

His first was in A. H. 925, when, after taking the fort of Bajour, he marched through Bunír, and, fording the Sind with his cavalry, camels and baggage, transported the infantry and camp followers over the river by rafts. He seems to have crossed above Attok. He had with him but an inconsiderable force, between fifteen hundred and two thousand men; having left part of his army in Kábul, part in Bajour,—and numbers, whose horses had been worn out by fatigue in some preceding excursions, had returned home. His chief object in entering the Penjáb was to collect plunder, the army not having been successful in that respect in their previous forays. He pushed on without delay to the country of Bhíra, which lay on the upper course of the Jilem or Behat, the Hydaspes of the ancients.

Penjáb held by Doulat Khan, A. H. 854, A. D. 1450.

The Penjáb, at the time of this first invasion, was subject to the kingdom of Delhi; and Sultan Ibráhím had but recently mounted the throne. We have seen that his grandfather, Sultan Behlúl, had been raised to the throne by a combination of six or seven great Afghán chiefs. Of these, Tátár Khan was one. This Tátár Khan held Sirhind, and all the countries of the Penjáb north of the Setlej. On his death, Sultan Sekander, who then reigned, probably jealous of the power of the family, had deprived them of that government. But, about two years before Báber mounted the throne of Kábul, the Sultan had restored to Doulat Khan, Tátár's son, the government of Lahúr alone; which, at the time of this invasion, he had therefore held about seventeen years.* Bhíra had been gained A. H. 908.

* Báber calls Tátár's son, Doulat Khan Tátár Khan Yusef Khail. Mem. p. 256. Ferishta calls him, Doulat Khan Lodi (vol. ii. p. 37, and vol. i. p. 597—8); as does the Nisáb-náma-e Afghánán, f. 79.;

BOOK III.

at a later period by Doulat Khan, who bestowed it on his eldest son, Ali Khan.

Báber occupies Bhíra,

Báber halted some time in Bhíra; and, as he intended to take permanent possession of the country, which he claimed,—as having for a series of years belonged to the House of Taimur, whose sole representative he now was,—he carefully prevented all pillage and outrage; instead of which he substituted a contribution of four hundred thousand shahrukhis from Bhíra alone.* Many of the neighbouring chiefs submitted, and sent him tribute; and he appointed some of his own officers to take charge of the more considerable districts. He then encamped on the low grounds, when a sudden and unexpected rain swelled the rivers, and threatened destruction to his whole army. The troops, however, with difficulty reached a higher situation, having effected a passage over the inundation, partly by wading through it, and partly by the assistance of boats. The whole country of Bhíra, Khusháb, and Chenáb, probably including the low lands along the course of the Jelem, from the Salt range to the junction of that river with the Chenab or Acesines, submitted to his authority, and received the civil and military officers whom he sent.

A.H. 925, Sefer 25, A.D. 1519. Feb. 26.

Returns by the Gáker's country;

Having made the needful arrangements, he took his way back to Kábul, by the table-land, which is buttressed by the Salt range; and passed througn the country of the Gakers. These were an old and independent people, who had long occupied the high broken ground, intersected by deep ravines and precipitous water-courses, that runs along the foot of the snowy mountains. The tribe had lately been divided into two

and gives the same epithet to his son Gházi Khan. Was Tátár really a Lodi? The Penjáb, and territory held by Tátár, are those that were held by Behlúl, before he ascended the throne. Did he transfer them to his relation, Tátár? Is Báber's addition of Yusef-khail a mistake of the copyist for Isa-Khan?

* This sum might amount to nearly 16,000*l.*, the shahrukhi being about nine pence half-penny.

factions. Háti Gaker possessed the higher and more inaccessible country, and retained his independence. Tátár Gaker, whose capital was Perháleh, had the less lofty and broken ground, and had yielded some sort of submission to Doulat Khan. At the very moment when Báber was in Bhíra, Háti Gaker had advanced on Tátár by surprise, had defeated and slain him, and seized his whole country and wealth. Báber was instigated by the Jenjúheh, a neighbouring tribe, who were old enemies of the Gáker, to attack them. He accordingly planned an expedition against Perháleh; and, though opposed by Háti Gaker with great gallantry and perseverance, defeated that chieftain's troops in the field, and, pursuing them closely, entered Perháleh along with him in his flight. Háti, indeed, effected his escape; but, in a few days, tendered his submission, which Báber willingly accepted, as it had now become expedient for him to march home. He received the submission of some other tribes, and then recrossed the Sind, having been six weeks beyond it.*

takes Perháleh.

Although, from the defenceless state of the country, and Báber's uncommon energy, this expedition had proved eminently successful, yet, in consequence of the small number of men engaged in it, and from other circumstances, it bore more the character of an inroad than an invasion. Báber was not able to leave a sufficient body of troops to retain the country he had acquired. Accordingly, he had not left Bhíra a month before he was overtaken by the governor and officers whom he had placed in charge of his new conquests, who had been compelled to abandon the country, by the return of its old masters, aided by a party among the inhabitants.†

Loses Bhíra.

It was in the course of this expedition that Báber dispatched Múlla Murshid as ambassador to Sultan

His embassy to Ibráhím

* Mem. of Báber, p. 253—263, also p. 310.

† Ibid. p. 267.

BOOK III. Ibráhím; most probably to congratulate him on his recent accession to the throne of Delhi, and, at the same time, to demand restitution of the countries in the Penjáb, which, he alleged, had long been held by Túrki families dependent on the House of Taimur. He also gave his ambassador letters for Doulat Khan at Lahúr, through whose territory it was necessary to pass. But that wary politician, after detaining the ambassador a long time at his capital, would not suffer him to proceed to Delhi; so that, about five months afterwards, the Múlla rejoined his master at Kábul, having effected nothing.*

frustrated.

Second invasion of India.

The particulars of Báber's second expedition are by no means clear. Kháfi Khan says, that, in the course of it, the Emperor advanced towards Lahúr, Multán and Sirhind, quelled the refractory Afgháns, carried off thirty thousand of the inhabitants as slaves, and levied a contribution of four hundred thousand shahrukhis. But the advance seems to be too great, compared with future expeditions, to have been made so early; and it is probable that the circumstances of the first and of some later expedition have been mixed up in this account. Ferishta, on the contrary, considers an expedition—undertaken in the same year as the last mentioned, and directed against the Yúsefzais; in which Báber advanced to Peshávwer, but did not cross the Indus,—as being the second invasion.†

Third invasion, A.H. 926, A.D. 1520.

The third invasion took place in A.H. 926. Having crossed the Indus, he marched through the country of the Gakers, and descended the Salt range into the low country of Bhíra; chastising those whom he considered as the authors of what he called the revolt. Thence, having crossed the Jelem, he advanced to Siálkót; an important town, which stands high up to the south of the Chenáb (or Acesines). As it submitted, the town

Siálkót taken.

* Mem. of Báber, p. 257. Briggs's Ferishta, vol. ii. p. 36.

† Kháfi Khan, MS. A, f. 25.

CHAP. I.

A. D. 1522.

was preserved from plunder. Syedpúr was not so fortunate; for, resistance being made, the garrison was put to the sword, and the inhabitants carried into captivity.

While thus engaged, he received the news of an inroad made into the territory of Kábul or Ghazni by the Arghúns of Kandahár; upon which he retraced his steps. He clearly perceived, that, if he would direct his whole strength, without interruption, against Hindustán, he must take means to relieve himself from such diversions on the west. He, therefore, employed his army between two and three years in completing the subjugation of Kandahár and the other provinces lying between Ghazni and Khorásán; which he effected, as has been already mentioned.*

A. H. 928, A. D. 1522.

Rebellion against Ibráhím.

In the interval between his third and fourth expedi-

* Kháfi Khan, as above; Ferishta, ii. p. 37. There is much difference among historians in regard to Báber's expeditions into India. All agree that they were five. I have chiefly followed Ferishta and Kháfi Khan, assisted by Báber himself—the best of authorities, where it is to be got. Abulfazl reckons the long and circuitous expedition which Báber made in the Afghán country (A. H. 910), immediately after conquering Kábul, as his first Indian expedition. Báber, no doubt, set out intending to enter India, but did not cross the Indus; though, in one part of his course, he came upon a portion of the territory of Multán, west of the Indus. His second expedition, Abulfazl places in A. H. 913, when Báber, alarmed at Sheibáni's approach, set out for Hindustán. But he halted before reaching the Indus, and turned back to Kábul. The third invasion of Abulfazl (A. H. 925) is that, which, in the text, is placed as the first, and which Báber himself considered as such. (Mem. p. 309.) Of the fourth, Abulfazl acknowledges that he could get no information—a singular admission regarding an important event, so near his own time, especially considering his means of information. (See Akbarnáma MS. A, f. 27—8.) The Kholáset-ul-Towárikh, f. 244., agrees with Abulfazl as to the three first expeditions; the fourth it very properly makes the expedition of A. H. 930, when Báber advanced to Lahúr. As to the fifth, there is no difficulty. What is reckoned the second, in the text, though resting on the authority of Ferishta and Kháfi Khan, is indistinct and uncertain. Indeed, there is hardly an interval of time sufficient to admit of its taking place. I would gladly discard it for one in the long interval between the third and fourth, were there any evidence of an inroad at that period.

BOOK III.

A. D. 1522-24.

tions, while Báber was employed in the reduction of Kandahár, in bringing the Afgháns into order, and in arranging the internal economy of his kingdom, events had daily become more and more favourable for his attempts on India. The civil wars, which had followed the accession of Sultan Ibráhím, had been renewed in an aggravated form, and threw the whole country into disorder. Alá-ed-dín, Ibráhím's uncle, who fled to Báber, now solicited that monarch to place him on the throne of Delhi. In the Penjáb, Doulat Khan of Lahúr, long an object of suspicion to Sultan Ibráhím, having joined the hostile confederacy of Afghán nobles, had been attacked by an army sent against him under Behár Khan Lodi. Finding himself unable, with his own resources, to resist this force, he sought assistance from Báber; offering in return to acknowledge him as his sovereign. This call the Emperor gladly obeyed, and soon put his troops in motion. He crossed the Sind, advanced through the country of the Gakers, passed the Jelem and the Chenáb, and speedily appeared within ten miles of Lahúr. Doulat Khan, meanwhile, on Behár Khan's approach, abandoning his capital, had fled to the country of the Balúches; that is, to some one of the Balúch tribes, which already occupied the banks of the Ghara, and much of the adjoining country. Báber was encountered near Lahúr, by the Lodi army, under Behár Khan, which he defeated with great slaughter; and his troops, entering the city in pursuit of the fugitives, plundered it and burned the bazár. He halted only four days in Lahúr, and then, with his accustomed celerity, advanced to Dibálpúr; which he assaulted and took by storm; the defenders being put to the sword and the town plundered.

Alá-ed-dín calls in Báber,

A. H. 930, A. D. 1524, who defeats the Lodis, and takes Lahúr,

and Dibálpúr.

Báber joined by Doulat,

Here Báber was joined by Doulat Khan and two of his sons, Ghází and Diláwer Khan. They were courteously received; but a misunderstanding soon arose between the protected and the protector. Instead of the wide province of Lahúr, Báber allotted to Doulat Khan only the districts of Jalinder and Sultanpúr, that lie between the Bíah and the Satlej (the classical rivers Hyphasis and Hesudrus) as his jágír. At this moment, that chieftain communicated information to Báber, that Ismael Jilwáni, a powerful Afghán chief, had collected a body of troops, about Tihára, to the south of the Satlej, with the intention of harassing his army, and opposing its progress towards Delhi; and suggested, that a strong detachment should be sent to beat up their quarters and disperse them. While the Emperor, who approved of the plan, was actively employed in forwarding the preparations for carrying it into execution, Diláwer Khan privately waited upon him, and informed him, in confidence, that his father's advice was given with the treacherous intention of inducing Báber to divide his army, so that Doulat and Gházi Khan might be enabled to attack and destroy it, when thus separated. Báber, roused by this notice, instituted inquiries, which convinced him of its truth. He placed Doulat Khan, and his son Gházi, in custody; but was soon after induced to set them at liberty, when he assigned to Doulat Khan the town of Sultanpúr (which that nobleman had built), along with its territory, as a jágír for the support of himself and his family.

whom he imprisons;

gives him a jágír.

Doulat Khan took leave of the Emperor to repair to his jágír, boiling with secret indignation. Soon after his arrival there, having privately sent off everything that could be serviceable to him in his meditated hostilities, he hastily withdrew from Sultánpúr into the hill-country of Himaláya on the east, attended by his son, Ghází Khan,—there, at once to escape the Emperor's power, and to watch a favourable season for pouring down his followers into the plains, and regaining his former authority.

Doulat flees to the hills.

With the real history of these events we can hardly hope to become accurately acquainted. On one side,

Báber delays his invasion of Delhi.

BOOK III. A.D. 1524.

Doulat Khan must have felt a natural resentment against Báber, who, when called in to his assistance, instead of restoring him to his government, had himself taken possession of it; and we may easily suppose a man of his ambition to have been ready to adopt any means, by which he could hope to recover the grand object of his wishes. On the other hand, little credit is due to a son who could stoop to exercise the trade of an informer against his father and brother, in the hope of founding his guilty greatness on the ruin of them both. Báber, who had advanced towards Sirhind, on his way to Delhi, as soon as he heard of their flight, thought it prudent to hasten back to Lahúr, to check any attempts at revolt, and to put the province into a state of defence against the designs of its late governor. This compelled him to give up, at that time, his expedition against Hindustán; and circumstances soon after obliged him to return to Kábul. The traitor, Diláwer Khan, was rewarded with the district of Sultánpúr, which his father had abandoned; and was honoured with the high title of Khan Khánán.*

Returns to Kábul.

Parcels out the Penjáb.

Báber, having now acquired an extensive territory beyond the Indus, intrusted the different provinces of his new conquest to some of his most distinguished officers. Sultan Alá-ed-dín Lodi, the competitor for the crown of Delhi, who had instigated this expedition, and who was still treated as a king, got Dibálpúr for his support,—Báber Kushkeh, a veteran Moghul officer, being appointed ostensibly to advise, but really to direct him; Mír Abdal-azíz, a near relative of Báber, had Lahúr; Khosrou Gokuldásh had Siálkót; and Muhammed Ali Tájík, Kila-núr, a district which lies high up between the Rávi and the Bíah.† Multán, it is to be observed, still belonged to the Balúch tribe of Langa;

* Lord of Lords. Báber's Mem. p. 360.; Briggs's Ferishta ii. p. 37—9.; Kholaset-ul-Towárikh, f. 244.

† Briggs's Ferishta, ii. p. 37.; Kháfi Khan.

CHAP. I.

A.D. 1525.

and it was probably at this time that Báber incited Shah Hasan to attack it.

Doulat enters the Penjáb.

As soon as Báber was fairly out of the Penjáb, on his return to Kábul, Doulat Khan, who retained great influence in the province which he had so long governed, issued from his mountain retreat, with a band of his faithful adherents; surprised, and threw into chains, Diláwer Khan, his perfidious son; seized Sultánpúr, and speedily collected a large army. His first operations were directed against Alá-ed-dín, in Dibálpúr, whom he defeated. Alá-ed-dín fled straight to Kábul, to Báber; while Báber Kushkeh retreated to Lahúr. Doulat Khan next detached a body of five thousand men to reduce Siálkót; but Báber's generals, concentrating their force, marched from Lahúr to protect the place; attacked the detachment, and defeated it.* Sultan Ibráhím of Delhi, meanwhile, wishing to avail himself of the favourable moment to recover the Penjáb, had sent another army to reduce it to obedience. But Doulat Khan, artfully availing himself of the discontents that prevailed among the Afgháns in Ibráhím's service, and of the factions by which the court and army were divided, contrived to gain over the general and a part of the troops, who deserted and joined him; upon which, the remainder of the army of Delhi broke up and retreated.†

Ibráhím also invades it.

His army disperses.

* A. H. 931, A. D. 1525.

† Ferishta, ii. p. 40.; Kháfi Khan. Considerable confusion exists among historians regarding Alim or Alá-ed-dín Khan Lodi. He is variously represented as the uncle, the brother, and the son of Sultan Ibráhím Lodi.

1. Ferishta calls him the brother of Ibráhím Lodi. (Vol. i. p. 598.; vol. ii. p. 39. twice; and p. 40.) This was about the time of Báber's last invasion; and he is uniformly so called by Kháfi Khan, perhaps following Ferishta. He could hardly, however, be a brother of Ibráhím's; for,

2. In the enumeration of the sons of Sekander (Ibráhím's father), on his accession, six are mentioned, but among them is no Alim or Aláeddín. (Vol. i. p. 564.)

3. Ibráhím's brother, Jilál Khan, having revolted and proclaimed himself King of Juánpúr (ibid. p. 591.), Ibráhím "confined his other brothers in the fort of Hansi, where they remained for life." (Ibid. p. 592.)

BOOK III.

A. D. 1525. Alá-ed-dín — his history.

When Alá-ed-dín, in his flight, had reached Kábul, he prevailed upon Báber to engage anew in an expedition

This would apply, even supposing Alim to have been born after his father's accession. See also Tar. Akber. shahi, f. 148.

4. The Taríkhe Nizámi gives the names of the brothers so confined, Ismael Khan, Husein Khan, Mahmúd Khan, and Sheikh Doulat. (f. 162.) It probably was intended to confine them for life; but some of them, at least, seem to have been released on their brother Ibráhím's death; for Mahmúd Khan was acknowledged by the Afgháns, and by Rána Sanga, as his successor, under the title of Sultan Mahmúd, and became King of Behár.

5. Ferishta himself mentions that Sultan Behlúl Lodi, *at the time of his accession*, had nine sons, among whom was "Alum, who also became king, under the appellation of Aláeddin." (Ibíd. p. 549.) This was A. H. 854. This Alim Khan received from his father the province of Karra-Mánikpúr (p. 560.), and, in the reign of his brother Sekander, having declared his independence, fled from Raberi-Chandwar, then his jágír, to his cousin, Isa Khan Lodi; and was afterwards reconciled to Sekander, who gave him Etáwa. (p. 566—7.)

6. After Sekander's death, Alim again aspired to the crown, fled to Báber, at Kábul, and entered the provinces of Delhi, in an attempt to dethrone his brother Ibráhím. His defeat, mentioned in the text, occurred when Báber was marching through the Penjáb, on his last invasion of India.

7. Báber, the best authority, never mentions who he was; the fact was too well known for a contemporary to think such information needed. But, in the rhetorical account of the battle of Kanwa (Mem. p. 362.), the prince in the command of the left of Báber's centre is called Sultan Alá-ed-dín Alim Khan, the son of Sultan Behlúl Lodi. This seems decisive. In a future passage, Jelál Khan and Kemál Khans are called "the sons of the Sultan Alá-ed-dín, who has been mentioned." (Ibid. p. 364.) Ferishta himself, in his account of the battle of Kanwa, following Báber, mentions "Prince Alim Khan, a son of Bheilole Lody," as commanding the left wing. (Vol. ii. p. 56.)

8. He was afterwards sent to Badakhshán, and, as will be mentioned, escaped to Gujrát, where, in the reign of Humáyún, he was encouraged by Sultan Behádar Shah to attempt the throne of Delhi. (Ferishta, vol. ii. p. 74, and vol. iv. p. 125.) At a later period Dandhúka is mentioned as his jágír in Gujrát, where he received and supported Mahmúd Shah III., of Gujrát (vol. iv. p. 146), A. H. 947; and even aspired again to the throne of Delhi; but finally joined Shír Shah.

Supposing Alim to have been only one year old at the time of his father Behlúl's accession (A. H. 854, A. D. 1450), he must have been about seventy-four or seventy-five when he marched against Dehli, before Báber attacked it; upwards of eighty when set up by Behádar Shah; and ninety when he supported Mahmúd Shah.

Ferishta and Kháfi Khan seem, therefore, to be mistaken in considering Alim Khan as Sultan Ibráhím's brother.

In the reign of Humáyún, new difficulties occur regarding this personage, from his being confounded with others of the same name.

for the reduction of Delhi. Alá-ed-dín, or, as he is generally called, Alim Khan, was the son of Sultan Behlúl Lodi, King of Delhi; and, consequently, was the brother of the late Sultan Sekander, and uncle of the reigning prince Ibráhím. After his father's death, one of Sultan Sekander's first acts was to deprive his brother, Alim Khan, of his jágír of Ráberi. Alim, who escaped, remained for some time hostile to him; but afterwards was reconciled, and received the jágír of Etáwa. He is said, however, to have fled to Gujrát, where he was protected by Sultan Mozeffer, who then reigned. On the death of his brother Sekander, Alim Khan openly aspired to the throne. In the distracted state of affairs that followed, he had secured a considerable number of partizans among the Afghán lords, who were disgusted with his nephew's cruel and imperious conduct. All these were prepared to favour his enterprise. He was willing to purchase the co-operation of Báber at a high price; and it seems to have been settled that, while the Sultan, Alá-ed-dín as he was called, was to be elevated to the throne of Delhi, Báber was to receive the formal cession of Lahúr and all the countries west of it, in full sovereignty. This formal confirmation of Báber's right of conquest was something gained, in the meanwhile, for public opinion; and, as political justice was not the virtue of the age, Báber probably calculated, that, if affairs turned out prosperously, it would be an easy matter to cast down the puppet king whom he had set up. He accordingly sent back Sultan Alá-ed-dín, to his generals who commanded at Lahúr, with a body of troops and a firmán, enjoining them to assist him in his expedition against Delhi. He intimated his intention to follow without delay.

He aspires to the throne.

Treaty with Báber,

who gives him troops.

It so happened, however, that Sultan Alá-ed-dín had scarcely taken leave of the court, when news reached Báber, that the whole Uzbek chiefs had assembled their forces and laid siege to Balkh,—which still belonged to

Uzbeks besiege Balkh.

BOOK III.

A.D. 1525.

Alim hastens to Lahúr.

his ally the King of Persia, and the possession of which was of such importance to them both that he resolved to march without loss of time to its relief. Sultan Alá-ed-dín, meanwhile, eager to avail himself of the advantage which he had gained from the Emperor's firmán, and apprehensive lest the change of affairs at Kábul might produce a new order for arresting the march of the troops that were devised to accompany him, hastened forward, by marches of twice the usual length, in spite of the scorching weather, and regardless of the sufferings of those who attended him. On reaching Lahúr, he insisted that Báber's generals should join him, in terms of the imperial firmán, and march at once on Delhi. Doulat Khan, when informed of the enterprise of Sultan Alá-ed-dín, seeing, in the diversion caused to Báber by the Uzbek war, and in the proposed expedition against Delhi, a reasonable prospect of recovering his power at Lahúr, made haste to arrange his differences with the Sultán, pretended to enter warmly into his views, and professed an earnest desire to be allowed to march with his army to assist in seating him on the throne of his father. This offer was most joyfully accepted by Alim Khan; but Báber's officers, with great justice, represented to him, that, situated as they were in regard to Doulat Khan, who was still in arms against the Emperor, as he had so recently been against Alá-ed-dín himself, it was impossible that they could, with any confidence, engage in concert with him in such an enterprise; nor did it appear to them that it would be prudent for Alá-ed-dín himself to do so; unless Ghází Khan, as a pledge of the good faith of the family, would consent to send his younger brother, Háji Khan, and his own son, to Báber's court; or at least leave them at Lahúr as hostages. To evade this demand, and to testify the sincerity of his professions, Doulat Khan presented to Alá-ed-dín a Deed of Accession and Allegiance, acknowledging him as his sovereign, authenti-

Doulat joins him.

Báber's officers object to his proceedings.

Union of the Afgháns of the Penjáb.

cated and guaranteed under the seals of the Kázis and leading men of the province. Alá-ed-dín, eager to gain so important an ally, and deaf to all the representations made to him by the Emperor's officers, sent his own son, Shír Khan, to confer with Doulat and Gházi; and, soon after, himself had a conference with them. Diláwer Khan, also, who had escaped from their custody, and arrived in Lahúr two or three months before, was now reconciled to them, and associated in the confederacy. Mahmúd Khan Jehán Khan, whom Báber describes as entrusted with the government of Lahúr, perhaps an Afghán chief to whom he had committed the civil charge of the country and the management of the native officers, was pressed into the service. In short, it was finally arranged among them, that Doulat Khan and Gházi Khan were to remain in the Penjáb, and to have the government of that country and the controul of all the officers whom Báber had left behind, and who were still stationed there; while Sultan Alá-ed-dín, attended by Diláwer Khan and Háji Khan, two sons of Doulat, was to lead the army against Delhi.*

CHAP. I.

A.D. 1525

March to Delhi.

In pursuance of this plan Alá-ed-dín, attended by these noblemen, put his army in motion, and was soon joined by Ismael Jilwáni, who had lately been his enemy, by Malik Baban Jilwáni, an able and powerful Afghán chief, and by a number of other Afgháns of rank. He hastened by forced marches to Delhi, new adherents joining him by the way; so that, on arriving before the city, to which he laid siege, his army amounted to thirty or forty thousand men.

Ibráhím opposes him.

Sultan Ibráhím, when informed of these operations, lost no time in advancing to meet his rival. On his approach, the siege was raised; and the invaders, retiring, took up a position, prepared to encounter him. Alá-ed-dín had a secret correspondence with some leading

* Báber's Mem. p. 295.

BOOK III.

A. D. 1525.

Treachery in his camp.

Afghán nobles in his rival's camp; but did not venture to attack him in the day-time, in consequence of a singular national point of honour, which hinders the Afgháns from deserting the army to which they belong in the face of day; while they are under little restraint in quitting it by night, which, they observe, covers many things. He therefore resolved to favour this feeling, by a night attack, which would allow them to follow their wishes. But there was a want of decision in his councils. The distance between the camps was only nine miles; yet, twice did the cavalry mount at noon, to be ready to march to the attack, and, after remaining under arms till past midnight, receive their dismissal, without having moved a step; the generals being unable to come to a resolution. The third time, however, they set out about three in the morning; the plan proposed being, merely, to set fire to the enemy's tents and huts, beat up their quarters, spread an alarm, and return. They succeeded in setting fire to the tents, at the same time shouting the war-cry. The enemy's troops, alarmed, fled in dismay. Some Afghán lords did join the assailants, and acknowledged Alá-ed-dín. During this confusion, Sultan Ibráhím remained immovable at the royal tent, surrounded by a small but chosen band of his tribesmen; and kept his ground steadily till the morning appeared. As the day dawned, he perceived Alá-ed-dín's troops, now dispersed, and employed in plundering on every side. He saw that they were not many in number, and that they were much scattered. Seizing the favourable moment, he put his followers in motion, accompanied by his only remaining elephant. But, no sooner was it seen moving along, than Alá-ed-dín's troops were struck with a panic, which, in their flight, they communicated to the rest of the army, who fled on every hand. That prince himself joined in the flight, and crossed the Jamma into the Doáb, recrossing at Panipat. His army dis-

Night attack,

which fails.

persed. His eldest son, Jilál Khan, with Ismael Jilwáni and Baban, sought shelter in the Doáb. Some of his chief officers, among whom was Mahmúd Khán Khán Jehán, had joined Sultan Ibráhím before the battle; so that there was treason in both armies. Alá-ed-dín himself retreated in confusion towards the Penjáb, attended by the two sons of Doulat Khan.*

CHAP. I. A.D. 1525. Alim's army dispersed.

At this important crisis, Báber himself was not far distant. No sooner had he disengaged himself from the affairs of Balkh and Kábul, than, leaving his son Kámrán, then a child, in the nominal charge of Kábul and Kandahár, he set out on his fifth and last invasion of India. He was joined on his march, first, by his eldest son Humáyun, with the troops from Badakhshán, and, the same day, by Khwája Kilán, with those from Ghazni. In about a month he passed the Sind, with a larger army than he had ever yet carried into India, though the whole, troops, servants, and camp followers of every description included, amounted only to twelve thousand men.† He hastened forward for Siálkót, keeping close to the eastern mountains, to secure a supply of grain, as there had been a deficiency of rain in the low lands. In the Gaker country he found some pools covered with ice, the only ice or snow, he remarks, that he had ever met with in India. After passing the Behat, he was joined by some officers of his Lahúr army, who had come from Siálkót, and learned, that Khosrou Gokuldásh, the governor, had abandoned that place to march for Lahúr, where Báber's officers had all formed a junction, for the purpose of counteracting the hostile intentions of Doulat Khan. Báber sent on expresses to that city to announce his approach, and to enjoin his generals not to

Báber's fifth invasion.

A.H. 932, Sefer 1, A.D. 1525, Nov. 17.

He passes the Sind, Rebi I. 1. Dec. 16.

Rebi I. 9, Dec. 24.

* Báber's Mem. p. 295, 296.; Nisabnáma-e Afgh. f. 79, 80. The Nisabnáma makes the number, who remained in the field with Sultan Ibráhím, amount to five or six thousand men.

† Ibid. p. 293.

BOOK III. A. D. 1525.

engage in action, but to meet him, either at Siálkót or Perserúr. Events had proved the soundness of their judgment in distrusting the intentions of Doulat Khan, and his son Gházi, who were eager to recover the rich government that they had lost. The latter, after Alá-ed-dín's departure on the expedition against Delhi, had, by strenuous exertions, collected a powerful army; and his father, old as he was, had girded on two swords, to intimate his defiance of Báber, and his determination to meet him in the field, there to conquer or die. In two marches more, Báber reached the Chináb, and was so much struck with the situation of Behlúlpúr, which stands on a ravine on the banks of that river, that he resolved to transfer the population of Siálkót to that place. On reaching Siálkót, he found that the inhabitants in the vicinity, who were chiefly composed of Játs and Gujers, according to their old rapacious habits, had harassed and plundered his garrison when on its retreat from Siálkót to Lahúr, which induced him to subject them to military execution, and to put to death some of the principal offenders. It was at Siálkót that he learned the disastrous result of Alá-ed-dín's expedition against Delhi.

reaches Siálkót, Rebi I. 14, Dec. 29.

hears of Alim's defeat,

Next morning, he continued his march to Perserúr, where he was joined by some of his troops from Lahúr. He sent out a party to reconnoitre the disposition of the enemy, who, to the number of forty thousand*, were encamped on the banks of the Rávi, near that capital; and, on their return, learned that the enemy, as soon as they were informed of his approach, had broken up and retreated in consternation. Báber, upon this, anxious to intercept them before they gained the mountains, leaving his heavy baggage to follow, pushed forward with a light force, and reached Kila-núr. He anticipated that the two Khans would attempt to

Rebi I. 15, Dec. 30.

Doulat's army breaks up in alarm.

A. H. 932,

Báber sets out in pursuit, Rebi I. 16, Dec. 31.

* This is the number given by Ferishta, vol. ii. p. 42.; and in the Kholáset-ul-Towárikh, p. 245. Báber seldom mentions numbers.

gain the strong fortress of Milwat, which lies close upon the mountains, and was eager to prevent them from strengthening themselves there. On the following morning, therefore, he again marched on; and, discovering along the road evident traces of the flight of Gházi Khan and his scattered followers, hurried forward a detachment of light troops, with orders to follow the fugitives without halting, and, if possible, to overtake them; but, at all events, as soon as they reached the fort of Milwat, to block up every passage and outlet from it, so that none who were in the place might escape. Gházi Khan was the person chiefly aimed at by these orders. Báber then proceeded to cross the Bíah; and three marches more brought him before Milwat.

Rebi I. 17, A. D. 1526, January 1.

reaches Milwat,

Being now joined by the rest of his troops, and by many of the Amírs of the country, he blockaded Milwat on every side. He sent a grandson of Doulat Khan's into the fort to offer terms. As the siege was pushed on with great vigour, Doulat Khan, seeing no hope of escape, was unwillingly forced to capitulate. He sent to say that his son, Gházi Khan, was not in the fort, having fled to the mountains, but that he himself was the Emperor's slave, and ready to wait upon him. Báber had soon after the satisfaction of seeing this powerful chief, who had so long governed Lahúr with regal power, come out from his fortress as a humble suppliant, having, suspended from his neck, as if ready to be used for his punishment, the two swords which he had boasted that he was to employ against his foe. The Emperor, who was deeply offended, and behaved to the old man with little courtesy, at the same time that he commanded the swords to be removed from his neck, reproached him with his perfidy; but he allowed him to retain the private estates of his family, and the authority which he held in his tribe. The whole rich property in the fort was seized; and Báber

which he blockades, Rebi I. 20, January 4.

Doulat surrenders.

Rich booty.

BOOK III. A.D. 1526. mentions in particular Ghází's library, as containing a number of valuable books, part of which he gave to Humáyun, and part to Kámrán, another of his sons. Doulat Khan was sent to be confined in a fort of Bhíra. but died on the road.

Alim reaches Ghási Khan, Meanwhile Alá-ed-dín, with Dilάwer and Háji Khan, having passed Sirhind in their flight to the Penjáb, were informed of Báber's approach, and of the fall of Milwat. Dilάwer Khan, who had always professed himself a partizan of Báber, separated from them and hastened to join the Emperor; while the other two, who were conscious in what an unfavourable light he must regard them, crossing the Satlej, entered the hills, and threw themselves into the strong castle of Kinkúteh, where they were instantly surrounded and besieged by a detachment of Hazáras and Afgháns from Báber's army. They contrived, however, to escape, on foot, during the darkness of the night; and, after excessive suffering, joined Ghází in the mountains. is ill received, That chief gave but a poor reception to Alá-ed-dín, who, in his present miserable circumstances, was no longer a tool that could be profitably employed. The detachment which Báber sent among the hills, with orders to use every exertion to seize Ghází Khan, succeeded in taking several hill forts (in the outer and inferior range) that had long been deemed impregnable, and reduced the surrounding districts; but Ghází himself eluded their vigilance.*

Lahúr, and its dependent provinces, being subdued and brought to some degree of quiet, Báber was now enabled to bend the whole force of his arms against Delhi itself, and its king, Sultan Ibráhím Lodi. The factions, among the Afghán chiefs, still continued; and several of them had invited the Emperor to advance, promising to join him when a favourable opportunity

* Báber's Mem. pp. 296—300.

CHAP. I.

A.D. 1526.

presented itself. As he was setting out, he was met by his detachment, which returned from the hills; and, at the same time, Alá-ed-dín, who had absconded from Gházi Khan, disgusted at the slight with which he was treated, arrived in the neighbourhood, destitute and on foot, and sent humbly soliciting to be allowed to wait upon his Majesty. Báber, who knew that the presence of the Afghán prince in his camp might facilitate his designs on Hindustán, sent out Mír Khalífa, his minister, and a deputation of his nobles, to receive him with honour, and furnished him with such an equipment as enabled him to appear in the camp in a manner suitable to his rank. He was received at court, and professed anew his attachment to the Emperor. But he was not long considered as of much consequence. He had the nominal command of a part of the army at the great battle with Ibráhím, the success of which in reality put an end to his hopes. He had also a division in the battle against Rána Sanga. But Báber, soon after, finding his claims or pretensions inconvenient, sent him to Badakhshán, where he was for some time confined in the strong fort of Kila-Zefer. From this custody he escaped, and, recrossing the lofty range of Hindú-kúsh, assisted by some Afghán merchants, whom he accompanied in disguise, found his way through Báber's dominions, and afterwards through some Afghán tribes, into Balúchistán, whence he passed into Sind, and finally took refuge in the court of Behâder Shah, then King of Gujrát. Here he was met by one of his sons, Tátár Khan, who had also effected his escape. They were well received; and, at a future period, were supported by Beháder in an attempt to expel Báber's son, Humáyun, from Agra.*

flees to Báber,

who receives him with honour.

His future history.

* In the account of all the preceding transactions, Báber's Memoirs have been chiefly followed. Abulfazl, in the Akbernáma; Nizam-ed-dín Ahmed Bakhshi, in the Tabakáte Akberi or Taríkhe-Nizámí;

BOOK III.

A.D. 1526. Báber reaches Ambála.

Báber, after passing the Satlej, advanced by Sirhind, and crossed the Gagar at Ambála. Here he learned, that Sultan Ibráhím was advancing from Delhi, and Hamíd Khan from Hissár-Firóza, to meet him. Having proceeded one march farther, he dispatched a select body of men, under his son Humáyun, to attack the latter — a service which was accomplished with great vigour, the troops of Hamíd being routed and dispersed. In order to inspire terror into the enemy, the Emperor, in compliance with the cruel policy of his age, ordered upwards of a hundred prisoners, who were brought to the camp, to be shot. Seven or eight elephants were also taken by the victors. A part of the detachment, following the fugitives, entered Hissár-Firóza along with them, and took and sacked the place. This being Humáyun's first exploit, the district of Hissár-Firóza, and its dependencies, were bestowed on him as a jágír.

A.H. 932, Jemádi I. 13, A.D. 1526, Feb. 25. Humáyun defeats Hamíd, Jemádi I. 16, Feb. 28.

Hissár-Firóza taken.

Malek Baban joins.

It was at this station that Báber was joined by Malek Baban Jilwáni, an Afghán chief of great weight, already mentioned; who, after the defeat of Alá-ed-dín near Delhi, had fled to the Doáb. He brought with him three thousand horse, and afterwards acted an important part in the history of the times. Báber was, from the first, offended with his Afghán independence and presumption, and especially with his pretensions to sit at the Derbár; though, the Emperor observes, neither Diláwer Khan, nor even the sons of Alá-ed-dín, had that privilege.*

Báber approaches Ibráhím's camp.

Báber now held on, on his way by Shahábád, where he halted some days; and, after two marches more, encamped on the Jamna, opposite Sirsáwa. Ibráhím's

and also Ferishta and Kháfi Khan, — follow the Memoirs more or less closely. Indeed, most of what we know of Báber's history is ultimately derived from his own Commentaries. It is surprising how difficult it is to supply, in a satisfactory manner, the blanks, sometimes of several years, that are found in them.

* Báber, p. 302.; Ferishta, vol. ii. p. 43.

camp was not far off. That prince had been advancing slowly, by three or four miles at a time, halting two or three days at each station. Báber continued his route, down the right bank of the river, for two marches more; when he was informed, by his scouts, that Ibráhím had sent Dáúd Khan across the Jamna, into the Doáb, with six or seven thousand horse, who were now encamped three or four kos in advance of Ibráhím's position. Against this advanced body, Báber sent a strong detachment, under Chín-Taimur Sultan and Mehdi Khwája*, with orders to cross over and attack them by surprise. They accordingly did cross the river, and, about the morning twilight, reached the ground where the Afgháns lay; when, though the enemy had time to march out to meet the assailants, and to form themselves, they were broken by the vigour of the charge, and pursued, with great keenness, to the very outskirts of Ibráhím's camp. Six or seven elephants were taken, and some prisoners, several of whom were put to death, as before, to strike terror into the enemy.†

defeats a detached force;

Jemádi II. 18. April 1.

Being now near the royal camp, Báber made every thing ready for the battle that was to decide the fate of India. To prevent the irruption of the enemy's cavalry, he connected the gun-carriages by twisted bull-hides, instead of chains; and, between every two guns, placed six or seven small movable breast-works‡, behind which the matchlock-men could load and fire their pieces in safety. He halted five or six days to prepare this apparatus; and called a council, in which it was agreed to advance as far as Panipat, a considerable town, at a convenient distance from the river, which, in case of a general action, might be very advantageously employed to cover one of the flanks of the

Prepares for battle,

* Chin-Táimur Sultan was a son of the younger Khan of the Moghuls, Báber's uncle.

† Báber, p. 303.

‡ The Táríkhe-Bedáuni says, bags filled with earth. (f. 136.)

BOOK III. A.D. 1526. occupies Panipat, Jemádi II. 29, April 12. A.H. 932, A.D. 1526.

army. Báber, therefore, moved forward two marches more, and occupied that town, near which the fate of India has so often been decided. Here he took up a strong position; the town and suburbs on his right, his centre secured by his cannon and the breast-works that had been prepared; the left and various other points were covered by ditches, and by defences made of the boughs of trees. In his line, at the distance of every bow-shot, he left a passage large enough for a hundred or a hundred and fifty men to march out abreast.

Great as was the confidence of Báber's army in their leader, apprehensions and alarm began to spread among them. They were now two or three months' march from their own homes; surrounded by a strange people, whose language they did not understand, and who did not understand theirs. They were comparatively few in number, and opposed to an army of a hundred thousand men, with nearly a thousand elephants. Sultan Ibráhím had in his possession the treasures of his father and grandfather, which, had he expended them liberally, might have brought into the field as many more. Báber acknowledges, however, that the enemies opposed to him here were very different from those veterans with whom he had had to contend in the north; and that Ibráhím was not only avaricious, but "an inexperienced young man, negligent in all his movements, who marched without order, halted or retired without plan, and engaged in battle without foresight."*

Skirmishes.

The Túrki warriors had greatly the advantage of their enemies, not only in experience, but in reputation and self-confidence. During the seven or eight days that the army remained at Panipat, a small party of the Emperor's troops, encouraged by the inactivity of the enemy, rode up to their very camp, and insulted them by shooting arrows among them; in spite of

* Báber, pp. 304, 305.

which they remained immovable; not even a sally was attempted. Báber was now prevailed upon to venture a night attack; which, against armies of that description, is so often effective. He sent four or five thousand men on this service, under able leaders. But, through some mistake, at the time of setting out, they fell into confusion, and did not get on well. The day had begun to dawn when they reached the enemy's camp; and then, instead of retiring at once, they imprudently lingered on till it was broad daylight; when the enemy beat their kettle-drums and issued out in force to assail them. In spite, however, of the cloud of troops that hung on their rear in the pursuit, Humáyun having been sent two or three miles forward to cover their retreat, and Báber drawing out the whole army ready for battle, they were enabled to retire without loss.*

CHAP. I.

A. D. 1526.

Rejeb 8, April 20.

This appearance of success probably roused and elated the Sultan. Next morning, at early twilight, the pickets reported that the enemy was advancing in battle array. All in the imperial camp prepared for action. Báber assigned commanders to each division. On the right and left of the whole line, he stationed strong flanking parties of Moghuls, who were to be ready, when ordered, at once to wheel round on the enemy and take them in the flank and rear, by the formidable charge of the *Tulughmeh*, the effects of which he had himself experienced in early days on the banks of the Soghd.†

A. H. 932, A. D. 1526. Rejeb 9, April 29. Battle.

* Báber, pp. 304, 305.

† Báber's chief officers at this time—at least such as were in India—appear as commanders of the various parts of his line. (Mem. p. 306.)

Right;—Khwája Kílan, Sultan Muhammed Duldai, Hindú Beg, Wáli Kházin, Pír Kuli Sistáni.

Left; Muhammed Sultán Mírza, Mehdi Khwája, Adel Sultán, Shah Mír Husein, Sultan Juneid Birlás, Katlek Kadam, Jan Beg, Muhammed Bakhshi, Shah Husein Bargi, Moghul Ghanchi

Right Centre; Chín Taimur Sultán, Muhammed Gokultásh, Shah Mansur Birlás, Yúnis Ali, Derwísh Muhammed Sárbán, Abdalla Kitábdár.

Left Centre; Mír Ali Khalífa, styled Nizám-ed-dín (the prime minister), Khwája Mír-Mírán, Ahmedi Perwánchi, Terdi Beg, Kúch Beg, Mohib Ali Khálífa, Mírza Beg Terkhán.

BOOK III.

A.D. 1526.

When the approach of the Afgháns was first descried, they appeared to be directing their attack against Báber's right. He, therefore, immediately sent orders to the reserve to march to its support. From the very first, the enemy never halted for an instant, but came right on at a quick pace. On arriving near the lines, and observing the defences that had been prepared, and the order of the troops, they were seen to stand still for a moment, as if hesitating how to act. They could not halt, as fresh bodies were pressing on them behind; yet they were unable to advance with the same speed as before. This occasioned some confusion or hesitation, of which Báber availed himself, by ordering the flankers on both extremes to wheel round and attack the enemy in rear, without loss of time; and the right and left wings to charge in front, at the same moment. The Moghuls, accordingly, wheeled into the enemy's rear, harassing them from behind with showers of arrows. Part of the Emperor's left wing, that advanced before the rest, under Mehdi Khwája, was roughly handled by the enemy; but he supported it by a strong detachment from the centre, and the Afgháns, in the end, were driven back. On the right, too, the battle was obstinately contested. Báber, meanwhile, ordered part of his centre to advance, and his artillery to open its fire, which was done with effect. The vast masses of the enemy were hemmed in, in front and rear, by the very inferior forces of the Túrki army. They were plied on all sides with arrows and artillery; and, though they made a few charges, attempting to break the adverse line, yet, in the end, they were huddled together

Advance; Khosrou Gokultásh, Muhammed Ali Jeng-jeng.

Reserve; Abdal-azíz (Mír Akhúr).

Flank of Right; Wáli Kazil, Malek Kásim, Bába Kushkeh (apparently Moghuls).

Flank of Left; Kara-kúzi, Abul Muhammed Nezeh-báz, Sheikh Ali, Sheikh Jemál Bárin, Mehdi, Tengri-kuli Moghul.

on their centre, unable to advance or even to retire. Still, however, they fought bravely. The battle began in the morning, and lasted till noon, when the Afgháns were thrown into inextricable confusion, and only thought of flight. The rest was mere pursuit and slaughter. The victors reckoned the number of slain, on the field of battle alone, at fifteen or sixteen thousand. Parties were sent out with orders to pursue the flying enemy as far as Agra; and, in particular, to spare no exertions to take Ibráhím. That prince, however, was found the same afternoon, stretched dead in the field; having five or six thousand of the slain lying in heaps in a small space around him. His head was cut off, and presented to Báber; who, after visiting his pavilion and camp, passed the night beside a stream a little beyond it.*

Ibráhím defeated, with great slaughter,

and slain.

On the very day of the battle, the Emperor pushed forward two detachments, the one to Delhi, the other to Agra, both to prevent the plunder, and to secure the public treasure in these cities. He himself followed, and reached Delhi on the third day after the battle; where, on the Friday following, his name, as Emperor, was read in the public prayers at the Grand Mosque, by Sheikh Zein-ed-dín, the Sadr or chief minister of religion. Having made the different treasuries at Delhi be sealed up, he hastened on to Agra.†

Báber at Delhi;

Rejeb 12, April 24,

Rejeb 15.

On arriving in that city, he found that the fort still held out; though Humáyun, who had been sent forward

At Agra. Rejeb 22, May 4.

* The impression made on the Afghâns by this disaster must have been very great. They long looked back with melancholy regret to the ruin of their empire, and to the fate of Sultan Ibráhím, whom they regarded as a martyr; and, for many years, continued to resort to his tomb as a place of pilgrimage. Nisáb-náma-e Afgh. f. 81. Sounds of wailing and of terror were long heard by night on the field of battle, which was haunted. Abdal Káder, the author of the Tárikhe Bedáuni, mentions (f. 136.) having himself heard them, while crossing it with a party, who, filled with awe, repeated the holy name of God as a preservative, and passed on.

† Báber's Mem. pp. 303—307.

BOOK III. A. D. 1526.

for the purpose, had blockaded it in such a way that, even had the treasuries been broken open, nothing could have been carried off. Bikermájít, the Rajah of Gualiár, had lately been compelled to surrender his principality to Ibráhím, after a long resistance; but had been called into his service, and had fought and fallen in his army in the late battle. His wives and children, with some of his chief followers, who were now in the fort of Agra, were seized in attempting to escape. Humáyun behaved generously to this ancient Hindu family, and prevented their being plundered. They, in return, had shown their gratitude, by making him a present of jewels and precious stones, among which was the celebrated diamond valued, by Tavernier, a jeweller and a competent judge, at nearly 880,000*l.* sterling.* On Báber's arrival, Humáyun presented it to his father, who returned it to him. The Emperor took up his residence in the palace of Sultan Ibráhím.†

Rejeb 28. May 10.

Báber's reflections on his conquest.

Báber now saw himself seated on the throne of Delhi, an object which had so long inflamed his ambition. Ever since the conquest of Kábul, two-and-twenty years before, he had never lost sight of it; and, in the course of the last seven or eight years, he had entered India five times at the head of an army, in furtherance of this, his favourite object. In the earlier portion of his residence at Kábul, his views had been thwarted,

* It weighed 8 miskals, or about 320 ratis. Tavernier says, that when *rough* it weighed 907 ratis, or 793 carats; when *cut* 319½ ratis or 279$\frac{9}{16}$ carats; and was worth 11,723,278 livres; which, taking the livre of the time at 18*d.*, would make about 879,245*l.* sterling. (Travels in India, pp. 148,143; English transl.) It had belonged to Sultan Alá-ed-dín Khilji, of Malwa. Tavernier remarks, that the apparently trifling fraction, $\frac{9}{16}$ adds upwards of 3,534*l.* to the price of the diamond.

† Báber's Mem. p. 308. Busy as Báber was with the concerns of kingdoms, he found time, with his usual activity, to visit the tombs of the saints and holy men in the vicinity of the city, as well as all the public buildings.

CHAP. I.

A.D. 1526.

sometimes by the turbulence of his Amírs, sometimes by the cabals of his brothers. As soon as these obstacles were removed, he had bent the whole powers of his mind to accomplish it. With just pride he remarks, that two foreign princes, besides himself, had conquered India, Sultan Mahmúd of Ghazni, and Sultan Shehábed-dín Ghúri *; but that he considered his own exploit as far surpassing either of theirs. That the former, a very powerful monarch, not only filled the throne of Ghazni, but that of Khorásán; and had the princes of Khwárazm subject to him, as well as the King of Samarkand; and had an army of between one and two hundred thousand men. While, as to Sultan Shehábed-dín Ghúri, though not himself sovereign of Khorásán, yet his elder brother was; and he himself is said, on one occasion, to have marched into India at the head of an hundred and twenty thousand cataphract horse. His enemies, too, were only petty Rais and Rajas; no single king governed Hindustán. That he, Báber, on the contrary, possessed only Badakhshán, Kunduz, Kábul, and Kandahár, countries which hardly supported themselves; and, though threatened by the Uzbeks on the north, who could bring into the field an hundred thousand brave soldiers, he had ventured, followed by only twelve thousand men, to attack Sultan Ibráhím, the monarch of all Hindustán from Bhíra to Behár, who had resources enough to have brought into the field five hundred thousand men, and had actually with him an army of an hundred thousand men, with a thousand elephants. "In consideration of my reliance on Divine aid," says the pious prince, "the Most High God did not suffer the distress and hardships that I had undergone to be thrown away, but defeated my formidable enemy, and made me conqueror of the noble country of

* This, as formerly observed, is the prince by Ferishta called Moiz-ed-dín Muhammed Ghúri.

BOOK III. A. D. 1526.

Hindustán. This success I do not ascribe to my own strength, nor did this good fortune flow from my own efforts, but from the fountain of the favour and mercy of God." *

He divides the spoil.

He now proceeded to examine and divide the spoil, which would appear to have been immense. To Humáyun he gave about seventy laks, in money; besides a palace, with all that it contained, of which no inventory had been taken. To several of his chief Amírs he presented sums of ten, eight, seven, and six laks †, according to their respective merits or claims. On every fighting man in his army, Afghán, Hazára, Arab or Balúch, he bestowed gratuities from the treasury. Nor were even the traders and men of letters, who had accompanied the camp, forgotten; all shared his bounty. Besides this, his sons and relations, even though not with the army, had magnificent presents, in gold and silver, jewels, rich cloths, and captive slaves, assigned to them. Nor were his friends in Samarkand, Khorásán, Káshghar, and Persia, forgotten. Rich presents were sent to them; which, while they were received with delight, spread the fame of the conqueror over those distant lands. The holy men of Khorásán and Samarkand, and the shrines of Mekka and Medina, participated in his prosperity. Finally, to every person in the country of Kábul, male or female, slave or free, young or old, he sent a shahrukhi, as a gift; to excite emulation, and perhaps to assist in recruiting his army. This magnificent distribution of the accumulated wealth of the Lodi kings, in which Báber seemed to retain nothing for himself, is said to have made him be familiarly called the Kalendar, from the name of that class

* Mem. pp. 309, 310.

† The amount of these sums is doubtful. See Appendix E. It is probable, however, that the donation to Humáyun was about 56,700*l.*; and the smaller ones, 8,100*l.*, 6,480*l.*, 5,670*l.*, and 4,860*l.* respectively; very large sums for the age.

CHAP. I.

A. D. 1526.

of religious mendicants who devoted themselves to voluntary poverty.*

Kingdoms in India.

At the time of Báber's conquest of Delhi, the political state of India was considerably different from what it has been in later ages. Besides the kingdom of Delhi, which reached from the Salt range and the mountains of Kashmír to Behár, and from Gualiár to the Himáláyas,—there were three kings and one Raja, north of the Nerbáda, who had very extensive power. The kingdom of Juánpúr (distinguished as the Sherki or Eastern, from its comprising the countries beyond the Ganges to the East of Delhi,) had indeed been subdued by the Lodis, though it was at this time in a state of revolt, under a king of its own; but Bengal, Gujrát, and Málwa were three formidable and independent kingdoms, governed respectively at this period by Nasret Shah, Sekander Shah, and Sultan Mahmúd. This last kingdom, that of Málwa, had latterly been on the decline. The Raja was Rána Sanga †, the brave and able prince of the Rájpút principality of Cheitúr; who, taking advantage of the civil wars in Málwa, had added to his hereditary dominions several of its provinces, such as Rantbór, Chándéri, and others; and was daily increasing in power. The princes to the south of the Nerbáda were altogether independent of Delhi.

Delhi,

Juánpúr,

Bengal, Gujrát, Málwa.

Rána Sanga.

The population hostile to the invaders.

But, though Báber had been victorious in the field, and was in possession of the two great capitals of the kingdom, it soon appeared that his situation, far from being one of safety or ease, was surrounded with difficulty and danger. He and his army were strangers

* Mem. p. 334.; Briggs's Ferishta, vol. ii. p. 49. note. For the amount of Báber's revenues, see Appendix D, p. 540.; and, for the value of his money of account, see Appendix E, p. 543.

† In the translation of Báber's Memoirs, following former writers, I gave this Prince the name of Sanka. I willingly adopt the correction of Colonel Tod, whose intimate acquaintance with Rájpút history and the Rájpúts, makes him an authority on such a subject. See Annals of Rájasthan, vol. ii. p. 23, and elsewhere.

BOOK III. A. D. 1526.

to the people whom he had subdued; and a mutual dislike soon manifested itself between his soldiers and the inhabitants of Agra, his head-quarters. The peasantry, as well as the fighting men of the country, shunned and fled from his followers. The north of India, at the time of Báber's conquest, still retained much of its original Hindu organisation; its system of village and district administration and government; its division into numerous little chieftainships, or petty local governments; and, in political revolutions, the people looked much more to their own immediate rulers, than to the prince who governed in the capital. Except at Delhi and Agra, the inhabitants everywhere fortified their towns, and prepared to resist. The invasion was regarded as a temporary inundation, that would speedily pass off. Every man in authority raised troops, and put himself in a condition to act. Those who held delegated authority or jágírs, being generally Afgháns, were consequently hostile to the new state of things. They soon came to an understanding among themselves, and took measures for mutual co-operation. Raja Hasan Khan of Mewát, in the neighbourhood of Agra, was the grand instigator of the opposition; which was supported by Nizám Khan, in Biána; Muhammed Zeitún, in Dhúlpúr; Tátár Khan Sarang-khání, in Gualiár; Husein Khan Lohani, in Raberi; Kutb Khan, in Etáwa; Alim Khan Jilál Khan Jighat, in Kalpi; Kásim Sambhali, in Sambhal; and Marghúb, a slave, in Maháwan, within twenty kos of Agra. Indeed, all of these chiefs were immediately around Agra, or close upon its borders. They looked for aid from Rána Sanga, the powerful chief of Cheitúr; who, on his part, laid claim to a great part of the right bank of the Jamna. These Western Afgháns wished to place Sultan Mahmúd Lodi, a brother of the late Sultan Ibráhím, on the throne of Delhi; and so to preserve the Afghán and the Lodi dynasty.

Combinations against them,

in the West.

In the East.

In the Eastern provinces of Juánpúr and Oud, the opposition presented even a more regular form. There, the confederacy of Afghán chiefs, who had been in open rebellion against Ibráhím for two years before his death, still continued. The revolt was originally headed by Násir Khan Loháni, Maarúf Fermuli, and others. The insurgents, we have seen, had elected Báber Khan Loháni, the son of Deriá Khan of Behár, for their king; and proclaimed him, under the name of Sultan Muhammed Shah. They now possessed, not only Behár, but nearly the whole territories of the old Sherki monarchy, especially the country on the left bank of the Ganges; and had even crossed to the right bank of the river, and taken possession of Kanauj, and advanced into the Doáb. Sultan Ibráhím had sent an army, under Mustafa Fermuli and Firúz Khan Sarang-kháni, to reduce the rebels to obedience. Mustafa had met the revolted chiefs, and defeated them in some well-contested actions. On his death, which occurred some time before the defeat of Sultan Ibráhím, he was succeeded in the command by Sheikh Bayezíd, his younger brother. The army under his orders was formidable; and it was naturally to be expected, that, changed as circumstances now were, the two armies opposed to each other in the field, being both Afgháns, would lay aside their mutual animosities, and, animated by national feelings, unite to expel Báber, the common enemy.

Sultan Muhammed Shah.

Army sent against him by Ibráhím.

It was clear that the Afghán chiefs, who till now had ruled with nearly unlimited authority both in Delhi and Behár, must be ruined if Báber settled in Hindustán. They, therefore, stirred up, with great success, the apprehensions of the natives, whether Musulman or Hindu, by the most false and groundless reports. The people of the country were told, that they had every thing to dread from their barbarous invaders; that they would be robbed of their property; that their wives and children would be dishonoured;

Difficulties of Báber.

BOOK III.

A. D. 1526.

their temples profaned or destroyed. Báber and his army had reached Agra in May, in that climate the hottest season of the year. The inhabitants, in terror, fled before them, and abandoned their dwellings, so that no grain or provender could be procured for man or beast. The villagers fled to the waste, and infested the highways, plundering and robbing on every side. The roads became impassable. Báber's force was so small that he was unable to send out detachments sufficient to protect the different districts. To add to these difficulties, the heats that year happened to be uncommonly intense, so that many of his men, who were from more temperate climates, unaccustomed to the burning sun of India, dropped down and died on the spot.

Discontent in his army.

The pressure of so many evils began to spread discontent even among Báber's best officers. Some lost heart, and many resolved to return. Murmurs rose on every hand. Even Khwája Kilán was impatient to go back. Amír Khwája Kilán was no common man. He was the son of Moulána Muhammed Sadr, who had been one of the most eminent counsellors of Báber's father, both in the religious and civil affairs of his kingdom of Ferghána. After Báber's accession he had continued to the son the same attachment he had shown to the father, and fell a sacrifice to his loyalty. The whole family had followed their young prince from his early days through every reverse of fortune. Six brothers had fallen by the Emperor's side in his various wars, and Khwája Kilán alone survived. He was a learned man, a hardy veteran, a distinguished general, and a wise counsellor.* The Emperor had owed much to his vigour in the recent conquest of Hindustán, and was sincerely attached to him as a private friend. Báber's situation was become peculiarly distressing.

* Tar. Resh. f. 364.

He had gained the long-cherished object of his ambition, which had floated before his eyes ever since the tales of his old hostess of Dehkát had fired his youthful imagination; and, now that it was in his possession, he was on the point of being compelled to let it slip from his grasp.

CHAP. I.

A. D. 1526.

His address to his council.

He called a council of his nobles, and addressed them on the present posture of his affairs. He told them, that after long years of toil, after many a weary march and many a bloody field, they had at last gloriously vanquished every difficulty, and were the masters of numerous rich and extensive provinces; that they never could expect that what was gained with toil was to be preserved by indolence; and that, to abandon their conquests and fly, though victorious, with every symptom of rout and discomfiture, from the scene of their glory, would brand them, in the eyes of all mankind, as mean and dastardly. "Let no such proposal," he added, "come from any friend of mine. But if among you there be found any one who does not wish to remain with me, let him depart; he has my full permission." The Emperor's address touched their point of honour. Even such as were most eager to return were ashamed to avail themselves of his offer. All declared their willingness to stand by him. Báber, however, who saw that his friend Khwája Kilán suffered, and believed that even the supposition of discontent in a man of his weight might have an unfavourable influence upon the troops, bestowed on him the government of Ghazni, Gurdíz, and the Masaúdi Afgháns, to which he added a valuable estate in India; and, appointing him to guard the presents which he was sending to Kábul and his more distant dominions, dismissed him with every mark of honour and regard; after which, he applied himself to support the spirit of his followers, by active employment and by new successes.*

* Báber's Mem. pp. 335 336.

BOOK III.

A.D. 1526

Change in his prospects;

He was speedily rewarded for his heroic firmness. It was no sooner known that his invasion was not to be a temporary inroad, like those of Mahmúd of Ghazni and the great Taimur, but that he was to remain permanently in the country, and to govern it on the spot, than new fears and new hopes began to operate, both on the natives and the Afgháns. His generous policy, his manly deportment, and known valour, inspired his friends with confidence, and struck terror into his enemies. The consequence was soon visible. His affairs began to brighten. Sheikh Kuren, an Afghán officer*, joined him, with two or three thousand Terkish-bend followers from Kol, in the Doáb. Two sons of Ali Khan Fermuli were accidentally taken, between Delhi and Agra, in a skirmish. Báber sent one of them back to their father, which led to that nobleman's now submitting and waiting on the Emperor, by whom he was graciously received. But a more important accession of strength speedily followed, when he was acknowledged by the Afghán army of Sultan Ibráhím, which, under Sheikh Bayezíd Fermuli and Firúz Khan, had been successfully employed, as already mentioned, against Sultan Muhammed Shah, of Behár, and the revolted chiefs of the East.† Both Bayezíd Fermuli and Firúz Khan now submitted to Báber, who bestowed on them, and the leading officers of their army, large assignments, chiefly in Juánpúr and Oudh, out of the revenues of the territories that were still in the hands of the insurgents, to whom they were opposed. This event added much to the security of Báber's government.‡

he is joined by Sheikh Kuren,

by Ali Khan Fermuli,

by the Afghán army under Sheikh Bayezíd.

* Second in music to none, says the Tárikhe-Bedáuni.

† Báber calls the Juánpúr provinces indiscriminately Sherki and Purabi. Indeed, Sherk and Purab are only the Persian or Arabic and Hindu names for the East. They are, therefore, equally applicable to that country and to Bengal; though historians seem generally to apply Sherki, the Musulman term, to Juánpúr and Behár; and Purabi, the Hindu form, to the Bengal kingdom.

‡ Báber's Memoirs, p. 337. I may here take an opportunity of

Kásim besieged in Sambhal.

Báber's first active operation, in the field, was to dispatch a force to the relief of Sambhal, a district lying beyond the Ganges, in what is now called Róhilkand. It was held by Kásim Sambhali, who had formerly shown himself hostile to Báber, but was glad to solicit his aid, when, at this time, besieged in his chief town, by Malek Baban Jilwáni. This powerful and active Afghán chief had, as we have seen, joined Báber after he had passed Sirhind, but subsequently left him, under circumstances which are not mentioned; but he probably was not satisfied with his reception, as Báber complains, with bitterness, of his presumption and pretensions, and of the rudeness and stupid forwardness of the Afgháns in general. However that may be, Baban had withdrawn himself from Báber's camp, had collected an army, and now besieged Kásim in Sambhal, which he had discovered was ill-garrisoned. Kásim, reduced to the last extremity, applied to Báber for assistance. The Emperor dispatched Hindú Beg, with a body of Túrks and Moghuls, along with Sheikh Kuren and his Doáb Terkish-bends, to his succour. Hindú Beg marched with all possible expedition till he reached the Ganges; and, while busily employed in conveying his other troops across that river, sent on in advance a Moghul officer with a body of his countrymen. Though the party did not exceed a hundred and fifty men, they rode forward till they reached the town, and such was the superiority which the invaders from the

Hindú Beg sent to his relief,

correcting what seems to be a mistake in the translation of Báber's Memoirs, p. 337. The assignment there made to Mahmúd Khan, the third in command, following the two copies of the original which I possessed, was only nine lacs, thirty-five thousand. In the Persian translation of a portion of the Memoirs already referred to, the assignments are stated as under, and apparently more correctly :—"To Firúz Khan, one krór, forty-six lak, and five thousand tankas, from Juánpúr; to Bayezíd, one krór, forty-eight laks, and fifty thousand tankas, from Oud; to Mahmúd Khan, ninety laks, thirty thousand tankas, from Gházipúr; and to Kázi Jia, twenty laks." Here, it will be observed, the computation is by tankas.

BOOK III.

A. D. 1526.

north had acquired over the troops of the country, that the Moghuls had no sooner got between the town and the besiegers than they resolutely turned and charged them, though already the alarm had been given, and Baban had had time to draw out his force. The attack was so vigorous, and probably the panic produced by the expected approach of the rest of the detachment so great, that Baban's whole army was routed and dispersed, several elephants taken, and a number of heads brought in. Next day Hindú Beg arrived with the rest of the troops, and had an interview with Kásim Sambhali, who made some difficulty about giving up the place. He had asked for succour, not for a master or successor. He was soon, however, seized by stratagem, and the fort itself taken possession of. His family and followers were allowed to retire to Biána.*

raises the siege,

but seizes the place.

Ráberi taken.

Báber's success did not end here. The fortress of Ráberi on the Jamna, was soon after abandoned by its garrison, and occupied by his troops; and he sent detachments to besiege Etáwa and Dhúlpúr, two places of the greatest importance, from their vicinity to Agra.

Rána Sanga takes Rantbór.

Meanwhile, Rána Sanga, the victorious chief of Cheitúr, and the most powerful and warlike prince of the West, had advanced from Rantbór, and taken the strong hill-fort of Kandar from Hasan Makan, who had applied to Báber for assistance; though probably not till he saw that he possessed no means, in his own resources, of making a successful defence. The Rájpút chief had exactly the same views with Báber,—to make the most of the ruin of the Afghán monarchy.

Council held.

The events that have been mentioned took place during the rainy monsoon, which was now nearly over, and the season for action in the field was at hand. Báber, therefore, held a grand council, to decide which

* Báber's Mem., pp. 338, 339.

CHAP. I.

A.D. 1526.

way he should turn his arms. On the west, Rana Sánga was fast advancing the limits of his already extensive dominions. On the east, the confederate Afghán chiefs, who acknowledged Sultan Muhammed of Behár, — after recovering the country beyond the Ganges and occupying Kanauj, — led by Násir Khan Lohani, and Maarúf Fermuli, had made two or three marches within the Doáb, with forty or fifty thousand men. As the Eastern, or Sherki, confederates were the enemy not only nearest at hand, but, from their connection with the country, most to be dreaded, it was agreed that the first attack should be directed against them. The Emperor's Amírs recommended that he should himself remain at Agra, to superintend the general system of affairs, while he sent his son Humáyun, at the head of an army, to meet the advancing enemy. This arrangement was agreed to, and Báber, fully aware that, if he was successful in the field, the various forts that now held out would rapidly fall, recalled the troops that he had sent to invest Etáwa and Dhúlpúr—a force chiefly composed of the followers of Sheikh Bayezíd, Firóz Khan, and the other Afghán chiefs, who had lately been opposed to the very army against which they were once more to march, — and ordered them to join Humáyun at head-quarters, at Chandwár on the Jamna.

Resolution to attack the Sherkis.

Humáyun sent in command.

The young prince, having collected his forces, and being attended by Mehdi Khwája and Muhammed Sultan Mírza, marched straight against the enemy; who, under Násir Khan and Maarúf, instead of advancing on Agra, seem to have marched down the Doáb to Jajmou. When he had arrived within twenty miles of them, he sent out parties to ascertain their position; intending to beat up their quarters by a sudden attack. But he could get no accurate account of their movements; and the Afghán army, on discovering his approach, broke up; and, retreating in disorder, re-

They recross the Ganges.

BOOK III. A.D. 1526.

He is joined by Fateh Khan.

crossed the Ganges. Humáyun, upon this, advanced and occupied the ground they had left. As he proceeded to Dilmou, farther down, he was met by Fateh Khan Sirwáni (the son of the late Azím Humáyun, and who had been the minister, first of the unfortunate Jilál Khan, and afterwards of the late Sultan Ibráhím,) who tendered his submission. This was an important acquisition, as he was a nobleman who had a perfect knowledge of the state of parties, as well as great personal influence. He was, therefore, sent without delay to attend the Emperor. Báber, highly pleased with his submission, confirmed him in all the estates that had been held by his father, and made considerable additions to them. He also seems to have borne the title of Azím Humáyun; but, as the Emperor did not mean that that style should in future belong to any one but his own son, he honoured Fateh Khan with the title of Khan-Jehán.*

Takes Juánpúr, and Kalpi.

Humáyun, after putting to flight the Afghán army, crossed the Ganges and took possession of Juánpúr. He next marched to Gházipúr, intending to attack Násir Khan's army, which had retired into that neighbourhood. But the Afgháns, on his approach, retired behind the Gogra, as it would appear, into the territory of Bengal; and a detachment that he sent to pursue them returned, after plundering the country of Kheríd and Behár. Having thus expelled them from the Juánpúr territory, he left Shah Mir Husein †, in the city of Juánpúr, supported by Sultan Juneid Birlás with some of his best troops; and Sheikh Bayezíd in Oud, with every means of maintaining the country; and then, in

* Báber's Mem. pp. 342, 343. Khan-Jehán signifies Lord of the World. Báber remarks, p. 344, that it was the custom of the kings of Hindustán to bestow on the Amírs in highest favour high-sounding titles; such as Azím Humáyun (the magnificently propitious), Khan-Jehán, and Khan-Khánán (Lord of Lords). Báber and his successors continued the practice.

† The Tabakáti Akberi, f. 142., and Táríkhe Bedáuni f. 137., call him Khwája Amír Shah Hasan.

compliance with orders which he received from his father, recrossed into the Doáb; and marching back by Kalpi, of which he gained possession by the submission of Alim Khan, rejoined the Emperor at Agra, bringing Alim Khan along with him.*

A. H. 933, A. D. 1527. Rejoins Báber, Rebi II. 3. Jan. 6.

Báber builds a palace.

When Báber, after despatching Humáyun to the eastward, remained behind in Agra, he was not idle. He devoted his chief attention to restoring the finances, and the military resources of the kingdom, to a healthy state. Influenced, not merely by his taste for all the fine arts, but by an earnest desire to reassure the minds and to confirm the confidence of his new subjects, he began to build a palace, and to lay out a garden, on the left bank of the Jamna, opposite to Agra; and encouraged his chief nobility to imitate his example. These improvements soon grew into the fine suburb which got the name of Kábul. But such peaceful occupations, much as he always delighted in them, did not absorb his attention. He was justly alarmed at the progress of Rana Sánga; who was in active correspondence with Hasan Khan Mewáti, the chief of the Afghán confederacy of the West; and had acknowledged as King of Delhi, Sultan Mahmúd, the brother of the late Sultan Ibráhím, whom the western Afgháns had proclaimed King, after his brother's death. Báber, therefore, sent orders to Humáyun to lose no time in returning to Agra with the bulk of his troops, as soon as he had settled Juánpúr, and the eastern provinces. Before his return, however, Báber despatched a small expedition against Biána, which was held by Nizám Khan, who refused to acknowledge him. From its vicinity to Agra, from its position between that town and the Rájpúts, and from its strength, Biána was a place of the utmost consequence. Desirous to gain possession of it, he sent a force under Terdi Beg, ac-

The Rana's progress;

Humáyun recalled. Sefer 22, A. D. 1526. Nov. 28.

Expedition against Biána,

* Báber's Mem. pp. 342—44.; Tabakáti Akberi, f. 142.

BOOK III. A. D. 1526. companied by some chosen officers; and instructed him to invite the garrison, by every assurance of indemnity and favour, to yield the place; but, if his efforts were fruitless, then he was to plunder and lay waste the whole country around, and to do all in his power to reduce those who held the fortress to the last extremity.

At this time, Alim Khan of Tehenger, an elder brother of Nizám Khan, the chief of Biána, offered to Báber to procure the surrender of the place, if he were entrusted with the direction of the troops sent against it. As he was possessed of a considerable jágír in the neighbourhood, had great local knowledge, and professed to be in correspondence with officers in the fort, Báber accepted of his services. "Though the men of Hindustán," says Báber, "are often brave swordsmen, yet they are extremely ignorant of the art of war, and of the disposition and conduct of troops as commanders." Alim seems to have been a man of this description. He would listen to nobody; and, in spite of the remonstrances of Báber's veteran officers, carried the which fails; detachment close up to the walls of Biána. The whole force did not consist of more than two or three hundred Túrks, and two thousand men of Hindustán and other countries. Nizám Khan had, within the place, a garrison of above four thousand cavalry and ten thousand foot, composed of Afgháns and others. Taking advantage of the error which Alim Khan had committed, he made a sally with his whole troops, charged him and his detachment furiously, threw them into confusion at the first onset, and pursued them in their retreat. Alim Khan himself was taken prisoner. But it was not long before the advance of Rana Sánga from Rantbór, showed Nizám Khan that he must choose between but Biána surrenders, two masters. He preferred the Musulman Báber, to whom the important fortress of Biána was soon after surrendered*, Nizám Khan being provided for by a jágír in the Doáb. And, about the same time, Muhammed Zeitun was induced, from similar motives, to surrender Dhúlpúr; which lies on the Chambal, between Agra and Gualiár, and which Baber converted into an imperial domain.†

and Dhúlpúr.

Báber invited to Gualiár;

But his good-fortune did not terminate here. The impregnable hill-fort of Gualiár has always been held by the natives of India to be of the greatest consequence. Tátár Khan Sarangkháni, — who held it, — though he had repeatedly conveyed to Báber professions of his attachment and submission, had always refused to admit the imperial troops into his territories. After Rana Sánga had taken Kándár, and when he was advancing to Biána, the hopes of the Hindus being revived, Raja Mankat Rái, who was of the ancient race of the hereditary Rajas of Gualiár, Khan Jehán Bandéli, and other Hindu chiefs, entered the province, the inhabitants of which they attempted to raise in support of their claims; so that they might expel the Musulman intruders, and recover possession of the fortress. Tátár Khan, finding himself hard pushed, and of two evils, wishing rather to submit to a Musulman, though an enemy to his race, than to a Pagan, the enemy of his religion, wrote once more to Báber with his usual professions, offering to give up the place. In consequence of the numerous demands for troops in different quarters, and the small number of which his army was composed, Báber happened at this time to have none of his superior Begs or more confidential servants near him. Eager, however, to avail himself of so favourable an opportunity, he dispatched Rahímdád, one of his adherents, with a party of Bhíra and Láhúr men, to his assistance, with Sheikh Kuren

* The Tabakáti Akberi says, by the intervention of Syed Rafia-ed-dín, a holy man who had many disciples in that age (f. 141.).

† Báber's Mem., f. 345.; Tabakáti Akberi, f. 141, 142.

BOOK III.

A. D. 1526.

which is taken by stratagem.

and some Afgháns; who, on reaching Gualiár, found that Tátár Khan would not admit them into the fort.*

There lived at this time in the place, one Sheikh Muhammed Ghús, a Derwísh, celebrated for his sanctity, who had a number of disciples and adherents. This man sent a private message to Rahímdád, to advise him to get into the fort, no matter how, and then to watch events; for, that Tátár Khan had changed his mind, and did not intend to give up the place. In compliance with this suggestion Rahímdád, affecting a dread of being attacked by the common enemy, who hovered around, begged that he himself, with a few of his immediate servants, might be admitted into the fort; and that his troops should be suffered to lie close under the walls for security. This was imprudently allowed. He next got permission to have certain of his followers stationed at the gate, along with Tátár's guard, to prevent quarrels and to point out who really were his servants, that they might be permitted to come and go without interruption. That same night, so many men were introduced, that Tátár Khan, seeing himself entirely in their power, gave up the fort and repaired to Agra; where Báber assigned him a different district as a provision for his support.†

* The Tabakáti Akberi calls him Khwája Rahímdád. It calls the Derwísh, Sheikh Muhammed Ghazali Ghús.

† Báber's Mem. pp. 345, 346.; Briggs's Ferishta, vol. ii. pp. 51, 52. Ferishta and Kháfi Khan add several circumstances to the details of this stratagem; but the simple account is contained in Báber's Commentaries, from which all borrow. Báber's account of the covered doolies, said to contain women, by which armed men were introduced into the fort, does not suit a hasty expedition like Rahímdád's, on which ladies never go. The author of the Tabakáti Akberi (f. 142.), who seems to have been well acquainted with the holy man's character, relates, that Sheikh Muhammed, being thoroughly versed in the science of the attributes and mysterious names of God, offered to utter a prayer in one of these names for the taking of the castle, which he doubted not would find acceptance; an offer that was gladly accepted. This is probably true, being quite in accordance with the mixture of superstition and artifice that characterises many of these Musulman saints. See also Tarikhi Bedáuni, f. 137.

Attempt on Báber's life.

About this time the Emperor had a narrow escape from a dangerous attempt upon his life. It happened that, when the late King's establishment was broken up, Báber had retained in his service four out of the numerous cooks of Sultan Ibráhím, for the purpose of preparing such dishes as were peculiar to the country. This had reached the ears of Ibráhím's mother, to whom Báber had assigned an estate for her maintenance. She sent for one Ahmed, who had been her son's taster, or bekáwal; and, communicating with him through a female slave, gained him over, and sent him some poison folded up in a paper. Ahmed, by the promise of great rewards, seduced one of the cooks, who had formerly been under him; delivered to him the poison; and instructed him to sprinkle it on some part of the food sent up to the Emperor. The cook, being watched by the tasters who attend for that purpose in the imperial kitchen, was not able to throw it into the cooking-pots; but, while dishing the meat, contrived unperceived to scatter a portion of it over some slices of bread on which the different meats were to be placed. Half of it, in the hurry, fortunately fell into the fire. On this bread he placed some meats fried in butter. The Emperor ate a piece of hare, and a good deal of fried carrot, without being sensible of any disagreeable taste. He next ate a morsel or two of smoked meat, and felt nausea. He thought little of it, at first; but by-and-by was seized with a violent retching, while the tray was still before him; and the usual effects of sickness followed. Never before having been sick after eating, nor even after the deep drinking bouts, in which the gaiety of his character had so often led him to indulge, the circumstance excited his suspicions. The cooks were placed in custody, and some of the meat was given to a dog, which swelled and became much distressed. Two young men, who had eaten part of the food, were also violently affected. An examination of the cooks

BOOK III. A. D. 1526. ensued, followed by that of the other persons concerned, when the whole conspiracy was brought to light. The guilty were subjected to the cruel punishments which even in polished times have continued to be inflicted on such crimes. The bekáwal was hewn in pieces; the cook flayed alive; of two female slaves who were implicated, one was shot, another was trampled to death by an elephant. With the necessary medical assistance, Báber, in a short time, was restored to health. The guilty queen was placed under custody, and her property confiscated.*

Multán submits.

Hardly twelve months had passed since Báber entered India, and only eight since the defeat of Sultan Ibráhím, yet the Emperor's sway now extended from Attok to Behár; and, from Kalpi and Gualiár, to the mountains of Himála. It was about this time, too, as is elsewhere mentioned, that Multán was added to his empire. When, on a previous occasion, he invaded the Penjáb, he had encouraged Shah Hasan Arghún, who was then in possession of Bheker, to attack that province. (A. H. 931, A. D. 1525.) This he willingly did; ravaged the country, and invested the capital. On this first occasion, the Arghún retired, on getting a cession of that part of the Multán territory which lay below the Ghara. But having not long after renewed his invasion, he once more sat down before the city of Multán; which, after a siege of fifteen months, he took by storm and plundered. (A. H. 932, A. D. 1526.) An end was thus put to the Langa dynasty in Multán; for, though Shah Hasan's troops were afterwards expelled by an insurrection of the inhabitants, the country submitted to the Emperor, and was annexed to the empire of Delhi.†

The Uzbeks invade Khorásán.

This important year was still farther distinguished by the operations of the Uzbeks against the Persians,

* Báber's Mem. pp. 347, 348. Briggs's Ferishta, vol. ii. pp. 396. 400, and 435, 436.

† Taríkhe Sind, f. 145—7.; Tabakáti Akberi, f. 140—142.;

both in Khorásán and Balkh. That brave and hardy people had now had time to recover from the alarm occasioned by their defeat near Merv; and the death of Shah Ismael, who some time before this period had been succeeded by his son Shah Tahmásp, then a boy, had relieved them from their dread of his talents and fortune.* All were eager to avail themselves of the favourable opportunity thus offered, to recover the country and reputation which they had lost; and Obeíd Khan of Bokhára, acting with the authority of his grand uncle, Kuchum Khan, then the great Khan of the Uzbeks, summoned all the Uzbek chiefs, on both sides of the Sirr, to an invasion of Khorásán. They accordingly entered that country, Durmish Khan Shámlú, the Atalik of Sám Mírza, Shah Tahmásp's son, Beglerbeg or governor of the province, retiring into Herát, where the Uzbeks besieged him for several months, but were finally compelled to raise the siege.

CHAP. I.

A.D. 1526.

A.H. 930, A.D. 1523.

In the course of the following year, Durmish Khan having died, and the governor of Meshhíd having been killed in a civil feud, there was no one left to take the chief management of affairs in the province; and, quarrels having arisen among the Amírs, the army and the country of Khorásán fell into complete confusion. This encouraged Obeíd Khan to renew his invasion. Crossing the Amu, at Charjú, he took Merv and Sirakhs; and, proceeding to the holy city of Meshhíd, made himself master of it, after a sharp resistance. Tús also fell into his hands, after sustaining a siege of eight months; when, in spite of the capitulation entered into, all the men in the place were massacred by the Uzbeks, and the females carried off into slavery.†

A.H. 931, A.D. 1524.

Take Meshhíd, A.H. 932, A.D. 1525.

and Tús.

* Towards the end of this year, an envoy from Shah Tahmásp reached Báber's court, bringing, we are told, among other presents, two Circassian slaves for the Emperor's haram. Báber's Mem. p. 346.

† Tar Alim-Arai Abáso, f. 22—23.; Báber's Mem. pp. 342, 343.

BOOK III.

A.D. 1526.

Desertion of Bishágheri and his brother.

The hostilities between the Persians and Uzbeks were not confined to Khorásán. We have seen that, before Báber left Kábul, they had laid siege to Balkh; and, that Báber was apprehensive of danger to his dominions beyond the mountains. The decline of the Persian, and rise of the Uzbek, power, roused such unquiet spirits, even in Báber's court, as hoped to rise by disorder and change. When Humáyun was on his way from Badakhshán to join Báber, then on his march from Kábul to the Indus, two of his officers, Múlla Bába Beshágheri, and Bába Sheikh, his younger brother, deserted, and went over to Kar Kitin, the Uzbek chief, who was besieging Balkh. It was not the first occasion on which these officers had proved faithless to Báber. Múlla Bába had been his particular favourite, and intrusted with the most distinguished commands. Yet both of them had formerly joined the Moghuls of Ghazni in their revolt under Shiram Ali Taghái. When that rebellion was quelled, they had been pardoned and placed in offices of trust in the Kunduz territory, which did not prevent them from now deserting again. Not long after they had joined the Uzbeks, Balkh surrendered, upon which an expedition was sent, under the two deserters, against Báber's northern dominions, which reduced Eibák, Sárabágh, and Khuram, places situated in the valley of the Khúlm river, among the mountains between Khúlm and Kahmerd. The garrison of Ghuri, an important town on the river of that name, panic-struck at the fall of Balkh, also surrendered to the Uzbeks. Mír Hámeh, who had a stronghold in the neighbourhood, saw nothing left for it but in like manner to declare for them. As soon as this was known, the Mír and his garrison were ordered to Balkh; and Bába Sheikh, one of the traitors, arrived with a party to take possession of the castle. The Mír received Bába within its walls, and artfully assigned to the rest of the party quarters for the night in

Balkh taken,

also Eibák, Ghuri, &c.

Affair cf Mír Hámeh.

houses rather remote from each other. He then availed himself of the unsuspecting security in which they all were, attacked Bába Sheikh, whom he wounded, made him and several of his followers prisoners, and dispatched an express to Báber's general in Kunduz, to inform him how matters stood. A detachment of troops was instantly hurried off to his relief, who, on their approach, found that a fresh party of Uzbeks had arrived to invest the castle. They succeeded, however, in bringing off Mír Hámeh and his men. As Bába Sheikh's wound did not admit of his accompanying them, they cut off his head, not to leave him behind alive. Báber, who was much, and justly, incensed against the brothers for their repeated treachery, rewarded Mír Hámeh with many marks of his favour.*

* Báber's Mem. p. 350.

CHAPTER II.

WAR OF RÁNA SÁNGA, AND OF CHÁNDÉRI.

RÁNA SÁNGA. — HIS DOMINIONS — CHARACTER. — PREVIOUS TRANSACTIONS WITH BÁBER. — MUTUAL RECRIMINATION. — HIS VIEWS OF AMBITION. — SUPPORTS THE WESTERN AFGHÁNS. — IS JOINED BY HASAN KHAN — MARCHES TO BIÁNA. — ADVANCE OF BÁBER TO SIKRI, TO OPPOSE HIM. — PROWESS OF THE RÁJPÚTS. — SKIRMISH. — DISCOURAGEMENT OF BÁBER'S TROOPS. — HE LAYS WASTE MEWÁT. — HIS MEASURES TO REANIMATE HIS ARMY. — HE RENOUNCES THE USE OF WINE. — REMITS THE TEMGHA. — ADDRESS TO HIS COUNCIL — ITS SUCCESS. — PROGRESS OF THE AFGHÁNS IN VARIOUS QUARTERS. — BÁBER MOVES ONWARDS. — PREPARES FOR BATTLE. — RÁJPÚT FORCES. — BATTLE OF KANWA. — BÁBER VICTORIOUS. — ASSUMES THE TITLE OF GHÁZI. — KOEL RETAKEN. — MEWÁT REDUCED. — HUMÁYUN SENT BACK TO BADAKHSHÁN. — THE LOST TOWNS IN THE DOÁB, AND COUNTRY BEYOND THE GANGES, RECOVERED — CAMPAIGN OF CHÁNDÉRI. — MEDÍNI RAO — HIS HISTORY. — REVOLUTIONS OF MALWA. — RÁNA SÁNGA CALLED IN — HIS VICTORY AND GENEROSITY. — BÁBER'S PROPOSALS TO MEDÍNI REJECTED. — HE TAKES THE OUTER TOWN AND FORT OF CHÁNDÉRI. — MASSACRE OF THE RÁJPÚTS. — DEATH OF RÁNA SÁNGA.

Rána Sánga.

BUT a formidable rival was now advancing to contest with Báber the sovereignty of India. Rána Sánga was the head of the Rájpút principality of Cheitúr, now known as Udipúr, and the representative of a family which, by the universal consent of the Rájpúts, is allowed the pre-eminence among all the Rájpút tribes as the most ancient and the noblest. Like Báber, he had been educated in the school of adversity. After overcoming the many difficulties and dangers of his early life, when he at length mounted the throne, he carried on successful wars with his neighbours on every side, and added largely to his own extensive hereditary

His dominions,

dominions. From Sultan Mahmúd Khilji, the king of Málwa,—whom he defeated in battle, took prisoner, and honourably entertained, in a spirit worthy of the best days of chivalry,—he had wrested the wide and valuable provinces of Bhílsa, Sárángpúr, Chándéri, and Rántbór.* He had engaged in hostilities with Sultan Ibráhím of Delhi, and twice had met the Sultan himself in pitched battles. To use the words of the historian of the Rájpúts, "Eighty thousand horse, seven Rájas of the highest rank, nine Raos, and one hundred and four chieftains bearing the titles of Ráwul and Ráwut, with five hundred war elephants, followed him into the field. The princes of Márwár and Ambér did him homage, and the Raos of Gualiár, Ajmér, Sikri, Raesen, Kalpec, Chándéri,' Boondi, Gagrown, Rampoora, and Aboo, served him as tributaries, or held of him in chief." His personal figure corresponded with his deeds. "He exhibited at his death but the fragments of a warrior; one eye was lost in the broil with his brother, an arm in an action with the Lodi King of Delhi, and he was a cripple owing to a limb being broken with a cannon-ball in another, while he counted eighty wounds from the sword or the lance on various parts of his body." And his rival, Báber, who loved in an enemy the qualities he himself possessed, pays him only a just tribute of respect when he says, that the high eminence he then held he had attained but recently by his valour and his sword.†

and character.

* Ferishta, vol. ii. p. 262.

† Tod's Annals and Antiquities of Rajasthan, vol. ii. pp. 229. and 307.; and Báber's Mem. p. 312. It is a general belief in Hindustán that the Rána's family is descended from Nushírwán the Just, and there are many legends on the subject. Kháfi Khan, in mentioning the report, adds, "The author of this work, when he was in the Rájpút country, ascertained from the Rána's divan or minister, and from other officers of his government, that the Ránas by no means considered themselves to be descended from Nushírwán; and that, on the contrary, in consequence of difference of religion, they being Hindus and he a fire-worshipper, they viewed his sect with abhorrence." This passage is curious,

BOOK III.

His previous transactions with Báber.

Rána Sánga was not now for the first time known to Báber. Before the Emperor had set out from Kábul on his last Indian expedition, he had received from the Rána an embassy conveying expressions of regard; and it seems to have been arranged, that, while Báber attacked Sultan Ibráhím by marching upon Delhi, Rána Sánga was to attack him on the side of Agra.

Mutual recrimination;

Báber, on his part, complains, that, while he advanced and occupied these two capitals, the Rána did not make a single movement. On the other hand the Rána complained of broken faith; and, in particular, claimed Kálpi, Dhúlpúr, and Biána, as his by agreement, all of which had been occupied by Báber. And, as Agra itself had, till recent times, been considered as only a dependency of Biána, that city might also have been understood to accompany it. But to an ambitious man no great excuse was required for marching to conquest. The empire of Delhi was in confusion; it had become the prey of the strongest; and the former successes and mighty power of the Rána might seem to justify at once his hopes of seating himself on the vacant throne of the Lodis, and his more

views of ambition.

reasonable and glorious ambition of expelling both the Afghán and Túrki invaders from India, and restoring her own Hindu race of kings, and her native institutions. In the meanwhile, however, he acknowledged Sultan Mahmúd Lodi, the son of Sultan Sekander Lodi, who had been set up by the Western Afgháns as the legal successor of Sultan Ibráhím.*

A. H. 933, A. D. 1527. He advances to Biána,

The preparations made by Rana Sánga, evidently with the intention of marching towards Biána, had induced Báber not only to collect a strong force near

though not very decisive for settling the question. It is not in every copy of Kháfi Khan. Indeed, the different manuscripts of that writer's history vary considerably from each other; there being, besides verbal alterations in the text, passages of considerable extent in some copies that are not in others. These were probably added on a revision of the work.

* Báber's Mem. p. 339.

CHAP. II.

A.D. 1527.

Agra for the purpose of repelling his attack, but hastily to recal Humáyun from Juánpúr. Soon after that prince's return, the Emperor received intelligence from Mehdi Khwája, the governor of Biána, that Rána Sánga was certainly on his march towards that place, that Hasán Khan of Mewát had declared for him; and that it was necessary that reinforcements should be sent to his assistance without loss of time. A light force was therefore instantly dispatched towards Biána, under Muhammed Sultan Mírza, and other officers of experience, who were instructed to hang upon the skirts of the approaching army, and to harass it in its movements. Part of them, accordingly, pushed on towards the enemy, and brought back some heads and a few prisoners, from whom they got authentic information that Hasan Khan had actually arrived in the Rána's camp.

Rebi II. 3, Jan. 6.

Joined by Hasan Khan.

This news was particularly unwelcome to the Emperor. The Khan was a chief of great power and influence. At the battle of Panipat, his son, Náher Khan, had been made prisoner, and he had ever since kept up a friendly correspondence with the Emperor, and a negociation for his release. Báber, hoping that if he set the son at liberty he would attach the father by the strongest ties of gratitude, invested Náher Khan with a dress of honour, and sent him back to his father. But though the son had made the fairest promises, no sooner did the old man hear that he was out of Báber's hands, and on his way to join him, than, without even waiting to see him, he marched from Alúr*, his capital, and joined the Rána.

Báber marches, Jemádi I. 9. Feb. 11.

On the 11th of February, 1527, the Emperor marched out of Agra to proceed against Rána Sánga, but halted a few days near the city to collect and review his troops, and to get in order his train of artillery, the

* Or Alwer.

BOOK III. A.D. 1527.

baggage, and camp followers. As, in this warfare, he had little reliance on the Afghán chiefs or the men of Hindustán who had joined him, he sent several of them to strengthen his various garrisons. He then marched westward to Medhákúr, where he had previously caused wells to be dug, and thence next day to Sikri, the present Fatehpúr, which, from its having plenty of water, he considered as a good situation for a camp; but being apprehensive that the Rána, who was now near at hand, might attempt to occupy the ground before his arrival, he marched out with his troops in order of battle, ready to attack the enemy should they appear, and took possession of the place which had been chosen for his encampment, close by a tank. He was now joined by Mehdi Khwája, and the troops from Biána, which he had called in, as well as by the detachment which had been sent out towards that place. They had had some sharp rencounters with the Rájpúts, in which they had been severely handled, and taught to respect their new enemy. A party from the garrison had some days before incautiously advanced too far from the fort, when the Rájpúts in great force fell upon them, and drove them in. All the troops that had been engaged in this affair united in bestowing unbounded praise on the gallantry and prowess of the enemy. Indeed, the Jaghatái Túrks found that they had now to contend with a foe more formidable than either the Afgháns, or any of the natives of India, to whom they had yet been opposed. The Rájpúts, energetic, chivalrous, fond of battle and bloodshed, animated by a strong national spirit, and led on by a hero, were ready to meet, face to face, the boldest veterans of the camp, and were at all times prepared to lay down their life for their honour. A small party being sent out to get notice of their motions, discovered that they were encamped at Bisáwer.*

to Sikri, Jemádi I. 14. Feb. 16.

Encamps.

Prowess of the Rájpúts.

* Báber's Mem. pp. 351, 352.

CHAP. II.

A.D. 1527.

Skirmish.

The Emperor was accustomed to commit to his principal Begs in turn the charge of the advance and pickets. When it was Mír Abdal-azíz's day, that rash and impetuous youth pushed on seven or eight miles from Sikri. The Rájpúts, hearing of this incautious forward movement, dispatched to meet him a body of four or five thousand horse, who, without hesitation, charged the instant they came up. His force did not exceed a thousand or fifteen hundred. Many of his men were killed, others taken prisoners and carried off the field on the very first onset. The moment the news of what was going on reached the camp, Mohib Ali Khalífa, the minister's son, and his followers, were pushed forward to their assistance; and, there being no room for delay, numbers of separate horsemen, as fast as they were equipped, were sent off at the best of their speed; while a regular detachment, under Muhammed Alí Jeng-jeng, moved forward to support them. Mohib Ali, who arrived first, found every thing in disorder, Abdal-azíz's horse-tail standard taken, and many excellent officers slain. Not only was he unable to turn the tide of success, but was himself unhorsed, though finally brought off by a desperate charge of his followers. The Emperor's troops were then pursued for about two miles; and it was only the arrival of the regular detachment, under Muhammed Ali, that checked the enemy. Meanwhile, when the alarm reached the camp, the whole troops were called out and marshalled in battle-order to meet the hostile army, which was thought to be approaching. But after the imperial line had advanced a mile or two, with all its artillery, it was found that the enemy, satisfied with their success, had returned back to their camp.

Báber's troops discouraged.

These repeated successes of the Rájpúts, the unexpected valour and good conduct they displayed, and their numbers, for they are said to have amounted to an

BOOK III. A.D. 1527.

hundred and twenty thousand horse *, had begun to spread a visible discouragement among the troops. Every precaution was employed by the Emperor, at once to strengthen his position and to give his men time to recover their confidence. The guns were now placed in battery, and connected by chains; ditches were run, and other means adopted, to fortify the camp. These operations were continued for three or four weeks, during which time the army kept within the trenches. Báber, at this crisis, received a small but acceptable reinforcement of five hundred volunteers from Kábul. Along with it arrived a long line of camels loaded with wine from Ghazni; and Muhammed Sheríf, a noted astrologer. This soothsayer, instead of assisting the Emperor, as was the duty of his craft, added to the depression and panic which prevailed in the camp by publishing, at a most unseasonable moment, his opinion, that as Mars was now in the west, whoever engaged, coming from the opposite quarter, would be defeated.†

Mewát wasted. Jemádi I. 22. Feb. 24.

To divert the attention of the enemy, and to revenge himself on Hasan Khan for joining the Rájpúts, Báber sent a predatory force into Mewát, with orders to plunder the country, to carry off the inhabitants into captivity, and to leave nothing undone to ruin the province. The ravages were extended into many of the neighbouring districts; but the result of this diversion did not answer his expectations.

Báber renounces wine.

Báber was now in some measure cooped up in his camp, while the enemy were in possession of the open country. The uneasiness which he, in consequence, experienced in this state of inaction appears, very naturally, to have excited feelings of religious compunction in his mind. When he reviewed his past life, he keenly felt that he had long and openly violated one of the strictest injunctions of his faith, by the use of wine.

* Tabakáti Akberi.

† Mem. of Báber. p. 353.

CHAP. II.

A. D. 1527.

Like other habitual offenders, he had all along firmly resolved to give up the evil custom at some future time; but that time had been constantly deferred. He now resolved to perform his vows. "Having sent for the gold and silver goblets and cups," says he, "with all the other vessels used at drinking parties, I directed them to be broken up, and renounced the use of wine, purifying my mind. The fragments of the goblets, and other gold and silver drinking vessels, I directed to be divided among derwíshes and the poor. The first person who followed me in my repentance was Asás, who also accompanied me in my resolution of ceasing to cut the beard, and of allowing it to grow." * This was a visible sign commonly adopted by such as were under the influence of a vow. Many nobles and others, to the number of three hundred, followed the example of their sovereign. Salt was thrown into the ample store of wine just arrived from Ghazni; all the rest found in the camp was poured upon the ground; and a well was ordered to be dug and an almshouse built on the spot, to commemorate this great religious event. As a boon to his Muhammedan followers and subjects, he gave up the Temgha or Stamp-tax in all his dominions, so far as concerned Musulmans, and published a firman to that effect. †

Remits the Temgha. Jemádi I. 24. Feb. 26.

Address to the council.

The dejection and alarm of Báber's troops had at this time reached their extreme point. The contagion had infected even his highest officers. He excepts only Mír Ali Khalífa, his prime minister; who, he says, all along behaved admirably. Báber, whose bold and elastic mind never gave admittance to despair, but, even in the lowest depths of danger, turned to any gleam of hope, saw that matters were fast advancing to a crisis, and that some stirring and energetic measures were indispensably required. He determined to make a bold

* Báber's Mem., p. 354.

† Ibid. p 355.

BOOK III. A. D. 1527.

exertion to infuse a portion of his own heroic ardour into the drooping spirits of his followers; and, for that purpose, he addressed himself to the religious feelings so powerful with all Moslems, but especially with such as are engaged in a holy war against infidels. "At length," says he, "observing the universal discouragement of my troops, and their total want of spirit, I came to a resolution. Having called a general assembly of my Amírs and officers*, I addressed them:—'Noblemen and soldiers! Every man that comes into the world is subject to dissolution. When *we* are passed away and gone, God survives, One and Unchangeable. Whoever sits down to the feast of life must, before it is over, drink of the cup of death. He who arrives at the inn of mortality, the world, must one day, without fail, take his departure from that mansion of sorrow. How much better, then, is it to die with honour, than to live with infamy;

> "'Give me but fame, and if I die I am contented.
> If fame be mine, let Death claim my body.'†

"'The most High God has been propitious to us. He has now placed us in such a crisis that if we fall in the field, we die the death of martyrs; if we survive, we rise victorious, the avengers of his sacred cause. Let us, therefore, with one accord swear on God's Holy Word, that none of us will for a moment think of turning his face from this warfare; or shrink from the battle and slaughter that ensue, till his soul is separated from his body.'" Master and servant, small and great, all with emulation seizing the blessed Korán in their hands, swore in the form that I had given. My attempt was completely successful, and the effects

Its effect.

* The Tabakáti Akberi, f. 142., asserts that, at this council, the grandees advised that Báber, having fortified and provisioned some castles and places of strength in Hindústan, should himself retire for a time into the Penjáb.

† A couplet from the Shahnáma of Ferdausi.

CHAP. II.

A.D. 1527.

were instantly visible far and near, on friend and foe." Báber, to improve this spirit, ordered an immediate advance from the entrenchments in which the army had so long been cooped up.*

Success of the Afgháns in the Doáb.

In truth he had no time to lose; the danger was thickening around him. Since he had left Agra, insurrection and revolt appeared on every hand. The towns and forts, of which with so much labour he had gained possession, were fast changing masters. Rábere and Chandwár on the Jamna, Koel in the Doáb, and Sambhal beyond the Ganges, but of all of them near Agra, had been retaken by the Afgháns. His troops had been obliged to abandon Kanáuj. Gualiár was blockaded by the Rájpúts of the vicinity. Alem Khan †, who was sent to relieve it, instead of executing his orders, had marched off to his own country. Many Hindu chiefs deserted the cause of the Emperor. Indeed, the previous conquests and recent success of Rána Sánga, a Hindu, had inspired all his countrymen with hopes that a change of dynasty was about to take place; and they hailed with joy the prospect of a native government.

Báber moves his camp, Jemádi II. 9. March 12.

It was on the 12th of March that Báber drew forward his guns, and a kind of defensive cover that moved on wheels, and which served as a breastwork; supporting them by his matchlock-men and all his army. He himself galloped along the line, animating his troops and officers, and giving them instructions how to conduct themselves in every emergency that could occur. The army having advanced a mile or two, halted to encamp. As soon as the Rájpúts heard that they were in motion, several bodies of them galloped close up to the guns. Báber, not intending to engage in a general action that day, quietly finished his intrenchments and ditches; and then sent out a few

* Báber's Mem. p. 357.

† This seems to be Alem Khan Jilál Khan Jighat of Kalpi, already mentioned. See Báber's Mem. pp. 349, 351, 358.

BOOK III. A. D. 1527.

horsemen to skirmish with them, and try the temper of his men. They took several prisoners, and returned with a number of heads elevated on their spears, or dangling from their saddle-bows; which had a wonderful effect in restoring the confidence of the troops.

and again advances.

He now threw up other trenches, in a position about a mile or two farther in advance, near the spot which he had pitched upon as favourable for a general engagement; and, when they were finished, advanced to occupy them, dragging forward his guns. His people, having reached their ground, were still busy in pitching their tents, when news was brought that the enemy was in sight. All were instantly ordered to their posts. Báber mounted, and drew up his troops, riding cheerfully along the ranks, and confidently assuring them of victory. The centre he took to himself, assisted by Chín Taimur Sultán*; the right wing he committed to Humáyun, who had under him Kásim Husein Sultan, Hindu Beg, and Khosrou Kokiltásh; the left he entrusted to Syed Mehdi Khwájeh, his son-in-law, with Muhammed Sultan Mírza, Abdal-azíz, and Muhammed Ali Jeng-jeng. He appointed strong reserves to carry succour wherever it was required; and, on the right and left, placed two flanking columns, chiefly composed of Moghul troops, who formed what is called the Tulúghma, and were, on a signal given, to wheel round on the enemy's flank and rear in the heat of battle. This arrangement he had learned, to his cost, in his early wars with the Uzbeks; and he had practised it, as we have seen, in his later wars with brilliant success. His Hindustáni troops appear to have been stationed chiefly in the left. His artillery, under Ustád Ali Kuli, was placed in the centre, in front; connected by chains,

Jemádi II. 13. March 16. Prepares for a general battle.

* Chin Taimur Sultan was a Moghul, son of the younger Khan of the Moghuls, and consequently Báber's cousin; Muhammed Sultan Mírza was, by his mother, a grandson of the great Sultan Husein Mírza, of Herát; Kásim Husein Sultán was an Uzbek of high rank.

and protected by the moveable defences or breastworks which he had constructed; behind which were placed matchlock-men; and, in their rear, a body of chosen troops, ready either to repel any attack from behind, or themselves to rush forward and charge the enemy, whenever the chains that connected the guns were dropped to permit their passage. The army abounded with veteran commanders, who had learned the art of war under the Emperor himself.

Rájpút force.

In the Rájpút army, the commanders under Rána Sánga were generally great chieftains, who, from their territorial possessions, could bring a large force into the field. Thus Siláheddín *, the Chief of Bhilsa, is rated at thirty thousand horse; Hasan Khan Mewáti, twelve thousand; Ráúl Udi Sing Nagari, of Dongerpúr, ten thousand; Medíni Rao, the Chief of Chánderi, ten thousand. The first and last of these had acted an important part in the history of Málwa. Sultan Mahmúd Lodi, a son of Sultan Sekander Lodi of Delhi, who was acknowledged by the Afgháns of the Delhi kingdom and by the Rána, as the successor of his brother Ibráhím, though he possessed no territory, yet had with him a body of ten thousand adventurers, who hoped to be liberally rewarded should fortune raise him to the throne. There were other chiefs, who could command each from four to seven thousand men; and all were animated by the most exalted hopes, and by hatred of the common enemy. A more gallant army could not be brought into the field.†

No sooner was the array of the Emperor's army

* Siláheddín, the Pagan, as he is called in the official account of the victory, is the Silhadi of Ferishta, who occupied Bhilsa, Raisen, and Sarangpúr. Briggs's Ferishta, vol. iv. p. 264. In one manuscript of the Akbernáma, A f. 32 *r.*, the name Siláheddín is corrected in the margin, Silhadi. The former, however, is the correct title given by one of the Sultans of Málwa to this great Hindu chief; the latter is the popular corruption of it.

† The official account (Mem. p. 361.) estimates the numbers which the different chiefs did or could bring into the field at two hundred and ten thousand men.

BOOK III. A.D. 1527.

completed, than, to guard against the evils that might be occasioned through the over-ardent forwardness of his troops, he sent strict commands on every side, that no man should move from his place, or dare to engage the enemy in any shape, till orders were given.

Battle of Kanwa.

The battle began about half-past nine in the morning, by a desperate charge made by the Rájputs on Báber's right. Bodies of the reserve were pushed on to its assistance; and Mustafa Rúmi, who commanded one portion of the artillery on the right of the centre, opened a fire upon the assailants. Still, new bodies of the enemy poured on undauntedly, and new detachments from the reserve were sent to resist them. The battle was no less desperate on the left, to which, also, it was found necessary to despatch repeated parties from the reserve. When the battle had lasted several hours, and still continued to rage, Báber sent orders to the flanking columns to wheel round and charge; and he soon after ordered the guns to advance, and, by a simultaneous movement, the household troops and cavalry stationed behind the cannon were ordered to gallop out on right and left of the matchlockmen in the centre, who also moved forward and continued their fire, hastening to fling themselves with all their fury on the enemy's centre. When this was observed in the wings, they also advanced. These unexpected movements, made at the same moment, threw the enemy into confusion. Their centre was shaken; the men who were displaced by the attack made in flank, on the wings and rear, were forced upon the centre and crowded together. Still the gallant Rájpúts were not appalled. They made repeated desperate attacks on the Emperor's centre, in hopes of recovering the day; but were bravely and steadily received, and swept away in great numbers. Towards evening, the confusion was complete, and the slaughter was consequently dreadful. The fate of the battle was decided. Nothing remained for the Rájpúts, but to force their way through the bodies of the enemy that were now in their rear, and to effect a retreat. The Emperor pursued them as far as their camp, which was about three or four miles from his own. On reaching it, he halted; but detached a strong body of horse, with orders to pursue the broken troops of the confederates without halting; to cut up all they met; and to prevent them from re-assembling. "In this," says he, "I acted wrong. I should myself have gone forward, and ought not to have entrusted the business to another. I had got about a kos beyond the enemy's camp when I turned back, the day being spent; and reached my own head-quarters at bed-time prayers." He adds a characteristic anecdote. "Muhammed Sheríf, the astrologer, whose perverse and seditious practices I have mentioned, came to congratulate me on my victory; I poured forth upon him a torrent of abuse; but, when I had relieved my heart by it, although he was a self-conceited fellow, heathenishly inclined, and an intolerable evil-speaker, yet, as he was my old servant, I gave him a lak in a present *, and dismissed him, commanding him to depart out of my dominions."

CHAP. II. A.D. 1527.

Báber victorious.

No victory could be more complete. The enemy were quite broken and dispersed. The whole fields around were strewed with the dead, as well as the roads to Biána and Alwar. Among the slain were Hasan Khan Mewáti, who fell by a matchlock shot; Ráúl Udi Sing, of Dongerpúr †; Rai Chanderbhan

* The transactions against Rána Sánga are given in detail by Báber himself, Mem. p. 349—368.; and by Abulfazl, Akbernáma, f. 31—33. The donation to the astrologer was probably a lak of tangas, or about 880*l*. See Appendix E.

† In the translation of the official account of the victory (Báber's Mem. p. 367.), this prince is called the Wali of Udipúr. Colonel Tod, to whom Indian history, but particularly that of the Rájpúts, owes so much (his valuable work having shed a new light on the manners of that remarkable people), remarked the error. (Hist. and Antiq. of Rajasthan, vol. i. p. 306. note.) On examining the manuscripts of Báber, I find that though the

BOOK III.

A. D. 1527.

Takes the title of Gházi.

Chohan; Manikchand Chohan, and many other chiefs of note. Báber directed a tower of heads to be erected, on a rising ground near the camp; and henceforth assumed the proud title of Gházi, Victorious in a Holy War. Rána Sánga himself escaped; it is said, by the devotion of some of his followers, who threw themselves in the way of the pursuers, and sacrificed their lives for his safety; and the regret expressed by Báber for not having urged the pursuit in person has reference probably to the escape of his illustrious rival. It is remarkable that, since this defeat of Rána Sánga, no Rána of Cheitúr has ever taken the field in person against any of the princes of the House of Taimur. When these princes were along with their armies, the Rána's troops have been entrusted to some eminent Rájpút chief, the Rána himself withdrawing to some one of the hill-forts of his country.

Sultan Mahmúd Lodi, deprived by the event of this battle of all immediate hope of filling the throne of Delhi, fled to Sultan Behády Shah, the King of Guzrát.*

Koel retaken, Jemádi II 14. March 17.

On the very day after the battle, Báber detached a strong force to chastise the insurgents in the Doáb, who had surprised Koel and made his governor prisoner. The fame of the victory preceded them; and, as they approached, the insurgents fled in all directions. Elías Khan, their leader, was taken some time after and flayed alive, with a barbarity which disgraced the age and country.

Three marches now brought the Emperor to Biána, through fields all the way strewed with the bodies of the slain. Here, being on the borders of the enemy's country, he called a council of his nobles, and consulted about invading it. But, as their march must have lain

manuscript which I generally followed as most correct has Udipúr, the Metcalfe MS. has Dongerpúr, confirming the Colonel's correction.

* Khafi Khan. In Báber's army, at the battle, we find an envoy from Persia; and Husein, ambassador from Sistán.

through a barren waste, deficient in water; and, as the heat had already become excessive, it was resolved to defer this enterprise to a more favourable time.

Mewát reduced.

Resolved, however, to improve his victory to the utmost, he marched into Mewát. That country had always hitherto yielded but an imperfect obedience to the kings of Delhi, though it lies close upon their capital. Whether from the hilly nature of the country and the bravery of the hardy inhabitants; from the constant diversions occasioned by the extent of the Delhi dominions, which distracted and drew off the attention of the kings; or from that principle, fortunate in many respects in some eastern countries, which leads the kings to govern rather by means of secondary princes and delegated authority, than directly and by their immediate servants; they had never fully subdued it. It had been in the possession of Hasan Khan's family for two hundred years. The Khan, as we have seen, had been able to bring twelve thousand horse into the field, and was at the head of the opposition made to Báber by the old dependents of the Lodi kings; for the Rána of Cheitúr, who led the grand confederation, was not in the rank of a dependent, never having owned the yoke of these princes. It would seem that the Khan, even for some time before this grand invasion, had begun to entertain apprehensions from the success of Báber's arms; and, in the year when that monarch conquered Lahúr and Dibálpúr, had left Tajara, the old capital, and built and fortified Alwar, in a stronger situation. The great defeat which the confederate army received at Kanwa, and in which he fell, crippled the strength, and still more had broken the confidence of the Mewátis. As the Emperor approached Alwar, he was met by a mission from Náher Khan, who had lately been his prisoner, and who had succeeded his father; deprecating the Emperor's resentment. The young prince was induced to visit the

BOOK III. A.D. 1527. camp, on the promise of security to his person, was graciously received, and allowed a Pergana for his support; an intimation that he had lost his hereditary dominions. It is probable that he had expected to be continued in the principality of his forefathers; for he soon after embraced an opportunity of withdrawing from the custody in which he was placed, and effected his escape from the camp. The Emperor appointed governors to the province and its chief forts, with ample allowances; and bestowed on Humáyun the whole treasure and property found in Alwar. He soon after dispatched him to Kábul, accompanied by the mountaineers of Badakhshán, whom the prince had led from their country, and who now longed for home; they, therefore, gladly availed themselves of a promise given by the Emperor before the great battle, that, after beating the enemy, he would discharge as many as chose to go. Báber accompanied his son a march or two on his route, and took an affectionate leave of him; but the young prince, soon after, in passing through Delhi, with an unpardonable levity, opened some of the chambers that contained the Emperor's treasure, and seized the contents by force,—a conduct that gave great pain to the Emperor, and led him to write in severe terms to his son. Báber, having made a slight circuit in Mewát, again visited Biáni and Sikri, and returned to Agra.*

Humáyun sent back to Badakhshán.

Rejeb 23. April 25.

The lost towns recovered.

Being now disengaged of his most formidable enemies, he was enabled to send a force to recover Chándwár and Ráberi; places not far distant from Agra, of which the insurgents had made themselves masters, during his operations against Rána Sánga. The consternation occasioned by his success was such that this object was effected with little difficulty; and, even Etáwa, lower down the Jamna, which had never yet

* Báber's Mem., pp. 368, 371.

submitted to his power, was surrendered by Kutb Khan, who held it.

CHAP. II.

A. D. 1527.

Success beyond the Ganges.

It has already been remarked, that the spirit of insurrection had not been confined to the neighbourhood of Agra, but had extended to the eastward. Beyond the Ganges, the restless Baban, ever on the watch, had availed himself of the difficulty in which the Emperor's affairs placed him, to occupy Laknáu; and Sultan Muhammed Duldái, Báber's governor, had been forced to abandon Kanáuj. Determined to regain what had been thus lost, the Emperor bestowed the government of these countries on Muhammed Sultan Mírza,—a grandson of the great Sultan Husein Mírza of Khorásán, and one of the Emperor's favourite officers,—and sent him, with a strong army, to recover the lost territory. Baban no sooner heard that Muhammed Sultan had crossed the Ganges, than he deserted Laknáu, and retired once more into the upper country.

The territories immediately around Agra being thus recovered, and the greater part of his former conquests regained, the Emperor had now leisure to make a distribution, among his faithful followers, of the various provinces and districts of which they were composed, and, as the rainy season was at hand, during which an army could not keep the field, he granted permission to his chiefs and officers to repair with their followers to their respective governments and jágírs, that they might be the better able to regulate their affairs, and to make the necessary preparations for rejoining him, when the rains were over.* A twelvemonth only had passed since the battle of Panipat; but his condition was already much improved. That battle had broken the power of the Afgháns in India, as that of Kanwa had since broken that of the Hindu confederacy. He had evinced, to every class of men in the country, the

* Báber's Mem., pp. 370—372.; Akbernáma, f. 33.

BOOK III. A.D. 1527.

decided superiority of his arms; and, with his mental resources, the awe inspired by his hardy northern troops, and his own bravery and conduct, the conquest of every part of India seemed to lie open to his arms.

It affords a curious proof of the active and unsettled life of Báber, that, as he himself informs us, he had never since his eleventh year, spent the grand festival observed on the termination of the Rámzán twice at one place. "Last year's festival," says he, "I spent at Agra. In order to keep up the usage, on Sunday

Rámzán 30. June 30.

the 30th, I proceeded to Sikri to keep the feast there."*

During the rains he visited Sikri, Dhúlpúr, and Bári, proceeding as far as the Chambal; he thence returned to Agra; and went to Kol or Koel in the Doáb, and on to Sambhal, beyond the Ganges, returning by a different route.

Campaign against Chándéri.

When the rainy monsoon was over, Báber's mind was divided between two plans of operation, which suggested themselves for the following campaign: the one, to march against the Afgháns of the East, who still held out, in considerable force, beyond the Ganges and in Behár; the other, to march against some of those Hindu chiefs in the West whose confederacy he had felt to be so formidable. He decided on the latter; not only thinking, probably, that under the guidance of such a leader as Rána Sánga they were most to be feared; but influenced by a vow which he had made, during his difficulties, that he would prosecute, to a prosperous termination, the holy war which he had begun, against the infidels. Medíni Rao, the chief of Chándéri, and one of the most formidable of them, was the first object of his vengeance. Chándéri, that chieftain's principal stronghold, lies on the south-east of Malwa; and towards it Báber bent his course.

A. H. 934. Rebi I. 14. Dec. 9.

Leaving Agra early in December, he marched down

* Báber's Mem., p. 373.

the left bank of the Jamna, and afterwards crossed that river below its junction with the Chambal. Having reason to entertain violent suspicions of the fidelity of Sheikh Bayezíd, — who had joined him after Sultan Ibráhím's death, with the army which that prince had sent against the revolted Afghán chiefs of the East, — Báber detached from his army Muhammed Ali Jeng-jeng, a veteran officer, with directions to proceed to Kanáuj, and to call upon Muhammed Sultan Mírza, the governor of the farther province, and the other generals and chiefs who were in that quarter, to meet him there; and, in conjunction with them, to march against the hostile Sherki Afgháns, who acknowledged Sultan Muhammed Shah of Behár. Báber, at the same time, instructed Jeng-jeng to summon Sheikh Bayezíd to join him in the expedition. If he came frankly when invited, they were all to proceed against the common enemy; but, if he did not, Muhammed Ali was instructed to consider him as ill-affected, and to take measures accordingly for bringing him to reason.

CHAP. II. A.D. 1527-8. Rebi II. 3. Dec. 27.

Jeng-jeng detached to the eastward.

Having made these arrangements, the Emperor continued his route down the Jamna, he himself generally proceeding by water. He reached Kalpi on the first day of January, A.D. 1528, and thence struck off, in the direction of Irej and Kechwa. Here, the country being little frequented was covered with jungle; so that it was necessary to send on pioneers to cut down the wood before them, and to form a road for the passage of cannon and waggons. On the 20th he reached Chándéri, the immediate object of his expedition.*

Báber's march.

Rebi II. 8. A.D. 1528, Jan. 1.

He reaches Chándéri. Rebi II. 27. Jan. 20.

Medíni Rao, who at this time possessed the town, was a Rájpút chief of great power. Chándéri had originally been subject to the Sultans of Málwa; but, during the civil wars that followed the accession of Sultan Mahmúd Khilji (the present King of Málwa),

Medíni Rao.

* Báber's Mem., pp. 374—376.

BOOK III.
A. D. 1528.

Muhammed Shah, one of his brothers, who aspired to the crown, had seized upon it, and made it the seat of his government. This pretender was supported by Sultan Sekander Lodi of Delhi, who sent several armies to his aid. On his death, in the reign of Sultan Ibráhím of Delhi, leaving a younger son named Ahmed Shah, Ibráhím carried off the young prince, his ally, and placed a dependent of his own in the government. Rána Sánga, in the course of his wars with Delhi, having given Sultan Ibráhím a great defeat at Dhúlpúr, many of the neighbouring Hindu chiefs, who till then had adhered to the King of Delhi, deserted him; Chándéri was one of several important places which fell into the hands of the Rána, who bestowed it on the present occupant, Medíni Rao.

His history.

Medíni Rao was a very distinguished personage in his time. He had been the means of placing and confirming the reigning King, Sultan Mahmúd Khilji, on the throne of Mandu; and, supported by his Rájpúts, had defeated various pretenders to the crown, in bloody battles. He had, for several years, the entire direction of Mahmúd's affairs; till the jealousy of the Musulman chiefs, whose pride was hurt at the supremacy of a Rájpút and a heathen, and probably disgusted by the overbearing habits often acquired by an all-powerful minister, produced intrigues at court; which, in the end, wrought upon the Sultan to escape from his thraldom, and take refuge in Gujrát. Here Mozaffer Shah, the sovereign of the country, received him honourably; and, at the head of a powerful army, restored Mahmúd to the throne of Mandu. But, as many districts, especially those held by Hindus, adhered to the minister, and refused to acknowledge a prince thus imposed on them by foreign force, and by a Musulman, a civil war was the consequence; and such of the Rájpút chiefs of Málwa as were hostile to Sultan Mahmúd called in Rána Sánga to their assistance. The restless impatience

Revolutions of Malwa.

Rána Sánga called in.

His victory.

CHAP. II. A.D. 1528.

of the Sultan led prematurely to a battle; in which the Gujrát auxiliary cavalry were destroyed by the Rájpút horse, and the Sultan himself wounded and taken prisoner. The conduct of Rána Sánga may illustrate the chivalrous character of the Rájpúts. "His enemy Rána Sánga of Cheitúr," says Ferishta, "caused him to be brought into his own tent, dressed his wounds, attended him in person, and showed him every mark of attention; and, after his recovery, furnished him with an escort of one thousand Rájpút horse, who conducted him back to Mando, where he resumed the reins of government."* The consequence, however, was, that the power of the kingdom of Málwa was broken; and a variety of nearly independent principalities rose, or rather revived, on its ruins. Besides Chándéri, Medíni Rao held also Gagrown, and several other districts. He was present with his troops in the Rána's army at the battle of Kanwa.†

and generosity.

When the Emperor's army approached Chándéri, Medíni Rao was himself in the place, with four or five thousand of his Rájpúts. Báber sent a friend of the Rao into the fort, to urge him to surrender; and to offer him Shemsábád in the Doáb in exchange for Chándéri. This negociation failing, the Emperor proceeded to construct his batteries, and to make preparations for an escalade. When every thing was in readiness, he gave orders for the camp to be moved nearer to the town, preparatory to making the attempt. That very morning, just as the army had reached its ground, Nizám-ed-dín Ali Khalífa, Báber's prime minister, brought him some letters which had that instant

Báber's proposals rejected.

Jemádi I. 6. Jan. 28. Alarming news from the East.

* Briggs's Ferishta, vol. iv. p. 263.

† Briggs's Ferishta, vol. iv. pp. 245—264.; Báber's Mem., pp. 375, 376. Báber mentions the captivity of Mahmúd, p. 385. Ferishta does not mention the defeat of Ibráhím, and fixes Medíni's possession of Chándéri from the former event; Báber from the latter. There can be no comparison between the weight of the two authorities.

BOOK III.

A.D. 1528.

arrived. They contained the disagreeable information that his army in the East, while marching in disorder, had been attacked and defeated; that his generals had been forced to abandon Laknáu, to recross the Ganges, and fall back upon Kanáuj. Báber, who saw that his minister was extremely agitated, preserving his own presence of mind, calmly remarked that all events were in the hands of Providence; desired him to conceal the intelligence; and to push on every preparation for making a grand attack on the citadel next morning. That night, the outer town, which was inadequately garrisoned, fell into his hands, the walls being escaladed by his troops, who entered it at the same moment on different sides.

Báber's presence of mind;

he takes the outer town,

and the fort.

Next morning, accordingly, the troops were ordered to their posts, and commanded to wait in readiness to make a general assault, the moment the royal standard should be raised and the sound of the kettle-drum heard. The Emperor then repaired to his battery, where the chief engineer discharged two or three shots; in that age a tedious operation. The citadel stands on the top of a hill; the outer fort and the town, which was built entirely of stone, lie below on the slope of the hill. The defences being strong, and cut out of the rock, the effect was trifling. There was a covered way, the wall of which ran from the citadel to connect it with a large tank at the bottom of the hill; and this was the point where the fort was judged to be most assailable. To distract the enemy, an attack was made on every part of the citadel at once; but against that point was the main assault directed; and, though the Rájpúts exerted themselves with the utmost bravery and vigour, hurling down rocks from above, and throwing flaming substances on the heads of the assailants, the storming parties persevered, and one of them at length succeeded in mounting where the wall of the outer fort was knit to the projecting works. Nearly at the same time the wall was scaled in two or three other places. The garrison stationed in the covered way fled, and that part of the works was occupied. The upper fort was less obstinately defended. The assailants scaled and entered it by storm. This success was followed by a dreadful sacrifice made to Rájpút honour. "In a short time," says the royal historian, "the Pagans rushed out, completely naked, to attack us; put numbers of my men to flight; and leaped over the ramparts. Some of our troops were attacked furiously, and put to the sword. The reason of this desperate sally from the works was, that, on giving up the place for lost, they had put to death all their wives and women, and being resolved not to survive, had stripped themselves naked, in which condition they rushed out to the fight, and engaging with ungovernable desperation, drove our people along the ramparts. Two or three hundred Pagans had entered Medíni Rao's palace, where numbers of them slew each other; one person taking his stand with a sabre in his hand, while the others pressed in one by one in succession, and stretched out their necks, eager to die. In this way many went to hell, and by the favour of God, in the space of two or three *geris* *, I gained this celebrated fort, without raising my standard or beating my kettle-drum, and without exerting the whole strength of my arms." †

Self-sacrifice of the Rájpúts.

It had been Báber's intention, after reducing Chándéri, to proceed against the neighbouring countries of Raisen, Bhilsa and Sarangpúr, which were part of the

* About an hour, the geri being twenty-four minutes.

† Báber's Mem., p. 377. Kháfi Khan gives (f. 36.) rather a different account of this affair. He affirms that the outer fort, which includes the town, was given up on condition that the lives of the inhabitants and garrison were to be spared; that, however, the Rájpúts, on leaving the place, had been guilty of some acts of hostility, in consequence of which Báber's troops cut three or four thousand of them in pieces; that upon this Medíni Rao and his followers took refuge in the citadel; where, after putting to death all the women and children, they slew each other, after the manner of Rájpúts.

BOOK III.

A. H. 934.
A. D. 1528.

territories of Siláh-ed-dín, also a Rájpút; and, after he had conquered them, to complete his operations by marching at once against Rána Sánga himself by Cheitúr. But the unfavourable news from the East interfered with these intentions. He therefore resolved to leave Ahmed Shah (the prince whose claims to Malwa had been supported by Sultan Ibráhím, and whom Báber now found it convenient to patronise,) in possession of Chándéri, with an auxiliary force of two or three thousand Chaghatáis and Hindustánis to maintain the country; and himself to direct his march without delay, to restore his affairs beyond the Ganges.*

Death of Rána Sánga.

It must have been soon after these events that the life of Báber's great opponent Rána Sánga came to a close. The account given of his death, like the story of his life, is mixed with something of the romantic and marvellous. It is said, that, having laid siege to Irej †, a town which had declared for Báber, one of the sages of ancient days ‡ appeared to him in a dream, under a terrific form, and with a menacing demeanour; that the Rána arose from his troubled sleep, trembling and shivering; that a violent fever succeeded; that he raised the siege, but died in his retreat; having survived the vision but a few days. His death, and the internal feuds that followed in Cheitúr, relieved Báber from any apprehensions of danger from that quarter. §

* Briggs's Ferishta, vol. ii. p. 60. It is at this period that Ferishta and Kháfi Khan (f. 36.) place the surrender of the important fortresses of Raisen, Sarangpúr, and Rantambór to Báber; who, it is said, gave them over to Ahmed Shah. The real history of the acquisition of Rantambór, which, at this time, was in the occupation of Rána Sánga, is given in a future page. It does not appear that Báber ever possessed either of the others.

† Or Erich.

‡ Perhaps one of the Ríshís.

§ Akbernáma, f. 33. v. Abulfazl makes Rána Sánga's death precede the fall of Chándéri, which does not agree with Báber's narrative. It probably took place soon after he had marched to the eastward. Báber, in his diary, 14 Moharrem, A. H. 935 (29 Sept. 1528), mentions that Rána Ruttonsi had succeeded his father, and that Bikermájit, his next brother, was in Rantambór. Mem., p. 385.

CHAPTER III.

BÁBER'S CAMPAIGNS ON THE GANGES.

BÁBER MARCHES TO THE EAST — PASSES THE GANGES AT KANÁUJ — DISPERSES THE ARMY OF BABAN AND BAYEZÍD — RETURNS TO AGRA. — TRANSACTIONS IN KHORÁSÁN. — INVASION OF THE UZBEKS. — OBEID KHAN BESIEGES HERÁT. — THE SHAH DEFEATS AN UZBEK ARMY — RAISES THE SIEGE OF HERÁT — ADVANCES TO MESHHÍD — DEFEATS THE UZBEKS WITH GREAT SLAUGHTER. — TEMPORARY REVIVAL OF BÁBER'S DESIGNS ON SAMARKAND — BALÚCH INROADS. — THE EASTERN AFGHÁNS ACKNOWLEDGE SULTAN MAHMÚD LODI. — RAPID INCREASE OF HIS POWER. — THREE COMPETITORS FOR THE EASTERN KINGDOM. — BÁBER TAKES THE FIELD — DISPERSES THE AFGHÁNS — OVERRUNS BEHÁR. — AFFAIRS OF BENGAL. — NEGOTIATIONS WITH THAT POWER. — BÁBER ATTACKS AND DEFEATS THE BENGAL ARMY. — SUBMISSION OF THE AFGHÁNS. — PEACE WITH BENGAL. — BÁBER RETURNS TO AGRA.

CHAP. III.

A.D. 1528.

Báber marches to the East. A.H. 934. Jemádi I. 11. Feb. 2.

BÁBER, having brought the war of Chándéri to a conclusion, lost no time in marching to meet the danger that threatened him in the East. Having repassed the Jamna, he proceeded without intermission towards Kanáuj. On the road, he learned that his suspicions of Sheikh Bayezíd's fidelity had not been unfounded. That chief had joined Baban and Maarúf, the leaders of the revolt, with his whole army; so that Báber's troops had been compelled to retreat across the Ganges, to evacuate even Kanáuj, and to fall back on Ráberi, — movements that had enabled the enemy to take Shemsábád, a rich town in the Doáb, by storm. The Emperor, having passed the Jamna, sent a light force in advance to gain intelligence of the motions of the Afgháns; but, while he was yet several marches off, the confederates having got notice of his approach, in alarm

BOOK III. A. D. 1528.

abandoned Kanáuj; and, retreating across the Ganges, took up a position on its left bank, opposite to that city, determined to dispute the passage of the river.

Constructs a bridge at Kanáuj. Jemádi II. 6. Feb. 27.

On the 27th of February, the imperial army having marched past Kanáuj, encamped on the right bank of the Ganges. Báber had resolved to force a passage, and ordered a bridge to be constructed across the river. About thirty or forty boats were collected, by means of which several skirmishing parties passed over. The chief engineer, Ustád Ali Kuli, planted a great gun to cover the workmen employed on the bridge; while a number of matchlockmen kept up a fire from a breastwork a little above, and others from an island somewhat below. The account given by Báber illustrates the nature of the clumsy massy guns of that age. "For several days," says he, "while the bridge was constructing, Ustád Ali Kuli played his gun remarkably well. The first day, he discharged it eight times; the second day, sixteen times; and for three or four days, he continued firing at the same rate. The gun which he fired was that called Díg Ghází (the victorious gun). It was the same that had been employed in the war with Rána Sánga, whence it got its name. Another gun," he adds, "larger than this, had been planted, but it burst at the first fire." * Such ponderous pieces of artillery must, in the open field, have produced effect chiefly by their novelty, and by the alarm they excited in minds not accustomed to the terrific effects of their explosions.

Passes the Ganges, Jemádi II. 21. March 13.

The Afgháns treated Báber's attempt to throw a bridge over the Ganges with ridicule. Yet, such was his success, that, on the 13th of March, it was completed; when part of his troops passed over, and had a skirmish with the enemy. He next marched over a considerable body of his best soldiers. These, the

* Báber's Mem., p. 379.

enemy advancing in all their force attacked with great vigour, while thus divided from the rest of the army; and succeeded, at one time, in driving the left from its position; but the centre and right, standing firm, repulsed that portion of the enemy to whom they were opposed. The action continued till late in the evening, and the night was employed in bringing the troops back to the right bank. Báber blames himself for not having rather carried over the rest of his army to join them on the other bank; but says that he was deterred from doing so by some superstitious fancy as to lucky times. Next day, however, he carried over his artillery; and the day following, all his army had orders to cross. But the enemy, in the meantime, had marched off. The Emperor sending Sultan Chín Taimur, with a strong force to pursue them, himself advanced and occupied Laknáu on the 21st, and passed the Gumti. Moving again in pursuit of the retreating enemy, he encamped, on the 28th, four or five miles above Oud, at the junction of the Gogra and Sirwu. Till then, Sheikh Báyezíd had maintained his ground beyond the Sirwu, and had prevented Sultan Chín Taimur, Báber's general, from crossing. Being now reinforced, however, Chín Taimur effected a passage, and found the Afgháns in full retreat. He followed them with great alacrity, slew numbers of them, and dispersed their army. Sheikh Báyezíd threw himself into a jungle and escaped. Chín Taimur, after a pursuit of sixty miles, reached a spot which the families of the fugitives had left but a short time before. The light force was now divided into several parties, who followed the flying enemy in different directions. Their baggage and families were overtaken and seized; and several Afgháns brought in as prisoners. The success was complete. But, as the heat was now become oppressive and the rainy season approaching, Báber, after making the ne-

The enem retreat.

He takes Laknáu Jemádi II. 29. March 21. Rejeb 7. March 28.

Bayezíd's army dispersed.

Báber returns to Agra.

BOOK III. A.D. 1528. cessary arrangements for the government of the country, returned to Agra.*

Acquires Rantambór. A. H. 935. Moharrem 5 to 24. Sept. 20 to Oct. 9. During all these operations, Báber's health had been considerably impaired, but his activity remained undiminished. At the close of the monsoon, he made a progress to Dhulpúr, Guáliár and Sikri. His rival, Rána Sánga, had been succeeded by his eldest son Ruttonsi; but his second son, Bikermájít, assisted by the intrigues of his mother Padmáwati, aspired to the throne, and possessed the strong fort of Rantambór. He sent, at this time, to court the assistance of Báber, in pursuing his pretensions; and, after some negotiation, it was settled that he should give up Rantambór to Báber, in exchange for Shemsábád in the Doáb, and that Báber should support his claims, and establish him as Rána in Cheitúr, in his father's room. It was in the course of these transactions that Bikermájít sent to the Emperor the crown † and rich girdle of Sultan Mahmúd Khilji of Málwa; which Rána Sánga had retained, when he released that king after his captivity. Báber dispatched a force to take possession of Rantambór, in pursuance of the treaty.‡

Increase of taxes. The Emperor's liberality, and the necessary expenses of supporting a large establishment, had now so completely exhausted the magnificent treasures of Sultan Sekander and Ibráhím Lodi, which he had found on his arrival at the capital, that he was at this time obliged to add about thirty per cent. to the ordinary taxes, in order to meet the great expenditure of his armies. His giving up the tamgha or stamp-tax on Musulman property, however popular that act may have been among those of his own religion, could not fail to make a large diminution in the amount of the ordinary revenue.§

* Mem., pp. 379—381.

† Táj-kuláh.

‡ Báber's Mem. pp. 385—387.

§ Báber's Mem., p. 387. Báber's expressions, in stating this fact, show that, on taking possession of Delhi

Important events, and deeply interesting to Báber, were in the meanwhile passing in Khorásán. We have seen that the Uzbeks, after the death of Shah Ismael, and during the minority of his son Shah Tahmasp, had twice entered that country, had even advanced to Herát, and were in possession of Meshhíd and Tús. After this success, Obeid Khan, who, though second to his grand-uncle Kuchum, the Grand Khan, in reality directed the affairs of the Uzbeks, advanced and took Asterábád, defeating the Persian generals who opposed him. Leaving his son, Abdal-azíz Sultan, to defend that province, he marched for Balkh; but soon after, large reinforcements from Azerbaiján having joined the Persians, Abdal-azíz was forced to fall back; and, his father joining him, they turned on the Persian generals and totally defeated them near Bostám. Obeid, having recovered Asterábád, committed the government of the city and province to Renish* Beh*á*der Khan, an officer of rank; and himself moved towards Herát, sending out detachments in different directions, and took up his winter-quarters at Ghurián.

CHAP. III.

A. D. 1528.

Transactions in Khorásán.

A. H. 932.

A. H. 933.

Next year, he laid siege to Herát, which was bravely defended by Husein Khan Shamlu, who had succeeded Dermish Khan as governor of Sam Mírza, the young prince, and of the province. When the siege had lasted seven months, provisions began to fail. Husein being in the greatest distress, seized, for the use of his garrison, whatever grain was left in the place. He was, however, reduced to the last extremity, when news arrived of the defeat of Renish Behåder.

Obeíd Khan besieges Herát.

A. H. 934.

The Persians had collected a large force, which was placed under their governors of Sebzáwár and Asterábád, who attacked Renish near Damghán, and at first defeated him; but he, having recovered the day, gained

Shah Tahmasp defeats Renish,

and Agra, he did not distribute among his troops *all* the treasures of these princes, as is affirmed by Ferishta and other historians.

* Or Zinish.

BOOK III. A.D. 1528.

a complete victory, in which both the Persian leaders fell. While Obeid was elated with this news, messengers arrived, bringing intelligence that the young King, with an army of forty thousand men, was on his march for Herát; that the advance had besieged Renish in Damghán; had defeated and put to the sword most of his army; and had slain himself, while attempting to escape. In their sweeping course, they routed a second Uzbek detachment, which, in consequence, hastily fell back on Obeid Khan, who was still employed in the siege of Herát. The approaching danger compelled him to decamp from Púl-Málán, and retreat by hasty marches to Merv, whither he invited the whole Uzbek chiefs to hasten to his aid. They, accordingly, repaired to his standard from Samarkand, Andeján, Táshkend, Hissár, and Balkh, to the number, according to the Uzbeks, of one hundred and five thousand men.* So great an army, say the Persians, had never crossed the Amu since the days of Chengíz Khan.

raises the siege of Herát;

Meanwhile, Tahmasp had advanced to Meshhíd, hoping to cut off Obeid's retreat from Herát. When he found that the Uzbeks had made good their way to Merv, after a short stay in Meshhíd, to visit the holy places, he proceeded to Jám, on his route to Herát. Hearing that the Uzbeks were fast assembling from all quarters, he intrenched himself strongly in the Auleng-Zingán †, where he then happened to be. The Uzbeks, when informed of this, concluded that the Kezelbashes were afraid; and despising their enemy, resolved to march for Meshhíd. Their plan of campaign is singularly illustrative of the superstition of their age and tribe. They proposed, that the main body of their

advances to Meshhíd;

attacked by the Uzbeks,

* Mír Yahía Saifi, the author of the Leb-al-Towárikh, gives them one hundred and twenty-one thousand. The Alim-arái Abási says eighty thousand veterans, exclusive of other troops. According to the Persian reports of the time, as brought to Báber, they were three hundred thousand.

† Or Zadegán, or perhaps Zághán.

army should encamp at Meshhíd, while a force of twenty thousand cavalry was to be pushed forward to scour the country round the enemy's camp, and not to suffer a man to show his head beyond the trenches. They were then to let their magicians work their enchantments; so that the enemy being, by that means, shut up spell-bound, and reduced to extremity, not a man of them was to be allowed to escape out of their hands. But they had not leisure to carry into effect this hopeful arrangement. As soon as Shah Tahmasp heard that the Uzbeks were fairly in motion, and approaching by Zorábád, he joyfully advanced to meet them. The two armies came in sight of each other, on the 25th September, near Jám, a town lying between Meshhíd and Herát. The Persians did not exceed forty or fifty thousand men*, but they were veterans, disciplined troops, trained to service in the Ottoman wars; and they possessed a fine artillery, a body of two thousand artillerymen to work the guns, and six thousand matchlockmen.

whom he defeats, A. H. 935. Moharrem 10. Sept. 26.

The battle began on the morning of the 26th September. The guns of the Persians were in their centre, protected behind by twenty thousand chosen troops, under the personal command of the King. The Uzbeks, following their usual tactics, made use of their flanking columns; which, as they moved on, drove in all the enemy's advanced posts, broke the extremities of their line, and wheeled round into their rear. Here they found the baggage and camels of the army, which soon became the prey of the robbers of the desert, and probably delayed their hostile operations. To common eyes the day was their own; but the Persian centre had stood unshaken; and, when the moment seemed favourable, the chains that connected the Kezelbash guns being dropped, the troops stationed behind them

* The author of the Alim-árái Abási gives them only twenty-four thousand regular troops.

BOOK III. A.D. 1528.

rushed forward, and a furious combat at close quarters ensued between the main bodies. There was, in particular, a body of three thousand Persian cuirassiers, a kind of body-guard, who charged with undaunted gallantry. Thrice were the Uzbeks broken, and thrice did they return undismayed to the charge. At length they were routed on all sides, with prodigious slaughter; fifty thousand of their numbers, it is said, covered the field; but beside them lay no fewer than twenty thousand of their enemies. The numbers are probably much exaggerated. Several of the leading Uzbek chiefs were slain. Kuchum, the Grand Khan, and Obeid, their great leader, escaped from the field, the latter wounded. Jáni Beg, the Uzbek chief of Andeján, who had pursued the flying troops of the Persian wings to a great distance, supposing the victory secure, returned back the same night, and, guided by the fires and lights of the camp, which he imagined to be that of Obeid, came upon the encampment of Tahmasp. The Persian warriors again took to horse and followed him; the fight was renewed, but he effected his escape. Soon after this victory the necessity of Tahmasp's affairs recalled him to his western dominions.*

With great slaughter.

Revival of Báber's views on Samarkand.

This great victory of the Persians revived Báber's hopes of conquest and dominion on the side of Samarkand; hopes which, to the close of his life, he always fondly cherished. He wrote therefore to Húmáyun, who was in Badakhshán, a letter of advice regarding his future operations; recommending to him to attempt to gain Balkh and Hissár, and if possible to march against Samarkand. The letter written on that occasion has been preserved to us, and is full of enlarged political

Rebi I. 31. Nov. 26.

* Tárikh-Alim-aria Abási, f. 23, 24. Báber's Mem., pp. 388, 389, et seq., and pp. 396, 397. The accounts brought to Báber, immediately after the battle, and recorded in his journal, were in some respects erroneous. Obeid Khan was not killed, as was supposed; but when Báber's messenger came from Khorásán, it was still believed that he had fallen.

views and sound sense; and, at the same time, indicates an elegant and refined critical taste. Húmáyun, meanwhile, had not neglected the favourable occasion. He collected an army of forty or fifty thousand men, and marched for Samarkand, accompanied by Sultan Weis, whose younger brother advanced and occupied Hissár, (which the Uzbek Sultan, who held it, had abandoned after the battle of Jám, leaving only a garrison behind); while another of Húmáyun's officers, marching from Turmez, occupied Kabádián, an important town in the same quarter.* In the course of these operations, various irregularities had been committed in the territories of Balkh, which belonged to Kitin Kara Sultan, an Uzbek, who at this time was on friendly terms with Báber, and had an envoy at his court. As, through this envoy, Kitin Kara sent strong remonstrances on the conduct and proceedings of Báber's Amírs, who had permitted much robbery and pillage to be committed on his frontiers, Báber, in return, dispatched instant orders to his officers to use every exertion to seize and punish all such pillagers and robbers, and to comport themselves towards the neighbouring friendly powers with perfect amity and good faith.† About this time he intimated an intention of marching in person to Kábul in the spring, to be near these movements,—an intention which the state of his affairs in Hindustán afterwards prevented his carrying into effect. The Uzbeks, who were numerous and brave, soon after recovered all that they had lost.‡ But his wish to revisit the countries beyond the mountains never forsook him; and, in writing, at a later period, to his friend Khwája Kilán, he informs him, that, as things were becoming more settled in India, he yet expected to be soon able to set out for his northern dominions, his desire to visit which, he says, was unbounded.§

CHAP. III. A.D. 1528.

Jemádi II. 1. A.D. 1529. Feb. 11.

* Báber's Mem. pp. 390. 399.
† Ibid. p. 403.
‡ Ibid. p. 388.
§ Ibid. p. 401.

BOOK III. A. D. 1528. Decline of Báber's health.

For some time past Báber's health had shown evident symptoms of decline. About this period he had frequent attacks of fever, which at each return lasted a month or six weeks. In addition to the usual remedies, he attempted, he tells us, to remove it by composing verses in honour of an eminent Musulman saint.

Rebi. I. 19. Dec. 2.

The rains being over, he once more summoned his army to join him. Early in December he held a council to deliberate in what direction he should march. It was arranged that his son Askeri Mírza should take the command of the army in the eastern provinces; and letters were addressed to Sultan Juneid Birlás, to whom had been committed the chief direction of affairs in that quarter, to inquire if the Emperor's presence was necessary, as, if not, he would turn his arms another way. The interval before an answer was received, Báber employed in giving a grand feast to his nobles and to the foreign ambassadors at his court *; and he then visited the improvements going on at

* Báber gives a particular account of this feast (Mem. p. 394—396.). It was held in a garden. He himself was seated in a temporary pavilion that was covered with khas-grass, for coolness. On his right were his cousin (Tokhtah) Bugha Sultan, a son of the younger khan of the Moghuls, his own son Askeri, and the family and dependents of Hazret Khwája, readers of the Koran, and Múllas; on his left were Muhammed Zeman Mírza, his son-in-law; Autenk Itmish Sultan (apparently a Moghul chief) with a number of Syeds. Thirty or forty yards to the right were the Persian ambassadors. There were also ambassadors from various Hindu chiefs. Before dinner, all the Amírs and grandees made their offerings of money, rich clothes, or other valuables. Fights of furious camels and elephants were succeeded by ram-fights and wrestling matches. During the dinner, numerous dresses of honour and presents of gold and silver, swords, richly embroidered sword-belts, and enamelled daggers were bestowed on the Khwájas, Múllas, and ambassadors, who were present, as well as on the courtiers and distinguished officers; and especially on all such of the Emperor's old servants as had accompanied him from Ferghána. The feats of skill of Hindustáni jugglers succeeded, with rope-dancing and tumbling; after which, dancing-girls were introduced. The whole was concluded, towards evening prayers, by scattering among the bystanders a quantity of gold, silver, and copper money. When the party broke up, Báber detained five or six of the most distinguished guests, who sat conversing with him till the end of the first watch of the night.

Dhúlpúr, where he was building a palace, laying out a garden and sinking wells. The return of the messenger assured him that all was quiet in the East; that Sultan Juneid had advanced with his army towards Kheríd, a province which lies chiefly on the left bank of the Gogra, and which was then in the occupation of the King of Bengal; and that there was nothing that required the Emperor's presence. It was, however, suggested that one of the Emperor's sons should be sent to the army, and orders issued to the Amírs and Jagírdars to attend him; and an ambassador, who returned about this time from Bengal, gave the most favourable report of the disposition of the king of that country.*

CHAP. III.

A.D. 1528-9. Rebi II. 16. Dec. 29.

Rebi II. 19, A.D. 1529. Jan. 1.

He resolves to march to the West.

Báber now, therefore, resolved to march to the West; where, since he was not to attack Bengal, he expected the richest booty and the best means of supporting his army. Before he set out, and to put his mind quite at ease respecting affairs to the eastward, he sent a confidential officer to the principal chiefs and Amírs in the provinces beyond the Ganges, to enjoin them to attend Askeri Mírza, wherever he should lead. This envoy was to lose no opportunity of reporting on the spot every kind of intelligence that could in any degree influence the Emperor's conduct.†

Balúch inroads.

At this crisis, news reached him that the Balúches had made an inroad into his territories and committed great devastation. That brave but barbarous race at that time possessed most of the country from Bheker in Sind to Multán and Samana. Báber entrusted the task of repressing and punishing these freebooters to his cousin Chín Taimur Sultan, Governor of Mewát; and, for that purpose placed under him some of his ablest generals, with all the forces of Sirhind, Samana and the adjoining provinces; commanding them to take

Chín Taimur sent agains them.

* Báber's Mem. p. 394—397.

† Ibid. p. 398.

BOOK III. A.D. 1529.

stores and provisions for six months' service, that they might do the business effectually.*

Sultan Mahmúd acknowledged by the Eastern Afgháns.

The Emperor then hastened to Dhúlpúr; that, before taking the field, he might enjoy some short relaxation, in superintending the extensive improvements he was himself carrying on at that place; where several of his nobles were also laying out grounds, and building country houses. But he had been there only four days, when intelligence reached him that Sultan Mahmúd, the brother of the late Sultan Ibráhím Lodi, who, as we have seen, had, after his brother's death, been acknowledged by the Western Afgháns and Rána Sánga as his lawful successor,—having now been invited from Gujrát by the Eastern Afgháns,—had arrived among them, assumed the crown, was at the head of an army, and already master of Behár.

Affairs of Behár.

The affairs of Behár will be better understood from the history of Shír Shah; with the events of whose early life they are intimately connected. Suffice it, at present, to remark that, on the death of Sultan Muhammed Shah Loháni, the Afghán king of Behár, of the new dynasty (an event which occurred some time

* Báber's Memoirs, p. 399. Ferishta (vol. ii. p. 62.) tells us that Askeri Mírza, who governed Multán, was ordered to court this year (A. H. 935) when Báber was about to march to the East. He adds, that towards the close of the year Báber received advice that the Balúches in Multán had raised the standard of revolt. Now, Báber mentions, that, before setting out against Chándéri, which was 14th Rebi I. A. H. 934 (Dec. 9, A. D. 1527), he had recalled Askeri, to confer with him on the affairs of Multán, and that that prince joined him in Moharrem 3, being the third day of the year 935, (Sept. 18. 1528); that Askeri took leave of him to proceed to the eastward on 8 Rebi II. of the same year (Dec. 21); and that news of the inroads of the Balúches reached him on the 28th of that month (Jan. 10, 1529). Báber's Mem. pp. 382. 396. 398. Askeri must, therefore, have been recalled from Multán, A. H. 934, and must have gone to that country either in A. H. 933 or early in 934; a fact of some consequence in settling the chronology of the reduction of Multán by Báber. The preparations for Chín Taimur's campaign are more like those for the conquest of a province, than for repelling an invasion. To secure the repose of Multán, which they had long governed, it was necessary to break the power of the Balúch tribes.

CHAP. III.

A.D. 1529.

Behár in the Bengal camp.

the Gogra joins the Ganges from the north-east; and where, apparently, the kingdom of Bengal commenced, on the left bank of that river. Here he learned that Sultan Mahmúd Lodi was in the Bengal camp at the junction of the two rivers, with a body of Afgháns, and, that when he and his followers wished to remove their families and baggage, they were not permitted, the Bengalis probably wishing to retain them as hostages. Sultan Jilál-ed-dín Loháni, his rival, who had lately sent his submission to Báber, was in like manner hindered from departing, in consequence of which he had come to blows with the Bengalis, had effected a passage over the Ganges into Behár with his followers, and was on his march to join the imperial army The Emperor, therefore, who considered that the position of the army of Bengal, and the conduct of its leaders, had violated their neutrality, prepared to call them to account.

Affairs of Bengal,

The transactions between Báber and Nasrat Shah, the King of Bengal*, are hinted at, but not explained, in the Emperor's commentaries. When Sultan Sekander Lodi overran the Sherki kingdom of Juánpúr, the reigning king took refuge with the King of Bengal. Sekander, having subdued Behár, entered Bengal; and his advance was stayed only by a convention, by which he was allowed to retain Behár, Tirhút, Sirkár, Sáran, and all that he had subdued, but was not to invade Bengal; and neither prince was to support the enemies of the other. The confusion occasioned by Báber's approach against Ibráhím Lodi, presented a favourable opportunity to the King of Bengal for recovering the ceded provinces. Nasrat Shah accordingly invaded and took possession of Tirhút, subdued Hájipúr, and,

A. H. 905.

A. H. 930-2.

* The complete title of Nasrat, according to Stewart, History of Bengal, p. 118., was "Sultan Nasrat Shah bin Sultan Alá-ed-dín Husein Shah." By many historians he is called Nasíb, a name by which he appears to have been familiarly known.

BOOK III. A.D. 1529.

crossing the Ganges, took the fort and district of Mongeir, which he entrusted to Kutb Khan, one of his best generals. After the defeat and death of Sultan Ibráhím, many Afgháns fled to Bengal; and Nasrat even married a daughter of that prince.* He now afforded a refuge to her uncle, Sultan Mahmúd, when driven from his dominions.

Báber's negotiation with Bengal.

Báber found the army of Kheríd, as the Bengal army was called, lying in what is at present the territory of Sáran, which Nasrat had recovered from the Afgháns. It was encamped near the junction of the Ganges and the Gogra †, so as to be able to defend both the course of the Gogra, and the left bank of the Ganges, after the union of the two rivers. He discovered, too, that the Bengal generals had collected about an hundred or an hundred and fifty vessels, on their side of the stream; by means of which they were able, at once to hinder the passage of an enemy and to facilitate their own. Such an army he could not safely leave behind; especially as the troops of Baban and Bayezíd had also taken refuge upon, and in strength occupied, the upper course of the Gogra. He was, indeed, at peace with Bengal; but the shelter afforded to his flying enemy, the position of the Kheríd army, and the equivocal conduct of its leaders, made it indispensable that he should have a categorical declaration as to the disposition and intention of the Bengal government. He,

* Stewart's History of Bengal, pp. 113—116.

† Some confusion arises from the various names given to this river, Gogar or Gogra, Siru or Sirju, and Dewah. The principal branch rises in the Himaláya mountains, where it is named Kali. At Swarga-dwára it meets and unites with the Saryu, Sirju or Sirjew; after which it is indiscriminately named Gogra, Siru, or Dewa.

There is another Surju or Suryu, which, from the map, appears to run parallel to it, and to branch off from it; and, passing Azímgar and Mow, falls into the Ganges.

It would appear that Kheríd, a division not now known by that name, included the country on both sides of the Gogra, near Sekanderpúr, and thence on its left bank down to the Ganges.

CHAP. III.

A.D. 1529.

therefore, dispatched an envoy to Nasrat Shah, the King of Bengal; and sent along with him an ambassador of that prince, who was in his camp, to remind the King that he had always carefully cultivated his friendship and preserved the relations of peace and amity that subsisted between them; but that these relations, as matters now stood, could be preserved only by his acceding to three conditions already sent him, but to which the Emperor had received no answer; that they should again be laid before the King, for his acceptance; that, in the meanwhile, Báber, until he received the King's answer, must follow his flying enemies wherever they went; that he would engage, however, that the subjects of Bengal should suffer no injury from his troops, either by land or water; but that the army of Kheríd must leave the track in which he was marching, and retire from its present position; that he was ready to afford safe-conducts to the Afghâns who had been in arms against him, to send troops to protect them on their march, and to allow them to return home with assurances of indemnity; that, if the road was not left open for the advance of his army, he could not be answerable for the consequences.*

Shábán 10. April 29. Báber's arrangements to attack the Bengal army,

Báber was now joined by Sultan Juneid Birlás, from Juánpúr, with about twenty thousand men. The tardy arrival of these troops subjected their commander to a temporary disgrace. Not having received a satisfactory answer to his demands, the Emperor resolved to compel the army beyond the Gogra to quit its strong position. He made the necessary arrangements for the intended attack. He formed his army into six divisions. Four of these, consisting of Askeri's army, which was already on the left bank of the Ganges, and of Sultan Juneid's, which had recently joined on the same side, were ordered to be prepared to cross the Gogra, either in boats

* Báber's Mem. pp. 411, 412.

BOOK III. A.D. 1529.

at Haldi, or by fording still farther up that river. The other two divisions were still on the right bank of the Ganges. One of these, under the Emperor's personal direction, was to effect the passage of that river, and then to cover the operations of Ustád Ali Kuli, his chief engineer; who was directed to plant a battery on the banks of the Siru or Gogra, above its union with the Ganges, directly opposite to the Bengal camp, which it would be able to cannonade,—and afterwards to cover the passage of the Emperor's division when it crossed the Gogra to attack the enemy. Mustafa, another engineer, who had a party of musqueteers and artillery, supported by Muhammed Zemán Mírza, and the sixth division, was to open a cannonade on the flank of the enemy's camp, from the Behár bank of the Ganges, below the junction of the rivers. The main body of the army, which was that under Askeri, after passing the Gogra at Haldi, was ordered to march down upon the enemy, so as to draw them from their camp, and induce them to march up that river; and, by this diversion, to keep them occupied until the two divisions of Báber and Muhammed Zemán, under cover of the fire of the artillery and matchlockmen, could be transported across.

The whole army was accordingly put in motion. Askeri's four divisions marched for Haldi. The batteries, both on the Gogra and Ganges, were constructed and commenced their fire. The Bengal army behaved with great bravery and pushed parties across to attack the Emperor's troops, both above and below the junction of the rivers. At length, after various movements, Báber received notice that Askeri had effected a passage over the Gogra at the Haldi-Ghát, and was now ready for action; and that he had been strengthened by the defection of Shah Muhammed Maarúf, an Afghán nobleman of the highest rank and consequence, who had deserted the confederacy with his followers, and now joined his camp. The general attack was therefore, fixed for next morning; but in the meanwhile, there was some fighting between the vessels in the river. CHAP. III. A. D. 1259.

On the morning of the 6th of May, as soon as Askeri's army was known to be in motion, the Bengal troops moved up to meet him; whereupon Báber ordered both his division and that of Muhammed Zemán to cross over without delay. This was effected bravely, though not without sharp resistance. The troops got across; some in boats, some by swimming, some floating on reeds. They were met with equal gallantry on landing; but kept together, formed, and made repeated vigorous charges. As Askeri advanced downwards, the enemy, finding themselves surrounded and driven in on three sides, finally quitted the field in confusion.* which he defeats. Shábán 27. May 6.

This victory was decisive in its consequences. Numbers of the Afgháns, who till now had been refractory, having lost all hope of re-establishing an Afghán government in the East, submitted; and Sultan Jilál-eddín Loháni, the late King of Behár, whose escape from the Bengal camp has been mentioned, arrived, with many of his principal Amírs, and acknowledged Báber. Other chiefs, imitating their example, petitioned to be received into the Emperor's service. Seven or eight thousand Loháni Afgháns had already joined him, and were now rewarded and employed. The feuds between the Loháni and Lodi factions in the Eastern provinces were fatal to the national interest. Many Afgháns submit. Ramzan 8. May 17.

The success of Báber's arms hastened the acceptance of the three propositions which had been sent to Nasrat Shah for his acceptance or refusal; for, the prince of Mongeir, a son of the King, and Hasan Khan Leshker, his minister, now took it upon them to write to Báber agreeing to them on his part. "As this expedition had been undertaken," says Báber, "for the Peace with Bengal. Ramzán 10. May 19.

* Báber's Mem. pp. 412—417.

BOOK III. A.D. 1529.

purpose of punishing the rebellious Afgháns, of whom many had gone off and disappeared, many had come in and entered my service, while the few that remained had taken shelter among the Bengális, who undertook to answer for their conduct; and as, besides, the rainy season was now close at hand, I wrote an answer in return, and sent my ratification of the terms of pacification." A few days after, the Emperor set out to chastise Baban and Bayezíd, the only Afghán chiefs of any consequence who were still in arms, and who were probably at this time in the Bharech country.*

Baban and Bayezíd flee to Mohóba.

No sooner was it known that a treaty was finally concluded with Bengal, and that the great Afghán leaders had submitted to Báber, than these two chiefs, who seem in general to have had more power and influence than the King whom they served, especially in the provinces to the east of the Ganges, no longer finding shelter in the Bengal territory, and seeing Behár occupied by the Emperor's troops, recrossed the Gogra and Siru, and marched upon Laknáu, in hopes of carrying it by a *coup-de-main*, in the absence of the regular army. On their arrival at that city, they made an assault and were repulsed; but some hay or straw that had been collected in the fort having been set on fire by combustible missiles, the heat became so intense that the garrison could not stand on the works; so that the assailants were enabled to enter and take possession of the place. As soon, however, as the Afgháns heard that Báber was on his return back, they abandoned it, and crossed the Ganges into the Doáb, near Dilmáu. Being pursued by a detachment sent after them, they next crossed the Jamna also. Part of their troops were overtaken and cut off; the remainder were followed as far as the borders of Bandélkand to Mahóba, which also they left hastily on the advance of the pursuing force.†

Ramzán 13. May 22.

* Báber's Mem. pp. 418, 419. † Ibid. ff. 421—423.

The Emperor, meanwhile, after this successful campaign, having set out on his return, had reached a ghát on the Gogra, opposite to Sekanderpúr; and the troops were busily employed in passing the river, when, on the night of the 26th of May, the rains set in with one of those violent tempests which often mark the opening of the monsoon; and so suddenly, that the Emperor's pavilion and the screens surrounding it were blown down over him, as he was writing, and his life endangered. In a few days, however, he was able to cross the Gogra; and, having sent out the main body of his army to Ghazipúr, himself marched up to Oud; whence, by way of Kórah, he once more returned to Agra.

CHAP. III.

A.D. 1529.

Báber returns to Agra.

Ramzán 17. May 26.

Shawál 17. June 24.

This is the last campaign of which we have the history from the pen of Báber himself; and of the military events of the next fifteen months, we know hardly any thing. The only occurrence transmitted to us is the disaffection and intended revolt of Rahím-dád, the governor of Gualiár; who was, however, prevailed upon by the influence and remonstrances of Sheikh Muhammed Ghus, the celebrated Musulman saint, who was still in that neighbourhood,—to restore that strong and important fortress into the hands of Báber.*

Moharrem 3. Sept. 7.

* Báber's Mem. p. 424.

CHAPTER IV.

BÁBER'S ILLNESS AND DEATH.

BÁBER'S HEALTH DECLINES. — HUMÁYUN LEAVES BADAKHSHÁN. — ALARM OF THE INHABITANTS. — SULTAN SAÍD CALLED IN — BESIEGES KILA-ZEFER — MAKES PEACE AND RETIRES. — SULEIMÁN MÍRZA SENT TO BADAKHSHÁN. — HUMÁYUN AT COURT. — HIS ILLNESS. — BÁBER'S SELF-DEVOTION. — BÁBER'S DANGEROUS ILLNESS. — INTRIGUES IN FAVOUR OF MEHDI KHWÁJA. — HIS ARROGANCE AND FALL. — BÁBER'S DYING ADVICE TO HIS SONS AND AMÍRS. — HIS DEATH. — TOMB. — CHARACTER. — COMMENTARIES. — PERSON. — CHILDREN. — DOMINIONS. — THEIR POLITICAL SITUATION — TAXES — LANDED PROPERTY — REVENUE — CUSTOMS — JEZÍA — POST-HOUSES — MEN OF LETTERS.

A. D. 1529.

Decline of Báber's health.

THE decline in the Emperor's health, which for some time past had become evident to all about him, excited in his eldest son, Humáyun Mírza, who had now resided for the greater part of nine years * in the distant government of Badakhshán, a natural anxiety to be near his father, for the purpose of counteracting the intrigues so common in the harams and the courts of all Eastern princes, under such circumstances. He accordingly set out, without leave, as it would appear, to proceed to Agra. Mírza Haider, indeed, affirms that Báber, at the same time that he placed Kámrán Mírza in Kandahár, recalled Humáyun into India; that, if any thing adverse happened, he might be at hand, to assume the reins of government. But, in this instance, the opposite assertion of other historians is more probable; as we cannot suppose that a prince of Báber's talents and experience would have recalled his son from so important a station as Badakhshán then was,

End of A. H. 935. Humáyan leaves Badakhshán.

* From A. H. 926 to 935, excepting when he attended his father on the conquest of India. Tar. Resh. f. 293.

collision with the Emperor Báber; he reminded them that they had invited him, from apprehension that they might fall into the hands of the Uzbeks,—an event which would have been equally injurious to all parties. After some mutual explanations, the siege was raised, and the Khan returned to Káshghar.

CHAP. IV.

A.D. 1530.

Perplexity of Báber,

The news of this invasion was particularly unpleasing to Báber in all its circumstances. Besides his displeasure with Humáyun for having left his government without leave, and his disappointment at the unfriendly invasion of Sultan Saíd, he was anxious not to lose a country which might be of so much consequence, in the event of any future operations on the Oxus. It is said that, in this emergency he was induced to ask Mír Ali Khalífa, his chief minister, to visit Badakhshán, and to settle the affairs of the province. That minister, who probably saw in the requisition only the result of some intrigue to remove him at an important moment from the presence, contrived to excuse himself. Humáyun was next asked to resume his government; but declined, unless commanded peremptorily and on his duty. Báber, thus disappointed and perplexed, resolved to confer the province on Suleimán Mírza, the son of his cousin, that Khan Mírza, who had governed it for so many years, and who, on the mother's side, was descended from the ancient kings of the country, who gloried in being sprung from Alexander the Great. Suleimán Mírza was the son-in-law of Sultan Weis, who had managed Badakhshán under Humáyun; and his appointment, it was thought, might be the means of restoring that powerful chief to his allegiance. The Emperor sent Suleimán off without delay. He carried with him an order recalling Hindál, and also a letter to Sultan Saíd Khan, in which Báber told that prince, that, whatever might be his hereditary claims, he felt surprise at what had occurred; that he had, however, recalled Hindál and sent Suleimán, whom, if the Khan

who appoints Mírza Suleimán to Badakhshán.

BOOK III.

A.D. 1530.

wished to favour the claims of hereditary right, he would cordially support, since both of them looked upon him as their son; he trusted, therefore, that the Khan would yield to the Mírza the possession of Badakhshán; if not, that the Emperor, having resigned to him his own claims, would know how to support him against the pretensions of others.

He assumes the government.

When Suleimán Mírza reached Kábul, he found that the Khan had retreated from Badakhshán some time before. Hindál, on the Mírza's arrival in that kingdom, resigned to him the government, as he had been ordered; and set out for Hindustán. The new governor, or rather King of Badakhshán, assumed the direction of affairs; and, his hands being strengthened by the confusion in Hindustán, which followed Báber's death, fixed himself permanently as Suleimán Sháh, in the country, which he transmitted to his descendants with nearly independent authority.*

Humáyun at court.

Humáyun, on leaving Kábul, had posted on to Agra. He arrived at the palace, as we are told by the courtly Abulfazl, at the very moment when his mother and the Emperor were sitting together conversing about him; and was most affectionately welcomed. It must be acknowledged that the whole course of his proceedings has much the air of a plan concerted between Humáyun and his mother, who saw the decline of her husband's health, and wished her son to be upon the spot, as there was a strong party, headed by Mír Ali Khalífa, the prime minister, who wished to set him aside from the succession. Humáyun, who had a cultivated mind, a sprightly wit, and polite and refined manners, rendered himself very agreeable in society to his father, who acknowledged that there could not be a more acceptable companion. Báber had just lost a young son, Alwer†; and the depression of spirits under

* Taríkhe Reshídi, f. 293—295.; Akbernáma, f. 33.; Briggs's Ferishta, vol. ii. p. 63, 64.

† Or, Anwar.

CHAP. IV.

A. D. 1530.

which he laboured, gave him the more lively relish for the company of Humáyun. When the prince had been some months at court, he was sent to his jágír or government of Sambal, beyond the Ganges, but at no great distance from Delhi. There he enjoyed himself for about six months, when he fell dangerously ill. His father, who was deeply affected by the news, directed that he should be removed to Delhi, and from thence by water to Agra. On his arrival there, the violence of the disease was such that his life was despaired of. No symptom of amendment appeared to result from the medical treatment, and the worst was apprehended. At this time, as the Emperor was one day sitting in the palace, which he had built beyond the Jamna, conversing with his Amírs, and some learned and pious men, on the subject that was nearest his thoughts, Mír Abul Baká, one of the personages then most celebrated for sanctity, happened to remark, that it was an observation handed down from olden times, that, in cases like the present, where all human assistance had failed, an offering made to the Almighty of the most valuable thing belonging to the person who laboured under the affliction, had been accepted, and the sufferer restored to health. Báber, excited by the hopeless situation of his son, and perhaps by his own increasing malady, exclaimed, that of all things, his life was what was dearest to Humáyun, as Humáyun's was to him; that his life, therefore, he cheerfully devoted as a sacrifice for his son's; and prayed the Most High to vouchsafe to accept it. Khwája Khalífa and his other friends attempted to divert his thoughts from the gloomy channel in which they flowed; and to comfort him by the hope that through the mercy of God, Humáyun had yet many happy years before him; they suggested that the offering made in such cases was not of life, but of some worldly goods, and that the diamond acquired some years before, being of immense value, might be sold

Sent to Sambal, A. H. 936.

Falls dangerously ill.

Báber's self-devotion.

BOOK III. A.D. 1530.

and the price devoted to charitable and pious uses. But Báber repelled the idea; affirming, that no earthly possession could be a suitable exchange for a life so precious as his son's, that he could not endure to witness his sufferings, and was resolved to devote himself in his stead. He then, we are told, retired into the private apartments, and having prayed earnestly, walked thrice round the dying prince, a solemnity corresponding to that used in waive offerings; and when, after a time, he fancied that he felt the influence of his vow visibly affecting both him and the prince, he was heard to call out, — "I have prevailed! I have saved him." Humáyun recovered, and was able to return to his government of Sambal; while the Emperor daily grew worse.

Intrigues in favour of Mehdi Khwája.

But though Humáyun was restored to health, his succession to his father was still by no means secure. The prime minister, Khwája Khalífa, had, for some unknown cause, conceived a dislike or apprehension of him; and, it is asserted, had resolved to exclude all the sons of Báber from the succession, and, in their room, to set up Mehdi Khwája, a young nobleman of high rank, probably a relation of his own, who had married a daughter of Báber's. Mehdi was brave, high-spirited, and generous; but wild and extravagant. Khalífa, his supporter, possessed the highest influence with all the older Túrki nobles, who had the chief authority at court, and in the army; and there was much reason to believe that the cause which he espoused must be successful. The ambitious youth entered eagerly into the intrigues that were to exalt him so high; and, while the Emperor lay at the last extremity, Khalífa, having given some intimation of his intentions, many of the principal men of the army, influenced by him, and eager to salute the rising sun, waited on Mehdi Khwája, as their future sovereign; to pay him their court by anticipation, and to secure his favour.

These brilliant prospects, and these attentions, seem to have turned his head He foolishly began already to assume the deportment of a monarch; and, though he continued to frequent the Derbár, the growing arrogance and overweening presumption that he discovered disgusted even his most attached partizans; so that Khalífa, we are told, was influenced by their remonstrances to alter his views, to return to his allegiance to his old master's family, and to transfer his interest to Humáyun, before his purposes had been manifested by any overt act. The consequence was that Mehdi Khwája was ordered into custody.* CHAP. IV. A. D. 1530.

Such is nearly the account given by Abulfazl; but an anecdote related by a contemporay historian throws farther light on this change of fortune.† "It so happened," says he, "that Mír Khalífa had gone to see Mehdi Khwája, whom he found in his pavilion. Nobody was present but Khalífa, Medi Khwája, and my father, Muhammed Mokím. Khalífa had hardly sat down an instant, when Báber, who was at the point of death, sent for him. When he left the pavilion, Mehdi Khwája accompanied him to the door to do him honour, and to take leave of him, and stood in the middle of the doorway; so that my father, who followed, but out of respect did not push by him, was immediately behind. The young man, who was rather flighty and hairbrained, forgetting that my father was present, as soon as Khalífa was fairly gone, stroking his beard, muttered to himself, 'Please God, I will soon flay off your hide, old boy;' and, turning round at the same instant, saw my father. He was quite confounded; but immedi- His arrogance and levity.

* Akbernáma, f. 34.; Kholáset-ul-Towáríkh, ff. 254, 255.

† Nizám-ed-dín Ahmed Bakhshi, the author of the Tabakáti Akberi, or Taríkhe Nizámi, was the son of Muhammed Mokím Hirvi, who was at this time Diwán Bintát to Báber. See Tabakáti Akberi, f. 134. v. Nizám-ed-dín himself rose to the highest offices of the state under Akber; he held the chief command in Gujrát, and was for some time minister of finance.

BOOK III. A.D. 1530.

ately seizing my father's ear, twisted it round, and said hurriedly, 'You Tájík, the red tongue often gives the green head to the winds.' My father, having taken his leave and left the tent, called upon Khalífa, and remonstrated with him on his line of conduct; telling him that, in violation of his allegiance, he was taking away the sovereignty from Muhammed Humáyun and his brothers, who were accomplished princes, to bestow it on the son of a stranger. And yet, how did this favoured man behave? He then repeated what had passed, just as it happened. Khalífa, on the spot, sent off an express to call Humáyun; and, at the same time, dispatched a body of yesáwels or special messengers to Mehdi Khwája, to inform him that the Emperor's orders were, that he should instantly retire to his own house. The young man by this time had sat down to dinner, which was still before him. The yesáwels communicated their orders, and forced him away to his house, reluctant as he was to go. Mír Khalífa then issued a proclamation, prohibiting all persons from resorting to Mehdi Khwája's house or waiting upon him; while Mehdi Khwája himself received orders forbidding him to appear at court." *

He is placed in custody.

Báber's dying advice.

In the midst of these intrigues, with which he was probably unacquainted, Báber, finding his strength fast declining, directed a council of his ministers and friends to be called, to receive his dying injunctions. Among those who were present were his minister Nizám-ed-dín Khwája Ali Khalífa; Kamber Alí Beg; Terdi Beg and Hindu Beg, who had attended him in all the many changes of his fortune. Taking in his own the hand of Humáyun, who had now returned, he formally declared him to be his lieutenant and successor in all his dominions, and commanded him to take his seat on the imperial throne, at the foot of which the Emperor him-

* Tabakáti Akberi, f. 144. See also Tar. Bedáuni, f. 139.

CHAP. IV.

A. D. 1530.

self lay, stretched on his couch. He then proceeded, with all the authority of a dying monarch, and of a man who had seen so much, and taken so large a share in the great events of his time, to recommend to them all a conscientious discharge of their duties to God and to man; above all, honestly and assiduously to administer justice to those over whom they were placed; but, while they punished the guilty, to extend their tenderness and mercy to the ignorant and the penitent, and their protection to the poor and the defenceless; and, addressing himself particularly to Humáyun, he besought him, as his most earnest and dying request, above all things to deal kindly and affectionately with his brothers, and, whatever their offences might be, never to permit his resentment to lead him to the last extremity against any of them.*

His death. A. H. 937. Jemádi I. 5. Dec. 26.

He soon after breathed his last, in his palace at the Charbagh near Agra, on the 26th of December, 1530, while yet only forty-eight †; having reigned, in all, upwards of thirty-six years,—and, of that time, twenty-six over Kábul, and about five over part of India. His body, at his own desire, was carried to Kábul, and buried in a beautiful spot marked out by himself, on a hill near the city, which still bears his name. "I lost no time," says a distinguished traveller, to whom the geography of all the kingdoms of Báber owes so much, and whose talents and misfortunes have rendered him eminent, "I lost no time in making excursions near Cabool, and chose the earliest opportunity to visit the tomb of the Emperor Baber, which is about a mile from the city, and situated in the sweetest spot of the neighbourhood." "I have a profound respect for the memory of Báber, which had been increased by a late perusal of his most interesting Commentaries. He had directed

He is buried at Kábul.

His tomb.

* Akbernáma, f. 34. MS. A.; Tarîkhe Bedáuni, f. 139.

† Reckoning by the Arab computation, he lived fifty, and reigned thirty-eight years.

BOOK III. A.D. 1530.

his body to be interred in this place, to him the choicest in his wide dominions. These are his own words regarding Cabool:—'The climate is extremely delightful, and there is no such place in the known world.' 'Drink wine in the citadel of Cabool, and send round the cup without stopping; for it is at once mountain and stream, town and desert.'

"The grave is marked by two erect slabs of white marble, and, as is common in the East, the different letters of a part of the inscription indicate the number of the year of the Hegira in which the Emperor died. The device in the present instance seems to me happy. 'When in heaven Roozvan asked the date of his death. I told him that heaven is the eternal abode of Baber Badshah.' Near the Emperor many of his wives and children have been interred; and the garden, which is small, has been once surrounded with a wall of marble. A running and clear stream yet waters the fragrant flowers of this cemetery, which is the great holiday resort of the people of Cabool. In front of the grave there is a small but chaste mosque of marble; and an inscription upon it sets forth that it was built in the year 1640, by order of the Emperor Shah Jehán, after defeating Mahommed Nuzzur Khan in Balkh and Badakhshán, that poor Mahommedans might here offer up their prayers. It is pleasing to see the tomb of so great a man as Báber honoured by his posterity.

"There is a noble prospect from the hill which overlooks Báber's tomb, and a summer-house has been erected upon it by Shah Zemán from which it may be admired. If my reader can imagine a plain, about twenty miles in circumference, laid out with gardens and fields in pleasing irregularity, intersected by three rivulets which wind through it in a serpentine course, and wash innumerable little forts and villages, he will have before him one of the meadows of Cabool. To the north lie the hills of Pughman, covered half way down with snow, and separated from the eye by a sheet of the richest verdure. On the other side the mountains, which are bleak and rocky, mark the hunting preserves of the kings; and the gardens of this city, so celebrated for fruit, lie beneath, the water being conducted to them with great ingenuity. I do not wonder at the hearts of the people being captivated with the landscape, and of Báber's admiration; for, in his own words, 'its verdure and flowers render Cabool, in spring, a heaven.' "*

His character.

Báber was certainly one of the most illustrious sovereigns that ever filled an eastern throne. His character was happily compounded of most of the qualities that go to form a great prince and a good man. He was bold, enterprising, full of ardour, and possessed of the commanding talents that sway and lead the minds of men. His temper was frank, confiding, and gay, and maintained through life the freshness of youth. He had strong affections, the warmest domestic feelings, was devotedly attached to his relations and friends, and ready to sympathise with the pleasures and the sufferings of human beings of every class. Keenly alive to whatever was grand or beautiful, he cultivated knowledge of every kind with unwearied assiduity and with proportional success. Glory in every shape inflamed his imagination, and he attained to a rare eminence of power and renown. Yet no man's success could be more entirely his own. When, as a boy, he mounted the throne of Ferghána, the neighbouring kingdoms were all held by sultans and sovereigns of his own race. While he was still only a youth, not one of them was left; they had all either fallen by domestic treason, or been swept away by foreign invasion, the torrent of which overwhelmed him also, and bore him into distant lands; but, by his native energy, he emerged

* Burnes's Travels into Bokhara, vol. ii. pp. 121—123. Lond. 1835. 2d ed.

from the sweeping inundation, and raised himself above it, the only remnant of the House of Taimur. Before the age of twenty he had experienced every diversity of fortune, having been by turns a petty prince, the conqueror of a renowned kingdom, and a houseless and hunted fugitive; but under no circumstances did his sanguine temper, and his determined resolution, forsake him; and, when in the lowest pitch of misery, expelled from his hereditary dominions, and wandering with a few ragged followers, the fame of his valour brought to his standard many thousand bold adventurers, aided by whom he conquered new and extensive kingdoms. In that age of confusion, to be able to reign it was necessary to be a soldier; and he became the first of his time.

His fondness for war did not lead him to neglect the arts of peace. The few intervals of repose from military operations which he enjoyed in his troubled life, he devoted, with his habitual ardour, to examining into and improving the state of his kingdom, and to bettering the condition of his subjects. His natural genius made him fond of all the fine arts, and among others of architecture* and gardening. He built palaces and

* The author of the Táríkhe-Sind, in enumerating the curiosities of Kábul and Kandahár, in which latter country he was stationed for three years, after mentioning some caves near Baba Hasan Abdál, describes (f. 120, 121.) the mansion (ímárat) of Pustak, excavated by Báber's orders in the hill of Biserlureh, out of the solid rock. It has a very lofty dome (or arch). Seventy stone-cutters were constantly employed on it for three years. It is described as a curious and beautiful work, commanding an extensive, rich and magnificent view over the water Azanderi (Ab-Azaanderi, *quære*, Ab-Arghandábi, the river Arghandab?), and numerous gardens and cultivated fields. It is, we are told, much frequented in the spring; though many, from the height of its situation, and the great difficulty of access, are prevented from reaching it. Our author informs us that there were tablets in it, containing the names of Báber, Kámrán, Askeri, and Hindál; but not of Humáyun, who had never been there; but, he adds, that he employed stone-cutters from Bheker to add the names of Humáyun and Akber, and a list of the numerous provinces of the wide empire of the latter. I know not if any British officer, during the late wars, has visited these excavations.

laid out gardens in several parts of his dominions; he delighted in flowers and in beautiful prospects. He was a horticulturist, and succeeded in naturalising some valuable fruits and plants in provinces to which they had formerly been strangers, and where they still flourish; and was as proud of his success, as of a victory in the field of battle. All this he did in the midst of turmoil and war. In the course of his most important expeditions, we find him inquiring after the progress of his improvements, and expressing an earnest longing to be restored to the scenes and friends that he loved. It is not surprising that, with so inherent a love of knowledge, he should have been a patron of learning and of learned men; or that, by his liberality, he should have drawn many of them around him; but the fact that, in a life so full of agitation and bustle as his, having from boyhood to age been in constant motion, he should himself have found time to cultivate the learning and knowledge of the age, is a proof how strong was the natural bias of his mind to useful and liberal studies. "He was," says "Haider Mírza, who knew him well, "a prince adorned with various excellences, and distinguished for his admirable qualities. Of all these qualities his generosity and humanity took the lead. In Túrki poetry, after Mír Ali Shír, none equalled him. He has composed a Túrki Diwán (or collection of Odes) of extreme elegance and vigour. He wrote an useful treatise on Law and Religion, which has met with general approbation. He also composed a tract on Túrki Prosody, superior in merit to any written before on the subject. The Resáleh e Walidíeh of Hazret Ishan, he versified.* His Commentaries, which he composed in Túrki, are remarkable for their easy and unaffected manner, and great purity of style. He was also skilled in music, and other arts. None of

* This is probably the Matiin, said to be a work of mystical divinity.

BOOK III. his family before him exceeded him in talents and accomplishments; and, in wonderful exploits and adventures, none of his descendants is soon likely to equal him." *

He was not only fond of music, but was himself a composer; and several of his airs are said to have been in a pleasing style, and to have survived him.

Besides his Túrki, he composed some Persian poetry; but, in the revolutions to which India has been subject since his time, little more than the names of his poetical productions have been preserved; though by the invariable consent of his countrymen, he still retains his place as the second Túrki poet.

As an appendage to literature, he had acquired great skill in penmanship,—an art held in high estimation in the East, where literary works are diffused only by the pen, and where it is generally considered as one of the fine arts, — a distinction which may seem to be justified by the uncommon style of elegance in which its productions are sometimes executed. Báber, we are told, wrote in great perfection the different hands then in use, and invented one which was distinguished by his name.

His Commentaries. But of all his literary works, his Commentaries are by much the most remarkable. The first part contains a continuous narrative of his early life and troubles; the latter portions consist of fragments of a journal, written from time to time, and often from day to day; some comprising accounts of his most celebrated exploits, others being merely short entries or jottings, as if to assist his future recollection, and frequently referring to the incidents of his private life. "His Memoirs," says the historian of India, "are almost singular in their own nature, and perfectly so if we consider the circumstances of the writer. They contain a minute

* Tar. Resh. f. 123, 124.

account of the life of a great Tartar monarch, along with a natural effusion of his opinions and feelings, free from disguise and reserve, and no less free from all affectation of extreme frankness and candour. The style is plain and manly, as well as lively and picturesque; and, being the work of a man of genius and observation, it presents his countrymen and contemporaries in their appearance, manners, pursuits, and actions, as clearly as in a mirror. In this respect, it is almost the only specimen of real history in Asia; for the ordinary writers, though they give pompous accounts of the deeds and ceremonies of the great, are apt to omit the lives and manners even of that class; while everything beneath their level is left entirely out of sight. In Báber, the figures, dress, tastes, and habits, of each individual introduced are described with such minuteness and reality, that we seem to live among them, and to know their persons as well as we do their characters. His description of the countries he visited, their scenery, climate, productions, and works of art and industry are more full and accurate than will, perhaps, be found, in equal space, in any modern traveller; and, considering the circumstances in which they were compiled, are truly surprising.

"But the great charm of the work is in the character of the author, whom we find, after all the trials of a long life, retaining the same kind and affectionate heart, and the same easy and sociable temper, with which he set out on his career, and in whom the possession of power and grandeur had neither blunted the delicacy of his taste, nor diminished his sensibility to the enjoyments of nature and imagination. 'It is a relief,' says his translator, 'in the midst of the pompous coldness of Asiatic history, to find a king who can weep for days, and tell us that he wept, for the playmate of his boyhood.' He speaks with as much interest of his mother and female relations, as if he had never quitted

BOOK III.

their fireside; and his friends make almost as great a figure in the personal part of his narrative as he does himself. He repeats their sayings, records their accidents and illnesses, relates their adventures, and sometimes jokes on their eccentricities.*

"It would have been fortunate if Báber had left off wine sooner, for there seems good reason to think his indulgence in it tended to shorten his days. Many a drinking party is recorded in his Memoirs, with at least as much interest as his battles or negotiations; and, unsuitable as they are to his station, they are not the least agreeable scenes in Báber's history. The perfect ease and familiarity among the company makes one forget the prince in the man; and the temptations that generally lead to those excesses, — a shady wood, a hill with a fine prospect, or the idleness of a boat floating down a river, — together with the amusements with which they are accompanied, extemporary verses, recitations in Túrki and Persian, with sometimes a song, and often a contest of repartee, take away all the coarseness that might attach to such scenes of dissipation." †

No part of his character is more admirable than his uniform humanity and kindliness of disposition. If, in the course of his Memoirs, some cruel executions appear, they belong to the age, not to the man. The historians of his reign remark, that, whenever any either of his nobles or brothers had revolted, or entered into

* Elphinstone's History of India, vol. ii. pp. 117—119.

† Ibid. p. 120. His commentaries were translated into Persian, in the reign and by command of his grandson Akber, by Mírza Abdal Rahím, the son of the celebrated Biram Khan, in the thirty-fourth year of Akber's reign, as the court returned from an expedition to Káshmír and Kábul. There seems to have been a previous version by Sheikh Zein Kháni, who, Abdal Kádir tells us, translated them in an eloquent style. Perhaps the fragment of the paraphrastic translation already quoted may be a portion of that production. Tar. Bedáuni, f. 138. They have also been translated into English under the title of "Memoirs of Zehír-ed-dín Muhammed Báber, translated partly by John Leyden, M.D., partly by Wm. Erskine, Esq. Lond. 1826. 4to."

cabals against him, no sooner did they acknowledge their offence and return to their duty than, to use the words of Kháfi Khan, "contrary to the custom of the princes of Persia, Arabia, or India, he not only forgave them, but never retained towards them any feeling of resentment."

His person.

In stature, he is represented as having been above the middle size; he was of great vigour of body, fond of field sports and athletic exercises, a skilful archer, and an excellent swordsman. On numerous occasions he distinguished himself by his prowess; in several instances by engaging and slaying his adversary hand to hand, in single combat. Such, indeed, was his bodily strength, that he is said at times to have run along the battlements of a fort, having a man under each arm, and, though thus encumbered, to have kept on, leaping over the embrasures that he met in his way.*

His family.

He left four sons. 1. Muhammed Humáyun Mírza, who succeeded him; born 4 Zikada, A.H. 913 (April 5, A.D. 1508). 2. Kámrán Mírza. 3. Hindál Mírza; born Sefer, A.H. 925 (February, A.D. 1525); and, 4., Askeri Mírza. He had another son, Anwar, who died young, not long before his father.

He had several daughters, some of whom married the leading nobles of his court; their ages are not well ascertained. Among them were,

1. A daughter by his cousin Aisha Sultán Begum, who lived only a few days.

2. Maasúma Sultán Begum, by his cousin Maasúma Sultán Begum, who died in childbed of her. This daughter married Muhammed Zemán Mírza, the son of Badi-ez-zemán Mírza, and grandson of the great Sultan Husein Mírza Backra of Herát.

3. Gúlbadan Begum, a sister of Humáyun, who mar-

* Akbernáma; Tabak. Akberi, f. 143.

BOOK III.

ried Khwája Khizer, a Sultan or Khan of the race of the Moghul Sultans.

4. Gúlrang Begum, another of Humáyun's sisters, who married Núr-ed-dín Muhammed Mírza. Their daughter, Selima Sultán Begum, married first the celebrated Biram Khan, and, after his death, her cousin the Emperor Akber.

5. Gúlchahreh Begum, Humáyun's youngest full sister, who, in her brother's reign, married Abás Sultán, one of the Sultans of the Uzbeks.

6. Sheher-bánu Begum, who married her cousin Yádgár Násir Mírza, the son of Báber's youngest brother Násir Mírza. She seems to have had a son, Mírza Sanjer.

There were probably some others, and among them one whose name is unknown, that married the Syed Mehdi Khwája, who aspired to the kingdom on the Emperor's death.*

Dominions.

The dominions of Báber at the time of his death were very extensive, stretching from the river Amu to Behár. Beyond the Hindú-kúsh range he possessed Badakhshán, with Kundúz; and all the districts to the south of the

* We have not a very distinct account of the wives or haram of Báber. The following are, however, mentioned as of the number:

1. Aisha Sultán Begum, daughter of his uncle Sultán Ahmed Mírza of Samarkand. She was betrothed to him when he was but five (A. H. 893). He had by her a daughter who lived only a few days. Mem. p. 22.

2. Zeináb Sultán Begum, fifth daughter of Sultan Mahmúd Mírza of Hissár, his uncle. He married her when he took Kábul. Two or three years after, she died of the small-pox. Mem. p. 30.

3. Maasúma Sultán Begum, the youngest sister of his first wife, Aisha. Báber saw her in Khorásán, after her sister's death, asked her in marriage, and married her at Kábul. She had a daughter Maasúma, mentioned above, of whom she died in child-bed. Mem. pp. 22. 208.

4. Maham Begum, a relation of Sultan Husein Mirza of Herát. Akbernáma, f. 35. She was the mother of Humáyun Mírza, and of Gúlrang, Gúlbadan, and Gulchehreh Begums.

5. Dildár Aghácha Begum, the mother of Hindál Mírza. Akbernáma.

6. Ráika Begum appears as one of Báber's widows. She lived at Kábul. Jouher, p. 82.

7. A daughter of Malek-shah Mansúr, a chief of the Yusef-záis. Mem. p. 250.

Oxus, as low down as the borders of Balkh. To the south of the mountains he had the kingdoms of Kábul, Ghâzni, and Kandahár, and much of the mountainous country of the Hindú-kúsh and Ghúri or Parapamisan ranges, inhabited by Afgháns, Aimáks, and other tribes, some of them migratory; as well as the hilly and desert tracts to the south as far as the borders of Balúchistán, in all of which the tribes, though self-governed, acknowledged his authority. To the east of Ghazni and Kábul, below the passes, the low-lands of Jilálábád, Pesháwer, the Kohdáman, as well as Swád and Bajour, and in general the more extensive and cultivated plains or accessible country, had submitted; but, over a great portion of what we now denominate Afghánistán, especially the more inaccessible hills and secluded valleys, his sway was hardly admitted by the rude tribes that traversed them; and prudence was satisfied with some easy acknowledgment which was treated as tribute. Occasional inroads were made into the territories of such as were refractory, or offered a tempting booty in cattle or other property; they, on their part, infested the roads, plundered the merchants or caravans, drove off the flocks, or carried away the harvests of their neighbours in the lower grounds. In Upper and Lower Sind the khutba was read in his name; but, though his supremacy was acknowledged, he had little direct power. To the east of the Indus all the Penjáb, including Multán,—and to the south and east of the Satlej the rich provinces of Hindustán lying between that river and Behár on the one side, and the Himaláya mountains and the countries of the Rájputs and of Málwa on the other,—were subject to him; the western boundary being nearly a line marked by the fortresses of Biána, Rantambór, Gualiár, and Chándéri. On the south towards Bengal, the limits of his authority are not well defined. Though he possessed the greater part of Behár, some portions of it, especially the hilly or

BOOK III. wooded parts of the country, were still held by the remains of the Afgháns or by native chiefs. On the frontier of his empire, the Rájpút principalities, the shattered kingdom of Malwa, Bandélkand, and Bengal were still independent states; though the language of overweening superiority used by Indian authors, who treat even foreign war as a rebellion, might often betray an incautious reader into the erroneous conclusion, that they were subject to Delhi.

Their political situation.

There was little uniformity in the political situation of the different parts of this vast empire. Hardly any law could be regarded as universal, but that of the unrestrained power of the prince. Each kingdom, each province, each district, and (we may almost say) every village, was governed, in ordinary matters, by its peculiar customs. There were no regular courts of law spread over the kingdom for the administration of justice. Such disputes as occurred in the Hindu parts of the country were settled by the village or district officers of the vicinity, or by a kind of conventional arbitration, subject to an irregular appeal or complaint to the superior chief or governor. Where Musulmans were concerned, though the Kázi was nominally a judge, his active jurisdiction appears to have been chiefly confined, in practice, to cases of marriage and divorce, claims arising out of marriage contracts, and to questions considered as properly religious. All differences relating to land, where they were not settled by the village officers, were decided by the district authorities, the collectors, the zemindárs or jágírdárs. The higher officers of government exercised not only civil, but criminal jurisdiction, even in capital cases, with little form and under little restraint.

Taxes.

We have very imperfect means of knowing what were the taxes then levied. The chief revenue of the state has always in India been a kind of land-tax, which, in the fully settled and quiet provinces, was raised directly on the land; but where the country remained under its native chiefs, or was not fully subdued, was drawn by the Emperor in the shape of an annual tribute.

Landed property in India.

The rights of landed property were considerably different from those that prevail in the west. There were two separate and legal rights in the land; that of the ryot or cultivator, who held it by hereditary succession; and that of the government, which could justly claim a fixed share of the produce. Both of these were permanent.

We frequently see the officers of the army or government rewarded by jágírs or estates. But these jágírs were not like our territorial possessions or landed estates in Europe. Though the larger ones implied a jurisdiction both civil and criminal, very much resembling that enjoyed by the greater feudal chiefs during the middle ages, or by barons holding of the crown in Scotland down to the abolition of the heritable jurisdictions in the last century, yet their legal power over the land itself did not extend to a property in the soil, but to the exercise of all such rights as belonged to the government; for instance, that of levying the government's share of the produce, and the government taxes. Though the Musulman conquerors claimed, in theory, an absolute right of property in the soil, the right was in practice restrained, in conformity with the ancient law and usage, to some fixed portion of the produce collected from villages, or smaller zemíndárs, or separate ryots. Their exactions were indeed often oppressively increased, but the ryot was rarely removed; and he considered the land as his by right, subject to the payment of a certain share of the produce, varying according to circumstances. The jágírdár or holder of the jágír, was properly, in Musulman times, merely an officer of government, and removable at pleasure, except where the grant had been made hereditary. The term zemíndár, or landholder, is ap-

Zemíndárs and tributaries.

BOOK III. plied by Musulman writers not only to persons who held lands granted by the Crown, but even to the great Hindu chiefs and rajas, who had possessed their lands unrestricted from the remotest times; though the more powerful of these chiefs considered themselves as of right independent, and yielded obedience, not to a law, the existence of which they denied, but to fear or the pressure of a superior force. India, in reality, was rather a congeries of little states under one prince, than one regular and uniformly-governed kingdom. Many of the hill and frontier districts yielded little more than a nominal submission.

Revenue, Besides the land-tax, or government share in the produce, there were other sources of revenue. There was a duty levied, on the frontier, on goods imported by Customs, caravans or otherwise. The tamgha, or stamp, was the mark by which, on cattle and in goods, the payment of the duties was ascertained. There were transit duties on merchandise transported from one part of the country to another; there was a shop-tax, chiefly in towns; and, in those parts of the country where the Muhammedans had a confirmed and safe ascendency, Jezía. the jezía, or poll-tax, was levied on all who were not Musulmen.

Measurement of marches. It may be remarked that Báber was the first prince who ordered all his marches to be regularly measured, as well as his journeys and hunting excursions; an operation which must have tended to improve the geography of a country then very imperfectly surveyed. Post-houses. He also established a regular series of post-houses from Agra to Kábul, at the distance of about fifteen miles from each other; and stationed relays of six horses and proper officers at each.*

Men of letters. In spite of the migratory nature of his court, during the greater part of his reign, several of his nobles cul-

* Báber's Mem. pp. 393, 394.

tivated letters with success, and several authors of eminence flourished there. Of these, the best known, at least in the present day, is Mír-Khánd (the son of Khand-emir, the author of the Rozet-es-Sefá), himself the author of two historical works of uncommon merit, the Habíb-es-Syar, and the Kholásd-al-Akhbár, as well as of some other literary productions. Abulfazl has given a list of the chief men of letters who adorned his court; but most of them, whatever may have been their real merit, are now nearly forgotten.*

* Akbernáma, end of Báber's reign. For a masterly view of the state of the Hindus, see Elphinstone's History of India, vol. i., and for the internal state of India under the Musulman rulers, vol. ii. pp. 230—250.

APPENDICES.

APPENDIX A. (p. 8.)

THE TARTAR TRIBES — THEIR RACES AND ORIGIN.

APPENDIX A.

It is only of late years, and chiefly aided by the observations of modern travellers, that we have acquired any correct knowledge of the different races inhabiting the north of Asia, which were so long confounded under the general name of Tartars. The most valuable work on the subject is that of the late M. Abel-Remusat, "Recherches sur les Langues Tartares," (Paris, 1820, 4to.), a production of singular industry, ingenuity and talent, in which he investigates the origin of the various races, not only from the authority of the Chinese writers, but, as far as his means allowed, from the more certain and enduring evidence of the structure and genius of their own languages. The view of the divisions of these races, taken in the Introduction to the "Memoirs of Báber," (London, 1826, 4to.) and derived from a comparison of the historical accounts of the writers of Southern Asia, especially of Báber, with those of the earlier European travellers, corresponds nearly, in the most important respects, with that taken by M. Abel-Remusat, who pursued a more sure and solid course of inquiry. It is much to be regretted that that learned writer did not possess ampler materials for examining the different dialects of the Túrki, an opportunity which he could have turned to so good account, and which would have led him to many important conclusions in his own peculiar line of research; and it is still deeper subject of regret, that an early death removed him in the midst of his successful career.

The origin of the name of Tartar, or more properly Tátár, is involved in some obscurity. There were unluckily no general names, by which the different great races which inhabited the wide regions of the north of Asia were distinguished, either by themselves or by their neighbours. The numerous smaller

APPENDIX A.

tribes of which they consisted, had each its separate name. Tátár, as a general appellation, is unknown to the Tartar tribes of the present day. In early times it distinguished one of the tribes of that race which Europeans generally denominate as Mongol, that inhabited the country on their eastern frontier, round the Buyur Lake, next to the tribes of Tungus or Manchú extraction. This tribe, called Tatars, which had distinguished itself and acquired a name previous to the time of Chengíz Khan, insomuch that several other tribes were proud to be ranked under it and called by the same name, was subdued by that great conqueror, who belonged to a different tribe (properly called Mongols) of the same race. These ancient Mongols inhabited the high grounds at the upper course of the Kerula, the Onon, and the Tula. (D'Ohsson, Hist. des Mongols, tom. 1. pp. 7. 62. 67., and the curious note from Rashíd's Jámi-ut Towárikh, p. 680.) After his time the desire of being called Tátárs, after what was then a conquered and subordinate tribe, of course ceased; and the inferior tribes, and even men belonging to no tribe at all, were in like manner eager to be called Mongols, after the tribe now become the dominant one.

Chengíz Khan's grand army was a mixed assemblage of many tribes and races. We are told that the Tátár tribe, after it was conquered, having accompanied him in his invasion and formed the advance, was consequently the first part of his immense army that entered the territories which he invaded; and being thus the earliest portion of the invading force known to strangers, their name of Tátár was applied to all the numerous bands that followed; and in Europe or to Europeans, from its similarity in sound to Tartarus, and the detestation and horror which the invaders everywhere inspired, was readily perverted into that of Tartari or Tartars. (See Introduction to Báber, pp. 22 and 23., and authors there quoted.) The traveller Carpini (A. D. 1246) gives the name of Tartar as the peculiar distinctive title of the Su-Mongols, or river Mongols, in which he seems to be correct; and Rubriquis (A. D. 1254) speaks of it as rejected by Chengíz Khan's grandson, as being the appellation of an inferior tribe, he himself claiming to be of the race of pure Mongols. (Hakluyt's Voyages, vol. i. pp. 30. and 93.)

The whole confusion has arisen, as already observed, from the want of general names known to the tribes themselves, by which to mark their division into great classes, according to their extraction. Hence it has happened that different nations give them different appellations; and that, while Europeans in general designate the whole northern races as Tartars, from the name of one of the tribes of the race called Mongols, the writers of Persia, — whose country not only borders on that occupied by the tribes of Túrki race, but is itself traversed in all directions by the Iliáts, or tribes of wandering Túrks,—have adopted the name of Túrk as the general appellation, and extend the name of Túrkistán over a great part of the northern regions, comprehending Mongol and other tribes in its bounds.

In like manner, in the grand Genealogies of the Túrks and Persians deduced from Adam, which contain their theories of the connection and affiliation of nations, and which present the names of their earliest patriarchs as marking out the various races supposed to be derived from them, Túrk the son of Yáfith (Japhet) the son of Nuh (Noah) is made the progenitor of all the northern nations, from the Sea of China to the remotest west. Yáfith is made the chief of Nuh's sons, and his progeny are Túrk, Khozar, Saklab, Rús, Mansik, Chín, Kaman, Kaimál, and Mázikh; apparently the ancestor of the Túrks, Khozars, Slavonians, Russians, Ghaz or Turkomans, Chinese and Komans*, with two unknown tribes, one of which seems to have lived on the borders of China. Túrk is declared to be the chief of all Yáfith's sons, and his legitimate successor. From Túrk, after some generations, comes Alanja or Almchana Khan, generally called the fifth in descent from him, who had twin sons, Tátár and Moghul, between whom his dominions were divided. From the latter are descended the Moghul tribes, while the different Túrki tribes are descended from the former; and thus both Túrks and Moghuls are represented as having their descent from Túrk. The whole genealogy evidently betrays the hand of a Musulman and a Túrk, and is consequently of a comparatively late age. It is probably subsequent to the time of Taimur. (See Abulghází, Hist. Geneal. pt. I. c. 2 and 3.; Shajrat-ul-Atrák, pp. 22—29.; Kháfi Khan, &c.) The Shajrat-ul-Atrák, or "Genealogy of the Túrks," is a work which contains the genealogy of the Moghuls even more than the Túrks.

As an additional proof of the confusion that prevails on this subject, it may be noted that many European writers, especially the Russian, perhaps misled by the above genealogy of Tátár and Moghul, confine the name of Tátár to the Túrki race; though there can be little doubt that originally and properly it belonged to one of the tribes of Mongols.

The subject of the origin and changes of language has, of late years, excited much and curious research, which the importance

* One might be tempted to suppose that the Kamari were the Cimbri; but, from the habitation assigned to them in the Shajrat, they appear rather to have been the Kamans (Comani).

APPENDIX A.

of the subject well merits. If the wide and early conquests of the Tartar nations be considered, it should seem that a better knowledge than we yet possess of the structure of the Mongol and Túrki tongues and of their influence on the languages of the south, as well as of the degree in which they have themselves been modified by these languages, is a very essential part of the general inquiry. The Persian and Hindustáni languages have, in particular, felt their influence; especially in terms of government and war. One can hardly say in how early times the influence of the Túrki on the Persian began. M. Quatremére has already done much to facilitate our acquaintance with the ancient Túrki tongue; and still more is expected from his learned labours in the same department.

It may be here remarked that the Genealogical History of the Túrks by Abulgházi Beháder Khan of Khwárazm, is unfortunately very imperfectly translated. We owe it to some Swedish officers of Charles XII., prisoners at Tobolzk, who purchased the original manuscript, had it translated into Russian "et le traduisirent ensuite eux-mêmes en diverses autres langues." (Avertissement au Lecteur.) These languages were probably Swedish or French or German. A whole year, we are told, was required to reconcile the various translations. Having gone through this process, the only wonder is that their meritorious labour is so distinct and intelligible as it is. It is said to be translated from the Moghul language, but is probably written in the Túrki of Khwárazm. Abulgházi is made to say, "The reason why I have written this book in the *Moghul or Túrki* language, is that it is everywhere in use." No Moghul or Túrk would have confounded these two languages; and the reason given, which in Khwárazm is true of the Túrki, is not so of the Moghul. (Pt. II. c. v. f.) The names, as might have been expected, are more particularly corrupt.*

* Since writing these remarks I find that Count Nicolas de Romanzow has published the original at Casan, in Russia (1825, folio), and that the work is in the Túrki, not the Mongol tongue.

APPENDIX B. (p. 43.)

(The following Lists of the Khans of the Moghuls and of the Amírs of Káshgar, which D'Herbelot and Deguignes were not able to procure, are chiefly extracted from the Táríkhe-Reshídi of Mírza Haider, who was himself descended from these princes, and who collected the materials for their history, which he wrote with much ability and research.)

KHANS OF MOGHULISTAN.

APPENDIX B.

Isan-bugha Khan seems to have been called into Moghulistán from Máwerannaher, about A. H. 721, and to have reigned till A. H. 730.

An interregnum.

Toghlak-Taimur Khan, son of Isan-bugha, born about A. H. 730, came to the throne about A. H. 748, died A. H. 764.

Ilías Khwája Khan, his son, murdered by Kamreddín, A. H. 766.

Usurpation of Amír Kamreddín. It was against him that the expeditions of Mír Taimur into the Jetteh country were directed, A. H. 768—794.

Khizer Khwája Khan, son of Toghlak-Taimur, raised to the throne in A. H. 791, before Kamreddín's death. He reigned thirty years, and was succeeded by his son,

Muhammed Khan, who was succeeded by his son,

Shír Muhammed Khan, who was succeeded by his nephew, Sultan Weis Khan, the son of Shír-Kúli, the brother of Shír-Muhammed. Sultan Weis was killed, A. H. 832.

On his death there was a division among the Moghuls, some adhering to Yúnis Khan, the eldest son of Sultan Weis, others to Isan-bugha, the younger son.

Yúnis Khan, who was expelled A. H. 832, returned A. H. 860, and regained the western part of Moghulistán. Hostilities were maintained between the Eastern and Western Moghuls, till the death of his grand-nephew, Kepek Sultan, when he reigned without a rival.

In the latter part of his life, the remoter tribes of the desert, displeased with his fondness for towns, separated from him,

Isan-bugha Khan raised to the throne in A. H. 832, and through life supported by the Eastern Moghuls, died A. H. 866: succeeded by his son,

Dost Muhammed Khan, who ruled to the eastward; died A. H. 873.

Kepek Sultan Ughlan, his son, ruled for a time, about Terfán, where he was murdered.

APPENDIX B.

and acknowledged his second son, Sultan Ahmed, or Iláchi Khan, as their Khan—so that the empire was again severed in two in his lifetime; he died A. H. 892.

Sultan Mahmúd Khan, Yunis's eldest son, succeeded his father in Tashkend and the Western Tribes. He was defeated by Sheibáni Khan, in A. H. 908, and lost Táshkend and Seiram, and finally was put to death, A. H. 914.

Sultan Ahmed Khan, second son of Yúnis, governed the Eastern Moghuls, with Aksu, Terfán, &c. He was generally known as Iláchi Khan, the slaughtering Khan. He was bent upon making himself absolute in the desert, and destroyed the chiefs, and lessened the power of many of the tribes. Defeated by Sheibáni Khan, A. H. 908; he died of grief, A. H. 909.

The death of Sultan Ahmed Khan was followed by many civil wars and much anarchy in Moghulistán. His elder brother, Sultan Mahmúd, invaded his dominions from the west. Sultan Ahmed's numerous sons contended with one another. Several tribes, and among others the Kirghiz, separated from the great body. The anarchy and civil wars lasted some years. The country was overrun by Ababeker of Káshghar, by the Kalimáks and Kara Kaizáks. The whole tribes of Moghulistán never again united under one head. Two Khanships, however, and the confederation of the Kinghiz-Kaizáks, seem to have arisen out of the ruins of the Khanship of the Moghuls. Sultan Mansúr, the eldest son of Sultan Ahmed, established himself in Aksú, Terfán, &c., and a new Khanship rose in Káshghar.

Mansúr Khan, Iláchi Khan's eldest son, was acknowledged and ruled in Terfán, and the farthest East. He died, A. H. 950; having reigned two years along with his father, and forty-one more by himself; he was succeeded by his son,

Shah Khan.

Sultan Saíd Khan, third son of Iláchi Khan, in Rejeb, A. H. 920, eleven years after his father's death, seized Káshghar, and expelled Ababeker Mírza. He died, A. H. 939, Zilhajeh 19; and was succeeded by his son,

Abdal-Rashíd Khan, who died, A. H. 893; and was succeeded by his son,

Abdal Kerím.

Meanwhile, in the Desert of Moghulistán, the Kirghiz established themselves under Khans of their own; and in process of time formed a kind of federative junction with the Kaizák-Uzbeks, which has in some degree lasted to the present day, and has been called the "Three Hordes of the Kirghiz."

This union of the Old Kirghiz, who were Moghuls, with the Uzbek-Kaizák, who were Túrks, accounts for the difference of origin and language in the present Kirghiz, which has puzzled modern inquirers. See Description des Hordes des Kirghiz-Kaizáks par Alexis de Leochine. Paris, 1840; a curious and valuable work.

AMÍRS OF KÁSHGHAR CONTEMPORARY WITH THE KHANS OF MOGHULISTÁN.

Amír Tuluk, Ulusbegi of the Moghul Khans, contemporary with Isan-bugha Khan; succeeded by

Amír Yúlaji (sometimes called Bolaji) his brother; raised Toghlak-Taimur to the throne; succeeded by his son,

Amír Khodáidád, who reigned about ninety years, in Káshgar. He succeeded his father, probably soon after A. H. 748.

In his time Amír Kamreddín, his uncle, usurped the Khanship of the Moghuls; and it would seem for a period, the greater part of the Káshghar territory. The chronology of Mír Khodáidád's life is very uncertain. He was succeeded by

Mír Syed Ali, grandson of Khodáidád by his son Amír Syed Ahmed. He reigned about twenty-four years, A. H. 838—861, and was succeeded by his sons,

Sániz Mírza, in Yárkend, who expelled his brother from Káshghar, and reigned seven years, died A. H. 868.	Muhammed Haider Mírza in Káshgar, expelled by his brother.

Muhammed Haider Mírza, on his brother's death, succeeded. He is said to have reigned six years, with imperfect, and eighteen years with full authority. In A. H. 885, he was expelled by his nephew and stepson Ababeker.

Ababeker Mírza, son of Sániz, reigned in all forty-eight years. The years of his reign are probably reckoned from the date of his taking possession of Yárkend, about A. H. 873. He was finally defeated and expelled by Sultan Saíd Khan, the third son of Sultan Ahmed Khan (Iláchi Khan), who changed the dynasty. See Khans of Moghuls. Ababeker, one of the most cruel and odious tyrants recorded in history, died A. H. 820.

APPENDIX C. (p. 67.)

KHANS OF THE CHAGHATAI WHO REIGNED IN MÁWERANNAHER, FROM THE TIME OF KÁZAN KHAN.

Appendix C.

Kázán Khan was slain A. H. 747, in a revolt headed by Mír Kazaghan.

Dánishmend-cheh Khan, who was of the race of Oktái Khan, was raised to the throne, but put to death A. H. 749.

Baián-kuli Khan, of the race of Chaghatái, raised by Kazaghan, murdered by that chieftain's son, Mír Abdalla.

Taimur-shah Khan, a descendant of Chaghatái, raised by Mír Abdalla, slain in battle.

Adel Khan, of the same race, set up in Badakhshán, and afterwards murdered.

Toghlak-Taimur Khan and Elías Khwája Khan } invaded Máwerannaher from Moghulistan, and overran it from A. H. 761 to 766.

To restore internal order, the Amírs of the country elected as Grand-Khan,

Kábul-shah Khan, of the race of Chaghatái, put to death A. H. 771.

Syurghatmish Khan, of the race of Oktái, raised by Mír Taimur, succeeded by his son,

Sultan Mahmúd Khan, who took Bajazet.

Tuman Kutluk Ughlan, probably his son, appears to have succeeded him.

APPENDIX D. (p. 441.)

AMOUNT OF BÁBER'S REVENUES.

Appendix D.

Báber, in the account which he gives of Hindustán, after the battle of Panipat, observes: "The countries from Bhíra to Behár, which are now under my dominion, yield a revenue of fifty-two krors, as will appear from the particular and detailed statement. Of this amount, Perganas to the value of eight or nine krors, are in the possession of some Rais and Rajas, who from old times have been submissive, and have received these Perganas for the purpose of confirming them in their obedience." —Memoirs, p. 334.

APPENDIX D.

In none of the copies of the Memoirs which I possessed, while translating this portion of them, was this statement (correctly?) given; but, in a manuscript translation or paraphrase of parts of Báber's Commentaries, now in my possession, I find this defect supplied. I subjoin the statement as there contained.

REVENUE OF THE PROVINCES OF THE EMPIRE.

		Tankas.
1.	The Sirkár on the other side of the Satlej, Bhíra, Lahúr, Siálkót, Dibálpúr, &c.	36,315,989
2.	Sirhend and its dependencies	12,931,985
3.	Hissár-Firúza	13,075,104
4.	The capital (Dár-ul-Mulk) Delhi, in the (Mián) Doab	36,950,254
5.	Mewát (not included in Iskander's Revenue-Roll (*der mián Iskandra*)	16,981,000
6.	Biána	14,414,930
7.	Agra	2,976,919
8.	Mián e Viláet	29,119,000
9.	Guáliar	22,357,450
10.	Kalpi, Sehindeh (?) &c.	42,855,950
11.	Kanáuj	13,063,358
12.	Sambala	13,844,000
13.	Laknáu and Baksar (Buxar?)	13,982,433
14.	Khairábád	1,265,000
15.	Oud and Behráich	11,721,369
16.	Juánpúr	40,088,333
17.	Karra and Mánikpúr	16,327,280
18.	Behár	40,560,000
19.	Sirwár	15,517,506½
20.	Sárán	11,018,679
21.	Chipáran	19,086,609
22.	Gondleh	4,330,300
23.	Tirhút. Tribute (Khidmatána) of the Tirhúti Raja 250,000 silver Tankas (tankeh-núkreh) and 2,750,000 black (or copper) tankas (tankeh siáh).	
24.	Rantanbór from Boli, Milarneh, and Chatsu (Q)	2,000,009
25.	Nagór	13,000,000
26.	Raja Bikermájít from Rantbor.	
27.	Raja Kalinjeri.	
28.	Raja Barsang-deo.	
29.	Raja Bikam-deo.	

APPENDIX D.

	Tankas.
30. Raja Bikam-chand.	
The amount of these sums, some of which are probably erroneous, would give - - -	443,783,457½
If the tankas of account are black tankas, add for Tirhút - - - - -	2,750,000
	446,533,457½

Besides 250,000 silver tankas of Tirhút Khidmatána, and the tribute of the various Rajas left blank.

The revenues of Agra, and perhaps of Khairábád, seem to be stated low, perhaps by a clerical error. The chief revenue of Delhi was perhaps derived from possessions in the Doáb. I know not if Mián-e-Viláet, is to be understood of any province in the Doáb. Laknáu and Baksír are classed together. The latter is unknown to me (Buxar?). Mewát is said not to have been included in Iskander (*keh der mián e Iskander dákhil nabúdeh*), by which I understand Sultan Sekander Lodi's revenue-roll.

The amount of the revenue given is nearly forty-five krors; the rest, amounting to about seven krors more, was probably made up of tribute.

The amount of this revenue, of fifty-two krors, if considered as represented in single dams, according to the mode of computation in Akber's reign, would be 1,300,000*l.*; if in double dams, according to the calculation of Ferishta, 2,600,000*l.*; if we adopted the mode of reckoning suggested by the facts stated by Mírza Haider, it would be 4,212,000*l.*; while, if we take the tanga at 7½*d.*, which is somewhat below the lowest rate it reached in the reign of Sultan Muhammed Toghlak, the amount would be 16,250,000*l.*; but, if at its full and proper value of a rupee, 52,000,000*l.* Every thing considered, I should incline to consider 4,212,000*l*, as the amount of Báber's nominal revenue; a very large sum, when the working of the American mines had not yet produced its full effect.

It is not easy to find any unobjectionable point of comparison. The statements of Akber's revenue given in the translation of the Ayín Akberi, have not been generalised, and are far from being always distinct.

In Catron's Histoire de l'Empire du Mogol, Paris, 1715, 4to. vol. i. p. 264., a statement of the revenue of Hindustán, &c., in Aurengzeb's time is given, probably from the papers of Manucci the Venetian traveller, and said to be drawn from the Archives of the Empire. It amounts in all to 38.71.94.000 rs. (p. 266.) But the greater part consists of the provinces of Bengal, Málwa

Gujrát, the Dekhan, &c.; so that the provinces acquired by Báber are but a small part. They are stated thus:— APPENDIX D.

				Rupees.
Delhi, 8 sirkars,	220 perganas	-	-	1.25.50.000
Agra, 14 „	278 „	-	-	2.22.03.550
Lahór, 5 „	314 „	-	-	2.35.05.000
Behár, 8 „	245 „	-	-	1.21.50.000
Illavás and dependencies -	-	-	-	77.38.000
				7.81.46.550

The revenue of the Old Provinces is therefore only seven krors, eighty-one laks, forty-six thousand five hundred and fifty rupees, or 7,814,655*l.* sterling. Catron adds, that the other taxes and duties equal or exceed the land-revenue. This does not make the amount of Báber's revenue improbable.

APPENDIX E. (p. 411.)

BABER'S MONEY OF ACCOUNT.

It is by no means easy to ascertain the intrinsic value of the coins and monies of account used at different periods of history. The usual tendency in all countries, except under very enlightened governments, is for the value of the current coin to become less and less; partly by waste from ordinary tear and wear, but chiefly from repeated debasements in the coin itself, from ill-judged financial operations affecting the mint, and diminishing the intrinsic value, but preserving the denomination of the currency. APPENDIX E.

Mr. Elphinstone observes, that the earlier Musulman princes used the dinár and the dirhim like the khalifs; that these coins were succeeded in India by tankas, divided into jitals or dams, equal to about the peise; and that Shír Shah changed the name of tanka to that of rupeia, or rupee, which was adopted by Akber in his coinage. (Hist. of India, vol. ii. p. 244.)

The state of the circulating medium at the period when Báber entered India is not very distinctly known. Báber does not in general mention the denomination of Indian coin by

APPENDIX E.

which he reckons, that being sufficiently fixed and known by universal use. In converting his sums into English money, in the notes to the translation of his Memoirs, I fear that I may have estimated them too low, having assumed that the Treasury Accounts were kept in dams, forty to the rupee. The tanka was the current coin in his time.

The silver tanka, in the reign of Sultan Aláeddín Khilji, was a tola in weight, and was equal to fifty jitals or peisas. (Briggs's Ferishta, vol. i. p. 360.) It was probably very nearly equal to Akber's rupee, or about two shillings.

In the prodigal reign of Sultan Muhammed Toghlak Shah, the coin was so much debased that the tanka was exchanged for only sixteen peisas (Ibid. p. 410.); less than a third of the proper standard, or about 7¾*d.* sterling, if we compute by jitals.

Ferishta, in relating the circumstances mentioned in the text, states that Báber gave Humáyun a donation of 350,000 rupees. (Ferishta, vol. ii. p. 48.) Now, the sum issued from the Treasury being 70 laks or 7,000,000 of some coin or denomination of money, this would make Báber's money of account equal to 2 dams only, or a double dam, supposing Ferishta to reckon by the Akberi rupee of 40 dams, as seems probable. The value of the donation to Húmáyun would thus be about 35,000*l.* sterling.

The Kholáset-ul-Akbár (f. 246.) makes the same donation seven laks of Sekanderi tankas. The value of the Sekanderi rupee I do not know, but if Ferishta's reckoning of 3½ laks of rupees be correct, this would make the Sekanderi tanka equal to half a rupee, and to ten pieces of the money used in account, or double dams.

Mírza Haider tells us (Tar. Reshídi, f. 365.) that his allowances, in the high situation which he filled at Lahúr, were at first 15 laks, but were afterwards increased to 50 laks; and adds, that one lak of Hindustán is equal to 20,000 shahrukhis. This was in Humáyun's reign, when Kámrán retook Kandahár, in A. H. 944. Now, at this rate, each shahrukhi is exactly equal to five pieces of the money of account of the time.

What was the value of the shahrukhi? It was a coin, the value of which probably remained uniform, as it is not likely that there were new coinages of it. Abulfazl tells us, that 8 laks of shahrukhis were equivalent to 1 kror, 28 laks of dams; so that 8 shahrukhis represented 128 dams, and 1 shahrukhi 16 dams.

Thus we have the shahrukhi represented by Mírza Haider as equal to five pieces of the money of account, and by Abulfazl as equal to sixteen pieces of that money; and the shahrukhi being the same, the money of account in Báber's time is rather more than three times more valuable than in Akber's. Appendix E.

Now, if the rupee of Akber be taken at 2*s.*, and the shahrukhi be considered as equal to 16 dams of Akber, or rather better than 9½*d.*, say 9¾*d.*, the lak of Humáyun (or 20,000 shahrukhis) would be equal to nearly 810*l.* sterling, and Báber's lak was probably the same.

One difficulty occurs, that, in several instances in Báber's Memoirs, payments are expressly stated to be made in tankas; and, in a Persian translation or paraphrase in my possession of a part of Báber's Commentaries, by I know not what author, but evidently old, all the large payments, and that now in question among the rest, are expressed as made in tankas, f. 67. v.*

If we take the value of the tanka, when Báber entered India, at that of the adulterated tanka of Toghlak Shah, or 7½*d.*, perhaps the lowest known in India, the lak would be 3125*l.*; and the donation to Humáyun of 70 laks would amount to 218,750*l.* which seems too high.

In the statement of the revenue of Hindustán contained in the same translation, and given p. 409. in the article of Tirhút, there is stated to be paid of khidmatána (tribute) by the Raja 2 laks and 50,000 tanke nukreh (silver tankas), and 27 laks 50,000 tanke siáh, (black or copper tankas). There would seem, therefore, to have been both silver and copper tankas. May not these black tankas have corresponded to the dams in which the treasury accounts were afterwards kept; or, perhaps, with the farther difference of the substitution of 40 dams for 50 jitals?

On the whole, if we suppose that in Báber's time the money of account was at 40 dams to the rupee, the lak would be of the value of 250*l.* sterling; if we take Ferishta's reckoning of double dams, it would be worth 500*l.*; and, if we follow the reckoning of Mírza Haider, as above deduced, something near 810*l.* We evidently cannot adopt even the most depreciated tanka of Toghlak-shah, which would make it about 3125*l.*; and, still less, the lak of rupees which succeeded tankas, and would bring it to 10,000*l.* sterling. I confess, I incline most to the lak of Mírza Haider, as being deduced from data given by a contemporary. The question, however, deserves to be decided on surer principles, and may perhaps be settled satisfactorily by an examination of some collection of older Indian coins.

* A present of seventy thousand tangs or tankas is made to Kuchum Khan's ambassador. Báber's Mem. p. 399.

APPENDIX E.

It may be added, that the word tanka or tanga is of Chaghatái Túrki origin, being derived from *tang*, which in that language means *white*; having the same origin as the asper (from *aspros*, white) of the modern Greeks, the *Ak-chia* of the Osmanli Turks, the *Tátari* of the Mingrelians, and many other monies, all originally signifying *white*. (Josafa Barbaro in Ramusio, vol. ii. p. 96.) The Tengi of Khwárazm would appear to have been worth the fourth of a crown. (Astley's Voyages, vol. iv. p. 484.) At the present day in Persia, the tanga seems to be worth only 6*d*. (J. B. Fraser's Travels in Persia, p. 81.)

INDEX

TO

THE FIRST VOLUME.

Ababeker, of Káshghar, *56*. His conquest of Káshghar, *57*. Defeats Yúnis Khan, *57*. Invades Ferghána, 90. Concludes a peace, and retires, 90. Seizes part of Badakhshán, 287. Besieges Andeján, 317. Defeated by Sultan Saíd, 318. Expelled from Káshghar, 332.

Ab-burden, Báber's description of, 164. He cuts verses on the rock at, 164.

Abdal Ali Terkhán (Mír), of Bokhára, protects Sheibáni, 134. His death, 137.

Abdal-azíz (Mír), appointed by Báber to Lahúr, 420. Defeated by the Rájpúts, *465*. His part in the battle of Kanwa, 470.

Abdal-azíz Sultan, son of Obeid Khan, left in charge of Asterábád, 489. Defeats the Persians near Bostám, 489.

Abdal Fitáh, son of Mír Fázil, his command in Sind, 384. His death, 384.

Abdal-Kadús (Amír), slays Sheikh Jemál-ed-dín, *55*. Releases Yúnis Khan, *55*.

Abdal-rizák Mírza, son of Ulugh Beg Mírza, king of Kábul, 210. Expelled by Mokim Arghún, 210. 216. Attempts to regain his kingdom, 216. Submits to Báber, 223. Joins Báber on his expedition to Kandahár, 2?7. Left by Báber in Kábul, 280. Receives Nangenhár, 282. Plan to restore him to the throne of Kábul, 284. Put to death, 286.

Abel Remusat, M., notice of his "Recherches sur les Langues Tartares," 533.

Abu Ali Hasan, ibn Ali, ibn Sina, the Avicenna of the West, 83, *note*.

Abul Baká (Mír), his remark on Humáyun's illness, 513.

Abul-fazl, his account of the battle at Kul-málek, 323. His account of the intrigue in favour of Mehdi Khwája, *515*.

Abulgházi Behádor Khan, prince of Khwárazm, his Genealogical History in Túrki, 81. *536*.

Abulkhair Khan, Khan of the Uzbeks, 29. His vigorous reign, 29. Places Abusaíd Mírza on the throne of Samarkand, 29. Marries a daughter of Ulugh Beg Mírza, 29. Offends his chieftains, 29. Is defeated by the Kalimáks, 30, *note*. Is defeated by the chiefs of Kipchák, and slain, 30.

Abul Makáram (Khwája), visits Báber, 114. His confidant, 167. 169. Is put to death by Sheibáni, 186.

Abusaíd Mírza, Sultan of Samarkand, 47. Defeats Isanbugha, 47. Resides at Herát, 48. Sets up Yúnis Khan, 49. His treaty with Yúnis Khan, 50. Bestows on him the territory of Masíkhi, 52. His disastrous expedition into Irák, 53. 74. His death, 53. 74.

Adínapúr (now Jelálábád), Báber arrives at, 223. Báber halts there, 281.

Afgháns (the), their original seat, 219. Their predatory habits near Kábul, 280. Dispersed by Báber, 281. The Mehmend tribe defeated by Báber, 284. The Yusef-záis make a convention with Báber, 338. Báber's periodical inroads, 338, 339, *note*. Their power at Delhi under the Lodis, 406. Their chiefs resolve to divide the empire, 407. Their union in the Penjáb, 424. Defeated by Chin-Taimur, 433. Defeated under Sultan Ibráhím at Panipat, 437. Their apprehensions from Báber's conquest, 443. Driven by Humáyun to Bengal, under Násir Khan, 450. Their confederacy in the West, 451. Their success in the Doáb, 469. Defeated with the Rájpúts at

Kanwa, 473. Their revolt in the East, 485. Engaged by Báber on the Ganges, 486. Their retreat, 487. Pursued and defeated by Chín-Taimur, 487.

Agha Rustam Roz-efzun, prince of Mazenderán, anecdote of, 304.

Agra occupied by Báber, 437. He builds a palace there, 451.

Ahmed, the bekáwal or taster, his attempt to poison Báber, 455. Is put to death, 456.

Ahmed (or Muhammed) ben Kothair, Al-Ferghání, a celebrated astronomer, 83, *note*.

Ahmed Kásim, nephew of Khosrou Shah, 202. Driven from his government of Kahmerd, 214. Is slain, 227.

Ahmed Kásim Kohbur (Mír), confidential officer of Báber, 247. Defends Kábul, 250. Appointed to Táshkend, 319. Driven out by the Uzbeks, 330. Rebels against Báber, 335. Defeated, 335.

Ahmed Keráwal (Sultan), joins Báber, 122.

Ahmed Khan (Sultan), "the younger Khan," son of Yúnis Khan, secedes from his father, 61. Becomes Khan of Moghulistán, 63. His character, 65. Defeats the Kalimáks, 66. Surnamed "Ilachi Khan," 66. His energetic reign, 66. Proceeds to meet his brother Sultan Mahmúd Khan, 168. His meeting with Báber, 168. And with his brother, 169. Taken prisoner by Sheibáni, 184. Released, 185. Returns to the Desert, 190. Dies, 190.

Ahmed Khan, of Mehwát, holds Mehroli and Mewát, 405.

Ahmed Khan Lodi, quells a revolt of Sultan Ibráhím's nobles, 411.

Ahmed Mírza (Sultan), son of Abusaíd, Sultan of Samarkand and Bokhára, 53. 74. His quarrels with his brother Umersheikh, 58. Peace between them dictated by Nasíreddín Obeidulla, 62. Defeated by Sultan Mahmúd Khan, 63. 136. Invades Ferghána, 87. Makes peace with Báber, 89. Dies, 89.

Ahmed Shah, left in charge of Chándéri, 484.

Ahmed Sultan Sefi, commands the Persian auxiliaries sent to Báber, 315.

Ahmed Tambol (Sultan). See Tambol.

Aimáks (the), a tribe of Moghuls, 14. Account of their origin, 221, *note*. They join Báber, 212. Their country, 220. Driven out of Lamghán, 227. Acknowledge Báber's authority, 239.

Ais-doulat Begum, grandmother of Báber, 51. Her lineage and character, 51, *note*. Instance of her spirited conduct, 55. Heads a party against Hasan Yákúb, 91. Notice of her daughters, 248.

Aisha Sultan Begum, her marriage with Báber, 128. 526, *note*.

Ak-Orda (the White Horde), 26.

Ak-Sakáls (Greybeards), 11.

Akhsi (or Akhsíkat), district and fort of, besieged by Sultan Mahmúd Khan, 89. Siege abandoned, 90. Demanded from Báber by Sultan Mahmúd Khan, and by Jehángír, 107. Surrendered to Ibráhím Saru, 117. The citadel defended by Uzun Hassan, 117. Surrendered to Báber, 118. Attacked by the "elder" and "younger" khans, 170. Báber received there, 174.

Aksu, battle of, 52.

Alá-ed-dín (Sultan) of Bengal, his convention with Sultan Sekander of Delhi, 406.

Alá-ed-dín Lodi (Sultan), or Alim Khan, son of Sultan Behlúl, deprived of Rabéri, 423. Receives Etáwa, 423. Aspires to the throne of Delhi, 412. Flies to Báber, and solicits his aid, 412. 418. Receives Dibálpúr, 420. Defeated by Doulat Khan, 421. Flies to Kábul, 421. His relationship to Sultan Ibráhím Lodi, 421, *note*. Engages Báber in an expedition to reduce Delhi, 422. His treaty with Báber, 423. Hastens to Lahúr, 424. Joined by Doulat Khan, 424. Is acknowledged by Doulat Khan as his sovereign, 424. Marches to Delhi, 425. Defeated by Sultan Ibráhím, 426. Flies to the Doáb, 426. Retreats to the Penjáb, 427. Takes shelter in Kinkúteh, 430. Escapes, and joins Gházi Khan, 430. Flies to Báber, who receives him with honour, 431. His future history, 431. Confined in Kila-Zefer, 431. Finds refuge at the Court of Behåder Shah of Gujrát, 431.

Alankáwa, ancestress of Chengíz Khan, and of Taimur, 23. 69. Her miraculous conception, 23.

Alatágh mountains, separate Ferghána from Kashgar and Tartary, 79.

Alengiz Núián, his compact with Dáwa Chichan, 71.

Al-Fárábi, a philosopher, 83, *note*.

Ali (Amír Sultan), brother of Zúlnún, made governor of Sistán, 273.

Ali Dost Taghái, governor of Andeján, 109. Surrenders it to Jehángír, 110. Invites Báber to Marghinán, 115. Makes peace between Báber and Jehángír, 125. Becomes Báber's prime minister, 127. His character and conduct, 127. His resignation, 132.
Ali Khalífa. See Nizám-ed-dín.
Ali Khan Fermuli, joins Báber, 446.
Ali Khan Istijlu, a commander of the Persian auxiliaries sent to Báber, 315.
Ali Mírza (Sultan), son of Sultan Mahmúd Mírza, retires from Uratippa, 94. Proclaimed King of Samarkand, 97. Made captive by Bayesanghar, and ordered to be blinded, 99. Escapes unhurt to Bokhára, 99. Defeats his brother Bayesanghar 99. Invades Samarkand, 100. His alliance with Báber, 100. Retains Samarkand, Bokhára, and the neighbouring districts, 105. Kept in restraint by his Terkhán nobles, 128. Calls in Sheibáni, 140. Is put to death, 141.
Ali Shír Núwai (Mír or Amír), a distinguished Túrki noble and poet, 81. Placed in charge of Herát, 270. Makes peace between Sultan Husein and his son, 271. His determined defence of Herát, 272.
Alim Khan. See Alá-ed-dín Lodi.
Alim Khan, of Kalpi, joins the confederacy against Báber, 442. Deserts Báber, 469.
Alim Khan, of Tehenger, offers to procure the surrender of Biána, 452.
Altamgha (the) of Tumana Khan, 70.
Alur, or Alwer, capital of Mewát, built and fortified by Hasan Khan, 475.
Amráni (Amír), brother of the Khankar, slain, 399.
Andeján, district and fort of, capital of Ferghána, 80. Taken by Isanbugha Khan, 48. Báber acknowledged there, 86. Besieged by Jehángír, 109. Its surrender, 110. Besieged by the "elder" and "younger" khans, 174. Siege abandoned, 175. Invaded by Sheibáni, 187. And taken, 189. Bestowed on Jani Beg, 189. 309. The Uzbeks driven out, 311. Given to Sultan Saíd Khan, 312. Besieged by Ababeker, 317. Threatened by the Uzbeks, 330.
Andekhúd, taken by Sheibáni, 258.
Angora, battle of, 68.
Ansaris (the), a race descended from, govern Sind, 358.
Anwar, or Alwer, son of Báber, dies, 512. 525.
Architecture, Báber's fondness for, 520. His excavations at Biserlureh, 520, *note.*
Arghúns (the), derive descent from a son of Chengís, 262. See Zúlnún, Shah Shujáa, Muhammed Mokím, Shah Hasan.
Arghún Khan, 25.
Arkhián, fortress of, Támbol retires to it, 125.
Artillery used by Báber, at Panipat, 436., at Kanwa, 470., at Kanáuj, 486.
Asfendek, castle of, Báber's residence there, 146.
Asfera, range of hills separating Ferghána from Karatigin, 79.
Asfera, district of Ferghána, 80. Fort of, suprised by Ibráhím Saru, and retaken by Báber, 92.
Askeri Mirza, son of Báber, 525. His command in the East, 494, 495. Joins Báber in Bengal, 503-505.
Asterábád, taken by the Uzbeks, 489. Abandoned and retaken, 489. Committed to Renish Beháder, 489.
Astrakhan, the Khanship of, formed, 27.
Astronomical tables of Ulugh Beg Mírza, 72. 105.
Attok, Báber crosses the Indus above, 413.
Avicenna of the West, 83, *note.*
Ayub Begchik (Mír), conspires against Báber, 327.
Azerbáiján, conquered by Shah Ismáel, of Persia, 6.
Azím Humáyún Sirwáni, besieges Gwaliar, 409. Joins Jilál Khan, 409. Deserts him, 409. Meaning of his name, 450, *note.*

Baba Ahmed, son of Mír Fázil, sent to oppose the Balúches, 382. Defeats them, 384. Is slain, 384.
Bába Bishágheri (Múlla), 247. Defends the fort of Kábul, 250. Joins the rebellion against Báber, 335. Deserts Humáyun, 458. Invades Báber's northern dominions, 458.
Baba Seirámi, his pursuit of Báber, 178.
Bába Sheikh, his desertion to the Uzbeks, 458. Invades Báber's northern dominions, 458. Slain by Mír Hameh, 459.
Baba Sultan, grandson of the younger Khan, with Báber at Kábul, 256.
Baban Jilwáni (Malek) joins Alim Khan, 425. Seeks shelter in the Doáb, 427. Joins Báber, 432. Withdraws from him, 447. Besieges Sambhal, 447. Routed, 448. Occupies

Laknáu, 477. Abandons it, 477. Is joined by Sheikh Bayezíd, 485. Driven to Bandélkand, 506.

Báber, Zehír-ed-dín Muhammed, son of Umersheikh Mírza, his birth and parentage, 78. Interpretation of his name, 79, *note*. His father's death, 85. His accession, 86. His territory invaded by his uncle Sultan Ahmed, 87. Andeján threatened, 87. Failure of the expedition, 88. Pacification, 89. Invasion of Sultan Mahmúd, 89. And of Ababeker, 90. His enemies expelled, 91. Hasan Yákúb, his protector, conspires against him, 91. Báber recovers the fort of Asfera, 92. And Khojend, 93. Visits Sultan Mahmúd, 93. Plunders the Jagrak tribe, 93. Invades Uratippa, 94. Accepts the services of the Uzbek and Moghul chiefs, 95. Determines to attack Samarkand, 99. His alliance with Sultan Ali Mírza, 100. Their interview in the river Kohik, 100. Deserted by his Uzbeks, 100. Blockades Samarkand, 101. Operations of the siege, 102. He huts his army, 103. Marches out to face Sheibáni, 103. Occupies Samarkand, 105. Discontent of his troops, 106. Their desertion, 107. His bother Jehángír claims from him Andeján and Akhsi, 107. His illness at Samarkand, 110. He abandons Samarkand, 110. His expedition to Andeján, 110. Its failure, 110. His distress, 111. Applies for succour to his uncle Sultan Mahmúd, 111. Who fails him, 112. Proceeds to Khojend, 112. His unsuccessful attempt to regain Samarkand, 113. He visits Sultan Mahmúd, 113. Captures the fort of Násukh, and returns to Khojend, 113. Removes to Bishágher, 114. Driven out by Sultan Ali, 114. Goes to the Iláks, 114. His interview with Khwája Abul Makáram, 114. Invited to Marghinán, 115. His entry into the city, 116. Besieged by Jehángír's party, 116. Recovers Andeján, 118. Takes Akhsi, 118. His imprudence, 119. Revolt of the Moghuls, 120. They defeat his army under Kásim Beg, 120. His defence of Andeján, 121. Marches to Ush, 121. Joined by Sultan Ahmed Keráwal, 122. Defeats Támbol at Khubán, 123. Winter campaign at Suárási, 123. Returns to Andeján, 123. His campaign of Kásán, 124. He makes peace with Jehángír and Támbol, 126. Returns to Andeján, 126. Kept in restraint by his minister Ali Dost Taghái, 127. Marries Aisha Sultán Begum, 128. Engages the services of Muhammed Mazíd Terkhán, 129. Marches against Samarkand, 129. Encamps at Yuret-khan, 131. Intrigues with Khwája Yahía, 132. Fails in his attempt to seize the city, 132. Flies towards Kesh on Sheibáni's approach, 141. Crosses the hills with difficulty to Kán, 143. Approaches Samarkand, 144. Fails to surprise Robát-Khwája, 144. Joined by Kamber Ali, 144. Fails in his attempt to surprise Samarkand, 145. His state of mind, 146. Succeeds in a second attempt, 147. Receives the submission of the surrounding provinces, 149. His difficulties, 150. Engages Sheibáni on the Kohik, 151. Is defeated, 152. Defends Samarkand, 153. Capitulates, after a siege of five months, 157. His account of his flight from Samarkand, 158. Proceeds to Uratippa, 159. His residence at Dekhat, 160. Comparison between him and Henri Quatre, 162. Sends presents to Jehángír and Támbol, 162. His grief on the death of Nevián Gokultásh, 163. His residence at Masíkhi, 164. His verses cut on the rock at Ab-burden, 164. Visited by the poet Múlla Hajári, 164. Visits his uncle at Táshkend, 165. Composes his first ode, 166. His life at Táshkend, 166. Schemes for the future, 167. Meets his uncle "the younger Khan," 168. Surprises and takes Ush, 171. Advances to Andeján, 171. Is surprised by Támbol, 172. His wound, and narrow escape, 172. He joins the Khans, 173. Is received into Akhsi, 174. Driven from Akhsi, 177. His flight, 177. He is overtaken, 179. Escapes, and joins the Khans, 183. His flight on their defeat, 184. He wanders as a fugitive in Andeján, 189. Sets out for Khorásán, 190. Enters the Hissár territory, 194. His motley band of attendants, 195. He crosses the Amu, 202. Is joined by Báki Cheghániáni, 202. And by many of Khosrou's dependents, 203. 207. Receives Khosrou's submission, 208. Sets out for Kábul, 211. First sees the star Soheil (Canopus), 211. Routs and takes prisoner Shirkeh Arghún, 211. Is joined by other tribes, whom he reduces to order, 212. Encamps near

Kábul, 213. Joined by his family, 213. Besieges Kábul, 214. Its surrender, 216. His repression of pillage, 217. Becomes King of Kábul and Ghazni, 217. His account of Kábul, 217. Rewards his followers, 222. Submission of Abdal-Rizák, 223. Báber's expedition to the Indus, 223. Arrives at Jelálábád, 223. His surprise at the climate and appearance of the country, 223. Takes a plundering circuit, and returns to Kábul, 224. Báki's plot against him, 225. Invades Kandahár, 229. Takes Kelát, but abandons it, 229. Báki's intrigues and resignation, 230. Peace in Kábul, 233. Báber receives Muhammed Husein Doghlat, 237. Invited by Sultan Husein, 238. Sets out from Kábul, 239. Hears of the death of Sultan Husein, 239. Defeats a body of Uzbeks at Sáf, 239. Acknowledged by the Aimáks, 239. Waited on by Jehángír, 240. Reaches the Murgháb, 240. Royally entertained in Khorásán, 240. Visits Herát, 242. Returns to Kábul, 243. Reaches the Zírín Pass, 244. Danger from the severity of the cold, 245. Reaches Yeke-Auleng, 246. Passes Bamián, 246. Plunders the Túrkomán Hazáras, 246. Muhammed Husein Mírza placed in charge of Kábul, during his absence, 247. Report spread of Báber's imprisonment in Khorásán, 248. Rebellion of Shah Begum and Muhammed Husein, 249. Báber hastens towards Kábul, 250. Communicates with the garrison, 250. Surprises and disperses the rebels, 252. His clemency, 252. His reflections on the conduct of the rebels, 254–257. Takes from his chiefs a bond of allegiance and fidelity, 258. Invited by Zúlnún's sons, 276. Marches to Kandahár, 276. Levies a contribution from an Indian caravan, 277. His aversion to plunder, 277. Defeats the Arghúns at the battle of Kandahár, 278. Takes the city, 278. Divides the rich spoil among his followers, 278. Bestows Kandahár on Násir Mírza, 279. Alarmed at the power of Sheibáni, 279. Leaves Kábul, and marches for India, 280. Proceeds by Khurd-Kábul and Jagdálik, 280. Defeats the Afghán robbers, 281. Halts before Adínapúr (now Jelálábád), 281. Returns to Kábul, 282. Assumes the title of "Padshah," 282. Conspiracy of his Moghuls, 283. His valour, 285. Quells the revolt, 286. His reception of Haider Mírza, 291. His amiable character described by Haider Mírza, and by Sultan Saíd, 294. Receives intelligence of the battle of Merv, 306. Anecdote of his kindness to Haider Mírza, 306, *note*. Marches to Kunduz, 306. Receives an embassy from Shah Ismael, of Persia, 308. Sends an embassy to the Shah, 309. Treachery of Báber's Moghuls, 311. His convention with Shah Ismael, 312. Invades Hissár, 312. Retreats before the Uzbeks, 312. Totally defeats the Uzbeks, 314. Joined by Persian auxiliaries, 315. Takes Bokhára and Samarkand, 315. Received triumphally at Samarkand, 316. Proclaimed King, 316. Dismisses his Persian auxiliaries, 316. Recovers Máwerannaher, 318. Extent of his dominions, 319. Adopts the Persian dress and cap, 319. Offends the Sunnis of Máwerannaher, 320. Decline of his popularity, 321. Invaded by the Uzbeks, 322. Defeated by them at Kúl-malek, 322. Abandons Samarkand, 322. Defends Hissár, 323. Joined by Amír Nijm Sáni, minister of Shah Ismael, 323. Takes Khozar, 324. Sacks Karshi, 324. Totally defeated by the Uzbeks at Ghazhdewán, 325. Flies to Hissár, 325. Attacked by his rebel Moghuls, 327. Escapes with difficulty into the fort of Hissár, 327. Retires to Kunduz, 328. Returns to Kábul, 329. Abandons all hope of regaining his native country, 332. Quells a rebellion of the Moghuls, 335. Subdues the hill tribes, 336. Takes Bajour, 337. Puts the male inhabitants to the sword, 337. Bestows the government on Khwája Kilán, 338. Plunders Penjkora, 338. Marries a daughter of Malek-shah Mansúr, 338. His convention with the Yusef-záis, 338. His forays into the country around Kábul, 339, *note*. Appoints his son Humáyun to Badakhshán, 341. His projected invasions of Kandahár and Hindustán, 341. Plans the conquest of Kandahár, 352. Attacked with illness on the march, 352. Makes peace, 353. Returns to Kábul, 353. Kindly receives Shah Hasan Arghún, 354. Invades the Penjáb, 354. Besieges Kandahár, 355. Surrender of the country to him, 355. Occupies Multán, 398. Extent of his dominions at the period of his invasion of India, 401. Invited to India by Alá-ed-dín, 412. His first invasion of India, 413. Crosses the Indus above Attock, and enters the Penjáb, 413. Occupies Bhíra, 414. Returns through the Gáker country, 414. Loses Bhíra, 415. Sends an embassy to Sultan Ibráhím, 415. His second invasion of India, 416. His third invasion, 416. Takes Siálkót, 416. Returns to complete the subjugation of Kandahár, 417. Again enters India, 418. Defeats the Lodis, and takes Lahúr, 418. Storms Dibálpúr, 418. Joined by Doulat Khan and his sons, 418. Imprisons Doulat and Gházi Khan, 419. Liberates them, and assigns Sultánpúr to Doulat, 419. Advances to Sirhind, 420. Returns to Lahúr and Kábul, 420. Parcels out the Penjáb, 420. His treaty with Alá-ed-dín Lodi, 423. Furnishes him with troops, 423. Determines to march against the Uzbeks, 424. Disengages himself from the affairs of Balkh and Kábul, 427. Leaves Kámrán in charge of Kábul and Kandahár, 427. His fifth invasion of India, 427. Joined by Humáyun and Khwája Kilán, 427. Passes the Sind, 427. Reaches Siálkót, 427. Hears of Alá-ed-dín's defeat at Delhi, 428. Pursues Doulat and Gházi Khans, 428. Takes Milwat, 429. Receives Doulat Khan's submission, 429. Receives Alá-ed-dín, 431. Imprisons him, 431. Reaches Ambála, 432. His cruelty, 432. Joined by Malek Baban, 432. Approaches Sultan Ibráhím's camp, 432. Prepares for battle, 433. Occupies Panipat, 434. Gains the battle of Panipat, 437. Reaches Delhi, 437. Proclaimed Emperor, 437. Proceeds to Agra, 437. His reflections on his conquest, 438. Divides the spoil, 440. Obtains the name of *the Kalendar*, 440. Hostility of the people, 441. Combinations against him, 442. His difficulties, 443. Discontent of his army, 444. His address to his council, 445. His prospects brighten, 446. Joined by various chiefs, 446. His operations in the field, 447. Sends Humáyun in command against the Sherki confederates, 449. Builds a palace at Agra, 451. Recalls Humáyun, 451. Sends an expedition against Biána, 451. Gains Biána and Dhúlpúr, 452, 453. Invited to Guáliár, 453. Guáliár taken, 454. Attempt on his life, 455. Submission of Multán, 456. Affair of Mír Hameh, 458. Báber's transactions with Rána Sánga, 462. Marches against him, 463. His troops discouraged, 466. He renounces wine, 466. He remits the Temgha, 467. His address to his council, 468. He moves his camp, 469. Again advances, 470. Gains a complete victory at Kanwa, 473. Assumes the title of Gházi, 474. Reduces Mewát, 475. Returns to Agra, 476. Recovers Chándwár and Ráberi, 476. His success beyond the Ganges, 477. Distributes the provinces, 477. Anecdote of his unsettled life, 478. His campaign against Chándéri, 478. He reaches Chándéri, 479. Alarming news from the East, 481. His presence of mind, 482. Takes Chándéri, 482. His campaigns on the Ganges, 485. Marches to the East, 485. Crosses the Ganges at Kanáuj, 486. His artillery, 486. Retreat of the enemy, 487. Báber takes Laknáu, 487. The army of the enemy dispersed, 487. Báber returns to Agra, 488. Acquires Rantambór, 488. Increases the taxes, 488. Revives his views on Samarkand, 492. Sends a letter of advice to Humáyun, 492. Represses pillage at Balkh, 493. His desire to revisit his native country, 493. Decline of his health, 494. Gives a grand feast to his nobles and ambassadors, 494. Resolves to march to the West, 495. Inroads of the Balúches, 495. Báber proceeds to Dhúlpúr, 496. Returns to Agra, 497. Assumes command of the eastern army, 498. Supports the pretensions of Sultan Jelál-ed-dín Sherki, 499. Occupies Behár, 500. Makes Muhammed Zemán Mírza governor of Behár, 500. Sends an envoy to Nasret Shah, 503. Is joined by Sultan Juneid Birlas, 503. Attacks and defeats the Bengal army, 504. Receives the submission of the Afgháns, 505. Makes peace with Bengal, 505. Expels Baban and Bayezíd, 506. Returns to Agra, 507. Decline of his health, 508. His perplexity respecting Badakhshán, 511. Appoints Suleimán Mírza to that country, 511. Death of his son Alwer, 512. Dangerous illness of Humáyun, 513. Báber's self-devotion, 513. His dying advice, 516. His death, 517. His interment at Kábul, 517. His character and accomplishments, 519—522. His fondness for architecture and gardening,

520. His literary talent, 521. His commentaries, 522. His person, 525. His family, 525. His harem, 526, *note*. His dominions, 526. Their political state, 528. His taxes, 528. State of landed property, 529. Sources of his revenue, 530. Customs, 530. The Jezía, 530. Posthouses, 530. Men of letters, 530.

Báber Kushkeh, appointed minister to Alá-ed-dín at Dibálpúr, 420.

Badakhshán, invested by Kamber-Bi, 226. Násir Mírza made king, 228. Ravaged by the Uzbeks, 228. Násir Mírza expelled, 229. Its troubled state, 286. Khan Mírza becomes king, 288. Invaded by Sultan Saíd, 340. Given by Báber to his son Humáyun on the death of Khan Mírza, 341. Deserted by Humáyun, 508. Alarm of the inhabitants, 509. Sultan Saíd called in, 509. Hindal assumes the government, 510. Suleimán Mírza made king, 511.

Badi-ez-zemán Mírza, son of Husein Mírza, attacks Kunduz, 96. 198. Retreats, 96. 198. Marches against Khosrou Shah, 198. Appointed to the government of Balkh, 198. Expelled from Balkh, 199. Hospitably received by Khosrou, 199. Joins Zúlnún Beg Arghún in Zemín-dáwer, 199. 268. Marries a daughter of Zúlnún, 269. Attempts to surprise the Khákán, 270. Invades Khorásán, 271. Makes peace, 271. Has Sistán and Farrah assigned to him, 271. Again invades Khorásán, 271. Peace concluded, 273. Receives Balkh with the title of Humáyun Khákáni, 273. Appointed joint King of Khorásán, 240. Conquered by Sheibáni, 259. Flies to Persia, 260. Dies, 260.

Bághbán, plundered by the Arghúns, 353. Submits to Shah Beg, 364.

Bajazet Ilderim, made prisoner at the battle of Angora, 68.

Bajour, governed by an independent Sultan, 337. Taken by Báber, 337. Given to Khwája Kilán, 338. Taken by Báber, 413.

Báki Cheghániáni, brother of Khosrou Shah, defends Hissár, 95. 198. Joins Báber, 202. Advises him to send Jehángír to Khorásán, 209. His plot against Báber, 225. His ambition and intrigues, 230. His resignation, 231. Sets out for India, 231. Is put to death by Yár Husein, 231.

Báki Terkhán, defeated by Sheibáni Khan, 132. Takes possession of Khozar and Karshi, 149.

Balance of Power, first idea of, 5.

Balkh, overrun by Chengíz Khan, 12. Bestowed on Badi-ez-zemán Mírza, 198. Besieged by Khosrou Shah, 200. Taken by Sheibáni, 238. 241. Besieged by the Uzbeks, 423. 458.

Balúches, massacre of, 375. Their war with Shah Hasan, 382. Routed by Abdal-Fitáh, 384. Chastised by Shah Hasan, 385. Made prisoners in Mou, 388. Defeated at Uch, 389. Their inroads into Báber's dominions, 495. Attacked by Chín Taimur, 495.

Bandeh Ali, his pursuit of Báber, 178.

Bárúj Ughlan, son of Abulkhair, Khan of the Uzbeks, 30. Surprises the Moghuls under Yúnis Khan, 31. Is defeated by Yúnis Khan, and slain, 32. 133.

Bátu Khan, his government of the Desht-Kipchák, 25. His invasion of Europe, 26.

Bayesanghar Mírza, son of Sultan Mahmúd Mírza, succeeds his father as Sultan of Samarkand, 92. Defeats the "Elder" Khan, near Kánbái, 96. Slaughters his prisoners, 97. Seized and imprisoned in the Gok-serái, 97. Escapes, 98. Regains the throne, 99. Defeated by his brother, Sultan Ali, 99. Blockaded by Báber, 101. Abandons Samarkand, 104. Received at Kunduz by Khosrou Shah, 104, 199. Made King of Hissár, 142, 200. Seized and strangled by Khosrou Shah, 142. 202.

Bayezíd (Jám), receives a portion of Multán, 387.

Bayezíd (Sheikh), brother of Tambol receives Báber at Akhsi, 174. Seized by Báber's followers, 177. Escapes, 177. Joins Sheibáni, 184. Báber suspects his fidelity, 479. He joins Baban and Maaruf, 485. Defeated by Chin-Taimur, 487. Driven to Bandélkand, 506.

Bayezíd Fermuli (Sheikh), succeeds his brother in command of Sultan Ibráhím's army, 443. Submits to Báber, 446. Left in Oud, 450.

Bechega Khalífa, escapes from Samarkand, 157.

Begchak, tribe of Chagatái Moghuls, 36.

Beháder Khan, nephew of Bátu Khan, governs the Ak-orda, or "White Horde," 26.

Beháder Shah (Sultan), King of Gujrát, receives Alá-ed-dín Lodi, 431.

Behá-ed-dín (Sheikh) of Multán, mediates a treaty with Shah Hasan, 391.
Behár, under the Ghúri dynasty, 404. Conquered by Sekander Lodi, 406. Revolt against Sultan Ibráhím, 412. Under Sultan Muhammed Shah, 443. Under the Lohánis, 496. Under Sultan Mahmúd Lodi, 497. Three competitors for the throne, 498. Occupied by Báber, 500. The government bestowed on Muhammed Zemán Mírza, 500.
Behár Khan Lodi, sent with an army against Doulat Khan, 418. Defeated by Báber, 418.
Behár Khan Loháni, son of Deria Khan, made king under the style of Sultan Muhammed Shah, 412. 443. His death, 496.
Behlúl Lodi, raised to the throne of Delhi, 405. His possessions and conquests, 405.
Behlúlpúr, its commanding situation, 428.
Benáres, occupied by Shír Khan, 498. Abandoned, 499.
Bengal, under the Ghúri dynasty, 404. Under Nasret Shah, 441. History of its affairs, 501. Its army defeated by Báber, 505. Peace concluded, 505.
Berenduk Khan, son of Gerai Khan, Khan of the Kaizák-Uzbeks, 33. 77. Attacked by Sheibáni, 296. Expelled by Kásim Khan, 331.
Beshkent, invaded by Sheibáni, 163.
Beshkhárán, fortress of, 125. Peace of, 126.
Bheker, left in charge of Sultan Muhammed Khan Kokiltash, 366. Made his capital by Shah Beg, 374. Improved and fortified by Shah Hasan, 381.
Bhíra, occupied by Báber, 414. Taken from him, 415.
Biána, under the rule of Daúd Khan Lodi, 405. Its surrender to Báber, 452.
Bikermájít, son of Rána Sánga, aspires to his father's throne, 488. Delivers Rantambór to Báber, 488. Sends to him the crown and girdle of Sultan Mahmúd Khilji, 488.
Bikermájít, rajah of Gwáliár, slain at Panipat, 438. His family present a diamond of immense value to Humáyun, 438.
Binái (Mouláná), a poet, slain at the sack of Karshi, 324.
Biram Khan Karamanlu, the Persian commander at Balkh, sends troops to Báber, 323. Defeated at Ghazhdewán, 325.
Bishágher, occupied by Báber, 114.
Bish-báligh, Chagatái's head-quarters, 37.
Bíst, taken by Sultan Husein, 200. 270.
Blinding by the fire pencil, 99.
Blood, the Muhammedan law of, 209.
Bloody Tower (the) of Bheker, so called from the murder of the Dharécha chiefs, 373.
Bokhára, taken by Sultan Ali Mírza, 105. Taken by Sheibáni, 133. Under Obeidulla Sultan, 309. Taken by Báber, 315.
Bosnia, overrun by the Moghuls, 13. 26.
Bostám, battle of, 489.
Brahminical religion, prevalent in India, 402.
Bridge, Báber's, over the Ganges, 486.
Buddhist religion (the), prevalent in India during the Hindu period, 402.
Bulgaria, conquered by the Moghuls, 13.
Burga Sultan, seizes part of the Uzbek dominions on Abulkhair's death, 30. Surprised and slain by Sheibáni, 136.
Burhán-ed-dín Ali (Sheikh), a writer on Muhammedan law, 83, *note*.
Burhán-ed-dín Kilij (Sheikh), a saint of renown, 86.
Burj-Khúni, the Bloody Tower of Bheker, 373.
Burnes, Sir A., his notice of the Hazáras, 221, *note*. His "Travels," 222, *note*. His description of Báber's tomb at Kábul, 517.

Carpini, on the word *Tartar*, 534.
Chaghatái (or Jaghatái), a race of Túrks, founded the Moghul empire, 14. The principal tribes of Chaghatái Moghuls, 36. Division of the khanship into Moghulistán and Máwerannaher, 37. 66.
Chaghatái Khan (son of Chengíz Khan), his dominions, 24. 35.
Chanderbhan Chohan (Rái), slain at the battle of Kanwa, 473.
Chándéri, obtained by Sultan Sekander Lodi, 406. Originally under the Sultans of Malwa, 479. Taken by Rána Sánga, and given to Medíni Rao, 480. Stormed by Báber, 482. Left in charge of Ahmed Shah, 434.
Chandwár, taken by the Afghans, 469. Retaken by Báber, 476.
Chárbágh, palace of, at Agra, Báber dies there, 517.

Cheghán-serái, a district of Laghmán, 219.

Chehár-bágh, palace of, at Kábul, 253.

Cheitúr (now Udipúr), under Rána Sánga, 460.

Chengíz Khan, chief of the Moghuls, 12. His conquests, 12. Those of his descendants, 13. Dissolution of their empire, 14. Religion of Chengíz, 18. His plan of government, 19. His descent, 23. Divides his empire among his sons, 24. Composition of his army, 534.

Chichektú plundered, 242.

China, conquered by the Manchús, 11. Assigned to Túli, son of Chengíz, 24.

Chín-Taimur Sultan, son of the "younger" Khan, with Báber at Kábul, 256. Defeats Daúd Khan, 443. His command at the battle of Kanwa, 470. Defeats the confederate Afghans on the Ganges, 487. Sent against the Balúches, 495.

Chirágh-kúsh, sect of; their tenets, 287, *note.*

Chirr, the battle of the, 65.

Commentaries (the) of Báber, 522.

Contaish, origin of the term, 30, *note.*

Cornish, ceremony of, 169.

Cossacks, Don. See Kaizáks.

Customs' duties, those in Báber's time, 530.

Dabúsi, fort of, taken by Sheibáni Khan, 150.

Dalmatia, overrun by the Moghuls, 13. 26.

Daúd Khan Lodi, governs Biána, 405. Defeated by Chín-Taimur Sultan, 433.

Dehr, a tribe of Baluches, their contests with Shah Hasan, 382. 384.

Dekhát, the district of, assigned to Báber, 160. Described, 160.

Delhi, conquered by Eibák, 403. Under the Khiljis, 404. Under the Toghlaks, 404. The Syeds, 404. Under Behlúl Lodi, 405. Under Sekander Lodi, 406. Great extent of the empire, 406. Under Ibráhím Lodi, 407. Conquered by Báber, 437. State of the kingdom when conquered, 441.

Dera Khan (probably Deria Khan), marches against Shah Beg, 364. Is defeated, and put to death, 365.

Deria Khan, minister of Sind, his retirement, 360. Joins Jám Firóz, 361. Replaces him on the throne, 362.

Deria Khan Lodi, ruler of Sambhal, 405.

Deria Khan Loháni, governor of Behár, 408. Elected king, 412. His death, 412.

Derwísh Muhammed Terkhán, rebels against Bayesanghar, 97. Is put to death, 99.

Desht of Jitteh, 41, *note.*

Desht Kipchák. See Kipchák.

Dharíchas (the), their revolt in Bheker, 371. Their chiefs put to death, 372, 373.

Dhúlpúr, taken by Báber, 448. 453.

Diamond, of immense value, 438.

Dibalpúr, under Behlúl Lodi, 405. Stormed by Báber, 418. Given to Alá-ed-dín, 420.

Díg Ghází, large cannon of Báber's, 486.

Diláwer Khan, son of Doulat Khan, joins Báber, 418. Informs him of his father's treachery, 419. Appointed to Sultánpúr, 420. Honored with the title of "Khan Khánán," 420. Seized and imprisoned by his father, 421. Escapes, and joins the Afghán confederacy against Báber, 425. Marches with them to Delhi, 425. Separates from them, and joins Báber, 430.

Dilázáks (the), expelled from Swád by the Yusef-záis, 337. Guide Báber in his expedition to Bajour, 337.

Dildár Aghácha Begum, mother of Hindal Mírza, 526, *note.*

Diráwel, besieged and taken by Shah Hasan, 391, 392.

Diwán, or collection of odes, in Túrki, by Báber, 521.

Dizák, massacre of Moghul chiefs in the castle of, 45.

Doáb, under the rule of Sultan Sekander, 406.

Doghlat, a tribe of Chagatái Moghuls, 36.

D'Ohsson's "Histoire des Mongols," reference to, 14.

Dost Muhammed Khan, of Moghulistán, succeeds his father Isanbugha, 53. His death, 53.

Doulat Khan, governor of Lahúr, rebels against Sultan Ibráhím, 412. 413. Attacked by Behár Khan, 418. Solicits the aid of Báber, 418. Flies from Lahúr, 418. Joins Báber, 418. Receives the districts of Jalinder and Sultánpúr, 419. Imprisoned by Báber, 419. Has Sultánpúr as his jágír, 419. Flies to the hills, 419. Invades the Penjáb, 421. Imprisons his son Diláwer Khan, 421. Seizes Sultánpúr, 421. Defeats Alá-ed-dín, 421. Arranges his differences with Alá-ed-

dín, and joins him, 424. Acknowledges him as his sovereign, 424. Collects an army to recover Lahúr, 428. Besieged in Milwát, 429. Surrenders to Báber, 429. Dies, 430.
Doulat Kitta, arranges the flight of Máh-chuchak, 349.
Dúdú, mother of Sultan Jilál-ed-dín of Behár, 497.
Durmish Khan Shamlu, besieged by the Uzbeks in Herát, 457. Dies, 457.

Earthquake, violent at Kábul, 229.
Egypt, added to the Ottoman empire, 5.
Eibák (Sultan), succeeds Muhammed Ghúri in Hindustán, 403.
Ekbál Khan, deserts to Shah Hasan, 391.
Ekhtiár-ed-dín, castle of, Muhammed Momín put to death there, 269.
Elías Khan, taken and flayed alive, 474.
Elías Khwája Khan, son of Toghlak Taimur, established in Máwerannaher, 40. Succeeds as Khan of Moghulistán, 41.
Elphinstone, the Honorable M., reference to his "History of India," 2. 522. To his "Account of Cabul," 222, *note.*
Etáwa, bestowed in jágír on Alim Khan, 423. Besieged by Báber, 448. Taken, 477.
Europe, state of, in the 15th and 16th centuries, 2.

Fakhr Ali, left in charge of Badakhshán, by Humáyun, 509.
Farrah, government of, conferred on Zúlnún, 264. Granted to Badi-ez-zemán, 371.
Farsang, a measure of length, 121, *note.*
Fateh Khan Sirwáni, prime minister of Jilál Khan, 407. Deserts his master, 409. Submits to Báber, 450. Honoured with the title of Khan-Jehán, 450. Joins Sultan Mahmúd Lodi, 498.
Fatehpúr, taken by Shah Beg, 347.
Fázil Beg Gokuldásh (Mír), wounds Ibn Husein Mírza, 274. Meets Shah Beg at Shál Mustung, 343. Proceeds with Shah Beg to Tatta, 364. Defeats the confederated Sindians, 367. Murders the Dharícha and other chiefs, 372. His death, 375.
Ferdausi, Báber's quotation from, 468.
Ferghána (now Kokán), description of, 79. Divided by the Sirr, or Seihun, 79. Famous as the birthplace of Báber, 80. Its districts, 80. Productions and climate, 80. Inhabitants, 80. Language, 81. State of society, 82. State of learning, 82. Religious families, 83. Knowledge of the art of war, 84. Government, 5. Invaded by Sultan Ahmed Mirza, 87. Invaded by the Moghuls, 89. Invaded by Ababeker of Káshghar, 90. Recovered by Báber, 118. The Uzbeks expelled by Syed Muhammed Mírza, 310. They again enter the country, 316.
Fire-pencil, used for blinding, 99.
Firóz (Jám), of Sind, civil wars during his minority, 353. Established on the throne, 360. His misgovernment, 360. Flies from Tatta, 361. Replaced on the throne, 362. His continued misrule, 363. Flies from Tatta, 365. Concludes a treaty with Shah Beg, 366. His continued misconduct, 367. Driven from Tatta by Siláh-ed-dín, 368. Recovers his throne, 369. His exultation on Shah Beg's death, 378. Sends a deputation to Shah Hasan, 379. Flies to Kach, 380. Re-enters Sind, 380. Defeated and flies to Gújrat, 381. Subsequent attempt to recover his throne, 381, *note.*
Firúz Khan Sarang-kháni, sent against Behár Khan, 443. 446. Submits to Báber, 446.
Firúz-koh, fort of, taken by Huláku Khan, 221, *note.*

Gakers (the), position of their territory, 414. Defeated by Báber, 415.
Gardening, Báber's fondness for, 520.
Gebrek, country of, its situation, 222.
Gerái, Khan of the Kaizák Uzbeks, secedes from Abulkhair, 29. Succeeded by his son Berenduk, 33.
Germsír, Zúlnún's influence established there, 264.
Ghazels, or odes, composed by Báber, 166.
Ghazhdewán, battle of, 325. Mírza Sekander's account of it, 326, *note.*
Ghází, title of, assumed by Báber, 474.
Ghází Khan, son of Doulat Khan, joins Báber, 418. Imprisoned, 419. Liberated, 419. Flies to the hills, 419. Collects a powerful army, 428. His army breaks up, 428. He flies to the mountains, 429.
Ghaznevi dynasty (the), in India, 403.
Ghazni, kingdom of, taken by Sebaktegín, 16. Bestowed on Jehángír by Báber, 222. Bestowed on Násir Mírza, 258. 282, Given to Khwája Kilán, 445.

Ghiás-ed-dín (Mír), gives up Kandahár to Báber, 355.
Ghúr, the government of, conferred on Zúlnún, 263.
Ghúri dynasty (the), in India, 403.
Ghuri, its surrender to the Uzbeks, 458.
Gibbon, his opinion on the authenticity of the "Institutes of Taimur," 71, *note*.
Gogra, river, Báber defeats the army of Bengal on the banks, 502.
Gokaldásh (or Kokiltásh), meaning of the word, 90, *note*.
Gok-Serái (or Green Palace), at Samarkand, description of, 98.
Gonds (the), take Jilál Khan, and deliver him to his brother, 410.
Guáliár, under the Ghúri dynasty, 404. Submits to Sultan Sekander Lodi, 406. Held by Tátár Khan Sarangkháni, 453. Surrendered to Báber, 454. Blockaded by the Rájputs, 469.
Gújrat, under Sekander Shah, 441.
Gúlbadan Begum, daughter of Báber, 525.
Gúlberg Begum, daughter of Khálifa, 385.
Gúlchahreh Begum, daughter of Báber, 526.
Gulistán, of Sheikh Sádi, quotation from, 240.
Gúlrang Begum, daughter of Báber, 526.

Habíb-es-Syar (the), historical work, 531.
Háde (Syed), marries Báber's sister, 308. Slain at the battle of Merv, 308.
Há-derwish, wind of, 163.
Haibat, son of Jám Siláh-ed-dín, slain in battle, 369.
Haider Mírza, author of the Tarikh-e-Reshídi, his account of Sheibáni, 137. Value of his history, 192, *note*. His account of his father's conduct, 249. And of Báber's clemency, 253. His escape from Sheibáni, 257. 290. His visit to Khan Mírza, 289. His reception by Báber at Kábul, 291. Báber's kindness to him, 292. Assists in expelling the Uzbeks from Samarkand, 314. His account of Báber's defeat at Kúl-malek, 323, *note*. And at Ghazhdewán, 325. Sent by Sultan Saíd into Badakhshán, 510. His character of Báber, 521.
Hajári (Mulla), the poet, his visit to Báber, 164.
Háji Khan, son of Doulat Khan, joins Alá-ed-dín Lodi, 425. Flies with Alá-ed-dín, 430.
Háji Vazír, defeats Jám Firóz, 362.
Hak Názer Chápa, plunders Chichektú, 242.
Haldi-Ghát, battle of, 505.
Hamad (Sheikh), shrine of, 388.
Hameh (Mír), surrenders to the Uzbeks, 458. Receives Bába Sheikh, 458. Attacks and puts him to death, 459. Rewarded by Báber, 459.
Hamíd Khan, advances to assist Sultan Ibráhím, 432. Defeated by Humáyun, 432.
Hasan Arghún (Shah), son of Shah Beg, flies from his father's court to Báber, 354. Returns home, 354. Sent by his father to assist Jám Firóz, 368. Defeats Siláh-ed-dín, and places Jám Firóz on the throne, 369. Returns to his father at Bághbán, 370. Succeeds to the throne of Upper Sind, 379. Has the Khutba read in Báber's name, 379. Receives an embassy from Jám Firóz, 379. Marches for Tatta, 379. Expells the Jám, 380. Defeats the Jám, and becomes sole master of Sind, 381. Attempts to settle the country, 381. His views on Multán, 384. Visits Síwí, 385. Plunders the Rind and Maksi Balúches, 385. Marries Máh-Chuchak Begum, 385. Marries Gúlberg Begum, 385. Marches from Bheker, 388. Takes Sewrái and Mou, 388. Advances to Uch, 389. Defeats the Langas, 389. Takes and destroys Uch, 390. Concludes a treaty with Husein Langa, 391. Rebuilds Uch, 391. Takes Dirável, 392. Returns to Bheker, 392. Invited to Multán, 393. Besieges Multán, 394. Takes it by storm, 395, 396, *note*, 456. Returns to Bheker, 397. Leaves Khwája Shems-ed-dín governor of Multán, 397. His governor expelled, 398. He resigns Multán to Báber, 398. Defeats the Khankar, 400. Extent of his dominions, 400.
Hasan Khan Leshker, makes peace between Báber and Bengal, 505.
Hasan Khan Mewáti (Raja), chief of the Sherki confederacy against Báber, 442. 451. Declares for Rána Sánga, 463. His force at Kanwa, 471. Slain in the battle, 473.
Hasan Yákúb, joins Báber, and is made master of the household, 86. Appointed Protector, 91. His treason, 91. His death, 92.

Hati Gaker, defeats and slays his brother Tátár, 415. Defeated by Báber, 415. Submits to him, 415.

Hazáras (the), descendants of a Moghul tribe, 14. 212. 216. 220. Sir A. Burnes' notice of them, 221, *note*. Reduced to order by Zúlnún Beg, 264. Sheibáni's campaign against them, 297.

Hazret Moulána, informs Moúlana Muhammed Kázi of Haider Mírza's danger, 290, *note*.

Henri Quatre, compared in his boyhood with Báber, 162.

Herát, the capital of Khorásán, its magnificence, 77. Shah Ismael's residence there, 305. 310. Besieged by the Uzbeks, 457. Again besieged by Obeid Khan, 489. The siege raised, 490.

Hezéber Alla, "the Lion of God," a title conferred on Zúlnún, 275.

Hindal Mírza, son of Báber, 525. Sent by Humáyun to Badakhshán, 510. Besieged in Kíla-zefer, 510. Recalled by Báber, 511.

Hindu Beg, sent to relieve Sambhal, 447. Seizes the fort, 448. His part at the battle of Kanwa, 470. Present at Báber's death-bed, 516.

Hindu (the), period of the government of India, 402.

Hindustán, its revolutions previous to Báber's conquest, 402. Its condition at that time, 442. The people hostile to the invaders, 442.

Hindustáni, origin of the language, 22.

Hissár, or Hissár Shádmán, held by Sultan Masáúd Mírza, 92. Invaded by Sultan Husein Mírza, 94. 197. Defended by Báki Cheghániáni, 95. 198. Bestowed on Bayesanghar by Khosrou Shah, 142. 200. Invaded by Sheibáni, 186. Besieged and taken by Sheibáni, 203. Taken by Báber, 315. Defended by Báber, 323. Abandoned to the rebel Moghuls, 328. Pestilence in the city, 328. The Moghuls expelled by the Uzbeks, 329.

Hissár-Firóza, taken by Humáyun, 432. Bestowed on him in jágír, 432.

Huláku Khan, 221, *note*.

Humáyun Khákáni, title conferred on Badi-ez-zemán, 273.

Humáyun Mírza, son of Báber, appointed to Badakhshán, 341. Joins Báber, 427. Defeats Hamíd Khan, 432. Takes Hissár-Firóza, 432. Receives Hissár-Firóza in jágír, 432. Blockades Agra, 438. Receives a diamond of immense value, 438. His share of Báber's Indian spoil, 440. Sent against the Sherki confederacy, 449. Puts their army to flight, 449. Is joined by Fateh Khan, 450. Takes Juánpúr and Kalpi, 450. Is recalled, 451. Commands the right wing at the battle of Kanwa, 470. Receives from his father the treasures of Alwar, 476. Seizes some of the emperor's treasure at Delhi, 476. Returns to Kábul, 476. Receives directions to attempt Balkh and Hissár, 492. Marches for Samarkand, 493. Leaves Badakhshán, 508. Reaches Kábul, 510. Sends Hindal Mírza to Badakhshán, 510. Arrives at Agra, 512. Desire to set him aside, 512. Sent to Sambal, 513. His dangerous illness, 513. His recovery, 514. Intrigues against his succession, 514. Acknowledged by Báber on his death-bed as his successor, 516.

Hungary overrun by the Moghuls, 13. 26.

Husein (Shah Mír), left by Humáyun in Juánpúr, 450.

Husein Khan Loháni, joins the confederacy against Báber, 442.

Husein Khan Shamlu, defends Herát against the Afgháns, 489.

Husein Langa, son of Sultan Kutb-ed-dín, succeeds his father at Multán, 387.

Husein Langa (Sultan), son of Sultan Mahmúd, succeeds his father at Multán, 391. Anarchy during his minority, 393. His capital taken by storm, 395. His death, 396.

Husein Mírza Baikera (Sultan), of Khorásán, conquers Khorásán, 74. His power, 77. 194. Splendour of his capital, Herát, 77. Invades Hissár, 94. 197. Hospitably receives Sultan Masáúd, 142. Raises the siege of Hissár, 198. Returns to Khorásán, 198. Revolt of his son Badi-ez zemán, 199. 268. Invasion of Kandahár, 200. 269. Takes Bíst, 200. 270. Retreats, 200. 270. Makes peace with Badi-ez-zemán, 271. Proceeds to Asterábád against another son, 271. Again attacked by Badi-ez-zemán and Zúlnún, 272. Again makes peace, 273. Sends one of his sons to invade Sistán, 273. Honourably receives Muhammed Husein Doghlat, 236. Calls in Báber against Sheibáni, 238. His death, 239 His character, 241.

Husein Shah Sherki (Sultan), driven from Juánpúr, 406.
Husein Súfi, his gallant defence of Khwárazm, 237. His death, 238.

Ibn Husein Mírza, a son of Sultan Husein, invades Sistán, 273. His defeat and escape, 274.
Ibráhím Chápuk, seizes Sheikh Bayezíd, 177.
Ibráhím Jamád (Mouláná), at Multán, 396, *note*.
Ibráhím Lodi (Sultan), succeeds to the throne of Delhi, 407. Consents to the division of the empire, 407. Marches against his brother Jilál, 409. Puts him to death, 410. Wishes to humble the Afghán nobles, 410. Their revolt, 411. Quelled, 411. Puts to death some of his Amírs, 411. They revolt in Behár, 411. His troops defeated by Deria Khan Loháni, 412. Invades the Penjáb, 421. Dispersion of his army, 421. Advances against Alá-ed-dín, 425. Defeats the Afgháns, 426. Advances from Delhi against Báber, 432. Defeated and slain at Panipat, 437. His immense army, 439.
Ibráhim Sáru, surprises the fort of Asfera, 92. Pardoned by Báber, 93. His mission to Akhsi, 116. His success, 117. Imprisoned by Mír Ali Dost, 127. Joins Báber near Samarkand, 132. Slain in battle, 152.
Ibráhím Terkhán, throws himself into Shiráz, 144. Slain in battle, 152.
Ilachi Khan, "the Slaughtering Khan," name given to Ahmed Khan, 66.
Iláks (the), occupied by Báber, 114.
Imám, the Seventh, the descent of Shah Ismael from, 298.
Imám Reza, shrine of, at Meshhíd, 300, *note*. Visited by Shah Ismael, 301.
India, division of its history into three periods, 1. Its condition at the time of Báber's invasion, 21. Reference to Vasco de Gama's passage to, 113. Báber's first expedition into, 223. Its early history, 402. Hindu period, 402. First Musulman period, 402. Dynasty of Ghazni, 403. Of Ghúr, 403. The Khiljis, 404. The Toghlaks, 404. Invasion of Taimur, 404. The Syeds, 404. The Lodis, 405. Divided state of India, 405. Conquests of Sultan Behlúl Lodi, 405. Sultan Sekander Lodi, 406. He extends the limits of the empire, 407. Ibráhím Lodi, 407. Intended division of the empire, 407. Báber called in, 412. His first invasion, 413. His second invasion, 416. His third invasion, 416. His fourth invasion, 418. His fifth invasion, 427. Conquered by Báber at Panipat, 437. State of the country at the time, 441.
Institutes of Taimur, question of their authenticity, 70, *note*.
Irák, the calamity of, 53. 74.
Irazan Beg, of the Khirás Moghuls, leads 30,000 families to Samarkand, 44. Their fate, 45. "The calamity of Irazan," 45.
Iron Gate, pass of the, 204.
Isa Khan Túrk, rules in the Doáb, 405.
Isa Terkhán (Mírza), married to Máhchuchak, 352.
Isakhail tribes, plundered by Báber, 339.
Isanbugha Khan, called from Máwerannaher to be Grand Khan of the Moghuls, 37, 38. His wife Sátelmish Khátún, 39.
Isanbugha Khan, son of Weis Khan, Khan of the Moghuls, succeeds his father as Khan of Moghulistán, 44. Expels his elder brother, Yúnis Khan, 44. Assassinates Taimur Oighur, 46. Abandoned by his tribes, 46. Received by Mír Syed Ali of Káshghar, 46. His contrition, 46. Re-establishes himself in Moghulistán, 47. Invades Táshkend, 47. Is defeated by Abusaíd, 47. Besieges and takes Andeján, 48. Relieves Káshghar and defeats Yúnis Khan, 51. His death, 52.
Isan-Taimur Sultan, son of the younger Khan, with Báber at Kábul, 256.
Ismáel Koreishi (Sheikh), of Multán, sent to conciliate Shah Hasan, 393. Retires to Tatta, 393.
Ismáel Jilwáni, collects troops to oppose Báber, 419. Joins the army of the Afgháns against Delhi, 425. Seeks shelter in the Doáb, 427.
Ismáel Sefvi (Shah), King of Persia, founder of the Sefvi dynasty, 6. Sketch of his ancestry, 297. His embassy to Sheibáni, 298. Sheibáni's answer, 299. His reply, 299. Marches to Meshhíd and Merv, 301. Defeats Sheibáni at the battle of Merv, 303. Massacres the garrison and inhabitants of Merv, 305. Winters at Herat, 305. Sends an embassy to Báber, 308. Invades Máwerannaher, 309. Makes peace with the Uzbeks, and returns to Herát, 310. His convention with Báber, 312. Assists Báber against the Uzbeks, 315. His bigotry as a

Shía, 320. His cruel persecution of the Sunnis in Khorásán, 305. 321. 327. Sends Amír Nijm Sáni with an army to assist Báber, 323. Returns to Khorásán, 326. Receives the submission of Shah Beg, 344. Imprisons him in the fort of Zefer, 345. His war with the Ottoman Sultan, Selím, 352. His death, 457.

Jadeh, a Máchi, his proceedings in Multán, 395.
Jagdálik, hill pass of, 281.
Jágírdár, application of the term, 529.
Jagraks (the), plundered by Báber, 93.
Jalinder, assigned to Doulat Khan, 419.
Jám, battle of, 491.
Jan Muhammed Atkeh, assists in the battle against the Uzbeks, 314.
Jan Vafa Mírza, left by Sheibáni at Herát, 300. Abandons Herát, 301. Defeated by the Persians, 301.
Jani Beg Khan, of the Kaizák Uzbeks, secedes from Abulkhair, 29. His son Kásim Beg Khan, 53.
Jani Beg Sultan, his birth, 136. Appointed by Sheibáni to the government of Andeján, 189. Slaughters the Moghuls, 311. Invades Ferghána, 317. His part in the battle of Jám, 492.
Januka (Mír), Sheibáni's conversation with, 235.
Játs (the), a question as to their origin, 42, *note*. Their predatory incursions, 383.
Jaxartes (the), its course, 79.
Jehan (Shah), his mosque at Kábul, 518.
Jehángír Mírza, a younger brother of Báber, 89. Claims Andeján and Akhsi, 107. Besieges Andeján, 109. Takes the city, 110. Invests Báber in Marghinán, 116. Joins Támbol, 117. Retires with him to Urkend, 118. Defeated by Báber, 123. Escapes to Urkend, 123. Makes peace with Báber, 126. Escapes from Támbol and joins Báber, 175. Present at Akhsi, 176. Appointed to the government of Ghazni, 222. Reveals the plot of Báki, 225. Flies from Kábul to Bámián 231. Flies on the approach of Báber, 239. Waits on Báber at Pái, 240. His excessive indulgence in wine, and consequent illness, 251. His death, 258. His family, 258, *note*.
Jelálábád. See Adínapúr.
Jemál-ed-dín Khan (Sheikh), governor of Táshkend, 54. Takes Yúnis Khan prisoner, 54. Slain by Abdal-kadús, 55.
Jenjúheh (the), induce Báber to attack Hati Gaker, 413.
Jezía, or poll-tax, 530.
Jilál Khan, son of Alim Khan, seeks shelter in the Doáb after his father's defeat, 427.
Jilál Khan Lodi, made governor of Juánpúr, 407. Makes Fateh Khan Sirwáni his prime minister, 407. Declines to return to his brother Sultan Ibráhím, 408. Proclaims himself king of Juánpúr, by the style of Sultan Jilál-ed-dín, 409. Attacked by his brother, 409. Driven from his kingdom, 410. Put to death, 410.
Jilál-ed-dín Lodi (Sultan). See Jilál Khan.
Jilál-ed-dín Lohání (Sultan), succeeds to the throne of Behár, 497. Rival competitors, 497. Takes refuge in Bengal, 497. Submits to Báber, 500. Escapes from the Bengal camp, 500. Joins Báber, 505.
Jílál-ed-dín Sherki (Sultan), a claimant of the throne of Behár, 498. Magnificently entertains Báber, 499.
Juánpúr, conquered by Sultan Behlúl, 405. Under Sultan Sekander, 406. Given to Jilál Khan, 407. Its condition at Báber's conquest of India, 441. Rebellion in, 443. Taken by Humáyun, 450.
Júji Khan, son of Chengíz, has the Desht-Kipchák allotted to him, 24. Dies before his father, 24.
Juneid Birlás (Sultan), invites Sultan Mahmúd to attack Samarkand, 96. Left by Humáyun in Juánpúr, 450. Has the chief direction in the east, 494. Advances towards Kheríd, 495. Joins Báber on the Gogra, 503.

Kabádián, occupied by Humáyun, 493.
Kábul, state of the kingdom of, at Sultan Abusaíd's death, 214. Factions at court, 215. Taken by Muhammed Mokim, 216. 274. Surrendered to Báber, 216. 274. Extent of the kingdom at this period, 217. Adjacent tribes, 220. Diversity of inhabitants and languages, 220. 222. Climate and productions, 222. Violent earthquake, 229. Given by Báber in charge of Muhammed Husein Doghlat, 247. Gallant defence of the fortress against Khan Mírza's party, 250. Báber's return to, 251. Famine, 258. 276. The government left with Abdal Rizák, 280. Given to Názir Mírza, 319. The government re-

assigned by him to Báber, 334. Báber's account of its delightful climate, 518. Báber is interred there, 517.
Kábul, an ancestor of Chengíz Khan, 70.
Kach, pillaged by the Arghúns, 400.
Kaferistán, its position, 221.
Kahan, plundered by the Arghúns, 353.
Kaizák-Uzbeks, not identical with the Don or other Russian Cossacks, 29, *note*. Their origin, 30. 331. They become formidable, 31. Become the ruling power in the Eastern Kipchák, 33. Their quarrel with the Moghuls, 64. They defeat the "elder" Khan, 64. Sheibáni's unsuccessful campaign against them, 296. Their ravages in the Desht-Kipchák, 331.
Kajuli, an ancestor of Taimur, 70.
Kalendar, name given to Báber from his liberality to holy men, 440.
Kalimáks, or Kalmuks (the), their invasion of the country of the Uzbeks, 30, *note*. Their position to the southeast of the Moghuls, 36. They defeat Yúnis Khan, 31. 54. Return to their own country, 55. Defeated by the "younger" Khan, 66.
Kaliún, fort of. See Nirehtu.
Kalmuks. See Kalimáks.
Kalpi, plundered, 410. Taken by Humáyun, 451.
Kamber Ali, leaves Báber's camp at Suárási, 123. Makes peace between Báber and Jehángír, 125. Proceeds to defend Yar-Ailák, 144. Flies from the battle on the Kohik, 153. Accompanies Báber from Samarkand, *158. Conspires against Támbol, 165. Proposes terms of peace on the part of Támbol, 176. Sent away from Báber's camp, 210.
Kamber Ali Kochín (Amír), son of Kásim Beg, quells a rebellion against Báber, 335. Attends Báber's deathbed, 516.
Kamber-Bi, of Merv, appointed by Sheibáni, governor of Kunduz, 226. Attacks Badakhshán, 226. Is beaten back, 226. Besieged in Kunduz by Khosrou Shah, 227. Whom he defeats and puts to death, 228. Advises Sheibáni to delay the battle at Merv, 304.
Kampila, under Raja Pertáb Sing, 405.
Kámrán Mírza, son of Báber, 525. Left in charge of Kábul and Kandahár, 427.
Kamreddín, brother of Yúlaji, claims the office of Ulús-begi, 40. Assassinates Elías Khwája Khan, 41. Usurps the throne of the Moghuls, 41. Defeated and expelled by Mír Taimur, 42. His death, 42.
Kámrúd, Báber passes through the valley of the, 143.
Kanáuj, abandoned by Báber's troops to the Afgháns, 469. 477. The government given to Muhammed Sultan Mírza, 477. Evacuated by Báber's troops, 485.
Kánbái, battle of, 96.
Kandahár, under the government of Zúlnún Beg, 215. 220. 266. Invaded by Báber, 229. Its affairs on Zúlnún's death, 261. Its unhealthy climate, 266. Nature of the country, 268. Invaded by Sultan Husein, 269. Taken by Báber, 278. Bestowed on Násir Mírza, 279. Besieged and taken by Sheibáni, 279. 281. Restored to the Arghúns, 282. Invaded by Báber, 352. He accepts terms of peace with Shah Beg, and retires, 353. Again invaded by Báber, 354. He besieges the town, 355. The tower and kingdom surrendered to Báber, 355.
Kandar, fort of, taken by Rana Sánga, 448.
Kanwa, battle of, 470—473.
Kar Kitin, besieges Balkh, 458.
Káráchár-Nevián, or Núián, minister of Chengíz, 37. And of Chagatái Khan, 71.
Karakorum, the residence of the Grand Khan, 25.
Karakúl, district of, seized by a force from Merv, 149. Taken by Sheibáni, 150.
Karshi, district of, taken possession of by Báki Terkhán, 149. Sacked by Amír Nijm Sáni, 324.
Kásán, the khanship of, formed, 27.
Kásán, district and town of Ferghána, 80. Delivered up to Sultan Mahmúd Khan, 89. Recovered by Báber, 118. Besieged by the Khan's son, who retreats, 124. Taken by the Uzbeks, 317.
Káshghar, description of, 35. Its inhabitants, 36. Overrun by Taimur, 41. Taken by Mír Syed Ali, 46. Besieged by Yúnis Khan, 51. Who is defeated, 52. Governed by Muhammed Haider Mírza Doghlat, 56. Seized by his nephew Ababeker, 57. 58. 77. Ababeker expelled, 332. The prosperous rule of Saíd Khan, 332. List of the Amírs of, 539.
Kásim (Mír), sent with the expedition against the Balúches, 384.
Kásim Beg Khan, Khan of the Kaizáks,

son of Jani Beg, extends his power over the Desht, 33. His immense army, 33. Defeats Sheibáni, 296. Called in by Kitteh Beg, 331. His great power, 331. Plunders the country, and withdraws, 331. Visited by Sultan Saíd, 332.

Kásim Beg Kochín, Báber's prime minister, 112. His mission to Táshkend, 112. Sent to raise Ferghána, 116. Defeated by the Moghuls, 120. Dismissed by Mír Ali Dost, 127. Detached to surprise Robát-Khwája, 144. Fails, 144. His successful sally from Samarkand, 156. Accompanies Báber in his flight, 158. Proceeds to Hissár, 165. Accompanies Báber from Khorásán to Kábul, 243. His sagacity, 279. 311.

Kásim Gokultásh, married to Máhchuchak, 348. Manner of his death, 351.

Kásim Husein Sultan, his position at the battle of Kanwa, 470.

Kásim Sambhali, besieged by Baban Jilwáni, 447. Relieved by Hindu Beg, 447. Deprived of the fort of Sambhal, 448.

Kattór, county of, its situation, 222.

Kaúrchik, Grand Khan of Kipchák, 27.

Kázán Khan, of Persia, 25.

Kázán Sultan Khan, Khan of Máweran-naher, his energetic reign, 67. Is slain in battle, 67. 540.

Kázi (Khwája). See Khwája Mouláma Kázi.

Kázi Káz, intercedes with Shah Beg to stop the pillage of Tatta, 365. Sent by Shah Beg as an envoy to the confederated Sindis, 367. Becomes a councellor of Shah Beg, 369. Advises the slaughter of the Dharícha and other chiefs, 372. Betrays Jám Firóz, 3'.9.

Kepek Sultan Ughlan, son of Dost Muhammed Khan, 53. His murder, 53.

Kesel-básh, the Persians so named, origin of the name, 320.

Keshtúd, destroyed and depopulated by the Uzbeks, 144.

Khadíja Begum, 251.

Khaiber-pass, Báber's passage through, 224.

Khákán, title of the Grand Khans, 25.

Khákán (the). See Husein Mírza Baikera.

Khákán e Mansúr, title of, 283, *note*.

Khalífa. See Nizám-ed-dín.

Khalifs of Bagdad, their Túrki mercenaries, 15.

Khalíl, brother of Támbol, taken prisoner, 122. Seizes Ush, 130. Slain in battle, 152.

Khalíl Khan, son of the "younger" Khan, his war against his uncle Mahmúd, 191.

Khamseh Sultan, leaves Báber's service for Sheibáni's, 145. Defeats Khosrou Shah at Kunduz, 227. Marches against Báber, 307. 309. Occupies Púl-Sangín, 312. Defeated by Báber, 314. His death, 315.

Khans, Grand, of Moghulistán, their fall, 25.

Khan Jehán, title of, 450, *note*. Conferred upon Fateh Khan, 450.

Khan Jehán Bandéli, attempts to drive the Musulmans from Guáliár, 453.

Khan Jehán Lodi, his advice to Sultan Ibráhím, 407.

Khan Khánán, title of, 420. 450, *notes*. Conferred upon Diláwer Khan, 420.

Khan Mírza. See Weis Mírza.

Khánd (Mír), author of the Rozet-es-Sefá, 531.

Khankar (the), defeated by Shah Hasan, 399.

Khanzádeh Begum, Báber's sister, marries Sheibáni, 157. Divorced, and married to Syed Háde, 308. Sent to Báber by Shah Ismáel, 308. Resides at Kábul, 308.

Kherid, the army of, that of Bengal so called, 502.

Khilji dynasty (the), in India, 404.

Khirás, a tribe of Chaghatái Moghuls, 36.

Khirilji Afgháns (the), plundered by Báber, 339, *note*.

Khizer Khwája, Khan of Moghulistán, 42, 43, *notes*.

Khizer-khail Afgháns (the), plundered by Báber, 339, *note*.

Khodáidád (Amír), son of Yúlaji, nominated Ulús-begi, 40. Raises Khizer Khwája to the Khanship, 42. Retains the government as Ulús-begi, 43. Calls in Ulugh Beg Mírza against Weis Khan, 44.

Khojend, district of Ferghána, 80. Taken by Sultan Ahmed, 87. Recovered by Báber, 93.

Kholáset-al-Akhbár (the), 531.

Khorásán, conquered by Shah Ismáel of Persia, 6. Ravaged by Chengíz Khan, 12. Conquered by Taimur, 17. Conquered by Sultan Husein Mírza, 74. 77. Its affairs on his death, 240. Two joint kings appointed, 240. Splendour of its capital, Herát, 241. Sheibáni's invasion and conquest, 258—260. Invaded by Badi-ez-zemán, 271. Overrun by Shah Ismáel, 301. Ravaged by the Uzbeks, 326. Invaded by the Uzbeks under Obeid Khan, 456. 489. Relieved by the Persians, 490.

Khosrou Gokuldásh, appointed by Báber to Siálkót, 420. His part at the battle of Kanwa, 470.

Khosrou Shah, minister of Samarkand, 92. 196. Sent to Sultan Masáúd at Hissár, 92. Defends Kunduz against Badi-ez-zemán, 96. 198. Makes himself independent at Kunduz, 104. 197. Receives Bayesanghar, 104. His early life, 196. Hospitably receives Badi-ez-zemán, 199. Seizes Hissár, 142. 290. Blinds Sultan Masáúd, 142. 201. Makes Bayesanghar king of Hissár, 142. 201. Causes him to be strangled, 142. 202. His power and character, 202. He quits Kunduz on the approach of Mahmúd Sultan, 204. Submits to Báber, 208. Is deserted by his followers, 208. Sets out for Khorásán, 208. Returns to Kahmerd, 214. 226. Proceeds to Herát, 226. Attempts to regain Kunduz, 226. Attaches himself to Násir Mírza, who shakes him off, 227. Besieges Kunduz, 227. Is taken prisoner and beheaded, 228.

Khozar, district of, taken by Báki Terkhán, 149. Taken by Báber and the Persians, 324.

Khozars (the), plains of, added to the dominions of Chengíz Khan, 13.

Khubán, battle of, 123.

Khurram, son of Sheibáni Khan, 158, *note*.

Khutba (the), uncertainty in whose name it was read in Máwerannaher, 321, *note*.

Khutlán, government of, bestowed on Wali, 200.

Khwájika Khwája, protects Bayesanghar, 98. His rivalry with his brother Khwája Yahía, 131.

Khwárazm, ravaged by Chengíz Khan, 12. Conquered by Taimur, 17. Besieged by Sheibáni, 237. Gallantly defended by Husein Súfi, 237. Taken by Sheibáni, 238. Ceded by the Uzbeks to Shah Ismael, 310.

Kila Báki, plundered by Jehángír, 232.

Kila-núr, assigned by Báber to Muhammed Ali Tájík, 420.

Kila-zefer, castle of, origin of its name, 289, *note*. Made the capital of Badakhshán, 289. The environs laid waste by Sultan Saíd, 510.

Kilán (Amír Khwája), made governor of Bajour, 338. Joins Báber, 427. Sketch of his life and character, 444. Made governor of Ghazni, 445. Báber's letter to him, 493.

Kilát, fort of, taken and abandoned by Báber, 229.

Kipchák (Desht), assigned to Júji Khan, 24, 25. Its extent, 24. The Musulman faith introduced there, 26. Civil wars and anarchy, 27. Taimur's invasion, 27. The Grand Khanship of, claimed by three Khans, 27. Rise of separate Khanships, 27. Destruction of their power by the Russians, 28. Political state of the, about the time of Báber's birth, 33. The language, 34. Overrun by the Kaizáks, 331.

Kitin Kara Sultan, 493.

Kitteh Beg, appointed to Seirám, 319. Besieged by the Uzbeks, 330. Calls in the Kaizáks, 330. Rebels against Báber, 335. Defeated, 335.

Kochín, or Konchi, a tribe of Chaghatái Moghuls, 36.

Koel taken by the Afgháns, 469. Retaken by Báber, 474.

Kohistán, or highlands of Kábul, described, 218.

Kokiltásh. See Gokaldásh.

Korkán, a title, its meaning, 90, *note*.

Krim, formation of the Khanship of, 28.

Kuch Beg, his valour at the siege of Samarkand, 155.

Kuchum Khan, son of Abulkhair, elected supreme Khan of the Uzbeks, 309. Invades Ferghána, 317. Defeated by the Persians at the battle of Jám, 492.

Kúl-malek, battle of, 322.

Kúl Nazer, rebels against Báber, 334.

Kuli Gokaltásh (Mírza), accompanies Báber in his flight from Akhsi, 178.

Kumans (the), plains of the, added to the Moghul dominions, 13.

Kunduz, defended against Badi-ez-zemán by Khosrou, 96. 108. Held independently by Khosrou, 104. Taken by Mahmúd Sultan, 204. Given by Sheibáni to Kamber-Bi, 226. Besieged by Khosrou, 227.

Kuren (Sheikh), joins Báber, 446. Sent against Guáliár, 453.

Kutb Khan, of Etáwa, joins the confederacy against Báber, 442.

Kútb Khan entrusted with the fort of Mongeir, 502.

Kutb Khan Afghán, in possession of

Rabéri and its dependencies under the house of Lodi, 405. Surrenders it to Báber, 447.
Kutb-ed-dín (Sultan), Rai Sipehra, seizes the throne of Multán, 387. His death, 387.
Kutluk-Nigár Khánum, daughter of Yúnis Khan, married to Sultan Umer-sheikh, 54. 74. Mother of Báber, 76. 78. Joins Báber at Khojend 112. Accompanies him in his flight from Samarkand, 157. With Báber at Táshkend, 168. Accompanies him in his expedition to Kábul, 195. 208. 213. Her death, 237.

Laghmán. See Lamghán.
Lahúr, under the house of Ghazni, 403. Under Behlúl Lodi, 405. Taken by Báber, 418. Assigned to Mír Abdalazíz, 420.
Laknáu, under Sekander Lodi, 406. Occupied by Malek Baban, 477. Bestowed by Báber on Muhammed Sultan Mírza, 477. Abandoned by his troops, 482.
Lamghán, or Laghmán, district of Kábul, description of, 218. Bestowed on Násir Mírza, 222.
Lamp extinguishers. See Chirágh-kush.
Landed property in India, in Báber's reign, 529.
Langas, tribe of, govern Multán, 387. Defeated by Shah Hasan, 389.
Langer Khan, or Leshker Khan, 391. Invites Shah Hasan to Multán, 393. Associated with Shems-ed-dín in the government, 397. Leaves Multán, 398. Sent by Báber to Multán with his son Askeri, 398. Afterwards nominated to the government of Kábul, 398.
Language, that of the Ottoman dominions, 20. Of the tribes of Kipchák, 34. Of the kingdom of Kábul, 220.
Leshker Khan. See Langer Khan.
Letters, men of, in Báber's reign, 530.
Lodi dynasty (the), in India, 405. Subverted by Báber at the battle of Panipat, 437.
Lohger, a district of Kábul, 219.
Lovers' cave (the), near Samarkand, ambush of, 101. Escalade of a fort near, 147.

Maaruf Fermuli, revolts against Sultan Ibráhím, 412. 443. Leads the Sherki confederates, 449.
Maasúma Sultán Begum, daughter of Báber, 525.
Maasuma Sultán Begum, wife of Báber, 526, *note*.
Máchi, razed to the ground, 370.
Machís (the), their predatory habits, 383.
Maham Begum, wife of Báber, 526, *note*.
Máh-chuchak Begum, niece of Shah Beg, married to Kásim Gokultásh, 348. Plan for her escape from Kábul, 349. It succeeds, 350. Reaches Kandahár, 351. Her second and third marriages, 352.
Mahdúm Bilál, 367.
Mahib Ali, son of Nizám-ed-dín Ali, marries Nahíd, daughter of Máh-chuchak, 352.
Mahmúd (Sultan), of Ghazni, son of Sebektigín, his conquest of India, 16. 439. His conquest of Multán, 386.
Mahmúd Khan (Sultan), son of Syurghatmish, defeats Bajazet Ilderim at Angora, 68.
Mahmúd Khan (Sultan), "The Elder Khán", son of Yúnis Khan, sent against his brother Sultan Ahmed, 62. Succeeds as Grand Khan, 62. Defeats the Sultan of Ferghána, 63. And of Samarkand, 63. 136. Makes Sheibáni governor of Túrkistán, 63. Decline of his power, 65. Seizes Uratippa, 90. Bestows it on Muhammed Husein Mírza, 90. Visited by Báber, 93. Defeated near Kánbái by Bayesanghar, 96. Assists Báber with a small reinforcement, 113. Assists Támbol against Báber, 124. Assists Weis Mírza with troops, 129. Visited by Báber at Táshkend, 160. Bestows Uratippa on him, 160. Meets his brother, 169. Their proposed arrangement, 173. They besiege Andeján, 174. They abandon the siege, 175. Made prisoner by Sheibáni, 184. Released, 185. Retires into Moghulistán, 186. Seized at Khojend, and put to death, with five sons, by Sheibáni, 192.
Mahmúd Khan Bhekeri (Sultan), son of Mír Fázil, placed in charge of Bheker, 371. His cruel disposition, 373. Afterwards mounts the throne of Bheker, 384. His gallantry at Sewrái, 388. Assists in defeating the Khankar, 400.
Mahmúd Khan Jehán Khan, joins the Afghán chiefs against Sultan Ibráhím, 425. Joins Ibráhím, 427.
Mahmúd Khan Kokiltásh (Sultan), son of Mír Fázil, left in charge of Bheker,

366. His government, 371. Presented to Shah Beg, 372.
Mahmúd Khan Loháni, submits to Báber, 500.
Mahmúd Khilji (Sultan), of Malwa, receives Jilál Khan, 410. Defeated by Rána Sánga, 461. 481. Restored to the throne of Malwa, 480. His crown and girdle given to Báber, 488.
Mahmúd Langa (Sultan), grandson of Sultan Kutb-ed-dín, his accession to the throne of Multán, 387. Defeated by his ministers, 387. Division of his kingdom, 387. Raises an army to oppose Shah Hasan, 390. His death, 390.
Mahmúd Lodi (Sultan). Design to raise him to the throne of Delhi, 442. Acknowledged by Rána Sánga, 451. 462. His force against Báber at Kanwa, 471. Flies to Gujrát, 474. Crowned in Behár, 496, 497. Rapid increase of his power, 498. His competitors for the throne, 499. Retreats on Báber's approach, 499. Takes refuge with the army of Bengal, 500.
Mahmúd Matin Khan, brings an army of Sammas against Shah Beg, 364.
Mahmúd Mírza (Sultan), son of Abusaíd, sovereign of Hissár. His dominions, 74. Succeeds his brother in Samarkand and Bokhára, 89. Intrigues to depose Báber, 91. His death and character, 92.
Mahmúd Sultan, brother of Sheibáni Khan, sent against Seirám, 138. Defeated and pardoned, 139. Sent against Kunduz, 204. Occupies Kunduz, 204. His death, 204.
Mahter Sambal. See Sambal.
Maláhida, a sect of heretics, 287, *note*.
Malek-shah Mansúr, Yusefzái, marriage of his daughter with Báber, 338.
Malik Baban Jilwáni. See Baban Jilwáni.
Malúke Tewáif, or government of tribes, 405.
Malwa, under the Ghúri dynasty, 404. Under Sultan Mahmúd, 441. Power of Rána Sánga, 441.
Mamelukes, their origin, 17. Usurp the government of Egypt, 17. Circassian Mamelukes, 18. Subdued by the Ottoman Turks, 18. Revival of the Mamelukes, 18. Their final destruction by Muhammed Ali Pasha, 18.
Mán (Raja), of Guáliár, receives Jilál Khan, 410.
Manchús (the), a race of Tartars, 9. Their conquest of China, 11.
Mandráur, a division of Lamghán, 219.
Mangu-Taimur Khan, bestows the Ak Ordo on Behádar, 26.
Mánik Vazír, opposes Shah Hasan in crossing the Indus, 379. Slain, 380.
Manikchand Chohan, slain at the battle of Kanwa, 474.
Manjaníls, used in sieges, 317.
Mankat Rái (Raja), attempts to expel the Musulmans from Guáliár, 453.
Manselík, mother of Toghlak Taimur, 39.
Mansúr Khan, son of Sultan Ahmed Khan, Khan of the Moghuls, 191.
Marghinán (or Marghilán), district of Ferghána, 80. Town taken by Sultan Ahmed, 87. Delivered to Báber, 116. Invested by Uzun Hassan, 116. Siege raised, 117. Declares for Báber, 171.
Marze-Vibâ (the), disease in Kandahár, 266, *note*.
Masáúd Mírza (Sultan), son of Sultan Mahmud Mírza, placed in Hissár, 92. Flies to his brother at Samarkand, 95. Returns to Hissár, 100. Invades Samarkand, 100. Driven from Hissár by Khosrou, 142. 200. Escapes to Herát, 142. 200. Marries daughter of Sultan Husein, 200. Returns to Khosrou, 142. 200. Blinded, 143. 201.
Masíkha, territory of, 52. Conferred on Yúnis Khan, 52. Báber's sojourn there, 164.
Masson's "Travels," notice of, 222, *note*.
Matchlocks, used by Báber at Bajour, 337.
Mátila (now Mír-púr), ravaged by the Balúches, 382.
Máwerannaher, or Transoxiana, overrun by Chengíz Khan, 12. Conquered by Taimur, 17. 67. The Khanship of, 38. Separated from Moghulistán, 66. Its extent, 66. Titular Khans, 67. Extinction of the Khanship, 68. Becomes the portion of Sháhrúkh Mírza, 72. Overrun by Sheibáni, 139. The Uzbeks expelled from, 316. 318. State of the country, 319. Religious zeal of the inhabitants, 320. Recovered by the Uzbeks, 326. List of the Chaghatái Khans of, 540.
Mazíd Wajkeh (Mír), rebels against Báber, 334.
Medína Rao, chief of Chánderi, joins Rána Sánga, 471. His power, 480. His history, 480. Besieged by Báber.

481. Slain at the capture of Chándéri, 483, *note*.

Mehdi Khwája (Syed), defeats Dáud Khan, 433. His part at the battle of Panipat, 436. Sent with Humáyun against the Sherki confederates, 449. Threatened by Rána Sánga, 463. Joins Báber, 464. His part in the battle of Kanwa, 470. Married to a daughter of Báber's, 514. 526. Intrigue for placing him on the throne of Hindustán, 514. His arrogance, 515. His fall, 516.

Mehdi Sultan, leaves Báber's service for Sheibáni's, 145. Attacked by Báber, 307. Holds Cheghánián, 309. Defeated and taken prisoner, 315. Put to death, 315.

Mehr, ravaged by the Balúches, 382.

Mehr-nigár Khanum, daughter of Yúnis Khan, married to Sultan Ahmed Mírza, 248. Married to Sheibáni Khan, 157. 248. Divorced, 158. 248. Accompanies Shah Begum to Hérat, 237. Her residence at Kábul, 248. Báber's reception of her, 253. Accompanies Shah Begum to Badakhshán, 287. Her death, 288.

Mehroli, under the rule of Ahmed Khan Mewáti, 405.

Merv, taken by Shah Beg, 273. Battle of, 303. Taken by Obeid Khan, 457.

Meshhíd, taken by Obeid Khan, 457. 489.

Mewát, under Ahmed Khan, 405. Ravaged by Báber, 466. Reduced by Báber, 475.

Miánkál, submits to Báber, 149.

Milwát, besieged and taken by Báber, 429.

Mingelik Gokultásh, her escape from Samarkand, 157.

Mír, application of the title, 87, *note*.

Mirán Shah (Mírza), son of Taimur, his share of Taimur's dominions, 72. Falls in battle, 72.

Mirán Shah Mírza, son of Ulugh Beg, flies to Khosrou Shah, 201. Receives assistance from him, 201. His end uncertain, 215.

Mírpúr. See Mátila.

Mírza, application of the title, 87, *note*.

Mírza Khan, son of Sultan Mahmúd Mírza, accompanies Báber in his expedition to Kábul, 195. Demands the death of Khosrou, 309.

Miskín Terkhán, leads an army into Multán, 393. Marries a sister of Sultan Husein, 396.

Mobárek Shah, acknowledges Násir Mírza, King of Badakhshán, 228. Expels him, 229. Defeats the Arghuns, 342.

Moghul, or Mongol, grand race of Tartars, 9. 11. Their conquests under Chengíz Khan, 12. Their excessive cruelty, 13. Their dissolution as one grand empire, 14. Their religion, 18. 61. Their principal tribes in the Chaghatái desert, 36. Division of the tribes on the death of Elías Khwája, 41. Separation of the tribes on the murder of Taimur Oighur, 46. Reunited under Isan-bugha, 47. Revolt of those in the service of Báber, 120. They join Támbol, 120. Under the elder and younger Khans, defeated by Sheibáni Khan, 184. Discontent of the chiefs in the service of Báber, 283. Their conspiracy, 284. Their defeat, 286. Those in Sheibáni's service desert the Uzbeks, 305. Their slaughter in Ferghána, 311. Their treachery to Báber, 311. Their conspiracy against him, 327. Obtain possession of Hissár, 328. Defeated by the Uzbeks, and expelled from Hissár, 329. Their rebellion in Ghazni, 334. Quelled, 335. Their part in the battle of Kanwa, 470. They form the Tulúghma, 470.

Moghulistán, definition of, 36. Khanship of, 38. Invaded by Ulugh Beg, 44. Abandoned by the tribes, 46. Its conquest by Taimur, 72. List of the Khans of, 537.

Mohib Ali Khan Khalífa, son of Khwája Khalífa, married to Nahíd Begum, 385. Sent to support Mír Abdal-azíz, 465.

Mohib Ali Korchi, assists in the defence of Kábul, 250.

Mohib Terkhán, his cruelty at Multán, 395.

Mokím Arghún. See Muhammed Mokím.

Money of account, Báber's, 543—545.

Mongeir, taken by Nasrat Shah, 502.

Mongols. See Moghuls.

Moravia, overrun by the Moghuls, 13.

Moscow, taken by the Tartars, under Bátu Khan, 26.

Mou, taken by Shah Hasan, 388.

Mouláná Kázi (Khwája), called also Mouláná Muhammed Sadr, Sheikh-ul-Islam, invites Báber into Andeján, 86, and *note*. Attempts ineffectually to make peace between Báber and Sultan Ahmed, 88. Intercedes for the life of Ibráhím Sáru,

93. Sent to Uzim Khan at Andeján, 107. Assists in defence of Andeján, 109. Is put to death, 111. Báber's character of him, 111.
Mozeffer Hussein Mírza, appointed joint king of Khorásán, 240. Conquered by Sheibáni, 259. His death, 260.
Mozeffer Shah, of Gujrát, receives Jám Siláh-ed-dín, 360. Assists him to gain the throne of Sind, 361. Assists him against Shah Beg, 368. Receives Alim Khan, 423. Restores Sultan Mahmúd to the throne of Malwa, 480.
Muhammed (Mír), conspires against Báber, 327.
Muhammed Alí Jengjeng, supports Mír Abdal-azíz, 465. His part in the battle of Kanwa, 470. Sent against the Sherki Afghans, 479.
Muhammed Ali Pasha, his destruction of the Mamelukes in Egypt, 18.
Muhammed Ali Tájík, appointed by Báber to Kila-núr, 420.
Muhammed Beg, son of Zúlnún, defeated by the Sindians and slain, 342.
Muhammed Berendúk Birlás, minister of Khorásán, 259.
Muhammed Duldái (Sultan), abandons Kanáuj, 477.
Muhammed Ghús (Sheikh), a derwísh, effects the surrender of Guáliár, 454. Induces Rahímdad to restore that fortress to Báber, 507.
Muhammed Haider Mírza Doghlat, Amír of Káshghar, 56. Driven out by Ababeker, 57. Presented with the government of Ush, 58. Expelled, 58.
Muhammed Hissári, his conspiracy against Tambol, 165.
Muhammed Humáyun Mírza. See Humáyun.
Muhammed Husein Mírza Doghlat, son of Muhammed Haider Mírza, receives the government of Uratippa, 90. Receives the title of "Korkán," 90. Lends Báber the village of Bisháger, 114. Prepares to defend Uratippa against Sheibáni Khan, 183. Abandons Uratippa, 185. Joins Sheibáni Khan, 188. His influence with the Moghuls at Samarkand, 234. His marriages, 234. Flies from Samarkand to Herát, 236. Goes to Kábul, 237. Is placed in charge of Kábul by Báber, 247. Joins in the rebellion of Shah Begum, 249. Secretes himself, 252. Is discovered and pardoned, 254. Allowed to go to Khorásán, 257. Received by Sheibáni, 257. Put to death, 257.
Muhammed Kázi (Moulána), his preservation of Haider Mírza, 290. His interview with Báber, 292.
Muhammed Khan, son of Khizer Khwája Khan, succeeds as Grand Khan, 43.
Muhammed Korchi, of Badakhshán, 228.
Muhammed Kúli Kochín, his gallantry, 155.
Muhammed Maaruf (Shah), his defection to Báber, 504.
Muhammed Mazíd Terkhán, of Turkistán, taken prisoner by Sultan Mahmúd, 63. Is minister of Sultan Ali Mírza, 128. Withdraws from Samarkand, 129. Joins Weis Mírza, 129. Flies from him, and offers his services to Báber, 129. Joins Báber at Yurat-Khan, 131. Accompanies him to Hissár, 141.
Muhammed Mírza (Syed), expels the Uzbeks from Ferghána, 310 His previous adventures, 310, 311. Receives Sultan Saíd Khan at Andeján, 316. Succeeds in saving the lives of 3,000 prisoners, 318.
Muhammed Mokím, son of Zúlnún Arghún, seizes Kábul, 210. 216. 274. Surrenders it to Báber, 216. Retires to Germsír, 217. His invitation to Báber, 274. Submits to Sheibáni, 277. Defeated by Báber at Kandahár, 278. Flies to Zemín-Dáwer, 278. Calls in Sheibáni, 279. Restored to his government, 282.
Muhammed Moním Mírza, son of Badiez-zemán Mírza, his unsuccessful rebellion in Asterábád, 269. Put to death, 269.
Muhammed Shah (Sultan). See Behár Khan, Lohání.
Muhammed Sheríf, the astrologer, arrives in Báber's camp, 466. Dismissed by Báber, 473.
Muhammed Sultan (Khwája), uncle of Sheibáni Khan, marries the widow of Burga, 136.
Muhammed Sultan (Sultan), son of Sultan Mahmúd, left to defend Ferghána, 183. Flies to Moghulistán after the disaster of Táshkend, 185. Flies on his father's death to the Kaizáks, 192.
Muhammed Sultan Mírza, sent with Humáyun against the Sherki confederates, 449. Sent against Rána Sánga, 463. His part at the battle of Kanwa, 470. Appointed to Laknáu and Kanáuj, 477.

Muhammed Turkistáni (Múlla), delivers Kunduz to Sheibáni Khan, 204.
Muhammed Zeitún, joins the confederacy against Báber, 442. Surrenders Dhúlpúr, 453.
Muhammed Zemán Mírza, invested with the government of Behár, 500. His part in the defeat of the Bengal army, 504. Marries a daughter of Báber, 525.
Muhammed-záis, plundered by Báber, 339, *note*.
Multán, views of Shah Hasan on, 384. State of the country, 386. First Muhammedan conquest of, 386. Under the Hindus, and under Delhi, 386. Sheikh Yusef chosen ruler of, 386. Its extent, 387. Factions, 387. Minority of the Sultan, 393. Anarchy, 393. Besieged by Shah Hasan, 394. Distress of the besieged, 394. The city taken by storm, 395. Pillaged, 395. Tyranny of the Arghún governor, 398. His expulsion, 398. The country occupied by Báber, 398. 456. Its future revolutions, 398, 399.
Munga Oighúr, his generosity, 135.
Muri Saturgái, name of a tract of country, 221.
Murshid (Múlla), sent by Báber as ambassador to Sultan Ibráhím, 415. Detained by Doulat Khan at Lahúr, 416.
Mustafa Ali, a commander of the Persian auxiliaries, 315.
Mustafa Fermuli, sent against Behár Khan, 412. 443. His death, 443.
Mustafa Rúmi, at the battle of Kanwa, 472. At the battle on the Gogra, 504.
Mustung, conquered by Zúlnún, 268.
Musulman religion, introduced into the Desht Kipchák, 26. First dynasty in India, 402.

Náder Shah, notice of his conquests, 6.
Naher Khan, son of Hasan Khan Mewáti, taken prisoner at Panipat, 462. Released by Báber, 462. Succeeds his father in Mewát, 475. Surrenders to Báber, 476. Escapes, 476.
Nahíd Begum, daughter of Máh-chuchak, 348. Marries Mahib Ali, 352. 385.
Nanda (Jám), of Sind, his war with the Arghúns, 342. His death, 353. His extensive territory, 358.
Nanda Dehr, submits to Shah Hasan, 389.
Nang-nihár, a division of Lamghán, 219.
Nasíb Shah. See Nasret Shah.
Násir Khan Lohâni, of Ghazipúr, 408 Revolts against Sultan Ibráhím, 412. 443. Leads the Sherki confederates, 449. Put to flight by Humáyun, 450.
Násir Mírza, third brother of Báber, 89. Committed to his uncle Sultan Ahmed, 89. Meets Báber at Akhsi, 174. Appointed to the government of Lamghán and Nijrow, 222. Invited to Badakhshán, 226. Joined by Khosrou Shah, whom he shakes off, 227. Becomes King of Badakhshán, 228. Driven from Badakhshán, and rejoins Báber at Kábul, 229. Appointed to Ghazni, 258. Appointed to Kandahár, 279. Besieged by Sheibáni, 282. Capitulates, 282. Retires to Ghazni, 282. Appointed by Báber to Kábul and Ghazni, 319. Besieges Kábul, 334. His death from intemperance, 334.
Nasír-ed-dín Obeidulla (Khwája), his account of Yúnis Khan, 60. Dictates a peace between Umersheikh, Ahmed Mírza, and Yúnis Khan, 62.
Nasret Shah, or Nasíb Shah, King of Bengal, 441. Loses several provinces to Sekander Lodi, 501. Retakes them, 501. Takes Mongeir, 502. Receives Sultan Mahmúd, 502. Is defeated by Báber, 505. Makes peace, 505.
Násukh, fort of, surprised and captured by Báber, 113.
Nazer Mírza, his part in the Moghul conspiracy against Báber, 327.
Nevián Gokultásh, Báber's foster-brother, 146. His death, 163.
Nijm Sáni (Amír), minister of Shah Ismáel, joins Báber with the Persian troops, 323. Massacres the garrison and inhabitants of Karshi, 324. Defeated at Ghazhdewán, made prisoner and put to death, 325.
Nirehtu, or Kaliún, fort of, its strong position, 282, *note*.
Nizám Khan, of Biána, joins the confederacy against Báber, 442. Besieged in Biána, 452. Defeats his brother Alim Khan, 452. Surrenders to Báber, 453.
Nizám-ed-dín Ahmed Bakhshi, notice of, 515, *note*.
Nizám-ed-dín Mír (or Khwája) Ali Khalífa, Báber's favourite officer, his escape at Uratippa, 94. Discharged by Mír Ali Dost, 127. Left at Kábul with Muhammed Husein, 247. Defends Kábul, 250. His connection with Shah Hasan, 385. Is Báber's prime minister, 385. His firmness in Báber's difficulties, 467. Brings Báber

news of reverses, 481. Declines to proceed to Badakhshán, 511. Wishes to set aside Humáyun, 512. Intrigues in favour of Mehdi Khwája, 514. Returns to his allegiance, 516. Attends Báber's death-bed, 516.
Noukend, castle of, taken by Báber, 174.
Nukderis (the), join Báber near Kábul, 212. 220. Their country, 220. 263. Reduced by Zúlnún, 264. Plundered by Báber, 354.
Núrgil, district of, included in Lamghán, 219.

Obeid Khan, of Bokhára. See Obeidulla Sultan.
Obeidulla Sultan, or Obeid Khan, of Bokhára, nephew of Sheibáni, carries off Sheibáni's harem after the battle of Merv, 305. Holds Bokhára, 309. Fortifies himself in Kárshi, 315. Abandons the city, 315. Invades Bokhára, 322. Defeats Báber at Kúl-malek, 322. Totally defeats Báber and his allies at Ghazhdewán, 325. Invades Hissár, 328. Invades Khorásán, 457. 489. Takes Merv, Sirakhs and Tús, 457. 489. Seizes Meshhíd, 457. 489. Takes Asterábád, 489. Besieges Herát, 489. Defeated by the Persians at Jám, 491. Escapes from the field wounded, 492.
Observatory, Ulugh Beg's, at Samarkand, 83. 105.
Odes composed by Báber, 166.
Ogre, of fable, origin of the, 13, *note.*
Oighurs (the), a tribe of Túrks, acknowledge the sway of Chengíz, 12. Their reckless cruelty gives rise to the name of "Ogre," 13, *note.*
Oktái, or Ogatái, Khan, son of Chengíz, his dominions, 24. Acknowledged as Grand Khan, 25.
Orda-Itzen, son of Júji Khan, presents 15,000 Tartar families to his brother Sheibáni, 26.
Osmanlis, empire of the, foundation, 16. Its wide extent, 17. Shah Ismáel's wars with them, 346. 352.
Othman, founder of the Ottoman empire, 16.
Oud, under Sekander Lodi, 406. Rebellion in, against Báber, 443. Under Sheikh Bayezíd, 450.
Oxus, the river, the ancient boundary between Irán and Turán, 81, *note.*

Padmáwati, widow of Rána Sánga, intrigues to place his son on the throne, 488.
Padshah, Emperor, title assumed by Báber, 282.
Panipat, battle of, 435.
Páp, fort of, taken by Báber, 174.
Patiáli, under Raja Pertáb Sing, 405.
Pekin, conquest of, by Chengíz Khan, 12.
Penjáb, invaded by Báber, 354. Under the Ghaznevi dynasty, 403. Under the Ghuri, 403. Under Sultan Sekander, 406. Held by Doulat Khan, 413. Invaded by Báber, 413. Parcelled out by Báber, 420. Entered by Doulat Khan, 421. Invaded by Sultan Ibráhím Lodí, 421. Union of the Afgháns of the Penjáb, 424.
Penjkora, plundered by Báber, 338.
Perháleh, taken by Báber, 415.
Perowli Birlás (Sultan), attacks Shah Beg at Futehpúr, 347. Defeated, 347.
Persia, government of the Túrks established in, 16. Anecdote illustrative of the barbarous manners of the Persians in the time of Shah Ismáel, 304.
Pertáb Sing (Raja), governs Kampila and Patiáli, 405.
Pesheng, fortress of, its strength, 269. Zúlnún retires to it, 269.
Peshkesh (the), sent by Báber to Shah Ismael, 322, *note.*
Pigeon-training in the East, 75.
Pishín, conquered by Zúlnún, 268.
Poetry, a favourite pursuit in the East, 83. Specimen of Báber's, 164. Notice of his compositions, 521.
Poles (the), conquered by the Moghuls, 13. And by Bátu, 26.
Poll-tax (the), 530.
Post houses, established by Báber, 530.
Púl-Málán, the river of Herát, 272, *note.*
Pustak, the Imárat of, 520, *note.*

Ráberi, under Kutb Khan Afghán, 405. Taken by Báber, 448. Taken by the Afgháns, 469. Retaken by Báber, 476.
Radhan (Jám), his reign in Sind, 359, *note.*
Rafia-ed-dín (Syed), 453, *note.*
Rahímdád, captures the fort of Guáliár, 454. Restores it to Báber, 507.
Rahmú-dehris (the), a tribe, pardoned by Shah Hasan, 389.
Raika Begum, wife of Báber, 526, *note.*
Rájpúts, their desperate warfare, 380. Their defeat in Sind, 381. Their prowess under Rána Sánga, 464. Defeat Mír Abdal-azíz, 465. Their swarms of cavalry, 466. Prepare for battle with Báber, 469. Their

forces, 471. Completely defeated at Kanwa, 473. Their self-sacrifice at Chandéri, 483.
Ran-mal Sodha, his command in Sind, 369.
Rantambór, surrendered to Báber, 488.
Rázi-ed-dín (Shah), the Chirágh-kush, his possessions near Khutlan, 287. Beheaded, 291.
Renish Behánder, entrusted with the government of Asterábád, 489. Defeats the Persians, 490. Is defeated by Shah Tahmasp, and slain, 490.
Resáleh e Walidíeh (the), versified by Báber, 521.
Revenue of Báber (the), 530. 541.
Robát-Khwája, surprised by Báber, 144.
Róhilkand, Báber's operations in, 447.
Rubriquis, on the word *Tartar*, 534.
Rúh-ulla (Sheikh), of Mou, 389.
Rupee (the), name of coin, 543.
Russia, conquered by the Moghuls, 13. 26. Held by them for 150 years, 14. Destroys the power of the Tartars, 28.
Ruttonsi (Rána), succeeds his father Rána Sánga, 488.

Saad-ulla Lahúri (Moulána), his account of the sack of Multán, 396, *note.*
Sádi (Sheikh), reference to, 240.
Saíd Khan, or Sultan Saíd, son of the "younger" Khan, his war against his uncle Mahmúd, 191. His account of the conduct of Sheibáni on the death of his brother Mahmúd Sultan, 204. His residence at Samarkand, 234. Flies from Samarkand, 236. Báber's kindness to him, 256. Visits Khan Mírza at Kila-zefer, 289. Proceeds to Kábul, 289. Visited by Haider Mírza, 292. His character of Báber, 294. Declines the offer of the Moghuls to place him on the throne, 311. Appointed to Andeján, 312. Received there by Syed Muhammed, 316. Defeats Ababeker, 318. Invades Táshkend, 330. Is defeated and wounded, 330. Defends Ferghána, 330. Calls in Kásim Khan, the chief of the Kaizáks, 331. Visits Kásim Khan, 332. Abandons Ferghána, 332. Expels Ababeker from Káshgar, 332. His long and prosperous rule, 332. His quarrel with Khan Mírza, 339. Invades Badakhshán, but retires, 341. Called in to Badakhshán, 509. Besieges Kila-zefer, but retires, 510.
Saíd Khan, governor of Oud, driven out of Oud, 409.
Samarkand, invaded by Sultan Mahmúd, 96. Attacked at once by three different princes, 99. Who withdraw, 100. Again blockaded by Báber, 101. Abandoned by Bayesanghar, 104. Occupied by Báber, 105. Báber's account of, 105. Its fertility, 105. Manufactures, 106. Learning and skill, 106. Abandoned by Báber, 110. Attempts to regain it, 113. Occupied by Sultan Ali, 114. Unsuccessfully invaded by Weis Mírza, 129. Báber marches against it, 129. Sheibáni's invasion, 131. 140. Influence of its religious men, 131. Taken by Sheibáni, 141. Surprised and taken by Báber, 147. Besieged by Sheibáni, 153. Surrenders to him, 157. Held by Taimur Sultan, 309. Taken by Báber, 316. Joy of the population, 316. Báber proclaimed King there, 316. Abandoned by Báber, 322.
Sambal (Mahter), his plot to deliver his master, Shah Beg, from prison, 345. Succeeds, 345. Throws provisions into Kandahár, 355. Assists Jám Firóz of Sind, 361. Proceeds to besiege Diráwel, 392.
Sambhal, under Deria Khan Lodi, 405. Besieged by Baban Jilwáni, 447. Taken by Hindú Beg, 448.
Sammas (the), expel the Sumras from Sind, 358. Termination of their rule in Sind, 370.
Sánga (Rána), his power in Málwa, 441. Takes the fort of Kandar, 448. His progress of conquest, 451. Acknowledges Sultan Mahmúd, 451. 462. His dominions, 461. His person and character, 461. His alleged descent from Nushírwán the Just, 461, *note.* His transactions with Báber, 462. Mutual recrimination, 462. His ambitious views, 462. He advances to Biána, 462. Joined by Hasán Khan Mehwáti, 463. Prowess of his Rájpúts, 464. His army, 471. Completely defeated at Kanwa, 473. Escapes from the battle, 474. Invited to Malwa, 480. His chivalrous conduct, 481. His romantic death, 484.
Sanjer (Jám), his reign in Sind, 359, *note.*
Sarang Khan, a commander of Siláh-ed-dín in Sind, 369.
Sátelmish Khátún, chief wife of Isanbugha, 39.
Sebaktegín, a Túrki slave, sovereign of Ghazni, 16.
Sehwán, reduced by Shah Beg, 366 The fort strengthened by Shah Beg, 370.

Seirám, invaded by the Moghuls, 47. Bestowed on Kitteh Beg, 319.
Sekander (Mírza), his account of Báber's defeat at Kúl-malek, 322, *note.* His account of the battle of Ghazhdewán, 326.
Sekander Lodi (Sultan), his long reign at Delhi, 406. Subdues Behár, 406. Threatens Bengal, 406. Extends his empire, 406. His death, 407, *note.*
Sekander Shah, King of Gújrat, 441.
Selím (Sultan), his war with Shah Ismáel, 352.
Selíma Sultán Begum, daughter of Báber, 526.
Seljúkis, a tribe of Turks, their conquests, 16. Their government overturned by Chengíz, 16.
Senjer Birlás (Sultan), engaged in the conspiracy against Báber, 249. Seized, and pardoned, 252.
Seráichak, Toktamish placed on the throne of, 27.
Sewrái, fort of, taken by Shah Hasan, and razed to the ground, 388.
Shah, a title bestowed on holy men, 87, *note.*
Shah Beg. See Shah Shujáa Beg.
Shah Begum, wife of Yúnis Khan, repairs to Samarkand, 234. Her relationship to Sheibáni, 234. Her character, 235. Sent to Khorásán, 236. Arrives at Herát, 237. Resides at Kábul, 248. Intrigues in favour of her grandson, Sultan Weis, 249. Gains the Moghuls, 249. Induces Muhammed Husein Mírza to join the rebels, 249. Forgiven by Báber, 253. His kindness to her, 256. Accompanies her grandson, Khan Mírza, to Badakhshán, 282. Her boasted descent from Alexander the Great, 286. Her imprisonment and death, 288.
Shah Sufi, his valour at Samarkand, 155.
Sháhi Beg. See Sheibáni.
Shahnáma, the poem, the universal taste for, 83.
Shahrokhía, district north of the Sirr, 93. Invaded and ravaged by Sheibáni, 163.
Sháhrukh Khan Afshár, a commander of the Kezelbashes with Báber, 315.
Sháhrukh Mírza, son of Taimur, king of Khorásán, 45. Brings up Yúnis Khan, 45. Civil wars at his death, 47.
Sháhrukh Sultan Moherdár, commander of the troops sent by Shah Ismáel to Báber, 315.
Shahrukhi, coin, the value of, 414, *note.*
Shajrat-ul-Atrák, account given in, of the origin of the Aimáks, 221, *note.* Notice of, 535.
Shál, conquered by Zúlnún, 268. 342.
Shamu-khail (the), plundered by Báber, 339.
Sheháb-ed-dín Muhammed Ghúri, founder of the Ghúri dynasty in India, 403. His conquest of India, 439.
Sheher-bánu Begum, daughter of Báber, 526.
Sheibák Khan, reference to his death in Merv, 256.
Sheibáni, son of Júji Khan. his dominions, 26.
Sheibáni Khan, or Sháhi Beg, son of Shah Bidágh, and grandson of Abulkhair, 32. Notice of his early life, 133. Leaves his father-land, 133. Received at Bokhára by Abdal Ali Terkhán, 134. Growth of his power, 134. Surprises and slays Burga Sultan, 135. Betrays Sultan Ahmed, 136. Obtains Túrkistán, 63. 137. His faithlessness, 137. Is supported by Sultan Mahmúd, 139. Overruns Transoxiana, 139. Joined by Báber's Uzbeks, 100. Assists Bayesanghar, 103. Returns to Turkistán, 104. Defeats the Terkháns, 131. Takes Bokhára, 133. 140., and Samarkand, 141. Loses Samarkand, 147. Retires to Bokhára, 149. Advances towards Samarkand, 150. Takes the fort of Dabúsi, 150. Defeats Báber on the Kohik, 151. Blockades Samarkand, 153. Which capitulates, 157. Marries Khanzádeh Begum, 157. Ravages Shahrokhía and Beshkent, 163. Advances towards Ferghána, 183. Defeats the Moghuls, 184. Takes the two Khans prisoners, 184. Conquers Táshkend, 184. Marries into the family of the Khans, 185. Releases the Khans, 185. Puts Kwája Abul Makáram to death, 186. Invades Hissár, 186. And Andeján, 187. Takes it, and puts Tambol and his brother to death, 188. Takes Hissár, 203. Sends his brother Mahmúd against Kunduz, 204. Kunduz taken, 204. His sternness and composure on hearing the death of his brother, 205. Returns to Samarkand, 206. Prepares to attack Khwárazm, 206. His troops defeated in Badakhshán by Násir Mírza, 228. His future projects, 233. Sets out for Khwárazm, 235. Destroys or disperses the Moghul chiefs, 236. Besieges and takes Khwárazm, 237. Besieges and takes Balkh, 238.

241. Receives Muhammed Husein Mírza, 257. Puts him to death, 257. Invades and conquers Khorásán, 258. 260. Extent of his dominions, 261. Receives the submission of Zúlnún's sons, 277. Besieges Kandahár, 279. Takes the city, 281. Completes the conquest of Khorásán, 295. Unsuccessful campaign against the Kaizáks, 296. Campaign against the Hazáras, 297. His reception of an envoy from Shah Ismáel of Persia, 298. The Shah's reply, 299. He retires to Merv, 301. Defeated and slain at the battle of Merv, 303. His body dismembered, and his skull formed into a drinking cup, 304.

Sheikhem Mírza, governor of Karshi, put to death, 324.

Sheikh-ul-Islám, office of, 86. Of Herát, murdered by Shah Ismáel, 321.

Sheikh-záda, of Oud and Laknau, 408.

Shemsábád, taken by the confederate Afgháns, 485. Given by Báber to Rána Bikermájít, 488.

Shems-ed-dín (Khwája), appointed governor of Multán, 397. His cruelties, 397. His expulsion, 398.

Shemshír Khan, expels the Arghúns from Multán, 398.

Sherfeddín Ali Shirázi (Mouláma), historian of Taimur, Yúnis Khan placed under his care, 45.

Shías, their ascendancy in Persia, 299. Badge of the sect, 320.

Shír Khan, son of Alá-ed-dín, sent by his father to confer with Doulat and Gházi Khan, 425.

Shír Khan Súr, has the chief management of Behár, 497. Occupies Benáres, 498. Tenders his submission to Báber, 500.

Shír Muhammed Khan, Grand Khan of Moghulistán, 43.

Shír Shah. See Shír Khan Súr.

Shiram Chehreh, his defence of Hissár, 203. His capitulation, 203.

Shiram Taghái, sent to conduct Khosrou Shah towards Khorásán, 214. Plans his seizure, 214. Brings Baber's family to Kábul, 214. Rebels against Báber, 334. Is pardoned, 335 His death, 335.

Shiram Ziker, minister of Abdal-rizák of Kábul, 215. Is murdered, 215.

Shirkeh Arghún, routed and taken prisoner by Báber, 211.

Shujáa Beg (Shah), or Shah Beg, son of Zúlnún Beg, his valour when a boy, 268. Appointed to defend Kandahár, 269. His unsuccessful attempt to surprise Sultan Husein, 270. Takes Merv, 273. Succeeds his father at Kandahár, 261. Invites Báber, 275. Submits to Sheibáni, 277. Defeated by Báber at the battle of Kandahár, 278. Flies to Shál and Mustung, 278. Recovers Kandahár, 282. His talents and character, 341. Takes Síwí, 342. Loses it, 342. Submits to Shah Ismáel, 344. Sends a mission to conciliate Báber, 344. Repairs to Herát, 344. Is imprisoned, 344. His escape, 346. Turns his views towards Sind, 346. Takes Síwí, 347. Defeats Sultan Perowli, 347. Returns to Kandahár, 348. Receives his brother's daughter, Máh-chuchak, 351. Attacked by Báber, who retires, 352. Plunders part of Sind, 353. Quarrels with his son, Shah Hasan, who flies to Báber, 354. Takes possession of Sind, 355. Cedes Kandahár to Báber, 355. Departs for Shál and Síwí, 355. Is invited to Sind, 363. Advances to Tatta, 364. Defeats the Sindis, and takes Tatta, 365. His treaty with Jám Firóz, 366. Reduces Sehwán, 366. Defeats the Sindis, 367. Sends his son, Shah Hasan, to assist Jám Firóz, 368. Strengthens his forts, 370. Orders the murder of the Dharícha chiefs at Bheker, 373. Makes Bheker his capital, 374. Settles the country, 375. Massacres the Balúches, 375. Deeply affected by the death of Mír Fázil, 375. His death, 376. His character, 376.

Shujáa, or Shujáa-ul-moolk, Bokhári (Sheikh), minister of Sultan Mahmúd Langa, 390. Governs Multán during the minority of his son, 393. Put to death by the Arghúns, 398.

Siálkót taken by Báber, 416. Given to Khosrou Gokuldásh, 420. Unsuccessfully attacked by Doulat Khan, 421.

Sídim Ali Derbán, a Hazára chief, his retainer, beaten to death for plundering, 213.

Siláh-ed-dín, chief of Bhilsa, at the battle of Kanwa, 471.

Siláh-ed-dín (Jám), aspires to the throne of Sind, 360. Flies to Gujrát, 360. Invited to the government, 361. Ascends the throne, 361. Abandons his capital, and retires to Gujrát, 362. Seizes the capital, 368. Is defeated and slain, 369.

Silesia overrun by the Moghuls, 13. 26.

Sind, civil wars in, 353. Shah Beg

projects the invasion of, 353. Subjugated by Shah Beg, 355. Its extent under Jám Nanda, 353. Confederacy of the tribes against Shah Beg, 366. Seized by Siláh-ed-dín, 368. Commencement of the Arghún rule in, 370. 381. Sind extended to the Ghára, 391. Extent of the kingdom under Shah Hasan, 400.
Sipehra Rai. See Kútb-ed-dín.
Sirakhs, taken by the Uzbeks, 457.
Sir-e-ták, pass of, Báber's passage of the, 143.
Sirhind, under Behlúl Lodi, 405. Under Tátár Khan, 413.
Sirr (the), or Seihun (Jaxartes), its course, 79.
Sistán, bestowed on Badi-ez-zemán, 271. Bestowed on Amír Sultan Ali, 273. Invaded by a son of Sultan Husein, 273.
Siúnjek Khan, son of Kuchum Khan, governs Táshkend, 309. Invades Ferghána, 317. Takes Táshkend, 330. Defeats Sultan Saíd, 330. Obtains possession of Andeján, 332.
Síwí, or Síwístan, the fort taken by Shah Beg, 342. Retaken by the Jám of Sind, 342. Position of the country, 347. The town taken by Shah Beg, 347. Visited by Shah Hasan, 385.
Sogdiana, probably the modern Soghd, 106.
Soghd, river and district of Samarkand, 105. Taimur's garden at, 106. Submits to Báber, 149.
Soheil (Canopus), the star, first seen by Báber, 211.
Suleimán Mírza, son of Weis Sultan, or Khan Mírza, 341. Appointed King of Badakhshán, 511. His ancestry, 511. Assumes the government, 512.
Sultán-nigár Khánum, wife of Sultan Mahmúd, 248. Afterwards married to two Uzbek Khans in succession, 249.
Sultánpúr, assigned to Doulat Khan, 419. Given to his son, Diláwer Khan, 420. Seized by Doulat Khan, 421.
Sumras (the), a native tribe governing Sind, 358.
Sunnis, persecuted by Shah Ismáel, of Persia, in Khorásán, 305. 320. Their detestation of the Shías, 320.
Surkháb, the river, 207.
Swád, the Dilázáks expelled from, 337.
Syed Ali (Amír), grandson of Khodáidád, becomes master of Káshghar, 46. Receives Isan-bugha Khan, 46. Is attacked by Yúnis Khan, 51. Whom he defeats, 52. His generous conduct, 52. His death, 52.
Syed dynasty (the), in India, 404.
Syedpúr, taken, and the garrison put to the sword by Báber, 417.
Syeds (the), of Bheker, their importance, 371. Forced to quit the town, 374.
Syria, re-establishment of the Túrki dominion in, 17.
Syurghatmish, titular Grand Khan of the Moghuls, 68.

Táher Duldái, governor of Dizak, his reception of Báber, 158.
Tahmasp (Shah), succeeds to the throne of Persia, 457. Attacked by the Uzbeks, 489. Defeats Renish Beháder, 490. Advances to Meshhíd, 490. Defeats the Uzbeks at Jám, 491.
Taimur (Mír), or Tamerlane, his conquests, 17. His inroad into India, 21. Fable of his lineage, 23. His interference in Kipchák, 27. His invasions into the Desht Jetteh, 41. His birthplace, 69. His descent, 69. His claim to the office of hereditary prime minister, 70. Question of the authenticity of his "Institutes," 71, *note*. His great talents, 71. His vast empire at his death, 72.
Taimur Beg, son of Sheibáni, marries a princess of the family of the Khans, 185.
Taimur Kutluk, Grand Khan of Kipchák, 27.
Taimur Oighur, assassinated by Isanbugha, 46.
Taimur Sultan, son of Sheibáni, marries a daughter of Shah Begum, 249. Flies after the battle of Merv, 305. Holds Samarkand, 309. Defeated by Báber in Hissár, 314. Present at the battle of Ghazhdewán, 325.
Táishi, title of the Chief of the Kalimáks, 30, *note*.
Tajara, the old capital of Mewát, 475.
Táj-ed-dín Muhammed (Khwája), his interview with the dying Sultan Ahmed, 190.
Tájík, a townsman or peasant, as distinguished from a tribesman, 20. 81, *note*. Those of Kábul, 220.
Takerábád, battle of, between the Persians and Uzbeks, 301.
Tambol (Sultan Ahmed), a Moghul nobleman, 107. Deserts from Báber, 107. Heads a party in favour of Jehángír, 107. 109. Besieges Báber in Marghinán, 116. Retreats to Ush, 117. Driven from Ush by

the inhabitants, 118. Retires to Urkend, 118. Joins Báber's revolted Moghuls, 120. Defeats Kásim Beg, 120. Threatens Andeján, 121, 122. Defeated by Báber, 123. Aided by Sultan Mahmúd, 124. Marches to Kásán, 125. Retreats to Arkhián, 125. Proceeds to Beshkárán, 125. Makes peace with Báber, 126. His connection with Mír Ali Dost, 128. Leads his army against the "elder" Khan, 165. Retires, 165. Attacked by both Khans at Akhsi, 170. Surprises and wounds Báber, 172. Attempts to gain Báber, 174. Asks aid of Sheibáni, 175. Occupies Akhsi, 176. Drives out Báber, 177. Besieged in Andeján by Sheibáni, 187. Surrenders and is put to death, 189.

Tamerlane. See Taimur (Mír).

Tanka (the), coin, its value, 544.

Táráz, Isan-bugha's defeat at, 47.

Taríkhi Reshídi, of Haider Mírza, notice of, 192, *note*.

Tartars, their conquest of India under Báber, 6. Position of their country, 8. Origin of the name Tartar, or Tátár, 9. 533. Their manners and customs, 10. Their government, 11. Their settlement in tribes, or as adventurers, 19. Empire of Chengíz, 24. Its division on his death, 24. The Grand Khans, 25. Order of succession to the Khanship, 25. Their ravages in Europe under Bátu Khan, 26. Their adoption of the Musulman faith in Kipchák, 26. Their races and origin 533, *et seq.*

Táshkend, invaded by Isan-bugha, 47. Conquered by Sheibáni, 185. Under Siúnjek, 309. Bestowed by Báber on Mír Ahmed Kásim Kohbur, 319. Attacked by the Uzbeks, 322. Besieged and taken by Siúnjek, 330. Invaded by Sultan Saíd, 330. Laid waste by Kásim Khan, 331.

Tátár. See Tartar.

Tátár Gaker, defeated and slain by his brother, Hati Gaker, 415.

Tátár-Hazára, the tribe of, 221, *note.*

Tátár Khan, holds Sirhind, 413.

Tátár Khan, son of Alá-ed-dín, joins his father at the court of Gújrat, 431.

Tátár Khan Sarang-kháni, joins the confederacy against Báber, 442. Holds Guáliár, 453. Invites Báber, 453. Loses Guáliár, 454.

Tatta, capital of Sind, taken by Shah Beg, 355. Sacked by Shah Beg, 365. Seized by Siláh-ed-dín, 368. Taken by Shah Hasan, 380.

Taxes, increased by Báber, 488. 538.

Tekríl, a tribe of Chaghatái Moghuls, 36.

Temgha, or stamp tax, given up by Báber to the Musulmans, 467.

Terdi Beg, attends at Báber's death-bed, 516.

Terkhán chiefs, their power, 97. Proclaim Sultan Ali Mírza king of Samarkand, and dethrone Bayesanghar, 97. Those of Bokhára defeated by Sheibáni, 131.

Tíka-sakaratha, battle of, 59.

Toghlak dynasty (the), in India, 404.

Toghlak-Taimur Khan, his history, 39. Becomes Khan of Moghulistán and Káshghar, 40. Is converted to Muhammedanism, 40. Conquers Máwerannaher, 40.

Tokhteh-bugha, Sultan, son of the younger Khan, with Báber at Kábul, 256.

Toktamish, Grand Khan of Kipchák, 27.

Transoxiana. See Máwerannaher.

Túgh, or horsetail standard, conferred on Zúlnún, 265.

Túli, son of Chengíz, China allotted to him, 24.

Tulughmeh, the charge of the, 435.

Tulun Beg, a partisan of Báber's, taken and put to death, 109.

Tumán Kutluk Uglan, Grand Khan, 68.

Tumana Khan, the Altamgha of, covenant, 70.

Tumluq, or Tutluq, the battle of, 318.

Tungus, a race of Tartars, 9.

Túrk, a race of Tartars, 9. Their range, 15. Their influence, 15. Found the Ottoman empire, 16. Vast extent of country subject to their dominion, 17. In Egypt as Mamelukes, 18. Their religion, 18. Their language, 20. Distinguished from the Tájíks, 20. Origin of the name, 535.

Túrki, language in use in Persia, &c., 20. Spoken in purity in Ferghána, 81.

Túrkistán, seized by Sultan Mahmúd, and conferred on Sheibáni, 63. Under Kuchum Khan, 309.

Túrkomán Hazáras, plundered by Báber, 246.

Tús, taken by the Uzbeks, 457. 489.

Túzúk, "Institutes" of Taimur, their claim to authenticity, 71, *note.*

Uch, taken and pillaged by Shah Hasan, 390. The fort rebuilt, 391.

Udi Sing (Raúl), of Dongerpoor, his force at Kanwa, 471. Slain in the battle, 473.

Ulugh Beg Mírza, son of Shahrukh Mírza, Sultan of Samarkand, invades Moghulistán, 44. Murders the Moghul chiefs at Dizak, 45. His wars with his sons, 47. Protects Abusaíd, 73. His Astronomical Tables, 72. 83. *note*, 105 and *note*.

Ulugh Beg Mírza (Sultan), son of Abusaíd, sovereign of Kábul and Ghazni, 74. 77. His death, 215.

Ulús, or tribe, 19. 24.

Ulús-begi, "Director of the tribe," an hereditary office, 43.

Umersheikh Mírza (Sultan), father of Báber, succeeds to Andeján and Ferghána, 54. 74. Marries a daughter of Yúnis Khan, 54. 74. His ambition and restlessness, 59. 74. Defeated by Yúnis Khan, 59. The Khan's generosity to him, 59. Gains possession of Uratippa, 64. 75. His dominions invaded by Sultans Mahmúd and Ahmed, 75. His singular death, 75. His children, 76.

Uratippa, or Ushrushna, given up to Umersheikh, 64. 75. Taken by Sultan Ahmed, 87. Taken by Sultan Mahmúd, 90. 94. Bestowed upon Muhammed Husein Mírza Doghlat, 90. Unsuccessfully invaded by Báber, 94. Bestowed on Báber by Sultan Mahmúd, but not given up by Muhammed Husein, 160. Ravaged by Sheibáni, 165. Taken by Sheibáni, 185.

Urkend, or Uzkend, submits to Báber, 171.

Urus Khan, Grand Khan of Kipchák, 27.

Ush, a district of Ferghána, 58. 80. Assigned to Umersheikh, 58. Under the government of Tambol, 117. Declares for Báber, 118. Threatened by the Moghuls, 121. The fortress seized by Khalíl, 130. Surprised and taken by Báber, 170.

Ushter, fort of, taken by Sultan Mahmúd, 63.

Ustád Ali Kuli, commands Báber's artillery at the battle of Kanwa, 470. And at Kanáuj, 486. And on the banks of the Gogra, 504.

Uzbek Khan, of Kipchák, embraces Muhammedanism, 26. Converts some tribes, who take his name, 26.

Uzbekistán, extent of, 77.

Uzbeks (the), their great invasion of Transoxiana, 6. 17. Origin of their name, 26. 28. Introduced by Taimur into Kipchák, 28. Their union with the Túrki tribes, 28. Governed by Abulkhair, 29. Secession of the Kaizáks, 29. Governed by Bárúj Ughlán, 30. Dispersed by the Kaizáks, 32. Reunite under Sheibáni Khan, 64. Occupy Samarkand, 140. Destroy Keshtúd, 144. Driven out by Báber, 147. Defeat Báber on the Kohik, 152. Blockade of Samarkand, 153—157. Their various successes under Sheibáni, 163—303. Their consternation at his death, 305. Great numbers put to death at Merv, 305. Retire from Khorásán, 305. Their state at that time, 309. Raise Kuchum to the dignity of Khan, 309. Make peace with Shah Ismáel, 309. Expelled from Ferghána, 310. Invaded by Báber in Hissár, 312. Their plan of campaign, 312. They attack Báber, 313. Their defeat, 314. Expelled from Transoxiana, 316. Besiege and take Kásán, 317. Expelled from Máwerrannaher, 318. Driven back to Turkistán and the Desert, 319. Invade Transoxiana, 322. Defeat Báber at Kúlmalek, 322. Attack Hissár, 323. Their massacre at Karshi, 324. Defeat Báber and the Persians at Ghazhdewán, 325. Recover Transoxiana, 326. Ravage Khorásán, 326. Recover Hissár and Táshkend, 330. Put Kásim Gokultásh to death, 351. Besiege Bálkh, 423. 450. Invade Khorásán, 457. Besiege Herát, 457. Take Merv, Shirakhs, Meshhid, and Tús, 457. Their transactions in Khorásán, 489. Defeated with great slaughter by the Persians at Jám, 491. They recover their losses, 493.

Uz-Taimur, Táishi of the Kalimáks, his invasion of the Uzbek country, 30, *note*.

Uzun Hassan, governor of Akhsi, sets up Jehángír, 107. Besieges Andeján, 109. Takes the city, 110. Invests Marghinán, 116. Retreats, 117. Surrenders Akhsi to Báber, 118. Retires to Hissár, 119. Joins Báber at Samarkand, 157.

Vasco de Gama, his arrival in India, 113, *note*.

Velvet, manufacture of, in Samarkand. 106.

Vienna, threatened by the Moghuls, 13.

Visits in the East, ceremonials observed in, 253, *note*.

Wais (Sultan), of Swád, submits to Báber, 338.

Wali, brother of Khosrou Shah, 95. Accompanies Sultan Masaúd to attack Samarkand, 100. Sent by Khosrou to support Sultan Masaúd, 197. Obtains Khutlan, 200. Defeated by the Aimáks, and beheaded by Sheibáni, 212.

War, art of, among the Tartars of Transoxiana, 84.

Waran-mal Sodha, slain in battle against Shah Beg, 367.

Weis (Sultan) of Khutlán, invites Sultan Saíd Khan to Badakhshán, 509.

Weis Khan (Sultan), elected Grand Khan, 44. Slain, 44.

Weis Mírza, or Khan Mírza, son of Sultan Mahmúd, his unsuccessful invasion of Samarkand, 129. His parentage, 248. Attempt of his grandmother to place him on the throne of Kábul, 249. Defeat of the rebellion, 252. Báber's clemency to him, 254. Permitted to proceed to Khorásán, 254. Joins Báber in his expedition to Kandahár, 277. Sets out with his grandmother, Shah Begum, for Badakhshán, 282. Becomes king of Badakhshán, 286. Makes Kilazefer his capital, 289. Visited by Sultan Saíd, and Mírza Haider, 289. His poverty, 290. Communicates to Báber the news of the battle of Merv, 306. Sent as ambassador to Persia, 309. Assists in driving the Uzbeks from Hissár, 313. Left by Báber in Badakhshán, 329. Quarrels with Sultan Saíd, 339. His death, 341.

Wine, the use of, renounced by Báber, 466.

Women, their position among the Tartars, 11.

Yádgár Mírza, conspires against Báber, 327.

Yádgár Nasír Mírza, son of Násir Mírza, 334, *note.*

Yahía (Khwája), his hospitality to Sultan Ali, 99. Intrigues with Báber, 132. Waits on Sheibáni, 140. Banished and murdered, 141.

Yar Husein, of Bhera, invites Báber into India, 223. Becomes a freebooter, 231. Robs and puts to death Báki Chegháníáni, 231.

Yar-ailák, fortified by Kamber Ali, 144.

Yárkend, description of, 35.

Yási-Kijet, battle of, 120.

Yeke-Auleng, people of, their hospitality to Báber, 246.

Yúlaji Doghlat (Mír), Khan of Káshghar, 39. Brings forward Toghlak-Taimur, as son of Isan-bugha, 39. His death, 40.

Yúnis Khan, son of Weis Khan, driven from Moghulistán by his brother, Isan-bugha, 44. Sent to Sháhrukh Mírza, 45. Placed under the care of the historian Mouláná Sherf-ed-dín Ali Shirázi, 45. Invited to Herát by Abusaíd, 49. His treaty with him, 50. His character, 50. Marries Aisdoulat Begum, 51. Re-enters Moghulistán, 51. His attempt on Káshghar, 51. Is defeated at Aksu, 52. The territory of Masíkhi conferred on him by Abusaíd, 52. His successes, 53. Marries his three daughters to three sons of Abusáid, 54. Defeated by the Kalimáks, 54. 31. Defeats Bárúj Ughlán, 54. 32. Made prisoner by Sheikh Jemál, 54. Released, 55. Becomes sole Khan of Moghulistán, 56. His campaigns in Káshghar, 56. Twice defeated by Ababeker, 57. His attachment to Umersheikh, 58. His quarrel with him, 59. Peace between them, 60. Khwája Nasír-ed-dín's account of him, 60. His son Ahmed Khan withdraws from him, 61. His death, 62. His character, 62. Notice of his children, 248.

Yusef (Sheikh) chosen ruler of Multán, 386. Expelled, 386.

Yusef Ali Gokuldásh, assassinates Zobeir, 288.

Yusef Darogha, his interview with Báber, 182.

Yusef-zái Afgháns, settle in Swád, 337. Their convention with Báber, 338.

Zefer, the fort of, Shah Beg imprisoned there, 345.

Zeináb Sultan Begum, wife of Báber, 526, *note.*

Zein-ed-dín, the Sadr of Delhi, 437.

Zemíndárs, application of the term, 529.

Zemín-Dáwer, government of, conferred on Zulnún, 264. Description of, 264.

Zir-efshán, or Kohik, river of Samarkand, 105.

Zírin, the pass, 244.

Zobeir, of Rágh, a chief of Badakhshán, 288. Receives Khan Mírza, 288. Is assassinated, 288.

Zuhri Begi Agha, mother of Sultan Ali Mírza, her intrigues and misery, 140, 141.

Zúlnún (Sheikh), governor of Uratippa, 94.

Zúlnún Beg Arghún (Mír), his descent, 262, *note*. His early life, 262. Repairs to Herát, 262. Appointed by Sultan Husein Mírza, governor of Ghúr, 263. Reduces the Hazáras and Nukderis, 264. Made governor of Zemín-Dáwer and Farrah, 264. Honoured with the Túgh, 265. Recalled to court, 265. Attaches himself to Badi-ez-zemán, 265. Appointed to Kandahár, 215. 220. 266. Leaves Herát privately, 267. Arrives at Kandahár, 267. Receives Badi-ez-zemán, 199. 268. Attacked by Sultan Husein, 269. Invades Khorásán, 271. Besieges Herát, 272. Peace concluded, 273. Defeats Ibn Husein Mírza, 273. His high reputation, 274. His advice to his son Mokím, 216. Becomes prime minister of Herát, 275. Entitled "Hezéber Alla," or "Lion of God," 275. Defeated, made prisoner, and slain by Sheibáni, 259. 275. His character, as given by Báber, 275.

END OF THE FIRST VOLUME.